Aldous Huxley
Complete Essays

Aldous Huxley c. early 1920s (Estate of Aldous Huxley)

ALDOUS HUXLEY COMPLETE ESSAYS

Volume I, 1920–1925

EDITED WITH COMMENTARY BY

Robert S. Baker

AND

James Sexton

IVAN R. DEE

Chicago 2000

COMPLETE ESSAYS OF ALDOUS HUXLEY, Volume I, 1920–1925. Copyright © 2000 by
Ivan R. Dee, Publisher. All rights reserved, including the right to reproduce this book
or portions thereof in any form. For information, address: Ivan R. Dee, Publisher, 1332 North
Halsted Street, Chicago 60622. Manufactured in the United States of America and printed on
acid-free paper.

The publishers gratefully acknowledge the assistance and support of the Estate of Aldous Huxley
in preparing this volume.

Library of Congress Cataloging-in-Publication Data:
    Huxley, Aldous, 1894–1963.
    [Essays]
    Complete essays / Aldous Huxley ; edited with commentary by Robert S. Baker and
James Sexton.
        p. cm.
    Includes bibliographical references and index.
    Contents: v. 1. 1920–1925
    ISBN 1-56663-322-2 (alk. paper)
    I. Baker, Robert S., 1940– II. Sexton, James. III. Title.
PR6015.U9 A6 2000
    824'.912—dc21

00-034564

For Elizabeth Baker and Richard Sexton

Contents

III. HISTORY, POLITICS, SOCIAL CRITICISM

IV. TRAVEL

Contents

A Note on This Edition

THE EDITORS have included all of Huxley's published essays as well as a generous selection of shorter reviews and brief occasional pieces. When an essay appeared in a periodical to be followed by a slightly revised version in a published collection, we have included the latter as Huxley's preferred text. We have adopted an austere policy regarding footnotes. Only minor figures are identified on their first occurrence in the text, and then only when their identification appears necessary to comprehend the essay. It has, however, been difficult to apply this policy as consistently as we would have liked. French passages have been translated when they were of considerable length or necessary to comprehend the argument of the essay. The essays have been placed in chronological order and divided by topic. The reader or scholar who wishes to read the essays in the original order as determined by Huxley will find the tables of contents of both *On the Margin* and *Along the Road* reproduced in an appendix.

James Sexton wishes to thank the Social Sciences and Humanities Research Council of Canada for the generous assistance it has afforded him with this project.

Introduction

ALDOUS HUXLEY was born on July 26, 1894, at Laleham, near Godalming, Surrey, England. He was the third son of Leonard Huxley, who, after teaching at Charterhouse, became the editor of *The Cornhill Magazine.* Aldous's mother was Julia Frances Arnold, the granddaughter of Thomas Arnold and the niece of Matthew Arnold. He was, on his father's side, the grandson of the naturalist and proselytizer of Darwin, T. H. Huxley. With such a background it is not surprising that the essay form should have come so naturally to Aldous. In 1910 he contracted an eye infection that left his sight permanently impaired. It was diagnosed as *keritatis punctata,* and the condition improved only gradually during the twenties. Huxley taught himself to read Braille and to type. Exhibiting his customary determination and absence of self-pity, he taught himself to play the piano with one hand on the Braille text and the other on the piano keys. He also wrote his first novel of about eighty thousand words, which has disappeared. After Eton, Huxley attended Balliol College, Oxford, graduating in 1916 with a first in English literature despite his troubled vision. While an undergraduate he became a member of Ottoline Morrell's circle at Garsington, where he met a number of artists and writers, including T. S. Eliot, Augustus John, D. H. Lawrence, Bertrand Russell, Lytton Strachey, and Virginia Woolf. It was also at Garsington that he met a Flemish refugee, Maria Nys, who in 1919 became his wife.

The essays in this volume were written at the beginning of the period (1919 to the early 1930s) that was Huxley's most creative. The first example of what he called the "novel of social history," *Crome Yellow,* was published in 1921, a brilliant satire of the Garsington circle and a sustained meditation on the nature of history. This was the period of high modernism, of Joyce's *Ulysses* and Eliot's *The Waste Land,* of what Huxley called "the violent disruption of almost all the standards, conventions, and values current in the previous epoch." Acutely conscious of the Great War and the generational conflict that colored its aftermath, Huxley saw himself as a member of the "war generation" whose novels and essays were shaped by searching reflections on postwar English society and a probing skepticism. This recognition that the world had changed in some profound and disturbing way after the war of 1914–1918 found support in the pages of John Middleton Murry's *Athenaeum*. In 1919 Murry invited Huxley to contribute to his journal and, after T. S. Eliot had declined the post, appointed Huxley as second assistant editor. Under Murry's editorship *The Athenaeum* was transformed into a "Journal of English and Foreign Literature, Science, the Fine Arts, Music and the Drama." Such a breadth of coverage doubtless appealed to Huxley's wide-ranging interests.

In his first editorial Murry embraced a policy that wavered between a muted affirmation of what he called a "republic of the spirit" and a darker realization that "the earthquake [the Great War of 1914–1918] has happened and we have to live among the debris. We had better make the most of it." *The Athenaeum* was not as vividly charged with modernist assumptions as *The Egoist* or *Blast* but, under Murry's editorship, open to new art forms and acutely aware of the need to assess the impact of the war, it helped mold the taste and influence the literary culture of London. Huxley wrote a series of weekly essays under the heading "Marginalia," many of which were collected in *On the Margin*, published in 1923. In his introduction to the series he characterized his perspective with typical irony, referring to his columns as literary notes and his observations as a form of "curio-hunting." Yet in his concluding paragraph he compares himself to John Aubrey, the seventeenth-century antiquarian and author of *Miscellanies* and the more famous *Brief Lives*. He quotes Aubrey's account of walking through Newgate Street and finding the salvaged head of a statue that had been mostly destroyed during the Great Fire of London. If we read the Great Fire as the apocalyptic Great War and the salvaged relic as a fragment of history, Huxley's purpose becomes clear: "How these curiosities would be quite forgott, did not such idle fellowes as I am putt them down!"

Huxley was overworked during this period. In the eight months he was employed at *The Athenaeum* he contributed more than two hundred articles and reviews. The strain shows in some of the early essays, yet taken as a whole they lucidly rehearse various issues that were continually invoked in his novels of social history. Art, music, the excesses of the imagination, the status of history, and, especially, the traumatic experiences of the Great War are pivotal points of reference in both the early reviews and essays, and the most charged issues in novels like *Crome Yellow* (1921), *Antic Hay* (1923), *Those Barren Leaves* (1925), and *Point Counter Point* (1928).

Art, Literature, and Music

Huxley's early essays are often occasional pieces, brief reviews, and short columns that in their precise focus on specific facts appear to support his contention in his introduction to *Marginalia* that such "concrete solid little facts ... cannot by any conceivable possibility be made to serve a theoretic purpose." While this statement is broadly true, the early essays do explore a number of theoretical issues that Huxley developed and refined in his later work. In some cases they set down fundamental views and judgments that he would never abandon or even modify.

The essays collected in *On the Margin* and *Along the Road*, and those on music from *The Weekly Westminster Gazette*, reveal a mind delighting in the classical restraint and ordered rationality of poets such as Ben Jonson and architects such as Sir Christopher Wren, who are held up as exemplary figures at the expense of romantic poets and composers such as Shelley or Brahms. In his essay on Ben Jonson, Huxley maintains that "a consciously practiced theory of art has never spoiled a good artist," and his own work was rooted in a theoretically ambivalent response to what he called in *Along the Road* the "baroque, romantic style." Jonson, he argues, like Wren and Chaucer, refused to indulge in the emotional histrionics and theatrical duplicities of baroque architects such as Bernini or Borromini, or romantic poets such as Shelley and Wordsworth. In painting and literature, however, Huxley placed great value on the carefully nuanced rendering of human experience. This mimetic emphasis on the necessary correspondence between the elements of a painting and some actual set of conditions, events, or objects in a "real" world was reinforced by his preference for mass and solidity. The paintings of Mantegna and Piero della Francesca were singled out for special praise in this regard. Huxley praised Chaucer for his poised acceptance of nature and the empirical order, especially for his unwillingness to "go to nature as the symbol of some further spiritual reality." Similarly, Wren is celebrated for his restraint, his intuitive grasp of how to achieve a refined and inventive monumentality without recourse to the romantic excesses of the prevailing baroque of his Italian contemporaries. But Huxley's insistence on representation in art was never naively proffered at the expense of formal values. Much of the world's art, he concedes, is abstract, and the rise of photography had encouraged an eclecticism of taste that he welcomed.

Huxley's music and art criticism was marked by an assiduously detailed attention to matters of structure and form. Nevertheless, in painting and literature he insisted on a mimetic relationship between the artwork and the real world, just as in his music criticism he was wary of a composition that depended too markedly on formal matters. And it is at this point, where the categories of aesthetic form and some kind of referential "truth" overlap, that the tension in Huxley's aesthetic becomes most evident. Ben Jonson, valued for the well-wrought sobriety and sound judgment of his poetry is, nevertheless, criticized for an overreliance on logical analysis and an insensitivity to the "supremely real world of the mystic," while Huxley claimed to discover in the finest music of Mozart and Beethoven a "truth" that he connected to an indefinable form of transcendent beauty.

In 1922 Huxley became the music critic for *The Weekly Westminster Gazette,* his column appearing regularly between February 1922 and June 1923. Following closely the *Marginalia* essays of 1920–1922, his music essays expand and refine many of his ideas not only about music but about aesthetics in general. One notable feature of his music criticism is his preference for Renaissance polyphony. He set Palestrina's music with its refined multivoiced flexibility against the monodic music of Verdi with its accented rhythms and recurring melodic themes and came down emphatically on the side of the former. Formalistic intricacy and polyphonic variations fascinated Huxley and eventually shaped his theory of the novel. The musical values he especially cherished were most evident in the work of Beethoven, including the *Mass in D,* the *Diabelli Variations,* the piano sonatas (particularly opus 111), and the late string quartets, opus 132 being an enduringly significant work for Huxley. A self-taught music critic, he was fascinated by formal musical technique, but he tended to privilege certain qualities of emotional expression and the refined representation of a "beauty-truth" that could only be expressed in music. In a letter to the French poet Paul Valéry (January 4, 1930), he claimed to discover an aesthetic meaning in music that could not be adequately formulated in discursive prose but which permitted him to judge a composition "true." This nebulous notion of truth was also, on occasion, present in his literary criticism, and it underscores Huxley's slowly developing need to locate in the artwork some manifestation of a spiritual significance that went beyond intricately ordered themes and variations or subtle formal arrangements of pictorial forms in a painting or words in a poem. This tendency in Huxley's theory of art is only suggestively emergent in the essays of the early twenties, but it assumed vastly more importance in succeeding essays and novels.

Huxley's endorsement of realism and representation was, as noted above, never exclusively narrow or simplistic in its formulations. One might generalize to the extent of describing his art criticism as somewhat conservative, an aesthetic grounded in classical values, realism, stylistic restraint, and a belief that the artwork is not only founded on empirical truth and the texture of actual experience but is inseparable from moral and spiritual truths. This faintly fluctuating tendency to locate a transcendental value in art is most often displaced in the early essays by a tempered skepticism born of the disillusionment that followed the Great War.

Philosophy, Science, and Religion

Huxley's aesthetic interests, despite their somewhat conservative core, tended to range very widely. He may have preferred Mozart and Chaucer, but he was tentatively responsive to Béla Bartók and T. S. Eliot. He would confidently assert a set of aesthetic values in one essay and concede in the next that final judgments were impossible and that the range of aesthetic creativity precluded canonical lists and self-evident valuations. This refusal finally to locate the truth of art in one style or one century is a manifestation of a central tenet of Huxley's view of human experience—the absence of any form of epistemological certitude. Throughout the twenties Huxley rejected any notion of metaphysical absolutes, whether in history, philosophy, religion, or politics. By the end of the decade he was fond of referring to himself as a Pyrrhonist, that is, a thinker who mistrusted all philosophical systems founded on notions of essential truth. Huxley was a rationalist always ironically dismissive of the excesses of rationalism and idealism, and, like the Greek philosopher Pyrrho (365–270 B.C.) who advocated the suspension of judgment on any matter involving the truth, he consistently rejected system and ideology in his work. Huxley's first satirical novel, *Crome Yellow* (1921), brilliantly dramatizes many of the philosophical reservations that he addressed in his early essays, particularly his doubts concerning historical truth. The individual facts of history may be susceptible to precise formulation, but once interpretation enters the picture (that is, the endeavor to place those facts in a broader narrative context that insists on history as immanently meaningful with a definable goal), Huxley expressed carefully considered doubts.

The interwar period was a time of contending ideologies, and Huxley did his best to rise above the most systematically conceived interpretations of history. His own perspective was somewhat elitist, the stance of a well-educated member of the English upper middle classes who admired classical art and, on occasion, was quite willing to invoke generalizations and universal values when defending certain aesthetic and philosophical positions. But, by and large, he remained a skeptic who attempted to balance what in *Along the Road* he called "the rational simplicities" of mind with "the pleasing confusion of untempered reality."

In his description of a drive through the Dutch landscape in "Views of Holland," one of the central features of Huxley's own mental topography comes sharply into focus:

Delightful landscape! I know of no country that it is more mentally exhilarating to travel in. No wonder Descartes preferred the Dutch to any other scene. It is the rationalist's paradise. One feels as one flies along in the teeth of one's own forty-mile-an-hour wind like a Cartesian Encyclopaedist flushed with mental intoxication, convinced that Euclid is absolute reality, that God is a mathematician, that the universe is a simple affair that can be explained in terms of physics and mechanics, that all men are equally endowed with reason and that it is only a question of putting the right arguments before them to make them see the errors of their ways and to inaugurate the reign of justice and common sense. . . . We are soberer now. We have learnt that nothing is simple and rational except what we ourselves have invented; that God thinks neither in terms of Euclid nor of Riemann; that science has "explained" nothing; that the more we know the more fantastic the world becomes and the profounder the surrounding darkness; that reason is unequally distributed; that instinct is the sole source of action; that prejudice is incomparably stronger than argument and that even in the twentieth century men behave as they did in the caves of Altamira and in the lake dwellings of Glastonbury.

I have quoted this passage at length because it functions as a synoptic index to Huxley's beliefs, despite his willingness, on occasion, to strike out in more positive directions. The early essays focus for the most part on art and literature, but as the decade progressed Huxley turned his attention to social and political problems in surprisingly constructive as well as more ironically dismissive ways. Huxley's essays and novels of the interwar period were aimed at exposing the turmoil of a society aimlessly adrift in the wake of the Great War. Yet the corrosive skepticism that animates his satire was always counterpointed by his search for a framework of moral conviction and social emancipation. In the early essays of this volume that theme is only barely discernible, but in the succeeding volumes it will become increasingly apparent.

ROBERT S. BAKER

Aldous Huxley
Complete Essays

I.

Architecture,
Painting,
Literature

Proust: The Eighteenth-Century Method

WHEN WE SAY of M. Proust's work that it is "eighteenth-century" in quality, we mean more than that it possesses (though it does in effect possess it) that porcelain exquisiteness, that absurd, beautiful formality, with which we are inclined, fallaciously perhaps, to endow this most civilized period of history. The eighteenth century of pretty formalism is mostly a thing of our own invention; for the past, as it exists in our mind, is largely a pleasing myth, created and re-created by each succeeding generation for its own peculiar necessities of propaganda or delectation. The Romantics saw the eighteenth century as an age of moral and intellectual depravity. We picture it very differently: to some of us it is the precious and fantastic embodiment of *Fêtes Galantes* or of Mallarmé's elaborately futile *Princesse à jalouser le destin d'une Hébé*; to others, in search of a stick with which to beat mysticism, rant, sentimentality, and moral earnestness, it presents itself as the age of supreme enlightenment and entire reasonableness. There is probably an element of truth in all these views, including that of the Romantics. But we are not concerned at the moment with the myth of the past in general, but only with the question of what we mean when we say that *Du côté de chez Swann* and *A l'ombre des jeunes filles en fleurs* are "eighteenth-century" in quality.

M. Proust, then, is "eighteenth-century" in both senses of the epithet as we apply it today. His comedy of manners deals, very elaborately, with the charming futilities of social or even "society" life. Mr. Wells has likened Henry James to a hippopotamus pursuing a pea round a room; at that rate M. Proust will be a diplodocus, for in these first two volumes of *A la recherche du temps perdus* he has already filled twelve hundred pages of solidly set small type, unrelieved, as Alice would have complained, by pictures or conversations; and there are still three more volumes to follow before the lost times are finally "retrouvés": a diplodocus, then, in weight of matter, as well as in weight of intelligence, pursuing the minute pea of social life in the Faubourg Saint-Germain and its upper-bourgeois and half-worldly fringes.

But this exquisite frivolity of theme—and what a pleasure it is in these days of artistic grimness to find such a theme being seriously treated by a serious artist!—is not the only "eighteenth-century" quality of M. Proust's work. He is "eighteenth-century" in that other sense as well—enlightened and very intellectual in all his ways. If we examine his methods we shall find that they are the eighteenth-century methods, much developed and elaborated, but fundamentally the same.

In the second volume of his history of the French novel, Mr. Saintsbury let fall the remark that "psychological realism is perhaps a more different thing from psychological reality than our clever ones for two generations have been willing to admit, or, perhaps, able to understand." Psychological reality, as opposed to psychological realism, was what the eighteenth-century delineators of character aimed at. There is something extraordinarily satisfying and convincing about a good piece of their analysis. One thinks with admiration of the firmness of outline, the bare precision of Alfieri's self-portrait, or of Benjamin Constant's *Adolphe,* so subtle and yet so simply and economically drawn. They produced their effects by a process of abstraction from the multifarious and generally rather confused facts of psychology. The "clever ones of the last two generations" have occupied themselves for the most part in exactly recording these muddled facts as they are actually observable. To them this psychological realism has seemed nearer the truth than the earlier abstractions and distillations of the real brute facts. But, as Mr. Saintsbury suggests, it may be that artistic truth and convincingness of character are arrived at more certainly by the other method. The invention and development of the modern science of psychology has made us regard as important and interesting a multitude of small odds and ends of thought, emotion and sensation which seemed to our ancestors almost negligible. They did not insist on the phenomena because they were interested primarily in what they regarded as the reality behind them. They did not record little facts about their heroes' sensations or fleeting velleities of thought; they rationalized and generalized the chaotic complex of psychological life into the unity of a character. It is quite conceivable that Mr. James Joyce should some day write a book on the same theme as *Adolphe.* He would present us, in place of Constant's clearly outlined hero, with a many-colored medley of sensations, memories, desires, thoughts, and feelings, leaving to our imagination the task of boiling them down into a consistent character. *Adolphe* or *Ulysses*—which is true? Both, we imagine, or neither, if you like. Each, in any case, represents a way of looking at the human soul, a different facet of reality.

M. Proust belongs in his methods to the older school. He does not give us psychology in its crude, undigested state. He rationalizes and distills and peptonizes his data, serving up finally, for the consumption of his readers, a finished product of exquisite clarity. M. Proust carries the process of digestion to the point of making generalizations about life and character in that grand manner, so authoritative and didactic, of which we are all so much afraid now. Here is a specimen of his aphorisms, called forth apropos of the character of the literary diplomatist, Monsieur de Norpois:

> Ma mère s'émerveillait qu'il fut si exact quoique si affairé, si aimable quoique si répandu, sans songer que les "quoique" sont toujours des "parce que" méconnus, et que (de même que les vieillards sont étonnants pour leur âge, les rois pleins de simplicité et les provinciaux au courant de tout) c'était les mêmes habitudes qui permettaient à M. de Norpois de satisfaire à tant d'occupations et d'être si ordonné dans ses réponses, de plaire dans le monde et d'être aimable avec nous.[1]

This is admirable, and it would be possible to find things like it, generalizations tinged with M. Proust's curious wit and wisdom, on almost every page of the book.

To read M. Proust as he deserves requires an almost unlimited amount of time—a great deal more than most of us, alas! can spare. For he goes slowly, very slowly, and he grinds exceeding small. In the first volume, *Du côté de chez Swann,* we were introduced to the hero in childhood, surrounded by his family; then, in the course of an astonishingly brilliant and witty study of social life, we were told how it came about that Swann—Swann of the Jockey Club and so successful a figure in the highest society—came to marry Odette, the would-be intellectual demi-mondaine. Now, in the second volume, the hero has grown to adolescence; his boyish passion for Swann's young daughter grows and perishes, and in the latter part of the book it is dissipated among a whole troop of "jeunes filles en fleurs," met or merely glimpsed at, by the seaside. Nothing happens in any conventional, novelistic sense of the word; a great many characters pass across the stage; we are taken for drives in the country and bathes in the sea. That is all, but we read on absorbed, fascinated by M. Proust's clear, intellectual handling of his material, by the acuteness and thoroughness of his analysis, by his wit, and above all by his appreciation of beauty and his power of expressing it in a style somewhat precious perhaps, but genuinely original and beautiful.

M. Proust is one of the most interesting phenomena in contemporary

1. "My mother marveled at his being so punctilious although so busy, so friendly although so much in demand, never realizing that 'although,' with such people, is invariably an unrecognized 'because,' and that, just as old men are always wonderful for their age, and kings extraordinarily simple, and country-cousins astonishingly well informed, it was the same system of habits that enabled M. de Norpois to meet so many social demands and to be so methodical in answering letters, to go everywhere and to be so friendly when he came to us" (*Remembrance of Things Past,* I).

literature, if only because he is so certain of himself, so secure in his brilliant development and elaboration of a grand traditional manner. We look forward with pleasant anticipation to the appearance of *Le côté de Guermantes,* the two parts of *Sodome et Gomorrhe,* and the final *Le Temps Retrouvé,* which will complete this massive work. We shall buy them all, and though we may not, perhaps, have time to read them at the time of their appearance, we shall keep them against a calm and leisured old age, when, sometime between seventy and eighty, we propose to sit down in the warm sun or beside a comfortable fire and spend a whole happy year *A la recherche du temps perdus.*

[*Athenaeum,* August 8, 1919]

A Ghost of the Nineties
(*Poems and Prose of Ernest Dowson.* With an introduction by Arthur Symons.)

THERE USED TO BE, and perhaps there still is, a kind of tea, of which the advertisements affirmed "that it recalled the delicious blends of forty years ago." This little volume from "The Modern Library of the World's Best Books" recalls blends of slightly more recent concoction, but no less delicious—the literary alcohol and hashish (for we will not insult the nineties by likening their productions to tea) of only thirty years gone by. We feel as we pass through the "exquisite limp croftleather" portals of our volume—even the publishers' style seems to be tinged with the rich exotic quality of the period—we feel like the hero of Dowson's own *Diary of a Successful Man,* who, revisiting the city where "it is always autumn," Bruges, "strolled into Saint Sauveur's, wandered a while through its dim, dusky aisles, and then sat down near the high altar, where the air was heaviest with stale incense, and indulged in retrospect." On every page we breathe that ghost of once keen incense, and our indulgence in retrospect almost brings the tears to our eyes when we read such lines as

> O red pomegranate of thy perfect mouth!
> My lips' life-fruitage, might I taste and die
> Here in thy garden, where the scented south
> Wind chastens agony;
>
> Reap death from thy live lips in one long kiss,
> And look my last into thine eyes and rest:
> What sweets had life to me sweeter than this
> Swift dying on thy breast?

Or, if that may not be, for Love's sake, Dear!
Keep silence still, and dream that we shall lie,
Red mouth to mouth, entwined, and always hear
The south wind's melody.

Stale incense and retrospect, we respire them even in Mr. Symons's charming introduction: "Even before that time I have a vague impression of having met him, I forget where, certainly at night; and of having been struck, even then, by a look and manner of pathetic charm, a sort of Keats-like face, the face of a demoralized Keats, and by something curious in the contrast of a manner exquisitely refined, with an appearance generally somewhat dilapidated. . . . I liked to see him occasionally, for a change, drinking nothing stronger than coffee or tea. At Oxford, I believe, his favorite form of intoxication had been hashish; afterwards he gave up this somewhat elaborate experiment in visionary sensations for readier means of oblivion. Always, perhaps, a little consciously, but at least always sincerely, in search of new sensations, my friend found what was for him the supreme sensation in a very passionate and tender adoration. . . ." We could go on quoting indefinitely for the sake of those "somewhats," those "a littles," those "exquisitely's" and those "infinitely's," the last conspicuous in the passages of our selection by their absence. Everything in the book, Mr. Symons's introduction, Dowson's poetry, and Dowson's prose, conspires to recall to our palates the flavor of those forgotten, delicious blends. So much so, indeed, that we are in danger of dwelling sentimentally on what we may call the eheu! fugacity of things instead of asking the question which it is the critic's business to ask: What right have Dowson's poems to figure among the World's Best Books? But perhaps we should not take the title of this series of reprints too seriously, for we note that among the World's Best Authors are to be found Ellen Key, Oscar Wilde, Lord Dunsany, and Woodrow Wilson. Let us frame our question rather more modestly: How is it, then, that after a lapse of five-and-twenty years, when the world is ruled by different and hostile literary fashions, Dowson's poetry is still sufficiently alive to make it worth a publisher's while to reprint it?

Dowson was a minor poet—"infinitely" minor, as he himself might have said. He could express only one emotion, he knew only one tune. But in his limitation lay his strength. For by piping continually in the same melancholy mode he arrived in the end at a small perfection of his own; and perfection, even in a little, limited thing, will always ensure for the poet who achieves it a more than temporary hearing.

Dowson was a sentimentalist of the school of Verlaine, the English apostle of nostalgia. He refined grief to homesickness—a sickness for what home one does not know; it was a *nostalgie de nostalgie,* a longing for some longing that should have a definite object. Beauty he decked out in fancy dress, accentuating its transience by the artificiality of its decorations. He evaporated, attenuated every sensation and emotion, till pain was somewhat dolorous and love a little passionate.

Art can express emotion in a variety of ways: simply and directly, as in folk-song, where the different modes have an immediate and almost physical effect; later on with the complexity of the symphony, in which the primitive emotion is enriched with all its intellectual and spiritual implications; and then decadently, by allusions to other works of art and by ringing the changes of a well-learned technique. Dowson was as incapable of writing folk-songs as of writing symphonies; he did not possess the spontaneous life or the mental capacity to do either. He gave expression to his sentimentalized grief in highly complicated forms, rich with associations. And the associations, the complexity of form themselves added to the sentimental effect, just as, in retrospect, the elaborate and artificial life of the French Court tinges the last days of the old régime with a perfectly factitious melancholy. It is, after all, no small achievement to have written

> I have forgot much, Cynara! gone with the wind,
> Flung roses, roses, riotously with the throng,
> Dancing, to put thy pale lost lilies out of mind;
> But I was desolate and sick of an old passion,
> Yea, all the time, because the dance was long:
> I have been faithful to thee, Cynara! in my fashion.

The images and metaphors are old, the technical devices are old, the whole thing is immensely artificial. And yet the lines are moving. Dowson has found the perfect expression for his own artificial emotion. He has discovered the elaborate "dying fall" that descends through the heart-breaking, discord-enriched dominant to a tonic diapason of pure silence—for it all ends in nothing, nothing at all.

There are moods in which these variations on a nonexistent theme are all that the mind desires or deserves—moments of physical fatigue and mental lassitude, the true parents of sentimentality, when Verlaine's nostalgia is too subtly vaporous and Laforgue's too intellectual to be appreciated, and when Dowson, with his dying falls, his slow elaborate rhythms, his restful absence of any serious significance, is the only poet. We all suffer at times from these attacks of sentimentality: let us prepare for the next by laying in, among other homoeopathic remedies, a copy of Dowson's poems.

[*Athenaeum,* October 10, 1919]

(On Essays)

HOW SHALL WE inaugurate this series of literary notes more suitably than by a few reflections on the species at large, by a literary note on literary notes? The subject is one that suggests many pleasant considerations, moral and psychological; it has a history and a sufficiency of odd and curious interest: in a word, a perfect subject for that peculiar form of literature known as the literary note.

To the man of action, intent on making money or war or mischief of some kind or other, as well as to the philosopher inhabiting the realms of pure abstraction, our literary preoccupations will appear profoundly trivial and irrelevant. They bring in no cash, they reveal no new facet of the eternal Truth. What is the good, then, of your literary tittle-tattle? Money-maker and truth-seeker, combined in unexpected alliance, confront us menacingly with this question. What is the good of it all?

What, indeed! There are many other human occupations for which it would be as difficult to give an adequate moral or rational justification. But for our literary gossip we have at least this justification, not, it may be, of a very exalted nature, but none the less wholly satisfying: that it occupies and entertains the mind. Mental occupation, the comfortable sense of being busy—that is what we are all of us always asking for. *Ennui* is a haunting terror. At any cost we must escape the anguish of being bored, we must find something to fill our leisure. But at the same time we have no intention of tiring ourselves. The first necessity hurries us forward into spiritual adventure, while the discreet, self-preservative *vis inertiae* restrains our ardors within reasonably trivial bounds. Thus, we might devote our leisure to reading higher mathematics or philosophy; we might occupy our minds by trying to solve the problems of the universe. But, oh! the agony of trying to think abstractedly, the pain of long-continued mental concentration! Our restraining idleness steps in with counsels of moderation. And so, in the end, we turn to stamp collecting, to bibliophily, to antiquarian research, to the curiosities of literature. In these we find our antidote to boredom, the sense of being busy without the sense of fatigue.

What occupation is pleasanter, what less exacting, than the absorption of curious literary information? Leisure, a relishing palate, and a moderately efficient memory are all we need bring with us. Thought and concentration are quite unnecessary. And there is a further satisfaction: our reading is not merely entertaining; it is instructive too. We flatter ourselves that we are learning something, we pretend that we are plunged in study, working furiously. Yes, working on *The Anatomy of Melancholy,* on the *Curiosities of Literature,* or the *Literary Recreations* of Sir E. T. Cook. Working, learning. . . . We have already discovered what was Lord Palmerston's solitary reference to the classics, what name Achilles assumed among the women, who wrote the flattest line in English, and a thousand more delightful, unnecessary facts.

There have been whole ages when this spiritual equivalent of stamp collecting was the principal form of culture. In the days when Burton's fantastic genius was turning the sweepings of the Bodleian into an immortal book, it was not the man who could compose the finest epic, but the scholar who could write the oddest and obscurest literary notes, to whom the world paid homage. Salmasius had the reputation of being the greatest man of genius of his day, because he had written a commentary on Orosius, stuffed with absurd information from every author who had lived since the invention of writing. Compared with him, Milton, who had only written two or three tracts on divorce, but thinly sown with citations, and a few poems in passably golden Latin, was a man of small note, an impertinent schoolboy. For anyone with a literary turn of mind, those were happy days. He could gain a very decent reputation in science and philosophy by merely indulging his favorite hobby of curio hunting in the books of the past. Now, since these subjects have become so deplorably hard of comprehension, the literary man contents himself with being frankly literary and nothing more. Let others perform the difficult and ungraceful task of distorting their minds into thinking abstractly. Our business and pleasure shall be, like Cousin Pons, to potter up and down our rich little mental museum, commenting playfully or respectfully on the masterpieces, furbishing up old anecdotes, arranging and re-arranging the innumerable little facts which crowd the shelves. If we play the collector's part with enough industry and patience we shall end by having the reputation of being learned men. And what a respectable reputation to have been won so pleasantly! To reach the same summit of reputation the men of science will have had to sweat and groan as we have never had to do.

To be a true relisher of literary curiosities one must have a nose and palate that can detect the mellow flavor of ridiculousness that lurks in the history of all human affairs. One must further bring a great respect for the fact-in-itself. "Here Nelson fell"; "In this bed Queen Elizabeth may have slept": if you are left cold by such affirmations as these, if you are one of those perverse persons who are interested in facts only in so far as they support or refute theories, then you will never make a good literary man. The more absurd, trivial, and useless the fact, the more tenderly should it be cherished. Of such stuff the choicest literary notes may be made.

Facts-in-themselves, concrete solid little facts that cannot by any conceivable possibility be made to serve a theoretic purpose—what pen will ever describe or explain their charm? Or who will analyze that queer emotion that stirs in every literary heart at the reading of such sentences as these?

"About 1676 or 5, as I was walking through Newgate Street" (the speaker is John Aubrey of happy memory), "I sawe Dame Venetia Digby's bust standing at a stall at the Golden Crosse, a brasier's shop. I perfectly remembered it, but the fire" (the Great Fire, which had destroyed, among other things, Venetia's "sumptuous and stately monument," from which this bust was a piece of salvage) "had gott-off the guilding; but taking notice of it to one that was with me, I could never see it afterwards exposed to the street. They melted it downe. How these curiosities would be quite forgott, did not such idle fellowes as I am putt them down!"

[*Marginalia,* February 20, 1920]

(Proust and Best-Sellers)

"THE REWARDS of literature"—there is something deliciously rotund and episcopal about the phrase. Invested with this swelling title, the thin occasional guineas assume an air of importance—factitious, alas! for when the guineas come to be turned into food and clothing, they prove to be just as scarce and as meager as they were before their ennoblement. For us—poor, but honest, or, rather, intelligent and therefore poor—it is adding ironic insult to injury to call the sweated wages of literature "rewards." But the real rewards of literature, the thousands and ten thousands of which we enviously hear tell, are they inevitably unattainable?

After all, we tell ourselves, we are intelligent enough, we have a sense of humor. Why shouldn't we be able to beat the authors of best-sellers at their own game? It ought not to be insuperably difficult to turn out a few "wholesome love stories" or a volume of Wilcoxian gems. It is only a question of trying.

The genius, whose "genial" works are despised and misunderstood, and who earns his living by writing best-sellers, is not an uncommon character in fiction. But, in real life, does he exist? We have some doubts. There are plenty of people who can counterbalance third-rate journalism with a passable novel; there are few, or none that we know of, who can produce simultaneously works of genuine merit and works of genuine badness. Would it have been possible for Henry James to have made a fortune by throwing off, in his leisure moments, the novels of Nat Gould? Or could Mr. Yeats have paid for the luxury of being a poet by writing "Laugh and the world laughs with you"? We can be morally certain that, however hard he had tried, he would have found the task impossible. But genius is exceptional; it has nothing to do with the case in point, which concerns only poor, but honest men of letters like ourselves, who are neither geniuses nor Garvices, but simply educated persons with a certain measure of intelligence, even of talent. Surely we might, by the expense of a little patience and ingenuity, hatch from our brains the literary geese that should in their turn lay a few golden eggs. But no; if nature has made it impossible for the man of genius to be *pompier*, education has done the same for the honest man of letters. Do what he may, he will never be able to write those wholesome love stories, his play will never run for a thousand and one nights, his rhymes will never be sold in cheap editions.

Readers of M. Proust's enchanting novel will remember how Swann, in what is perhaps the finest episode in the book, finds himself drawn by his unfortunate love affair into a social system revolving round the dinner-table of the Verdurins. The Verdurins—how well we know their English equivalents!—are rich, move in circles that are not the highest, and have intellectual pretensions. Lion-hunters excluded from the best-stocked game preserves, they have collected a menagerie of the mangiest specimens—a second-rate man of science, a professor or two, an indifferent infant prodigy, a bad painter, with a few members of that section of the bourgeoisie which believes itself to be the *intelligentsia*. Into this dismal coterie Swann's deplorable weakness for the fair sex has lured him—Swann, the exquisitely cultured Swann, the aristocrat, Swann, whose intellectual refinement is as sensitive as that of the princess who could not sleep for the crumpled rose-leaf under her mountainous feather-beds. M. Proust has expended all his delicate and elaborate art in describing the discomforts of the situation. We are shown poor Swann faintly and painfully smiling at the Professor's puns, trying not to be too ironic at each exhibition of bad taste, wincing at the crudity (compared with the half-words, the mere suggestions by which his own over-cultured intimates are in the habit of communicating their thoughts) of completed statements, repetitions, and the laboring of obvious ideas.

In the presence of what is really popular in literature and drama, most of us feel rather like Swann among the Verdurins. We suffer from the education which it has been our fortune, or, perhaps, our mischance, to receive. Accustomed to all manner of reticences and restraints, we are constantly and profoundly shocked by the immodesty of the best-sellers and the stage successes. Our delicate mental constitutions are aped by the orgies of sentiment; we shrink as the obvious is rubbed into us, like salt into an open wound. It may be, indeed it almost certainly is the case, that our susceptibilities are too tender. It is true, as Wordsworth said in his Preface to "Lyrical Ballads," that "the human mind is capable of being excited without the application of gross and violent stimulants; and he must have a very faint perception of its beauty and dignity who does not know this, and who does not further know, that one being is elevated above another in proportion as he possesses this capability." But it is also true that a human being may become so much elevated above his fellows that he will finally shrink, not merely from the gross and violent emotions, but from all the obvious primary emotions of whatever sort. He will, in fact, become a highbrow. At the present time we see only too many of these persons, self-elevated to an enormous height above the ordinary level of humanity.

But this is a divagation from our theme. What we have to ask ourselves is this: Is it possible for a Swann to imitate a Verdurin well enough to escape detection? Can a person of high, or even of medium brow suppress his natural susceptibilities, overcome all his disgusts, and write a bestseller? It seems very doubtful. For even if he has successfully made the moral effort, has braved an ordeal which will cost him as much as for a shy man it would to take off his clothes in the street, even if he has brought himself to handle the unpleasant slush of popular sentiment, will he be able to prevent a cloven hoof of irony from peeping through? No; to be done well, these things must be done with love and conviction. And within their category these things must be well done, or else, to the great credit of those who buy, they will not succeed. Love and conviction must go into the work, and love and conviction are precisely the things that the highbrow cannot by any possibility put into it. It looks, alas! as though those glittering rewards of literature were fated to remain for most of us a mirage on our horizon, seductive and unattainable.

[*Marginalia*, March 12, 1920]

(Godwin and Bailey)

TO READ THROUGH the old *Athenaeum*s of ninety years ago is to discover that ours is not the only age in which the proportion of bad books to good ones has been overwhelmingly high. In only one respect had the reviewer of 1830 any advantage over his descendant of 1920: there were fewer books to review. The ratio of bad to good has remained, I should imagine, fairly constant; but where the reviewer of ninety years ago calculated in hundreds we have to think more imperially in terms of thousands and tens of thousands. But even with the comparatively tiny output of those days, the literary journalist of 1830 had his fair share of nonsense to wade through. Looking through the old files of *The Athenaeum*, one is astonished at the dismal quality, the depressing quantity of the bad books.

It was, therefore, with a thrill of pleased recognition that I came upon the name of William Godwin. *Cloudesley: A Tale*, by the author of *Caleb Williams*, was one of the features of the spring list of 1830. *The Athenaeum* greeted the book with a tempered enthusiasm. Godwin in principle and theoretically is admired and respected. He was very nearly a great man. He was a historical figure, a link with the noble past, and though *Political Justice* might have come, in the course of mellowing years, to look a little comic, its author could at least write a fine pure English style:

> The announcement of a new novel by so distinguished a writer as Mr. Godwin [says the reviewer] was welcomed with more indifference than we looked for by the reading world. To us it gave great pleasures of expectation, and we even hoped that the vigor of thought and style which makes "St. Leon" and "Caleb Williams" so delightful, might to some degree reclaim the public taste from those foolish idolatries that now degrade it, when a host of gentlemen, with no materials save effrontery and the Court Guide, undertake to teach the mob how the great live and the wise talk in fashionable and political novels. We remember the breathless interest with which we first hung over Mr. Godwin's pages; the harrowing pathos with which he told the sufferings of the humblest and least attractive characters, the Aeschylean power with which he painted some wretched man struggling against irresistible necessity, condemned, though innocent, to all the pains of guilt, and above all the fervid eloquence that cast a burning splendor around these magnificent conceptions.

Godwin in principle, then, was admirable, and his novel might give the intensest "pleasures of expectation." But when it came to reading *Cloudesley* . . . alas! the reviewer, being an honest man, has to admit that it is an atrocious novel. I have never read *Cloudesley;* nor, unless the secret of indefinitely prolonging human life is discovered within the next few years, do I propose to waste an hour of my brief existence in such a profitless occupation. *St. Leon,* which so much delighted the reviewer of 1830, is one of the books I have tried to read, miserably failing in the attempt. But *Caleb Williams* I have read, and read with pleasure, though not perhaps with all the transports of the reviewer of 1830. Godwin's total inability to draw a character, the impotence of his imagination to comprehend and enter into the chaos of human life—these were defects that made it impossible for him to be a good novelist. But he made up to some extent for these defects by the intensity of his political convictions. *Caleb Williams* is a dramatized essay on the evils of the tyranny of one class over another. "Zounds, how I have been deceived!" cries honest Thomas, when he sees Caleb Williams chained up like a wild beast in the county gaol. "They told me what a fine thing it was to be an Englishman, and about liberty and property and all that there; and I find it is all a flam."

The intensity with which Godwin believed that social life was "all a flam," his passion to show up "Things as they are" (the subtitle of his book), carried him on in triumph: It is the warmth of this intellectual fire that makes the book still readable.

In 1830, when *Cloudesley* made its appearance Godwin was a totally extinct volcano. Forty years before he had been a prophet, a voice, the inspiration of noble spirits; now he was just a harmless and cheerful old gentleman. There are few fates more melancholy and at the same time more absurd than that of the once famous man who lives on to see his ashes carried to the Pantheon and there duly buried and forgotten. Godwin's case reminds one of that even more remarkable example of a man who outlived by a generation the death of his early fame. Philip James Bailey published his *Festus* in 1839, when he was twenty-three years of age; he died in 1902.

Bailey had many of the attributes of greatness, not least among which was his appearance. His bust, taken in 1848, shows us a young man with a more than Shakespearean brow, wide, high and precipitous, large rapt eyes, a mouth set obstinately firm and a mass of hyacinthine hair. (One of the causes, by the way, of the apparent lack, at the present time, of great men lies in the poverty of the contemporary male coiffure. Rich in whiskers, beards, and leonine manes, the great Victorians never failed to look the part; nowadays it is impossible to know a great man when you see one.) Besides the grand appearance, Bailey possesses the grand outlook and the heroic energy of greatness. He was at home in interstellar space, he was familiar with angels and devils; he had spacious views about Man and Destiny, he was not afraid of being didactic ("Where true philosophy presides/Pleasure it is to teach," he remarks with a rather pleasing ingenuousness); and he was not afraid of length. But there was something not quite right about his imagination. Transmuted into verse, his grand ideas and his energy became highly colored fustian. At its best this fustian was very good fustian. There are great gaudy similes and purple passages which, in certain moods, are a pleasure to read. One enjoys, every now and then, to hear of "liquescent plains/Of ever seething flame, where sink and rise/Alp-blebs of fire, vast, vagrant."

At the same time one can easily have too much of this kind of thing. In tenderer and more lyrical moments Bailey could display a luscious facility that makes Moore seem exquisitely refined. Here is one of his songs:

I dreamed of thee, love, in the morn,
And a poet's bright dreamings drew nigh:
I woke, and I laughed them to scorn;
They were black by the blink of thine eye.

I dreamed of thee, love, in the day.
And I wept as I slept o'er thy charms:

I awoke as my dreams went away,
And my tears were all wet on my arms.

It makes one blush to commit such lines, even at secondhand, to paper.

Festus was received with transports by the public of 1839. (*The Athenaeum* raised almost the only inharmonious voice in the general chorus of praise: "The idea is a mere plagiarism of 'Faust' with all its impiety and scarcely any of its poetry.") People might still look at the work if Bailey had been content to leave it as it originally appeared. But no, in the course of a long and leisured life he set himself to make a hundred Miltonic lines grow where only one grew before, so that, when the jubilee edition was published in 1889, *Festus* was a work of forty thousand lines. Thenceforward it was in vain that Bailey adjured humanity in his Envoi:

Read this, world! He who writes is dead to thee,
But still lives in these leaves. He spoke inspired
Night or day, thought came unhelped and undesired
Like blood to the heart. The course of study he
Went through was of the soul-rack. The degree
He took was high.

[*Marginalia*, April 16, 1920]

(Balzac and Social History)

FOR SOME MONTHS NOW, with a few intermissions occasioned by pressure of other business or satiety, I have been devouring the works of Balzac. But "devouring" is too noble and leonine a word. Confronted with the *Comédie Humaine*, one feels like a very small mouse in presence of an enormous moon-like cheese. One gnaws and nibbles, loses courage, sharpens one's teeth, and returns heroically to one's task, and finally, after a long, long time, one has the satisfaction of seeing that the monstrous moon is perceptibly smaller. Another six years, one ventures to hope, and the feat will have been accomplished. But the accomplishment will have required unflagging patience and an undiminished appetite.

But it is not so much of Balzac that I wish to write as of the Balzacian novel in general. Why is it, one wonders, that there have been so few attempts since Balzac's day to imitate the *Comédie Humaine*? In France, practically the only novelist who has set to work with any degree of system to write a social history of his epoch is Zola. In England there has been nobody remotely answering to Balzac. Why? we ask again. One reason is sufficiently obvious. To write a *Comédie Humaine* one needs to have a mind that possesses an enormous, superficial area of sensitiveness. Balzac's most remarkable mental quality was this: that he was sensitive to an extraordinary number of different phases of life at the same time. Minds of this type are not common. Nor are Comédies Humaines. But it is possible, I believe, to find in external circumstances another explanation for the fewness of the attempts to rival Balzac, and an explanation, at the same time, of the fact that England has produced no system of social novels that comes anywhere near to rivaling the Frenchman's grandiose plan.

Balzac's favorite novelist was Sir Walter Scott; and the fact is of some significance. For Balzac's method in the *Comédie Humaine* is the method of the historical novel applied to contemporary life. Looking back over the annals of the past, it is easy to detect the significant form of any given epoch; it is easy, when one can telescope years into seconds, to make slow and obscure changes seem vivid to emphasize the picturesque contrasts between age and age. It is far easier to write an account of England in 1520 than of England in 1920. Of the earlier England one knows everything of significance; of the other almost nothing. But there occur every now and again periods of history when change is so violent and rapid, contrasts so palpably gross, that even contemporaries cannot fail to see what is significant in their own epoch. Such an age invites a social novelist to turn it into historical fiction; it forces upon him the conception of a complete picture. He cannot but think historically.

The age of Balzac was precisely one of those periods. Born a year before the new century, he learned from his elders the story of the Revolution and of the life that preceded it; with his own eyes he saw the glory and downfall of Napoleon. He lived through the Restoration and the Monarchy of July, and in his latest years beheld the birth of the Second Republic. In his half-century of life he had witnessed the invention of the steam engine with its industrial consequences, the discovery of advertisement, the re-discovery of Christianity, and many other new and surprising things. For a man like Balzac, for whom the essence of art was chiaroscuro, violent and picturesque contrast, the first half of the nineteenth century in France was a perfect subject. He and his epoch between them produced the *Comédie Humaine*. But suppose Balzac had been an Englishman. Would he, one wonders, have found in the comparatively calm and undramatic development of England in the nineteenth century the necessary stimulus? The fact that no English novelist of the nineteenth century attempted to do what Balzac did seems to point to the conclusion that to an Anglicized Balzac the notion of the *Comédie Humaine* would never have occurred.

Nothing is unsafer, but nothing, at the same time, is more amusing, than to lay down the law. Shall we then hazard the generalization that in times of slow development the social historian-novelist of the Balzac type will be unknown. In times of rapid and dramatic change he will find the stimulus required to bring him into existence. Even in Zola's time French history, though it lacks the picturesqueness of the Napoleonic era, is still a great deal more dramatic and highly colored than the contemporary history of England.

By every right, according to our modest little literary law, the war of 1914 and the revolutions by which there seems every prospect of its being followed should produce a new Balzac who shall record in fiction the whole social history of this astonishing period. Already the war, making history, as it did, with a dramatic violence which nobody but a blind and paralytic deaf-mute could fail to be conscious of, has produced a vast crop of novels that have recorded, with more or less subtlety, the changes in our habits of life and thought brought about by the catastrophe of 1914. The shock was so rude that every novelist became, for the time being, a social novelist; it was impossible to avoid taking the historical point of view. Sooner or later there will arise a larger mind—tentacular as it were, with feelers spreading far and wide over the whole face of this epoch—and we shall get from it a new *Comédie Humaine*. It will give us the history of our time written from within, a history that shall be true in the intimate immediate details and true in the broad significant outlines. It was possible to write such a history in France between 1830 and 1850. It has once more begun to be possible today, and possible not only in France but throughout all Europe. If Russia should ever again get enough food to allow her to think of anything but immediate animal needs, what fabulous reincarnations of Balzac may we not expect from her! A Balzac interested in the human soul, as the original Balzac, too easily content with the picturesque spectacle, with mere political movement, never was. Meanwhile there is nothing to do but to wait—patiently.

[*Marginalia*, July 23, 1920]

(Aristocracy and Literature)

HISTORIANS, literary and political, always dwell with a peculiar complacence on the achievement of those great men in the past who have in any way, and however shadowily, anticipated our modern discoveries. Milton was somehow an evolutionist before Darwin, Roger Bacon invented the motor-car, Shakespeare foresaw the British Empire, Tennyson had prophetic visions of the Zeppelin. These are facts over which we love to linger. And I remember a certain quatercentenary lecture on Leonardo. A large and highly polished audience had listened in polite apathy to an analysis of one of the most extraordinary intellects that have ever existed. The lecturer then let fall the fact that Leonardo had forestalled Mr. Churchill in the invention of the Tank. Applause, sudden, spontaneous, loud, and prolonged, burst from the whole assembly. The incident impressed me unforgettably. Why do we like to linger over these prophecies and foreshadowings? Surely, because it satisfies a rather childish vanity. For it was of us that these great men were prophetically thinking; we are the fulfilment of their dreams. We feel ourselves superior to them. Leonardo dimly dreamed of Tanks; we go for joy-rides in them at Southend. Argal, we are better than Leonardo. Mr. H. G. Wells is better informed than Shakespeare. Argal. . . . And so on and so forth. We are the bright consummate flower of ages of growth; these wise magians of the past scented our fragrance from afar and had a glimpse of our splendor.

I have been reading recently what seems to me one of the most somberly prophetic books of the nineteenth century, I mean Balzac's *Les Paysans*. Many of the problems that seemed to Balzac of prime importance have become, in the twentieth century, little more than historical curiosities. But the problem of *Les Paysans* is still very much with us, grown huger and a hundred times more complicated than it was when Balzac wrote of it in the faraway thirties and forties of last century. This story of the peasants' hatred of the rich landed proprietor and of the incessant secret guerrilla war they wage against him is the classic of its type, the first and best of the novels that have taken the conflict of the classes as their theme. It abounds with defect. The proportion of political tract to work of art is far too high; the author's asides and commentaries are infuriatingly copious. But the book is none the less a prodigious piece of work. Balzac has seen the whole problem in all its significance, and dramatized it with an unrivaled force.

Unlike almost every other writer who has touched the theme of the struggle between the rich and the poor, Balzac is wholeheartedly on the side of the rich. From Godwin to Mr. Galsworthy the sociologists have always espoused the cause of the oppressed many against the oppressing few. Caleb Williams has been reincarnated and re-martyred a hundred times over. But Balzac reverses the medal. He shows us the traditional tyrant being tyrannized over, the rich landlord persecuted by the peasants, and in the end destroyed by them. And he demands that we shall sympathize with the bloodsucker and beware of his traditional victim.

Balzac was not a democrat. His royalistic conservatism was due partly to his upbringing, partly to his native snobbishness. But chiefly he desired to preserve the old aristocratic order of things for the sake of what an aristocracy makes possible, namely culture, civilization. When General Montcornet is forced to abandon Les Aigues the peasants fall upon the property and divide it up among themselves. The great old house is pulled down, and what were once the gardens and the noble park become a patchwork of small gardens. Something grand and splendid is destroyed, and something sordid and small takes its place. Balzac feared and hated democracy because he loved culture and art and grandeur and the other luxuries of the leisured rich. Culture and the beautiful amenities of civilization have always been paid for by slavery in one form or another. Balzac, who heartily despised the philanthropists of his age, considered that the price was not excessive, and that it was right that a lower class should exist and work in order that culture might concomitantly exist in the higher class. The guerrilla fighting of 1840 has become an open class war, and the many, as was inevitable, are steadily gaining ground against the few. Les Aigues and its inhabitants, with all their peculiar culture, are doomed, as Balzac foresaw. It remains to be seen what new form of culture, if any, will take its place.

The most important function of an aristocracy is to be so secure in its position that it is impervious to general public opinion, so secure that it can afford to tolerate eccentricity and be hospitable to new and unusual ideas. The American plutocracy is not an aristocracy because its position is precarious. It cannot afford to tolerate eccentricity; heresy means excommunication. But in Europe the tradition of eccentricity still survives, though with ever-decreasing strength, in the leisured class. Its members do not risk serious persecution for nonconformity; their secure position protects them from ordinary public opinion, so that they can think, and to a great extent act, how they like with impunity. Not many of them do, of course; but that there should at least be an attitude of tolerance to heresy is of prime importance. Moreover, they actually extend their protection to eccentric and heretical members of other classes. The aristocracy is a sort of Red Indian Reservation, where the savages of the mind are permitted to live in their own way, untroubled and relatively free from persecution. In a little while the advancing armies of democracy will sweep across their borders and these happy sanctuaries will be no more. Les Aigues—the big house, the gardens, the park, the spacious and leisured life, the polite conversations and platonic passion, between the literary man and the lady of the manor—will utterly disappear, and the small holder will inherit the land. And eccentricity, new ideas, culture—one doesn't see much room in the new world for these occupations of prigs and madmen. The prospect is melancholy, dims one's liberal ardors.

In a characteristic article that appeared in a recent number of the *Yale Review,* Mr. H. L. Mencken deplores the absence in America of anything approaching an aristocracy. He puts down all the defects in American literature to "the lack of a civilized aristocracy, secure in its position, animated by an intelligent curiosity, skeptical of all facile generalizations, superior to the sentimentality of the mob and delighting in the battle of ideas for its own sake." There are in America no spiritual Reservations for the Red Indians of the spirit. Hemmed in on one side by the plutocracy and on the other side by the mob, the intelligent are driven either into feeble anarchy or else become tame Professors. The anarchists are futile wasters of spirit; the Professors too readily believe that whatever is, is right. (New England, says Mr. Mencken, true to his inveterate hatred of the Professor, "began its history as a slaughter-house of ideas, and it is today not easily distinguishable from a cold-storage plant.") Mr. Mencken is always the controversialist, and as such a little inclined to picturesqueness and an over-statement of his case. But his main contention is sound—that intellectual life has hitherto always depended on the existence of an aristocracy.

[*Marginalia*, August 27, 1920]

(Alfieri)

IS IT POSSIBLE for a man to say, like the little boy in Lewis Carroll's poem, "I want to be a poet, I want to write in rhyme," and, by wanting hard enough, to succeed, not merely in writing in rhyme, but also in being a poet? Can one become an artist by sheer force of will? If the universe were in the least moral, it certainly would be possible. For, morally, "la volonté peut et doit être un sujet d'orgueil bien plus que le talent." It is profoundly shocking that a man, casually endowed with talent and wholly lacking in self-discipline, should be able to do far greater things than one who has will and faith and patience and industry, but has not had the luck to be endowed with natural aptitude. There is almost nothing that concentrated will cannot accomplish; if we are to believe certain spiritualists it is possible to move furniture by will-power and to float in the air by simply desiring it. But nobody has yet succeeded in becoming a great artist by dint of will alone. The burning desire and faith of Benjamin Robert Haydon were of no avail against the inexorable fact of his second-rateness. And if will were enough, Ben Jonson would be as great as Shakespeare. But there is no more extraordinary instance of a man trying to will his way to literary greatness than that of Alfieri, who came very near to making himself into a tragic poet.

The life of Victor Alfieri by himself is one of the great autobiographies of the world. It is a sharp, firmly drawn picture of a very interesting and very eccentric character. In his delineation of himself Alfieri displays all the cool precision of the eighteenth-century psychologists. He studies himself in his strength and his weaknesses, subjects all his actions to the analysis of reason and explains them, generalizes them into sage reflections on the relationship between the instincts and passions and the higher faculties.

Alfieri was born in 1746 at Asti in Piedmont, then a part of the kingdom of Sardinia. His parents were noble and rich, but like many others of their class, both before and since that time, were of the opinion that gentlemen have no need to be pedants, and that wealth and nobility are qualities sufficiently brilliant in themselves to be able to dispense with the added graces of education. They were, however, persuaded into sending young Victor to the principal educational establishment in Piedmont, the Academy at Turin. In this institution Alfieri passed eight years and emerged into the world at the age of eighteen in a state of almost pre-lapsarian ignorance. He was incapable of speaking or writing correctly any language, whether ancient or modern. Latin, of course, he had studied continuously during those eight years; but then we have all studied Latin for eight years, and we know what that means. As for a native language, he did not possess one. A barbarous un-Tuscan Italian, streaked with French, was his vehicle of expression. Of real Italian and pure French he was ignorant. The Royal Academy of Turin had let loose upon the world a very formidable young barbarian—a savage with fierce yearnings towards some unknown civilization, a minor poet whose legitimate channel of expression was dammed up and who could only give vent to his emotions by violent and restless action. And vent them he did.

Throughout the sixties and seventies of the eighteenth century the inhabitants of every country in Europe were astonished by the spectacle of a ferocious young Italian with long red hair posting along through their midst as though the devil were after him. The faster he could go, the more he was delighted. In England he spent eight hours a day in the saddle or on the box of a chaise with the finest trotters of the country between the shafts. In Sweden he delighted in sledging, not only for speed, but also because the intense cold of the Northern winter exhilarated him like a strange wine; for he loved extremes and could not abide anything middling. Proud as a fiend and dumb as a beast, he associated with his fellow-creatures as rarely as he could, preferring, whenever he was absolutely forced to halt for a while, to sit bearishly alone, plunged in a melancholy stupor. At heart he was ashamed of the black ignorance that made him fear to associate with his equals; but the shame generally took the form of hatred and contempt for those who possessed the acquirements which he lacked. When he emerged from his solitude it was generally to associate with women, towards whom he was drawn with such a violence of desire that in later years, when he wanted to devote himself to study, he had to order his servant to tie him to his chair for fear he should break loose in pursuit of unworthy loves.

Time passed, and gradually this insensate restlessness abated. Alfieri began to see a little more clearly what he wanted to make of his life; he wanted at any cost and in any way to be a great man. Plutarch's *Lives,* which he took to reading when he was nearly twenty-five, intoxicated him. "Reading of the fine actions of these great men, I would start up with tears of rage and grief streaming from my eyes at the mere thought that I had been born in Piedmont, under such a Government and a time when nothing great could be done or said, and when, at the most, a man might only barrenly think or feel great things." Heroic action in the Italy of 1770 was unthinkable. There was nothing for it but to be heroic in literature. Alfieri decided to be a tragic poet. It was necessary, first of all, to have a language in which to write; Alfieri settled in Florence and applied himself to the task of learning Tuscan. It was necessary to have a certain culture; he hired masters to teach him the Latin he was supposed to have learned at the Turin Academy. It was finally necessary to study the Grand Passion in its more heroic aspects at first hand, and it was at this moment, almost providentially, that the Countess of Albany made her appearance on Alfieri's horizon. At the time when they met, her husband, the Young Pretender, was an old and disgusting man, who had little or nothing to do but to drink and maltreat his wife. Alfieri came as a liberator and a consoler. The story of their love is well known.

Meanwhile, Alfieri was writing tragedies with extraordinary industry and perseverance. He had found a language and mastered the art of versification. Fourteen dramas, written and rewritten, hammered, filed, and polished again and again, testified to his determination to be a great man. Once started upon the poetical road, he did not turn back; the old barbarian was dead. But not quite dead, for once, in the midst of his studies, he was seized by an irresistible longing to go back for a moment to the old life. So urgent was the desire that he was forced to rush incontinently to England, where he purchased fourteen magnificent horses—one for each of his tragedies which he proceeded, with infinite pains and expense, to lead back with him to Italy. Horses, women, and the Muse of tragedy— these were his three great passions, and the passion for horses was probably the strongest. But the passion for the Muse was a rational, a voluntary passion, and Alfieri had the strength to make it triumph. "I want to be a poet, I want to write in rhyme." But, alas! who reads these fourteen tragedies now? I have tried, but, it must be confessed, without marked success.

[*Marginalia*, October 8, 1920]

(Bacon's Symbolism)

ALL THINGS are profoundly symbolical to those who are ready to believe they are. Men have no tails; neither have guinea-pigs. Death's-heads appear to grin ironically. The stars of heaven fall into patterns of strange and dubious significance; the Great Bear is also a plough, a wain, and a dipper. In the Bestiaries the leopard is made the symbol of Christ because of his habit of sleeping in his den and only waking up after three days, when he exhales a breath so piercingly sweet that all living creatures are drawn towards him and so become his prey. In some Bestiaries the lion also symbolizes the founder of our religion; in others both lion and leopard stand for the devil. All is profoundly mysterious in symbology, and the art of parable and allegory is hard to learn, because there are so many masters, each interpreting the same phenomenon in his own way. Stones will preach as many sermons as there are Jaqueses to contemplate them; the running brooks contain a whole Bodleian. To see the world in terms of symbolism is one of humanity's chronic weaknesses. One must be immensely sophisticated to believe that things are what they seem to be— opaque objects, interesting in themselves and for themselves, and not transparent windows through which to gaze on further and more significant realities beyond.

If men have always loved to find symbols in inanimate things, how much more have they tried to allegorize literature! Not long ago I had occasion to quote the complaint of one of the Obscure Men: that these new-fangled Humanists understood nothing of the spiritual, allegorical, anagogical, and symbolical meanings of the ancient text they professed so much to admire. They were content with the mere muddy literal sense of what they had before them. How much more exciting Ovid's *Metamorphoses* become when you know that under all these tales lies some profound theological truth! How edifying is the Song of Solomon when the commentators have made apparent its real meaning! The Middle Ages abounded in symbologists. Nor was the Renaissance exempt from the symbolizing tendency, for all the Obscure Man's complaints. The symbolical view of the universe still prevailed, and much of the science of the period is unduly complicated and unduly simplified by the pleasing microcosm theory, which insists that man is the symbol and equivalent in miniature of the universe. Nor did the men of the Renaissance neglect to look for symbol and allegory in the literature of the past. Holy and classical writ were still the object of the symbologist's close scrutiny. Even the most enlightened men indulged in the delightful occupation of making two meanings grow where only one grew before—among them the greatest English apostle of enlightenment, Francis Bacon himself.

Bacon's *De Sapientia Veterum* is a book to which I have always been

particularly attached. I have a great weakness for wisdom. The sage's attitude of grave detachment from the world on which he comments with so
mature a justness of judgment is, to me, profoundly sympathetic. From
Solomon to Anatole France, all the sages are dear to me, and none dearer
than Bacon, whose Sapience of the Ancients is a fruit of wisdom so ripe
that it seems to drop from his mind spontaneously like a monster mulberry
grown weary of hanging on its tree. It was Bacon's modesty that made him
call his book the "Wisdom of the Ancients"; for the wisdom in it is entirely his own. All that the ancients contribute is a series of entertaining
myths, which Bacon allegorizes into sapience. It is unfortunate that Bacon
should have chosen to write this book in Latin. "I do conceive," he said of
his own Essays, "that the Latin volume of them (being in the universal language) may last as long as books last." He conceived wrongly and today
the ordinary reader will prefer to study *De Sapientia Veterum* in Spedding's admirable translation.

Like almost everyone else in the world before the invention of scientific
history and anthropology, Bacon believed that a great primordial civilization had existed in prehistoric times—a civilization whose accumulated
wisdom has been passed down to Greece and Rome in the veiled form of
allegorical fables. As an interpreter of these myths, he was only restoring
the ancient wisdom. But he is not a fanatical partisan of his theory. "Upon
the whole," he says, "I conclude with this: the wisdom of the primitive
ages was either great or lucky: great if they knew what they were doing
and invented the figure to shadow the meaning; lucky, if without meaning
or intending it they fell upon matter which gives occasion to such worthy
contemplations." Nor is he unaware of the dangers of allegorical interpretation:

> I know very well what pliant stuff fable is made of, how freely it will
> follow any way you please to draw it, and how idly with a little dexter
> ity and discourse of wit meanings which it was never meant to bear
> may be plausibly put upon it. Neither have I forgotten that there has
> been old abuse of the thing in practice; that many, wishing only to gain
> the sanction and reverence of antiquity for doctrines and inventions of
> their own, have tried to twist the fables of the poets into that sense;
> and that this is neither a modern vanity nor a rare one, but old of
> standing and frequent in use, that Chrysippus long ago, interpreting
> the oldest poets after the manner of an interpreter of dreams, made
> them out to be Stoics.

If he had lived today, Bacon might have added a further instance of the
perverse ingenuity of interpreters of past literature—the ingenuity of those
who interpret Shakespeare so as to make him out to be Bacon.

Bacon's interpretation of the classical myths is sometimes moral and political, sometimes scientific. The scientific interpretations are more curious than interesting. "Cupid, or the Atom," and "Proteus, or Matter," have become, in the course of time, simply fantastic. But the moral and political interpretations are still admirably wise. Some of the shorter interpretations are the prototype of those "Characters" of which seventeenth-century writers from Overbury to Flecknoe produced so many. Here, for example, is the character of Narcissus, symbol of self-love:

> In this fable are represented the dispositions, and the fortunes too, of those persons who from consciousness either of beauty or some other gift with which nature, unaided by any industry of their own, has graced them, fall in love as it were with themselves. For with this state of mind there is commonly joined an indisposition to appear much in public or engage in business; because business would expose them to many neglects and scorns, by which their minds would be dejected and troubled. Therefore they commonly live a solitary, private and shadowed life; with a small circle of chosen companions, all devoted admirers, who assent like as echo to everything they say, and entertain them with mouth-homage; till being by such habits gradually depraved, and besotted with self-admiration, they fall into such a sloth and listlessness that they grow utterly stupid and lose all vigor and alacrity. And it was a beautiful thought to choose the flower of spring as an emblem of characters like this: characters which, in the opening of their career, flourish and are talked of, but disappoint in maturity the promise of their youth.

Among the more elaborate and ingenious interpretations "Dionysus, or Desire," must be mentioned. Dionysus is represented as being always accompanied by satyrs. Why?

There is a humor in making those ridiculous demons dance about the chariot: for every passion produces motions in the eyes, and, indeed, in the whole countenance and gesture, which are uncomely, unsettled, skipping, and deformed: insomuch that when a man under the influence of any passion, such as anger, scorn, love, or the like, seems most grand and imposing in his own eyes, to the lookers-on he appears unseemly and ridiculous.

[*Marginalia*, November 19, 1920]

The Cry for a Messiah in the Arts

IT IS SEVEN MONTHS since I left London for Italy. Seven months—and here I am, a week or two after my return, as much at home in the place, as deeply involved, body and mind, in it as ever I was. I have the impression already that I have never been away; the long delightful months of life in Italy might never have been. The gap between London and London has magically closed and I feel as though I had been continuously here.

It is a feeling which is encouraged by the fact that everything in London—the London of literature and literary journalism, of painting and the theater—is exactly the same as when I left it in March. No, not exactly the same; for I have the impression that everything has just a little decayed, has advanced a little further down that road of deterioration on which it had already started when I left. Take the literary papers, for example: they are perceptibly worse and duller than they were. It was the old *Athenaeum* that Stevenson apostrophized with his "Golly, what a paper!" Today the *London Mercury* evokes the same pained exclamation—"Golly, *what* a paper!" There is no more to be said—except, perhaps, that its editor, Mr. J. C. Squire, has sailed for America on a missionary journey to convert the inhabitants of Those States into readers of the *London Mercury.* As for the *Athenaeum,* that venerable journal, after passing through phases of brilliance and phases of the profoundest dullness—and its penultimate phase, from 1919 to 1921, under the editorship of John Middleton Murry, was one of the brightest moments in its long career—has now withered into the literary supplement of the *Nation.*

London decays slowly. That, at least, is my impression. There is nobody large enough in literature or in painting to do the large simple obvious things, and do them well. It takes a Shakespeare to turn the feuilleton theme of *Romeo and Juliet* into a masterpiece. In London today we have nothing between the people who turn feuilleton themes of love, ambition, jealousy, and sin into feuilletons, and the sensitive, talented artists who know themselves too small to treat the feuilleton themes well, and so take refuge in the minor unimportant second-hand themes provided by culture and an undue introspection. There is no Shakespeare to fill the gulf; there is only H. G. Wells. . . . Living in these circumstances, one finds oneself haunted by the expectant hope of a messiah, of somebody new and prodigious, who will appear suddenly, out of nowhere, pronouncing a new unheard-of word of illumination. I have been feeling these messianic longings vaguely for a long time past, ever since President Wilson proved by emphatic demonstration that he was not the man we wanted. And now returning from a six-months' sojourn in the intellectual desert of Italy to a civilization that seems to be steadily decaying, I find the messianic expectation stirring more than ever impatiently within me. In the eastern skies of literature there is not a sign of a new strange star. Young poets and novelists, worthy, respectable, intelligent, sensitive, make their constant appearance. But none of them are so much as second cousins of the expected messiah. Perhaps the nearest approach to that surely not impossible personage is a youthful prodigy, a certain Peter Quennell, whose poems in the recently published *Anthology of Public School Verse* open a new chapter in the history of infant phenomenalism. Whether this prodigy is to ripen into maturity or to perish green, time alone will show.

Infant Phenomena are not, in themselves, particularly interesting; their potentialities are what matter. The history of child art teems with genius. One might even generalize and assert that all children are geniuses up to the age of, say, six or seven. A very few—Peter Quennell is one of them— retain their genius till they are fifteen or sixteen, while at most only one in five million grows up to be a genius at thirty.

So much for literature. What of the theater and the plastic arts? I can think of nothing of tremendous significance. The little band of Russian entertainers, whose banner bears the strange device of *Chauve-Souris,* have come over from Paris and have roused some of our dramatic critics to a loud enthusiasm. In due time, no doubt, M. Balieff and his troupe will cross the Atlantic and you will have an opportunity of judging them for yourselves. Personally, I find the *Chauve-Souris* an overrated institution. Its merits are the great good taste of the décors and the grouping, the admirable stage management, and the almost machine-like perfection of the performers. But, when all is said, the *Chauve-Souris* has only done well what the Russian Ballet has done a good deal better. Take the décors, for example. The Russian scenes designed for the *Chauve-Souris* by Soudeikine are certainly charming and tasteful and amusing; but as works of art they cannot be compared with the really grandiose creations of Goncharova and Larionov[2] for the *Children's Tales.*

Again, the historical reconstructions of the *Chauve-Souris* are often brilliant; but there is nothing so finely imaginative on M. Balieff's stage as the Italian eighteenth century of *The Good-Humoured Ladies,* or Picasso's astounding evocation of Spain in *The Three-Cornered Hat.*

The fundamental defect of the *Chauve-Souris* lies in its remoteness from real emotion of any kind. It makes art out of art instead of out of life. It is sophisticated and literary to the last and most hopeless degree. It lives, not on genuine emotions, but on allusions and evocations. Let us take a concrete example. Two young ladies come on to the stage and sing some of the sentimental songs of Glinka.[3] Excellent! The sentimental songs of Glinka are the expression of a quite genuine emotion. But M. Balieff insists on complicating and weakening the emotion by dressing up the ladies in *mil huit cent trente* dresses, setting them against a romantic back-

2. Natalia Goncharova (1881–1962). Russian-born French painter and set designer for Diaghilev's ballets. Mikhail Larionov (1881–1964). Russian painter and set designer.
3. Mikhail Glinka (1800–1857). Russian composer.

ground, and adding as a piece of furniture in one corner of the stage a whiskered young man, clothed in a waisted black coat and tight trousers, as a symbol of the George-Sandian romanticism which it has now begun to be fashionable to laugh at and admire. As a result, no emotion comes over but a faint literary amusement tempered with a slightly sloppy touch of sentimentality.

The best things are undoubtedly the frankly comic items, such as the parade of Wooden Soldiers, the Italian Opera, played by marionettes, Katinka dancing the polka, and the Three Huntsmen. But "good" and "bad" are not the right terms in which to criticize the *Chauve-Souris*. At its best it is "amusing," at its worst it is "tiresome." Those are the two poles on which, like so much of modern art, it turns.

The other theatrical events have been the production of Bernard Shaw's *Heartbreak House* at the Court and of Oscar Asche's[4] *Cairo* at His Majesty's. Both, I believe, have already appeared in New York.

Shaw's comedy has met with a good deal of disapproval from the critics, and it is true that these gentlemen have this much justification for their harsh judgments, that the play was not particularly well acted at the Court. But *Heartbreak House* is not one of the plays that bad actors can destroy. It triumphantly got the better of its interpreters—so, at least, it seemed to me.

As for *Cairo*—well, you know all about *Cairo*. It is the old, old story, old as the remote first night of *Chu Chin Chow*—the story of Oscar Asche in the Gorgeous East.

The art exhibitions are beginning again. Nevinson[5] has finally given himself away as a painter in a one-man show at the Leicester Galleries. His pictures in this exhibition are nothing but a series of facile essays in a dozen different styles of painting. Nevinson's artistic qualities are vigor, ease, and a knowledge of how to be effective. As an illustrator of battlefields, a war correspondent working in paint, he was admirable.

But as a painter of pictures that are not illustrations, he is a failure. One comes away from this exhibition wishing that he would stick to artistic journalism and the designing of posters.

The London Group exhibition at the Mansard Gallery was also a rather depressing affair. Several of the best painters in the group—such as Anrep and Gertler—were not exhibiting, and the pictures that were shown, competent and serious and well intentioned though they were, were mostly a little lifeless and uninteresting. The world of painting awaits its messiah, like all the other worlds of today. The French theorists, for all

---

4. John Oscar Asche (1872–1936). Australian actor and playwright.
5. Christopher Richard Nevinson (1880–1946). English artist.

their prodigious skill and knowledge and intelligence, do not give us what we want. Still less do their English followers, such as Duncan Grant, Vanessa Bell, and Roger Fry.[6] Still less again, the painters who have not even the French tradition to help in some sort to compensate for their fundamental lack of genius. The best things at the London Group were the Grants, the Bells, and the Thérèse Lessores. The best—but when one compares them in one's mind with some really good picture, they look, alas, a little foolish. But then we all look foolish if we start the comparison game.

[*Vanity Fair,* January 1922]

The Modern Spirit and a Family Party

"IT IS ONLY in literature that the academic tradition survives. No one dreams of taking the academic seriously in painting, sculpture or music." Mr. Osbert Sitwell,[7] the author of this remark, is one of those who make it their business not to take the academicians seriously. He throws stones at the singing birds whose nest is in the *London Mercury* and elsewhere: he waves loud indecorous rattles at them while they are warbling.

Mr. Sitwell's latest bird-scaring exploits are recorded in the pages of a little tract called *Who Killed Cock Robin?*—a pamphlet in which the academics and the nature-and-water poets are dealt with in an agreeably lively fashion. Read, for example, his paragraphs on the dreary, derivative nature poetry which still gets poured out in such enormous quantities, for no better reason than that Wordsworth once wrote some very beautiful poems about natural objects. Leading off with a quotation from one of the song-birds of the *London Mercury,* "The Nightjar spins his pleasant note," he goes on:

> Poetry is not the monopoly of the lark-lovers nor of those who laud the nightjar, any more than it belongs to the elephant or the macaw. Because a good poem has grown out of the emotion felt by a poet who realized a lark or a green tree, it does not follow that other verse writers, by babbling continually of larks and green trees, will write good poems. The lark has outstayed its welcome and migrated. It may return again one day. Many young poets have a bird in their bonnet. One swallow does not make a poem.

6. Duncan James Grant (1885–1978). Scottish painter and member of Roger Fry's Omega Workshops and the later London Group. Roger Eliot Fry (1866–1934). English artist and critic. Vanessa Bell (1879–1961). English painter and elder sister of Virginia Woolf.

7. Sir Osbert Sitwell (1892–1969). English author.

This is admirably put. *Who Killed Cock Robin?* is the brightest piece of anti-academic propaganda that has appeared for a long time. Propaganda is important and the Sitwells—for Mr. Osbert Sitwell has a brother and a sister—have a special significance as propagandists. But propaganda is only theoretical doctrine and the tree is known by its fruit, the artistic creed by its works. The Sitwells practice the anti-academism that they preach, and from their rival eyrie in *Wheels* they whistle a counterblast to the strains that issue from the *Mercury*. Their poetry has an intrinsic significance quite apart from any propagandist values. It is worthwhile examining it in some special detail; for it is in many respects very typical of the contemporary spirit. But before we go any further, we must ask ourselves a question: What is this contemporary spirit?

We live today in a world that is socially and morally wrecked. Between them, the war and the new psychology have smashed most of the institutions, traditions, creeds, and spiritual values that supported us in the past. Dadaism represents, in the sphere of art, that complete disintegration of values. Dada denies everything; even art itself, that last idol which we all tried so pathetically hard to keep standing when everything else—the soul, morality, patriotism, religion—has been laid low, even art itself was assaulted by Dada and smashed.

Dada was an exhilarating spectacle when it first appeared on the scene. One enjoyed it as one enjoys the sight of crockery being smashed by a music hall comedian; it gratified that childish love of destruction which lurks in the hearts of all of us. But after a while this crockery smashing grew a little tedious. It was time to pick up the bits and make something new. The only question was: what? The question still hangs over us. What is the new artistic synthesis going to be? It is too early to be able to answer definitely. But one can guess. The work of the Sitwells and a few others in England, of Cocteau, Morand, Aragon, MacOrland,[8] and the rest of them in France, helps one to make that guess. The new synthesis that will reassemble, in an artistic whole, the shattered values of our post-war world, the synthesis that will reflect the disintegration in an artistic unity, will surely be a comic synthesis. The social tragedy of these last years has gone too far and in its nature and origin is too profoundly stupid to be represented tragically. And the same is true of the equally complicated and devastating mental tragedy of the breakup of old traditions and values. The only possible synthesis is the enormous farcical buffoonery of a Rabelais or an Aristophanes—a buffoonery which, it is important to note, is capable of being as beautiful and as grandiose as tragedy. For the great comics,

8. Paul Morand (1889–1975). French writer and diplomat. Louis Aragon (1897–1983). French writer and Surrealist. Pierre MacOrland, pseud. of Pierre Dumarchey (1881–1970). French novelist and poet.

like the two already mentioned, like Chaucer, like the Shakespeare of
Falstaff, and the Balzac of *Contes Drôlatiques,* like Goya and Daumier,
are those who, almost miraculously, combine the hugely, the earthily
grotesque with the delicately and imaginatively beautiful. One of these
days we shall see the new Rabelais putting all the broken bits together in
an enormous comic whole. Meanwhile, we have his forerunners who are
already adumbrating the nature of his future achievement.

In the light of this digression into generalities, let us proceed to examine the particular case of the Sitwells. The best, the most finished writer of
the three is certainly the sister, Miss Edith Sitwell.[9] She has evolved and
brought to queer, disquieting perfection a very individual style of her own.
One can think of nothing that is quite comparable to her glassy brilliance,
her wit, her beautifully grotesque expression of thought and emotion. On
a small scale—for Miss Sitwell is a minor poet who does not attempt to be
universal in scope—she has achieved that comic synthesis of which we
have spoken. Read for example the astonishing nonsense rhymes in her
last published work *Façade.*

Jumbo asleep!
Grey leaves, thickfurred,
At his ears keep
Conversations blurred.
Thicker than hide
Is the trumpeting water;
Don Pasquito's bride
And his youngest daughter
Watch the leaves
Elephantine grey;
What is it grieves
In the torrid day?
Is it the animal
World that snores,
Harsh and inimical
In sleepy pores?
And why should the spined flowers
Red as a soldier
Make Don Pasquito
Seem still mouldier?

9. Dame Edith Sitwell (1887–1964). English poet.

All Leconte de Lisle[1] is in that nonsense tropical forest and what a wealth of Wordsworthian philosophy is telescoped into those four last lines! "Why should the spined flowers red as a soldier make Don Pasquito seem still mouldier?" This is the twentieth-century version of:

Sweet is the lore which Nature brings;
Our Meddling intellect
Mis-shapes the beauteous forms of things—
We murder to dissect.

These poems in her little *Façade* volume were written by Miss Sitwell for recitation through a megaphone to musical accompaniment; and they are consequently less polished, have less literary brilliance than other works intended for perusal in the calm of the library. Read, for example, her "Lady with the Sewing Machine":

Across the fields as green as spinach,
Cropped as close as Time to Greenwich,
Stands a high house: if at all,
Spring comes like a Paisley shawl
Patternings meticulous
And youthfully ridiculous.
In each room the yellow sun
Shakes like a canary, run
On run, roulade and watery trill—
Yellow, meaningless and shrill.
Face as white as any clock's.
Cased in parsley-dark curled locks,
All day long you sit and sew,
Stitch life down for fear it grow,
Stitch life down for fear we guess
At the hidden ugliness.
Dusty voice that throbs with heat,
Hoping with its steel-thin beat
To put stitches in my mind,
Make it tidy, make it kind;
You shall not! I'll keep it free,
Though you turn earth, sky and sea
To a patchwork quilt to keep
Your mind snug and warm in sleep.

1. Charles Marie Leconte de Lisle (1818–1894). French poet.

There is still much in Miss Sitwell's work which is merely the contemporary disintegration unsynthesized. There are poems which are no more than records of sensations, poems that are compounded merely of colored lights and restlessness. But there are others, and a respectable number of them, in which the broken bits have been worked, by a process of intellectual or emotional unification, into a patterned whole—fantastic, grotesque, and beautiful.

Mr. Sacheverell Sitwell[2] is potentially a more considerable poet than his sister; but his achievement still lags behind his conceptions. He aims at nothing short of a huge comic synthesis of Rabelaisian dimensions. That is, at any rate, what one would gather from his recently published *Dr. Donne and Garguntua* and *Parade Virtues for a Dying Gladiator*. A certain diffuseness of speech and of thought prevents these poems from completely "coming off." His most successful achievements have been in minor poems. I cannot refrain from quoting his beautiful "Fountains":

> This night is pure and clear as thrice refinéd silver.
> Silence, the cape of Death, lies heavy
> Round the bare shoulders of the hills.
> Faint throbs and murmurs
> At moments growing to mutter, then subsiding,
> Fill the night with mystery and panic.
> The honey-tonguéd arguings of fountains
> Stir the air with flutes and gentle voices.
>
> The graven fountain-masks suffer and weep—
> Curved with a smile, the poor mouths
> Clutch at a half-remembered song,
> Striving to forget the agony of ever laughing—
> Laughing while they hear the secrets
> Echoed from the depths of Earth beneath them.
>
> This half-remembered song,
> This flow of sad-restrained laughter
> Jars with the jets of youthful water
> Springing from the twisted masks;
> For this is but the birth of water;
> And singing joyfully
> It springs upon the world
> And wanders ceaselessly

2. Sacheverell Sitwell (1897–1988). English writer and art critic.

Along its jewelled valleys to the sea,
Rattling like rolls of drums
The shells and pebbles down its bed.

The endless argument of water ceases
A few drops fall heavily, splashing on the marble:
A sultan with his treasures
Seeking to gain the goodwill of his love
Pouring before her chains of crackling pearls
And weeping heavy jealous tears
Because she will not hear him.

This and a few other short poems are perhaps the most complete works of art Mr. Sacheverell Sitwell has produced. But the later long poems aiming, as they do, at a large, philosophical, comic synthesis are more important in design and conception, if not so completely finished as works of art. When Mr. Sitwell completely realizes these conceptions, something of real importance will have been achieved.

Mr. Osbert Sitwell, the principal propagandist of anti-academism, is at his best in what we may call Applied Poetry—in satire, in occasional pieces, in wit and diatribe. It is a long time since satire has been practiced in England, but the author of *Mrs. Kinfoot* and the political pieces has shown that it is not a lost art. I quote a few lines from his admirable *Sheep-Song*.

We are the greatest sheep in the world,
There are no sheep like us.
We come of an imperial bleat;
Our voices,
Trembling with music,
Call to our lambs oversea.
With us they crash across continents.

We will not heed the herdsman
For they warned us,
"Do not stampede."
Yet we were forced to do so.
Never will we trust a herdsman again.

Then the black lamb asked,
Saying, "Why did we start this glorious Gadarene descent?"
And the herd bleated angrily,
"We went in with clean feet,

And we will come out with empty heads . . .
We are stampeding to end stampedes.
We are fighting for lambs who are never likely to be born."

[*Vanity Fair,* August 1922]

Marie Laurencin: A Woman of Genius

IT IS IN the purely decorative applied arts that women have done most. In early times it was the women who stayed at home to practice the useful arts and crafts, while the men were abroad in the fields or at the chase.

Such arts as weaving, pottery, embroidery, and the like undoubtedly owe much of the beauty and elegance they possess to the inspiration of the women who originally practiced them. One may safely say, indeed, that in all the applied arts woman's influence has made itself directly or indirectly felt; in all of them her contribution of elegance and grace and charm has been considerable.

But in the fine, the unapplied arts, women have, so far at any rate, done little. Whether, as a result of increased liberty and a more satisfactory education, we shall see in the future a great increase in the amount and importance of feminine art is a question which we need not discuss here. We must admit that her actual achievement in the arts has been up till now inconsiderable. There have been no great feminine personalities in the history of the arts, no creators of types, no inventors, among the woman painters, of new elegances and unexplored graces to say nothing of new grandeurs and strengths. Rosalba, Vigée Lebrun, Angelica Kauffmann, Rosa Bonheur, Berthe Morisot[3]—they do not amount to very much, the women painters of the past.

One finds, on the whole, more talent among such contemporaries as Goncharova, Therese Lessore, Tour Donas, Nina Hamnett, and several more whom one might mention. And in one of these contemporaries, surely we find what we have vainly looked for in the past—the personality, the creator, the inventor of new and essentially feminine elegance. Her name is Marie Laurencin and in Paul Rosenberg's galleries in the Rue de la Boétie you may see, in a few weeks' time, a representative exhibition of her works.

Marie Laurencin is not a painter to whom one can attach a convenient descriptive label. She belongs to no school, she is determinedly and egotis-

---

3. Angelica Kauffmann (1741–1807). Swiss painter. Rosa Bonheur (1822–1899). French painter of animals. Berthe Morisot (1841–1895). French painter.

tically herself. She is, of course, vaguely "modern," inasmuch as she does not try to paint realistically nor to illustrate particular dramatic incidents. But that is about as far as one can go in the way of labeling and pigeonholing. The cubists were her friends; she lived and worked amongst them, listened to their firmly pedantic theories of art—and did not allow herself to be influenced by them in the smallest degree. While her friends were busy with their austerely geometrical arrangements of planes and lines, Marie Laurencin went on quietly recording on canvas her own fantastic visions. And what curious and exquisite things she saw in the world that lay behind her vague myopic eyes! How individually she portrayed them! Cats with the faces of women and women with the faces of cats, horses and birds and monkeys of a fabulous elegance, delicate white girls with disquieting black and beadlike eyes, imaginary dogs and flowers—these are the fauna and flora of her universe. Her pictures are like the illustrations to some fantastic story of which we do not know the plot; they are subject pictures painted round themes unknown and exquisitely absurd.

The austere cubistic critics would have us ignore in every work of art, all qualities but the purely plastic. Born of a reaction against the too literary standards of academism, this doctrine has done good work in reminding people that there are other things in art besides sentiment and drama, that art has other functions than the pointing of a moral or the accurate description of a scene.

But, like every other creed that has issued from a polemic, this doctrine of the purely aesthetic function of art has been carried too far. It is absurd to try and ignore the other-than-plastic qualities of art; you are ignoring facts if you do. Michelangelo's statuesque conception of form moves us; but so does his amazing *terribiltà*. Raphael's sweetness affects us as intimately as his beautifully studied compositions. The brooding reflectiveness and the dramatic force are as integral a part of Rembrandt's work as is the open composition and the new sense of space. And so it is with Marie Laurencin. It is not only the composition, the coloring, the method of painting that please us in her pictures; it is also the feminine charm, the dim and beautiful fantasy. The literary qualities of her work—if anything so indefinite and vague and undramatic can be called "literary"—are quite as important as its aesthetic qualities.

Taken as purely aesthetic phenomena her pictures are certainly curious and interesting. Her universe of forms is a queer shallow place, not completely flat, but possessing, so to speak, only a rudimentary third dimension. It consists generally of only two or three planes lying quite close to the surface and, more often than not, parallel with the picture plane. There are no deep vistas and no statuesque masses standing solidly in a surrounding space. Her world, in fact, is the closely bounded world of the very short-sighted person who is only aware of the immediately surrounding reality. In this shallow universe there is no chiaroscuro, no sharply defined modeling. The paint is laid on flatly and unbrokenly. The color is always soft and very subtly harmonized. The best of her compositions have a pleasing and generally simple rhythmic pattern.

The final impression which her work leaves upon us is one of exquisitely graceful elegance. Her pictures are the most charming of decorations. And in that word "decoration" we are surely assessing the nature and value of her contribution, her essentially feminine contribution, to art. She has invented a new and subtle form of adornment, which takes its place with all the other things that have been invented in the past for the enrichment of daily life. Hers is certainly not the grandest form of art; but it is one of the most gracious.

[*Vanity Fair,* September 1922]

A Film with a Warning

ALL SOCIAL REFORMERS will agree with me that the moral turpitude of the Twentieth Century is becoming more and more manifest, menacing, and unprecedented. I have been asked by the Ethical Society if I cannot, as a publicist, do something about it. I can; and, what is more, I have done something. Here it is—a Cautionary Film. The point of all cautionary stories consists in showing that Providence always visits upon the committers of sin a condign punishment—visits it punctually, efficiently, and with a sense of dramatic fitness. The children who mocked Elisha for his baldness were very properly eaten by bears. That is the ideal cautionary story upon which all subsequent writers of this class of literature have modeled their efforts. So much by way of introduction. Let me leave this film-drama of a man's great sin and its prompt and providential punishment to point its own moral.

Mr. Jonas carries on business as a stockbroker in the heart of the city of London. He is a man with two great passions, a love for his club and a love for orchestral music. A photograph of the Bank of England is flashed on to the screen to indicate the hero's financial stability, and we are then shown the interior of Mr. Jonas's office, with Mr. Jonas himself, stoutish, baldish, middle-aged, and well-preserved, seated at his roll-top desk, the picture of self-respecting burgess honesty.

He strolls to the window; the street below, with its incessant, jerkily moving river of traffic, its ant-like throngs of foot passengers, is revealed. Mr. Jonas's attention is fixed by a deplorable old beggar woman standing in the gutter, proffering matches to the passers-by. Benevolence dawns on Mr. Jonas's broad countenance; he opens the window, dips a hand into his waistcoat pocket for a sixpence, and throws it down into the street. He closes the window again and walks back to his desk. A charitable man as well as an honest one. This incident is meant to impress us favorably with Mr. Jonas's character. His pristine virtue makes the story of his single sin and its punishment even more cautionary.

Meanwhile, in the street below, we are shown the fall of the sixpence. Dropping close to the old woman's feet, it rolls away into the gutter. The old woman totters painfully in pursuit, but before she can stoop down to recover it, an able-bodied hooligan darts forward from a doorway, picks it up, and runs off. Mr. Jonas's broad face is shown once more, virtuously smiling.

The scene changes to the drawing-room of Mr. Jonas's house in Portman Square. Mrs. Jonas is taking tea. A childless woman, she lavishes her maternal instinct on her husband and her two black tom-cats, Albert-Edward and Belial. She is shown pouring rich, glutinous cream into a saucer. Belial and Albert-Edward lap at it slowly and with the serene, unhurried dignity of animals accustomed to eating more than enough.

Back in Mr. Jonas's office. The hands of the clock on the mantel point to six o'clock. Mr. Jonas prepares to leave the building. He puts on his hat and steps out on to the landing. The descending lift stops to take him down. Its only other occupant besides the lift boy is Miss Topsy Trelawny who makes her living *faute de mieux,* by doing typing on one of the upper floors. A close-up shows the roll of a bold eye, the all-too-modest fluttering droop of a long-lashed lid. In an X-ray close-up we see Mr. Jonas's heart pumping with a sudden spasmodic violence.

The lift disgorges its burden. Mr. Jonas and Miss Topsy walk across the hall; they stand for a moment hesitatingly in the doorway. Outside it is pouring with rain—a typical English summer day. Mr. Jonas unfurls his umbrella. Improvident Miss Topsy has come without hers. One of the Foolish Virgins evidently: but not, perhaps, quite so foolish as the parable would have us suppose. She looks appealingly at Mr. Jonas. Benevolently gallant, flattered in his middle-aged vanity, he responds to the appeal. They go out together under the one protecting umbrella. The old beggar woman, standing sodden in the gutter, holds out her damp match boxes. Mr. Jonas shakes his head. "I have already given," he explains. "From my window. . . ."

Mr. Jonas hails a taxi. After a vivid pantomime of coy refusal, Miss Topsy consents to enter it. Broad in the beam, Mr. Jonas dives through the door after her. The landscape whizzes past the windows—the Bank of England, St. Paul's, the Law Courts, Trafalgar Square, Piccadilly, Hyde Park

Corner, the Albert Memorial. Miss Topsy has a little flat in South Kensington. The taxi comes to a halt; they say good-bye—Miss Topsy with dropped eyelids, Mr. Jonas beamingly flirtatious. But the farewell is only temporary. Mr. Jonas has asked if he may call again, this very evening, at nine-thirty.

The Jonas's dining-room. On the floor, in the foreground, Belial and Albert-Edward are eating, fastidiously, Sole Meunière. Mr. and Mrs. Jonas have reached the dessert stage. Mr. Jonas looks at his watch; it is twenty past nine. He rises abruptly. He has to see a man on most important and urgent business at half past. Solicitous, Mrs. Jonas follows him into the hall. It is so wet and cold tonight; she implores him just to run upstairs and put on his red flannel chest protector. Mr. Jonas refuses, a little irritably. This anxious coddling which, ordinarily, he rather enjoys, seems to him, somehow, curiously out of place at the present moment. Connubial affection is all right on ordinary days. But holidays, but ferial interludes— one needs a little change every now and then. He darts down the steps into the street. Standing in the lighted doorway, Mrs. Jonas cries a last word of farewell advice into the dank darkness.

It is one o'clock; Mr. Jonas is returning. Trains and buses have ceased running, and he cannot find a cab. The rain pours down; he has forgotten his umbrella at Miss Topsy's flat. He trudges on, splashing through puddles at every step. Taxis whiz past; Mr. Jonas frantically waves at them, desperately shouts. They are always engaged. It is a lugubrious and sodden figure that finally mounts the stairs at Portman Square.

The Jonas's dining room on the following morning. Mrs. Jonas is preparing the cats' breakfast. Two bowls of warm milk, two plates of grilled kidneys and bacon are set out on the floor. Calmly and without enthusiasm, Belial and Albert-Edward settle down to their meal, while Mrs. Jonas looks on, affectionately. The door opens and Mr. Jonas comes in, looking perceptibly the worse for his evening's adventure. He settles down rheumatically into his chair and is just unfolding the *Times,* when he gives vent to an appalling cough. The cups on the table are seen to jump; so does Mrs. Jonas; and even Albert-Edward, even Belial lift for a moment their yellow pin-pupiled eyes and look with surprise in Mr. Jonas's direction. Mr. Jonas coughs again—a frightful tearing noise, a final stupendous crash. There is a fade-out and we are shown a group of Californian lumbermen in the act of felling a giant sequoia. The huge tree shudders a little, leans, leans and impends, at first almost imperceptibly, then faster and faster. A frightful tearing, a final shattering crash. The sequoia is down— Mr. Jonas has coughed again.

"If only you had put on your red flannel chest protector as I told you."

Mr. Jonas growls and buries his head in the *Times.* Every now and then another sequoia is brought in hideous ruin to the ground. At every crash Mrs. Jonas starts nervously, and the cats look up with a vague apprehension from their warm milk and their grilled kidneys and bacon. Providence has begun to move; we have a sense of impending catastrophe.

A few scenes from Mr. Jonas's life during the next few months are now shown. We see him first at the door of his office looking out at the incessant summer rain and unfolding his umbrella. He begins to cough. While he is still doubled up by the paroxysm, Miss Topsy, leaning on the arm of an elegant young man, passes him in the hall and is handed by her companion into a large Rolls-Royce. Fade-out and terrifying close-up of the face of *Desmodus Rufus,* the blood-sucking vampire of Ecuador.

In Mr. Jonas's club. The majestic library recedes away from the eye in impressive perspective. Sunk in huge arm-chairs, several old gentlemen are sleeping or somnolently reading. Mr. Jonas crosses the room. Just as he is slipping out through the further door, he coughs. It is quite a small sequoia that falls; but the noise is enough to make all the old gentlemen spring up in panic from their seats. They glower angrily about them to see who is responsible for the outrage. Each suspects the other of having tried to be funny. One of them, putting his hand to his heart, rings the bell for a waiter and orders a brandy and soda.

In an eminent physician's consulting room. Mr. Jonas is being sounded. After ten minutes listening-in on the stethoscope, the eminent physician straightens himself up, smiles, pats Mr. Jonas on the shoulder, and assures him that there is nothing wrong with his lungs and that there is no reason why he should go on coughing. Mr. Jonas gives him a check for five guineas and goes out.

Sunday morning in the Park. Mr. and Mrs. Jonas are taking the air together. Mr. Jonas wears a gloomy expression and his wife looks haggard and careworn. Mr. Jonas coughs. A baby in a passing perambulator is seized with convulsions.

At the Jonas's house on Christmas Day. In her boudoir, Mrs. Jonas is showing the cats their Christmas Tree. But the ceremony which, in previous years, used always to be such a joyous affair is but the mockery of merriment now. Gaunt and pale, her bright feverish eyes ringed with dark shadows, Mrs. Jonas stands by the glittering tree, whose branches bend with the weight of the pots of caviar and cream, the dried herrings, the raw veal cutlets hanging from them. Belial and Albert-Edward, grown as gaunt and thin as their mistress, prowl tigerishly round about. Belial is prematurely grey about the muzzle and Albert-Edward has grown a little mangy. Every now and then, from the floor below, there comes a sound, muffled a little by the intervening walls and ceilings, but still loud, still appalling—the sound of Mr. Jonas coughing. And when it comes, the two cats look at one another significantly and nod their heads, the woman shudders.

Below, in his study, sits Mr. Jonas, surrounded by ineffectual medicaments—linctuses, cough mixtures, inhalers, gargles, sprays. Fade out. On the bleak ridges of the Sierra Nevada the immense sequoias come tearing and crashing, one after another, to the ground. Mrs. Jonas and the gaunt cats appear again. She is just giving Belial his raw veal cutlet, when suddenly she starts, she listens. We have another glimpse of Mr. Jonas coughing uncontrollably. Then back to Mrs. Jonas, listening, with wide fixed eyes that take on an ever wilder expression. Another view of Mr. Jonas in the throes, and then back once more to the boudoir and the listening woman. All at once something seems to give way. Mrs. Jonas begins to rave. Howling, the cats rush round and round the room and the lunatic woman pursues them, fiendishly laughing. . . .

A few months later at Mr. Jonas's Club. A glimpse of poor Mrs. Jonas behind the bars of her asylum and of the house in Portman Square, standing gloomy, neglected, and empty, gives us to understand that Mr. Jonas is now making the club his home. He is sitting in the smoking room reading *Punch* in a state of profound depression which the perusal of that journal does nothing to alleviate. Occasionally he coughs. A footman brings him a note. He opens it and reads.

"Dear Mr. Jonas. At their meeting this afternoon the Committee have decided, regretfully but unanimously, to ask you to resign your membership. Your unfortunate affliction has been the cause of considerable discomfort among the members of this Club and the Committee feel that, in the best interests of the majority, they have no alternative but to request your resignation. The Committee, I may add, think it only right that your entrance fee should be returned, and I am enclosing a check for the amount. Believe me, in all sympathy, yours very sincerely, T. J. Dodder. (Secretary.)"

Mr. Jonas folds up the letter and without a word, without a gesture, walks out into the hall, puts on his hat and coat and slowly leaves the club—the dear old club of which he has been for twenty years a member—for ever. On the steps he coughs. Pall Mall is filled with the sound of falling redwood.

At the Aeolian Hall; the world-renowned Herzogovinian Quartet are giving a concert. They are playing the first movement of the Ravel quartet. Incomparable Petulengro, the First Violin, sways as he plays and his black bobbed hair swings like a voiceless bell. Bojanus, the Second Fiddle, is bluff and stout and business-like. Moschopulos, the Viola, has a way of closing his eyes through long half minutes, and his face wears an expression of voluptuous pain. Peperkoek caresses his cello as though it were a woman crouching between his knees. And from the conjunction of their grimaces an exquisite music is born.

In the middle of the eighth row, just at the perfect distance from the platform, Mr. Jonas sits in ecstasy, oblivious for the moment of all his troubles. Everything else may go; his wife, his club may be taken from him; but music, divine music remains. Hauntingly, the refrain returns and returns, like a friend, like a gentle comforter. Mr. Jonas is positively happy. All at once a look of frightful apprehension crosses his face; he realizes that he is about to cough. He makes a tremendous effort of the will; he swallows hard, he sets his teeth. The tickling in the throat grows gradually more and more intolerable. All unconscious of what is to come, the players go on grimacing, the public placidly listens. Mr. Jonas struggles on in agony, struggles vainly. Tear and crash—it is as though a cyclone had descended upon Mariposa or Calaveras and were uprooting the entire forest of ancient trees. Not a note of the music can be heard. The audience is in an uproar; all turn towards Mr. Jonas. There are threatening gestures; the players abandon their vain efforts to make themselves audible and shake their bows at the offender. An attendant comes and touches Mr. Jonas on the shoulder: the management must request him to leave the building immediately. Still coughing, he staggers out into the night. The last thing that made life worth living has been taken away. Providence is claiming its pound of flesh.

Mr. Jonas splashes along through the chill summer rain. The nineteenth-century Gothic of the Houses of Parliament looms up over him. He walks on to Westminster Bridge. In the middle of the bridge he halts and looks over at the black waters beneath. Fade out: Forbes Robertson as Hamlet reciting: To be or not to be. . . . Mr. Jonas decides not to be. He is just hoisting himself on to the parapet to throw himself into the river, when he is overtaken by another violent fit of coughing. The sequoias go crashing into the Thames. A policeman standing by the Boadicea statue is startled by the unfamiliar sound. Slowly and with dignity he walks in the direction from which it comes. In the middle of the bridge he finds Mr. Jonas doubled up against the parapet, incapable of doing anything but cough. The policeman takes him by the arm and leads him gently back to dry land. Again, the cough has been too much for him. The vision of Mr. Jonas and the policeman fades slowly out and we are left, somehow, with the impression that, while Mr. Jonas may want to make an end, Providence has only just begun.

[*Vanity Fair,* October 1922]

The Salzburg Festival

IF IT WERE NOT for its climate, which is proverbially beastly, and its cooking, which is sound but a little monotonous, the town of Salzburg would be as pleasant a place to spend a summer in as you could hope to find in Central Europe. At a first glimpse this city of domes and towers, set in a curving valley between high hills, and bestriding with its bridges a green erratic mountain-river, reminds one of Florence—a Florence in miniature and absurdly, delightfully Teutonic. The austere elegance of the Tuscan landscape has given place to prospects of meadowy plains and distant peaked mountains that are as wholeheartedly and unashamedly sentimental as a German song—as for example *Roslein* or *Ringlein* or *Tannenbaum*.

As you look at the picture-book view from the fortifications on the hill above the town, you seem to hear those lusciously plaintive notes oozing out of the landscape; and then you look down at the town. For the incomparable beauty and grandeur of Brunelleschi's dome we have the jolly baroque cupolas of the Collegienkirche and the cathedral, merrily parodying grandeur. We have the queer charm of their narrow streets, the oddity of tunneled passages that lead under archways through dark burrows into sudden unexpected courtyards open to the sky and surrounded by arcaded terraces, almost like Spanish patios, then on again through further mazes of mole work out into the street again. And then there are the fountains that mimic the fountains of Rome, the rose path of true Italian beauty in the Kapitel Platz, with others more or less ridiculously charming in the gardens which lend their loveliness to the place.

But best and most Italian of all Salzburg's beauties—not Florentine this, but Roman in its baroque magniloquence—is the thing they call the New Gate, which is nothing less than a great tunnel bored through the perpendicular crag; a superlative tunnel such as only a Prince Bishop of the Seventeenth Century would have dreamed of boring; forty feet high and, at either end, stupendous arches of triumph carved out of the living rock. It is worth going to Salzburg for that tunnel alone.

It was not, however, for the sake of this baroque Simplon, not for the semi-Italian splendors of churches and fountains, not for the German beauties of the mountains as seen from the beer terraces of the various Aussichtspunkten—it was for none of these things that so many of us made the Salzburg pilgrimage this autumn. It was the festival of modern chamber music that brought us thither from the distant corners of the earth.

Twice a day, at half past ten in the morning and at seven at night—for one must be an early worm in Salzburg if one would listen to the singing of the musical birds—we repaired to the great hall of the Mozarteum to have contemporary music administered to us in generous three-and-a-half-hour doses. The end of the feast found most of us rather weary; listening to one's contemporaries is not undilutedly pleasurable or interesting.

In the course of the last four hundred years there have been not more than a dozen composers indisputably of the first rank. This is a fact which forbids us to expect too much from a single generation of composers, even when the men of that generation happen to be our contemporaries. By no means are the musicians of our age men of genius. It follows, therefore, that the greater part of the music performed at Salzburg was not immensely interesting, that some of it was even downright boring. In passing judgment upon any work of art, the man of sense is neither a *passéiste* nor a futurist. He is consistently a talentist—an admirer of genius wherever and in whatsoever form he finds it.

The fact that the greater number of the composers represented at Salzburg were, like most of the rest of us, poor devils without enough talent to make themselves particularly interesting, is not to be wondered; neither has it anything to do with the goodness or badness of modern music in general. And the fact that the prevailing mediocrity of the concerts at the Mozarteum was relieved by compensatory thrills, that there were *bons quarts d'heure* which made up for the bad hours, amply justified the existence of the festival and the music performed at it.

The programs at this first Salzburg festival of modern chamber music were not so thoroughly representative of contemporary talent as they might have been—not so representative as, let us hope, they will be in future years. Strauss, for example, appeared only as the author of some very feeble sentimental songs; Elgar and Delius did not appear at all. There was no sign of Mahler, none of Ornstein,[4] none of Boyle, whose cello concerto, even with the orchestral part arranged for piano, is an interesting work and a great deal better worth listening to than much that was played at Salzburg.

There was hardly enough Pizetti and rather too much of the Parisian Six. The English were too exclusively represented by songs, the French by pieces for combinations of wind instruments. Altogether, there was much which might with advantage have been altered. None the less, in spite of all its failings, the festival was very well worth attending. It gave one a bird's-eye view of contemporary music which was most instructive. The city of modern music lay outspread below one—a collection of dwellings of every size and style with here and there a noble monument outstanding.

4. Leo Ornstein (1895–). Russian-born American composer.

It was, so to speak, the view over Salzburg from the beer-terrace at the top of the funicular.

And which were the noble monuments? What corresponded in this view over the city of music to the dome of the Collegienkirche and the cupolas of the cathedral, to the Kapitelbrunnen and the Newthar as they appear in the beer-terrace prospect of Salzburg? For me, at any rate, there were three or four works that stood out like domes and towers from the low Salzburg valley: Schönberg's *Steich Quartett mit Gesang,* Béla Bartók's violin sonata, The Quartet of Paul Hindemith, and, less unequivocally monumental, Kodály's Serenade for strings and the Violin Sonata of Ernest Bloch.[5]

Some of these names are already sufficiently familiar; one expects something of interest when one sees them on a program. From Schönberg, for example, one always expects profound musical learning and an intellectual subtlety that provokes and satisfies the mind. What one does not so much expect of him and what, in this *Steich Quartett mit Gesang,* one is delighted to find, is a quality of intense emotion. The third and fourth movements, in which the voice makes its appearance, are extraordinarily stirring. Across all the intricacy and subtlety of the writing, the emotions of the *Litanei* and *Entrückung* come through, clear and piercingly. Schönberg's Op. 10, as played by the admirable Amar-Hindemith Quartet and sung by Fräulein Huni, was one of the things that justified this festival of contemporary music.

So was Paul Hindemith's Quartet. This work, for me, was one of the surprises; the name did not make me expect anything in particular. I knew of Hindemith as the man who plays the violin in the string combination which goes under his name, but not as a composer. His quartet introduced what amounts to a new musical personality.

Rooted firmly in the classical past, this work of Hindemith's is yet essentially contemporary and original; it blossoms and fruits, so to speak, in the present. His technical framework is a development, a logical extension of the old framework. He does not, like Bartók, make a violent break with the past; he prefers to carry the traditional argument a step further. Listening to Hindemith's Quartet one is made aware that it has been written by someone who knows all there is to know about string quartets from the inside, the player's point of view; it is full of an ingenuity that makes the best of all the given material. But what is more remarkable and much more important is the fact that it is full of the most beautiful invention. It

---

5. Zoltan Kodály (1882–1967). Hungarian composer. Ernest Bloch (1880–1959). Swiss-born American composer.

abounds with new, surprising themes and melodies; and the writing of the parts, which move with a fine independence, is rich and subtle. Altogether, it is a highly admirable work.

The Bartók violin sonata is a very different piece of music. Bartók, as I have said before, does not attempt to carry the old argument a step further; he breaks violently with the past. His harmonic system is based on no known, accepted relations. At his weakest—in many of his piano pieces, for example—he uses his "unrelated sonorities" merely to make a disagreeable barbaric noise. But at his best, as in the violin sonata, he succeeds in producing new and beautiful effects of energy and passion.

Of Bloch, I find it rather hard to speak. He is obviously a good musician and a serious artist who aspires towards the grand and the noble—a laudable aspiration in these days when so many of us do our best to make of art a music-hall festival. And yet, somehow, his music does not give me complete satisfaction. The tragic emotions of his "Schelomo," which ought to be so fine, are somehow clothed and, as it were, rank. There is a sort of emotional impurity about it all very difficult to describe but which nevertheless prevents the work from achieving the greatness at which it aims.

One has the impression that Bloch derives his idea of greatness, not from Michelangelo or Beethoven in the original, but from M. Roman Rolland's portraits of these artists—portraits which all those who have stood among the Medici tombs at Florence or have listened to one Finale of Op. 131 will know to be singularly inadequate as representations of greatness. Bloch's violin sonata is altogether a finer work; it would be completely admirable if it were not for a trace of the clothed theatrical impurity of emotion which spoils "Schelomo."

And what of the other musicians represented at Salzburg? What of the common dwellings of the city from among which the monuments stood grandly out? There were the young Frenchmen with their fatiguing wit and their thin subject matter; and there was the later Stravinsky removed from his native seriousness and force by too long a sojourn in Paris. There were the Spaniards; De Falla at his most brilliant, making one forget the dreary composer of "The Gardens of Aranjuez"; Salazar sophisticating luxuriantly round the full-blooded vulgarity of a dance tune. There were the English; Bliss, empty and rather pretentious; Box, badly represented by romantic songs that didn't come off; Holst[6] in some pure archaistic settings of old religious work.

6. Sir Arthur Bliss (1891–1975). English composer. Box is probably a misprint for Sir Arnold Bax (1883–1953). English composer who called his work "romantic." Gustav Theodore Holst (1874–1934). English composer.

There were the Austrians; Wellesz,[7] as earnestly modern and boring as a second-rate exhibitor at the Salon des Indépendents; Webern who might be quite good, but whose quartet performed at Salzburg was written down to such an infinite pianissimo as to be completely inaudible; Reti, richly exotic; Marx, romantic; with others, none of them exceptionally interesting. There were the Germans; mathematically intellectual Busoni was almost the only good one, except Hindemith, represented. Hungary contributed, besides the sonata of Bartók, the beautifully limpid Serenade by Kodály. There were various Czechs who contributed songs of an interesting wildness. There was Willem Pijper[8] from Amsterdam, whose violin sonata sounded as though it had been written for performance in a very high-class cinema, so refined was it and so bottomlessly commonplace.

There were also several Scandinavian composers, whose works I was unable to hear as I had previously been driven from the concert hall by the portentously ill-written and pretentious violin sonata of Mr. Leo Sowerby[9] of New York. Two movements of it were enough for me. I left the building regardless of the Scandinavians who were to follow. Perhaps the Beethoven of the twentieth century lurked among that little band of Danes and Swedes—I missed hearing him! Who knows? But somehow, I feel pretty confident that I didn't miss very much.

[*Vanity Fair*, December 1922]

The Portraits of Augustus John

FEW THINGS are more pathetic than the spectacle of earnest and intelligent industry coming to nothing for lack of natural talent. The universe is not a particularly moral machine; or at any rate its morality, if it has one, is not the morality of the Sunday School. In this world the really important things are not achieved by hard work and high principles, or even by higher education. They are achieved by that native talent which is born in a man and for the possession of which he has to thank, not his own efforts, but the mere mysterious luck of heredity.

Nothing is more unfair and immoral and undemocratic than genius. There are thousands and millions of virtuous folk who thoroughly deserve the gift; they do not receive it. Of the few to whom it is vouchsafed how many can be said to have earned it? Some, no doubt; but many not at all.

---

7. Egon Joseph Wellesz (1885–1974). Austrian composer.
8. Ferruccio Busoni (1866–1924). Italian composer. Willem Pijper (1894–1947). Dutch composer.
9. Leo Sowerby (1895–1968). American composer.

The really delightful thing about genius is that, like the order of the Garter, there is "no damned merit about it." In their sermons about great men, the Sunday School teachers insist rather on those moral qualities which can be imitated than on the national gifts which, alas! cannot; they feel safer with the virtues than with their talents. If the thing were not so palpably ridiculous, they would like to put Alfieri above Shakespeare—Alfieri who, at thirty, resolved to make himself, by sheer hard work and strength of will, a great tragic poet and who came, what is more, surprisingly near (all things considered) to the fulfilment of his desire; Shakespeare who "never blotted a line" and never felt the need of doing so. Alfieri can be used, like the ant or the beaver, to point the most salutary moral. But Shakespeare—no: he is one of those exquisite monsters who have no place in Aesop.

One fact there is, however, on which the Sunday School teachers might dwell with a certain justifiable satisfaction: the greatest and most inimitable gifts are in many cases (I will not say all, for generalizations of this sort are altogether too dangerous) improved and developed by a systematic application to them of the ordinary imitable virtues. Schubert had perhaps a greater natural gift than Beethoven; his native woodnotes came to him almost too easily—so easily, indeed, that Beethoven's slower, more laborious methods of composition seemed to him incomprehensible. These painful efforts of concentration and selection and arrangement—were they, he could ask himself, worthwhile? With the most complete confidence we can answer: they were. Decidedly, the imitable virtues have scored a point.

Of all contemporary artists, Augustus John is perhaps the man to whom nature has been most prodigal with her gifts. Flowing and beautiful forms, subtle combinations of color come as spontaneously from him as melodies and delicate modulations came from Schubert. He thinks naturally in terms of visual beauty, and for him to draw or paint thoroughly badly would be as difficult as it is for the mere pedantic and laborious theorist of art to do the same things thoroughly well. John's first thoughts and fancies are always exquisitely right—witness the host of beautiful drawings in which he has recorded, with lines that have the streaming elegance of a living form, gestures of significant shapeliness and power; witness, too, the many canvases in which landscape and figures have been brought harmoniously together in brilliant and delicate combinations of color; the portraits so strikingly placed on the canvas, so lively painted. It is a beautiful, rare, and precious talent.

And yet, though the thing we have is so good—and, indeed, precisely because of its excellence—we long for something more. We should like to see Schubert turning into Beethoven. For we find that much of John's work is too like a brilliant improvisation of wonderful power; it possesses the freshness, the spontaneity, the quality of energetic life which belong to the sketches of an artist of genius. But besides the qualities, it possesses also the defects of the sketch. Much of John's painting seems to lack that solidity, that rich elaborate logic of construction which give to the finest pictures of the masters their permanent and unfailing interest. Michelangelo, El Greco, Rubens—here are three painters about as unlike one another as three men could well be. But their pictures have this, at least, in common: that they are full of that quality of life which is the sign of a natural genius, but of a life strictly controlled, ordered, analyzed, so to speak, and composed by a great labor of thought. In the finest of John's works we see, I think, this same finely ordered vitality; the *Smiling Woman,* for instance (now in the Tate Gallery), is a noble example of the way in which the natural, spontaneous genius can be improved and cultivated and developed, somehow, beyond itself by means of the laborious imitable virtues. The pulsing immediate life of the improvisation is there; but it informs an elaborate and logical intellectual system. There is something in this picture to satisfy every part of the mind; and because this is so, it remains one of the works of art which will never grow old, will never fatigue or irritate, however often it is seen.

But before many of John's other pictures we remain, somehow, incompletely satisfied, or satisfied, it may be, only for a time. There is a brilliance here, there is an ample life; but it is the brilliance, it is the life of a sketch. A complete, a truly finished picture should be something like the philosophical system of a mystic—at once emotional and intellectual, logical and passionate.

It is in a large and very chilly bedroom of the Albergo Fiorentius at San Sepolcro that I write these words. A couple of hundred yards up the street stands the Palazzo Comunale; on the wall of its great hall Piero della Francesca painted his fresco of the Resurrection. The best picture in the world? This afternoon, at any rate, I am ready to believe it. But whatever else it may be, it is a complete and finished picture. It contains everything, it satisfies the whole spirit. It is as passionately alive as the most brilliantly improvised sketch and it has the beautiful, inevitable logic of a proposition of Euclid. It is emotionally moving; it gives to the sense an exquisite and subtle pleasure; it presents itself to the mind as a wonderfully accurate and convincing argument. It is, in a word, beautiful in every possible way.

John's pictures are also beautiful—but not, with certain exceptions, in every possible way. Many of them are beautiful only up to a certain point, on one side, so to speak, of a dividing line. They delight the spectator, but not entirely; a part of him—and it is generally the intellectual, logical part of him—remains unaffected. The pictures at the John Exhibition at the

Alpine Club Galleries were the last works of art I saw before leaving England. Piero's *Resurrection* has been almost the first I have seen since my arrival in Italy. Inevitably, I find myself comparing *this* with the memory of those. The style, the technique, the medium—all these things, of course, are vastly dissimilar. But the fundamental points of resemblance and of difference are none the less easily appreciated. Life, energy, the brilliant national gift—these are common to both the painters. But logic, but the laborious power of construction and systematization—these are enormously much more developed in the painter of the *Resurrection* than in the painter of *Symphonie Espagnole*. And it is precisely this which makes him so much the greater artist.

But when all is said, when the Devil's Advocate has given vent to all his objections, how immensely preferable is John's rich natural gift to the drearily pedantic intellectualism which takes the place of talent in so much of the "young" painting of the present time! Life without logic may not be able to achieve everything in art; but it can at any rate go a long way. Logic without the natural talent, which expresses itself in the peculiar quality of life, can get nowhere at all and achieves nothing. If I wanted to be rude I should give a few examples, which prove this rule, from the annals of contemporary painting. I should cite the names of Messrs. So-and-So and Un-Tel as living proofs of the hopeless incapacity of intellectual theory and hard work to arouse anything but *ennui* in the mind of onlookers. But I have no desire to be rude. I will content myself by asking the reader to think of all the pictures by earnest *jeunes* he has ever seen and remember, with as little acrimony as possible, the exact amount of boredom evoked in him by each.

More deplorable even than the pedantic theorists, because louder and vulgarer and more pretentious than they, are the talentless painters who wildly simulate life in the hope of persuading the world that they have talent. How different again is the real talent, when one sees it in John, from this sham talent, the natural vitality from this galvanic artificial life. The futurists and their followers in England and elsewhere have almost all been of this kind—"protesting too much" that they may be noticed, wildly and violently gesticulating that people may believe them to be really alive. A picture by John, where the life comes from within and is not artificially forced into it from the outside, puts them all to shame, reveals the essential deadness of this galvanic violence.

No, when all is said, John remains a large and important and valuable figure. He emerges from the not very noble army of contemporary artists as one of the few great natural talents of the present day. With his few fellows of genius he stands apart, reminding us in the most salutary fashion that it is the gift of God, not the correct education, that produces genuine art; that though by thinking a great man may be able to add a cubit to his stature, it is necessary to start with a respectable stature; that art is as large and variable as human genius; that most of what the theorists of aesthetics have to say is nonsense, because they try to limit art and make it fit into their particular theory.

[*Vanity Fair,* July 1923]

Royalty and a Caricature

GREATLY, I imagine, to his astonishment, Mr. Max Beerbohm found himself, not long ago, at the vortex of one of those newspaper tornadoes which are periodically let loose for the devastation of public opinion. Not that the public opinion is ever very seriously devastated. Those Gods of the Winds—or should they not rather be called Gods of Wind, *tout court?*—whose home is in Fleet Street, are too liberal with their hurricanes. Familiarity breeds contempt, and the newspaper reader walks through the howling whirlwinds serenely and unheedingly as though the barometer were set at Mild Breezes.

This particular tornado which, for the space of about a week, whirled furiously around Mr. Beerbohm, to subside again, as all these winds of journalism do subside, as suddenly as it had arisen, was unleashed for reasons that seemed, goodness knows, queer enough even in England, but which must have struck the American mind as wonderfully fantastic.

It was an affair of *lèse majesté.*

In his latest exhibition of caricatures Mr. Beerbohm had exposed a picture of the Prince of Wales—of the Prince of Wales as he might be expected to appear fifty years hence and after the English Revolution. Old Mr. Edward Windsor, who now lives very quietly in most respectable lodgings at "Balmoral," Lenin Avenue, Ealing, is shown in the act of espousing his landlady's middle-aged daughter. It was a charming drawing and a piece, it seemed to me when I saw it, of delightful and entirely inoffensive fun.

But that, evidently, was not how it struck the journalist. With a splendid unanimity the Gods of Wind uncorked the inflated bladders, and for days it furiously blew. Mr. Max Beerbohm was accused of bad taste, boorishness, disloyalty, calumny, *lèse majesté,* and, almost, blasphemy. The royal family, we were told, had been insulted, the throne bemuddied—goodness knows what else.

For the philosophic onlooker, the spectacle was not uninteresting. Not that there was anything about the press campaign itself that was in the least curious or remarkable—it was as stupid as any other press campaign.

It was what the campaign represented. For genuinely, even after all the necessary discounts had been made, it did represent something. It really reflected—in a mirror, of course, that vastly magnified and distorted—the opinion of considerable sections of the English public. It voiced—through a megaphone—the feelings of those very numerous people in England who revere the royal family, as Ben Jonson loved Shakespeare, "this side idolatry"; and who feel that it is a piece of very bad taste, that it is all but blasphemy, to abuse or ridicule a member of the sacred clan. They would have us speak of royal personages as they would have us speak of the dead—nothing but good.

Now that this should be the case in Peru before the coming of the Spaniards, or in Constantinople before the coming of the Turks—or after it, for that matter—would be very comprehensible. For the Peruvian Inca was divine, a direct descendant of the Sun; the Emperor of Byzantium was the Viceroy of Christ, and his successor, the Sultan, was Mahomet's representative on earth. The subjects of these potentates were brought up from earliest infancy to regard their kings as sacred beings. Loyalty was a tenet of their religion, and to lampoon the king was a piece of horrid blasphemy.

There were, moreover, purely practical and material reasons for behaving respectfully. The royal personage could have you drawn like a chicken, quartered at a moment's notice like a carcass of beef, if you did not. If you were a believer in Safety First, you spoke of your prince with nothing but the profoundest respect. It is surprising to what sincerity one can arise with the thumb-screw before him.

Turn the clock back four hundred years, and imagine Mr. Beerbohm poking fun, shall we say, at the son of Pope Alexander VI. Then, if you like, one might expect a fuss. For not only would the prince be called Cesare Borgia, Duke of Valentinois; but his father, the old Borgia, would be sitting on the throne of St. Peter, would have been chosen in conclave by the advice of the Holy Spirit, and would be the holder of those formidable keys which open and close the gates of Paradise. In ridiculing, however mildly, the first-born son, however natural, of God's vice-regent upon earth, Mr. Beerbohm would have been risking an act whose consequences might have been serious, not merely in this world, but throughout all eternity.

But this is mere fancy. In point of fact the clock still stands at 1923 and Mr. Beerbohm has done no more than make a little joke about the marriage of the heir to an extremely constitutional monarchy. He runs no risk either in this or the next world. For the king of England has little or no power over the bodies of his subjects; and though by law he is head of their Church, he is no Pope to bind or loose the soul; he is no worshipped Inca, no deified Emperor of Rome. The English monarchy today is one of those up-to-date, hard-working, hand-shaking monarchies which seem to be the only ones that manage to survive in democratized Europe. And yet the fact remains that Mr. Beerbohm's joke did strike large numbers of English people as being slightly *risqué*, a little blasphemous. It seems, paradoxically, that the monarchy is more religiously revered now that it has no temporal power and lays no claim to spiritual authority, than when, in the past, it claimed a divine right to bully its subjects as much as it pleased.

Read, for example, what contemporary satirists wrote of Charles the Second—or rather don't read, of the process as I know by experience, having once devoted long months of my life to this sort of thing, is really rather a waste of time—wrote, that is to say, of a king who really did rule his country and who had a whole bench of bishops to say that he did it by divine right.

> Dunkirk was sold; but why we do not know,
> Unless to erect a new Seraglio—

says one anonymous writer, for example. And the poet Andrew Marvell, more indignantly and, for the nonce, less wittily, protested that it was a shameful thing

> To see Deo Gratias writ on the Throne,
> And the King's wicked life say: God there is none.

George III was mercilessly handled by the caricaturists and the pamphleteers. As regent and as king, his son was ridiculed and abused in a manner that would now be considered wholly outrageous. It would be easy, but tedious, to show that even the most absolute monarchs, even Popes, have been regarded as fair game by the pasquinaders of past ages.

It may be objected that most of the monarchs of the past deserved all the ridicule and all the denunciation that they got, and that the present royal family of England does not. Those were bad; these are good. But to that we would answer that even the blameless Prince Albert, during the first years of his marriage while he and Baron Stockmar were gradually taking into their hands the reins of government, was treated very much more rudely than Mr. Beerbohm, who was not rude at all, has treated the Prince of Wales.

And yet he has been abused for his little joke with a show of righteous indignation which nobody, except those whose interest it was to feel it, felt towards the caricaturists of George the Third or the satirists of Charles the Second. We can only conclude that, with the decay of the royal power, there has been a corresponding increase in the reverence felt for the throne. At first sight, as I have said, this seems paradoxical. But when we come to consider the matter more closely, we shall find that this process is altogether in the natural order of things. For it is obvious that a king who really does rule his people must be held responsible by them for the effects of his rule. And since in the nature of things no government can satisfy the desires of all the governed; since, indeed, a ruler must consider himself lucky as well as virtuous if he can content even half his subjects, it is clear that a king who is really the head of the government will have to put up with a good deal of unpopularity. Not even a monarch can expect to get something for nothing; the joys of power have to be paid for with the sound of complaints and curses, with abuse, denunciation and—most galling because so hopelessly unanswerable—ridicule.

Conversely, the sorrows—the boredoms, rather—of political impotence have their pleasing compensations. A monarch who does not govern is not held responsible by his subjects for the discomforts which almost every act of government must inevitably bring down upon some of them. So it comes about that what a constitutional monarch loses in power, he gains in respect and popularity. Ceasing to be the ruler of his country, he becomes, in a curious way, the symbol of it. And since to the human mind, which finds abstraction difficult and does not feel at home among entities on a more than human scale, a concrete symbol is something welcome and satisfying, it follows that the man who contrives to symbolize in his own person the whole national idea possesses a real importance, even though he may have no power or direct authority. Like the flag, like the national colors, the national heraldic animal or totem, the national anthem, the national allegoric personification, he becomes a simple and convenient sign for an idea immensely large and complex.

It is one thing to abuse the head of the government: even in these days of almost excessive politeness, the prime minister gets duly lampooned and caricatured. It is quite another thing to make fun of a national emblem. There are countries where you can get arrested for not saluting the flag; and I remember, in the Piazza at Venice, seeing an unfortunate individual, who remained seated and who laughed while the Italian anthem was being played, so mercilessly drubbed by the Fascists that he must have been thankful when the police closed round him and dragged him off to jail. Nobody can afford to laugh at an emblem. By a British subject, Britannia must be represented as Bernard Partridge has been representing her, weekly, for the last how many years? in the pages of *Punch*—as an infinitely respectable Greek goddess of the dullest and most classic period. A royal family which has become a national symbol must be treated with the respect due to all such sacred emblems. Mr. Beerbohm made the mistake of treating a member of our symbolical House of Windsor as one might treat the head of a government—humorously. The burgesses of England, who revere that House because it conveniently symbolizes not merely the Empire but also themselves and their ideals, resented it.

Americans, I know, find it difficult to understand how this effete "king business" contrives to go on in England. It goes on primarily, of course, because we are an exceedingly conservative people, tenaciously attached to our old customs even when they are most palpably absurd. It will be hundreds of years before England ceases to measure in rods and perches; to weigh with ounces that vary according to the material weighed; to calculate quantities in terms of firkins, hogsheads, cords, chaldrons, and kilderkins. It will also, I trust, be hundreds of years before England ceases to be a monarchy. For constitutional monarchy is an institution which, besides being respectably old, is also of great political value. We have arrived at it in England gradually, and as it were unconsciously. But what we have devised more or less by luck and accident, a Machiavelli, I am convinced, would have invented by the light of reason as being, in the circumstances, the most subtly perfect form of government imaginable. A state which possesses a nominal head, who does not in fact govern, possesses a permanent living symbol of itself to which its people can pay an unmixed devotion such as no real ruler can hope to have paid to him. To any government there is always an opposition. But government and opposition alike profess to have the interests of the country at heart; they differ only in their methods of serving these interests. The king who does not rule— who stands apart from the government and all its acts—is a living symbol of those national interests, like the country's flag—but more useful, because human and alive.

In a small community, such as the city-states of ancient Greece or medieval Italy, a symbolical figure of this kind is superfluous; the state is small enough for every citizen of it to be able to realize it completely and to feel a direct local patriotism towards it. But a great modern state is too large to be realized as a whole and directly felt for in this way. But if you can make one man into the symbol of the national idea, you at once endow your large state with many of the advantages belonging to the small one. For a direct local you substitute a direct personal patriotism. The human symbol can be sent round the great state to shake hands and, so to speak, to collect for the central authority the necessary tribute of personal patriotism. In the collection of this tribute the members of the House of Windsor work with an industriousness which I, for one, would be sorry to imitate. Poor symbols! Let us all be thankful that we stand only for ourselves.

[*Vanity Fair,* December 1923]

Centenaries

FROM BOCCA DI MAGRA to Bocca d'Arno, mile after mile, the sandy beaches smoothly, unbrokenly extend. Inland from the beach, behind a sheltering belt of pines, lies a strip of coastal plain—flat as a slice of Holland and dyked with slow streams. Corn grows here and the vine, with plantations of slim poplars interspersed and fat water-meadows. Here and there the streams brim over into shallow lakes, whose shores are fringed with sodden fields of rice. And behind this strip of plain, four or five miles from the sea, the mountains rise, suddenly and steeply: the Apuan Alps. Their highest crests are of bare limestone, streaked here and there with the white marble which brings prosperity to the little towns that stand at their feet: Massa and Carrara, Serravezza, Pietrasanta. Half the world's tombstones are scooped out of these noble crags. Their lower slopes are grey with olive trees, green with woods of chestnut. Over their summits repose the enormous sculptured masses of the clouds.

> From cape to cape, with a bridge-like shape,
> Over a torrent sea,
> Sunbeam-proof, I hang like a roof,—
> The mountains its columns be:[1]

The landscape fairly quotes Shelley at you. This sea with its luminous calms and sudden tempests, these dim blue islands hull down on the magical horizon, these mountains and their marvelous clouds, these rivers and woodlands are the very substance of his poetry. Live on this coast for a little and you will find yourself constantly thinking of that lovely, that strangely childish poetry, that beautiful and child-like man. Perhaps his spirit haunts the coast. It was in this sea that he sailed his flimsy boat, steering with one hand and holding in the other his little volume of Aeschylus. You picture him so on the days of calm. And on the days of sudden violent storm you think of him, too. The lightnings cut across the sky, the thunders are like terrible explosions overhead, the squall comes down with a fury. What news of the flimsy boat? None, save only that a few days after the storm a young body is washed ashore, battered, unrecognizable; the little Aeschylus in the coat pocket is all that tells us that this was Shelley.

I have been spending the summer on this haunted coast. That must be my excuse for mentioning in so up-to-date a paper as *Vanity Fair* the name of a poet who has been dead these hundred years. But be reassured. I have

---

1. Shelley, "The Cloud" (lines 63–66).

no intention of writing an article about the ineffectual angel beating in the void his some-or-other wings in vain. I do not mean to add my croak to the mellifluous chorus of centenary-celebrators. No; the ghost of Shelley, who walks in Versilia and the Lunigia, by the shores of the gulf of Spezia and below Pisa where Arno disembogues, this ghost with whom I have shaken hands and talked, incites me, not to add a supererogatory and impertinent encomium, but rather to protest against the outpourings of the other encomiasts, of the honey-voiced centenary-chanters.

The cooing of these persons, ordinarily a specific against insomnia, is in this case an irritant; it rouses, it exacerbates. For annoying and disgusting it certainly is, this spectacle of a rebellious youth praised to fulsomeness, a hundred years after his death, by people who would hate him and be horrified by him, if he were alive, as much as the Scotch reviewers hated and were horrified by Shelley. How would these persons treat a young contemporary who, not content with being a literary innovator, should use his talent to assault religion and the established order, should blaspheme against plutocracy and patriotism, should proclaim himself a Bolshevik, an internationalist, a pacifist, a conscientious objector? They would say of him that he was a dangerous young man who ought to be put in his place; and they would either disparage and denigrate his talent, or else—if they were a little more subtly respectable—they would never allow his name to get into print in any of the periodicals which they controlled.

But seeing that Shelley was safely burnt on the sands of Viarreggio a hundred years ago, seeing that he is no longer a live dangerous man but only a dead classic, these respectable supporters of established literature and established society join in chorus to praise him, and explain his meaning, and preach sermons over him. The mellifluous cooing is accompanied by a snuffle, and there hangs over these centenary celebrations a genial miasma of hypocrisy and insincerity. The effect of these festal anniversaries in England is not to rekindle life in the great dead; a centenary is rather a second burial, a reaffirmation of deadness. A spirit that was once alive is fossilized and, in the midst of solemn and funereal ceremonies, the petrified classic is duly niched in the temple of respectability.

How much better they order these things in Italy! In that country—which one must ever admire more the more one sees of it—they duly celebrate their great men; but celebrate them not with a snuffle, not in black clothes, not with prayer-books in their hands, crape round their hats and a hatred, in their hearts, of all that has to do with life and vigor. No, no; they make their dead an excuse for quickening life among the living; they get fun out of their centenaries.

Last year the Italians were celebrating the six hundredth anniversary of Dante's death. Now, imagine what this celebration would have been like in

England. All the oldest critics and all the young men who aspire to be old would have written long articles in all the literary papers. That would have set the tone. After that some noble lord, or even a Prince of the Blood, would have unveiled a monument designed by Frampton or some other monumental mason of the Academy. Imbecile speeches in words of not more than two syllables would then have been pronounced over the ashes of the world's most intelligent poet. Of his intelligence no reference would, of course, be made; but his character, ah! his character would get a glowing press. The most fiery and bitter of men would be held up as an example to all Sunday School children.

After this display of reverence, we should have had a lovely historical pageant—in the rain. A young female dressed in white bunting would have represented Beatrice and for the Poet himself some actor manager with a profile and a voice would have been found. Guelfs and Ghibellines in fancy dress of the period would go splashing about in the mud and a great many verses by Louis Napoleon Parker would be declaimed. And at the end we should all go home with colds in our heads and suffering from septic *ennui,* but with, at the same time, a pleasant feeling of virtuousness, as though we had been at church.

See now what happens in Italy. The principal event in the Dante celebration is an enormous military review. Hundreds of thousands of wiry little brown men parade the streets of Florence. Young officers of a fabulous elegance clank along in superbly tailored riding breeches and glittering top boots. The whole female population palpitates. It is an excellent beginning. Speeches are then made, as only in Italy they can be made—round, rumbling, sonorous speeches, all about Dante the Italianissimous poet, Dante the irredentist, Dante the prophet of Greater Italy, Dante the scourge of Jugo-Slavs and Serbs. Immense enthusiasm. Never having read a line of his works, we feel that Dante is our personal friend, a brother Fascist.

After that the real fun begins; we have the *"manifestazioni sportive"* of the centenary celebrations. Innumerable bicycle races are organized. Fierce young Fascisti with the faces of Roman heroes pay their homage to the Poet by doing a hundred and eighty kilometers to the hour round the Circuit of Milan. High-speed Fiats and Ansaldos and Lancias race one another across the Apennines and round the bastions of the Alps. Pigeons are shot, horses gallop, football is played under the broiling sun. Long live Dante!

How infinitely preferable this is to the stuffiness and the snuffle of an English centenary. Poetry, after all, is life, not death. Bicycle races may not have very much to do with Dante—though I can fancy him, his thin face set like metal, whizzing down the spirals of Hell on a pair of twinkling wheels or climbing laboriously the one-in-three gradients of Purgatory Mountain on the back of his trusty Sunbeam. No, they may not have much to do with Dante; but pageants in Anglican cathedral closes, boring articles by old men who would hate and fear him if he were alive, speeches by noble lords over monuments made by Royal Academicians—these, surely, have even less to do with the author of the *Inferno.*

It is not merely their great dead whom the Italians celebrate in this gloriously living fashion. Even their religious festivals have the same jovial warm-blooded character. This summer, for example, a great feast took place at Loreto to celebrate the arrival of a new image of the Virgin to replace the old one which was burnt some little while ago. The excitement started in Rome, where the image, after being blessed by the Pope, was taken in a motor-car to the station amid cheering crowds who shouted "Evvia Maria" as the Fiat and its sacred burden rolled past. The arrival of the Virgin in Loreto was the signal for a tremendous outburst of jollification. The usual bicycle races took place; there were football matches and pigeon shooting competitions and the Olympic games. The fun lasted for days. At the end of the festivities two cardinals went up in aeroplanes and blessed the assembled multitudes—an incident of which the Pope is said to have remarked that the blessing, in this case, did indeed come from heaven.

Rare people! If only we Anglo-Saxons could borrow from the Italians some of their realism, their love of life for its own sake, of palpable, solid, immediate things. In this dim land of ours we are accustomed to pay too much respect to fictitious values; we worship invisibilities and in our enjoyment of immediate life we are restrained by imaginary inhibitions. We think too much of the past, of metaphysics, of tradition, of the ideal future, of decorum and good form; too little of life and the glittering noisy moment. The Italians are born Futurists. It did not need Marinetti[2] to persuade them to celebrate Dante with bicycle races; they would have done it naturally, spontaneously, if no Futurist propaganda had ever been issued. Marinetti is the product of modern Italy, not modern Italy of Marinetti. They are all Futurists in that burningly living Italy where we from the North seek only an escape into the past. Or rather, they are not Futurists: Marinetti's label was badly chosen. They are Presentists. The early Christians preoccupied with nothing but the welfare of their souls in the life to come were Futurists, if you like.

We shall do well to learn something of their lively Presentism. Let us hope that our great-grandchildren will celebrate the next centenary of Shelley's death by aerial regattas and hydroplane races. The living will be

2. Emilio Marinetti (1876–1944). Italian writer and one of the founders of Futurism.

amused and the dead worthily commemorated. The spirit of the man who delighted, during life, in wind and clouds, in mountain tops and waters, in the flight of birds and the gliding of ships, will be rejoiced when young men celebrate his memory by flying through the air or skimming, like alighting swans, over the surface of the sea.

> The rocks are cloven, and through the purple night
> I see cars drawn by rainbow-winged steeds
> Which trample the dim winds; in each there stands
> A wild-eyed charioteer urging their flight.
> Some look behind, as fiends pursued them there,
> And yet I see no shapes but the keen stars;
> Others, with burning eyes, lean forth, and drink
> With eager lips the wind of their own speed,
> As if the thing they loved fled on before,
> And now, even now, they clasped it.[3]

The man who wrote this is surely more suitably celebrated by aeroplane or even bicycle races than by seven-column articles from the pens of Messrs.—well, perhaps we had better mention no names. Let us take a leaf out of the Italian book.

[*On the Margin*, 1923]

On Re-reading *Candide*

THE FURNITURE VANS had unloaded their freight in the new house. We were installed, or, at least, we were left to make the best of an unbearable life in the dirt and the confusion. One of the Pre-Raphaelites, I forget at the moment which, once painted a picture called "The Last Day in the Old Home." A touching subject. But it would need a grimmer, harder brush to depict the horrors of "The First Day in the New Home." I had sat down in despair among the tumbled movables when I noticed—with what a thrill of pleased recognition—the top of a little leather-bound book protruding from among a mass of bulkier volumes in an uncovered case. It was *Candide,* my treasured little first edition of 1759, with its discreetly ridiculous title-page, "*Candide ou L'Optimisme,* Traduit de l'Allemand de Mr. le Docteur Ralph."

Optimism—I had need of a little at the moment, and as Mr. le Docteur Ralph is notoriously one of the preachers most capable of inspiring it, I

3. Shelley, *Prometheus Unbound* (act 2, scene 5 lines 29–38).

took up the volume and began to read: "Il y avait en Westphalie, dans le Château de Mr. Le Baron de Thunder-ten-tronckh. . . ." I did not put down the volume till I had reached the final "Il faut cultiver nôtre jardin." I felt the wiser and the more cheerful for Doctor Ralph's ministrations.

But the remarkable thing about re-reading *Candide* is not that the book amuses one, not that it delights and astonishes with its brilliance; that is only to be expected. No, it evokes a new and, for me at least, an unanticipated emotion. In the good old days, before the Flood, the history of Candide's adventures seemed to us quiet, sheltered, middle-class people only a delightful fantasy, or at best a high-spirited exaggeration of conditions which we knew, vaguely and theoretically, to exist, to have existed, a long way off in space and time. But read the book today; you feel yourself entirely at home in its pages. It is like reading a record of facts and opinions of 1922; nothing was ever more applicable, more completely to the point. The world in which we live is recognizably the world of Candide and Cunégonde, of Martin and the Old Woman who was a Pope's daughter and the betrothed of the sovereign Prince of Massa-Carrara. The only difference is that the horrors crowd rather more thickly on the world of 1922 than they did on Candide's world. The maneuverings of Bulgare and Abare, the intestine strife in Morocco, the earthquake and *auto-da-fé* are but pale poor things compared with the Great War, the Russian Famine, the Black and Tans, the Fascisti, and all the other horrors of which we can proudly boast. "Quand Sa Hautesse envoye un vaisseau en Egypte," remarked the Dervish, "s'embarrasse-t-elle si les souris qui sont dans le vaisseau sont à leur aise ou non?" No; but there are moments when Sa Hautesse, absent-mindedly no doubt, lets fall into the hold of the vessel a few dozen of hungry cats; the present seems to be one of them.

Cats in the hold? There is nothing in that to be surprised at. The wisdom of Martin and the Old Woman who was once betrothed to the Prince of Massa-Carrara has become the everyday wisdom of all the world since 1914. In the happy Victorian and Edwardian past, Western Europe, like Candide, was surprised at everything. It was amazed by the frightful conduct of King Bomba,[4] amazed by the Turks, amazed by the political chicanery and loose morals of the Second Empire—(what is all Zola but a prolonged exclamation of astonishment at the goings-on of his contemporaries?). After that we were amazed at the disgusting behavior of the Boers, while the rest of Europe was amazed at ours. There followed the widespread astonishment that in this, the so-called twentieth century,

4. "King Bomba" was the name given to Ferdinand II, King of Naples, for the bombing of Messina in 1848.

black men should be treated as they were being treated on the Congo and the Amazon. Then came the war: a great outburst of indignant astonishment and afterwards an acquiescence as complete, as calmly cynical as Martin's. For we have discovered, in the course of the somewhat excessively prolonged *histoire à la Candide* of the last seven years, that astonishment is a supererogatory emotion. All things are possible, not merely for Providence, whose ways we had always known, albeit for some time rather theoretically, to be strange, but also for men.

Men, we thought, had grown up from the brutal and rampageous hobbledehoyism of earlier ages and were now as polite and genteel as Gibbon himself. We now know better. Create a hobbledehoy environment and you will have hobbledehoy behavior; create a Gibbonish environment and every one will be, more or less, genteel. It seems obvious, now. And now that we are living in a hobbledehoy world, we have learnt Martin's lesson so well that we can look on almost unmoved at the most appalling natural catastrophes and at exhibitions of human stupidity and wickedness which would have aroused us in the past to surprise and indignation. Indeed, we have left Martin behind and are become, with regard to many things, Pococurante.

And what is the remedy? Mr. le Docteur Ralph would have us believe that it consists in the patient cultivation of our gardens. He is probably right. The only trouble is that the gardens of some of us seem hardly worth cultivating. The garden of the bank clerk and the factory hand, the shopgirl's garden, the garden of the civil servant and the politician—can one cultivate them with much enthusiasm? Or, again, there is my garden of literary journalism. In this little plot I dig and delve, plant, prune, and finally reap—sparsely enough, goodness knows!—from one year's end to another. And to what purpose, to whom for a good, as the Latin Grammar would say? Ah, there you have me.

There is a passage in one of Chekov's letters which all literary journalists should inscribe in letters of gold upon their writing desks, "I send you," says Chekov to his correspondent, "Mihailovsky's article on Tolstoy. . . . It's a good article, but it's strange: one might write a thousand such articles and things would not be one step forwarder, and it would still remain unintelligible why such articles are written."

Il faut cultiver nôtre jardin. Yes, but suppose one begins to wonder why?

[*On the Margin,* 1923]

Subject-Matter of Poetry

IT SHOULD theoretically be possible to make poetry out of anything what-soever of which the spirit of man can take cognizance. We find, however, as a matter of historical fact, that most of the world's best poetry has been content with a curiously narrow range of subject-matter. The poets have claimed as their domain only a small province of our universe. One of them now and then, more daring or better equipped than the rest, sets out to extend the boundaries of the kingdom. But for the most part the poets do not concern themselves with fresh conquests; they prefer to consolidate their power at home, enjoying quietly their hereditary possessions. All the world is potentially theirs, but they do not take it. What is the reason for this, and why is it that poetical practice does not conform to critical theory? The problem has a peculiar relevance and importance in these days, when young poetry claims absolute liberty to speak how it likes of whatsoever it pleases.

Wordsworth, whose literary criticism, dry and forbidding though its aspect may be, is always illumined by a penetrating intelligence. Wordsworth touched upon this problem in his preface to *Lyrical Ballads*—touched on it and, as usual, had something of value to say about it. He is speaking here of the most important and the most interesting of the subjects which may, theoretically, be made into poetry, but which have, as a matter of fact, rarely or never undergone the transmutation: he is speaking of the relations between poetry and that vast world of abstractions and ideas—science and philosophy—into which so few poets have ever penetrated. "The remotest discoveries of the chemist, the botanist, or mineralogist, will be as proper objects of the poet's art as any upon which he is now employed, if the time should ever come when these things shall be familiar to us, and the relations under which they are contemplated shall be manifestly and palpably material to us as enjoying and suffering beings." It is a formidable sentence; but read it well, read the rest of the passage from which it is taken, and you will find it to be full of critical truth.

The gist of Wordsworth's argument is this. All subjects—"the remotest discoveries of the chemist" are but one example of an unlikely poetic theme—can serve the poet with material for his art, on one condition: that he, and to a lesser degree his audience, shall be able to apprehend the subject with a certain emotion. The subject must somehow be involved in the poet's intimate being before he can turn it into poetry. It is not enough, for example, that he should apprehend it merely through his senses. (The poetry of pure sensation, of sounds and bright colors, is common enough nowadays; but amusing as we may find it for the moment, it cannot hold the interest for long.) It is not enough, at the other end of the scale, if he apprehends his subject in a purely intellectual manner. An abstract idea must be felt with a kind of passion, it must mean something emotionally significant, it must be as immediate and important to the poet as a personal relationship before he can make poetry of it. Poetry, in a word, must be written by "enjoying and suffering beings," not by beings exclusively dowered with sensations or, as exclusively, with intellect.

Wordsworth's criticism helps us to understand why so few subjects have ever been made into poetry when everything under the sun, and beyond it, is theoretically suitable for transmutation into a work of art. Death, love, religion, nature; the primary emotions and the ultimate personal mysteries—these form the subject-matter of most of the greatest poetry. And for obvious reasons. These things are "manifestly and palpably material to us as enjoying and suffering beings." But to most men, including the generality of poets, abstractions and ideas are not immediately and passionately moving. They are not enjoying or suffering when they apprehend these things only thinking.

The men who do feel passionately about abstractions, the men to whom ideas are as persons—moving and disquietingly alive—are very seldom poets. They are men of science and philosophers, preoccupied with the search for truth and not like the poet, with the expression and creation of beauty. It is very rarely that we find a poet who combines the power and the desire to express himself with that passionate apprehension of ideas and that passionate curiosity about strange remote facts which characterize the man of science and the philosopher. If he possessed the requisite sense of language and the impelling desire to express himself in terms of beauty, Einstein could write the most intoxicating lyrics about relativity and the pleasures of pure mathematics. And if, say, Mr. Yeats understood the Einstein theory which, in company with most other living poets, he presumably does not, any more than the rest of us—if he apprehended it exultingly as something bold and profound, something vitally important and marvelously true, he too could give us, out of the Celtic twilight, his lyrics of relativity. It is those distressing little "ifs" that stand in the way of this happy consummation. The conditions upon which any but the most immediately and obviously moving subjects can be made into poetry are so rarely fulfilled, the combination of poet and man of science, poet and philosopher, is so uncommon, that the theoretical universality of the art has only very occasionally been realized in practice. Contemporary poetry in the whole of the Western world is insisting, loudly and emphatically through the mouths of its propagandists, on an absolute liberty to speak of what it likes how it likes. Nothing could be better; all that we can now ask is that the poets should put the theory into practice, and that they should make use of the liberty which they claim by enlarging the bounds of poetry.

The propagandists would have us believe that the subject-matter of contemporary poetry is new and startling, that modern poets are doing something which has not been done before. "Most of the poets represented in these pages," writes Mr. Louis Untermeyer in his *Anthology of Modern American Poetry,* "have found a fresh and vigorous material in a world of honest and often harsh reality. They respond to the spirit of their times; not only have their views changed, their vision has been widened to include things unknown to the poets of yesterday. They have learned to distinguish real beauty from mere prettiness, to wring loveliness out of squalor, to find wonder in neglected places, to search for hidden truths even in the dark caves of the unconscious." Translated into practice this means that contemporary poets can now write, in the words of Mr. Sandburg, of the "harr and boom of the blast fires," of "wops and bohunks." It means, in fact, that they are at liberty to do what Homer did: to write freely about the immediately moving facts of everyday life. Where Homer wrote of horses and the tamers of horses, our contemporaries write of trains, automobiles, and the various species of wops and bohunks who control the horse-power. That is all. Much too much stress has been laid on the newness of the new poetry; its newness is simply a return from the jeweled exquisiteness of the eighteen-nineties to the facts and feelings of ordinary life. There is nothing intrinsically novel or surprising in the introduction into poetry of machinery and industrialism, of labor unrest and modern psychology: these things belong to us, they affect us daily as enjoying and suffering beings; they are a part of our lives, just as the kings, the warriors, and chariots, the picturesque were part of Homer's life. The subject-matter of the new poetry remains the same as that of the old. The old boundaries have not been extended. There would be real novelty in the new poetry if it had, for example, taken to itself any of the new ideas and astonishing facts with which the new science has endowed the modern world. There would be real novelty in it if it had worked out a satisfactory artistic method for dealing with abstractions. It has not. Which simply means that that rare phenomenon, the poet in whose mind ideas are a passion and a personal moving force, does not happen to have appeared.

And how rarely in all the long past he has appeared! There was Lucretius, the greatest of all the philosophic and scientific poets. In him the passionate apprehension of ideas, and the desire and ability to give them expression, combined to produce that strange and beautiful epic of thought which is without parallel in the whole history of literature. There was Dante, in whose soul the medieval Christian philosophy was a force that shaped and directed every feeling, thought, and action. There was Goethe, who focused into beautiful expression an enormous diffusion of knowledge and ideas. And there the list of the great poets of thought comes to an end. In their task of extending the boundaries of poetry into the remote and abstract world of ideas, they have had a few lesser assistants—Donne, for example, a poet only just less than the greatest; Fulke Greville, that strange, dark-spirited Elizabethan; John Davidson, who made a kind of poetry out of Darwinism; and, most interesting poetical interpreter of nineteenth-century science, Jules Laforgue.

Which of our contemporaries can claim to have extended the bounds of poetry to any material extent? It is not enough to have written about locomotives and telephones, "wops and bohunks," and all the rest of it. That is not extending the range of poetry; it is merely asserting its right to deal with the immediate facts of contemporary life, as Homer and as Chaucer did. The critics who would have us believe that there is something essentially unpoetical about a bohunk (whatever a bohunk may be), and something essentially poetical about Sir Lancelot of the Lake, are, of course, simply negligible; they may be dismissed as contemptuously as we have dismissed the pseudo-classical critics who opposed the freedoms of the Romantic Revival. And the critics who think it very new and splendid to bring bohunks into poetry are equally old-fashioned in their ideas.

It will not be unprofitable to compare the literary situation in this early twentieth century of ours with the literary situation of the early seventeenth century. In both epochs we see a reaction against a rich and somewhat formalized poetical tradition expressing itself in a determination to extend the range of subject-matter, to get back to real life, and to use more natural forms of expression. The difference between the two epochs lies in the fact that the twentieth-century revolution has been the product of a number of minor poets, none of them quite powerful enough to achieve what he theoretically meant to do, while the seventeenth-century revolution was the work of a single poet of genius, John Donne. Donne substituted for the rich formalism of nondramatic Elizabethan poetry a completely realized new style, the style of the so-called metaphysical poetry of the seventeenth century. He was a poet-philosopher-man-of-action whose passionate curiosity about facts enabled him to make poetry out of the most unlikely aspects of material life, and whose passionate apprehension of ideas enabled him to extend the bounds of poetry beyond the frontiers of common life and its emotions into the void of intellectual abstraction. He put the whole life and the whole mind of his age into poetry.

We today are metaphysicals without our Donne. Theoretically we are free to make poetry of everything in the universe; in practice we are kept within the old limits, for the simple reason that no great man has appeared to show us how we can use our freedom. A certain amount of the life of the twentieth century is to be found in our poetry, but precious little of its mind. We have no poet today like that strange old Dean of St. Paul's three hundred years ago—no poet who can skip from the heights of scholastic philosophy to the heights of carnal passion, from the contemplation of divinity to the contemplation of a flea, from the rapt examination of self to an enumeration of the most remote external facts of science, and make all, by his strangely passionate apprehension, into an intensely lyrical poetry.

The few poets who do try to make of contemporary ideas the substance of their poetry, do it in a manner which brings little conviction or satisfaction to the reader. There is Mr. Noyes,[5] who is writing four volumes of verse about the human side of science—in his case, alas, all too human. Then there is Mr. Conrad Aiken.[6] He perhaps is the most successful exponent in poetry of contemporary ideas. In his case, it is clear, "the remotest discoveries of the chemist" are apprehended with a certain passion—all his emotions are tinged by his ideas. The trouble with Mr. Aiken is that his emotions are apt to degenerate into a kind of intellectual sentimentality, which expresses itself only too easily in his prodigiously fluent, highly colored verse. One could lengthen the list of more or less interesting poets who have tried in recent times to extend the boundaries of their art. But one would not find among them a single poet of real importance, not one great or outstanding personality. The twentieth century still awaits its Lucretius, awaits its own philosophical Dante, its new Goethe, its Donne, even its up-to-date Laforgue. Will they appear? Or are we to go on producing a poetry in which there is no more than the dimmest reflection of that busy and incessant intellectual life which is the characteristic and distinguishing mark of this age?

[*On the Margin*, 1923]

Water Music

THE HOUSE in which I live is haunted by the noise of dripping water. Always, day and night, summer and winter, something is dripping somewhere. For many months an unquiet cistern kept up within its iron bosom a long, hollow-toned soliloquy. Now it is mute; but a new and more formidable drip has come into existence. From the very summit of the house

---

5. Alfred Noyes (1880–1958). English poet whose *The Torchbearers*, celebrating men of science, was published between 1922 and 1930.
6. Conrad Aiken (1889–1973). American poet and novelist.

a little spout—the overflow, no doubt, of some unknown receptacle under the roof—lets fall a succession of drops that is almost a continuous stream. Down it falls, this all but stream, a sheer forty or fifty feet on to the stones of the basement steps, thence to dribble ignominiously away into some appointed drain. The cataracts blow their trumpets from the steep; but my lesser waterfalls play a subtler, I had almost said a more "modern" music. Lying awake at nights, I listen with a mixture of pleasure and irritation to its curious cadences.

The musical range of a dripping tap is about half an octave. But within the bounds of this major fourth, drops can play the most surprising and varied melodies. You will hear them climbing laboriously up small degrees of sound, only to descend at a single leap to the bottom. More often they wander unaccountably about in varying intervals, familiar or disconcertingly odd. And with the varying pitch the time also varies, but within narrower limits. For the laws of hydrostatics, or whatever other science claims authority over drops, do not allow the dribblings much license either to pause or to quicken the pace of their falling. It is an odd sort of music. One listens to it as one lies in bed, slipping gradually into sleep, with a curious, uneasy emotion. Drip drop, drip drap drep drop. So it goes on, this watery melody, forever without an end. Inconclusive, inconsequent, formless, it is always on the point of deviating into sense and form. Every now and then you will hear a complete phrase of rounded melody. And then—drip drop, di-drep, di-drap—the old inconsequence sets in once more. But suppose there were some significance in it! It is that which troubles my drowsy mind as I listen at night. Perhaps for those who have ears to hear, this endless dribbling is as pregnant with thought and emotion, as significant as a piece of Bach. Drip drop, di-drap, di-drep. So little would suffice to turn the incoherence into meaning. The music of the drops is the symbol and type of the whole universe; it is forever, as it were, asymptotic to sense, infinitely close to significance, but never touching it. Never, unless the human mind comes and pulls it forcibly over the dividing space. If I could understand this wandering music, if I could detect in it a sequence, if I could force it to some conclusion—the diapason closing full in God, in mind, I hardly care what, so long as it closes in something definite—then, I feel, I should understand the whole incomprehensible machine, from the gaps between the stars to the policy of the Allies. And growing drowsier and drowsier, I listen to the ceaseless tune, the hollow soliloquy in the cistern, the sharp metallic rapping of the drops that fall from the roof upon the stones below; and surely I begin to discover a meaning, surely I detect a trace of thought, surely the phrases follow one another with art, leading on inevitably to some prodigious conclusion. Almost I have it, almost, almost. . . . Then, I suppose, I fall definitely to sleep. For the next thing I am aware of is that the sunlight is streaming in. It is morning, and the water is still dripping as irritatingly and persistently as ever.

Sometimes the incoherence of the drop music is too much to be borne. The listener insists that the asymptote shall somehow touch the line of sense. He forces the drops to say something. He demands of them that they shall play, shall we say, "God Save the King," or the Hymn to Joy from the Ninth Symphony, or *Voi che Sapete*. The drops obey reluctantly; they play what you desire, but with more than the ineptitude of the child at the piano. Still they play it somehow. But this is an extremely dangerous method of laying the haunting ghost whose voice is the drip of water. For once you have given the drops something to sing or say, they will go on singing and saying it forever. Sleep becomes impossible, and at the two or three hundredth repetition of "Madelon"[7] or even of an air from *Figaro* the mind begins to totter towards insanity.

Drops, ticking clocks, machinery, everything that throbs or clicks or hums or hammers, can be made, with a little perseverance, to say something. In my childhood, I remember, I was told that trains said, "To Lancashire, to Lancashire, to fetch a pocket handkercher" and da capo ad infinitum. They can also repeat, if desired, that useful piece of information: "To stop the train, pull down the chain." But it is very hard to persuade them to add the menacing corollary: "Penalty for improper use Five Pounds." Still, with careful tutoring I have succeeded in teaching a train to repeat even that unrhythmical phrase.

Dadaist literature always reminds me a little of my falling drops. Confronted by it, I feel the same uncomfortable emotion as is begotten in me by the inconsequent music of water. Suppose, after all, that this apparently accidental sequence of words should contain the secret of art and life and the universe! It may; who knows? And here am I, left out in the cold of total incomprehension; and I pore over this literature and regard it upside down in the hope of discovering that secret. But somehow I cannot induce the words to take on any meaning whatever. Drip drop, di-drap, di-drep— Tzara and Picabia[8] let fall their words and I am baffled. But I can see that there are great possibilities in this type of literature. For the tired journalist it is ideal, since it is not he, but the reader who has to do all the work. All he need do is to lean back in his chair and allow the words to dribble out through the nozzle of his fountain pen. Drip, drop. . . .

[*On the Margin,* 1923]

---

7. "La Madelon" was a favorite song of French soldiers in World War I.
8. Tristan Tzara (Sami Rosenstock, 1896–1963). Romanian poet and Surrealist writer. One of the founders of the Dada movement. Francis Picabia (1879–1953). French Dadaist painter.

Bibliophily

BIBLIOPHILY is on the increase. It is a constatation which I make with regret; for the bibliophile's point of view is, to me at least, unsympathetic and his standard of values unsound. Among the French, bibliophily would seem to have become a kind of mania, and, what is more, a highly organized and thoroughly exploited mania. Whenever I get a new French book I turn at once—for in what disgusts and irritates one there is always a certain odious fascination—to the fly-leaf. One had always been accustomed to finding there a brief description of the "vingt exemplaires sur papier hollande Van Gelder"; nobody objected to the modest old Dutchman whose paper gave to the author's presentation copies so handsome an appearance. But Van Gelder is now a back number. In this third decade of the twentieth century he has become altogether too simple and unsophisticated. On the fly-leaf of a *dernière nouveauté* I find the following incantation, printed in block capitals and occupying at least twenty lines:

> Il a été tiré de cet ouvrage, après impositions spéciales, 133 exemplaires in-4. Tellière sur papier-vergé pur-fil Lafuma-Navarre, au filigrane de la *Nouvelle Revue Française,* dont 18 exemplaires hors commerce, marqués de A à R, 100 exemplaires réservés aux Bibliophiles de la *Nouvelle Revue Française,* numérotés de I à C, 15 exemplaires numérotés de CI à CXV; 1040 exemplaires sur papier vélin pur-fil Lafuma-Navarre, dont dix exemplaires hors commerce marqués de a à j, 800 exemplaires réservés aux amis de l'Édition originale, numérotés de 1 à 800, 30 exemplaires d'auteur, hors commerce, numérotés de 801 à 830 et 200 exemplaires numérotés de 831 à 1030, ce tirage constituant proprement et authentiquement l'Édition originale.

If I were one of the hundred Bibliophiles of the *Nouvelle Revue Française* or even one of the eight hundred Friends of the Original Edition, I should suggest, with the utmost politeness, that the publishers might deserve better of their fellow-beings if they spent less pains on numbering the first edition and more on seeing that it was properly produced. Personally, I am the friend of any edition which is reasonably well printed and bound, reasonably correct in the text and reasonably clean. The consciousness that I possess a numbered copy of an edition printed on Lafuma-Navarre paper, duly watermarked with the publisher's initials, does not make up for the fact that the book is full of gross printer's errors and that a whole sheet of sixteen pages has wandered, during the process of binding, from one end of the volume to the other—occurrences which are quite unnecessarily frequent in the history of French book production.

With the increased attention paid to bibliophilous niceties, has come a great increase in price. Limited editions de luxe have become absurdly common in France, and there are dozens of small publishing concerns which produce almost nothing else. Authors like Monsieur André Salmon and Monsieur Max Jacob[9] scarcely ever appear at less than twenty francs a volume. Even with the exchange this is a formidable price; and yet the French bibliophiles, for whom twenty francs are really twenty francs, appear to have an insatiable appetite for these small and beautiful editions. The War has established a new economic law: the poorer one becomes, the more one can afford to spend on luxuries.

The ordinary English publisher has never gone in for Van Gelder, Lafuma-Navarre, and numbered editions. Reticent about figures, he leaves the book collector to estimate the first edition's future rarity by guesswork. He creates no artificial scarcity values. The collector of contemporary English first editions is wholly a speculator; he never knows what time may have in store.

In the picture trade for years past nobody has pretended that there was any particular relation between the price of a picture and its value as a work of art. A magnificent El Greco is bought for about a tenth of the sum paid for a Romney that would be condemned by any self-respecting hanging-committee. We are so well used to this sort of thing in picture dealing that we have almost ceased to comment on it. But in the book trade the tendency to create huge artificial values is of a later growth. The spectacle of a single book being bought for fifteen thousand pounds is still sufficiently novel to arouse indignation. Moreover, the book collector who pays vast sums for his treasures has even less excuse than has the collector of pictures. The value of an old book is wholly a scarcity value. From a picture one may get a genuine aesthetic pleasure; in buying a picture one buys the unique right to feel that pleasure. But nobody can pretend that *Venus and Adonis* is more delightful when it is read in a fifteen thousand pound unique copy than when it is read in a volume that has cost a shilling. On the whole, the printing and general appearance of the shilling book is likely to be the better of the two. The purchaser of the fabulously expensive old book is satisfying only his possessive instinct. The buyer of a picture may also have a genuine feeling for beauty.

The triumph and the *reductio ad absurdum* of bibliophily were witnessed not long ago at Sotheby's, when the late Mr. Smith of New York bought eighty thousand pounds' worth of books in something under two

---

9. André Salmon (1881–1969). French poet and novelist. Max Jacob (1876–1944). French poet, novelist, and artist.

hours at the Britwell Court sale. The War, it is said, created forty thousand new millionaires in America; the New York bookseller can have had no lack of potential clients. He bought a thousand guinea volume as an ordinary human being might buy something off the sixpenny shelf in a second-hand shop. I have seldom witnessed a spectacle which inspired in me an intenser blast of moral indignation. Moral indignation, of course, is always to be mistrusted as, wholly or in part, the disguised manifestation of some ignoble passion. In this case the basic cause of my indignation was clearly envy. But there was, I flatter myself, a superstructure of disinterested moral feeling. To debase a book into an expensive object of luxury is as surely, in Miltonic language, "to kill the image of God, as it were in the eye" as to burn it. And when one thinks how those eighty thousand pounds might have been spent. . . . Ah, well!

[*On the Margin*, 1923]

Accumulations

IN THE BREVITY OF LIFE and the perishableness of material things the moral philosophers have always found one of their happiest themes. "Time, which antiquates Antiquities, hath an Art to make dust of all things." There is nothing more moving than those swelling elegiac organ notes in which they have celebrated the mortality of man and all his works. Those of us for whom the proper study of mankind is books dwell with the most poignant melancholy over the destruction of literary treasures. We think of all the pre-Platonic philosophers of whose writings only a few sentences remain. We think of Sappho's poems, all but completely blotted from our knowledge. We think of the missing fragments of the "Satyricon," and of many other precious pages which once were and are now no more. We complain of the holes that time has picked in the records of history, bewailing the loss of innumerable vanished documents. As for buildings, pictures, statues, and the accumulated evidence of whole civilizations, all destroyed as though they had never been, they do not belong to our literary province, and, if they did, would be too numerous to catalogue even summarily.

But because men have once thought and felt in a certain way it does not follow that they will forever continue to do so. There seems every probability that our descendants, some two or three centuries hence, will wax pathetic in their complaints, not of the fragility, but the horrible persistence and indestructibility of things. They will feel themselves smothered by the intolerable accumulation of the years. The men of today are so

deeply penetrated with the sense of the perishableness of matter that they
have begun to take immense precautions to preserve everything they can.
Desolated by the carelessness of our ancestors, we are making very sure
that our descendants shall lack no documents when they come to write our
history. All is systematically kept and catalogued. Old things are carefully
patched and propped into continued existence; things now new are
hoarded up and protected from decay.

To walk through the bookstores of one of the world's great libraries is
an experience that cannot fail to set one thinking on the appalling indestructibility of matter. A few years ago I explored the recently dug cellars
into which the overflow of the Bodleian pours in an unceasing stream. The
cellars extend under the northern half of the great quadrangle in whose
center stands the Radcliffe Camera. These catacombs are two storeys deep
and lined with impermeable concrete. "The muddy damps and ropy
slime"[1] of the traditional vault are absent in this great necropolis of letters;
huge ventilating pipes breathe blasts of a dry and heated wind, that makes
the place as snug and as unsympathetic to decay as the deserts of Central
Asia. The books stand in metal cases constructed so as to slide in and out
of position on rails. So ingenious is the arrangement of the cases that it is
possible to fill two-thirds of the available space, solidly, with books.
Twenty years or so hence, when the existing vaults will take no more
books, a new cellar can be dug on the opposite side of the Camera. And
when that is full—it is only a matter of half a century from now—what
then? We shrug our shoulders. After us the deluge. But let us hope that
Bodley's Librarian of 1970 will have the courage to emend the last word
to "bonfire." To the bonfire! That is the only satisfactory solution of an
intolerable problem.

The deliberate preservation of things must be compensated for by their
deliberate and judicious destruction. Otherwise the world will be overwhelmed by the accumulation of antique objects. Pigs and rabbits and wa-
tercress, when they were first introduced into New Zealand, threatened to
lay waste the country, because there were no compensating forces of destruction to put a stop to their indefinite multiplication. In the same way,
mere things, once they are set above the natural laws of decay, will end by
burying us, unless we set about methodically to get rid of the nuisance.
The plea that they should all be preserved—every novel by Nat Gould,
every issue of the *Funny Wonder*—as historical documents is not a sound
one. Where too many documents exist it is impossible to write history at

---

1. Taken from Robert Blair's "The Grave" (1753), this should read "the mouldy damps
and ropy slime."

all. "For ignorance," in the felicitous words of Mr. Lytton Strachey, "is the first requisite of the historian—ignorance which simplifies and clarifies, which selects and omits, with a placid perfection unattainable by the highest art." Nobody wants to know everything—the irrelevancies as well as the important facts—about the past; or in any case nobody ought to desire to know. Those who do, those who are eaten up by an itch for mere facts and useless information, are the wretched victims of a vice no less reprehensible than greed or drunkenness.

Hand in hand with this judicious process of destruction must go an elaborate classification of what remains. As Mr. Wells says in his large, opulent way, "the future world-state's organization of scientific research and record compared with that of today will be like an ocean liner beside the dug-out canoe of some early heliolithic wanderer." With the vast and indiscriminate multiplication of books and periodicals our organization of records tends to become ever more heliolithic. Useful information on any given subject is so widely scattered or may be hidden in such obscure places that the student is often at a loss to know what he ought to study or where. An immense international labor of bibliography and classification must be undertaken at no very distant date, if future generations of researchers are to make the fullest use of the knowledge that has already been gained.

But this constructive labor will be tedious and insipid compared with the glorious business of destruction. Huge bonfires of paper will blaze for days and weeks together, whenever the libraries undertake their periodical purgation. The only danger, and, alas! it is a very real danger, is that the libraries will infallibly purge themselves of the wrong books. We all know what librarians are; and not only librarians, but critics, literary men, general public—everybody, in fact, with the exception of ourselves—we know what they are like, we know them: there never was a set of people with such bad taste! Committees will doubtless be set up to pass judgment on books, awarding acquittals and condemnations in magisterial fashion. It will be a sort of gigantic Hawthornden competition. At that thought I find that the flames of my great bonfires lose much of their imagined luster.

[*On the Margin*, 1923]

On Deviating into Sense

THERE IS A STORY, very dear for some reason to our ancestors, that Apelles, or I forget what other Greek painter, grown desperate at the failure of his efforts to portray realistically the foam on a dog's mouth, threw his sponge at the picture in a pet, and was rewarded for his ill temper by discovering that the resultant smudge was the living image of the froth whose aspect he had been unable, with all his art, to recapture. No one will ever know the history of all the happy mistakes, the accidents and unconscious deviations into genius, that have helped to enrich the world's art. They are probably countless. I myself have deviated more than once into accidental felicities. Recently, for example, the hazards of careless typewriting caused me to invent a new portmanteau word of the most brilliantly Laforguian quality. I had meant to write the phrase "the Human Comedy," but, by a happy slip, I put my finger on the letter that stands next to "C" on the universal keyboard. When I came to read over the completed page I found that I had written "the Human Vomedy."

Was there ever a criticism of life more succinct and expressive? To the more sensitive and queasy among the gods the last few years must indeed have seemed a vomedy of the first order.

The grossest forms of mistake have played quite a distinguished part in the history of letters. One thinks, for example, of the name Criseida or Cressida manufactured out of a Greek accusative, of that Spenserian misunderstanding of Chaucer which gave currency to the rather ridiculous substantive "derringdo." Less familiar, but more deliciously absurd, is Chaucer's slip in reading "naves ballatrices" for "naves bellatrices," "ballet-ships" instead of "battle-ships"—and his translation "shippes hoppesteres." But these broad, straightforward howlers are uninteresting compared with the more subtle deviations into originality occasionally achieved by authors who were trying their best not to be original. Nowhere do we find more remarkable examples of accidental brilliance than among the post-Chaucerian poets, whose very indistinct knowledge of what precisely was the meter in which they were trying to write often caused them to produce very striking variations on the staple English measure.

Chaucer's variations from the decasyllable norm were deliberate. So, for the most part, were those of his disciple Lydgate, whose favorite "brokenbacked" line, lacking the first syllable of the iambus that follows the caesura, is metrically of the greatest interest to contemporary poets. Lydgate's characteristic line follows this model:

For speechéless nothing maist thou speed.

Judiciously employed, the brokenbacked line might yield very beautiful effects. Lydgate, as has been said, was probably pretty conscious of what he was doing. But his procrustean methods were apt to be a little indiscriminate, and one wonders sometimes whether he was playing variations on a known theme or whether he was rather tentatively groping after the beautiful regularity of his master Chaucer. The later fifteenth- and sixteenth-century poets seem to have worked very much in the dark. The poems of such writers as Hawes and Skelton abound in the vaguest parodies of the decasyllable line. Anything from seven to fifteen syllables will serve their turn. With them the variations are seldom interesting. Chance had not much opportunity of producing subtle metrical effects with a man like Skelton, whose mind was naturally so full of jigging doggerel that his variations on the decasyllable are mostly in the nature of rough skeltonics. I have found interesting accidental variations on the decasyllable in Heywood, the writer of moralities. This, from the *Play of Love,* has a real metrical beauty:

> Felt ye but one pang such as I feel many,
> One pang of despair or one pang of desire,
> One pang of one displeasant look of her eye,
> One pang of one word of her mouth as in ire,
> Or in restraint of her love which I desire—
> One pang of all these, felt once in all your life,
> Should quail your opinion and quench all our strife.

These dactylic resolutions of the third and fourth lines are extremely interesting. But the most remarkable example of accidental metrical invention that I have yet come across is to be found in the Earl of Surrey's translation of Horace's ode on the golden mean. Surrey was one of the pioneers of the reaction against the vagueness and uncertain carelessness of the post-Chaucerians. From the example of Italian poetry he had learned that a line must have a fixed number of syllables. In all his poems his aim is always to achieve regularity at whatever cost. To make sure of having ten syllables in every line it is evident that Surrey made use of his fingers as well as his ears. We see him at his worst and most laborious in the first stanza of his translation:

> Of thy life, Thomas, this compass well mark:
> Not aye with full sails the high seas to beat;
> Ne by coward dread in shunning storms dark
> On shallow shores thy keel in peril freat.

The ten syllables are there all right, but except in the last line there is no recognizable rhythm of any kind, whether regular or irregular. But when Surrey comes to the second stanza—

> Auream quisquis mediocritatem
> Diligit, tutus caret obsoleti
> Sordibus tecti, caret invidenda
> Sobrius aula—

some lucky accident inspires him with the genius to translate in these words:

> Whoso gladly halseth the golden mean,
> Void of dangers advisedly hath his home;
> Not with loathsome muck as a den unclean,
> Nor palace like, whereat disdain may gloam.

Not only is this a very good translation, but it is also a very interesting and subtle metrical experiment. What could be more felicitous than this stanza made up of three trochaic lines, quickened by beautiful dactylic resolutions, and a final iambic line of regular measure—the recognized tonic chord that brings the music to its close? And yet the tonelessness of the first stanza is enough to prove that Surrey's achievement is as much a product of accident as the foam on the jaws of Apelles' dog. He was doing his best all the time to write decasyllables with the normal iambic beat of the last line. His failures to do so were sometimes unconscious strokes of genius.

[*On the Margin*, 1923]

Polite Conversation

THERE ARE SOME PEOPLE to whom the most difficult to obey of all the commandments is that which enjoins us to suffer fools gladly. The prevalence of folly, its monumental, unchanging permanence and its almost invariable triumph over intelligence are phenomena which they cannot contemplate without experiencing a passion of righteous indignation or, at the least, of ill temper. Sages like Anatole France, who can probe and anatomize human stupidity and still remain serenely detached, are rare. These reflections were suggested by a book recently published in New York and entitled *The American Credo*. The authors of this work are those *enfants terribles* of American criticism, Messrs. H. L. Mencken and George Jean Nathan.[2] They have compiled a list of four hundred and eighty-eight articles of faith which form the fundamental Credo of the American people, prefacing them with a very entertaining essay on the national mind:

> Truth shifts and changes like a cataract of diamonds; its aspect is never
> precisely the same at two successive moments. But error flows down

---

2. Henry Louis Mencken (1880–1956). American journalist and satirist. George Jean Nathan (1882–1958). American editor and drama critic.

the channel of history like some great stream of lava or infinitely lethargic glacier. It is the one relatively fixed thing in a world of chaos.

To look through the articles of the Credo is to realize that there is a good deal of truth in this statement. Such beliefs as the following—not by any means confined to America alone—are probably at least as old as the Great Pyramid:

> That if a woman, about to become a mother, plays the piano every day, her baby will be born a Victor Herbert.
> That the accumulation of great wealth always brings with it great unhappiness.
> That it is bad luck to kill a spider.
> That water rots the hair—and thus causes baldness.
> That if a bride wears an old garter with her new finery, she will have a happy married life.
> That children were much better behaved twenty years ago than they are today.

And most of the others in the collection, albeit clothed in forms distinctively contemporary and American, are simply variations on notions as immemorial.

Inevitably, as one reads *The American Credo,* one is reminded of an abler, a more pitiless and ferocious onslaught on stupidity, I mean Swift's *"Complete Collection of Genteel and Ingenious Conversation, according to the most polite mode and method now used at Court and in the Best Companies of England. In three Dialogues. By Simon Wagstaff, Esq."* I was inspired after reading Messrs. Mencken and Nathan's work to refresh my memories of this diabolic picture of the social amenities. And what a book it is! There is something almost appalling in the way it goes on and on, a continuous, never-ceasing stream of imbecility. Simon Wagstaff, it will be remembered, spent the best part of forty years in collecting and digesting these gems of polite conversation:

> I can faithfully assure the reader that there is not one single witty phrase in the whole Collection which has not received the Stamp and Approbation of at least One Hundred Years, and how much longer it is hard to determine; he may therefore be secure to find them all genuine, sterling, and authentic.

How genuine, sterling, and authentic Mr. Wagstaff's treasures of polite conversation are is proved by the great number of them which have withstood all the ravages of time, and still do as good service today as they did in the early seventeen-hundreds or in the days of Henry VIII: "Go, you

Girl, and warm some fresh Cream." "Indeed, Madam, there's none left; for the Cat has eaten it all." "I doubt it was a Cat with Two Legs." "And, pray, What News, Mr. Neverout?" "Why, Madam, Queen Elizabeth's dead." (It would be interesting to discover at exactly what date Queen Anne took the place of Queen Elizabeth in this grand old repartee, or who was the monarch referred to when the Virgin Queen was still alive. Aspirants to the degree of B. or D. Litt. might do worse than to take this problem as a subject for their thesis.) Some of the choicest phrases have come down in the world since Mr. Wagstaff's day. Thus, Miss Notable's retort to Mr. Neverout, "Go, teach your Grannam to suck Eggs," could only be heard now in the dormitory of a preparatory school. Others have become slightly modified. Mr. Neverout says, "Well, all Things have an End, and a pudden has two."

I think we may flatter ourselves that the modern emendation, "except a roly-poly pudding, which has two," is an improvement. Mr. Wagstaff's second dialogue, wherein he treats of Polite Conversation at meals, contains more phrases that testify to the unbroken continuity of tradition than either of the others. The conversation that centers on the sirloin of beef is worthy to be recorded in its entirety:

LADY SMART. Come, Colonel, handle your Arms. Shall I help you to some Beef?

COLONEL. If your Ladyship please; and, pray, don't cut like a Mother-in-law, but send me a large Slice; for I love to lay a good Foundation. I vow, 'tis a noble Sir-loyn.

NEVEROUT. Ay; here's cut and come again.

MISS. But, pray; why is it call'd a Sir-loyn?

LORD SMART. Why, you must know that our King James the First, who lov'd good Eating, being invited to Dinner by one of his Nobles, and seeing a large Loyn of Beef at his Table, he drew out his Sword, and, in a Frolic, knighted it. Few people know the Secret of this.

How delightful it is to find that we have Mr. Wagstaff's warrant for such gems of wisdom as, "Cheese digests everything except itself," and "If you eat till you're cold, you'll live to grow old." If they were a hundred years old in his day they are fully three hundred now. Long may they survive! I was sorry, however, to notice that one of the best of Mr. Wagstaff's phrases has been, in the revolution of time, completely lost. Indeed, before I had read Aubrey's *Lives,* Lord Sparkish's remark, "Come, box it about; 'twill come to my Father at last," was quite incomprehensible to me. The phrase is taken from a story of Sir Walter Raleigh and his son.

Sir Walter Raleigh [says Aubrey] being invited to dinner to some great person where his son was to goe with him, he sayd to his son, "Thou art expected today at dinner to goe along with me, but thou art so quarrelsome and affronting that I am ashamed to have such a beare in my company." Mr. Walter humbled himselfe to his father and promised he would behave himselfe mighty mannerly. So away they went. He sate next to his father and was very demure at least halfe dinner time. Then says he, "I this morning, not having the feare of God before my eies, but by the instigation of the devill, went. . . ."

At this point Mr. Clark, in his edition, suppresses four lines of Aubrey's text; but one can imagine the sort of thing Master Walter said. Sir Walter, being strangely surprized and putt out of countenance at so great a table, gives his son a damned blow over the face. His son, as rude as he was, would not strike his father, but strikes over the face the Gentleman that sate next to him and sayd, "Box about: 'twill come to my father anon." 'Tis now a common used proverb.

And so it still deserves to be; how, when, and why it became extinct, I have no idea. Here is another good subject for a thesis. There are but few things in Mr. Wagstaff's dialogue which appear definitely out of date and strange to us, and these superannuations can easily be accounted for. Thus the repeal of the Criminal Laws has made almost incomprehensible the constant references to hanging made by Mr. Wagstaff's personages. The oaths and the occasional mild grossnesses have gone out of fashion in mixed polite society. Otherwise their conversation is in all essentials exactly the same as the conversation of the present day. And this is not to be wondered at; for, as a wise man has said:

Speech at the present time retains strong evidence of the survival in it of the function of herd recognition. . . . The function of conversation is ordinarily regarded as being the exchange of ideas and information. Doubtless it has come to have such a function, but an objective examination of ordinary conversation shows that the actual conveyance of ideas takes a very small part in it. As a rule the exchange seems to consist of ideas which are necessarily common to the two speakers and are known to be so by each. . . . Conversation between persons unknown to one another is apt to be rich in the ritual of recognition. When one hears or takes part in these elaborate evolutions, gingerly proffering one after another of one's marks of identity, one's views on the weather, on fresh air and draughts, on the Government and on uric acid, watching intently for the first low hint of a growl, which will show one belongs to the wrong pack and must withdraw, it is impossible not to be reminded of the similar maneuvres of the dog and to be thankful that Nature has provided us with a less direct, though perhaps a more tedious, code.

[*On the Margin, 1923*]

Nationality in Love

THE HAZARDS of indiscriminate rummaging in bookshops have introduced me to two volumes of verse which seem to me (though I am ordinarily very skeptical of those grandiose generalizations about racial and national characteristics, so beloved of a certain class of literary people) to illustrate very clearly some of the differences between the French and English mind. The first is a little book published some few months back and entitled *Les Baisers*. . . . The publisher says of it in one of those exquisitely literary puffs which are the glory of the Paris book trade: "Un volume de vers? Non pas! Simplement des baisers mis en vers, des baisers variés comme l'heure qui passe, inconstants comme l'Amour lui-même. . . . Baisers, baisers, c'est toute leur troublante musique qui chante dans ces rimes." The other volume hails from the antipodes and is called *Songs of Love and Life*. No publisher's puff accompanies it; but a colored picture on the dustwrapper represents a nymph frantically clutching at a coy shepherd. A portrait of the authoress serves as a frontispiece.

Both books are erotic in character, and both are very indifferent in poetical quality. They are only interesting as illustrations, the more vivid because of their very second-rateness, of the two characteristic methods of approach, French and English, to the theme of physical passion.

The author of *Les Baisers* approaches his amorous experiences with the detached manner of a psychologist interested in the mental reactions of certain corporeal pleasures whose mechanism he has previously studied in his capacity of physiological observer. His attitude is the same as that of the writers of those comedies of manners which hold the stage in the theaters of the boulevards. It is dry, precise, matter-of-fact, and almost scientific. The comedian of the boulevards does not concern himself with trying to find some sort of metaphysical justification for the raptures of physical passion, nor is he in any way a propagandist of sensuality. He is simply an analyst of facts, whose business it is to get all the wit that is possible out of an equivocal situation. Similarly, the author of these poems is far too highly sophisticated to imagine that every spirit as it is is most pure,

And hath in it the more of heavenly light,
So it the fairer body doth procure

To habit in, and it more fairly dight
With cheerful grace and amiable sight.
For of the soul the body form doth take
For soul is form and doth the body make.[3]

He does not try to make us believe that physical pleasures have a divine justification. Neither has he any wish to "make us grovel, hand and foot in Belial's gripe." He is merely engaged in remembering "des heures et des entretiens" which were extremely pleasant—hours which strike for everyone, conversations and meetings which are taking place in all parts of the world and at every moment.

This attitude towards *volupté* is sufficiently old in France to have made possible the evolution of a very precise and definite vocabulary in which to describe its phenomena. This language is as exact as the technical jargon of a trade, and as elegant as the Latin of Petronius. It is a language of which we have no equivalent in our English literature. It is impossible in English to describe *volupté* elegantly; it is hardly possible to write of it without being gross. To begin with, we do not even possess a word equivalent to *volupté*. "Voluptuousness" is feeble and almost meaningless; "pleasure" is hopelessly inadequate. From the first the English writer is at a loss; he cannot even name precisely the thing he proposes to describe and analyze. But for the most part he has not much use for such a language. His approach to the subject is not dispassionate and scientific, and he has no need for technicalities. The English amorist is inclined to approach the subject rapturously, passionately, philosophically—almost in any way that is not the wittily matter-of-fact French way.

In our rich Australian *Songs of Love and Life* we see the rapturous-philosophic approach reduced to something that is very nearly the absurd. Overcome with the intensities of connubial bliss, the authoress feels it necessary to find a sort of justification for them by relating them in some way with the cosmos. God, we are told,

looking through His hills on you and me,
Feeds Heaven upon the flame of our desire.

Or again:

Our passions breathe their own wild harmony,
And pour out music at a clinging kiss.
Sing on, O Soul, our lyric of desire,
For God Himself is in the melody.

3. From Edmund Spenser's "An Hymne in Honour of Beautie."

Meanwhile the author of *Les Baisers,* always elegantly *terre-à-terre,* formulates his more concrete desires in an Alexandrine worthy of Racine:

Viens. Je veux dégrafer moi-même ton corsage.

The desire to involve the cosmos in our emotions is by no means confined to the poetess of *Songs of Love and Life.* In certain cases we are all apt to invoke the universe in an attempt to explain and account for emotions whose intensity seems almost inexplicable. This is particularly true of the emotions aroused in us by the contemplation of beauty. Why we should feel so strongly when confronted with certain forms and colors, certain sounds, certain verbal suggestions of form and harmony—why the thing which we call beauty should move us at all—goodness only knows. In order to explain the phenomenon, poets have involved the universe in the matter, asserting that they are moved by the contemplation of physical beauty because it is the symbol of the divine. The intensities of physical passion have presented the same problem. Ashamed of admitting that such feelings can have a purely sublunary cause, we affirm, like the Australian poetess, that "God Himself is in the melody." That, we argue, can be the only explanation for the violence of the emotion. This view of the matter is particularly common in a country with fundamental puritanic traditions like England, where the dry, matter-of-fact attitude of the French seems almost shocking. The puritan feels bound to justify the facts of beauty and *volupté.* They must be in some way made moral before he can accept them. The French un-puritanic mind accepts the facts as they are tendered to it by experience, at their face value.

[*On the Margin,* 1923]

How the Days Draw In

THE AUTUMN EQUINOX is close upon us with all its presages of mortality, a shortening day, a colder and longer night. How the days draw in! Fear of ridicule hardly allows one to make the melancholy constatation. It is a conversational gambit that, like fool's mate, can only be used against the simplest and least experienced of players. And yet how much of the world's most moving poetry is nothing but a variation on the theme of this in-drawing day! The certainty of death has inspired more poetry than the hope of immortality. The visible transience of frail and lovely matter has impressed itself more profoundly on the mind of man than the notion of spiritual permanence.

Et l'on verra bientôt surgir du sein de l'onde
La première clarté de mon dernier soleil.[4]

That is an article of faith from which nobody can withhold assent. Of
late I have found myself almost incapable of enjoying any poetry whose inspiration is not despair or melancholy. Why, I hardly know. Perhaps it is
due to the chronic horror of the political situation. For heaven knows, that
is quite sufficient to account for a taste for melancholy verse. The subject
of any European government today feels all the sensations of Gulliver in
the paws of the Queen of Brobdingnag's monkey—the sensations of some
small and helpless being at the mercy of something monstrous and irre-
sponsible and idiotic. There sits the monkey "on the ridge of a building
five hundred yards above the ground, holding us like a baby in one of his
fore paws." Will he let go? Will he squeeze us to death? The best we can
hope for is to be "let drop on a ridge tile," with only enough bruises to
keep one in bed for a fortnight. But it seems very unlikely that some "honest lad will climb up and, putting us in his breeches pocket, bring us down
safe." However, I divagate a little from my subject, which is the poetry of
melancholy.

Some day I shall compile an Oxford Book of Depressing Verse, which
shall contain nothing but the most magnificent expressions of melancholy
and despair. All the obvious people will be in it and as many of the obscure
apostles of gloom as vague and miscellaneous reading shall have made
known to me. A duly adequate amount of space, for example, will be allotted to that all but great poet, Fulke Greville, Lord Brooke. For dark
magnificence there are not many things that can rival that summing up
against life and human destiny at the end of his "Mustapha."

Oh wearisome condition of humanity,
Born under one law to another bound,
Vainly begot and yet forbidden vanity,
Created sick, commanded to be sound.
What meaneth nature by these diverse laws,
Passion and reason, self-division's cause?
Is it the mark or majesty of power
To make offenses that it may forgive?
Nature herself doth her own self deflower
To hate those errors she herself doth give. . . .
If nature did not take delight in blood,
She would have made more easy ways to good.

4. From F. Maynard's *Poesies* (1646).

Milton aimed at justifying the ways of God to man; Fulke Greville gloomily denounces them. Nor shall I omit from my anthology the extraordinary description in the Prologue to "Alaham" of the Hell of Hells and of Privation, the peculiar torment of the place:

> Thou monster horrible, under whose ugly doom
> Down in eternity's perpetual night
> Man's temporal sins bear torments infinite,
> For change of desolation must I come
> To tempt the earth and to profane the light.
> A place there is, upon no center placed,
> Deep under depths as far as is the sky
> Above the earth, dark, infinitely spaced,
> Pluto the king, the kingdom misery.
> Privation would reign there, by God not made,
> But creature of uncreated sin,
> Whose being is all beings to invade,
> To have no ending though it did begin;
> And so of past, things present and to come,
> To give depriving, not tormenting doom.
> But horror in the understanding mixed. . . .

Like most of his contemporaries in those happy days before the notion of progress had been invented, Lord Brooke was what Peacock would have called a "Pejorationist." His political views (and they were also Sidney's) are reflected in his *Life of Sir Philip Sidney*. The best that a statesman can do, according to these Elizabethan pessimists, is to patch and prop the decaying fabric of society in the hope of staving off for a little longer the final inevitable crash. It seems curious to us, who have learnt to look at the Elizabethan age as the most splendid in English history, that the men who were the witnesses of these splendors should have regarded their time as an age of decadence.

The notion of the Fall was fruitful in despairing poetry. One of the most remarkable products of this doctrine is a certain "Sonnet Chrétien" by the seventeenth-century writer Jean Ogier de Gombauld, surnamed "le Beau Ténébreux."

> Cette source de mort, cette homicide peste,
> Ce péché dont l'enfer a le monde infecté,
> M'a laissé pour tout être un bruit d'avoir été,
> Et je suis de moi-même une image funeste.
> L'Auteur de l'univers, le Monarque céleste
> S'était rendu visible en ma seule beauté.

Ce vieux titre d'honneur qu'autrefois j'ai porté
Et que je porte encore, est tout ce qui me reste.

Mais c'est fait de ma gloire, et je ne suis plus rien
Qu'un fantôme qui court après l'ombre d'un bien,
Ou qu'un corps animé du seul ver qui le ronge.

Non, je ne suis plus rien quand je veux m'éprouver,
Qu'un esprit ténébreux qui voit tout comme en songe
Et cherche incessament ce qu'il ne peut trouver.[5]

There are astonishing lines in this, lines that might have been written by a Baudelaire, if he had been born a Huguenot and two hundred years before his time. That "carcase animated by the sole gnawing worm" is something that one would expect to find rotting away among the somber and beautiful Flowers of Evil. An amusing speculation. If Steinach's rejuvenating operations on the old become the normal and accepted thing, what will be the effect on poetry of this abolition of the depressing process of decay? It may be that the poetry of melancholy and despair is destined to lose its place in literature, and that a spirit of what William James called "healthy-mindedness" will inherit its kingdom. Many "eternal truths" have already found their way on to the dust-heap of antiquated ideas. It may be that this last and seemingly most inexorable of them—that life is short and subject to a dreadful decay—will join the other great commonplaces which have already perished out of literature.

The flesh is bruckle, the fiend is slee:
Timor mortis conturbat me:—[6]

---

5. This source of death, this murdering plague,
   This sin with which hell has infected the world
   Has left me for all beings a noise to have been
   And I am a deathly image of myself.
   The Author of the Universe, the heavenly Monarch,
   Was Himself visible only in my beauty.
   This old title of honor which I formerly bore
   And which I still bear, is all that's left to me.

   But it's done to my glory, and I am nothing more than
   A ghost who runs after the shade of some good,
   Or than a carcase animated by the sole gnawing worm.

   No, I am nothing more, when I want to blame myself,
   Than a gloomy spirit who sees everything as in a dream
   And who seeks incessantly what he can never find.

6. These lines are taken from the Scottish poet William Dunbar's (1460–1520) "Lament for the Makaris Quhen He was Sek" (1508).

Some day, it may be, these sentiments will seem as hopelessly superannu-ated as Milton's cosmology.

[*On the Margin*, 1923]

Beauty in 1920

TO THOSE who know how to read the signs of the times it will have be-come apparent, in the course of these last days and weeks, that the Silly Season is close upon us. Already—and this in July with the menace of three or four new wars grumbling on the thunderous horizon—already a monster of the deep has appeared at a popular seaside resort. Already Mr. Louis McQuilland has launched in the *Daily Express* a fierce onslaught on the younger poets of the Asylum. Already the picture-papers are more than half filled with photographs of bathing nymphs—photographs that make one understand the ease with which St. Anthony rebuffed his temp-tations. The newspaper-men, ramping up and down like wolves, seek their prey wherever they may find it; and it was with a unanimous howl of de-light that the whole Press went pelting after the hare started by Mrs. Asquith[7] in a recent installment of her autobiography. Feebly and belat-edly, let me follow the pack.

Mrs. Asquith's denial of beauty to the daughters of the twentieth cen-tury has proved a god-sent giant gooseberry. It has necessitated the calling in of a whole host of skin-food specialists, portrait-painters, and photog-raphers to deny this far from soft impeachment. A great deal of space has been agreeably and inexpensively filled. Everyone is satisfied, public, edi-tors, skin-food specialists and all. But by far the most interesting contribu-tion to the debate was a pictorial one, which appeared, if I remember rightly, in the *Daily News*. Side by side, on the same page, we were shown the photographs of three beauties of the eighteen-eighties and three of the nineteen-twenties. The comparison was most instructive. For a great gulf separates the two types of beauty represented by these two sets of pho-tographs.

I remember in *If,* one of those charming conspiracies of E. V. Lucas and George Morrow,[8] a series of parodied fashion-plates entitled "If Faces get any Flatter. Last year's standard, this year's Evening Standard." The faces of our living specimens of beauty have grown flatter with those of

7. Emma Margaret (Margot) Asquith (1864–1945). Wife of the English prime minister Herbert Asquith. Her *Autobiography* was published in two volumes (1920–1922).

8. Edward Verrall Lucas (1868–1938). English essayist and biographer. He was an as-sistant editor of *Punch*.

their fashion-plate sisters. Compare the types of 1880 and 1920. The first is steep-faced, almost Roman in profile; in the contemporary beauties the face has broadened and shortened, the profile is less noble, less imposing, more appealingly, more alluringly pretty. Forty years ago it was the aristocratic type that was appreciated; today the popular taste has shifted from the countess to the soubrette. Photography confirms the fact that the ladies of the eighties looked like Du Maurier drawings. But among the present young generation one looks in vain for the type; the Du Maurier damsel is as extinct as the mesozoic reptile; the Fish girl and other kindred flat-faced species have taken her place.

Between the thirties and fifties another type, the egg-faced girl, reigned supreme in the affections of the world. From the early portraits of Queen Victoria to the fashion-plates in the *Ladies' Keepsake* this invariable type prevails—the egg-shaped face, the sleek hair, the swanlike neck, the round, champagne-bottle shoulders. Compared with the decorous impassivity of the oviform girl our flat-faced fashion-plates are terribly abandoned and provocative. And because one expects so much in the way of respectability from these egg-faces of an earlier age, one is apt to be shocked when one sees them conducting themselves in ways that seem unbefitting. One thinks of that enchanting picture of Etty's,[9] "Youth on the Prow and Pleasure at the Helm." The naiads are of the purest egg-faced type. Their hair is sleek, their shoulders slope and their faces are as impassive as blanks. And yet they have no clothes on. It is almost indecent; one imagined that the egg-faced type came into the world complete with flowing draperies.

It is not only the face of beauty that alters with the changes of popular taste. The champagne-bottle shoulders of the oviform girl have vanished from the modern fashion-plate and from modern life. The contemporary hand, with its two middle fingers held together and the forefinger and little finger splayed apart, is another recent product. Above all, the feet have changed. In the days of the egg-faces no fashion-plate had more than one foot. This rule will, I think, be found invariable. That solitary foot projects, generally in a strangely haphazard way as though it had nothing to do with a leg, from under the edge of the skirt. And what a foot! It has no relation to those provocative feet in Suckling's ballad:

Her feet beneath her petticoat
Like little mice stole in and out.[1]

9. William Etty (1787–1849). English painter.
1. From Sir John Suckling's "A Ballad Upon a Wedding" (1641).

It is an austere foot. It is a small, black, oblong object like a tea-leaf. No living human being has ever seen a foot like it, for it is utterly unlike the feet of nineteen-twenty. Today the fashion-plate is always a biped. The tea-leaf has been replaced by two feet of rich baroque design, curved and florid, with insteps like the necks of Arab horses. Faces may have changed shape, but feet have altered far more radically. On the text, "the feet of the young women," it would be possible to write a profound philosophical sermon.

And while I am on the subject of feet I would like to mention another curious phenomenon of the same kind, but affecting, this time, the standards of male beauty. Examine the pictorial art of the eighteenth century, and you will find that the shape of the male leg is not what it was. In those days the calf of the leg was not a muscle that bulged to its greatest dimensions a little below the back of the knee, to subside, decrescendo, towards the ankle. No, in the eighteenth century the calf was an even crescent, with its greatest projection opposite the middle of the shin; the ankle, as we know it, hardly existed. This curious calf is forced upon one's attention by almost every minor picture-maker of the eighteenth century, and even by some of the great masters, as, for instance, Blake. How it came into existence I do not know. Presumably the crescent calf was considered, in the art schools, to approach more nearly to the Platonic Idea of the human leg than did the poor distorted Appearance of real life. Personally, I prefer my calves with the bulge at the top and a proper ankle at the bottom. But then I don't hold much with the *beau idéal*.

The process by which one type of beauty becomes popular imposes its tyranny for a period and then is displaced by a dissimilar type is a mysterious one. It may be that patient historical scholars will end by discovering some law to explain the transformation of the Du Maurier type into the flat-face type, the tea-leaf foot into the baroque foot, the crescent calf into the normal calf. As far as one can see at present, these changes seem to be the result of mere hazard and arbitrary choice. But a time will doubtless come when it will be found that these changes of taste are as ineluctably predetermined as any chemical change. Given the South African War, the accession of Edward VII, and the Liberal triumph of 1906, it was, no doubt, as inevitable that Du Maurier[2] should have given place to Fish as that zinc subjected to sulphuric acid should break up into $ZnSO_4 + H_2$. But we leave it to others to formulate the precise workings of the law.

[*On the Margin,* 1923]

2. George Louis Du Maurier (1834–1896). French-born British illustrator and novelist.

Great Thoughts

TO ALL LOVERS of unfamiliar quotations, aphorisms, great thoughts, and intellectual gems, I would heartily recommend a heavy volume recently published in Brussels and entitled *Pensées sur la Science, la Guerre et sur des sujets très variés*. The book contains some twelve or thirteen thousand quotations, selected from a treasure of one hundred and twenty-three thousand great thoughts gleaned and garnered by the industry of Dr. Maurice Legat—an industry which will be appreciated at its value by anyone who has ever made an attempt to compile a commonplace book or private anthology of his own. The almost intolerable labor of copying out extracts can only be avoided by the drastic use of the scissors; and there are few who can afford the luxury of mutilating their copies of the best authors.

For some days I made Dr. Legat's book my *livre de chevet*. But I had very soon to give up reading it at night, for I found that the Great often said things so peculiar that I was kept awake in the effort to discover their meaning. Why, for example, should it be categorically stated by Lamennais that "si les animaux connaissaient Dieu, ils parleraient"? What could Cardinal Maury have meant when he said, "L'éloquence, compagne ordinaire de la liberté [astonishing generalization!] est inconnue en Angleterre"? These were mysteries insoluble enough to counteract the soporific effects of such profound truths as this, discovered, apparently, in 1846 by Monsieur C. H. D. Duponchel, "Le plus sage mortel est sujet à l'erreur."

Dr. Legat has found some pleasing quotations on the subject of England and the English. His selection proves with what fatal ease even the most intelligent minds are lured into making generalizations about national character, and how grotesque those generalizations always are. Montesquieu informs us that "dès que sa fortune se délabre, un anglais tue ou se fait voleur." Of the better half of this potential murderer and robber Balzac says, "La femme anglaise est une pauvre créature vertueuse par force, prête à se dépraver." "La vanité est l'âme de toute société anglaise," says Lamartine. Ledru-Rollin is of opinion that all the riches of England are "des dépouilles volées aux tombeaux."[3]

The Goncourts risk a characteristically dashing generalization on the national characters of England and France: "L'Anglais, filou comme peu-

---

3. Montesquieu informs us that "as soon as his money runs out, an English kills or steals." Of the better half of this potential murderer and robber Balzac says, "The English woman is a poor virtuous creature by necessity, ready to deprave herself." "Vanity is the soul of all English society," says Lamartine. Ledru-Rollin is of opinion that all the riches of England are "the stolen remains of graveyards."

ple, est honnête comme individu. Il est le contraire du Français, honnête comme peuple, et filou comme individu." If one is going to make a comparison Voltaire's is more satisfactory because less pretentious. Strange are the ways of you Englishmen, qui, des mêmes couteaux, Coupez la tête au roi et la queue aux chevaux. Nous Français, plus humains, laissons aux rois leurs têtes, Et la queue à nos bêtes.[4]

It is unfortunate that history should have vitiated the truth of this pithy and pregnant statement.

But the bright spots in this enormous tome are rare. After turning over a few hundred pages one is compelled, albeit reluctantly, to admit that the Great Thought or Maxim is nearly the most boring form of literature that exists. Others, it seems, have anticipated me in this grand discovery.

"Las, de m'ennuyer des pensées des autres," says d'Alembert, "j'ai voulu leur donner les miennes; mais je puis me flatter de leur avoir rendu tout l'ennui que j'avais reçu d'eux." Almost next to d'Alembert's statement I find this confession from the pen of J. Roux (1834–1906): "Emettre des pensées, voilà ma consolation, mon délice, ma vie!" Happy Monsieur Roux![5]

Turning dissatisfied from Dr. Legat's anthology of thought, I happened upon the second number of *Proverbe*, a monthly review, four pages in length, directed by M. Paul Eluard and counting among its contributors Tristan Tzara of *Dada* fame, Messrs. Soupault, Breton, and Aragon, the directors of *Littérature,* M. Picabia, M. Ribemont-Dessaignes, and others of the same kidney.[6] Here, on the front page of the March number of *Proverbe,* I found the very comment on Great Thoughts for which I had, in my dissatisfaction, been looking. The following six maxims are printed one below the other: the first of them is a quotation from the *Intransigeant;* the other five appear to be the work of M. Tzara, who appends a footnote to this effect: je m'appelle dorénavant exclusivement Monsieur Paul Bourget.[7] Here they are:

4. "The English, crooked as a people, are honest as individuals. It is the opposite with the French, honest as a people, and crooked as individuals." Voltaire: Strange are the ways of you Englishmen, who, with the same blade, cut off the king's head and the tails of their horses. We French, more human, leave to the kings their heads, and to the beasts their tails.

5. "Tired of boring myself with the thoughts of others," says D'Alembert, "I wanted to give them mine, but I can flatter myself that I've given them back as much boredom as I have received from them." J. Roux: "To think thoughts, voilà my consolation, my delight, my life!"

6. Paul Eluard, pseud. of Eugène-Emile Grindel (1895–1952). French Surrealist poet. Philippe Soupault (1897–). French poet, novelist, and critic. André Breton (1896–1966). French poet and member of the Dadaist group. Louis Aragon (1897–1983). French writer and Surrealist. Georges Ribemont-Dessaignes (1874–1974). French dramatist and novelist.

7. Paul Bourget (1852–1935). French novelist and critic.

Il faut violer les règles, oui, mais pour les violer il faut les connaître.

Il faut régler la connaissance, oui, mais pour la régler il faut la violer.

Il faut connaître les viols, oui, mais pour les connaître il faut les régler.

Il faut connaître les règles, oui, mais pour les connaître il faut les violer.

Il faut régler les viols, oui, mais pour les régler il faut les connaître,

Il faut violer la connaissance, oui, mais pour la violer il faut la régler.[8]

It is to be hoped that Dr. Legat will find room for at least a selection of these profound thoughts in the next edition of his book. "Le passé et La pensée n'existent pas," affirms M. Raymond Duncan on another page of *Proverbe*. It is precisely after taking too large a dose of "Pensées sur la Science, la Guerre et sur des sujets très variés" that one half wishes the statement were in fact true.

[*On the Margin*, 1923]

Advertisements

I HAVE ALWAYS been interested in the subtleties of literary form. This preoccupation with the outward husk, with the letter of literature, is, I dare say, the sign of a fundamental spiritual impotence. Gigadibs, the literary man, can understand the tricks of the trade; but when it is a question, not of conjuring, but of miracles, he is no more effective than Mr. Sludge. Still, conjuring is amusing to watch and to practice; an interest in the machinery of the art requires no further justification. I have dallied with many literary forms, taking pleasure in their different intricacies, studying the means by which great authors of the past have resolved the technical problems presented by each. Sometimes I have even tried my hand at solving the problems myself—delightful and salubrious exercise for the mind. And now I have discovered the most exciting, the most arduous literary form of all, the most difficult to master, the most pregnant in curious possibilities. I mean the advertisement.

8. One must break the rules, yes, but in order to break them, one must know them.
One must govern knowledge, yes, but in order to govern it, one must violate it.
One must understand transgressions, yes, but in order to understand them, one must govern them.
One must know the rules, yes, but to know them, one must break them.
One must govern transgressions, yes, but in order to govern them, one must know them.
One must go beyond knoweldge, yes, but in order to go beyond it, one must govern it.

Nobody who has not tried to write an advertisement has any idea of the delights and difficulties presented by this form of literature—or shall I say of "applied literature," for the sake of those who still believe in the romantic superiority of the pure, the disinterested, over the immediately useful? The problem that confronts the writer of advertisements is an immensely complicated one, and by reason of its very arduousness immensely interesting. It is far easier to write ten passably effective Sonnets, good enough to take in the not too inquiring critic, than one effective advertisement that will take in a few thousand of the uncritical buying public. The problem presented by the Sonnet is child's play compared with the problem of the advertisement. In writing a Sonnet one need think only of oneself. If one's readers find one boring or obscure, so much the worse for them. But in writing an advertisement one must think of other people. Advertisement writers may not be lyrical, or obscure, or in any way esoteric. They must be universally intelligible. A good advertisement has this in common with drama and oratory, that it must be immediately comprehensible and directly moving. But at the same time it must possess all the succinctness of epigram.

The orator and the dramatist have "world enough and time" to produce their effects by cumulative appeals; they can turn all round their subject, they can repeat; between the heights of their eloquence they can gracefully practice the art of sinking, knowing that a period of flatness will only set off the splendor of their impassioned moments. But the advertiser has no space to spare; he pays too dearly for every inch. He must play upon the minds of his audience with a small and limited instrument. He must persuade them to part with their money in a speech that is no longer than many a lyric by Herrick. Could any problem be more fascinatingly difficult? No one should be allowed to talk about the *mot juste* or the polishing of style who has not tried his hand at writing an advertisement of something which the public does not want, but which it must be persuaded into buying. Your *boniment* must not exceed a poor hundred and fifty or two hundred words. With what care you must weigh every syllable! What infinite pains must be taken to fashion every phrase into a barbed hook that shall stick in the reader's mind and draw from its hiding-place within his pocket the reluctant coin! One's style and ideas must be lucid and simple enough to be understood by all; but at the same time, they must not be vulgar. Elegance and an economical distinction are required; but any trace of literariness in an advertisement is fatal to its success.

I do not know whether anyone has yet written a history of advertising. If the book does not already exist it will certainly have to be written. The story of the development of advertising from its infancy in the early nineteenth century to its luxuriant maturity in the twentieth is an essential chapter in the history of democracy. Advertisement begins abjectly, crawling on its belly like the serpent after the primal curse. Its abjection is the oily humbleness of the shopkeeper in an oligarchical society. Those nauseating references to the nobility and clergy, which are the very staple of early advertisements, are only possible in an age when the aristocracy and its established Church effectively ruled the land. The custom of invoking these powers lingered on long after they had ceased to hold sway. It is now, I fancy, almost wholly extinct. It may be that certain old-fashioned girls' schools still provide education for the daughters of the nobility and clergy; but I am inclined to doubt it. Advertisers still find it worthwhile to parade the names and escutcheons of kings. But anything less than royalty is, frankly, a "wash-out."

The crawling style of advertisement with its mixture of humble appeals to patrons and its hyperbolical laudation of the goods advertised, was early varied by the pseudo-scientific style, a simple development of the quack's patter at the fair. Balzacians will remember the advertisement composed by Finot and the Illustrious Gaudissard for César Birotteau's "Huile Céphalique."[9] The type is not yet dead; we still see advertisements of substances "based on the principles established by the Academy of Sciences," substances known "to the ancients, the Romans, the Greeks and the nations of the North," but lost and only rediscovered by the advertiser. The style and manner of these advertisements belonging to the early and middle periods of the Age of Advertisement continue to bear the imprint of the once despicable position of commerce. They are written with the impossible and insincere unctuousness of tradesmen's letters. They are horribly uncultured; and when their writers aspire to something more ambitious than the counting-house style, they fall at once into the stilted verbiage of self-taught learning. Some of the earlier efforts to raise the tone of advertisements are very curious. One remembers those remarkable full-page advertisements of Eno's Fruit Salt, loaded with weighty apophthegms from Emerson, Epictetus, Zeno the Eleatic, Pomponazzi, Slawkenbergius,[1] and other founts of human wisdom. There was noble reading on these strange pages. But they shared with sermons the defect of being a little dull.

The art of advertisement writing has flowered with democracy. The lords of industry and commerce came gradually to understand that the right way to appeal to the Free Peoples of the World was familiarly, in an

---

9. Characters in Balzac's *L'Illustre Gaudissart* (1833) and *César Birouteau* (1837).

1. Pietro Pomponazzi (1462–1525). Italian Aristotelian philosopher. Slawkenbergius was a fictional author in Sterne's *Tristram Shandy*.

honest man-to-man style. They perceived that exaggeration and hyperbole do not really pay, that charlatanry must at least have an air of sincerity. They confided in the public, they appealed to its intelligence in every kind of flattering way. The technique of the art became at once immensely more difficult than it had ever been before, until now the advertisement is, as I have already hinted, one of the most interesting and difficult of modern literary forms. Its potentialities are not yet half explored. Already the most interesting and, in some cases, the only readable part of most American periodicals is the advertisement section. What does the future hold in store?

[*On the Margin*, 1923]

Euphues Redivivus

I HAVE RECENTLY been fortunate in securing a copy of that very rare and precious novel *Delina Delaney*, by Amanda M. Ros, authoress of *Irene Iddesleigh* and *Poems of Puncture*. Mrs. Ros's name is only known to a small and select band of readers. But by these few she is highly prized; one of her readers, it is said, actually was at the pains to make a complete manuscript copy of *Delina Delaney*, so great was his admiration and so hopelessly out of print the book. Let me recommend the volume, Mrs. Ros's masterpiece, to the attention of enterprising publishers.

Delina Delaney opens with a tremendous, an almost, in its richness of vituperative eloquence, Rabelaisian denunciation of Mr. Barry Pain, who had, it seems, treated *Irene Iddesleigh* with scant respect in his review of the novel in *Black and White*. "This so-called Barry Pain, by name, has taken upon himself to criticize a work, the depth of which fails to reach the solving power of his borrowed, and, he'd have you believe, varied talent." But "I care not for the opinion of half-starved upstarts, who don the garb of a shabby-genteel, and fain would feed the mind of the people with the worthless scraps of stolen fancies." So perish all reviewers! And now for Delina herself.

The story is a simple one. Delina Delaney, daughter of a fisherman, loves and is loved by Lord Gifford. The baleful influence of a dark-haired Frenchwoman, Madame de Maine, daughter of the Count-av-Nevo, comes between the lovers and their happiness, and Delina undergoes fearful torments, including three years' penal servitude, before their union can take place. It is the manner, rather than the matter, of the book which is remarkable. Here, for instance, is a fine conversation between Lord Gifford and his mother, an aristocratic dame who strenuously objects to his connection with Delina. Returning one day to Columba Castle she hears an unpleasant piece of news: her son has been seen kissing Delina in the conservatory.

> "Home again, mother?" he boldly uttered, as he gazed reverently in her face.
>
> "Home to Hades!" returned the raging high-bred daughter of distinguished effeminacy.
>
> "Ah me! what is the matter?" meekly inquired his lordship.
>
> "Everything is the matter with a brokenhearted mother of low-minded offspring," she answered hotly.... "Henry Edward Ludlow Gifford, son of my strength, idolized remnant of my inert husband, who at this moment invisibly offers the scourging whip of fatherly authority to your backbone of resentment (though for years you think him dead to your movements) and pillar of maternal trust."

Poor Lady Gifford! Her son's behavior was her undoing. The shock caused her to lose first her reason and then her life. Her son was heart-broken at the thought that he was responsible for her downfall:

> "Is it true, O Death," I cried in my agony, "that you have wrested from me my mother, Lady Gifford of Columba Castle, and left me here, a unit figuring on the great blackboard of the past, the shaky surface of the present and fickle field of the future to track my lifesteps, with gross indifference to her wished-for wish?" ... Blind she lay to the presence of her son, who charged her death-gun with the powder of accelerated wrath.

It is impossible to suppose that Mrs. Ros can ever have read *Euphues* or the earlier romances of Robert Greene. How then shall we account for the extraordinary resemblance to Euphuism of her style? How explain those rich alliterations, those elaborate "kennings" and circumlocutions of which the fabric of her book is woven? Take away from Lyly his erudition and his passion for antithesis, and you have Mrs. Ros. Delina is own sister to Euphues and Pandosto. The fact is that Mrs. Ros happens, though separated from Euphuism by three hundred years and more, to have arrived independently at precisely the same stage of development as Lyly and his disciples. It is possible to see in a growing child a picture in miniature of all the phases through which humanity has passed in its development. And, in the same way, the mind of an individual (especially when that individual has been isolated from the main current of contemporary thought) may climb, alone, to a point at which, in the past, a whole generation has rested. In Mrs. Ros we see, as we see in the Elizabethan novelists, the result of the discovery of art by an unsophisticated mind and of its first conscious attempt to produce the artistic. It is remarkable how late in the history of every literature simplicity is invented.

The first attempts of any people to be consciously literary are always productive of the most elaborate artificiality. Poetry is always written before prose and always in a language as remote as possible from the language of ordinary life. The language and versification of *Beowulf* are far more artificial and remote from life than those of, say, *The Rape of the Lock*. The Euphuists were not barbarians making their first discovery of literature; they were, on the contrary, highly educated. But in one thing they were unsophisticated: they were discovering prose. They were realizing that prose could be written with art, and they wrote it as artificially as they possibly could, just as their Saxon ancestors wrote poetry. They became intoxicated with their discovery of artifice. It was some time before the intoxication wore off and men saw that art was possible without artifice. Mrs. Ros, an Elizabethan born out of her time, is still under the spell of that magical and delicious intoxication.

Mrs. Ros's artifices are often more remarkable and elaborate even than Lyly's. This is how she tells us that Delina earned money by doing needlework:

> She tried hard to keep herself a stranger to her poor old father's slight income by the use of the finest production of steel, whose blunt edge eyed the reely covering with marked greed, and offered its sharp dart to faultless fabrics of flaxen fineness.

And Lord Gifford parts from Delina in these words:

> I am just in time to hear the toll of a parting bell strike its heavy weight of appalling softness against the weakest fibers of a heart of love, arousing and tickling its dormant action, thrusting the dart of evident separation deeper into its tubes of tenderness, and fanning the flame, already unextinguishable, into volumes of burning blaze.

But more often Mrs. Ros does not exceed the bounds which Lyly set for himself. Here, for instance, is a sentence that might have come direct out of *Euphues:*

> Two days after, she quit Columba Castle and resolved to enter the holy cloisters of a convent, where, she believed she'd be dead to the built hopes of wealthy worth, the crooked steps to worldly distinction, and the designing creaks [sic] in the muddy stream of love.

Or again, this description of the artful charmers who flaunt along the streets of London is written in the very spirit and language of *Euphues:*

Their hair was a light-golden color, thickly fringed in front, hiding in
many cases the furrows of a life of vice; behind, reared coils, some of
which differed in hue, exhibiting the fact that they were on patrol for
the price of another supply of dye. . . . The elegance of their attire had
the glow of robbery—the rustle of many a lady's silent curse. These
tools of brazen effrontery were strangers to the blush of innocence that
tinged many a cheek, as they would gather round some of God's or-
dained, praying in flowery words of decoying Cockney, that they
should break their holy vows by accompanying them to the halls of
adultery. Nothing daunted at the staunch refusal of different divines,
whose modest walk was interrupted by their bold assertion of loath-
some rights, they moved on, while laughs of hidden rage and defeat
flitted across their doll-decked faces, to die as they next accosted some
rustic-looking critics, who, tempted with their polished twang, their
earnest advances, their pitiful entreaties, yielded, in their ignorance of
the ways of a large city, to their glossy offers, and accompanied, with
slight hesitation, these artificial shells of immorality to their homes of
ruin, degradation, and shame.

[*On the Margin,* 1923]

The Author of *Eminent Victorians*

A SUPERLATIVELY CIVILIZED Red Indian living apart from the vulgar
world in an elegant and park-like reservation, Mr. Strachey rarely looks
over his walls at the surrounding country. It seethes, he knows, with
crowds of horribly colonial persons. Like the hosts of Midian, the innumerable "poor whites" prowl and prowl around, but the noble savage
pays no attention to them.

In his spiritual home—a neat and commodious Georgian mansion in
the style of Leoni or Ware[2]—he sits and reads, he turns over portfolios of
queer old prints, he savors meditatively the literary vintages of centuries.
And occasionally, once in two or three years, he tosses over his park pal-
ings a record of these leisured degustations, a judgment passed upon his library, a ripe rare book. One time it is Eminent Victorians; the next it is
Queen Victoria herself. Today he has given us a miscellaneous collection of
Books and Characters.

If Voltaire had lived to the age of two hundred and thirty instead of

2. Leone Leoni (1509–1590). Italian sculptor. Isaac Ware (d. 1776). English architect.

shuffling off at a paltry eighty-four, he would have written about the Victorian epoch, about life and letters at large, very much as Mr. Strachey has written. That lucid common sense, that sharp illuminating wit which delight us in the writings of the middle eighteenth century—these are Mr. Strachey's characteristics. We know exactly what he would have been if he had come into the world at the beginning of the seventeen hundreds; if he is different from the men of that date it is because he happens to have been born towards the end of the eighteens.

The sum of knowledge at the disposal of the old Encyclopaedists was singularly small, compared, that is to say, with the knowledge which we of the twentieth century have inherited. They made mistakes and in their ignorance they passed what we can see to have been hasty and very imperfect judgments on men and things. Mr. Strachey is the eighteenth century grown-up; he is Voltaire at two hundred and thirty.

Voltaire at sixty would have treated the Victorian era, if it could have appeared in a prophetical vision before his eyes, in terms of "La Pucelle"—with ribaldry. He would have had to be much in knowledge and inherited experience before he could have approached it in that spirit of sympathetic irony and ironical sympathy which Mr. Strachey brings to bear upon it. Mr. Strachey makes us like the old Queen, while we smile at her; he makes us admire the Prince Consort in spite of the portentous priggishness—duly insisted on in the biography—which accompanied his intelligence. With all the untutored barbarity of their notions, Gordon and Florence Nightingale are presented to us as sympathetic figures. Their peculiar brand of religion and ethics might be absurd, but their characters are shown to be interesting and fine.

It is only in the case of Dr. Arnold that Mr. Strachey permits himself to be unrestrainedly Voltairean; he becomes a hundred and seventy years younger as he describes the founder of the modern Public School system. The irony of that description is tempered by no sympathy. To make the man appear even more ridiculous, Mr. Strachey adds a stroke or two to the portrait of his own contriving—little inventions which deepen the absurdity of the caricature. Thus we read that Arnold's "outward appearance was the index of his inward character. The legs, perhaps, were shorter than they should have been; but the sturdy athletic frame, especially when it was swathed (as it usually was) in the flowing robes of a Doctor of Divinity, was full of an imposing vigor." How exquisitely right those short legs are! how artistically inevitable! Our admiration for Mr. Strachey's art is only increased when we discover that in attributing to the Doctor this brevity of shank he is justified by no contemporary document. The short legs are his own contribution.

Voltaire, then, at two hundred and thirty has learned sympathy. He has learned that there are other ways of envisaging life than the common-sense, reasonable way and that people with a crack-brained view of the universe have a right to be judged as human beings and must not be condemned out of hand as lunatics or obscurantists. Blake and St. Francis have as much right to their place in the sun as Gibbon and Hume. But still, in spite of this lesson, learned and inherited from the nineteenth century, our Voltaire of eleven score years and ten still shows a marked preference for the Gibbons and the Humes; he still understands their attitude towards life a great deal better than he understands the other fellow's attitude.

In his new volume of *Books and Characters* Mr. Strachey prints an essay on Blake (written, it may be added parenthetically, some sixteen years ago), in which he sets out very conscientiously to give that disquieting poet his due. The essay is interesting, not because it contains anything particularly novel in the way of criticism, but because it reveals, in spite of all Mr. Strachey's efforts to overcome it, in spite of his admiration for the great artist in Blake, his profound antagonism towards Blake's view of life.

He cannot swallow mysticism; he finds it clearly very difficult to understand what all this fuss about the soul really signifies. The man who believes in the absoluteness of good and evil, who sees the universe as a spiritual entity concerned, in some transcendental fashion, with morality, the man who regards the human spirit as possessing a somehow cosmic importance and significance—ah no, decidedly no, even at two hundred thirty Voltaire cannot wholeheartedly sympathize with such a man.

And that, no doubt is the reason why Mr. Strachey has generally shrunk from dealing, in his biographies and his criticisms, with any of these strange incomprehensible characters. Blake is the only one he has tried his hand on, and the result is not entirely satisfactory. He is more at home with the Gibbons and Humes of this world, and when he is not discussing the reasonable beings he likes to amuse himself with the eccentrics, like Mr. Creevey or Lady Hester Stanhope.[3] The portentous, formidable mystics he leaves severely alone.

One cannot imagine Mr. Strachey coping with Dostoevsky or with any of the other great explorers of the soul. One cannot imagine him writing a life of Beethoven. These huge beings are disquieting for a Voltaire who has learned enough sympathy to be able to recognize their greatness, but whose temperament still remains unalterably alien. Mr. Strachey is wise to have nothing to do with them.

The second-rate mystics (I use the term in its widest and vaguest sense), the men who believe in the spirituality of the universe and in the queerer

---

3. Thomas Creevey (1768–1838). English politician and author of the *Creevey Papers*. Lady Hester Stanhope (1776–1839). English traveller and confidante of William Pitt.

dogmas which have become tangled in that belief, without possessing the genius which alone can justify such notions in the eyes of the Voltaire-ans—these are the objects on which Mr. Strachey likes to turn his calm and penetrating gaze. Gordon and Florence Nightingale, the Prince Con-sort, Clough—they and their beliefs are made to look rather absurd by the time he has done with them. He reduces their spiritual struggles to a series of the most comically futile series of gymnastics in the void. The men of genius who have gone through the same spiritual struggles, who have be-lieved the same sort of creeds, have had the unanswerable justification of their genius. These poor absurd creatures have not. Voltaire in his third century gives them a certain amount of his newly learned sympathy; but he also gives them a pretty strong dose of his old irony.

[*On the Margin*, 1923]

Edward Thomas

THE POETRY of Edward Thomas affects one morally as well as aestheti-cally and intellectually. We have grown rather shy, in these days of pure aestheticism, of speaking of those consoling or strengthening qualities of poetry on which critics of another generation took pleasure in dwelling. Thomas's poetry is strengthening and consoling, not because it justifies God's ways to man or whispers of reunions beyond the grave, not because it presents great moral truths in memorable numbers, but in a more subtle and very much more effective way. Walking through the streets on these September nights, one notices, wherever there are trees along the street and lamps close beside the trees, a curious and beautiful phenomenon. The light of the street lamps striking up into the trees has power to make the grimed, shabby, and tattered foliage of the all-but autumn seem brilliantly and transparently green. Within the magic circle of the light the tree seems to be at that crowning moment of the spring when the leaves are fully grown, but still luminous with youth and seemingly almost immaterial in their lightness. Thomas's poetry is to the mind what that transfiguring lamplight is to the tired trees. Our minds grown weary in the midst of the intolerable turmoil and aridity of daily wage-earning existence, it falls with a touch of momentary rejuvenation.

The secret of Thomas's influence lies in the fact that he is genuinely what so many others of our time quite unjustifiably claim to be, a nature poet. To be a nature poet it is not enough to affirm vaguely that God made the country and man made the town, it is not enough to talk sympathetically about familiar rural objects, it is not enough to be sonorously poetical about mountains and trees; it is not even enough to speak of these things with the precision of real knowledge and love. To be a nature poet a man must have felt profoundly and intimately those peculiar emotions which nature can inspire, and must be able to express them in such a way that his reader feels them. The real difficulty that confronts the would-be poet of nature is that these emotions are of all emotions the most difficult to pin down and analyze and the hardest of all to convey. In "October" Thomas describes what is surely the characteristic emotion induced by a contact with nature—a kind of exultant melancholy which is the nearest approach to quiet unpassionate happiness that the soul can know. Happiness of whatever sort is extraordinarily hard to analyze and describe. One can think of a hundred poems, plays, and novels that deal exhaustively with pain and misery to one that is an analysis and an infectious description of happiness. Passionate joy is more easily recapturable in art; it is dramatic, vehemently defined. But quiet happiness, which is at the same time a kind of melancholy—there you have an emotion which is inexpressible except by a mind gifted with a diversity of rarely combined qualities. The poet who would sing of this happiness must combine a rare penetration with a rare candor and honesty of mind. A man who feels an emotion that is very difficult to express is often tempted to describe it in terms of something entirely different. Platonist poets feel a powerful emotion when confronted by beauty, and, finding it a matter of the greatest difficulty to say precisely what that emotion is in itself, proceed to describe it in terms of theology which has nothing whatever to do with the matter in point. Groping after an expression of the emotions aroused in him by the contemplation of nature, Wordsworth sometimes stumbles doubtfully along philosophical byways that are at the best parallel to the direct road for which he is seeking. Everywhere in literature this difficulty in finding an expression for any undramatic, ill-defined emotion is constantly made apparent.

Thomas's limpid honesty of mind saves him from the temptation to which so many others succumb, the temptation to express one thing, because it is with difficulty describable, in terms of something else. He never philosophizes the emotions which he feels in the presence of nature and beauty, but presents them as they stand, transmitting them directly to his readers without the interposition of any obscuring medium. Rather than attempt to explain the emotion, to rationalize it into something that it is not, he will present it for what it is, a problem of which he does not know the solution. In "Tears" we have an example of this candid confession of ignorance:

It seems I have no tears left. They should have fallen—
Their ghosts, if tears have ghosts, did fall—that day
When twenty hounds streamed by me, not yet combed out
But still all equals in their rage of gladness
Upon the scent, made one, like a great dragon
In Blooming Meadow that bends towards the sun
And once bore hops: and on that other day
When I stepped out from the double-shadowed Tower
Into an April morning, stirring and sweet
And warm. Strange solitude was there and silence.
A mightier charm than any in the Tower
Possessed the courtyard. They were changing guard,
Soldiers in line, young English countrymen,
Fair-haired and ruddy, in white tunics. Drums
And fifes were playing "The British Grenadiers."
The men, the music piercing that solitude
And silence, told me truths I had not dreamed,
And have forgotten since their beauty passed.

The emotion is nameless and indescribable, but the poet has intensely felt it and transmitted it to us who read his poem, so that we, too, feel it with the same intensity. Different aspects of this same nameless emotion of quiet happiness shot with melancholy are the theme of almost all Thomas's poems. They bring to us precisely that consolation and strength which the country and solitude and leisure bring to the spirits of those long pent in populous cities, but essentialized and distilled in the form of art. They are the light that makes young again the tattered leaves.

Of the purely aesthetic qualities of Thomas's poetry it is unnecessary to say much. He devised a curiously bare and candid verse to express with all possible simplicity and clarity his clear sensations and emotions.... "This is not," as Mr. de la Mare[4] says in his foreword to Thomas's *Collected Poems,* "this is not a poetry that will drug or intoxicate.... It must be read slowly, as naturally as if it were prose, without emphasis." With this bare verse devoid of any affectation, whether of cleverness or a too great simplicity, Thomas could do all that he wanted. See, for example, with what extraordinary brightness and precision he could paint a picture:

Lichen, ivy and moss
Keep evergreen the trees
That stand half flayed and dying,

4. Walter de la Mare (1873–1956). English poet and novelist.

And the dead trees on their knees
In dog's mercury and moss:
And the bright twit of the goldfinch drops
Down there as he flits on thistle-tops.

The same bare precision served him well for describing the interplay of emotions, as in "After You Speak" or "Like the Touch of Rain." And with this verse of his he could also chant the praises of his English countryside and the character of its people, as typified in Lob-lie-by-the-fire:

He has been in England as long as dove and daw,
Calling the wild cherry tree the merry tree,
The rose campion Bridget-in-her-bravery;
And in a tender mood he, as I guess,
Christened one flower Love-in-idleness. . . .

[*On the Margin*, 1923]

A Wordsworth Anthology

TO REGARD Wordsworth critically, impersonally, is for some of us a rather difficult matter. With the disintegration of the solid orthodoxies Wordsworth became for many intelligent, liberal-minded families the Bible of that sort of pantheism, that dim faith in the existence of a spiritual world, which filled, somewhat inadequately, the place of the older dogmas. Brought up as children in the Wordsworthian tradition, we were taught to believe that a Sunday walk among the hills was somehow equivalent to church-going: the First Lesson was to be read among the clouds, the Second in the primroses; the birds and the running waters sang hymns, and the whole blue landscape preached a sermon "of moral evil and of good." From this dim religious education we brought away a not very well-informed veneration for the name of Wordsworth, a dutiful conviction about the spirituality of Nature in general, and an extraordinary superstition about mountains in particular—a superstition that it took at least three seasons of Alpine Sports to dissipate entirely. Consequently, on reaching man's estate, when we actually came to read our Wordsworth, we found it extremely difficult to appraise his greatness, so many veils of preconceived ideas had to be pushed aside, so many inveterate deflections of vision allowed for. However, it became possible at last to look at Wordsworth as a detached phenomenon in the world of ideas and not as part of the family tradition of childhood.

Like many philosophers, and especially philosophers of a mystical tinge of thought, Wordsworth based his philosophy on his emotions. The conversion of emotions into intellectual terms is a process that has been repeated a thousand times in the history of the human mind. We feel a powerful emotion before a work of art, therefore it partakes of the divine, is a reconstruction of the Idea of which the natural object is a poor reflection. Love moves us deeply, therefore human love is a type of divine love. Nature in her various aspects inspires us with fear, joy, contentment, despair, therefore Nature is a soul that expresses anger, sympathy, love, and hatred. One could go on indefinitely multiplying examples of the way in which man objectifies the kingdoms of heaven and hill that are within him. The process is often a dangerous one. The mystic who feels within himself the stirrings of inenarrable emotions is not content with these emotions as they are in themselves. He feels it necessary to invent a whole cosmogony that will account for them. To him this philosophy will be true, in so far as it is an expression in intellectual terms of these emotions. But to those who do not know these emotions at first hand, it will be simply misleading. The mystical emotions have what may be termed a conduct value; they enable the man who feels them to live his life with a serenity and confidence unknown to other men. But the philosophical terms in which these emotions are expressed have not necessarily any truth value. This mystical philosophy will be valuable only in so far as it revives, in the minds of its students, those conduct-affecting emotions which originally gave it birth. Accepted at its intellectual face value, such a philosophy may not only have no worth; it may be actually harmful.

Into this beautifully printed volume Mr. Cobden-Sanderson has gathered together most of the passages in Wordsworth's poetry which possess the power of reviving the emotions that inspired them. It is astonishing to find that they fill the best part of two hundred and fifty pages, and that there are still plenty of poems—"Peter Bell," for example, that one would like to see included. "The Prelude" and "Excursion" yield a rich tribute of what our ancestors would have called "beauties." There is that astonishing passage in which the poet describes how, as a boy, he rowed by moonlight across the lake:

> And, as I rose upon the stroke, my boat
> Went heaving through the water like a swan
> When, from behind that craggy steep till then
> The horizon's bound, a huge peak, black and huge,
> As if with voluntary power instinct,
> Upreared its head. It struck and struck again,
> And growing still in stature the grim shape
> Towered up between me and the stars, and still,

For so it seemed, with purpose of its own
And measured motion, like a living thing,
Strode after me.
There is the history of that other fearful moment when
I heard among the solitary hills
Low breathings coming after me, and sounds
Of undistinguishable motion, steps
Almost as silent as the turf they trod.

And there are other passages telling of Nature in less awful and menacing aspects, Nature the giver of comfort and strong serenity. Reading these we are able in some measure to live for ourselves the emotions that were Wordsworth's. If we can feel his "shadowy exaltations," we have got all that Wordsworth can give us. There is no need to read the theology of his mysticism, the pantheistic explanation of his emotions. To Peter Bell a primrose by a river's brim was only a yellow primrose. Its beauty stirred in him no feeling. But one can be moved by the sight of the primrose without necessarily thinking, in the words of Mr. Cobden-Sanderson's preface, of "the infinite tenderness of the infinitely great, of the infinitely great which, from out the infinite and amid its own stupendous tasks, stoops to strew the path of man, the infinitely little, with sunshine and with flowers." This is the theology of our primrose emotion. But it is the emotion itself which is important, not the theology. The emotion has its own powerful conduct value, whereas the philosophy derived from it, suspiciously anthropocentric, possesses, we should imagine, only the smallest value as truth.

[*On the Margin*, 1923]

Verhaeren

VERHAEREN[5] was one of those men who feel all their life long "l'envie" (to use his own admirably expressive phrase), "l'envie de tailler en drapeaux l'étoffe de la vie." The stuff of life can be put to worse uses. To cut it into flags is, on the whole, more admirable than to cut it, shall we say, into cerecloths, or money-bags, or Parisian underclothing. A flag is a brave, a cheerful and a noble object. These are qualities for which we are prepared to forgive the flag its over-emphasis, its lack of subtlety, its touch of childishness. One can think of a number of writers who have marched through literary history like an army with banners. There was Victor Hugo, for ex-

5. Emile Verhaeren (1855–1916). Belgian poet and dramatist.

ample—one of Verhaeren's admired masters. There was Balzac, to whose view of life Verhaeren's was, in some points, curiously akin. Among the minor makers of oriflammes there is our own Mr. Chesterton, with his heroic air of being forever on the point of setting out on a crusade, glorious with bunting and mounted on a rocking-horse.

The flag-maker is a man of energy and strong vitality. He likes to imagine that all that surrounds him is as large, as full of sap and as vigorous as he feels himself to be. He pictures the world as a place where the colors are strong and brightly contrasted, where a vigorous chiaroscuro leaves no doubt as to the true nature of light and darkness, and where all life pulsates, quivering and taut, like a banner in the wind. From the first we find in Verhaeren all the characteristics of the tailor of banners. In his earliest book of verse, *Les Flamands,* we see him already delighting in such lines as "Leurs deux poings monstrueux pataugeaient dans la pâte."

Already too we find him making copious use—or was it abuse?—as Victor Hugo had done before him, of words like "vaste," "énorme," "infini," "infiniment," " infinité," "univers." Thus, in "L'Ame de la Ville," he talks of an "énorme" viaduct, an "immense" train, a "monstrueux" sun, even of the "énorme" atmosphere. For Verhaeren all roads lead to the infinite, wherever and whatever that may be.

> Les grand'routes tracent des croix
> A l'infini, à travers bois;
> Les grand'routes tracent des croix lointaines
> A l'infini, à travers plaines.

Infinity is one of those notions which are not to be lightly played with. The makers of flags like it because it can be contrasted so effectively with the microscopic finitude of man. Writers like Hugo and Verhaeren talk so often and so easily about infinity that the idea ceases in their poetry to have any meaning at all.

I have said that, in certain respects, Verhaeren, in his view of life, is not unlike Balzac. This resemblance is most marked in some of the poems of his middle period, especially those in which he deals with aspects of contemporary life. *Les Villes tentaculaires* contains poems which are wholly Balzacian in conception. Take, for example, Verhaeren's rhapsody on the Stock Exchange:

> Une fureur réenflammé
> Au mirage du moindre espoir
> Monte soudain de l'entonnoir
> De bruit et de fumée,

Ou l'on se bat, à coups de vols, en bas.
Langues sèches, regards aîgus, gestes inverses,

Et cervelles, qu'en tourbillons les millions
traversent,
Echangent là leur peur et leur terreur. . . .
Aux fins de mois, quand les débâcles se décident
La mort les paraphe de suicides,
Mais au jour même aux heures blêmes,
Les volontés dans la fièvre revivent,
L'acharnement sournois
Reprend comme autrefois.

One cannot read these lines without thinking of Balzac's feverish money-makers, of the Baron de Nucingen, Du Tillet, the Kellers and all the lesser misers and usurers, and all their victims. With their worked-up and rather melodramatic excitement, they breathe the very spirit of Balzac's prodigious film-scenario version of life.

Verhaeren's flag-making instinct led him to take special delight in all that is more than ordinarily large and strenuous. He extols and magnifies the gross violence of the Flemish peasantry, their almost infinite capacity for taking food and drink, their industry, their animalism. In true Rooseveltian style, he admired energy for its own sake. All his romping rhythms were dictated to him by the need to express this passion for the strenuous. His curious assonances and alliterations—*Luttent et s'entrebuttent en disputes*—arise from this same desire to recapture the sense of violence and immediate life.

It is interesting to compare the violence and energy of Verhaeren with the violence of an earlier poet—Rimbaud, the marvellous boy, if ever there was one. Rimbaud cut the stuff of life into flags, but into flags that never fluttered on this earth. His violence penetrated, in some sort, beyond the bounds of ordinary life. In some of his poems Rimbaud seems actually to have reached the nameless goal towards which he was striving, to have arrived at that world of unheard-of spiritual vigor and beauty whose nature he can only describe in an exclamatory metaphor:

Millions d'oiseaux d'or, ô future vigueur!

But the vigor of Verhaeren is never anything so fine and spiritual as this "million of golden birds." It is merely the vigor and violence of ordinary life speeded up to cinema intensity.

It is a noticeable fact that Verhaeren was generally at his best when he took a holiday from the making and waving of flags. His Flemish bucolics and the love poems of *Les Heures,* written for the most part in traditional form, and for the most part shorter and more concentrated than his poems of violence and energy, remain the most moving portion of his work. Very interesting, too, are the poems belonging to that early phase of doubt and depression which saw the publication of *Les Débacles* and *Les Flambeaux Noirs.* The energy and life of the later books is there, but in some sort concentrated, preserved, and intensified, because turned inwards upon itself. Of many of the later poems one feels that they were written much too easily. These must have been brought very painfully and laboriously to the birth.

[*On the Margin,* 1923]

Edward Lear

THERE ARE few writers whose works I care to read more than once, and one of them is certainly Edward Lear. Nonsense, like poetry, to which it is closely allied, like philosophic speculation, like every product of the imagination, is an assertion of man's spiritual freedom in spite of all the oppression of circumstance. As long as it remains possible for the human mind to invent the Quangle Wangle and the Fimble Fowl, to wander at will over the Great Gromboolian Plain and the hills of the Cnankly Bore, the victory is ours. The existence of nonsense is the nearest approach to a proof of that unprovable article of faith, whose truth we must all assume or perish miserably: that life is worth living. It is when circumstances combine to prove, with syllogistic cogency, that life is not worth living that I turn to Lear and find comfort and refreshment. I read him and I perceive that it is a good thing to be alive; for I am free, with Lear, to be as inconsequent as I like.

Lear is a genuine poet. For what is his nonsense except the poetical imagination a little twisted out of its course? Lear had the true poet's feeling for words—words in themselves, precious and melodious, like phrases of music; personal as human beings. Marlowe talks of entertaining divine Zenocrate; Milton of the leaves that fall in Vallombrosa; Lear of the Fimble Fowl with a corkscrew leg, of runcible spoons, of things meloobious and genteel. Lewis Carroll wrote nonsense by exaggerating sense—a too logical logic. His coinages of words are intellectual. Lear, more characteristically a poet, wrote nonsense that is an excess of imagination, coined words for the sake of their color and sound alone. His is the purer nonsense, because more poetical. Change the key ever so little and the "Dong with a Luminous Nose" would be one of the most memorable romantic poems of the nineteenth century. Think, too, of that exquisite "Yonghy Bonghy Bo"! In one of Tennyson's later volumes there is a charming little lyric about Catullus, which begins

> Row us out from Desenzano,
> To your Sirmione row!
> So they row'd, and there we landed—
> O *venusta Sirmio!*

Can one doubt for a moment that he was thinking, when he wrote these words, of that superb stanza with which the "Yonghy Bonghy" opens:

> On the coast of Coromandel,
> Where the early pumpkins blow,
> In the middle of the woods,
> Dwelt the Yonghy Bonghy Bo.

Personally, I prefer Lear's poem; it is the richer and the fuller of the two. Lear's genius is at its best in the Nonsense Rhymes, or Limericks, as a later generation has learned to call them. In these I like to think of him not merely as a poet and a draughtsman—and how unique an artist the recent efforts of Mr. Nash[6] to rival him have only affirmed—but also as a profound social philosopher. No study of Lear would be complete without at least a few remarks on "They" of the Nonsense Rhymes. "They" are the world, the man in the street; "They" are what the leaderwriters in the twopenny press would call all Right-Thinking Men and Women; "They" are Public Opinion. The Nonsense Rhymes are, for the most part, nothing more nor less than episodes selected from the history of that eternal struggle between the genius or the eccentric and his fellow-beings. Public Opinion universally abhors eccentricity. There was, for example, that charming Old Man of Melrose who walked on the tips of his toes. But "They" said (with their usual inability to appreciate the artist), "It ain't pleasant to see you at present, you stupid old man of Melrose." Occasionally, when the eccentric happens to be a criminal genius, "They" are doubtless right. The Old Man with a Gong who bumped on it all the daylong deserved to be smashed. (But "They" also smashed a quite innocuous Old Man of White-haven merely for dancing a quadrille with a raven.) And there was that Old Person of Buda, whose conduct grew ruder and ruder; "They" were justified, I dare say, in using a hammer to silence his clamor. But it raises

---

6. Ogden Nash (1902–1971). American light versifier.

the whole question of punishment and of the relation between society and the individual.

When "They" are not offensive, they content themselves with being foolishly inquisitive. Thus, "They" ask the Old Man of the Wrekin whether his boots are made of leather. "They" pester the Old Man in a Tree with imbecile questions about the Bee which so horribly bored him. In these encounters the geniuses and the eccentrics often get the better of the gross and heavy-witted public. The Old Person of Ware who rode on the back of a bear certainly scored off "Them." For when "They" asked: "Does it trot?" He replied, "It does not." (The picture shows it galloping *ventre à terre*.) "It's a Moppsikon Floppsikon bear." Sometimes, too, the eccentric actually leads "Them" on to their discomfiture. One thinks of that Old Man in a Garden, who always begged everyone's pardon. When "They" asked him "What for?" he replied, "You're a bore, and I trust you'll go out of my garden." But they probably ended up by smashing him.

Occasionally the men of genius adopt a Mallarméen policy. They flee from the gross besetting crowd.

La chair est triste, hélas, et j'ai lu tous les
livres.
Fuir, là-bas, fuir. . . .

It was surely with these words on his lips that the Old Person of Bazing (whose presence of mind, for all that he was a Symbolist, was amazing) went out to purchase the steed which he rode at full speed and escaped from the people of Bazing. He chose the better part; for it is almost impossible to please the mob. The Old Person of Ealing was thought by his suburban neighbors to be almost devoid of good feeling, because, if you please, he drove a small gig with three owls and a pig. And there was that pathetic Old Man of Thermopylae (for whom I have a peculiar sympathy, since he reminds me so poignantly of myself) who never did anything properly. "They" said, "If you choose to boil eggs in your shoes, you shall never remain in Thermopylae." The sort of people "They" like do the stupidest things, have the vulgarest accomplishments. Of the Old Person of Filey his acquaintance was wont to speak highly because he danced perfectly well to the sound of a bell. And the people of Shoreham adored that fellow-citizen of theirs whose habits were marked by decorum and who bought an umbrella and sat in the cellar. Naturally; it was only to be expected.

[*On the Margin*, 1923]

Sir Christopher Wren

THAT AN ENGLISHMAN should be a very great plastic artist is always rather surprising. Perhaps it is a matter of mere chance; perhaps it has something to do with our national character—if such a thing really exists. But, whatever may be the cause, the fact remains that England has produced very few artists of first-class importance. The Renaissance, as it spread, like some marvellous infectious disease of the spirit, across the face of Europe, manifested itself in different countries by different symptoms. In Italy, the country of its origin, the Renaissance was, more than anything, an outburst of painting, architecture, and sculpture. Scholarship and religious reformation were, in Germany, the typical manifestations of the disease. But when this gorgeous spiritual measles crossed the English Channel, its symptoms were almost exclusively literary. The first premonitory touch of the infection from Italy "brought out" Chaucer. With the next bout of the disease England produced the Elizabethans. But among all these poets there was not a single plastic artist whose name we so much as remember.

And then, suddenly, the seventeenth century gave birth to two English artists of genius. It produced Inigo Jones and, a little later, Wren. Wren died, at the age of more than ninety in the spring of 1723. We are celebrating today his bi-centenary—celebrating it not merely by antiquarian talk and scholarly appreciations of his style but also (the signs are not wanting) in a more concrete and living way: by taking a renewed interest in the art of which he was so great a master and by reverting in our practice to that fine tradition which he, with his predecessor, Inigo, inaugurated.

An anniversary celebration is an act of what Wordsworth would have called "natural piety"; an act by which past is linked with present and of the vague, interminable series of the days a single comprehensible and logical unity is created in our minds. At the coming of the centenaries we like to remember the great men of the past, not so much by way of historical exercise, but that we may see precisely where, in relation to their achievement, we stand at the present time, that we may appraise the life still left in their spirit and apply to ourselves the moral of their example. I have no intention in this article of giving a biography of Wren, a list of his works, or a technical account of his style and methods. I propose to do no more than describe, in the most general terms, the nature of his achievement and its significance to ourselves.

Wren was a good architect. But since it is important to know precisely what we are talking about, let us begin by asking ourselves what good architecture is. Descending with majesty from his private Sinai, Mr. Ruskin dictated to a whole generation of Englishmen the aesthetic Law. On monolithic tables that were the Stones of Venice he wrote the great truths that had been revealed to him. Here is one of them:

> It is to be generally observed that the proportions of buildings have nothing to do with the style or general merit of their architecture. An architect trained in the worst schools and utterly devoid of ill meaning or purpose in his work, may yet have such a natural gift of massing and grouping as will render his structure effective when seen at a distance.

Now it is to be generally observed, as he himself would say, that in all matters connected with art, Ruskin is to be interpreted as we interpret dreams—that is to say, as signifying precisely the opposite of what he says. Thus, when we find him saying that good architecture has nothing to do with proportion or the judicious disposition of masses and that the general effect counts for nothing at all, we may take it as more or less definitely proven that good architecture is, in fact, almost entirely a matter of proportion and massing, and that the general effect of the whole work counts for nearly everything. Interpreted according to this simple oneirocritical method, Ruskin's pontifical pronouncement may be taken as explaining briefly and clearly the secrets of good architecture. That is why I have chosen this quotation to be the text of my discourse on Wren.

For the qualities which most obviously distinguish Wren's work are precisely those which Ruskin so contemptuously disparages and which we, by our process of interpretation, have singled out as the essentially architectural qualities. In all that Wren designed—I am speaking of the works of his maturity; for at the beginning of his career he was still an unpracticed amateur, and at the end, though still on occasion wonderfully successful, a very old man—we see a faultless proportion, a felicitous massing and contrasting of forms. He conceived his buildings as three-dimensional designs which should be seen, from every point of view, as harmoniously proportioned wholes. (With regard to the exteriors this, of course, is true only of those buildings which can be seen from all sides. Like all true architects, Wren preferred to build in positions where his work could be appreciated three-dimensionally. But he was also a wonderful maker of façades; witness his Middle Temple gateway and his houses in King's Bench Walk.) He possessed in the highest degree that instinctive sense of proportion and scale which enabled him to embody his conception in brick and stone. In his great masterpiece of St. Paul's every part of the building, seen from within or without, seems to stand in a certain satisfying and harmonious relation to every other part. The same is true even of the smallest works belonging to the period of Wren's maturity. On its smaller scale and different plane, such a building as Rochester Guildhall is as beautiful, because as harmonious in the relation of all its parts, as St. Paul's.

Of Wren's other purely architectural qualities I shall speak but briefly. He was, to begin with, an engineer of inexhaustible resource; one who could always be relied upon to find the best possible solution to any problem, from blowing up the ruins of old St. Paul's to providing the new with a dome that should be at once beautiful and thoroughly safe. As a designer he exhibited the same practical ingenuity. No architect has known how to make so much of a difficult site and cheap materials. The man who built the City churches was a practical genius of no common order. He was also an artist of profoundly original mind. This originality reveals itself in the way in which he combines the accepted features of classical Renaissance architecture into new designs that were entirely English and his own. The steeples of his City churches provide us with an obvious example of this originality. His domestic architecture—that wonderful application of classical principles to the best in the native tradition—is another.

But Wren's most characteristic quality—the quality which gives to his work, over and above its pure beauty, its own peculiar character and charm—is a quality rather moral than aesthetic. Of Chelsea Hospital, Carlyle once remarked that it was "obviously the work of a gentleman." The words are illuminating. Everything that Wren did was the work of a gentleman; that is the secret of its peculiar character. For Wren was a great gentleman: one who valued dignity and restraint and who, respecting himself, respected also humanity; one who desired that men and women should live with the dignity, even the grandeur, befitting their proud human title; one who despised meanness and oddity as much as vulgar ostentation; one who admired reason and order, who distrusted all extravagance and excess. A gentleman, the finished product of an old and ordered civilization.

Wren, the restrained and dignified gentleman, stands out most clearly when we compare him with his Italian contemporaries. The baroque artists of the seventeenth century were interested above everything in the new, the startling, the astonishing; they strained after impossible grandeurs, unheard-of violences. The architectural ideals of which they dreamed were more suitable for embodiment in theatrical cardboard than in stone. And indeed, the late seventeenth and early eighteenth centuries was the golden age of scene-painting in Italy. The artists who painted the settings for the elder Scarlatti's operas, the later Bibienas and Piranesis, came nearer to reaching the wild Italian ideal than ever mere architects like Borromini or Bernini, their imaginations cramped by the stubbornness of stone and the unsleeping activities of gravitations, could hope to do.

How vastly different is the baroque theatricality from Wren's sober restraint! Wren was a master of the grand style; but he never dreamed of building for effect alone. He was never theatrical or showy, never pretentious or vulgar. St. Paul's is a monument of temperance and chastity. His great palace at Hampton Court is no gaudy stage-setting for the farce of absolute monarchy. It is a country gentleman's house—more spacious, of course, and with statelier rooms and more impressive vistas—but still a house meant to be lived in by someone who was a man as well as a king. But if his palaces might have housed, without the least incongruity, a well-bred gentleman, conversely his common houses were always dignified enough, however small, to be palaces in miniature and the homes of kings.

In the course of the two hundred years which have elapsed since his death, Wren's successors have often departed, with melancholy results, from the tradition of which he was the founder. They have forgotten, in their architecture, the art of being gentlemen. Infected by a touch of the baroque *folie de grandeur,* the architects of the eighteenth century built houses in imitation of Versailles and Caserta—huge stage houses, all for show and magnificence and all but impossible to live in.

The architects of the nineteenth century sinned in a diametrically opposite way towards meanness and a negation of art. Senselessly preoccupied with details, they created the nightmare architecture of "features." The sham Gothic of early Victorian times yielded at the end of the century to the nauseous affectation of "sham-peasantry." Big houses were built with all the irregularity and more than the "quaintness" of cottages; suburban villas took the form of machine-made imitations of the Tudor peasant's hut. To all intents and purposes architecture ceased to exist; Ruskin had triumphed.

Today, however, there are signs that architecture is coming back to that sane and dignified tradition of which Wren was the great exponent. Architects are building houses for gentlemen to live in. Let us hope that they will continue to do so. There may be sublimer types of men than the gentleman: there are saints, for example, and the great enthusiasts whose thoughts and actions move the world. But for practical purposes and in a civilized, orderly society, the gentleman remains, after all, the ideal man. The most profound religious emotions have been expressed in Gothic architecture. Human ambitions and aspirations have been most colossally reflected by the Romans and the Italians of the baroque. But it is in England that the golden mean of reasonableness and decency—the practical philosophy of the civilized man—has received its most elegant and dignified expression. The old gentleman who died two hundred years ago preached on the subject of civilization a number of sermons in stone. St. Paul's and Greenwich, Trinity Library and Hampton Court, Chelsea, Kilmainham, Blackheath and Rochester, St. Stephen's Wallbrook and St.

Mary Abchurch, Kensington orangery and Middle Temple gateway—these
are the titles of a few of them. They have much, if we will but study them,
to teach us.

[*On the Margin*, 1923]

Ben Jonson

IT COMES as something of a surprise to find that the niche reserved for
Ben Jonson in the "English Men of Letters" series has only now been
filled. One expected somehow that he would have been among the first of
the great ones to be enshrined; but no, he has had a long time to wait; and
Adam Smith, and Sydney Smith, and Hazlitt, and Fanny Burney have gone
before him into the temple of fame. Now, however, his monument has at
last been made, with Professor Gregory Smith's qualified version of "O
rare Ben Jonson!" duly and definitively carved upon it.

What is it that makes us, almost as a matter of course, number Ben
Jonson among the great? Why should we expect him to be an early candi-
date for immortality, or why, indeed, should he be admitted to the "English Men of Letters" series at all? These are difficult questions to answer;
for when we come to consider the matter we find ourselves unable to give
any very glowing account of Ben or his greatness. It is hard to say that one
likes his work; one cannot honestly call him a good poet or a supreme
dramatist. And yet, unsympathetic as he is, uninteresting as he often can
be, we still go on respecting and admiring him, because, in spite of everything, we are conscious, obscurely but certainly, that he was a great man.

He had little influence on his successors; the comedy of humors died
without any but an abortive issue. Shadwell, the mountain-bellied "Og,
from a treason tavern rolling home," is not a disciple that any man would
have much pride in claiming. No raking up of literary history will make
Ben Jonson great as a founder of a school or an inspirer of others. His
greatness is a greatness of character. There is something almost alarming
in the spectacle of this formidable figure advancing with tank-like irre-
sistibility towards the goal he had set himself to attain. No sirens of romance can seduce him, no shock of opposition unseat him in his career. He
proceeds along the course theoretically mapped out at the inception of his
literary life, never deviating from this narrow way till the very end—till the
time when, in his old age, he wrote that exquisite pastoral, *The Sad Shepherd*, which is so complete and absolute a denial of all his lifelong principles. But *The Sad Shepherd* is a weakness, albeit a triumphant weakness.
Ben, as he liked to look upon himself, as he has again and again revealed

himself to us, is the artist with principles, protesting against the anarchic absence of principle among the geniuses and charlatans, the poets and ranters of his age.

> The true artificer will not run away from nature as he were afraid of her; or depart from life and the likeness of truth; but speak to the capacity of his hearers. And though his language differ from the vulgar somewhat, it shall not fly from all humanity, with the Tamerlanes and Tamer-Chams of the late age, which had nothing in them but the scenical strutting and furious vociferation to warrant them to the ignorant gapers. He knows it is his only art, so to carry it as none but artificers perceive it. In the meantime, perhaps, he is called barren, dull, lean, a poor writer, or by what contumelious word can come in their cheeks, by these men who without labor, judgment, knowledge, or almost sense, are received or preferred before him.

In these sentences from *Discoveries* Ben Jonson paints his own picture-portrait of the artist as a true artificer—setting forth, in its most general form, and with no distracting details of the humors or the moral purpose of art, his own theory of the artist's true function and nature. Jonson's theory was no idle speculation, no mere thing of words and air, but a creed, a principle, a categorical imperative, conditioning and informing his whole work. Any study of the poet must, therefore, begin with the formulation of his theory, and must go on, as Professor Gregory Smith's excellent essay does indeed proceed, to show in detail how the theory was applied and worked out in each individual composition.

A good deal of nonsense has been talked at one time or another about artistic theories. The artist is told that he should have no theories, that he should warble native wood-notes wild, that he should "sing," be wholly spontaneous, should starve his brain and cultivate his heart and spleen; that an artistic theory cramps the style, stops up the Helicons of inspiration, and so on, and so on. The foolish and sentimental conception of the artist, to which these anti-intellectual doctrines are a corollary, dates from the time of romanticism and survives among the foolish and sentimental of today. A consciously practiced theory of art has never spoiled a good artist, has never dammed up inspiration, but rather, and in most cases profitably, canalized it. Even the Romantics had theories and were wild and emotional on principle.

Theories are above all necessary at moments when old traditions are breaking up, when all is chaos and in flux. At such moments an artist formulates his theory and clings to it through thick and thin; clings to it as the one firm raft of security in the midst of the surrounding unrest. Thus, when the neoclassicism, of which Ben was one of the remote ancestors, was crumbling into the nothingness of *The Loves of the Plants* and *The Triumphs of Temper*, Wordsworth found salvation by the promulgation of a new theory of poetry, which he put into practice systematically and to the verge of absurdity in *Lyrical Ballads*. Similarly in the shipwreck of the old tradition of painting we find the artists of the present day clinging desperately to intellectual formulas as their only hope in the chaos. The only occasions, in fact, when the artist can afford entirely to dispense with theory occur in periods when a well-established tradition reigns supreme and unquestioned. And then the absence of theory is more apparent than real; for the tradition in which he is working is a theory, originally formulated by someone else, which he accepts unconsciously and as though it were the law of Nature itself.

The beginning of the seventeenth century was not one of these periods of placidity and calm acceptance. It was a moment of growth and decay together, of fermentation. The fabulous efflorescence of the Renaissance had already grown rank. With that extravagance of energy which characterized them in all things, the Elizabethans had exaggerated the traditions of their literature into insincerity. All artistic traditions end, in due course, by being reduced to the absurd; but the Elizabethans crammed the growth and decline of a century into a few years. One after another they transfigured and then destroyed every species of art they touched. Euphuism, Petrarchism, Spenserism, the sonnet, the drama—some lasted a little longer than others, but they all exploded in the end, these beautiful iridescent bubbles blown too big by the enthusiasm of their makers.

But in the midst of this unstable luxuriance voices of protest were to be heard, reactions against the main romantic current were discernible. Each in his own way and in his own sphere, Donne and Ben Jonson protested against the exaggerations of the age. At a time when sonneteers in legions were quibbling about the blackness of their ladies' eyes or the golden wires of their hair, when Platonists protested in melodious chorus that they were not in love with "red and white" but with the ideal and divine beauty of which peach-blossom complexions were but inadequate shadows, at a time when love-poetry had become, with rare exceptions, fantastically unreal, Donne called it back, a little grossly perhaps, to facts with the dry remark:

Love's not so pure and abstract as they use
To say, who have no mistress but their muse.

There have been poets who have written more lyrically than Donne, more fervently about certain amorous emotions, but not one who has formulated so rational a philosophy of love as a whole, who has seen all the facts so clearly and judged them so soundly. Donne laid down no literary theory. His followers took from him all that was relatively unimportant—the harshness, itself a protest against Spenserian facility, the conceits, the sensuality tempered by mysticism—but the important and original quality of Donne's work, the psychological realism, they could not, through sheer incapacity, transfer into their own poetry. Donne's immediate influence was on the whole bad. Any influence for good he may have had has been on poets of a much later date.

The other great literary Protestant of the time was the curious subject of our examination, Ben Jonson. Like Donne he was a realist. He had no use for claptrap, or rant, or romanticism. His aim was to give his audiences real facts flavored with sound morality. He failed to be a great realist, partly because he lacked the imaginative insight to perceive more than the most obvious and superficial reality, and partly because he was so much preoccupied with the sound morality that he was prepared to sacrifice truth to satire; so that in place of characters he gives us humors, not minds, but personified moral qualities.

Ben hated romanticism; for, whatever may have been his bodily habits, however infinite his capacity for drinking sack, he belonged intellectually to the party of sobriety. In all ages the drunks and the sobers have confronted one another, each party loud in derision and condemnation of the defects which it observes in the other. "The Tamerlanes and Tamer-Chams of the late age" accuse the sober Ben of being "barren, dull, lean, a poor writer." Ben retorts that they "have nothing in them but the scenical strutting and furious vociferation to warrant them to the ignorant gapers." At another period it is the Hernanis and the Rollas who reproach that paragon of dryness, the almost fiendishly sober Stendhal, with his grocer's style. Stendhal in his turn remarks: "En paraissant, vers 1803, le *Génie* de Chateaubriand m'a semblé ridicule." And today? We have our sobers and our drunks, our Hardy and our Belloc, our Santayana and our Chesterton. The distinction is eternally valid. Our personal sympathies may lie with one or the other; but it is obvious that we could dispense with neither. Ben, then, was one of the sobers, protesting with might and main against the extravagant behavior of the drunks, an intellectual insisting that there was no way of arriving at truth except by intellectual processes, an apotheosis of the Plain Man determined to stand no nonsense about anything. Ben's poetical achievement, such as it is, is the achievement of one who relied on no mysterious inspiration, but on those solid qualities of sense, perseverance, and sound judgment which any decent citizen of a decent country may be expected to possess. That he himself possessed, hidden somewhere in the obscure crypts and recesses of his mind, other rarer spiritual qualities is proved by the existence of his additions to *The Spanish Tragedy*—if, indeed, they are his, which there is no cogent reason to doubt—and his last fragment of a masterpiece, *The Sad Shepherd*. But these qualities, as Professor Gregory Smith points out, he seems deliberately to have suppressed; locked them away, at the bidding of his imperious theory, in the strange dark places from which, at the beginning and the very end of his career, they emerged. He might have been a great romantic, one of the sublime inebriates; he chose rather to be classical and sober. Working solely with the logical intellect and rejecting as dangerous the aid of those uncontrolled illogical elements of imagination, he produced work that is in its own way excellent. It is well wrought, strong, heavy with learning and what the Chaucerians would call "high sentence." The emotional intensity and brevity excepted, it possesses all the qualities of the French classical drama. But the quality which characterizes the best Elizabethan and indeed the best English poetry of all periods, the power of moving in two worlds at once, it lacks. Jonson, like the French dramatists of the seventeenth century, moves on a level, directly towards some logical goal. The road over which his great contemporaries take us is not level; it is, as it were, tilted and uneven, so that as we proceed along it we are momently shot off at a tangent from the solid earth of logical meaning into superior regions where the intellectual laws of gravity have no control. The mistake of Jonson and the classicists in general consists in supposing that nothing is of value that is not susceptible of logical analysis; whereas the truth is that the greatest triumphs of art take place in a world that is not wholly of the intellect, but lies somewhere between it and the inenarrable, but, to those who have penetrated it, supremely real, world of the mystic. In his fear and dislike of nonsense, Jonson put away from himself not only the Tamer-Chams and the fustian of the late age, but also most of the beauty it had created.

With the romantic emotions of his predecessors and contemporaries Jonson abandoned much of the characteristically Elizabethan form of their poetry. That extraordinary melodiousness which distinguishes the Elizabethan lyric is not to be found in any of Ben's writing. The poems by which we remember him—"Cynthia," "Drink to Me Only," "It Is Not Growing Like a Tree"—are classically well made (though the cavalier lyrists were to do better in the same style); but it is not for any musical qualities that we remember them. One can understand Ben's critical contempt for those purely formal devices for producing musical richness in which the Elizabethans delighted.

Eyes, why did you bring unto me these
graces,
Grac'd to yield wonder out of her true
measure,

Measure of all joyes' stay to phansie traces
Module of pleasure.

The device is childish in its formality, the words, in their obscurity, almost devoid of significance. But what matter, since the stanza is a triumph of sonorous beauty? The Elizabethans devised many ingenuities of this sort; the minor poets exploited them until they became ridiculous; the major poets employed them with greater discretion, playing subtle variations (as in Shakespeare's sonnets) on the crude theme. When writers had something to say, their thoughts, poured into these copiously elaborate forms, were molded to the grandest poetical eloquence. A minor poet, like Lord Brooke, from whose works we have just quoted a specimen of pure formalism, could produce, in his moments of inspiration, such magnificent lines as:

The mind of Man is this world's true dimension,
And knowledge is the measure of the mind;

or these, of the nethermost hell:

A place there is upon no center placed,
Deepe under depthes, as farre as is the skie
Above the earth; darke, infinitely spaced
Pluto the king, the kingdome, miserie.

Even into comic poetry the Elizabethans imported the grand manner. The anonymous author of

Tee-hee, tee-hee! Oh sweet delight
He tickles this age, who can
Call Tullia's ape a marmosite
And Leda's goose a swan

knew the secret of that rich, facile music which all those who wrote in the grand Elizabethan tradition could produce. Jonson, like Donne, reacted against the facility and floridity of this technique, but in a different way. Donne's protest took the form of a conceited subtlety of thought combined with a harshness of meter. Jonson's classical training inclined him towards clarity, solidity of sense, and economy of form. He stands, as a lyrist, half-way between the Elizabethans and the cavalier song-writers; he has broken away from the old tradition, but has not yet made himself entirely at home in the new. At the best he achieves a minor perfection of point and neatness. At the worst he falls into that dryness and dullness with which he knew he could be reproached.

We have seen from the passage concerning the true artificer that Jonson fully realized the risk he was running. He recurs more than once in *Discoveries* to the same theme, "Some men to avoid redundancy run into that [a "thin, flagging, poor, starved" style] and while they strive to have no ill-blood or juice, they lose their good." The good that Jonson lost was a great one. And in the same way we see today how a fear of becoming sentimental, or "chocolate-boxy," drives many of the younger poets and artists to shrink from treating of the great emotions or the obvious lavish beauty of the earth. But to eschew a good because the corruption of it is very bad is surely a sign of weakness and a folly.

Having lost the realm of romantic beauty—lost it deliberately and of set purpose—Ben Jonson devoted the whole of his immense energy to portraying and reforming the ugly world of fact. But his reforming satiric intentions interfered, as we have already shown, with his realistic intentions, and instead of recreating in his art the actual world of men, he invented the wholly intellectual and therefore wholly unreal universe of Humors. It is an odd new world, amusing to look at from the safe distance that separates stage from stalls; but not a place one could ever wish to live in—one's neighbors, fools, knaves, hypocrites, and bears would make the most pleasing prospect intolerable. And over it all is diffused the atmosphere of Jonson's humor. It is a curious kind of humor, very different from anything that passes under that name today, from the humor of *Punch,* or *A Kiss for Cinderella.* One has only to read *Volpone*—or, better still, go to see it when it is acted this year by the Phoenix Society for the revival of old plays—to realize that Ben's conception of a joke differed materially from ours. Humor has never been the same since Rousseau invented humanitarianism. Syphilis and broken legs were still a great deal more comic in Smollett's day than in our own. There is a cruelty, a heartlessness about much of the older humor which is sometimes shocking, sometimes, in its less extreme forms, pleasantly astringent and stimulating after the orgies of quaint pathos and sentimental comedy in which we are nowadays forced to indulge. There is not a pathetic line in *Volpone;* all the characters are profoundly unpleasant, and the fun is almost as grim as fun can be. Its heartlessness is not the brilliant, cynical heartlessness of the later Restoration comedy, but something ponderous and vast. It reminds us of one of those enormous, painful jokes which fate sometimes plays on humanity. There is no alleviation, no purging by pity and terror. It requires a very hearty sense of humor to digest it. We have reason to admire our ancestors for their ability to enjoy this kind of comedy as it should be enjoyed. It would get very little appreciation from a London audience of today.

In the other comedies the fun is not so grim; but there is a certain hardness and brutality about them all—due, of course, ultimately to the fact that the characters are not human, but rather marionettes of wood and metal that collide and belabor one another, like the ferocious puppets of the Punch and Judy show, without feeling the painfulness of the proceeding. Shakespeare's comedy is not heartless, because the characters are human and sensitive. Our modern sentimentality is a corruption, a softening of genuine humanity. We need a few more Jonsons and Congreves, some more plays like *Volpone,* or that inimitable *Marriage à la Mode* of Dryden, in which the curtain goes up on a lady singing the outrageously cynical song that begins

> Why should a foolish marriage vow,
> That long ago was made,
> Constrain us to each other now
> When pleasure is decayed?

Too much heartlessness is intolerable (how soon one turns, revolted, from the literature of the Restoration!), but a little of it now and then is bracing, a tonic for relaxed sensibilities. A little ruthless laughter clears the air as nothing else can do; it is good for us, every now and then, to see our ideals laughed at, our conception of nobility caricatured; it is good for solemnity's nose to be tweaked, it is good for human pomposity to be made to look mean and ridiculous. It should be the great social function— as Marinetti has pointed out—of the music halls, to provide this cruel and unsparing laughter, to make a buffoonery of all the solemnly accepted grandeurs and nobilities. A good dose of this mockery, administered twice a year at the equinoxes, should purge our minds of much waste matter, make nimble our spirits and brighten the eye to look more clearly and truthfully on the world about us.

Ben's reduction of human beings to a series of rather unpleasant Humors is sound and medicinal. Humors do not, of course, exist in actuality; they are true only as caricatures are true. There are times when we wonder whether a caricature is not, after all, truer than a photograph; there are others when it seems a stupid lie. But at all times a caricature is disquieting; and it is very good for most of us to be made uncomfortable.

[*On the Margin,* 1923]

Chaucer

THERE ARE few things more melancholy than the spectacle of literary fossilization. A great writer comes into being, lives, labors, and dies. Time passes; year by year the sediment of muddy comment and criticism thickens round the great man's bones. The sediment sets firm; what was once a

living organism becomes a thing of marble. On the attainment of total fossilization the great man has become a classic. It becomes increasingly difficult for the members of each succeeding generation to remember that the
stony objects which fill the museum cases were once alive. It is often a
work of considerable labor to reconstruct the living animal from the fossil
shape. But the trouble is generally worth taking. And in no case is it more
worth while than in Chaucer's.

With Chaucer the ordinary fossilizing process, to which every classical
author is subject, has been complicated by the petrifaction of his language.
Five hundred years have almost sufficed to turn the most living of poets
into a substitute on the modern sides of schools for the mental gymnastic
of Latin and Greek. Prophetically, Chaucer saw the fate that awaited him
and appealed against his doom:

> Ye know eke that, in form of speech is change
> Within a thousand years, and wordes tho
> That hadden price, now wonder nice and strange
> Us thinketh them; and yet they spake them so,
> And sped as well in love as men now do.

The body of his poetry may have grown old, but its spirit is still young
and immortal. To know that spirit—and not to know it is to ignore something that is of unique importance in the history of our literature—it is
necessary to make the effort of becoming familiar with the body it informs
and gives life to. The antique language and versification, so "wonder nice
and strange" to our ears, are obstacles in the path of most of those who
read for pleasure's sake (not that any reader worthy of the name ever reads
for anything else but pleasure); to the pedants they are an end in themselves. Theirs is the carcass, but not the soul. Between those who are
daunted by his superficial difficulties and those who take too much delight
in them Chaucer finds but few sympathetic readers. I hope in these pages
to be able to give a few of the reasons that make Chaucer so well worth
reading.

Chaucer's art is, by its very largeness and objectiveness, extremely difficult to subject to critical analysis. Confronted by it, Dryden could only exclaim, "Here is God's plenty!"—and the exclamation proves, when all is
said, to be the most adequate and satisfying of all criticisms. All that the
critic can hope to do is to expand and to illustrate Dryden's exemplary
brevity.

"God's plenty!"—the phrase is a peculiarly happy one. It calls up a vision of the prodigal earth, of harvest fields, of innumerable beasts and
birds, of teeming life. And it is in the heart of this living and material
world of Nature that Chaucer lives. He is the poet of earth, supremely

content to walk, desiring no wings. Many English poets have loved the earth for the sake of something—a dream, a reality, call it which you will—that lies behind it. But there have been few, and, except for Chaucer, no poets of greatness, who have been in love with earth for its own sake, with Nature in the sense of something inevitably material, something that is the opposite of the supernatural. Supreme over everything in this world he sees the natural order, the "law of kind," as he calls it. The teachings of most of the great prophets and poets are simply protests against the law of kind. Chaucer does not protest, he accepts. It is precisely this acceptance that makes him unique among English poets. He does not go to Nature as the symbol of some further spiritual reality; hills, flowers, sea, and clouds are not, for him, transparencies through which the workings of a great soul are visible. No, they are opaque; he likes them for what they are, things pleasant and beautiful, and not the less delicious because they are definitely of the earth earthy. Human beings, in the same way, he takes as he finds, noble and beastish, but, on the whole, wonderfully decent. He has none of that strong ethical bias which is usually to be found in the English mind. He is not horrified by the behavior of his fellow-beings, and he has no desire to reform them. Their characters, their motives interest him, and he stands looking on at them, a happy spectator. This serenity of detachment, this placid acceptance of things and people as they are, is emphasized if we compare the poetry of Chaucer with that of his contemporary, Langland, or whoever it was that wrote *Piers Plowman.*

The historians tell us that the later years of the fourteenth century were among the most disagreeable periods of our national history. English prosperity was at a very low ebb. The Black Death had exterminated nearly a third of the working population of the islands, a fact which, aggravated by the frenzied legislation of the Government, had led to the unprecedented labor troubles that culminated in the peasants' revolt. Clerical corruption and lawlessness were rife. All things considered, even our own age is preferable to that in which Chaucer lived. Langland does not spare denunciation; he is appalled by the wickedness about him, scandalized at the openly confessed vices that have almost ceased to pay to virtue the tribute of hypocrisy. Indignation is the inspiration of *Piers Plowman,* the righteous indignation of the prophet. But to read Chaucer one would imagine that there was nothing in fourteenth-century England to be indignant about. It is true that the Pardoner, the Friar, the Shipman, the Miller, and, in fact, most of the Canterbury pilgrims are rogues and scoundrels; but, then, they are such "merry harlots" too. It is true that the Monk prefers hunting to praying, that, in these latter days when fairies are no more, "there is none other incubus" but the friar, that "purse is the Archdeacon's hell," and the Summoner a villain of the first magnitude; but Chaucer can only regard these things as primarily humorous. The fact of people not practicing what they preach is an unfailing source of amusement to him. Where Langland cries aloud in anger, threatening the world with hellfire, Chaucer looks on and smiles. To the great political crisis of his time he makes but one reference, and that a comic one:

> So hideous was the noyse, ah *benedicite!*
> Certes he Jakke Straw, and his meyné,
> Ne maden schoutes never half so schrille,
> Whan that they wolden eny Flemyng kille,
> As thilke day was mad upon the fox.

Peasants may revolt, priests break their vows, lawyers lie and cheat, and the world in general indulge its sensual appetites; why try and prevent them, why protest? After all, they are all simply being natural, they are all following the law of kind. A reasonable man, like himself, "flees fro the pres and dwelles with soothfastnesse." But reasonable men are few, and it is the nature of human beings to be the unreasonable sport of instinct and passion, just as it is the nature of the daisy to open its eye to the suit and of the goldfinch to be a spritely and "gaylard" creature. The law of kind has always and in everything domination; there is no rubbing nature against the hair.

> For God it wot, there may no man embrace
> As to destreyne a thing, the which nature
> Hath naturelly set in a creature.
> Take any brid, and put him in a cage,
> And do all thine entent and thy corrage
> To foster it tendrely with meat and drynke,
> And with alle the deyntees thou canst bethinke,
> And keep it all so kyndly as thou may;
> Although his cage of gold be never so gay,
> Yet hath this brid, by twenty thousand fold,
> Lever in a forest, that is wyld and cold,
> Gon ete wormes, and such wrecchidnes;
> For ever this brid will doon his busynes
> To scape out of his cage when that he may;
> His liberté the brid desireth aye. . . .
>
> Lo, heer hath kynd his dominacioun,
> And appetyt flemeth [banishes] discrescioun.
> Also a she wolf hath a vilayne kynde,
> The lewideste wolf that she may fynde,
> Or least of reputacioun, him will sche take,

In tyme whan hit lust to have a make.
Alle this ensaumples tell I by these men
That ben untrewe, and nothing by wommen.

(As the story from which these lines are quoted happens to be about an unfaithful wife, it seems that, in making the female sex immune from the action of the law of kind, Chaucer is indulging a little in irony.)

For men ban ever a licorous appetit
On lower thing to parforme her delit
Than on her wyves, ben they never so faire,
Ne never so trewe, ne so debonaire.

Nature, deplorable as some of its manifestations may be, must always and inevitably assert itself. The law of kind has power even over immortal souls. This fact is the source of the poet's constantly expressed dislike of celibacy and asceticism. The doctrine that upholds the superiority of the state of virginity over that of wedlock is, to begin with (he holds), a danger to the race. It encourages a process which we may be permitted to call dysgenics—the carrying on of the species by the worst members. The Host's words to the Monk are memorable—

Allas! why wearest thou so wide a cope?
God give me sorwe! and I were a pope
Nought only thou, but every mighty man,
Though he were share brode upon his pan [head]
Should ban a wife; for all this world is lorn
Religioun hath take up all the corn
Of tredyng, and we burel [humble] men ben shrimpes;
Of feble trees there cometh wrecchid impes.
This maketh that our heires ben so sclendere
And feble, that they may not wel engendre.

But it is not merely dangerous; it is anti-natural. That is the theme of the Wife of Bath's Prologue. Counsels of perfection are all very well when they are given to those "That waide lyve parfytly; But, lordyngs, by your leve, that am not I." The bulk of us must live as the law of kind enjoins.

It is characteristic of Chaucer's conception of the world, that the highest praise he can bestow on anything is to assert of it, that it possesses in the highest degree the dualities of its own particular kind. Thus of Cressida he says:

She was not with the least of her stature,
But all her limbes so well answering

Weren to womanhood, that creature
Nas never lesse mannish in seeming.

The horse of brass in the "Squire's Tale" is

So well proportioned to be strong,
Right as it were a steed of Lombardye,
Thereto so *horsely* and so quick of eye.

Everything that is perfect of its kind is admirable, even though the kind
may not be an exalted one. It is, for instance, a joy to see the way in which
the Canon sweats:

A cloote-leaf [dock leaf] he had under his hood
For sweat, and for to keep his head from heat.
But it was joye for to see him sweat;
His forehead dropped as a stillatorie
Were full of plantain or of peritorie.

The Canon is supreme in the category of sweaters, the very type and
idea of perspiring humanity; therefore he is admirable and joyous to behold, even as a horse that is supremely horsely or a woman less mannish
than anything one could imagine. In the same way it is a delight to behold
the Pardoner preaching to the people. In its own kind his charlatanism is
perfect and deserves admiration:

Mine handes and my tonge gon so yerne,
That it is joye to see my busynesse.

This manner of saying of things that they are joyous, or, very often,
heavenly, is typical of Chaucer. He looks out on the world with a delight
that never grows old or weary. The sights and sounds of daily life, all the
lavish beauty of the earth fill him with a pleasure which he can only express by calling it a "joy" or a "heaven." It "joye was to see" Cressida and
her maidens playing together; and

So aungellyke was her native beauté
That like a thing immortal seemede she,
As doth an heavenish parfit creature.

The peacock has angel's feathers; a girl's voice is heavenly to hear:

Antigone the shene
Gan on a Trojan song to singen clear,
That it an heaven was her voice to hear.

One could go on indefinitely multiplying quotations that testify to Chaucer's exquisite sensibility to sensuous beauty and his immediate, almost exclamatory response to it. Above all, he is moved by the beauty of "young, fresh folkes, he and she"; by the grace and swiftness of living things, birds and animals; by flowers and placid, luminous, park-like landscapes.

It is interesting to note how frequently Chaucer speaks of animals. Like many other sages, he perceives that an animal is, in a certain sense, more human in character than a man. For an animal bears the same relation to a man as a caricature to a portrait. In a way a caricature is truer than a portrait. It reveals all the weaknesses and absurdities that flesh is heir to. The portrait brings out the greatness and dignity of the spirit that inhabits the often ridiculous flesh. It is not merely that Chaucer has written regular fables, though the "Nun's Priest's Tale" puts him among the great fabulists of the world, and there is also much definitely fabular matter in the *Parliament of Fowls*. No, his references to the beasts are not confined to his animal stories alone; they are scattered broadcast throughout his works. He relies for much of his psychology and for much of his most vivid description on the comparison of man, in his character and appearance (which with Chaucer are always indissolubly blended), with the beasts. Take, for example, that enchanting simile in which Troilus, stubbornly anti-natural in refusing to love as the law of kind enjoins him, is compared to the corn-fed horse, who has to be taught good behavior and sound philosophy under the whip:

> As proude Bayard ginneth for to skip
> Out of the way, so pricketh him his corn,
> Till he a lash have of the longe whip,
> Then thinketh he, "Though I prance all biforn,
> First in the trace, full fat and newe shorn,
> Yet am I but an horse, and horses' law
> I must endure and with my feeres draw."

Or, again, women with too pronounced a taste for fine apparel are likened to the cat:

> And if the cattes skin be sleek and gay,
> She will not dwell in housé half a day,
> But forth she will, ere any day be dawet
> To show her skin and gon a caterwrawet.

In his descriptions of the personal appearance of his characters Chaucer makes constant use of animal characteristics. Human beings, both beautiful and hideous, are largely described in terms of animals. It is interesting to see how often in that exquisite description of Alisoun, the carpenter's wife, Chaucer produces his clearest and sharpest effects by a reference to some beast or bird:

> Fair was this younge wife, and therewithal
> As any weasel her body gent and small. . . .
> But of her song it was as loud and yern
> As is the swallow chattering on a barn.
> Thereto she coulde skip and make a game
> As any kid or calf following his dame.
> Her mouth was sweet as bragot is or meath,
> Or hoard of apples, laid in hay or heath.
> Wincing she was, as is a jolly colt,
> Long as a mast and upright as a bolt.

Again and again in Chaucer's poems do we find such similitudes, and the result is always a picture of extraordinary precision and liveliness. Here, for example, are a few:

> Gaylard he was as goldfinch in the shaw,

or,

> Such glaring eyen had he as an hare,

or,

> As piled [bald] as an ape was his skull.

The self-indulgent friars are

> Like Jovinian,
> Fat as a whale, and walken as a swan.

The Pardoner describes his own preaching in these words:

> Then pain I me to stretche forth my neck
> And east and west upon the people I beck,
> As doth a dove, sitting on a barn.

Very often, too, Chaucer derives his happiest metaphors from birds and beasts. Of Troy in its misfortune and decline he says: Fortune

> Gan pull away the feathers bright of Troy from day to day.

Love-sick Troilus soliloquizes thus:

He said: "O fool, now art thou in the snare
That whilom japedest at lovés pain,
Now art thou hent, now gnaw thin owné chain."

The metaphor of Troy's bright feathers reminds me of a very beautiful simile borrowed from the life of the plants:

And as in winter leavés been bereft,
Each after other, till the tree be bare,
So that there nis but bark and branches left,
Lieth Troilus, bereft of each welfare,
Ybounden in the blacke bark of care.

And this, in turn, reminds me of that couplet in which Chaucer compares a girl to a flowering pear-tree:

She was well more blissful on to see
Than is the newe parjonette tree.

Chaucer is as much at home among the stars as he is among the birds and beasts and flowers of earth. There are some literary men of today who are not merely not ashamed to confess their total ignorance of all facts of a "scientific" order, but even make a boast of it. Chaucer would have regarded such persons with pity and contempt. His own knowledge of astronomy was wide and exact. Those whose education has been as horribly imperfect as my own will always find some difficulty in following him as he moves with easy assurance through the heavens. Still, it is possible without knowing any mathematics to appreciate Chaucer's descriptions of the great pageant of the sun and stars as they march in triumph from mansion to mansion through the year. He does not always trouble to take out his astrolabe and measure the progress of "Phebus, with his rosy cart"; he can record the god's movements in more general terms that may be understood even by the literary man of nineteen hundred and twenty. Here, for example, is a description of "the colde frosty seisoun of Decembre," in which matters celestial and earthly are mingled to make a picture of extraordinary richness:

Phebus wox old and hewed like latoun,
That in his hoté declinacioun
Shone as the burned gold, with streames bright
But now in Capricorn adown he light,
Where as he shone full pale; I dare well sayn
The bitter frostes with the sleet and rain
Destroyed hath the green in every yerd.

Janus sit by the fire with double beard,
And drinketh of his bugle horn the wine
Beforn him stont the brawn of tusked swine,
And *"noel"* cryeth every lusty man.

In astrology he does not seem to have believed. The magnificent passage in the "Man of Law's Tale," where it is said that

In the starres, clearer than is glass,
Is written, God wot, whose can it read,
The death of every man withouten drede,

is balanced by the categorical statement found in the scientific and educational treatise on the astrolabe, that judicial astrology is mere deceit.

His skepticism with regard to astrology is not surprising. Highly as he prizes authority, he prefers the evidence of experience, and where that evidence is lacking he is content to profess a quiet agnosticism. His respect for the law of kind is accompanied by a complementary mistrust of all that does not appear to belong to the natural order of things. There are moments when he doubts even the fundamental beliefs of the Church:

A thousand sythes have I herd men telle
That there is joye in heaven and peyne in helle;
And I accorde well that it be so.
But natheless, this wot I well also
That there is none that dwelleth in this countree
That either hath in helle or heaven y-be.

Of the fate of the spirit after death he speaks in much the same style:

His spiryt changed was, and wente there
As I came never, I cannot tellen where
Therefore I stint, I nam no divinistre;
Of soules fynde I not in this registre,
Ne me list not th' opiniouns to telle
Of hem, though that they witten where they dwelle.

He has no patience with superstitions. Belief in dreams, in auguries, fear of the "ravenes qualm or schrychynge of thise owles" are all unbefitting to a self-respecting man:

To trowen on it bothe false and foul is;
Alas, alas, so noble a creature
As is a man shall dreaden such ordure!

By an absurd pun he turns all Calchas's magic arts of prophecy to ridicule:

> So when this Calkas knew by calkulynge,
> And eke by answer of this Apollo
> That Grekes sholden such a people bringe,
> Through which that Troye muste ben fordo,
> He cast anon out of the town to go.

It would not be making a fanciful comparison to say that Chaucer in many respects resembles Anatole France. Both men possess a profound love of this world for its own sake, coupled with a profound and gentle skepticism about all that lies beyond this world. To both of them the lavish beauty of Nature is a never-failing and all-sufficient source of happiness. Neither of them are ascetics; in pain and privation they see nothing but evil. To both of them the notion that self-denial and self-mortification are necessarily righteous and productive of good is wholly alien. Both of them are apostles of sweetness and light, of humanity and reasonableness. Unbounded tolerance of human weakness and a pity, not the less sincere for being a little ironical, characterize them both. Deep knowledge of the evils and horrors of this unintelligible world makes them all the more attached to its kindly beauty. But in at least one important respect Chaucer shows himself to be the greater, the completer spirit. He possesses what Anatole France does not, an imaginative as well as an intellectual comprehension of things. Faced by the multitudinous variety of human character, Anatole France exhibits a curious impotence of imagination. He does not understand characters in the sense that, say, Tolstoy understands them; he cannot, by the power of imagination, get inside them, become what he contemplates. None of the persons of his creation are complete characters; they cannot be looked at from every side; they are portrayed, as it were, in the flat and not in three dimensions. But Chaucer has the power of getting into someone else's character. His understanding of the men and women of whom he writes is complete; his slightest character sketches are always solid and three-dimensional. The Prologue to the *Canterbury Tales,* in which the effects are almost entirely produced by the description of external physical features, furnishes us with the most obvious example of his three-dimensional drawing. Or, again, take that description in the "Merchant's Tale" of old January and his young wife May after their wedding night. It is wholly a description of external details, yet the result is not a superficial picture. We are given a glimpse of the characters in their entirety:

> Thus laboureth he till that the day gan dawe,
> And then he taketh a sop in fine clarré,

And upright in his bed then sitteth he.
And after that he sang full loud and clear,
And kissed his wife and made wanton cheer.
He was all coltish, full of ragerye,
And full of jargon as a flecked pye.
The slacké skin about his necké shaketh,
While that he sang, so chanteth he and craketh.
But God wot what that May thought in her heart,
When she him saw up sitting in his shirt,
In his night cap and with his necke lean;
She praiseth not his playing worth a bean.

But these are all slight sketches. For full-length portraits of character we must turn to *Troilus and Cressida,* a work which, though it was written before the fullest maturity of Chaucer's powers, is in many ways his most remarkable achievement, and one, moreover, which has never been rivaled for beauty and insight in the whole field of English narrative poetry. When one sees with what certainty and precision Chaucer describes every movement of Cressida's spirit from the first moment she hears of Troilus's love for her to the moment when she is unfaithful to him, one can only wonder why the novel of character should have been so slow to make its appearance. It was not until the eighteenth century that narrative artists, using prose as their medium instead of verse, began to rediscover the secrets that were familiar to Chaucer in the fourteenth.

Troilus and Cressida was written, as we have said, before Chaucer had learnt to make the fullest use of his powers. In coloring it is fainter, less sharp and brilliant than the best of the *Canterbury Tales.* The character studies are there, carefully and accurately worked out; but we miss the bright vividness of presentation with which Chaucer was to endow his later art. The characters are all alive and completely seen and understood. But they move, as it were, behind a veil—the veil of that poetic convention which had, in the earliest poems, almost completely shrouded Chaucer's genius, and which, as he grew up, as he adventured and discovered, grew thinner and thinner, and finally vanished like gauzy mist in the sunlight. When *Troilus and Cressida* was written, the mist had not completely dissipated, and the figures of his creation, complete in conception and execution as they are, are seen a little dimly because of the interposed veil.

The only moment in the poem when Chaucer's insight seems to fail him is at the very end; he has to account for Cressida's unfaithfulness, and he is at a loss to know how he shall do it. Shakespeare, when he rehandled the theme, had no such difficulty. His version of the story, planned on much coarser lines than Chaucer's, leads obviously and inevitably to the fore-ordained conclusion; his Cressida is a minx who simply lives up to her character. What could be more simple? But to Chaucer the problem is not so simple. His Cressida is not a minx. From the moment he first sets eyes on her, Chaucer, like his own unhappy Troilus, falls head over ears in love. Beautiful, gentle, gay; possessing, it is true, somewhat "tendre wittes," but making up for her lack of skill in ratiocination by the "sudden avysements" of intuition; vain, but not disagreeably so, of her good looks and of her power over so great and noble a knight as Troilus; slow to feel love, but once she has yielded, rendering back to Troilus passion for passion; in a word, the "least mannish" of all possible creatures—she is to Chaucer the ideal of gracious and courtly womanhood. But, alas, the old story tells us that Cressida jilted her Troilus for that gross prize-fighter of a man, Diomed. The woman whom Chaucer has made his ideal proves to be no better than she should be; there is a flaw in the crystal. Chaucer is infinitely reluctant to admit the fact. But the old story is specific in its statement; indeed, its whole point consists in Cressida's infidelity. Called upon to explain his heroine's fall, Chaucer is completely at a loss. He makes a few half-hearted attempts to solve the problem, and then gives it up, falling back on authority. The old clerks say it was so, therefore it must be so, and that's that. The fact is that Chaucer pitched his version of the story in a different key from that which is found in the "olde bokes," with the result that the note on which he is compelled by his respect for authority to close is completely out of harmony with the rest of the music. It is this that accounts for the chief, and indeed the only, defect of the poem—its hurried and boggled conclusion.

I cannot leave Cressida without some mention of the doom which was prepared for her by one of Chaucer's worthiest disciples, Robert Henryson, in some ways the best of the Scottish poets of the fifteenth and sixteenth centuries. Shocked by the fact that, in Chaucer's poem, Cressida receives no punishment for her infidelity, Henryson composed a short sequel, *The Testament of Cresseid,* to show that poetic justice was duly performed. Diomed, we are told, grew weary as soon as he had "all his appetyte and mair, fulfillit on this fair ladie" and cast her off, to become a common drab.

> O fair Cresseid! the flour and *A per se*
> Of Troy and Greece, how wast thow fortunait!
> To change in filth all thy femininitie
> And be with fleshly lust sa maculait,
> And go amang the Grekis, air and late
> So giglot-like.

In her misery she curses Venus and Cupid for having caused her to love only to lead her to this degradation:

The seed of love was sowen in my face
And ay grew green through your supply and grace.
But now, alas! that seed with frost is slain,
And I fra lovers left, and all forlane.

In revenge Cupid and his mother summon a council of gods and condemn the *A per se* of Greece and Troy to be a hideous leper. And so she goes forth with the other lepers, armed with bowl and clapper, to beg her bread. One day Troilus rides past the place where she is sitting by the roadside near the gates of Troy:

Then upon him she cast up both her een,
And with ane blenk it cam into his thocht,
That he some time before her face had seen,
But she was in such plight he knew her nocht,
Yet then her look into his mind it brocht
The sweet visage and amorous blenking
Of fair Cresseid, one sometime his own darling.

He throws her an alms and the poor creature dies. And so the moral sense is satisfied. There is a good deal of superfluous mythology and unnecessary verbiage in *The Testament of Cresseid*, but the main lines of the poem are firmly and powerfully drawn. Of all the disciples of Chaucer, from Hoccleve and the Monk of Bury down to Mr. Masefield, Henryson may deservedly claim to stand the highest.

[*On the Margin*, 1923]

How to Write a Tragedy

THE SIZE of the house; the family butler, who was so perfectly the genuine and traditional thing that you knew at once he could only be an unemployed actor repeating in private life his most successful role; the cooking and the wine; the strawberries that are as big as peaches; and the peaches larger than melons; the length of the cigars; the comfortable depth of the armchairs—all these, and a thousand other signs, testified to the grace of my generous host. There are certain classes of artists—fashionable portrait painters, for example; tenors, cinema stars, and the like—who are as grossly overpaid for their talents and their industry as others in less popular lines are grossly sweated. My old friend, Sophocles Robinson, was one of these; he was a playwright. His were the stage butler and the mansion; his the giant strawberries and the interminable cigars.

"It must be very agreeable," I said to him after dinner, thinking as I lighted Robinson's superb collector's-piece, of the sort of cigars I myself was occasionally able to afford; "it must be very agreeable to be rich."

"It is," Sophocles answered, with candor. He had not been rich long, and he was still immensely enjoying the sensation.

"I wish I knew how you did it," I said, enviously. "I never succeeded in writing a play myself. Or rather, I did once, when I was eighteen. But it was in blank verse and about King Arthur."

"I assure you," said Sophocles, "nothing could be easier."

"Tell me how it's done, and I'll give you a ten percent commission on all my royalties."

"Don't think of it, my dear boy," he said generously. "I'll tell you how it's done; but out of pure affection. Keep your ten percent." He patted me on the shoulder. "After the three-hundredth performance, if you like, you can give me a little souvenir."

"What shall it be?" I was touched by his kindness.

We hesitated for a long time between an electric player-piano and a first folio of Shakespeare. In the end, he decided for the electric piano. The fact was, he confided, that he never had any time nowadays to read Shakespeare; and besides, if he ever did want to, he had the old family Bowdler lying about somewhere. I confess that I was stingy enough to be relieved; an electric piano is a good deal cheaper than a First Folio. We discussed the merits of various makes of player-pianos.

"But I'm forgetting," said Robinson at last, when he had finally made his choice; "I'm forgetting about the play. We must teach you to write it before we can get to the three-hundredth night." He became very business-like. "Now, listen carefully."

I listened. Sophocles got up from his chair and began to pace up and down the room. He found it much easier to talk like that. After a moment of pensive silence, he began.

"We'll start," he said, "with tragedy—the noblest form of Drama, though by no means always the most profitable. Still, judiciously handled, it can be made to pay. I speak from experience. These cigars," he indicated the magnificent specimens we were smoking, "come out of the royalties of *Bathsheba's Husband.*"

I nodded respectfully.

"The first essential," Robinson went on, "is a good tragic theme. Plenty of conflict, plenty of problem. The Old Order against the New. The Younger Generation against the Old. The Aristocracy against the Plutocrats. The Workers against the Idle Rich. And so on—you know the sort of stuff. And in all cases, of course, you use the love element to emphasize and exacerbate the social conflict.

"The simplest method is to put the young man on one side and the young woman on the other. But perhaps the choicest theme of all is religion. A good mix-up of religion and sex—there's nothing like it. I know people who have made thousands and thousands a year on that, alone. But, personally, I think it wiser to alter one's themes as often as possible. It's no good getting known as a man who can write only one sort of play. That's why I never write the same sort of piece twice running. My last was a farce. So this time I'm doing a religious tragedy. You see the notion?"

"Perfectly," I said.

"Well, now, if you like," Sophocles went on, "I'll give you an outline of the plot, with comments as I go along, just to show you how this sort of thing is managed. One practical example is worth a hundred pages of theory." He halted, with his back to the empty fireplace, and from that strategical position began.

"The First Act," he said, "is extremely novel and impressive. Old Dr. Bradlaugh Bone is giving one of his famous anti-superstition dinner parties. Dr. Bone is a grand old relic of the nineteenth century—one of those stern, unbending atheists of the seventies, in whom the fires of anti-clerical hatred still continue to burn with all their pristine fury. It is a grand dinner. There are thirteen at table, including the skeleton of Jeremy Bentham, who sits at the head of the festive board, a benign though silent Chairman. The table ornaments are peacock's feathers, the ladies wear unlucky jewels; and at intervals during the meal, a servant comes in and spills some salt or breaks a looking glass.

"Dr. Bone sits in the middle of the table, facing the audience. On his right is a Neapolitan nobleman, renowned for his possession of the evil eye; on his left, another distinguished foreigner, a Frenchman—the senior guillotinist of the Republic. The rest of the party consists, for the most part, of Dr. Bone's contemporaries and disciples—a renegade Jesuit, two or three escaped nuns—forgotten controversialists of the old school. The youngest persons at the table are Dr. Bone's son, Voltaire Bone, and his ward, Maria Monk Mathers.

"The curtain rises on the tail end of the meal, and we start with a grand dialogue, over the nuts and wine, on the follies of superstition, the wickedness of clericalism, and the appealing charms of atheism. It is an agape of pure reason. Enlivened by occasional little knockabouts, such as the spilling of salt and the smashing of looking glasses, this dialogue goes on for some little time, until we have thoroughly evoked the spiritual atmosphere in which the characters have their being. Voltaire Bone and

Maria Monk Mathers remain conspicuously gloomy all this time, and not even the genial blasphemies of the renegade Jesuit can rise a smile to their pale lips.

"Old Dr. Bone at last calls for silence, and rising to his feet, begins a speech. 'Bones of Jeremy Bentham, ladies and gentlemen. . . .' And he goes on, in fine oratorical style, to remind his audience that they are the only true disbelievers left. The dragon that was hewed to pieces in the seventies has come to life again, and every fragment is a new and poisonous serpent. Let them hold fast to their principles of incredulity, let them propagate the true miscreance, let them bring up their children, as he has done, in the faithlessness of their fathers.

" 'But,' he continues, 'we have come together, not merely in the name of our common religion, but to celebrate also a happy family event.' There is applause. All eyes are turned towards young Voltaire and Maria Monk Mathers, who try to conceal their embarrassment. Old Dr. Bone goes on, his voice trembling with emotion, to describe how he has brought up his son and his ward on sound atheistical and rationalistic principles, with the intention, when they should come to a suitable age, of uniting them, not in the superstitious and antiquated bonds of unholy matrimony, but with the more rational ties of free love. He himself has composed a little secular service for the occasion, and he invites his guests to witness, in the auspicious presence of Jeremy Bentham's skeleton, the joining of their hands. The stage is set for an impressive secular ceremony which will glorify the freedom of an ideal, untrammeled, and innocent love.

"There is renewed applause. Everything seems in a blissful state of harmony, when Voltaire Bone springs to his feet, makes the sign of the cross, and cries, in a terrible voice: 'Silence!' All are struck dumb with amazement. The young man then proceeds in a rousing tirade which will fairly bring the house down, I may say, if it's well spoken—to denounce his father as an agent of the devil on earth and his doctrines as wholly satanic.

"It transpires, to the astonishment and horror of all present, that he has been in the habit for the past year or more of secretly reading forbidden literature. 'What!' cries his father, 'not the obscene works of a pietist?' And when young Voltaire admits that he has read À Kempis and St. Augustine, he covers his face and shudders. Voltaire winds up by declaring that he is now a convinced Catholic. And much as he loves and esteems Miss Maria—indeed, precisely because he does love and esteem her—he cannot entertain the idea of entering into any relation with her that has not been sanctioned by the blessing of the Church. Tableau!"

Sophocles Robinson paused dramatically.

"What next?" I asked.

"Well, now, as you can imagine," he said, "we have a tremendous scene. Old Dr. Bone breaks out in imprecations. Unnatural, ungrateful, and disobedient son! The other guests join in roaring like hungry lions in the amphitheater. But young Voltaire stands fast; pale, a Christian martyr." And in his enthusiasm, Sophocles crossed his hands over his chest and turned his large red disk of a face up towards the ceiling. "Oh, it's a wonderful scene!" he said.

"Splendid!" I agreed with him.

"Well, threats and vituperation having failed, old Dr. Bone becomes pathetic. Is a poor old father's heart to be broken? 'Wait, at least, till I am dead. It will not be long.' Voltaire is shaken by this appeal to his better feelings. Tears flow on both sides. The other guests join in. 'Respect an old man's simple creed.' 'How can you treat your old father so cruelly?' 'What, bring down his white hairs in dishonor and unhappiness to the grave?' Weeping, Voltaire protests how much he loves, honors, and respects his old dad; how gladly he would do anything to please him—except this one thing. He cannot give up his convictions. The eloquence in this scene rises to extraordinary heights. The stronger the emotions, the more purple you can make the writing. That's a point to remember. Make a note of it."

I made a note.

"Well," Sophocles went on, "Young Bone, as I say, stands firm. Tears, curses, cajolery are of no avail. Old Bone is completely broken down. In the end, he staggers from the room, followed by all his guests. The young people are left together. There is a long silence. Voltaire Bone remains plunged in a dolorous meditation; Maria Monk Mathers watches him with anxious and affectionate eyes. At last she approaches him." Sophocles advances on tip-toe, his finger to his lips, across the hearth rug.

"'Dear Voltaire!' she says. He starts. They look at one another for a long time, earnestly. He shudders, places his hand to his forehead, and averts his eyes. She tells him how much she admires his courage. She, too, she confesses, has been reading forbidden books. Secretly, in the watches of the night, she has convinced herself of the truth of Christian Science. She can sympathize with Voltaire; she will be only too happy, she protests, to go through any form of marriage he likes.

"Voltaire covers his face with his hands; he sobs. She begs him to tell her what is the matter. He confesses, at last, that in his recent pronouncement he dared not admit to his father to what lengths his apostasy from the family miscreance had really gone. He has determined to become a priest; there can be no question, now, even of marriage. He must sacrifice everything; even his love.

"The curtain comes down on them, weeping in one another's arms. The interest of the plot is thus transferred from the old-young conflict to the still more thrilling conflict between sex and religion. In the next act, we proceed to exploit this to the limit of its possibilities." Sophocles rubbed his hands together. "I hope you are learning something from this," he said, turning to me.

I assured him that it was being a liberal education.

"The action of the second," he said, "takes place two or three years later. Maria Monk Mathers still lives in the house of her guardian; but Voltaire Bone has left it, to enter a seminary. We start with a dialogue between old Bone and Maria, both in the depths of misery; one at the loss of a son, the other of a lover.

"They try to console one another; but there is no consolation. The old man finally unfolds a plan. The only person who can possibly rescue young Voltaire from the jaws of salvation is Maria Monk Mathers. He loves her; she must play on his weakness. Let her exert all her powers of seduction, and she may yet win him back before it is too late. He is to come this very evening to say farewell before setting out on a mission to the Cannibal Islands. Old Bone implores her, for her own, for his, for the young man's sake, to employ all her arts to make him break his vows.

"After some conscientious demurring not very serious in a young woman brought up on the sound irreligious principles of Dr. Bone, she agrees. She goes up to her room to prepare herself for the campaign. The doctor is left alone. He picks up a copy of the *Rationalist Press Year Book* and composes himself to read. After a short time, young Bone is ushered in. He is dressed in a black clerical costume; his face is emaciated and pale from his ascetic life; the eyes ringed with dark circles, are large and burning. He presents a most romantic appearance. There follows a long conversation between father and son. The old man tries to dissuade him from going to the Cannibal Islands; but the dangers of the mission, so far from repelling, actually attract the fervent neophyte. The futility of the old man's efforts are insisted upon at some length, in order to throw into more brilliant relief the complete success of the young lady's.

"She, in effect, now makes her appearance, doubly dazzling, inasmuch as, up till now, we have always seen her in rather dowdy costume approved by pure reason for the envelopment of the female form. She is dressed in the most gaudy creation of Poiret, and encrusted with jewels— of all kinds; not merely the unlucky varieties. Her face is scientifically made-up; her décolletage is extreme; her ankles captivate the eyes. Old Dr. Bone and his son regard her with astonishment. The former soon makes an excuse to leave her alone with the victim.

"The scene which follows is too familiar to all of us to require much description. On the stage, of course, it will be dragged out, relentlessly, to the bitter end, and beyond it. For remember that, on the stage, there is nothing like harping on the obvious. You must never be tempted, on the stage, to do anything subtly, or quickly, or airily. You must insist on all your points; make them twice over, if necessary; underline them three times. To you, I can describe the scene between young Voltaire and Maria Monk Mathers in sixteen words. Temptation; weakness; a moral reaction; more temptation; relapse; another rally; more temptation, and the final collapse. But on the stage, the scene will drag on excruciatingly for half an hour.

"She harps on those fatal phrases, 'goodbye,' 'for the last time'—phrases which reverberate in one's heart with such infinitely dolorous significance, when one happens to be parting with someone to whom one is attached, and which one hears or reads with such complete indifference—sometimes, even, positively with glee—when they are spoken or written by a person whose affection for us, outliving ours for him or her, has become for us merely tiresome and importunate. 'For the last time, for the last time. . . .' Terrible and unbearable words!

"In the end, he gives away; he falls. Passionately he kisses her. She seems to flee, to resist. His ardor is redoubled. Conquered at last, swooningly, she makes an assignation. He is to pretend to leave the house, but not to go farther than the garden. There he must hide; when the coast is clear, she will signal to him from her balcony. Curtain on the second act. Pretty soul-stirring, I flatter myself," said Robinson, addressing himself directly to me. I agreed.

"The scene of the last act," he continued, "is laid in the garden. It is night; the moon is shining. To the left is the house with the fatal balcony. The rest of the stage is a maze of lawns and boskage, black shadows, and moony light. Voltaire Bone walks, distraught, under the green limelight. And here, taking into account the troubled state of his mind and the very romantic character of the scene, I give him a soliloquy. Daring, I admit; but justifiable, I claim, in the circumstances. Moreover, it gives one an opportunity for some very poetical writing.

"He compares the calm of the night with the turmoil within his own breast; envies the remoteness and indifference of the celestial luminaries; contrasts the unhappy fate of Man who knows good and evil, who looks before and after, with that of unconscious Nature. Shall he; shall he not? He persuades himself that, after all, love being in accordance with nature, can hardly be offensive to the creator of the natural order. But then he reminds himself that this is mere casuistry. Religion, which transcends nature and stands apart from it, pronounces love a sin. He is on the brink of damnation; he must flee. But . . . there must be no but. And yet . . . the prohibition is categorical.

"He makes up his mind to flee. He is on the point of fleeing when admitting into the green aquarium light of the garden a yellow beam, a French window opens and Maria Monk Mathers steps onto the balcony. 'Voltaire!' With a word, she calls him back; his doom is sealed. There follows a bit of *Romeo and Juliet* put into prose. At the end of which, hurling himself with glee to his destruction, he attempts to scale the balcony. He is just hoisting himself over the balustrade when old Dr. Bone appears in the garden below, to feast his eyes upon the triumph of pure reason over superstition. Seeing the young man in the act of climbing towards pure reason, he cannot control a movement of delight.

" 'Victory!' he exclaims.

"Startled by the sound, the young man looks round and, as he does so, misses his footing. He falls with a thump to the ground, where he lies, pitifully groaning. Dr. Bone rushes to his assistance. Maria Monk Mathers darts in from the balcony and reappears an instant later below in the garden. While the doctor administers restoratives, applies the stethoscope, and feels his skull, she kneels beside him and, as a good Christian Scientist, ardently tries to bring spiritual powers to bear on the case. But Christian and non-Christian science are alike unavailing. After making an exceedingly pathetic speech, in which he repents of the sin from which this accident mercifully preserved him, Voltaire expires. Dr. Bone and Maria Monk Mathers are left with their dead. Slowly and impressively the curtain descends."

Robinson's voice, as he spoke these last words, had sunk almost to a whisper. He helped himself to some brandy and another nine-inch cigar, and sat down. "Have I taught you anything?" he asked. I shook his hand. "In eighteen months' time," I said, "we shall be listening to your electric piano."

[*Vanity Fair*, May 1924]

The Importance of the Comic Genius

THE HISTORY of literature and art provides us with more examples of fine serious than fine comic achievements. A list of the world's great creators of comedy turns out, when one takes the trouble to compile it, to be surprisingly small. Aristophanes, Chaucer, Rabelais, the Shakespeare of Falstaff, the Balzac of the *Contes Drôlatiques*, Dickens; and among the pictorial artists, Daumier, Rowlandson, Doré, when he was not wasting his talents on horrible and unsuccessful religious compositions, and Goya, in certain moods. These are the names that first occur to one; and though it would, of course, be possible to lengthen the list, there would not be so very many more to add.

True, we might compile a very long list of the writers and draftsmen who make us laugh; but a few of them would be what may be styled makers of pure comedy. The number of our physiological reactions to emotion is strictly limited, and we go through the same bodily convulsions in response to very different stimuli. Laughter, for example, is provoked in us by a number of quite distinct emotions. There is the laughter of mockery—the laughter that is a social punishment, applied by the sane majority to those whose crime it is to be unlike their fellow-beings. Go out in an exceptionally large hat or an exceptionally bright tie, and you will hear plenty of that kind of laughter. Satire, whether in art or literature, provokes this cruel laughter. The fact that it is generally written by the exceptional man against the only too sane majority does not prevent it from having fundamentally the same source of mockery of the majority against the exception. And then, there is the laughter that is our response to the smoking-room story—the laughter that is a safety valve for letting off innocuously a part of our somewhat excessive interest in the blushful mysteries. There is, also, the laughter released in us by sudden surprise—the loud and rather nervous laughter of children when they hide and pounce out on one another from dark recesses; the hysterical, involuntary laughter that seizes one when stout old Uncle Ebenezer slips on a banana skin and comes thudding to the pavement. Its surprising, startling quality is perhaps the principal reason why verbal wit makes us laugh.

Satire, sex, wit—all these things make us laugh, and they may all be present in a work of pure comedy. But they are not, themselves, pure comedy. It is not right to include in one's list of pure comic geniuses the savage satirist, such as Swift; or the mild satirist, like Congreve; the hardy pornographers of Wycherley's stamp; or the subtler, sniggering suggesters, like Sterne. Your great comic genius is much more copious, much larger, and more inclusive than a mere satirist, or writer of comedy of manners, or a creator of wit. And he is, accordingly, much rarer than the satirist or the wit. He is as rare as the great tragic genius—and, perhaps, even rarer than he.

The pure comic genius must be a great inventor. That is why he is so rare; the gift of invention is not a common one. You can be an admirable satirist or a fine serious writer, and not be an inventor—only an interpreter of actual life. Tolstoy is a supreme example of the latter class. But to create a coherent, satisfying, comic universe, you must be an inventor. You cannot stick very close to reality—particularly, the inward, spiritual reality—and make pure comedy. And the same applies to pure tragedy—though with this difference, that pure tragedy moves in the internal world, and largely ignores the externals from which pure comedy starts in flight. The characteristic creations of pure comedy, as well as of pure tragedy, are really not human beings at all. They are inventions of the poet's mind, living not in our world, but in a parallel world; similar, but not the same. The Wife of Bath, Panurge, Falstaff, Mr. Pecksniff, Medea, Macbeth, Ivan Karamasov—these are all creatures of fable, larger than life, as befits mythological beings; and living, not with the everyday life of men, but more intensely—with the prodigious and god-like life infused into them by their creators. Serious realistic art is not creative, like pure tragedy. It depends on actual life, of which it is a picture and practical interpretation. Similarly, satire, the comedy of manners, and wit are not creative, like pure comedy. Satire and the comedy of manners depend on the actual life they portray and mock at, with greater or less ferocity; while wit is an affair of verbal ingenuity. The difference is important.

All these varieties of what we may call contingent art are less eternally interesting than the two great creative and absolute types of art. For though, to contemporary readers, a book which deals directly, and so to speak scientifically, with life they know may be immensely valuable, it will lose much of its interest and value when the conditions of life on which it is based have changed. Only the ideal, perfected world, that is parallel to the real world, remains forever comprehensible and fresh. It is difficult not to believe, for example, that Dickens will outlast Tolstoy; though Tolstoy, in certain respects, is much more interesting and valuable to us at the present time.

It would be absurd, of course, to pretend that the great comic creations are as profoundly significant as the great creations of tragedy. Comedy necessarily leaves out of account some of the most important elements of man's spiritual life. It is of the earth, earthy—its strength, its size, its colossal energy—and these are the essential characteristics of all great comic creations, from Gargantua to Micawber, from Falstaff to the fabulous Burgesses of Daumier's impassioned invention. There are the strength, size, and energy of earth-born things; there is something superbly animal, something sappy, full-blooded, and earthily unself-conscious in pure comedy. We seem to be looking on at the gamboling of mastodons, the playing of young whales, the tumbling of a litter of dinosaur puppies. The mind, the troubled spirit of man, have but little place in comedy; the stage is occupied by his healthy body and its natural instincts. But this does not prevent a comic creation from being, in its own sphere, a delightful, and even a grand, magnificent, and beautiful, thing. Comedy deserves to be taken seriously.

This is a fact too frequently forgotten; a fact that is not even understood by the second-rate practitioners of comedy. These lesser exponents of comedy humiliate their art to an association with triviality, ugliness, and vulgarity. The great mass of what passes nowadays (or that has passed, for that matter, at any other period) for comic literature or art is stamped with this pettiness and vulgar hideousness. The average comic drawings, comic novels, comic plays, comic films—how small and grubby they all are! One has only to compare these little horrors with the creations of the genuine comic geniuses to see how miserably debased, how unworthy of the name of comedy, they are. A great comic work can be as large, as magnificent, and, in its own way, as beautiful, as a work of serious art.

The fact is that the *beau idéal* and the grand style are not exclusive possessions of serious art. There is also a comic *beau idéal* and a comic grand style. Comic poetry can be genuine poetry; that is to say, beautiful poetry. Comic art can be grand. A huge scale, a colossal, earthy energy, are, as we have seen, the characteristics of comedy. The comic grand style is accordingly, a rich, emphatic style, that chiefly differs from the grand style of serious art by being too rich and too emphatic.

The step is short from the sublime to the ridiculous—and in much art that is intended to be serious, that short step has been taken. The baroque style in the plastic arts, for example, is essentially a comic grand style; its extravagance is unfitted for use in serious, tragic art. The rich, turgid prose of the seventeenth century is essentially prose for the expression of comedy. The best passages in Milton's prose works are those in which he is making some enormous joke (the portentous phenomenon occurs more than once in the *Areopagitica,* and produces overwhelming effects). This clotted, extravagant style of prose, which the critics have agreed to call "poetic," is seen in Urquhart and Motteaux's translation of Rabelais to be the most perfect medium for comic expression. And the gorgeous rhetoric of the Elizabethans, which, when employed in serious passages, trembles perilously all the time on the verge of the ludicrous, is seen, when used for comic purposes, to be perfectly suitable.

Returning to pictorial arts, we find that practically the only good artist produced by the romantic movement is Gustave Doré; and he is good, not when he is being romantically serious, but in his masterly comic works (the illustrations to Balzac's *Contes Drôlatiques* are a typical and noble example). The romantic style, with its extravagance, its picturesqueness, its violent contrasts, is like baroque, an essentially comic grand style. Briefly to sum up, we may say that the principal difference between the comic grand style and the tragic is that the comic grand style is the grander. It is ludicrous in its exaggerated vehemence, but beautiful.

The great comedians have all combined comedy with beauty and magnificence. Aristophanes was one of the finest of Greek poets. In the *Canterbury Tales,* you will find the richest comedy, expressed in terms of a limpid beauty hardly rivaled in all literature. Ben Jonson's *Volpone* and *The Alchemist* are positively heroic in scale; in them, the sublime is fused indissolubly with the ridiculous.

We see the same beauty, the same grand style, in the works of the great comic artists. All Goya's sense of beauty appears in his comic work. He was, in his comedy, an intensely serious artist: witness his admirable series of "Caprices." Daumier, in the world of comic art, is what Michaelangelo is in the world of tragic art. His comic conceptions are on the same grand scale, and exhibit the same prodigious energy, as the frescoes on the roof of the Sistine Chapel. Doré, as we have seen, makes the grotesque romantic. And the best of Rowlandson's drawings and engravings—for example, the marvelous *Soirée at Burlington House*—are marked by a force and grandeur of scale that would do credit to a great tragic creation.

It is unnecessary to speak here of our contemporaries. A few men of real comic talent are producing books and pictures at the present time. Not many, however. Most of our comic literature is mere satire, mere comedy of manners, mere wit. Most of our comic art is either not intrinsically comic at all—it is a mere accurate illustration of a funny scene, corresponding to the comedy of manners in literature—or else, when it tries, by distortion and an energetic exaggeration to become intrinsically comic, it achieves only a petty ugliness and a mean and irritating vulgarity.

[*Vanity Fair,* July 1924]

A Ballet in the Modernist Manner

EDITOR'S NOTE: *In this burlesque ballet, Mr. Huxley follows, with a gesture of absurdity, the familiar method created by the choreographers of the Russian Ballet, as in "Coq d'Or," by providing a narrative setting for some specific musical composition. Jean Cocteau's "Les Mariés de la Tour Eiffel," which was first published in* Vanity Fair *a year ago was conceived in something the same way. Mr. Huxley here follows the same technique but, of course, enlarges his effects out of their normal proportion and reduces the whole to the level of satire.*

THERE IS no orchestra; but two and thirty players perform in unison upon as many harpsichords the most brilliant compositions of Domenico Scarlatti. The dry glitter of the instruments fills and exhilarates the air. It is a music that might cure phthisis.

The scene represents a flat and almost limitless plain, quite bare except for a few small Italian houses, miles away on the horizon, and a vast oak tree which rises a little to the right of the center and within a few feet of the back of the stage. There are no leaves on the tree. It is winter; and the grey, intense light of a northern day illumines the scene.

In the foreground and to the left, a company of vagabond actors are grouped around their hooded wagon. Here are Guarsetto and Mestolino in their linen coats and baggy trousers, their shovel hats stuck with parrot's feathers, their goat's beards, and paper noses. Razullo in tights, tattered jerkin, and page's cap plays on a guitar, the little belly and interminable long neck of which make it the very antithesis of Curcurucu, who carries—cautiously, carefully, tremulously, on a poor, thin, pair of legs—a great paunch, hunched shoulders, and a jutting rump. Fracischina and Signora Lucia are dressed in long flowing skirts, tight bodices, and sleeves like a bishop's fluttering ringlets.

Opposite, on the right of the stage, a group of ladies and gentlemen, gypsies, beggars, idiots, stand watching them. In the open space between, the actors step out and dance.

They dance, alone, in pairs and trios, in every variety of combination. Now it is Franca Trippa and Fratellino kicking up their heels at one another in a sly, low jog. Now Signora Lucia steps nobly and gracefully through a pavane, while Razullo postures over his guitar, showing off the elegance of his legs in a series of lunging steps. Curcurucu walks behind him, trying to imitate, as well as his belly and his feeble legs will allow, these heroical attitudes. They are followed by Fracischina and the two satyr-pantaloons. They dance as though intoxicated; not with wine or any of the grosser joys, but with some more rarefied poison. They dance as though they were philosophers who had succeeded at last in picking the lock of the Absolute's back door. They dance as though they had discovered, in a sudden flash, that life is what it is. The Pantaloons dance with their arms akimbo, their hands twisted back downwards, jutted rump answering to jutted belly—a bounding hornpipe. Arms upstretched and beating a tambourine above her head, Fracischina is all aspiring lines and vertical leaping. She is the living, leaping may-pole; and the pantaloons, Guarsetto and Mestolino, go leaping round her. They dance, they dance as though they would never stop.

In the midst of their dancing, across the dry and glittering music of the harpsichords, is heard, far off, the sound of drums beating a march. It grows louder and louder, till at last, at the back of the stage, there files in a company of pikemen. Behind the dancing philosophers, the soldiers maneuvre. Their long pikes come together, fall apart, making arithmetical patterns against the sky. It is a grave Pythagorean dance of pure Number.

When, panting, Fracischina and the Pantaloons have made an end, the leaders of this troop, redoubtable Captain Malagamba, redoubtable Buon-avita, dressed, like all the other gentlemen, in the romantic uniform of Puss-in-Boots, come striding forward. Theirs is a stamping dance of swashbucklers. The pikes maneuvre against the colorless sky.

A scene of descriptive pantomime follows the dance. The Captains point up towards the branches of the oak tree; then, turning to their pike-men, make a signal of command. The ranks divide; we see a pinioned pris-oner kneeling at the feet of a friar who holds aloft a crucifix and with choreographic gestures exhorts to repentance. The ranks close again.

It is a little matter of hanging.

The company applauds: Bravissimo. Then in a ring, actors, idiots, gen-try, beggars, and gypsies—all hand in hand dance round the two Captains, who blow kisses and bow their appreciation of the compliment.

The ring breaks up. Six acrobats enter with a long ladder and a rope. They balance the ladder on end, climb up, slide down. All the tricks that one can do with a ladder are done. It is set up at last against the tree and the rope is fastened to the principal branch, so that the noose hangs at a point immediately above the center of the stage.

The ranks reopen. Slowly the prisoner and the gesticulating friar ad-vance. All crowd forward, turning their backs on the audience, to witness the spectacle. Captain Malagamba takes the opportunity to embrace the Signora Lucia. She, at the imminence of his amorous whiskers, starts away from him. Malagamba follows; there is a brief dance of retreat and pur-suit. The Captain has driven her into a corner, between the shafts of the wagon, and is about to ravish an embracement in good earnest, when Razullo, happening to look around, sees what is going on. Brandishing his long-necked guitar, he bounds across the stage and with one magistral blow lays out the Captain along the floor. Then, pirouetting, he skips off with the delivered Signora. Meanwhile the prisoner has been led forward to the foot of the ladder, on the rungs of which, like a troop of long-limbed monkeys, gambol the playful acrobats. The spectators have eyes for noth-ing else.

One of the village idiots, who lacks the wits to appreciate the charms of the spectacle, sees as he gapes vacantly about him the prostrate carcass of Malagamba, approaches and bends over it in imbecile sympathy. Malagamba utters a groan; someone in the crowd looks round, calls the attention of the rest. There is a rush. The imbecile is seized, Malagamba raised to his feet, plied with strong waters from a bottle. Buonavita inter-rogates the idiot, who is held, smiling and driveling, between two harque-busiers.

While, in the foreground, the descriptive pantomime of the idiot's ex-amination, trial, and condemnation is being danced through, behind and above the heads of the spectators, the acrobats are hauling the prisoner up the ladder; they have slipped the noose over his head, they have turned him off. His feet dance a double shuffle on the wind, then gradually are still.

Captain Buonavita has by this time duly sentenced the idiot to execution. Still smiling, he is led down stage towards the foot of the ladder. The friar proffers him the crucifix.

Everybody dances. Malagamba has by this time sufficiently recovered to seize the vaulting Fracischina by the waist and toss her up into the air. The beggars, the Puss-in-Boots gentlemen, the actors, the idiots even— each seizes a partner, throws her up, brings her floating slowly down, as though reluctant to come to earth again. Fratellino and Franca Trippa jog in and out among the couples, slapping at them with their wooden swords. And the two pantaloons, who know that the world is what it is and are intoxicated with a truth that is forty-three percent above proof, go leaping and leaping, back and forth, across the front of the stage.

Still smiling, the idiot is coaxed up the rungs of the ladder. Like the most debonair of black spider-monkeys, the acrobats frisk around him; and in the extreme background the moving pikes come together, break apart, asserting unanswerably that two and two make four and that five over blue beans is the number of blue beans that make five.

As the spider-monkeys drop the noose over the idiot's head there is a long commanding roll of drums. All turn round towards the ladder, forming up in an ordered line across the stage; they stand quite still. Only the two Pantaloons, intent on their hornpipe, dance on to the glittering phrases of the harpsichords.

The drums roll on. The noose is tightened. For the last time the Friar raises his crucifix towards the idiot's lips; the idiot roars with laughter. Then the whole fantastic troupe move off.

The Puss-in-Boots captains and the gentlemen, the actors, the beggars, the gypsies, and the idiots stare after the retreating procession in an openmouthed astonishment. And well they may; for the impresario has made an absurd mistake. The music belongs, strange as it may seem, to an entirely different ballet.

[*Vanity Fair*, April 1924]

Fashions in Visual Imagery

THE POWER of mentally visualizing varies, as Galton was the first to point out, in every human being. Some people are so completely devoid of it that they cannot conjure up the faintest mental image of a familiar scene or face. In some the faculty is so acute that the forms of memory or fancy are as vivid as those of reality, while every idea, down to numbers and historical dates, is seen as something concrete occupying a definite position in space before the mental eye.

The majority of human beings do not conform to either of these extreme types. We are for the most part neither visionaries nor abstract intelligences. We are just moderately good visualizers. When we want to remember what Mr. Jones looked like, we can shut our eyes and see, if not the living image of that gentleman, at least a recognizable likeness. If we desire to conjure up out of our fancy some fairy scene, we can produce something which, if a little hazy in patches, is at least as good in its general effect as a transformation scene at the pantomime. And when we read a novel or a poem we find no difficulty in transforming the words into more or less definite images. It is of the reader's visualizations of what he reads that I propose to speak in this place.

One of the qualities of good writing that is not of a purely abstract character is its power to stimulate the reader to visualize to the limits of his capacity. For bad writing it is difficult to make equivalent mental images, and the reader is not easily tempted to do so. Much is written, indeed, which cannot be visualized at all, either because the writer himself had no clear image in his mind when he wrote or because he lacked the power of giving a verbal equivalent to what he saw. The greatest part of what we read belongs to this category. All those millions of words of journalism and ephemeral fiction which we skim through every year are read by us with the eye alone, not with the visualizing mind. They are not susceptible of being read otherwise. It is this habit of reading vast masses of ill-written and uninteresting stuff that makes us read even good books carelessly and with the outward eye only. We read a great deal more than our ancestors did; but I doubt whether we mark, learn, and inwardly digest so thoroughly as they. But this is by the way. Our business is with visualization.

When we read a fine piece of imaginative literature, that has the power of calling up bright or somber images before the mind's eye, how far does the thing we see correspond with what the writer saw, with what he desired his readers to see? That was the question I put to myself the other day while I was reading the young Marcel Proust's first volume, *Les Plaisirs et les jours,* published some thirty years ago. It is a question the complete and methodical answer to which would be a full-dress History of Taste. I have no intention, however, of being either complete or methodical. But it may be amusing to sport for a little with the flying fringes of the subject.

That it should have been *Les Plaisirs et les jours* that provoked me to ask this question is not due to any special quality in the writing of Marcel Proust's first book. At twenty, Proust did not write particularly well or particularly badly; he wrote, as a matter of fact, much as one would expect a very young, highly cultured, and talented Frenchman to write in the nineties of the last century. No, it was not Proust's part of the volume that set me pondering; it was the illustrations. These last were by a woman artist, much esteemed in Paris at the period, called Madeleine Lemaire. And they are, to our eyes, so penetratingly horrible that one marvels how so delicate a creature as Proust could have chosen her for his collaborator and how Anatole France, in his preface to the book, could have lavished on her the charming and laudatory phrases which we there read. Another little fact for the History of Taste.

But it was not so much the horror of the drawing that set me thinking as the style of them, the convention in which they were executed, the social and aesthetic ideals that they expressed. Looking at these drawings of moustached young beaux, frock-coated or dressed in evening clothes of an astonishing stiffness and correctitude, admiring these lovely young heroines with their puffed sleeves, their frizzy coiffures glittering with tiaras and the proud, austere Roman profiles, I reflected that these were the people about whom Proust had written in his later book; that all of those charming people out of this huge interminable novel were not in the least as I had pictured them, but resembled, in point of historical fact, these creatures of Madeleine Lemaire's imagination. And Madeleine Lemaire's vision of them was much the same as Proust's; her ideas of elegance, of manly and womanly beauty, of luxury, of art, were his, were the ideals of that elegant world of the nineties which he describes. My mental reconstruction of these scenes and people is utterly unlike the idea of them originally formed in the mind of Proust.

That this should actually be the case is, when we come to think of it, sufficiently obvious. Tastes change, ideals have their vogue and pass; it would be surprising, therefore, if those of us who were in our cradles when Madeleine Lemaire was drawing her horrible pictures could see the world as she saw it and feel as she felt. Our visualization of Proust cannot correspond to what Proust himself had in mind when he wrote. But that is not to say that Proust failed as a writer. The fact that he stimulates our visualizing faculty at all proves him to be a *good* writer. No power can make us visualize things of which we are absolutely ignorant. Visions of Christian saints do not appear to Buddhists. Fancy depends on experience and education for the raw material of its images.

The works of the great writers of the past cause us to visualize; but we may be certain that the visions we conjure up seldom or never bear much resemblance to those whose likeness the writer was trying to project upon his page. What ancient writers actually did see when they wrote certain passages, which to us are still magical and evocative of visions, can only be inferred. The artistic history of the period at which they wrote will give us the best clue. And what queer things, according to the taste and judgment of these times, some of them must have seen! Keats, for example—what was in his mind when he wrote his luxuriant *Endymion?* There were certain elements of Hellenic beauty, no doubt. (And we may note parenthetically here that whatever uniformity of visual fancy there has been for the last few centuries has been due to the existence of an ancient art which every educated person has been taught in youth to admire.) But Greek beauty is not the main or even a considerable part of *Endymion.* The poem is far too rococo to have come out of a Greek imagination. What Keats saw when he wrote it may be guessed by studying the art and decoration of his period—the Regency. Brighton Pavilion, the furniture and decoration of some of the State Apartments at Windsor Castle—these give us the clue. Artistically the beginning of the nineteenth century was a strange period. It witnessed the ever-accelerated breakup of the great tradition that had flourished ever since the Renaissance, and the growth of a new art, florid, opulent, undisciplined, and without austerity. If we want to know what Keats had in mind when he wrote *Endymion,* we must study this art.

The literature of the Romantic period is full of spirits, angels, nymphs, and the like. Visualizing them today we would probably see the austerer spirits as beings having the faces of Italian primitives; while to the gayer, more frivolous, and voluptuous variety we should attribute the form and features of the charmers who smile at us out of the pages of the *Vie Parisienne.* But what the Romantics themselves beheld is another question. Their good angels, we may be sure, would owe nothing to the Italian primitives, since the Italian primitives were regarded, at that time, as merely barbarous. More likely they would wear the delicious forms invented by Guido Reni or Carlo Dolci. As for the less exalted spirits—their likeness can be seen in any of Etty's charming compositions. Delicious creatures, with sleek hair, egg-shaped faces, champagne bottle shoulders, and a nudity the more prettily voluptuous in our eyes since we cannot imagine this pure, egg-faced type of the earlier nineteenth century as being anything but copiously and flowingly clothed.

Our visualizations from the works of earlier writers than the Romantics diverge even more widely from their original imaginings. The case of animals is an obvious example. When an ancient author wrote of lions, or elephants, or "fretful porpentines," he had before his mind's eye the vision of fantastic, improbable, and positively heraldic beasts. Not only were their shapes extraordinary, but their moral and allegorical qualities, as laid down in the pages of the Bestiary, were even more striking. To us, familiar from earliest childhood with menageries and zoological gardens, the most far-fetched beasts are just ordinary animals, like dogs or sheep. It is only by an effort of will and on condition that we possess a certain amount of historical knowledge that we can conjure up anything remotely resembling the rich and complex imagery that was evoked, shall we say, in Shakespeare's mind by the word "pelican" or "panther." The surprising thing is that ancient literature should still mean as much to us as it does.

[*Vanity Fair,* October 1924]

Popular Literature

LET NO ONE IMAGINE, after reading the title of this article, that I am going to reveal the secret for infallibly concocting best-sellers. If I knew that interesting recipe, I should be by this time the Corona-smoking owner of a Hispano-Suiza. But I do not know it—alas. Nor, I venture to affirm, does anyone else. For, if anyone really did know what the public wanted, would there—I ask—be as many impecunious authors as there actually are? Would there be any but supremely successful publishers? Would theatrical managers ever go bankrupt?

That all authors fail to be prosperous is not, perhaps, a completely cogent argument in favor of my hypothesis; for authors may remain poor on principle, for the love of their art and other frivolous and irrelevant reasons. But the love of art has rather less weight, I fancy, with the majority of publishers and theatrical managers. Most of them would be only too glad to know the secret of popularity; and most of them quite honestly profess to be looking for nothing else.

And yet they never find it. No publishers, no theatrical manager, ever ventures to prophesy with confidence. This novel, that play—will it be a success? They really cannot tell. And yet it is their business to know, they may be ruined for their lack of knowing. A producer will sometimes stake a fortune on his opinion—and lose the fortune. The piece which, he felt certain, was going to run three hundred nights, has to be ignominiously taken off after a week. And, less spectacularly, the same is true of novels. Publishers are incessantly making mistakes; it is notorious. They reject in manuscript books which afterwards turn out to be best-sellers; and they print other books in huge quantities which have subsequently to be remaindered, or reduced to pulp—to pulp, from which paper will again be made; paper on which yet other balderdash will be printed; balderdash that in its turn will once more be reduced to pulp. Solemn and profoundly symbolical process! On this deep theme one could meditate at length. But I refrain. . . .

We see, then, that the experts—the people whose business it is to know what the public wants—are constantly making mistakes. A man can spend a lifetime publishing, or producing plays, and be, at the end of it, just as liable to error—and to enormous error—as he was at the beginning. In a case where the most experienced cannot but confess their ignorance, it would be folly and presumption for a mere amateur, like myself, to lay down the law. It is impossible to give a recipe for the making of popular literature. Popular writers are born, not made. To be a popular writer, a man must be born with just the right sort of vulgar mind, just the adequate amount of talent. For talent is necessary; let us make no mistake about that. Your highbrow, who, after reading a novel by Mrs. Barclay or Nat Gould, declares derisively that he himself could do that sort of thing in his spare time, if he wanted to, is not telling the truth. He couldn't write that sort of thing; he couldn't write anything, in all probability, half so good. The fact that he can read Henry James is no guarantee of his being able to write Charles Garvice. In order to write anything—anything, that is to say, that other people will spend money to read—one must be born with a well-developed power of self-expression. The soul that you express may be perfectly commonplace and vulgar; that makes no difference to your power of expressing it. Wordsworth's mind was more interesting and beautiful than Miss Wilcox's; but their powers of expression were about equal. Miss Wilcox, it may be, expressed Wilcoxism more effectively and completely than Wordsworth expressed Wordsworth. Her audience was wider than Wordsworth's, because more people have minds like that of the authoress of *Laugh and the World Laughs with You* than minds like that of the author of *The Prelude*. That is the difference between a popular and an unpopular artist. For every ten people with Henry-Jamesian minds there are several hundred with Nat-Gouldian minds. But from out of these two classes of people it is only the rare Goulds and Jameses, gifted with a literary talent, who know how to express themselves and, consequently, the other members of their class.

The highbrow may have sense and modesty enough to realize that, in no circumstances, could he conceivably write a short story like one of Chekhov's; but he often imagines that it would be easy for him to turn out something in the style of the *Saturday Evening Post*. But lacking the requisite gift, he would find the one as impossible as the other.

Those people who have ever had anything to do with the editing of a periodical know how rare a thing is a talent that enables a human being to express what is within him. For every manuscript that is accepted, how many hundreds are returned with perfunctory thanks! Once, when I was working on the staff of the *Athenaeum*—Golly, what a paper! but I am sorry, none the less, that it is no more—the business manager took it into his head that a competition with prizes might send up the circulation. A small check was accordingly dangled before the noses of the British intelligentsia, who were given a chance of proving their intelligence by writing about the state of modern English literature. I forget how many hundreds of them were tempted. The number at any rate was considerable; a third of the resultant lucubrations fell to my share—I had to read them through and select those that were to go before the judges who finally awarded the prize. I did my duty conscientiously and read all the essays through from beginning to end; drearier hours I never remember to have passed in all my life. The best of the essays aspired to a dim mediocrity; the worst were beneath all criticism.

The production which finally won the prize was of the sort that one of the regular contributors might have written against time and extenuated with fatigue—the sort of article for which he would have excused himself to the editor and which the editor would have printed reluctantly and because there was no other copy on hand. The whole affair was a striking proof that there are more people who can read modern literature than can write even passable modern journalism.

A certain native talent, then, and a mind that is more Wilcoxian than Wordsworthian—these are the indispensable qualifications of the popular author. The things that please such a mind will be the things the public likes; and the talent will make it possible for the mind to express itself. Formulas cannot replace talent nor induce a frame of mind. There are no recipes for making popular literature; no shortcuts to becoming a bestseller. The best one can do is to analyze the sort of literature that is popular, so as to show what are the more or less invariable elements on which individual writers work.

The first generalization that must be made is so obvious that I am almost ashamed to make it. It is this. No literature can be popular that deals with anything but the primary instincts and the emotions dependent upon them. All intellectual interests are ruled out. Popular literature must be "human"—that is to say it must deal with men and women in so far as they resemble the brutes. The heroes and heroines of best-sellers feel, but never think; thinking is a chilly, uncomfortable process—it is essentially "inhuman." The all-too-human themes of popular novels are the instincts of reproduction, self-preservation, and gregariousness; with their dependent emotions, love—sacred and profane—and the parental emotions; anger, fear, the love of danger, acquisitiveness and its corollaries; conscience, the sense of honor, pride, ambition, emulation, and all the other emotions which we feel because we live in herds, like dogs, and not, like cats, in solitude.

Such, then, is the stuff on which the author of the best-seller must work. The pattern on which he cuts it will vary with his temperament, the epoch in which he happens to live, his nationality and education. Thus, it is sufficiently notorious that love, in the Latin and the Anglo-Saxon countries, is treated rather differently. All that concerns the reproductive instinct is treated by the French best-sellers with an almost scientific matter-of-factness. In England and across the ocean the majority of popular novels leave one to suppose that there is nothing to be matter-of-fact about.

Of recent years, this has somewhat changed, and the facts of nature have been freely admitted in more than one work having sale of more than fifty thousand copies. We are still, however, a long way away from the dry precision of the characteristic Parisian comedy. It is a significant fact that your French popular writer, when he wishes to talk about the reproductive instinct, finds an elegant and almost technical vocabulary ready to hand, a vocabulary in which he can go into the most intimate details with precision and yet with elegance and decorum. An English writer desirous of imitating him is compelled to be gross for lack of that vocabulary. Those who have at any time been rash enough to undertake the translation of a French novel will know the fearful difficulty of finding merely decent equivalents for what in the original was perfectly polished and urbane. Shall one be gross, or bowdlerize? I must confess that, confronted by that dilemma, I have bowdlerized.

Even the other less scabrous instincts are treated in different fashions in different countries. Take, for example, ambition and the love of money. It may be a mere fancy, but my impression is that these passions are more frequently, more fully and unequivocally treated in French literature than in the Anglo-Saxon. Balzac's Rastignac brooding over Paris is one of a large family of ambitious young men who are prepared to go to any length to make their fortune. Rastignac has a score of brothers in the works of Balzac himself, dozens more in Zola; and when the lesser novelists can spare a moment from love, they like to bring in some Machiavellian personage of the same clan. Ambition and acquisitiveness figure largely, it is true, in English and American fiction. But it will be found, I think, that the Anglo-Saxon counterparts for Rastignac are rarely so ruthless, so logical, so frankly immoral as Balzac's hero. In the fiction magazines, young men make good and acquire large lumps of cash; but they do it in a very genteel way, without infringing the moral code, or doing harm to anyone except the villain, who is, of course, fair game.

The young man who makes a great deal of money in a perfectly honorable fashion, marries the heroine in the last chapter and lives happy ever after, is, of course, the ideal hero of popular fiction. For he represents what we should all like to be and what so few of us are; he compensates by his virtue and his happiness for the chronic inclemency and the incurable moral weakness of the reader's life. A perfectly good and happy people would have no need of literature. One of the principal functions of the popular literature in the present state of society is to do ideal justice and to make dreams come true.

Popular literature fulfils on this earth the function of heaven. It is there that good men are rewarded and the bad punished; it is there that we seem to other people what we imagine ourselves to be or fondly wish that we were. Those extraordinary novels of Mrs. Barclay's in which luscious young men of five and twenty fall wildly in love with sexagenarian females constitute the heaven—the world where wishes are fulfilled and justice done—of all the unmarried and superannuated women in the miserable world of reality. Every best-seller has something of this heavenly quality of compensations for the harshness of reality.

But heaven would not be heaven if it were not for hell; we appreciate the good and the delicious only in contrast with what is horrible and bad. That is why the heroes and heroines of every melodrama pass through four and a half acts of unmerited persecution before emerging from the imbroglio into serenity. *All's Well That Ends Well*—it is difficult to think of any best-seller that might not have had that title.

[*Vanity Fair*, November 1924]

Art and Life

EVERY NOW AND THEN there appears on my breakfast table an envelope addressed to me, care of my publishers, in an unknown handwriting. I open it and find that it contains a letter from some unknown admirer or detester of my works—generally the former (for the haters don't take the trouble to write, preferring not to soil their note paper with an epistle addressed to such a monster as myself) and generally, also, from admirers of the female sex. I read these letters with interest; and my ardent fancy conjures up the most ravishing visions of their writers. I imagine them very young, brilliantly clever, and exquisitely beautiful. But sober reason intervenes, quoting to my overheated fancy that terrible saying of the painter Degas, who, when reproached by a lady for always making the women in his pictures look so ugly replied: "Mais, madame, les femmes en général *sont* laides." Not very gallant, but alas, too true. My imagination cools and I put the letter aside, to be answered in a brief and business-like manner when occasion offers.

Years ago, at the very beginning of my literary career, when I was writing impassioned love poems to nobody, I should have responded to such letters, if I had ever received them, in a very different, a much more tender, rapturous, and romantic style. At that time it was the height of my ambition to write works which should provoke correspondence with the feminine readers of them. It seemed to me, then, that nobody was more to be envied than the writer who receives letters from lady admirers and who answers them in long letters of his own, full of an intellectual and idealistic sensuality. My views are a little different now. Correspondence with fair strangers seems to me less desirable, if only because correspondence generally leads, in the long run, to personal meetings. Tschaikowsky, it is true, managed to keep up a correspondence for twenty years with a rich admirer, whom he never saw, and who made him a handsome cash allowance; that was an ideal state of affairs. But it is difficult, generally, not to meet one's correspondents. Balzac's case is a terrible example. Ladies were constantly writing to him; and he, with that ardent and romantic boyishness which went hand in hand with his rather cynical knowingness, responded enthusiastically. The result was that he was always engaged in the most tiresome love affairs. The last of these correspondence-affairs with female strangers was the death of him. After years of letter writing he actually married the romantic countess who had written to him years before from her palace in Little Russia. A few months later he was dead. The moral of that is: don't enter into entangling alliances, even at long range. Forewarned by his fate, I make my answers to such letters as brief and as formal as courtesy will permit.

Some little while ago, I received a particularly engaging letter—so engaging that I was tempted to throw discretion to the winds, to forget the fate of Balzac and the embittered wisdom of the painter of women, and reply in nineteen sheets of tender, wise, and witty badinerie in the style of the letters of Alfred de Musset to Aimée d'Alton. In the end, however, reason prevailed and I did nothing of the kind. But the letter continued to preoccupy me. There were one or two sentences in it that made me pensive. For the writer had remarked, among other things, that my works had had a profound influence on her life and that she was firmly intending to put my "charming principles" into practice. Now, what she imagined my principles to be, and why she should have thought them charming, I do not know. My principles, as a matter of fact, happen to be identical with those of St. Augustine; but I could not help feeling that the authoress of the letter had made some mistake and was anxious to put my principles into practice because she imagined them to be something very different from what in reality they are. Not that I minded being misunderstood; indeed, it would be horrible and humiliating to think that one had been perfectly comprehended. But I was somewhat oppressed by the thought, which had never occurred to me before, that I might be exercising an influence over anyone in any direction. To have to be in any way responsible for other people, when one can hardly assume responsibility for oneself, is dreadful. That letter disquieted me and made me pensive. In the future, I felt, I should be well advised to preface my books with a little notice, similar to that which Galileo appended to his astronomical writings, to the effect that whatever I say must be taken merely as a mathematical hypothesis and must not be held to commit the writer, or allowed to influence the reader, in any way.

From my own case, which is after all an exceedingly trivial and unimportant one, I went on to consider the case of other artists and of the influence which art in general has exercised and still exercises on life. Many laborious and boring critics have devoted all their deplorable energies to investigating the influence on art of surrounding life. Few have considered the opposite tendency—the reactions of art on contemporary life; and none, so far as I know, at length or systematically. And yet the subject, when one comes to think of it, is exceedingly interesting. For the effects that artists have had on the life around them have often been considerable and in the greater number of cases of a rather curious character, tending towards the creation in society of extreme and exaggerated types.

The effect produced by an artist on his contemporaries is not at all proportional to his intrinsic merit as an artist. Many of the greatest artists, indeed, have exercised little or no influence on the habits of their contemporaries, while men whom we now see to have been mere charlatans and mountebanks, have enormously affected the social life around them. Shakespeare, for example, had no direct influence on social life in the reigns of Elizabeth and James I—nor, for that matter on life at any subsequent period. He has no particular "principles," such as my young correspondent discovers in my writing. He did not discuss ideas that were fashionable at the moment or emphasize one particular human tendency at the expense of the rest. He was universal and of all time. Hence he created no special social tendency.

Oscar Wilde, on the other hand, who was a specialist artist, insisting on one side of life and having peculiar "principles," had a profound effect on the social life of his age. With Beardsley, he invented decadence as a social stunt. Society during the last years of Victoria's reign would have been different if Wilde and Beardsley had never lived. Shakespeare on the contrary inaugurated no stunt, and Elizabethan life would have gone on just the same if he had never existed. The social effects of Marlowe and of Donne were very much greater than were those of Shakespeare.

To enumerate all the artists who have exercised a direct influence on the social life of their contemporaries would be tedious. Vast erudition and unlimited space would be required in order to do the job properly; and I possess neither. I shall confine myself to giving a few fairly obvious instances from the past and from contemporary history.

Of all the great artists who have had a social influence, none, I imagine, can have had a greater influence than Byron. He popularized world-weariness, made romantic misanthropy fashionable, created a vogue in diabolism. The number of young men who, in the early years of the last century, were turned, for a shorter or longer period, into insupportable young cubs under the direct influence of Lord Byron's poetry must have been enormous. Fortunately for the young cubs, he also created a large audience of young ladies all ready to regard the aforesaid Y.C.'s as the last word in romantic attractiveness.

Among the great French writers who have had a similar social effect we may mention Balzac. The fact which I have already mentioned—that he was the recipient of a copious correspondence from female strangers— might have led us to guess as much. But we have it on the direct authority of Sainte-Beuve that there were cliques in the most fashionable Parisian society which deliberately took the parts of Balzac's heroes and heroines and acted them in real life. The effects must have been most interesting, seeing that Balzac's characters are always extreme types, whether of vice or virtue, ingenuousness or cynicism, and almost monomaniacal in the fixity and unity of their several purposes.

Of the world's absolutely first class and universal writers, none have had so much influence during their own time and in subsequent years as Dostoevsky. The effect of *The Brothers Karamasov* and *The Possessed,* especially on adolescents, is generally of a somewhat disastrous nature. Much violence, many quite supererogatory beastlinesses, and unnecessary suicides of young people have been due to Dostoevsky. The fault lies less in the writer than in his readers, who failing to understand the inwardness of his method, have tried to put his books literally into practice. Just as in the laboratory the chemists discover the intimate secrets of matter by submitting it to extreme heats and colds, to chemical disintegration and recombination, so Dostoevsky examines the intimate constitution of the human soul by putting his characters into situations that test them as severely as matter is tested in a furnace. What he discovers is extraordinary. No man has ever seen further. But it is not necessary to repeat laboratory experiments in real life.

Painters and draftsmen have had their influence as well as writers. It is the painters and, above all, the popular draftsmen who determine the fashionable style of beauty at any given period. The egg-faced, smooth-tressed, champagne-bottle-shouldered young lady of early Victorian times is the invention of artists such as Etty and of a host of fashion-plate draftsmen and illustrators. Du Maurier was influential in creating that type of classical and queenly beauty popular in England during the eighties. All the photographs of society beauties belonging to that period conform to the type he created. What happened to the snub-faced young women who have been popular of more recent years I do not know. Du Maurier condemned them to outer darkness. In the early twentieth century we had the Gibson girl,[7] who degenerated into the pretty little shop girl type of the fashion plate. This type has remained popular till quite recently, when a new type has been imported from France. Its inventor is Marie Laurencin. The draftsmen of *Vogue* have popularized it out of France. Marie Laurencin, moreover, is responsible for that wave of imitation manliness which is somewhat perversely invading female fashions at the present time. Her delicate little Amazons may be seen, translated into flesh and blood, in the streets of Paris, London, and New York.

Another contemporary artist who has been immensely influential, in England at any rate, is Augustus John. His influence was at its height some years ago, when he positively called into being the young woman from Chelsea. Mr. John is a most admirable painter; but he is also responsible for short hair, brilliantly colored jumpers, a certain floppiness and untidiness, and a deplorable tendency to pose against cosmic backgrounds on the top of hills or by the sea. The "arty" young lady, who was once a living Rossetti, is now a John.

On cultured society no contemporary writer has had a more penetrating effect than Marcel Proust. Since the publication of *A la recherche du temps perdu,* love is made, in the best drawing rooms, in a new and Proustian fashion. His interminable analyses of the passion have enabled somewhat jaded young men and women to love once more at greater length, more self-consciously and with a more damning knowledge of what is going on in their partner's mind than was possible in the past. Without such occasional renewings, love tends to become rather stale in those sections of society where it is the staple occupation. Writers like Proust are real benefactors to humanity, or at any rate to certain sections of it. Another great renewer of love is Mr. D. H. Lawrence, who, magnificent writer though he is, is responsible for much in certain sections of contem-

---

7. A reference to the drawings of an idealized American woman published in various periodicals by the American cartoonist and illustrator Charles Gibson (1867–1944).

porary society that is exceedingly tiresome. It is certainly true that one can have a great deal too much of love and hate, loins and solar plexuses.

[*Vanity Fair,* February 1925]

The Spread of Bad Art

I KNEW A YOUNG MAN once who committed suicide, not for any of the ordinary, classical reasons—love, debt, impending disgrace, or mortal disease—but simply because he found the world too intolerably second-rate to be put up with any longer. I regretted his death; for though he was never exactly a friend of mine—indeed, I doubt whether he was ever anyone's friend—I found him a delightful companion. He was intelligent, he was erudite, he was variously talented, he had faultless taste—such good taste, indeed, that there was practically nothing that did not strike him as vulgar; just enough talent to enable him to do many things charmingly, as an amateur, and none really well; learning in sufficient quantity to make him realize his own and all other men's bottomless ignorance, and so much intelligence, coupled with so little enthusiasm that nothing whatever seemed to him worth doing. There was nothing left but to commit suicide. He was logical; and he had the courage of his convictions.

What distressed him most was the fearful mediocrity of contemporary art. He complained that there were more bad artists in modern times than there had ever been in the past. Bad art, in the shape of silly novels, driveling plays, sentimental music, and vulgar, or dully pretentious pictures, haunted him like a guilty conscience. Another man would simply have been at pains to avoid these manifestations of bad art. But just as, when one suffers physically, one cannot resist fingering the half-cicatrized wound, or touching the aching tooth which is the source of the pain, so he, who suffered so acutely from bad art, could not ignore it, but was perpetually lacerating his spirit by the contemplation of what he so much detested. He read all the popular favorites, never missed a first night, spent whole days in the Royal Academy and all the various Salons, from the official to that of the independents, assisted at every performance of a work by Saint-Saëns or Rachmaninoff. What he suffered—he who was distressed by the stupidity of Swift, the vulgarity of Shakespeare, the platitude of Goya and the coarseness of Mozart—what he suffered, reading those books, seeing those plays and pictures, listening to that music, cannot be imagined. Only one thing is certain; he killed himself.

I used to listen to his jeremiads with amusement—for he could denounce wittily. But I never took what he said very seriously; for at that time I had not yet taken to literary journalism. I had no knowledge of what bad contemporary art really was. Since then I have reviewed several thousand books, attended professionally some hundreds of first nights, private views, and concerts. What my poor friend did out of a morbid love of self-laceration, I have since done in order to earn money. *Le borborygme d'un estomac qui souffre,* was my excuse; but he was an amateur of independent means. I swam in the muddy tide of bad art in order that I might live; he, in order that he might die. But, for whatever reason, I too swam where he had swum. If he were alive today I should listen to his complaints and denunciations with a great deal more sympathy and understanding than I listened in my days of innocence. And I should have, moreover, certain reflections to offer him—reflections which, while they might not have consoled him for the badness of contemporary art, might at least have explained why that badness took precisely the form it did; and by turning his mind from the contemplation of the thing itself to the contemplation of its causes, might have changed his passion for self-laceration into a passion for scientific enquiry.

But these reflections were not made, alas, till after he was dead—for the good reason that it was not till after his death that review copies and free tickets had forced the problem of bad art on my attention. So far as he is concerned, these reflections are a piece of *esprit d'escalier* that has come to me some five or six years too late. Still, such as it is, the *esprit* has come. And it seems a pity to waste it, the more so as the subject is not uninteresting. "Why is bad art—or at any rate, why does bad art seem to be—more copious now and of worse quality than it was in the past?" Without being a matter of life and death, as it was to my poor friend, that question is one that must have presented itself in one form or another to all who occupy themselves at all consciously with the arts.

Let us being with the obvious. There is more bad art in 1925 than there was in 1625 for the simple reason that there are many more people in the world than there were then, and these people can almost all read and write and that they dispose of a, comparatively speaking, ample leisure. That leisure has got to be made tolerable. The traditional arts of self-amusement have been mostly lost; education and a snobbish desire to imitate the rich and cultured have killed the morris, the maypole, the folk-song, the mummers. Nor is it possible, as a matter of fact, to practice most of these entertainments in the crowded cities in which the great mass of human beings now live.

The supplying of diversions ready made has become a profitable industry. To own a merry-go-round is profitable; to have written a successful novel is still more profitable. Playwrights can earn more than company promoters, composers can afford large motor-cars, a skillful draftsman can make enough to support three wives in luxury. Not all of them do, of course; but all have a chance. Millions and millions of human beings, terrified of boredom and enjoying a leisure which they are powerless to fill themselves, are hungrily craving for distraction, are begging to be relieved from their own intolerable company and to be given substitutes for thought. The man who can give what the greatest number of his fellow beings require is made for life. All the worst works of art are created to supply the hunger of the greatest number. Incidentally, a few of the best do the same.

Education and leisure have enlarged the public which patronizes the arts; and the greater public's increased demand for art has correspondingly enlarged the circle of those who, by purveying what it requires, live professionally on its patronage. But education has had a further effect; it has caused an enormous number of people who, in the past, would either have done nothing at all, or done some useful work, to profess themselves "artists" and produce "works of art." The decay of formal religion has had many deplorable effects, of which perhaps the worst is the exaltation of the idea of patriotism and the most harmlessly absurd cult of High Art. Earnest young people who would in the past have been regular church goers, now devote themselves to art and imagine that they themselves are artists.

Many, it is true, abandon their artistic aspirations once they are fairly grown up and launched into the world; but many, very many (particularly of those who have a small independent income) go on imagining themselves to be artists to the day of their death. To them is due that vast mass of dull, respectable, flabby art which goes trickling, like a semi-liquid mass of unleavened dough, over the face of our modern world. All the flat novels, all the boring, competent poems, all the blank verse tragedies, all the insipid performances of Bach, all the dim water colors and the dreary still lives are their work. It is they who, with heavy-footed enthusiasm, follow in the track of the pioneers, strewing the world with lifeless imitations of living art.

It is better that they should do these things than that they should spend their lives between the race course and the night club (though I am not perfectly sure even of this). But it would be much better still if they blew off steam as their ancestors did, by going to church, praying, and doing good works.

The artists who are artists because it pays them to be, and the artists who are artists because they no longer believe in an organized religion and must have something to satisfy their higher feelings—these are responsible for all that is peculiarly vulgar and peculiarly dull in contemporary art. Neither class was anything like so numerous in the past.

It might be remarked in passing that the spread of education has had yet another result, which is a great raising of the level of technical accomplishment in most classes of art. The average popular novel is far better written and put together than it was in the past. All that can be taught about art has now been learnt by its practitioners. But bad work is no better for being technically well done. Indeed, I am inclined to think it is rather worse. There is a certain charm about ingenuous and untutored badness. But when bad artists are like the average French novelist of the present day—accomplished, knowing all the tricks of the trade, working according to the best recipes in the literary cookery books—then they are utterly insupportable. The untutored bad sometimes achieve a kind of excellence by mistake. The tutored never make mistakes, they are consistently and efficiently bad all the time.

It would be easy to enumerate other factors in modern life which have made contemporary bad art; bad in a peculiar, unique twentieth-century way. Thus, our habit of hurrying has killed the long book, our bourgeois way of life has killed the large and grandiose picture, our widely diffused knowledge has led to eclecticism and catholicity of taste, with consequent pastiching of every kind of ancient or far-fetched style. Particularly striking is the influence of the camera on the visual arts. Daguerre's invention has reacted on painting in a number of curious and unexpected ways.

In the first place, photography has tended to make the modern painter much less interested in the exact imitation of nature than he was in the past. The camera can do the job so much more quickly and easily that it seems hardly worth his while to strain after exact likeness. Cubism, expressionism, post-impressionism, and all the other brands of non-realistic art, together with the whole modern theory of aesthetics have been made possible by the camera.

The making of exact (and beautiful) imitations of nature was one of the principal functions of the second-rate artists of other days. The camera has now robbed these worthy second-rate artists of their occupation. Modern theory tells them that they ought to produce something purely aesthetic and formally significant. They do their best—and the result is that unspeakably dismal second-rate "advanced" art which fills the galleries of the contemporary world.

In pre-photographic, pre-"process" days, the work of engraving occupied the energies of a very large number of conscientious, technically competent, and entirely unoriginal artists of the second rank. The public wanted reproductions, both of pictorial documents, and of the original works of the great masters. The engravers supplied them. They did useful work, which was often, incidentally, beautiful in itself. Then came "process"—the photographic reproduction first of line drawings, then of half-tones. The engravers were doomed. For a few years the American wood block makers struggled heroically against the machines. But it was no good. For all practical purposes there are now no engravers. In a certain sense we have gained by their extermination. Pictorial documents of perfect accuracy can be made and multiplied with ease; the works of genuine, original artists can be reproduced by mechanical means, without having to pass through the refracting medium of the engraver's personality.

The labor which, in a happier age, they would have expended in the reproduction of Rubenses and Raphaels, in making steel engravings of Turner, in neatly scratching architecture, landscape, animals, figures on copper plates is now devoted to the playing of "original" five-finger exercises on canvas. No wonder, then, that the great mass of modern painting is in general so appallingly dull.

[*Vanity Fair*, March 1925]

What, Exactly, Is Modern?

AT A CAFÉ in Siena I once got into conversation with an Italian medical student. Like most of his compatriots, he was very open and confiding. We had not known one another half an hour before he told me the whole story of his life. Among other things he informed me that he had spent a year as a student at the University of Rome, but that he had been compelled to remove to Siena because it was impossible for him to learn anything at Rome; there were too many distractions in the capital, too many feminine distractions in particular. He knew that he would never get a degree if he stayed at Rome. "In a little town like Siena," I said, "I suppose there are no distractions of that sort?" "Not so many," he admitted, "as at Rome. All the same," he added, and smiled a smile of male fatuity, "you'd be surprised by the young women of Siena. They're really very modern." And he went on to tell me of his adventures with the local shop girls.

I laughed, not at his stories, which were exceedingly tedious and commonplace, but at his peculiar use of the word "modern." It was the first time I had heard it employed in such a context. Since then I have heard it similarly used, more than once. I remember, in London, hearing one of those scrubby camp-followers of the arts who make their "artistic temperament" the excuse for leading an idle, sordid, and perfectly useless life, loudly and proudly boasting that he was absolutely modern: anyone might have his wife, so far as he was concerned. And he gave it to be understood that the lady in question thought just as little of promiscuous infidelity—was, in a word, just as modern—as he.

Now, as a grammarian and a literary pedant, I strongly object to the improper use of words. Every word possesses some single, definite meaning. It should always be used in its accepted sense and not forced to signify something it was never meant to signify. Thus, when one wants to say of a person that he or she is lascivious and insensitive to the point of indulging promiscuously in what is technically known as "love," one should state the fact in so many words and not say that he or she is "modern." For such a person is not modern, but on the contrary, antique and atavistic. To behave like the Romans under Caracalla, the Asiatic Greeks, the Babylonians, is not a bit modern. In point of historical fact it is monogamous love and chastity that are the modern inventions. My Italian friend and the young camp-follower of the arts were terribly old-fashioned, if only they had known it. They were eighteenth-century in their outlook, they were Roman-Empire, they were Babylonian. Really modern people love like the Brownings.

My Italian friend and the camp-follower of the arts had, it is true, a certain justification for their employment of the epithet "modern" in this particular context: the state of mind which they thus qualified does happen to be fairly common, in certain circles, at the present time. But a thing may be fashionable without necessarily being modern. There is a great difference between mere fashionableness or contemporaneity on the one hand and modernity on the other. For things and ideas which were fashionable in the past may become fashionable again. Crinolines and clinging draperies, waists high, or low, tight or loose, alternately come and go. But it would be absurd to call any one of them modern merely because it happens to be in vogue at the particular moment when you are speaking. Only that which is really new, which has no counterpart in antiquity, is modern. Thus, our mechanical civilization, with the conditions of life and the ideas begotten by it are modern. But sexual promiscuity is not modern at all; it is a very ancient and anachronistic habit which happens, at the moment and in certain limited circles, to be fashionable.

We talk of modern art just as loosely and inaccurately as we talk of modern manners. Some contemporary art is genuinely modern, inasmuch as it is typical of our civilization alone and different from ancient art. Much, on the other hand, is not modern, but merely something old, *réchauffé* which we call modern only because it happens to be in vogue. Thus, the barbaric music of Stravinsky is fundamentally not modern at all. It is merely an ingenious, scholarly, and more efficient development of the noises made up by savage people to work themselves up into a state of emotional excitement. Those who heard the transcriptions of Tibetan music brought back by members of the Everest expedition must have been struck by the close resemblance which this savage music bore to Stravinsky's. Without excessive vanity we can say, I think, that the Tibetans are several thousand years behind us in mental development; the music of Stravinsky and his imitators is therefore only a cultured and conscious atavism. In their intellectuality and idealism, Bach and Beethoven are incomparably more modern than Stravinsky. Among contemporary musicians Schönberg may be regarded as modern; for unlike the fashionably atavistic Stravinsky, he is doing something which our savage ancestors couldn't do—appealing to the intellect and the spirit, not to the primary emotions and the nerves. Schönberg, though not, perhaps, a greatly inspired artist, is at any rate moving forward in the direction of all human development—towards more and more mind and spirit. Stravinsky is going backwards, away from mind, toward physiology.

In speaking of the visual arts, we make a somewhat similar mistake. For we are accustomed to call "modern" almost any picture or sculpture which happens to be unlike the object which it is supposed to represent. Now distortion as such is not at all modern. All primitive art is non-realistic. So is all incompetent art (which does not mean of course, that all non-realistic art is incompetent). Non-realism in itself is no criterion of modernity. It is only an accident that we happen to be living in an age when many artists cultivate a deliberate naivism, when the technical practice (though not the subject matter and the symbolism) of the primitives is freely imitated and art is simplified and conventionalized to the utmost. There is obviously nothing remarkably modern in imitating the primitives. What is modern—and deplorably so—is the contemporary habit of emptying the primitives of their content and significance. Art for art's sake and the theory of pure aesthetics are modern products, due to the divorce of art from religion. The majority of contemporary painters, one feels when looking at their works, haven't the faintest notion what to paint. They exercise their art in the void, so to speak, making no contact with the life and the ideas around them. Plenty of admirable artists have shown, in the past, that it is possible to combine pure aesthetics with story telling and the expression of ideas. Few of the most talented artists of the present day make any attempt to accomplish this union or there would be more really modern art.

It is the same in literature as in painting and music. What is commonly called modern, by journalists and other thoughtless people, is either trivially eccentric, like the literature of the dadaists; smartly cynical and heartless in a minor eighteenth-century way, like the novels of Mr. Firbank; or obstreperously gross and blasphemous, like *Ulysses* which is simply the reaction of its author against his medieval catholic education. The blasphemies in *Ulysses* are precisely like those of Marlowe in the sixteenth century and their grossnesses are those of a Father of the Church, who having emerged from his hermitage, enlarges on the horrors of the sin-ridden world. None of these literary manifestations are modern. For they are not new; they do not represent what is most typical of our civilization, they are off the main line of progress, which is towards increasing subtlety of mind, increasing sensitiveness of emotion, increasing toleration and understanding. An enormously enhanced mental elasticity and freedom distinguish this age from past ages. The most modern work of literature is the most intelligent, the most sensitive and spiritual, the freest and most tolerant, the most completely and widely comprehending. Thus, the most modern novelist who ever wrote is certainly Dostoevsky. That he happened to die in 1881 makes no difference to his modernity. His subtlety, his sensitiveness, his intelligence and comprehension remain unsurpassed and hardly approached. His novels are still the most complete and characteristic product of the modern mind. It may be hoped, it may even be expected, that, in the course of evolution, the mass of human beings will grow to be as intelligent, as deeply and as widely comprehending, as exquisitely sensitive as was Dostoevsky. He has been dead for more than forty years. But he was so excessively and abnormally modern that it will probably be several centuries before the rest of us have come abreast with him.

To distinguish what is modern in recent literature from what is not modern requires only a little reflection. Thus, Anatole France, however delightful an author, is not modern; he is a contemporary ancient, a sort of Lucian brought up to date. Marcel Proust, on the other hand, is decidedly modern; his sensitiveness and his acute, though somewhat limited, understanding of character, are things to which we can find no parallel in antiquity. D. H. Lawrence is partly extremely modern, partly atavistic, in the manner of Stravinsky. As a poet, Thomas Hardy, in spite of his age, is a great deal more modern than, shall we say, Jean Cocteau. It would be easy, but tedious, to multiply such examples. They would all point to the same conclusion: not all that is fashionable is modern. Let us not, therefore, abuse a very useful and significant word by applying it indiscriminately to everything that happens to be contemporary.

[*Vanity Fair,* May 1925]

Where Are the Movies Moving?

IN THE COURSE of one of his adventures, my favorite dramatic hero, Felix the Cat, begins to sing. He thrums his guitar, he rolls up his eyes, he opens his mouth. A stream of crotchets and semi-quavers comes gushing out of his throat. The little black notes hang in the air above him. Looking up, Felix sees them suspended there. With his usual quick resourcefulness, he realizes at once that these crotchets are exactly the things he has been looking for. He reaches up, catches a few handfuls of them, and before you can say *Knife!* he has fitted them together into the most ingenious little trolley or scooter, of which the wheels are made out of the round heads of the notes, the framework of their tails. He helps his companion into her seat, climbs in himself, seizes by its barbs the semi-quaver which serves as the lever of propulsion, and, working it vigorously backwards and forwards, shoots away, out of the picture, towards some unknown region of bliss to which we are not privileged to follow him.

Seen on the screen, this conversion of song into scooters seems the most natural, simple, and logical thing in the world. The cat opens his mouth and the written symbols of sound appear, by a familiar convention, in the air above him. Forgetting their symbolical significance and concentrating exclusively on their shape, we perceive that the notes are circles attached to lines—or, more concretely, wheels and rods, the raw material of the engineer. Out of these wheels and rods, Felix, cat of all trades, makes a scooter. There is no improbability, no flaw in the artistic logic. One image easily and naturally suggests the other. For the dramatist of the screen, this sort of thing is child's play.

As a mere word-monger and literary man, I envy him. For if I tried to do the same thing in terms of words, the result would be very nearly nonsense. I might write like this, for example: "Don Giovanni touched his guitar and began to sing, *Deh, vieni alla finestra*. The notes floated out and hung in the soft warm air of the Spanish night, like the component parts of a Ford car waiting to be assembled." At a first reading, this simile would seem quite incomprehensible, not to say deliberately and perversely idiotic. Prolonged reflection might at last extract from the phrase its meaning; the resemblance between printed notes and the parts of a motor-car might finally suggest themselves to the imagination. But the process would certainly be slow; and, being slow, would be unsatisfactory. A simile that is understood with difficulty is a bad simile. In a good simile or striking metaphor the terms, however remote from one another, must be made to come together in the reader's mind with, so to speak, a smart click. Now, to the average mind the connection between notes and spare parts is not immediately obvious. (To begin with, the idea suggested by the word "notes" is primarily an idea of sound; it is only on second thoughts that one recalls the printed symbol.) Hence the inadequacy and ineffectiveness of the simile when expressed in words. On the screen, where it is expressed in visual images, it is perfectly satisfactory.

I have dwelt at some length on Felix's song and scooter—but not, I think, unduly. For the example indicates very clearly what are the most pregnant potentialities of the cinema; it shows how cinematography differs from literature and the spoken drama and how it may be developed into something entirely new. What the cinema can do better than literature is to be fantastic. An artist who uses words as his medium finds himself severely limited in the expression of his fantasy by the fact that the words he uses are not his own invention, but traditional and hereditary things, impregnated by centuries of use with definite meanings and aureoled with certain specific associations. To a certain extent, a writer must employ clichés in order to be understood at all. He cannot dissociate long-united ideas, or bring together ideas which have never previously been joined, without appearing to his readers to be talking nonsense.

We have seen for example, how difficult it would be for a writer to associate, without a long preliminary explanation, the ideas of musical notes and the parts of a motor-car—and how easy for the maker of films, who can almost arbitrarily associate any two ideas, simply by bringing together a pair of suitable images. "Young" writers, especially in France, have for some years been in revolt against the tyrannies of language. They have tried forcibly to dissociate old ideas, to use words in a new and revolutionary way. It cannot be said that the results have been very successful. To the general public their writing seems nonsensical; and even their admirers have to admit that their books make difficult reading. The fact is that these "young" writers are rebelling, not against effete literary conventions, but against language itself. They are trying to make words do what they cannot do, in the nature of things. They are working in the wrong medium. You cannot do silversmith's work in terms of Egyptian granite. In the same way, the most extravagant flights of fancy cannot be rendered in words; on the screen however, it is easy to give them form. *Super-realism* is the name of the most recent of these "young" French schools. The aim of the *super-realists* is to free literature completely from logic and to give it the fantastic liberty of the drama. What they attempt to do—not very successfully—the cinema achieves brilliantly. The adventures of Felix the Cat are *super-realistic* in the highest degree. And not only Felix. Many of our best films are *super-realistic* or dream-like in their fantasy. Think, for example, of those hilarious and subtle nightmares invented by Charlie Chaplin; think of the adventure films of Douglas Fairbanks.

In future, I am sure, the tendency will be to exploit this potentiality of the cinema to an ever-increasing extent. It is inevitable; the medium lends itself so well to *super-realism* that it would be extraordinary if this were not to be the case. On the screen, miracles are easily performed; the most incongruous ideas can be arbitrarily associated; the limitations of time and space can be largely ignored. Moreover, the very imperfections of the cinema are, in this respect, an important asset. The absence of color is already a bold and arbitrary simplification of reality. The silence in which even the most violent action takes place is strangely nightmarish. (How fantastic it is to look on at some furious fight, in which mortal blows are given and exchanged without a sound! It is like watching a battle of fishes through the glass of an aquarium.) And then the darkness of the theater, the monotonous music—inducing, as they do, a kind of hypnotic state—enhance in the minds of the spectators the dream-like quality of what they see on the screen.

In future, then, the fantastic, *super-realistic* qualities of the cinema will be more deliberately exploited than they are now. This does not mean, of course, that ordinary realism will be ousted from the screen. The cinema will continue to unfold its everyday epics. Realism will persist side by side with *super-realism*—but a little leavened by it, let us hope, and a little enlivened by its efforts to compete with its fantastical rival.

Broadly speaking, there are two ways in which a story, depending on human character, can be told on the screen. The first method is what I may call the Behaviorist method. The story is told in terms of psychological details. The film abounds in significant close-ups of faces, hands, or even feet moving under the stress of emotion. The method is an excellent one, provided that the actors can act. In the hands of unimaginative producers and bad actors it leads to the most horribly dreary results. (Oh, those heroes and heroines who gradually look over their shoulders towards the camera and smile, or make a face that is meant to be one of agony! Those huge, close-up smiles of tenderness, eight feet from ear to ear! One shudders at the recollection.)

The second method, which is favored by the Germans and, more recently, by the Italians, may be called the Expressionist or Pictorial method. For the producers belonging to this school, the small details of human behavior under emotional stress are not so important as the general pictorial effect of the scene regarded as an expressive, symbolical composition. Where the Behaviorists would present a close-up of a face gone suddenly rigid, a nervously twitching hand, the Pictorialists build up a more or less fantastic scenic picture, the general effect of which is expressive of horror, fear, or whatever the emotion to be rendered may be. The great defect of this expressionism has consisted, so far, in its pretentiousness, its melodramatic ponderosity. Touched with a lighter fancy, the method might be used much more successfully than it actually is. A study of *Felix the Cat* would teach the German producers many valuable lessons. My own hope and belief is that the Behaviorist school of producers will borrow hints from the Expressionists, that they will learn to touch their realism with a certain picturesque *super-realism*. Those dismal stories of millionaires, adultery, heavy fathers, true love, and all the rest would become much more tolerable if they were treated in a less prosaically direct way. No five-reel drama would be any the worse for having a little nightmare put into it.

[*Vanity Fair*, July 1925]

The Pleasant and the Unpleasant

THE LIFE of a newspaper editor resembles the discouraging eternity of those who, in hell, try to fill sieves with water. Twelve pages, twenty-four pages—and as, with every advance of civilization, every acquisition of leisure, universal boredom and the urgent need of distraction grow and grow, the number will gradually increase—must daily be filled with reading matter. Every day, every damned day, from forty thousand to a quarter of a million words have to be poured into the bottomless waste-paper baskets, the dustbins, the insatiable sewers of the world. And there is no respite; there can be no slackening off. However little there is to say, the pages must be filled.

Sisyphus had to push a stone up a hill; when it got to the top, the stone rolled irresistibly down and he had to begin again. But at any rate the stone was always there; Sisyphus was not expected to produce it and reproduce it each time, like a rabbit, out of his empty hat. The newspaper man has to push just as hard as Sisyphus and just as hopelessly; he must also conjure up his stone, every day, out of nothing. Hence the silliness that is in newspapers. Reading it, we should feel, not irritation, but pity for the miserable wretches who have been reduced to such desperate shifts.

I caught a pathetic note of desperation in recent comments in England on Mr. Noel Coward's play *Fallen Angels*. Here was a little dramatic anecdote, skillfully and amusingly told; a trifle scabrous, perhaps—but after all, since ladies have taken to tobacco, the smoking-room story, as we all know, has found its way into the drawing-room; why pretend that it hasn't? And in any case, *Fallen Angels* is very mild smoking indeed—hardly tobacco even; the merest grass; but very pleasantly scented withal, and of an indubitably contemporary flavor. Nobody but a harassed journalist, driven to his wit's end to find food for our waste-paper baskets, would have dreamed of making much ado about this graceful nothing. But the waste-paper baskets gaped; desperately, the ado was made. Mr. Coward was reproached for having falsified life by presenting nothing but its sordid side, for having libeled humanity by showing only unpleasant characters. (As if it were necessary, or even possible, to put the whole of life and every sort of humanity into a brief and witty anecdote! But let that pass.) His taste and his morals were impugned; he was accused of sapping the foundations of society. And so on and so on. A lot of space was easily filled.

In the circumstances, the fuss was ridiculous; for Mr. Coward's play is not in the least unpleasant. The professional moralists of the evening papers made a bad choice. If they had hit on something that was really unpleasant, a fuss might have been worth making. Or rather, not a fuss; for fusses don't get anyone anywhere; a critical enquiry, shall we say. For the subject, after all, is an interesting one. Should plays and novels always be pleasant? Do readers and spectators in general want their entertainments to be pleasant? Do they object to unpleasantness?

If we are to believe the evening papers, the public doesn't like unpleasantness. It wants the characters in its books and plays to be good; or if unpleasant people must be brought in, it demands that they should be counterbalanced, conquered, and put to shame by the virtuous. And if it doesn't want these things—well, it ought to. Are these papers right?

It will be as well to leave the moral question out of account; people ought, no doubt, to do a great many things that they don't do. Let us confine ourselves to facts. Do people, as a matter of fact, like unpleasantness? Or don't they? To me it seems sufficiently obvious that they do, if not exactly like it, at least take a profound interest in unpleasantness. We are interested in the hundredth straying sheep, not merely because we want to bring it back into the fold with the other ninety-nine, but for its own sake, just because it has strayed. Evil fascinates us as such. (And don't the journalists know it? What sells their paper is not the grave, more-sorrowful-than-angry denunciation of unpleasant authors; it is the lively and lengthy descriptions of murder, fraud, lust, and cruelty on the other pages.) We like police news and unpleasant fiction for the same reason as we like chatty items about actresses and the Prince of Wales, happy endings, and the lives of saints. We like them because they show us what we might be, potentially or ideally, but in dull fact are not. Actresses and the Prince of Wales, unbelievably happy endings and holiness—what are they but our dramas made actual? We would all like to be popular, rich, powerful, extraordinarily lucky and—the longing is quite as intense—extraordinarily good. There are other moments, however, when, tired of being respectable, we wish that we had the courage of our instincts, when we long to carry every velleity of vice in us to its logical conclusion in action. Stavrogin and

Leopold and Loeb, Nero and Mme. Marneffe are as much fulfilments of our dreams as Prince Mishkin and St. Francis, Alexander the Great and the heroes and heroines of all the fairy tales. Even the lowest, the most disgusting villains are dream fulfilments of a part of our potential selves. True, we may never actually desire to be like the hero of Dostoevsky's *Letters from the Underground,* the most repulsively unpleasant character, with the possible exception of Little Judas in Shchedrin's *Golovieff Family,* in all fiction; but the fact that we can recognize in him certain of our own weaknesses makes us take the deepest interest in him. We see what, but for the grace of God, we might be. We are excused, by this vicarious actualization of our worst potentialities, from making the personal experiment of total depravity. Little Judas and his kind are scapegoats. We live respectable lives and they sin for us. And since we also live dull lives, worldly and perhaps furtively vicious lives, we must have Prince Charming and actresses to lead us out of the drabness into fairylands, we must have saints to shame us into going heavenwards.

We like unpleasant characters, then; we are deeply interested in them. But there is much truth in the contention of the evening paper moralists that we don't like them alone and by themselves. Things exist only in virtue of their opposites. Significance is begotten by the coupling of extremes. A single extreme, isolated, has no meaning. True, we can and do mentally supply the deficiencies of a book or play which isolates a single moral extreme from the opposite that gives it its meaning. But it would be better if the work had no deficiencies. The painter of a complete picture illuminates unpleasantness by pleasantness, and vice versa. Moreover, the uniformly unpleasant work, like the uniformly pleasant, tends to be dull, because it suppresses that element of conflict which is the soul of all drama. It is impossible for us, being what we are, to envisage the material world, except in terms of space and time; and similarly, being what we are, we cannot think of that other world—the world of the spirit—except in terms of conflicting good and evil. Unpretentious little anecdotes, like *Fallen Angels* or the *novelle* of Boccacio, can bombinate gracefully in the moral void; all that is required of them is that they should be self-consistent and deftly told. But serious drama ought in some sort to represent symbolically our view—our unescapably, inevitably moral view—of life. A play, a novel, in which there is no conflict, no crucial alternative between good and evil, strikes us as dull. Mr. Joyce's *Ulysses* is an obvious example.

In spite of its very numerous qualities—it is, among other things, a kind of technical handbook, in which the young novelist can study all the possible and many of the quite impossible ways of telling a story—*Ulysses* is one of the dullest books ever written, and one of the least significant.

This is due to the total absence from the book of any sort of conflict and to the absolutely static nature of the characters. Bloom is consistently and statically unpleasant. At no point in the course of that interminable narrative does he make anything in the nature of a choice between pleasantness and unpleasantness. He is just a Theophrastian character: "The Nasty Man." Theophrastus would have described him in a page. Mr. Joyce has taken six or seven hundred to produce a portrait no more significant. The unrelievedly pleasant, obviously enough, is as unsatisfactory from the point of view of completeness and significance as the unrelievedly unpleasant. To those who find actual life too overwhelmingly depressing it may be medicinally valuable as a sedative and restorative—just as unrelieved unpleasantness may be good for those who live too shelteredly and comfortably.

So far, I have looked at the matter only from the reader's point of view. Writers are also readers (sometimes) and they have the same general reason for taking an interest in unpleasantness. But it seems to me that they have a further reason—a special, almost technical reason—for liking bad characters. For it is a curious, but undeniable fact, that, just as joy is far harder to express in words than grief or pain, so goodness is more difficult to describe than evil. Of the well-drawn, completely realized characters of fiction, more are on the whole unpleasant than pleasant. Convincing examples of positively holy characters are exceedingly rare. Dostoevsky's "Idiot" and "Aloysha" are among the very few of them who really live.

Why should it be so hard to express pure joy without sinking into insipidity, or to describe unalloyed and perfect virtue without seeming to cant and snuffle through the nose and tell lies? It is not easy to say. The difficulty of achieving these things in art seems to be exactly proportional to the difficulty of achieving them in life.

[*Vanity Fair*, September 1925]

Books for the Journey

ALL TOURISTS cherish an illusion, of which no amount of experience can ever completely cure them; they imagine that they will find time, in the course of their travels, to do a lot of reading. They see themselves, at the end of a day's sight-seeing or motoring, or while they are sitting in the train, studiously turning over the pages of all the vast and serious works which, at ordinary seasons, they never find time to read. They start for a fortnight's tour in France, taking with them *The Critique of Pure Reason*,

Appearance and Reality, the complete works of Dante, and the *Golden Bough*. They come home to make the discovery that they have read something less than half a chapter of the *Golden Bough* and the first fifty-two lines of the *Inferno*. But that does not prevent them from taking just as many books the next time they set out on their travels.

Long experience has taught me to reduce in some slight measure the dimensions of my traveling library. But even now I am far too optimistic about my powers of reading while on a journey. Along with the books which I know it is possible to read, I still continue to put in a few impossible volumes in the pious hope that some day, somehow, they will get read. Thick tomes have traveled with me for thousands of kilometers across the face of Europe and have returned with their secrets unviolated. But whereas in the past I took nothing but thick tomes, and a great quantity of them at that, I now take only one or two and for the rest pack only the sort of books which I know by experience can be read in a hotel bedroom after a day's sight-seeing.

The qualities essential in a good traveling-book are these. It should be a work of such a kind that one can open it anywhere and be sure of finding something interesting, complete in itself and susceptible of being read in a short time. A book requiring continuous attention and prolonged mental effort is useless on a voyage; for leisure, when one travels, is brief and tinged with physical fatigue, the mind distracted and unapt to make protracted exertions.

Few traveling-books are better than a good anthology of poetry in which every page contains something complete and perfect in itself. The brief respites from labor which the self-immolated tourist allows himself cannot be more delightfully filled than with the reading of poetry, which may even be got by heart; for the mind, though reluctant to follow an argument, takes pleasure in the slight labor of committing melodious words to memory.

In the choice of anthologies every traveler must please himself. My own favorite is Edward Thomas's[8] *Pocket Book of Poems and Songs for the Open Air*. Thomas was a man of wide reading and of exquisite taste, and peculiarly gifted, moreover, to be an anthologist of the Open Air. For out of the huge tribe of modern versifiers who have babbled of green fields, Thomas is almost the only one whom one feels to be a "nature poet" (the expression is somehow rather horrible, but there is no other) by right of birth and the conquest of real sympathy and understanding. It is

8. Edward Thomas (1878–1917). English poet, nature writer, and novelist.

not everyone who says Lord, Lord, that shall enter into the kingdom of heaven; and few, very few of those who cry Cuckoo, Cuckoo, shall be admitted into the company of nature poets. For proof of this I refer my readers to the various volumes of Georgian Poetry.

Equally well adapted, with poetry, to the traveler's need, are collections of aphorisms or maxims. If they are good—and they must be very good indeed; for there is nothing more dismal than a "Great Thought" enunciated by an author who has not himself the elements of greatness—maxims make the best of all reading. They take a minute to read and provide matter upon which thought can ruminate for hours. None are to be preferred to La Rochefoucauld's. Myself, I always reserve my upper left-hand waistcoat pocket for a small sexto-decimo reprint of the Maximes. It is a book to which there is no bottom or end. For with every month that one lives, with every accession to one's knowledge, both of oneself and of others, it means something more. For La Rochefoucauld knew almost everything about the human soul, so that practically every discovery one can make oneself, as one advances through life, has been anticipated by him and formulated in the briefest and most elegant phrases. I say advisedly that La Rochefoucauld knew "almost" everything about the human soul; for it is obvious that he did not know all. He knew everything about the souls of human beings in so far as they are social animals. Of the soul of man in solitude—of man when he is no more interested in the social pleasures and successes which were, to La Rochefoucauld, so all-important—he knows little or nothing. If we desire to know something about the human soul in solitude—in its relations, not to man, but to God—we must go elsewhere: to the Gospels, to the novels of Dostoevsky, for example. But man in his social relationships has never been more accurately described, and his motives never more delicately analyzed than by La Rochefoucauld. The aphorisms vary considerably in value; but the best of them and their number is surprisingly large—are astonishingly profound and pregnant. They resume a vast experience. In a sentence La Rochefoucauld compresses as much material as would serve a novelist for a long story. Conversely, it would not surprise me to learn that many novelists turn to the Maximes for suggestions for plots and characters. It is impossible, for example, to read Proust without being reminded of the Maximes, or the Maximes without being reminded of Proust. "Le plaisir de l'amour est d'aimer, et l'on est plus heureux par la passion que l'on a que par celle que l'on donne." "Il y a des gens si remplis d'eux-mêmes, que, lorsqu'ils sent amoureux, ils trouvent moyen d'être occupés de leur passion sans l'être de la personne qu'ils aiment." What are all the love stories in *A la recherche du temps perdu* but enormous amplifications of these aphorisms? Proust is La Rochefoucauld magnified ten thousand times.

Hardly less satisfactory as travel books are the aphoristic works of Nietzsche. Nietzsche's sayings have this in common with La Rochefoucauld's, that they are pregnant and expansive. His best aphorisms are long trains of thought, compressed. The mind can dwell on them at length because so much is implicit in them. It is in this way that good aphorisms differ from mere epigrams, in which the whole point consists in the felicity of expression. An epigram pleases by surprising; after the first moment the effect wears off and we are no further interested in it. One is not taken in twice by the same practical joke. But an aphorism does not depend on verbal wit. Its effect is not momentary, and the more we think of it, the more substance we find in it.

Another excellent book for a journey—for it combines expansive aphorisms with anecdotes—is Boswell's *Life of Johnson,* which the Oxford Press now issues, on India paper, in a single small octavo volume. (All travelers, by the way, owe much to the exertions of Henry Frowde, of the Oxford Press, the inventor, or at least the European reinventor, of that fine rag paper, impregnated with mineral matter to give it opacity, which we call India paper.) What the aphorism is to the philosophical treatise, the India paper volume is to the ponderous editions of the past. All Shakespeare, perfectly legible, gets into a volume no bigger than a single novel by the late Charles Garvice. All Pepys, or as much of him as the British public is allowed to read, can now be fitted into three pockets. And the Bible, reduced to an inch in thickness, must surely be in danger of losing those bullet-stopping qualities which it used, at any rate in romantic novels, to possess. Thanks to Henry Frowde one can get a million words of reading matter into a rucksack and hardly feel the difference in its weight.

India paper and photography have rendered possible the inclusion in a portable library of what in my opinion is the best traveler's book of all—a volume (any one of the thirty-two will do) of the twelfth, half-size edition of the *Encyclopaedia Britannica.* It takes up very little room (eight and a half inches by six and a half by one is not excessive), it contains about a thousand pages and an almost countless number of curious and improbable facts. It can be dipped into anywhere, its component chapters are complete in themselves and not too long. For the traveler, disposing as he does only of brief half-hours, it is the perfect book, the more so, since I take it that, being a born traveler, he is likely also to be one of those desultory and self-indulgent readers to whom the *Encyclopaedia,* when not used for some practical purpose, must specially appeal. I never pass a day away from home without taking a volume with me. It is the book of books. Turning over its pages, rummaging among the stores of fantastically varied facts which the hazards of alphabetical arrangement bring together, I wallow in my mental vice. A stray volume of the *Encyclopaedia* is like the mind of a learned madman stored with correct ideas, between which, however, there is no other connection than the fact that there is a B in both; from orach, or mountain spinach, one passes directly to oracles. That one does not oneself go mad, or become, in the process of reading the *Encyclopaedia,* a mine of useless and unrelated knowledge is due to the fact that one forgets. The mind has a vast capacity for oblivion. Providentially; otherwise, in the chaos of futile memories, it would be impossible to remember anything useful or coherent. In practice, we work with generalizations, abstracted out of the turmoil of realities. If we remembered everything perfectly, we should never be able to generalize at all; for there would appear before our minds nothing but individual images, precise and different. Without ignorance we could not generalize. Let us thank Heaven for our powers of forgetting. With regard to the *Encyclopaedia,* they are enormous. The mind only remembers that of which it has some need. Five minutes after reading about mountain spinach, the ordinary man, who is neither a botanist nor a cook, has forgotten all about it. Read for amusement, the *Encyclopaedia* serves only to distract for the moment; it does not instruct, it deposits nothing on the surface of the mind that will remain. It is a mere time-killer and momentary tickler of the mind. I use it only for amusement on my travels; I should be ashamed to indulge so wantonly in mere curiosity at home, during seasons of serious business.

[*Along the Road,* 1925]

Sabbioneta

"THEY CALL IT the Palazzo del Te," said the maid at the little inn in the back street where we had lunch, "because the Gonzaga used to go and take tea there." And that was all that she, and probably most of the other inhabitants of Mantua, knew about the Gonzaga or their palaces. It was surprising, perhaps, that she should have known so much. Gonzaga—the name, at least, still faintly reverberated. After two hundred years, how many names are still remembered? Few indeed. The Gonzaga, it seemed to me, enjoy a degree of immortality that might be envied them. They have vanished, they are as wholly extinct as the dinosaur; but in the cities they once ruled their name still vaguely echoes, and for those who care to listen they have left behind some of the most eloquent sermons on the vanity of human wishes and the mutability of fortune that stones have ever mutely preached.

I have seen many ruins and of every period. Stonehenge and Ansedonia, Ostia and medieval Ninfa (which the duke of Sermoneta is busily

turning into the likeness of a neat suburban park), Bolsover and the gruesome modern ruins in Northern France. I have seen great cities dead or in
decay: Pisa, Bruges, and the newly murdered Vienna. But over none, it
seemed to me, did there brood so profound a melancholy as over Mantua;
none seemed so dead or so utterly bereft of glory; nowhere was desolation
more pregnant with the memory of splendor, the silence nowhere so richly
musical with echoes. There are a thousand rooms in the labyrinthine Reggia at Mantua—Gothic rooms, rooms of the renaissance, baroque rooms,
rooms rich with the absurd pretentious decorations of the first empire,
huge presence chambers and closets and the horribly exquisite apartments
of the dwarfs—a thousand rooms, and their walls enclose an emptiness
that is the mournful ghost of departed plenitude. It is through Mallarmé's
creux néant musicien[9] that one walks in Mantua.

And not in Mantua alone. For wherever the Gonzaga lived, they left
behind them the same pathetic emptiness, the same pregnant desolation,
the same echoes, the same ghosts of splendor.

The Palazzo del Te is made sad and beautiful with the same melancholy as broods in the Reggia. True, the stupid vulgarity of Giulio Romano was permitted to sprawl over its wall in a series of deplorable
frescoes (it is curious, by the way, that Giulio Romano should have been
the only Italian artist of whom Shakespeare had ever heard, or at least the
only one he ever mentioned); but the absurdities and grossnesses seem actually to make the place more touching. The departed tenants of the palace
became in a manner more real to one, when one discovers that their taste
ran to trompe l'oeil pictures of fighting giants and mildly pornographic
scenes out of pagan mythology. And seeming more human, they seem also
more dead; and the void left by their disappearance is more than ever musical with sadness.

Even the cadets of the Gonzaga house enjoyed a power of leaving behind them a more than Pompeian desolation. Twenty miles from Mantua,
on the way to Cremona, is a village called Sabbioneta. It lies near the Po,
though not on its banks; possesses, for a village, a tolerably large population, mostly engaged in husbandry; is rather dirty and has an appearance—probably quite deceptive—of poverty. In fact it is just like all other
villages of the Lombard plain, but with this difference: a Gonzaga once
lived here. The squalor of Sabbioneta is no common squalor; it is a
squalor that was once magnificence. Its farmers and horse-copers live,
dirtily and destructively, in treasures of late renaissance architecture. The
town hall is a ducal palace; in the municipal school, children are taught

9. From Mallarmé's *Poésies* (1898).

under carved and painted ceilings, and when the master is out of the room they write their names on the marble bellies of the patient, battered caryatids who uphold the scutcheoned mantel. The weekly cinema show is given in an Olympic theater, built a few years after the famous theater at Vicenza, by Palladio's pupil, Scamozzi. The people worship in sumptuous churches, and if ever soldiers happen to pass through the town, they are billeted in the deserted summer palace.

The creator of all these splendors was Vespasiano, son of that Luigi Gonzaga, the boon companion of kings, whom, for his valor and his fabulous strength, his contemporaries nicknamed Rodomonte. Luigi died young, killed in battle; and his son Vespasiano was brought up by his aunt, Giulia Gonzaga, one of the most perfectly courtly ladies of her age. She had him taught Latin, Greek, the mathematics, good manners, and the art of war. This last he practiced with distinction, serving at one time or another under many princes, but chiefly under Philip II of Spain, who honored him with singular favors. Vespasiano seems to have been the typical Italian tyrant of his period—cultured, intelligent, and only just so much of an ungovernably ferocious ruffian as one would expect a man to be who had been brought up in the possession of absolute power. It was in the intimacy of private life that he displayed his least amiable characteristics. He poisoned his first wife on a suspicion, probably unfounded, of her infidelity, murdered her supposed lover and exiled his relations. His second wife left him mysteriously after three years of married life and died of pure misery in a convent, carrying with her into the grave nobody knew what frightful secret. His third wife, it is true, lived to a ripe old age; but then Vespasiano himself died after only a few years of marriage. His only son, whom he loved with the anxious passion of the ambitious parvenu who desires to found a dynasty, one day annoyed him by not taking off his cap when he met him in the street. Vespasiano rebuked him for this lack of respect. The boy answered back impertinently. Whereupon Vespasiano gave him such a frightful kick in the groin that the boy died. Which shows that, even when chastising one's own children, it is advisable to observe the Queensberry rules.

It was in 1560 that Vespasiano decided to convert the miserable village from which he took his title into a capital worthy of its ruler. He set to work with energy. In a few years the village of squalid cottages clustering round a feudal castle had given place to a walled town, with broad streets, two fine squares, a couple of palaces, and a noble Gallery of Antiques. These last Vespasiano had inherited from his father, Rodomonte, who had been at the sack of Rome in 1527 and had shown himself an industrious and discriminating looter. Sabbioneta was in its turn looted by the Austrians, who carried off Rodomonte's spoils to Mantua. The museum remains; but there is nothing in it but the *creux néant musicien* which the Gonzaga alone, of all the princes in Italy, had the special art of creating by their departure.

We had come to Sabbioneta from Parma. In the vast Farnese palace there is no musically echoing void—merely an ordinary, undisturbing emptiness. Only in the colossal Estensian theater does one recapture anything like the Mantuan melancholy. We drove through Colorno, where the last of the Este built a summer palace about as large as Hampton Court. Over the Po, by a bridge of boats, through Casalmaggiore and on, tortuously, by little by-roads across the plain. A line of walls presented themselves, a handsome gate. We drove in, and immediately faint ghostly oboes began to play around us; we were in Sabbioneta among the Gonzaga ghosts.

The central piazza of the town is oblong; Vespasiano's palace stands at one of the shorter ends, presenting to the world a modest façade, five windows wide, once rich with decorations, but now bare. It serves at present as town hall. In the waiting-room on the first floor, stand four life-sized equestrian figures, carved in wood and painted, representing four of Vespasiano's ancestors. Once there was a squadron of twelve; but the rest have been broken up and burned. This crime, together with all the other ravages committed by time or vandals in the course of three centuries, was attributed by the mayor, who personally did us the honors of his municipality, to the socialists who had preceded him in office. It is unnecessary to add that he himself was a fascista.

We walked round in the emptiness under the superbly carved and gilded ceilings. The porter sat among decayed frescoes in the Cabinet of Diana. The town council held its meetings in the Ducal Saloon. The Gallery of the Ancestors housed a clerk and the municipal archives. The deputy mayor had his office in the Hall of the Elephants. The Sala d'Oro had been turned into an infants' classroom. We walked out again into the sunlight fairly heart-broken.

The Olympic Theater is a few yards down the street. Accompanied by the obliging young porter from the Cabinet of Diana, we entered. It is a tiny theater, but complete and marvelously elegant. From the pit, five semicircular steps rise to a pillared loggia, behind which—having the width of the whole auditorium—is the ducal box. The loggia consists of twelve Corinthian pillars, topped by a cornice. On the cornice, above each pillar, stand a dozen stucco gods and goddesses. Noses and fingers, paps and ears have gone the way of all art; but the general form of them survives. Their white silhouettes gesticulate elegantly against the twilight of the hall.

The stage was once adorned with a fixed scene in perspective, like that which Palladio built at Vicenza. The mayor wanted us to believe that it was his Bolshevik predecessors who had destroyed it; but as a matter of fact it was taken down about a century ago. Gone, too, are the frescoes with which the walls were once covered. One year of epidemic the theater was used as a fever hospital. When the plague had passed, it was thought that the frescoes needed disinfecting; they were thickly whitewashed. There is no money to scrape the white-wash off again.

We followed the young porter out of the theater. Another two or three hundred yards and we were in the Piazza d'Armi. It is an oblong, grassy space. On the long axis of the rectangle, near one end there stands, handsomely pedestaled, a fluted marble column, topped by a statue of Athena, the tutelary goddess of Vespasiano's metropolis. The pedestal, the capital, and the statue are of the late renaissance. But the column is antique, and formed a part of Rodomonte's Roman booty. Rodomonte was evidently no petty thief. If a thing is worth doing it is worth doing thoroughly; that, evidently, was his motto.

One of the long sides of the rectangle is occupied by the Gallery of Antiques. It is a superb building, architecturally by far the finest thing in the town. The lower storey consists of an open-air arcade, and the walls of the gallery above are ornamented with blind arches, having well-proportioned windows at the center of each and separated from one another by Tuscan pilasters. A very bold projecting cornice, topped by a low roof, finishes the design, which for sober and massive elegance is one of the most remarkable of its kind with which I am acquainted.

The opposite side of the piazza is open, a hedge separating it from the back gardens of the neighboring houses. It was here, I fancy, that the feudal castle originally stood. It was pulled down, however, during the eighteenth century (busy Bolsheviks!) and its bricks employed, more usefully but less aesthetically, to strengthen the dykes which defend the surrounding plain, none too impregnably, from the waters of the Po.

Its destruction has left Vespasiano's summer palace, or Palace of the Garden, isolated (save where it joins the Gallery of the Antiques), and rather forlorn at the end of the long piazza. It is a long, low building of only two storeys, rather insignificant from outside. It is evident that Vespasiano built it as economically as he could. For him the place was only a week-end cottage, a holiday resort, whither he could escape from the metropolitan splendor and bustle of the palace in the market-place, a quarter of a mile away. Like all other rulers of small states, Vespasiano must have found it extremely difficult to take an effective holiday. He could not go ten miles in any direction without coming to a frontier. Within his dominions it was impossible to have a change of air. Wisely, therefore, he decided to concentrate his magnificences. He built his Balmoral within five minutes' walk of his Buckingham Palace.

We knocked at the door. The caretaker who opened to us was an old woman who might have gone on to any stage and acted Juliet's Nurse without a moment's rehearsal. Within the first two minutes of our acquaintance with her she confided to us that she had just got married—for the third time, at the age of seventy. Her comments on the connubial state were so very Juliet's Nurse, so positively Wife-of-Bath, that we were made to feel quite early-Victorian in comparison with this robustious old gammer from the quattrocento. After having told us all that can be told (and much that cannot be told, at any rate in polite society) about the married state, she proceeded to do us the honors of the house. She led the way, opening the shutters of each room in the long suite, as we entered it. And as the light came in through the unglazed windows, what Gonzagesque ravishments were revealed to us. There was a Cabinet of Venus, with the remains of voluptuous nudes, a Hall of the Winds with puffing cherubs and a mantel in red marble; a Cabinet of the Caesars, floored with marble and adorned with medallions of all the ruffians of antiquity; a Hall of the Myths on whose ceiling, vaulted into the likeness of a truncated pyramid seen from within, were five delightful scenes from Lemprière[1]—an Icarus, an Apollo and Marsyas, a Phaeton, an Arachne and, in the midst, a to me somewhat mysterious scene: a naked beauty sitting on the back, not of a bull (that would have been simple enough), but of a reclining horse, which turns its head amorously towards her, while she caresses its neck. Who was the lady and who the travestied god I do not rightly know. Vague memories of an escapade of Saturn's float through my mind. But perhaps I am slandering a respectable deity.

But in any case, whatever its subject, the picture is charming. Vespasiano's principal artist was Bernardino Campi[2] of Cremona. He was not a good painter, of course; but at least he was gracefully and charmingly, instead of vulgarly mediocre, like Giulio Romano. About the Palazzo del Te there hangs a certain faded frightfulness; but the Giardino is all sweetness—mannered, no doubt, and rather feeble—but none the less authentic in its ruinous decay.

The old caretaker expounded the pictures to us as we went round—not out of any knowledge of what they represented, but purely out of her imagination, which was a good deal more interesting. In the Hall of the

---

1. John Lemprière (1765–1824). English scholar, author of the *Classical Dictionary* (1788).
2. Bernardino Campi (1522–1592). Italian artist.

Graces, where the walls are adorned with what remains of a series of very pretty little grotteschi in the Pompeian manner, her fancy surpassed itself. These, she said, were the records of the Duke's dreams. Each time he dreamed a dream he sent for his painter and had it drawn on the walls of this room. These—she pointed to a pair of Chimaeras he saw in a night-mare; these dancing satyrs visited his sleep after a merry evening; these four urns were dreamt of after too much wine. As for the three naked Graces, from whom the room takes its name, as for those—over the Graces she once more became too Wife-of-Bath to be recorded.

Her old cracked laughter went echoing down the empty rooms; and it seemed to precipitate and crystallize all the melancholy suspended, as it were, in solution within those bleared and peeling walls. The sense of des-olation, vaguely felt before, became poignant. And when the old woman ushered us into another room, dark and smelling of mold like the rest, and threw open the shutters and called what the light revealed the "Hall of the Mirrors," I could almost have wept. For in the Hall of the Mirrors there are no more mirrors, only the elaborate framing of them on walls and ceil-ing. Where the glasses of Murano once shone are spaces of bare plaster that stare out like blind eyes, blankly and, it seems after a little, reproach-fully. "They used to dance in this room," said the old woman.

[*Along the Road*, 1925]

Breughel

MOST OF OUR MISTAKES are fundamentally grammatical. We create our own difficulties by employing an inadequate language to describe facts. Thus, to take one example, we are constantly giving the same name to more than one thing, and more than one name to the same thing. The re-sults, when we come to argue, are deplorable. For we are using a language which does not adequately describe the things about which we are argu-ing.

The word "painter" is one of those names whose indiscriminate appli-cation has led to the worst results. All those who, for whatever reason and with whatever intentions, put brushes to canvas and make pictures, are called without distinction, painters. Deceived by the uniqueness of the name, aestheticians have tried to make us believe that there is a single painter-psychology, a single function of painting, a single standard of criti-cism. Fashion changes and the views of art critics with it. At the present time it is fashionable to believe in form to the exclusion of subject. Young people almost swoon away with excess of aesthetic emotion before a Matisse. Two generations ago they would have been wiping their eyes before the latest Landseer. (Ah, those more than human, those positively Christ-like dogs—how they moved, what lessons they taught! There had been no religious painting like Landseer's since Carlo Dolci[3] died.)

These historical considerations should make us chary of believing too exclusively in any single theory of art. One kind of painting, one set of ideas are fashionable at any given moment. They are made the basis of a theory which condemns all other kinds of painting and all preceding critical theories. The process constantly repeats itself.

At the present moment, it is true, we have achieved an unprecedentedly tolerant eclecticism. We are able, if we are up-to-date, to enjoy everything, from negro sculpture to Lucca della Robbia and from Magnasco to Byzantine mosaics. But it is an eclecticism achieved at the expense of almost the whole content of the various works of art considered. What we have learned to see in all these works is their formal qualities, which we abstract and arbitrarily call essential. The subject of the work, with all that the painter desired to express in it beyond his feelings about formal relations, contemporary criticism rejects as unimportant. The young painter scrupulously avoids introducing into his pictures anything that might be mistaken for a story, or the expression of a view of life, while the young *Kunstforscher* turns, as though at an act of exhibitionism, from any manifestation by a contemporary of any such forbidden interest in drama or philosophy. True, the old masters are indulgently permitted to illustrate stories and express their thoughts about the world. Poor devils, they knew no better! Your modern observer makes allowance for their ignorance and passes over in silence all that is not a matter of formal relations. The admirers of Giotto (as numerous today as were the admirers of Guido Reni a hundred years ago) contrive to look at the master's frescoes without considering what they represent, or what the painter desired to express. Every germ of drama or meaning is disinfected out of them; only the composition is admired. The process is analogous to reading Latin verses without understanding them—simply for the sake of the rhythmical rumbling of the hexameters.

It would be absurd, of course, to deny the importance of formal relations. No picture can hold together without composition and no good painter is without some specific passion for form as such—just as no good writer is without a passion for words and the arrangement of words. It is obvious that no man can adequately express himself, unless he takes an interest in the terms which he proposes to use as his medium of expression.

3. Carlo Dolci (1616–1686). Italian painter.

Not all painters are interested in the same sort of forms. Some, for example, have a passion for masses and the surfaces of solids. Others delight in lines. Some compose in three dimensions. Others like to make silhouettes on the flat. Some like to make the surface of the paint smooth and, as it were, translucent, so that the objects represented in the picture can be seen distinct and separate, as through a sheet of glass. Others (as for example Rembrandt) love to make a rich thick surface which shall absorb and draw together into one whole all the objects represented, and that in spite of the depth of the composition and the distance of the objects from the plane of the picture. All these purely aesthetic considerations are, as I have said, important. All artists are interested in them; but almost none are interested in them to the exclusion of everything else. It is very seldom indeed that we find a painter who can be inspired merely by his interest in form and texture to paint a picture. Good painters of "abstract" subjects or even of still lives are rare. Apples and solid geometry do not stimulate a man to express his feelings about form and make a composition. All thoughts and emotions are interdependent. In the words of the dear old song,

> The roses round the door
> Make me love mother more.

One feeling is excited by another. Our faculties work best in a congenial emotional atmosphere. For example, Mantegna's faculty for making noble arrangements of forms was stimulated by his feelings about heroic and god-like humanity. Expressing those feelings, which he found exciting, he also expressed—and in the most perfect manner of which he was capable—his feelings about masses, surfaces, solids, and voids. "The roses around the door"—his hero worship—"made him love mother more" made him, by stimulating his faculty for composition, paint better. If Isabella d'Este had made him paint apples, table napkins and bottles, he would have produced, being uninterested in these objects, a poor composition. And yet, from a purely formal point of view, apples, bottles, and napkins are quite as interesting as human bodies and faces. But Mantegna—and with him the majority of painters—did not happen to be very passionately interested in these inanimate objects. When one is bored one becomes boring.

> The apples round the door
> Make me a frightful bore.

Inevitably; unless I happen to be so exclusively interested in form that I can paint anything that has a shape; or unless I happen to possess some measure of that queer pantheism, that animistic superstition which made Van Gogh regard the humblest of common objects as being divinely or devilishly alive. "Crains dans le mur aveugle un regard qui t'épie." If a painter can do that, he will be able, like Van Gogh, to make pictures of cabbage fields and the bedrooms of cheap hotels that shall be as wildly dramatic as a Rape of the Sabines.

The contemporary fashion is to admire beyond all others the painter who can concentrate on the formal side of his art and produce pictures which are entirely devoid of literature. Old Renoir's apophthegm, "Un peintre, voyez-vous, qui a le sentiment du téton et des fesses, est un homme sauvé," is considered by the purists suspiciously latitudinarian. A painter who has the sentiment of the pap and the buttocks is a painter who portrays real models with gusto. Your pure aesthete should only have a feeling for hemispheres, curved lines and surfaces. But this "sentiment of the buttocks" is common to all good painters. It is the lowest common measure of the whole profession. It is possible, like Mantegna, to have a passionate feeling for all that is solid, and at the same time to be a stoic philosopher and a hero-worshipper; possible, with Michelangelo, to have a complete realization of breasts and also an interest in the soul or, like Rubens, to have a sentiment for human greatness as well as for human rumps. The greater includes the less; great dramatic or reflective painters know everything that the aestheticians who paint geometrical pictures, apples, or buttocks know, and a great deal more besides. What they have to say about formal relations, though important, is only a part of what they have to express. The contemporary insistence on form to the exclusion of everything else is an absurdity. So was the older insistence on exact imitation and sentiment to the exclusion of form. There need be no exclusions. In spite of the single name, there are many different kinds of painters and all of them, with the exception of those who cannot paint, and those whose minds are trivial, vulgar, and tedious, have a right to exist.

All classifications and theories are made after the event; the facts must first occur before they can be tabulated and methodized. Reversing the historical process, we attack the facts forearmed with theoretical prejudice. Instead of considering each fact on its own merits, we ask how it fits into the theoretical scheme. At any given moment a number of meritorious facts fail to fit into the fashionable theory and have to be ignored. Thus El Greco's art failed to conform with the ideal of good painting held by Philip the Second and his contemporaries. The Sienese primitives seemed to the seventeenth and eighteenth centuries incompetent barbarians. Under the influence of Ruskin, the later nineteenth century contrived to dislike almost all architecture that was not Gothic. And the early twentieth century, under the influence of the French, deplores and ignores, in painting, all that is literary, reflective, or dramatic.

In every age theory has caused men to like much that was bad and reject much that was good. The only prejudice that the ideal art critic should have is against the incompetent, the mentally dishonest, and the futile. The number of ways in which good pictures can be painted is quite incalculable, depending only on the variability of the human mind. Every good painter invents a new way of painting. Is this man a competent painter? Has he something to say, is he genuine? These are the questions a critic must ask himself. Not, Does he conform with my theory of imitation, or distortion, or moral purity, or significant form?

There is one painter against whom, it seems to me, theoretical prejudice has always most unfairly told. I mean the elder Breughel. Looking at his best paintings I find that I can honestly answer in the affirmative all the questions which a critic may legitimately put himself. He is highly competent aesthetically; he has plenty to say; his mind is curious, interesting, and powerful; and he has no false pretensions, is entirely honest. And yet he has never enjoyed the high reputation to which his merits entitle him. This is due, I think, to the fact that his work has never quite squared with any of the various critical theories which since his days have had a vogue in the aesthetic world.

A subtle colorist, a sure and powerful draftsman, and possessing powers of composition that enable him to marshal the innumerable figures with which his pictures are filled into pleasingly decorative groups (built up, as we see, when we try to analyze his methods of formal arrangement, out of individually flat, silhouette-like shapes standing in a succession of receding planes), Breughel can boast of purely aesthetic merits that ought to endear him even to the strictest sect of the Pharisees. Coated with this pure aesthetic jam, the bitter pill of his literature might easily, one would suppose, be swallowed. If Giotto's dalliance with sacred history be forgiven him, why may not Breughel be excused for being an anthropologist and a social philosopher? To which I tentatively answer: Giotto is forgiven, because we have so utterly ceased to believe in Catholic Christianity that we can easily ignore the subject-matter of his pictures and concentrate only on their formal qualities; Breughel, on the other hand, is unforgivable because he made comments on humanity that are still interesting to us. From his subject-matter we cannot escape; it touches us too closely to be ignored. That is why Breughel is despised by all up-to-date *Kunstforschers.*

And even in the past, when there was no theoretical objection to the mingling of literature and painting, Breughel failed, for another reason, to get his due. He was considered low, gross, a mere comedian, and as such unworthy of serious consideration. Thus, the *Encyclopaedia Britannica,* which in these matters may be safely relied on to give the current opinion of a couple of generations ago, informs us, in the eleven lines which it parsimoniously devotes to Peter Breughel that "the subjects of his pictures are chiefly humorous figures, like those of D. Teniers;[4] and if he wants the delicate touch and silvery clearness of that master, he has abundant spirit and comic power."

Whoever wrote these words—and they might have been written by any one desirous, fifty years ago, of playing for safety and saying the right thing—can never have taken the trouble to look at any of the pictures painted by Breughel when he was a grown and accomplished artist.

In his youth, it is true, he did a great deal of hack work for a dealer who specialized in caricatures and devils in the manner of Hieronymus Bosch. But his later pictures, painted when he had really mastered the secrets of his art, are not comic at all. They are studies of peasant life, they are allegories, they are religious pictures of the most strangely reflective cast, they are exquisitely poetical landscapes. Breughel died at the height of his powers. But there is enough of his mature work in existence—at Antwerp, at Brussels, at Naples, and above all at Vienna—to expose the fatuity of the classical verdict and exhibit him for what he was—the first landscape painter of his century, the acutest student of manners, and the wonderfully skillful pictorial expounder or suggester of a view of life. It is at Vienna, indeed, that Breughel's art can best be studied in all its aspects. For Vienna possesses practically all his best pictures of whatever kind. The scattered pictures at Antwerp, Brussels, Paris, Naples, and elsewhere give one but the faintest notion of Breughel's powers. In the Vienna galleries are collected more than a dozen of his pictures, all belonging to his last and best period. *The Tower of Babel,* the great Calvary, the Numbering of the People at Bethlehem, the two Winter Landscapes and the Autumn Landscape, the Conversion of Saint Paul, the Battle between the Israelites and the Philistines, the Marriage Feast and the Peasants' Dance—all these admirable works are here. It is on these that he must be judged.

There are four landscapes at Vienna: the Dark Day (January) and Huntsmen in the Snow (February), a November landscape (the Return of the Cattle), and the Numbering of the People at Bethlehem which in spite of its name is little more than a landscape with figures. This last, like the February Landscape and the Massacre of the Innocents at Brussels, is a study of snow. Snow scenes lent themselves particularly well to Breughel's style of painting. For a snowy background has the effect of making all dark or colored objects seen against it appear in the form of very distinct, sharp-edged silhouettes. Breughel does in all his compositions what the snow does in nature. All the objects in his pictures (which are composed in a manner that reminds one very much of the Japanese) are paper-thin sil-

---

4. David Teniers the Elder (1582–1649). Flemish painter. The allusion would also fit David Teniers the Younger (1610–1690). Flemish painter.

houettes arranged, plane after plane, like the theatrical scenery in the depth of the stage. Consequently in the painting of snow scenes, where nature starts by imitating his habitual method, he achieves an almost disquieting degree of fundamental realism. Those hunters stepping down over the brow of the hill towards the snowy valley with its frozen ponds are Jack Frost himself and his crew. The crowds who move about the white streets of Bethlehem have their being in an absolute winter, and those ferocious troopers looting and innocent-hunting in the midst of a Christmas card landscape are a part of the very army of winter, and the innocents they kill are the young green shoots of the earth.

Breughel's method is less fundamentally compatible with the snowless landscapes of January and November. The different planes stand apart a little too flatly and distinctly. It needs a softer, bloomier kind of painting to recapture the intimate quality of such scenes as those he portrays in these two pictures. A born painter of Autumn, for example, would have fused the beasts, the men, the trees, and the distant mountains into a hazier unity, melting all together, the near and the far, in the rich surface of his paint. Breughel painted too transparently and too flatly to be the perfect interpreter of such landscapes. Still, even in terms of his not entirely suitable convention he has done marvels. The Autumn Day is a thing of the most exquisite beauty. Here, as in the more somberly dramatic January Landscape, he makes a subtle use of golds and yellows and browns, creating a sober yet luminous harmony of colors. The November Landscape is entirely placid and serene; but in the Dark Day he has staged one of those natural dramas of the sky and earth—a conflict between light and darkness. Light breaks from under clouds along the horizon, shines up from the river in the valley that lies in the middle distance, glitters on the peaks of the mountains. The foreground, which represents the crest of a wooded hill, is dark; and the leafless trees growing on the slopes are black against the sky. These two pictures are the most beautiful sixteenth-century landscapes of which I have any knowledge. They are intensely poetical, yet sober and not excessively picturesque or romantic. Those fearful crags and beetling precipices of which the older painters were so fond do not appear in these examples of Breughel's maturest work.

Breughel's anthropology is as delightful as his nature poetry. He knew his Flemings, knew them intimately, both in their prosperity and during the miserable years of strife, of rebellion, of persecution, of war and consequent poverty which followed the advent of the Reformation in Flanders.

A Fleming himself, and so profoundly and ineradicably a Fleming that he was able to go to Italy, and, like his great countryman in the previous century, Roger van der Weyden, return without the faintest tincture of Italianism—he was perfectly qualified to be the natural historian of the Flemish folk. He exhibits them mostly in those moments of orgiastic gaiety with which they temper the laborious monotony of their daily lives: eating enormously, drinking, uncouthly dancing, indulging in that peculiarly Flemish scatological waggery. The Wedding Feast and the Peasants' Dance, both at Vienna, are superb examples of this anthropological type of painting. Nor must we forget those two curious pictures, the Battle between Carnival and Lent and the Children's Games. They too show us certain aspects of the joyous side of Flemish life. But the view is not of an individual scene, casually seized at its height and reproduced. These two pictures are systematic and encyclopaedic. In one he illustrates all children's games; in the other all the amusements of carnival, with all the forces arrayed on the side of asceticism. In the same way he represents, in his extraordinary *Tower of Babel,* all the processes of building. These pictures are handbooks of their respective subjects.

Breughel's fondness for generalizing and systematizing is further illustrated in his allegorical pieces. The Triumph of Death, at the Prado, is appalling in its elaboration and completeness. The fantastic "Dulle Griet" at Antwerp is an almost equally elaborate triumph of evil. His illustrations to proverbs and parables belong to the same class. They show him to have been a man profoundly convinced of the reality of evil and of the horrors which this mortal life, not to mention eternity, hold in store for suffering humanity. The world is a horrible place; but in spite of this, or precisely because of this, men and women eat, drink, and dance; Carnival tilts against Lent and triumphs, if only for a moment; children play in the streets, people get married in the midst of gross rejoicings.

But of all Breughel's pictures the one most richly suggestive of reflection is not specifically allegorical or systematic. Christ carrying the Cross is one of his largest canvases, thronged with small figures rhythmically grouped against a wide and romantic background. The composition is simple, pleasing in itself, and seems to spring out of the subject instead of being imposed on it. So much for pure aesthetics.

Of the Crucifixion and the Carrying of the Cross there are hundreds of representations by the most admirable and diverse masters. But of all that I have ever seen this Calvary of Breughel's is the most suggestive and, dramatically, the most appalling. For all other masters have painted these dreadful scenes from within, so to speak, outwards. For them Christ is the center, the divine hero of the tragedy; this is the fact from which they start; it affects and transforms all the other facts, justifying, in a sense, the horror of the drama and ranging all that surrounds the central figure in an ordered hierarchy of good and evil. Breughel, on the other hand, starts from the outside and works inwards. He represents the scene as it would have appeared to any casual spectator on the road to Golgotha on a certain spring morning in the year 33 A.D. Other artists have pretended to be angels, painting the scene with a knowledge of its significance. But Breughel resolutely remains a human onlooker. What he shows is a crowd of people walking briskly in holiday joyfulness up the slopes of a hill. On the top of the hill, which is seen in the middle distance on the right, are two crosses with thieves fastened to them, and between them a little hole in the ground in which another cross is soon to be planted. Round the crosses, on the bare hill top stands a ring of people, who have come out with their picnic baskets to look on at the free entertainment offered by the ministers of justice. Those who have already taken their stand round the crosses are the prudent ones; in these days we should see them with camp stools and Thermos flasks, six hours ahead of time, in the vanguard of the queue for a Melba night at Covent Garden. The less provident or more adventurous people are in the crowd coming up the hill with the third and greatest of the criminals whose cross is to take the place of honor between the other two. In their anxiety not to miss any of the fun on the way up, they forget that they will have to take back seats at the actual place of execution. But it may be, of course, that they have reserved their places, up there. At Tyburn one could get an excellent seat in a private box for half a crown; with the ticket in one's pocket, one could follow the cart all the way from the prison, arrive with the criminal, and yet have a perfect view of the performance. In these later days, when cranky humanitarianism has so far triumphed that hangings take place in private, and Mrs. Thompson's[5] screams are not even allowed to be recorded on the radio, we have to be content with reading about executions, not with seeing them. The impresarios who sold seats at Tyburn have been replaced by titled newspaper proprietors who sell juicy descriptions of Tyburn to a prodigiously much larger public. If people were still hanged at Marble Arch, Lord Riddell[6] would be much less rich.

That eager, tremulous, lascivious interest in blood and beastliness which in these more civilized days we can only satisfy at one remove from reality in the pages of our newspapers, was franklier indulged in Breughel's day; the naive ingenuous brute in man was less sophisticated, was given longer rope, and joyously barks and wags its tail round the appointed victim. Seen thus, impassively, from the outside, the tragedy does not purge or uplift; it appalls and makes desperate; or it may even inspire a kind of gruesome mirth. The same situation may often be either tragic or

5. Edith Thompson (d. 1923). English murderess executed in 1923 for the murder of her husband.

6. George Riddell, 1st Baron (1865–1934). Scottish lawyer and newspaper proprietor.

comic, according as it is seen through the eyes of those who suffer or those who look on. (Shift the point of vision a little and Macbeth could be paraphrased as a roaring farce.) Breughel makes a concession to the high tragic convention by placing in the foreground of his picture a little group made up of the holy women weeping and wringing their hands. They stand quite apart from the other figures in the picture and are fundamentally out of harmony with them, being painted in the style of Roger van der Weyden. A little oasis of passionate spirituality, an island of consciousness and comprehension in the midst of the pervading stupidity and brutishness. Why Breughel put them into his picture is difficult to guess; perhaps for the benefit of the conventionally religious, perhaps out of respect for tradition; or perhaps he found his own creation too depressing and added this noble irrelevance to reassure himself.

[Along the Road, 1925]

Rimini and Alberti

RIMINI WAS HONORED, that morning, by the presence of three distinguished visitors—ourselves and the Thaumaturgical Arm of St. Francis Xavier. Divorced from the rest of the saint's remains, whose home is a jeweled tabernacle in the church of Jesus at Old Goa, the Arm, like ourselves, was making an Italian tour. But while we poor common tourists were spending money on the way, the Thaumaturgical Arm—and this was perhaps its most miraculous achievement—was raking it in. It had only to show itself through the crystal window of the reliquary in which it traveled—a skeleton arm, with a huge amethyst ring still glittering on one of the fingers of its bony hand—to command the veneration of all beholders and a copper collection, thinly interspersed with nickel and the smallest paper. The copper collection went to the foreign missions; what happened to the veneration, I do not venture to guess. It was set down, no doubt, with their offered pence, to the credit of those who felt it, in the recording angel's book.

I felt rather sorry for St. Francis Xavier's arm. The body of the saint, after translation from China to Malacca and from Malacca to India, now reposes, as I have said, in the gaudy shrine at Goa. After a life so extraordinarily strenuous as was his, the great missionary deserves to rest in peace. And so he does, most of him. But his right arm has had to forgo its secular quiet; its missionary voyages are not yet over. In its gold and crystal box it travels indefatigably through catholic Christendom collecting pence—"for spoiling Indian innocence," as Mr. Matthew Green[7] tersely and rather tartly put it, two hundred years ago. Poor Arm!

We found it, that morning, in the church of San Francesco at Rimini. A crowd of adorers filled the building and overflowed into the street outside. The people seemed to be waiting rather vaguely in the hope of something thaumaturgical happening.

Within the church, a long queue of men and women shuffled slowly up into the choir to kiss the jeweled bone-box and deposit their soldi. Outside, among the crowd at the door of the church, stood a number of hawkers, selling picture postcards of the Thaumaturgical Arm and brief but fabulous biographies of its owner. We got into conversation with one of them, who told us that he followed the Arm from town to town, selling his wares wherever it stopped to show itself. The business seemed a tolerably profitable one; it enabled him, at any rate, to keep a wife and family living in comfort at Milan. He showed us their photographs; mother and children—they all looked well nourished. But, poor fellow! his business kept him almost uninterruptedly away from home. "What does one marry for?" he said as he put the photographs back into his pocket. "What?" He sighed and shook his head. If only the Arm could be induced to settle down for a little!

During the lunch hour the Arm was taken for a drive round Rimini. Red and yellow counterpanes were hung out of all the windows in its honor; the faithful waited impatiently. And at last it came, driving in a very large, very noisy, and dirty old Fiat, accompanied, not, as one might have expected, by the ecclesiastical dignitaries of the city, but by seven or eight very secular young men in black shirts, with frizzy hair, their trouser pockets bulging with automatic pistols—the committee of the local fascio, no doubt.

The Arm occupied the front seat, next the driver: the fascists lolled behind. As the car passed, the faithful did a very curious thing; mingling the gestures of reverence and applause, they fell on their knees and clapped their hands. The Arm was treated as though it were a combination of Jackie Coogan and the Host. After lunch, it was driven rapidly away to Bologna. The vendors of sacred pictures followed as fast as the Italian trains would take them, the crowd dispersed, and the church of San Francesco reverted to its habitual silence.

For this we were rather glad; for it was not to see a fragment of St. Francis Xavier that we had come to Rimini; it was to look at the church of St. Francis of Assisi. Sight-seeing, so long as the Arm was there, had been

7. Matthew Green (1696–1737). English poet.

impossible; its departure left us free to look round at our ease. Still, I was very glad that we had seen the peripatetic relic and its adorers in San Francesco. In this strange church which Malatesta founded a Christian temple, rebuilt in pagan form, and rededicated to himself, his mistress, and the humanities, the scenes we had just witnessed possessed a certain piercing incongruousness that provoked—the wit of circumstances—a kind of meditative mirth. I tried to imagine what the first St. Francis would have thought of Sigismondo Malatesta, what Sigismondo thought of him, and how he would have regarded the desecration of his Nietzschean temple by this posthumous visit of a bit of the second St. Francis. One can imagine a pleasant little Gobinesque or Lucianic dialogue between the four of them in the Elysian Fields, a light and airy skating over the most fearful depths of the spirit. And for those who have ears to hear, there is eloquence in the dumb disputation of the stones. The Gothic arches of the interior protest against the Roman shell with which Alberti enclosed St. Francis's church; protest against Matteo de'Pasti's pagan decorations and Malatesta's blasphemous self-exaltation; protest, while they commend the missionary's untiring disinterestedness, against the excessive richness of his Jesuit reliquary. Grave, restrained, and intellectual, Alberti's classical façade seems to deplore the naïveté of the first St. Francis and the intolerant enthusiasms of the second, and, praising Malatesta's intelligence, to rebuke him for his lusts and excesses. Malatesta, meanwhile, laughs cynically at all of them. Power, pleasure, and Isotta—these, he announces, through the scheme of decorations which he made Matteo de'Pasti carry out, these are the only things that matter.

The exterior of the church is entirely Alberti's. Neither St. Francis nor Malatesta are allowed to disturb its solemn and harmonious beauty. Its façade is a triumphal arch, a nobler version of that arch of Augustus which spans the street at the other end of Rimini. In the colossal thickness of the southern wall, Alberti has pierced a series of deep arched niches. Recessed shadow alternates harmoniously down a long perspective with smooth sunlit stone; and in every niche, plain and severe like the character of an early Roman in the pages of Plutarch, stands the sarcophagus of a scholar or a philosopher. There is nothing here of St. Francis's pre-lapsarian ingenuousness. Alberti is an entirely conscious adult; he worships, but worships reason, rationally. The whole building is a hymn to intellectual beauty, an exaltation of reason as the only source of human greatness. Its form is Roman; for Rome was the retrospective Utopia in which such men as Alberti, from the time of the renaissance down to a much later date, saw the fulfilment of their ideals. The Roman myth dies hard, the Greek harder still; there are certain victims of a classical education who still regard the Republic as the home of all virtues and see in Periclean Athens the unique repository of human intelligence.

Malatesta would have got a better personal apotheosis if he had lived in a later century. Alberti was too severe and stoical an artist to condescend to mere theatrical grandiosity. Nor, indeed, was the art of being grandiose really understood till the seventeenth century, the age of baroque, of kingly and clerical display. The hard-working missionary, whose arm we had seen that morning in Malatesta's temple, reposes at Goa in the sort of surroundings that would be perfectly suitable in a tyrant's self-raised shrine. Alberti's monument, on the contrary, is a tribute to intellectual greatness. As a memorial to a particularly cunning and murderous ruffian it is absurd.

In the interior of the church, it is true, Malatesta had things all his own way. Alberti was not there to interfere in his scheme of decoration, so that Sigismondo was able to dictate to Matteo de'Pasti and his colleagues all the themes of their carving. The interior is consequently one vast personal tribute to Malatesta and Isotta, with an occasional good word in favor of the pagan gods, of literature, art, and science. The too-expressive theatrical gesture of the baroque architects and decorators had not yet been invented; Sigismondo's vulgar tyranny is consequently celebrated in the most perfect taste and in terms of a delicate and learned fantasy. Sigismondo got better than his deserts; he deserved Borromini, the Cavaliere Arpino, and a tenth-rate imitator of Bernini. What he actually got, owing to the accident of his date, was Matteo de'Pasti,[8] Piero della Francesca, and Leon Battista Alberti.

Alberti's share in the monument, then, is a kind of hymn to intellectual beauty, a paean in praise of civilization, couched in the language of Rome—but freely and not pedantically employed, as the philosophers and the poets of the age employed the Latin idiom. To my mind, he was almost the noblest Roman of them all. The exterior of San Francesco at Rimini, the interior of Sant'Andrea at Mantua (sadly daubed about by later decorators and with Juvara's absurd high-drummed cupola in the midst instead of the saucer dome designed by Alberti himself) are as fine as anything in the whole range of renaissance architecture. What renders them the more remarkable is that they were without precedent, in his age. Alberti was one of the re-inventors of the style. Of his particular Roman manner, indeed (the manner which became the current idiom of the later renaissance) he was the sole re-discoverer. The other early renaissance manner, based, like Alberti's, on the classics—the manner of Brunelleschi—was doomed, so far at any rate as ecclesiastical architecture was

8. Matteo Di Pasti (1420–1467/68). Italian medalist, sculptor, and architect.

concerned, to extinction. Sant'Andrea at Mantua is the model from which the typical churches of the later renaissance were imitated, not Brunelleschi's Florentine San Lorenzo or Santo Spirito.

A comparison between these nearly contemporary architects—Brunelleschi was born some twenty-five years before Alberti—is extremely interesting and instructive. Both were enthusiastic students of the antique, both knew their Rome, both employed in their buildings the characteristic elements of classical architecture. And yet it would be difficult to discover two architects whose work is more completely dissimilar. Compare the interiors of Brunelleschi's two Florentine churches with that of Alberti's Sant'Andrea. Brunelleschi's churches are divided into a nave and aisles by rows of tall slender pillars supporting round arches. The details are classical and so correct that they might have been executed by Roman workmen. But the general design is not Roman, but Romanesque. His churches are simply more spidery versions of eleventh-century basilicas, with "purer" details. All is airiness and lightness; there is even a certain air of insecurity about these church interiors, so slender are the pillars, so much free space is to be seen. What a contrast with Alberti's great church! It is built in the form of a Latin cross, with a single nave and side chapels. The nave is barrel-vaulted; over the crossing is a dome (Juvara's, unfortunately, not Alberti's); the altar is placed in an apse. The chapels open on to the central nave by tall, and proportionately wide, round-headed arches. Between each of the chapels is a gigantic pier of masonry, as wide as the arches which they separate. A small door is pierced in each of these piers, giving access to subsidiary chapels hollowed out of their mass. But the doors are inconspicuous and the general effect is one of void and solid equally alternating. Alberti's is essentially the architecture of masses, Brunelleschi's of lines. Even to the enormous dome of Santa Maria del Fiore, Brunelleschi contrives to impart an extraordinary lightness, as of lines with voids between them. The huge mass hangs aerially from its eight ribs of marble. A miracle is effortlessly consummated before our eyes. But a dome, however light you make it, is essentially an affair of masses. In designing his cupola for Santa Maria del Fiore, Brunelleschi found the plastic view of things imposed upon him. That is why, it may be, the dome is so incomparably the finest thing he ever made. He was not permitted by the nature of the architectural problem to be solved to give free play to his passion for lightness and the fine line. He was dealing here with masses; it could not be escaped. The result was that, treating the mass of the dome as far as was possible in terms of light, strong, leaping lines, he contrived to impart to his work an elegance and an aerial strength such as have never been equaled in any other dome. The rest of Brunelleschi's work, however charming and graceful, is, to my mind at any rate, far less satisfying, precisely because it is so definitely an affair of lines. Brunelleschi studied the architecture of the Romans; but he took from it only its details. What was essential in it—its majestic massiveness—did not appeal to him. He preferred, in all his church designs, to refine and refine on the work of the Romanesque architects, until at last he arrived at a slender and precarious elegance that was all vacuum and outline.

Alberti, on the other hand, took from the Romans their fundamental conception of an architecture of masses and developed it, with refinements, for modern, Christian uses. To my mind, he was the better and truer architect of the two. For I personally like massiveness and an air of solidity. Others, I know, prefer lines and lightness and would put the interior of San Lorenzo above that of Sant'Andrea, the Pazzi chapel above San Francesco at Rimini. We shall never be reconciled. All who practice the visual arts and, presumably, all who appreciate them must have some kind of feeling for form as such. But not all are interested in the same kind of forms. The lovers of pure line and the lovers of mass stand at opposite ends of an aesthetic scale. The aesthetic passion of one artist, or one art lover, is solidity; another is moved only by linear arabesques on a flat surface. Those formal passions may be misplaced. Painters may be led by their excessive love of three-dimensional solidity quite beyond the field of painting; Michelangelo is an obvious example. Sculptors with too great a fondness for mere linear effect cease to be sculptors, and their work is no more than a flat decoration in stone or metal, meant to be seen from only one point of view and having no depth; the famous Diana attributed to Goujon (but probably by Benvenuto Cellini) is one of these statues conceived in the flat. Just as painters must not be too fond of solidity, nor sculptors too much attached to flatness, so, it seems to me, no architect should be too exclusively interested in lines. Architecture in the hands of a linear enthusiast takes on the too slender, spidery elegance of Brunelleschi's work.

The psychoanalysts, who trace all interest in art back to an infantile love of excrement, would doubtless offer some simple fecal explanation for the varieties in our aesthetic passions. One man loves masses, another lines the explanation in terms of coprophily that is so obvious that I may be excused from giving it here. I will content myself by quoting from the works of Dr. Ernest Jones,[9] the reason why the worship of form should come to be connected in so many cases with the worship of a moral ideal; in a word, why art is so often religious. "Religion," says Dr. Jones, "has always used art in one form or another, and must do so, for the reason

---

9. Ernest Jones (1879–1958). Welsh psychoanalyst, disciple of Freud, and founder of the British Psycho-Analytical Society in 1913.

that incestuous desires invariably construct their fantasies out of the material provided by the unconscious memory of infantile coprophilic interests; that is the inner meaning of the phrase, 'Art is the handmaid of Religion.' "
Illuminating and beautiful words! It is a pity they were not written thirty years ago. I should have liked to read Tolstoy's comments in *What is Art?* on this last and best of the aesthetic theories.

[*Along the Road*, 1925]

Conxolus

TO KNOW what everybody else knows—that Virgil, for example, wrote the *Aeneid*, or that the sum of the angles of a triangle is equal to two right angles—is rather boring and undistinguished. If you want to acquire a reputation for learning at a cheap rate, it is best to ignore the dull and stupid knowledge which is everybody's possession and concentrate on something odd and out of the way. Instead of quoting Virgil quote Sidonius Apollinaris, and express loudly your contempt of those who prefer the court poet of Augustus to the panegyrist of Avitus, Majorianus, and Anthemius.[1] When the conversation turns on *Jane Eyre* or *Wuthering Heights* (which of course you have not read) say you infinitely prefer *The Tenant of Wildfell Hall*. When Donne is praised, pooh-pooh him and tell the praiser that he should read Gongora. At the mention of Raphael, make as though to vomit outright (though you have never been inside the Vatican); the Raphael Mengses at Petersburg, you will say, are the only tolerable paintings. In this way you will get the reputation of a person of profound learning and the most exquisite taste. Whereas, if you give proof of knowing your Dickens, of having read the Bible, the English classics, Euclid, and Horace, nobody will think anything of you at all. You will be just like everybody else.

The extreme inadequacy of my education has often led me, in the course of my journalistic career, to adopt these tactics. I have written airily of the remote and odd in order to conceal my ignorance of the near and the classical. The profession of a literary journalist is not one that greatly encourages honesty. Everything conspires to make him a charlatan. He has no leisure to read regularly or with purpose; at the same time reviewing makes him acquainted with a mass of fragmentary and miscellaneous in-

1. Sidonius Apollinaris (c. 430–c. 490). Gallo-Roman poet and Christian writer of Merovingian France. Flavius Avitus (d. 456). Western Roman Emperor (455–456). Julius Majorianus (d. 461). Western Roman Emperor (457–461). Anthemius (d. 472). Western Roman Emperor (467–472).

formation. He would be a prodigy of intellectual integrity if he did not reproduce it in his own articles, casually and with confidence, as though
each queer item were an outlying promontory of the vast continent of his
universal knowledge. Moreover the necessity under which he labors of always being readable tempts him at all costs to be original and unusual. Is
it to be wondered at if, knowing five lines each of Virgil and Apollinaris,
he prefers to quote the latter? Or if, knowing none of Virgil, he turns his
ignorance into a critical virtue and lets it be understood that the best
minds have now gone on from Maro to Sidonius?

In the monastery of Subiaco, which lies in that remote back of beyond
behind Tivoli, there are, among many other things of beauty and historical
interest, a number of frescoes by a thirteenth-century master, unknown except as the author of these works, called Conxolus. The name is superb
and could not be improved. Majestic and at the same time slightly grotesque, uncommon (indeed, for all I know, unique) and easily memorable,
it is a name which seems by right to belong to a great man. Conxolus:[2] at
the sound of those rich syllables the cultured person has a vague uncomfortable feeling that he ought to know what they connote. Is it a battle? or
scholastic philosophy? or a heresy? or what? Learning, after a moment's
agonizing suspense (during which he is uncertain whether his interlocutor
will let out the secret or force him to confess his ignorance) that Conxolus
was a painter, the cultured person confidently plunges. "Such a marvellous
artist!" he rapturously exclaims.

The old journalistic Adam is not quite dead within me, and I know my
cultured society. The temptation was strong. I would preach Conxolus to a
benighted world and, exalting him as an artist, exalt myself at the same
time as an art critic. And how cheaply! For the price of three gallons of
petrol, ten francs of postcards and tips, and an excellent lunch, with trout,
at Tivoli, I should have made myself completely master of my subject and
established my *Kunstforscher*'s reputation. No tiresome journeys to faraway galleries in search of the master's minor works, no laborious reading
of German monographs. Just this one extremely agreeable trip to the
upper Anio, this forty minutes' walk uphill, this little trot round Saint
Benedict's first hermitage and that was all. I would go back to London, I
would write some articles, or even a little book, with handsome reproductions, about the master. And when, in cultured society, people talked of
Duccio or Simone Martini, I should smile from the height of my superiority. "They are all very well, no doubt. But when one has seen Conxolus."
And I should go on talking of his tactile and olfactory values, his magistral
treatment of the fourth dimension, his exquisitely subtle use of repoussoirs

2. Conxolus was a thirteenth-century Italian painter known for his frescoes in Subiaco.

and that extraordinary mastery of color which enabled him to paint all the flesh in his pictures in two tones of ocher, impure purple and goose-turd green. And my auditors (terrified, as all the frequenters of cultured society always are, of being left behind in the intellectual race), would listen with grave avidity. And they would leave me, triumphantly conscious that they had scored a point over their rivals, that they had entered a new swim from which all but the extremely select were excluded, that their minds were dressed in a fashion that came straight from Paris (for of course I should give them to understand that Derain and Matisse entirely agreed with me); and from that day forth the name of Conxolus, and with it my name, would begin to reverberate, crescendo, with an overgrowing rumor of admiration, in all the best drawing-rooms, from Euston to the World's End.

The temptation was strong; but I wrestled with it heroically and at last had the mastery. I decided that I would not pervert the truth for the sake of any reputation, however flattering, for critical insight and discrimination. For the truth, alas, is that our unique and high-sounding Conxolus is an entirely negligible painter. Competent and well trained; but no more. His principal merit consists in the fact that he lived in the thirteenth century and worked in the characteristic style of his period. He painted in the decadent Byzantine manner which we, arguing backwards from sixteenth-century Florence instead of forwards from sixth-century Ravenna, miscall "primitive." It is in this, I repeat, that his principal merit consists—at any rate for us. For a century ago his primitiveness would only have aroused derision and pity. We have changed all that nowadays; and so thoroughly that there are many young people who, in their anxiety not to be thought old-fashioned, regard all pictures bearing a close resemblance to their subjects as highly suspicious and, unless guaranteed chemically pure by some recognized aesthetic authority, a priori ridiculous. To these ascetics all natural beauty, when reproduced by art, is damnable. A beautiful woman accurately painted is "chocolate boxy"; a beautiful landscape mere poetry. If a work of art is obviously charming, if it moves at first sight, then, according to these people, it must also necessarily be bad. This doctrine applied to music has led to the exaltation of Bach, even Bach in his most mechanical and soulless moments, at the expense of Beethoven. It has led to the dry "classical" way of playing Mozart, who is supposed to be unemotional because he is not vulgarly emotional, like Wagner. It has led to steam organ-like performances of Handel and senseless bellowings of Palestrina. And the absurd young, in reaction against the sentimentalities and lachrymose idealisms which they imagine to have characterized the later Victorian age, being left absolutely unmoved by these performances, have for that very reason applauded them as in the highest degree artistic.

It is the same in painting. The muddier the colors, the more distorted the figures, the higher the art. There are hundreds of young painters who dare not paint realistically and charmingly, even if they could, for fear of losing the esteem of the young connoisseurs who are their patrons. True, good painters paint well and express all they have to say whatever convention they may use; and indifferent painters paint indifferently in all circumstances. It ought, therefore, to give us no concern whatever if indifferent young painters do prefer distortion and muddy coloring to gaiety, realism, and charm. It does not seriously matter how they paint. At the same time the world did get a certain amount of entertainment out of its indifferent painters in the past, when they did their best to imitate nature and tell stories. It got faithful copies of beautiful objects, it got documents and pictorial notes, it got amusing anecdotes and comments on life. These things might not be great pictures; but they were at any rate worth something, for they had an other than aesthetic value. Aiming as he does at some mythical ideal of pure aestheticism, to which all but form is sacrificed, the young talentless painter of the present time gives us nothing but boredom. For his pictures are not good pictures, and they do not make amends for their badness by reminding us of pleasing objects; they have not even the merit of being documents or comments, they do not even tell a story. In a word they have nothing to recommend them. From being an entertainer, the second-rate artist (if he happens also to be "advanced") has become an intolerable bore.

The young's mistrust of realism does not apply only to contemporary art; it is also retrospective. Of two equally untalented artists of the past, youth unhesitatingly prefers the man who is least realistic, most "primitive." Conxolus is admired above his seventeenth-century counterpart, simply because his figures remind one of nothing that is charming in nature, because he is innocent of light and shade, because the composition is rigidly symmetrical, and because the emotional content of his ardently Christian pictures has, for us, completely evaporated, leaving nothing that can evoke in our bosoms the slightest sentiment of any kind, with the single exception of those famous aesthetic emotions which the young so studiously cultivate.

True, the convention in which the seventeenth-century Italian painters worked was an intolerable one. The wild gesticulations with which they filled their pictures, in the hope of artificially creating an atmosphere of passion, is fundamentally ludicrous. The baroque style and the kindred romantic style are the two styles best fitted in the nature of things for the expression of comedy. Aristophanes, Rabelais, Nashe, Balzac, Dickens, Rowlandson, Goya, Doré, Daumier, and the nameless makers of grotesques all over the world and at every period—all practitioners of pure comedy, whether in literature or in art—have employed an extravagant, baroque, romantic style. Naturally; for pure comedy it is essentially extravagant and enormous. Except in the hands of prodigious men of genius (such as Marlowe and Shakespeare, Michelangelo and Rembrandt) this style, when used for serious purposes, is ludicrous. Almost all baroque art and almost all the kindred romantic art of a later epoch are grotesque because the artists (not of the first order) are trying to express something tragic in terms of a style essentially comic. In this respect the works of the "primitives"—even of the second-rate primitives—are really preferable to the works of their seicento descendants. For in their pictures there is no fundamental incongruity between the style and subject. But this is a negative quality; second-rate primitives are decent but they are extraordinarily dull. The work of the later realists may be vulgar and absurd as a whole; but it is redeemed, very often, by the charm of its details. You can find, in the pictures of second-rate artists of the seventeenth century, charming landscapes, interesting physiognomies, studies of curious effects of light and shade—things which do nothing, it is true, to redeem these works, viewed as wholes, from badness, but are nevertheless agreeable and interesting in themselves. In the Conxoluses of an earlier epoch the work as a whole is respectable; but its dullness is not relieved by any curious or delightful details. By their absurdly ascetic distrust of the obviously delightful, the young have deprived themselves of a great deal of pleasure. They bore themselves by second-rate Conxoluses when they might amuse themselves by equally second-rate Fetis and Caravaggios and Rosa da Tivolis and Carpionis and Guercinos and Luca Giordanos[3] and all the rest of them. If one must look at second-rate pictures at all—and there are so few good pictures that one inevitably must—it is surely more reasonable to look at those which give one something (even though the plums be embedded in a suet of horror) than those which give one absolutely nothing at all.

[*Along the Road*, 1925]

The Best Picture

BORGO SAN SEPOLCRO is not very easy to get at. There is a small low-comedy railway across the hills from Arezzo. Or you can approach it up the Tiber valley from Perugia. Or, if you happen to be at Urbino, there is a

---

3. The reference here is probably to Domenico Fetti (1588/89–1623). Italian baroque painter. Luca Giordano (1632–1705). Italian painter.

motor bus which takes you to San Sepolcro, up and down through the Apennines, in something over seven hours. No joke, that journey, as I know by experience. But it is worth doing, though preferably in some other vehicle than the bus, for the sake of the Bocca Trabaria, that most beautiful of Apennine passes, between the Tiber valley and the upper valley of the Metauro. It was in the early spring that we crossed it. Our omnibus groaned and rattled slowly up a bleak northern slope, among bald rocks, withered grass, and still unbudded trees. It crossed the col and suddenly, as though by a miracle, the ground was yellow with innumerable primroses, each flower a little emblem of the sun that had called it into being.

And when at last one has arrived at San Sepolcro, what is there to be seen? A little town surrounded by walls, set in a broad flat valley between hills; some fine renaissance palaces with pretty balconies of wrought iron; a not very interesting church, and finally, the best picture in the world.

The best picture in the world is painted in fresco on the wall of a room in the town hall. Some unwittingly beneficent vandal had it covered, some time after it was painted, with a thick layer of plaster, under which it lay hidden for a century or two, to be revealed at last in a state of preservation remarkably perfect for a fresco of its date. Thanks to the vandals, the visitor who now enters the Palazzo dei Conservatori at Borgo San Sepolcro finds the stupendous Resurrection almost as Piero della Francesca left it. Its clear, yet subtly sober colors shine out from the wall with scarcely impaired freshness. Damp has blotted out nothing of the design, nor dirt obscured it. We need no imagination to help us figure forth its beauty; it stands there before us in entire and actual splendor, the greatest picture in the world.

The greatest picture in the world. . . . You smile. The expression is ludicrous, of course. Nothing is more futile than the occupation of those connoisseurs who spend their time compiling first and second elevens of the world's best painters, eights and fours of musicians, fifteens of poets, all-star troupes of architects, and so on. Nothing is so futile because there are a great many kinds of merit and an infinite variety of human beings. Is Fra Angelico a better artist than Rubens? Such questions, you insist, are meaningless. It is all a matter of personal taste. And up to a point this is true. But there does exist, none the less, an absolute standard of artistic merit. And it is a standard which is in the last resort a moral one. Whether a work of art is good or bad depends entirely on the quality of the character which expresses itself in the work. Not that all virtuous men are good artists, nor all artists conventionally virtuous. Longfellow was a bad poet, while Beethoven's dealings with his publishers were frankly dishonorable. But one can be dishonorable towards one's publishers and yet preserve the kind of virtue that is necessary to a good artist. That virtue is the virtue of integrity, of honesty towards oneself. Bad art is of two sorts: that which is merely dull, stupid, and incompetent, the negatively bad; and the positively bad, which is a lie and a sham. Very often the lie is so well told that almost everyone is taken in by it—for a time. In the end, however, lies are always found out. Fashion changes, the public learns to look with a different focus and, where a little while ago it saw an admirable work which actually moved its emotions, it now sees a sham. In the history of the arts we find innumerable shams of this kind, once taken as genuine, now seen to be false. The very names of most of them are now forgotten. Still, a dim rumor that Ossian once was read, that Bulwer was thought a great novelist and "Festus" Bailey[4] a mighty poet still faintly reverberates. Their counterparts are busily earning praise and money at the present day. I often wonder if I am one of them. It is impossible to know. For one can be an artistic swindler without meaning to cheat and in the teeth of the most ardent desire to be honest.

Sometimes the charlatan is also a first-rate man of genius and you have such strange artists as Wagner and Bernini, who turn what is false and theatrical into something almost sublime.

That it is difficult to tell the genuine from the sham is proved by the fact that enormous numbers of people have made mistakes and continue to make them. Genuineness, as I have said, always triumphs in the long run. But at any given moment the majority of people, if they do not actually prefer the sham to the real, at least like it as much, paying an indiscriminate homage to both.

And now, after this little digression we can return to San Sepolcro and the greatest picture in the world. Great it is, absolutely great, because the man who painted it was genuinely noble as well as talented. And to me personally the most moving of pictures, because its author possessed almost more than any other painter those qualities of character which I most admire and because his purely aesthetic preoccupations are of a kind which I am by nature best fitted to understand. A natural, spontaneous, and unpretentious grandeur—this is the leading quality of all Piero's work. He is majestic without being at all strained, theatrical, or hysterical—as Handel is majestic, not as Wagner. He achieves grandeur naturally with every gesture he makes, never consciously strains after it. Like Alberti, with whose architecture, as I hope to show, his painting has certain affinities, Piero seems to have been inspired by what I may call the religion of Plutarch's *Lives*—which is not Christianity, but a worship of what is ad-

4. Philip James Bailey (1816–1902). English poet.

mirable in man. Even his technically religious pictures are paeans in praise of human dignity. And he is everywhere intellectual.

With the drama of life and religion he is very little concerned. His battle pictures at Arezzo are not dramatic compositions in spite of the many dramatic incidents they contain. All the turmoil, all the emotions of the scenes have been digested by the mind into a grave intellectual whole. It is as though Bach had written the 1812 Overture. Nor are the two superb pictures in the National Gallery—the Nativity and the Baptism—distinguished for any particular sympathy with the religious, emotional significance of the events portrayed. In the extraordinary Flagellation at Urbino, the nominal subject of the picture recedes into the background on the left-hand side of the panel, where it serves to balance the three mysterious figures standing aloof in the right foreground. We seem to have nothing here but an experiment in composition, but an experiment so strange and so startlingly successful that we do not regret the absence of dramatic significance and are entirely satisfied. The Resurrection at San Sepolcro is more dramatic. Piero has made the simple triangular composition symbolic of the subject. The base of the triangle is formed by the sepulchre; and the soldiers sleeping round it are made to indicate by their position the upward jet of the two sides, which meet at the apex in the face of the risen Christ, who is standing, a banner in his right hand, his left foot already raised and planted on the brim of the sepulchre, preparing to set out into the world. No geometrical arrangement could have been more simple or more apt. But the being who rises before our eyes from the tomb is more like a Plutarchian hero than the Christ of conventional religion. The body is perfectly developed, like that of a Greek athlete; so formidably strong that the wound in its muscular flank seems somehow an irrelevance. The face is stern and pensive, the eyes cold. The whole figure is expressive of physical and intellectual power. It is the resurrection of the classical ideal, incredibly much grander and more beautiful than the classical reality, from the tomb where it had lain so many hundred years.

Aesthetically, Piero's work has this resemblance to Alberti's: that it too is essentially an affair of masses. What Alberti is to Brunelleschi, Piero della Francesca is to his contemporary, Botticelli. Botticelli was fundamentally a draftsman, a maker of supple and resilient lines, thinking in terms of arabesques inscribed on the flat. Piero, on the contrary, has a passion for solidity as such. There is something in all his works that reminds one constantly of Egyptian sculpture. Piero has that Egyptian love of the smooth rounded surface that is the external symbol and expression of a mass. The faces of his personages look as though they were carved out of some very hard rock into which it had been impossible to engrave the details of a human physiognomy—the hollows, the lines and wrinkles of real life. They are ideal, like the faces of Egyptian gods and princes, surface meeting and marrying with curved unbroken surface in an almost geometrical fashion. Look, for example, at the faces of the women in Piero's fresco at Arezzo: The Queen of Sheba recognizing the Holy Tree. They are all of one peculiar cast: the foreheads are high, rounded, and smooth; the necks are like cylinders of polished ivory; from the midst of the concave sockets the eyelids swell out in one uninterrupted curve into convexity; the checks are unbrokenly smooth and the subtle curvature of their surfaces is indicated by a very delicate chiaroscuro which suggests more powerfully the solidity and mass of the flesh than the most spectacular Caravaggioesque light and shade could do.

Piero's passion for solidity betrays itself no less strikingly in his handling of the dresses and drapery of his figures. It is noticeable, for example, that wherever the subject permits, he makes his personages appear in curious head-dresses that remind one by their solid geometrical qualities of those oddly-shaped ceremonial hats or tiaras worn by the statues of Egyptian kings. Among the frescoes at Arezzo are several which illustrate this peculiarity. In that representing Heraclius restoring the True Cross to Jerusalem, all the ecclesiastical dignitaries are wearing enormously high head-dresses, conical, trumpet-shaped, even rectangular. They are painted very smoothly with, it is obvious, a profound relish for their solidity. One or two similar head-dresses, with many varieties of wonderfully rounded helmets, are lovingly represented in the battle-pieces in the same place. The Duke of Urbino, in the well-known portrait at the Uffizi, is wearing a red cloth cap whose shape is somewhat like that of the "Brodrick" of the modern English soldier, but without the peak—a cylinder fitting round the head, topped by a projecting disk as the crown. Its smoothness and the roundness of its surfaces are emphasized in the picture. Nor does Piero neglect the veils of his female figures. Though transparent and of lawn, they hang round the heads of his women in stiff folds, as though they were made of steel. Among clothes he has a special fondness for pleated bodices and tunics. The bulge and recession of the pleated stuff fascinates him and he likes to trace the way in which the fluted folds follow the curve of the body beneath. To drapery he gives, as we might expect, a particular weight and richness. Perhaps his most exquisite handling of drapery is to be seen in the altar-piece of the Madonna della Misericordia, which now hangs near the Resurrection in the town hall at San Sepolcro. The central figure in this picture, which is one of the earliest of Piero's extant works, represents the Virgin, standing, and stretching out her arms, so as to cover two groups of suppliants on either side with the folds of her heavy blue mantle. The mantle and the Virgin's dress hang in simple perpendicular folds, like the flutings on the robe of the archaic bronze charioteer at the Louvre.

Piero has painted these alternately convex and concave surfaces with a peculiar gusto.

It is not my intention to write a treatise on Piero della Francesca; that has been done sufficiently often and sufficiently badly to make it unnecessary for me to bury that consummnate artist any deeper under layers of muddy comment. All I have meant to do in this place is to give the reasons why I like his works and my justifications for calling the Resurrection the greatest picture in the world. I am attracted to his character by his intellectual power; by his capacity for unaffectedly making the grand and noble gesture; by his pride in whatever is splendid in humanity. And in the artist I find peculiarly sympathetic the lover of solidity, the painter of smooth curving surfaces, the composer who builds with masses. For myself I prefer him to Botticelli, so much so indeed, that if it were necessary to sacrifice all Botticelli's works in order to save the Resurrection, the Nativity, the Madonna della Misericordia, and the Arezzo frescoes, I should unhesitatingly commit the Primavera and all the rest of them to the flames. It is unfortunate for Piero's reputation that his works should be comparatively few and in most cases rather difficult of access. With the exception of the Nativity and Baptism at the National Gallery, all the really important works of Piero are at Arezzo, San Sepolcro, and Urbino. The portraits of the Duke and Duchess of Urbino with their respective triumphs, in the Uffizi, are charming and exceedingly "amusing"; but they do not represent Piero at his best. The altar-piece at Perugia and the Madonna with saints and donor at Milan are neither of them first-rate. The St. Jerome at Venice is goodish; so too is the damaged fresco of the Malatesta, at Rimini. The Louvre possesses nothing, and Germany can only boast of a study of architecture, inferior to that at Urbino. Anybody, therefore, who wants to know Piero, must go from London to Arezzo, San Sepolcro, and Urbino. Now Arezzo is a boring sort of town, and so ungrateful to its distinguished sons that there is no monument within its walls to the divine Aretino. I deplore Arezzo; but to Arezzo, nevertheless, you must go to see Piero's most considerable works. From Arezzo you must make your way to San Sepolcro, where the inn is only just tolerable, and to which the means of communication are so bad that, unless you come in your own car, you are fairly compelled to stay there. And from San Sepolcro you must travel by bus for seven hours across the Apennines to Urbino. Here, it is true, you have not only two admirable Pieros (the Flagellation and an architectural scene), but the most exquisite palace in Italy and very nearly a good hotel. Even on the most wearily reluctant tourist Urbino imposes itself, there is no escaping it; it must be seen. But in the case of Arezzo and San Sepolcro there is no such moral compulsion. Few tourists, in consequence, take the trouble to visit them.

If the principal works of Piero were to be seen in Florence, and those of Botticelli at San Sepolcro, I do not doubt that the public estimation of these two masters would be reversed. Artistic English spinsters would stand in rapturous contemplation before the story of the True Cross, instead of before the Primavera. Raptures depend largely upon the stars in Baedeker, and the stars are more freely distributed to works of art in accessible towns than to those in the inaccessible. If the Arena chapel were in the mountains of Calabria, instead of at Padua, we should all have heard a good deal less of Giotto.

But enough. The shade of Conxolus rises up to remind me that I am running into the error of those who measure merit by a scale of oddness and rarity.

[*Along the Road*, 1925]

The Pierian Spring

"A LITTLE LEARNING," said Pope, "is a dangerous thing." And who, indeed, should have known its dangers more intimately than the man who had undertaken to translate Homer without (for all practical purposes) knowing a word of Greek? "Drink deep"—the exhortation, you feel, comes from the translator's very heart—"or taste not the Pierian spring."

Drink deep. The advice is good, provided always that the liquor be a sound one. But is the Pierian spring sound? That is the question. Not all medicinal waters are good for every drinker. People who can profitably drink deep of Carlsbad or Montecatini may die of a surfeit of Bath. Similarly the Pierian spring is not for everybody. The philosopher and the man of science may drink of it as deeply as they like and it will do them nothing but good. To the poet it can certainly do no harm; his native woodnotes are enriched by a little learning. The politician would do well to drink of this spring more often and more copiously than he actually does. The man of business may find profit in the draft, while the dilettante drinks for mere pleasure. But there is at least one class of men to whom the Pierian spring seems to be almost fatal. On no account should the artist be allowed to drink of it.

Two centuries have passed since Pope warned his readers against the dangers of a little learning. The history of those two centuries, and especially of the last fifty years, has proved that, so far as the artist is concerned, much learning is quite as dangerous as little learning. It is, in fact, a great deal more dangerous.

I can best explain what happens when artists drink deep of the Pierian spring by describing a kind of Arts and Crafts exhibition which I happened to see, a summer or two since, in Munich. It was a huge affair. Furniture, jewelry, ceramics, textiles—every kind of applied art was copiously represented.

And all the exhibits were German. All German—and yet these pots and pans, these chairs and tables, these weavings, paintings, carvings, forgings spoke a hundred languages besides the native Teuton. Aryan, Mongolian, Semitic, Bantu, Polynesian, Maya—the stocks and stones of Munich were fluent in all the tongues. Here, for example, stood a Mexican pot, decorated with Moorish arabesques; here a statuette that was sixth-century Greek, subtly mingled with Benin. Here was a Black Forest peasant's table standing on Egyptian legs; here a crucifix that might have been carved by a T'ang artist who happened to have spent a year in Italy as the pupil of Bernini. Goat, woman, lion, and griffin here were chimeras and empusas at every turn. And none of them (that was the real horror, for success justifies everything) none of them were good.

Germany, it is true, is the country where the dangers of too much learning have made themselves most apparent. It is the country that has drunk most deeply of the Pierian spring. For the last fifty years German publishers have brought out six illustrated monographs to every one produced in France, and a dozen at least to every one that we have published in England. With untiring industry and an enthusiasm which nothing—not the War, not even the Peace—has been able to damp, the Germans have photographed the artistic remains of every people that has ever flourished on the face of the earth. And they have published these photographs, with learned prefaces, in little books, which they sold, once upon a time, for a mark apiece, and which even now do not cost more than, shall we say, fifteen or twenty thousand millions. The Germans know more about the artistic styles of the past than any other people in the world—and their own art, today, is about as hopelessly dreary as any national art could well be. Its badness is, in mathematical terms, a function of its learnedness.

What has happened in Germany has happened, though to a slightly less marked degree, in every country of the world. We all know too much, and our knowledge prevents us—unless we happen to be artists of exceptional independence and talent—from doing good work.

Up till quite recently no European artist knew, or thought it worthwhile to know, anything about any forms of art except those which had been current in his own continent. And even of those he knew precious little. A sixteenth-century sculptor, for example, knew something about Greek carving—or something, at any rate, about Roman copies of carvings belonging to a certain period of Greek art. But of the works which the sculptors of the Gothic past had produced, even in his own country, he knew very little; and what he knew, he was disposed to deride as being merely barbarous. There were no photographs then; there were even very few engravings. The renaissance sculptor worked in an almost total ignorance of what had been done by other sculptors, at other periods or in countries other than his own. The result was that he was able to concentrate on the one convention that seemed to him good—the classical—and work away at it undisturbed, until he had developed all its potential resources.

The case of architecture is still more remarkable. For three hundred years the classical orders reigned supreme in Europe. Gothic was forgotten and despised. Nobody knew anything of any other styles. Generation after generation of architects worked away uninterruptedly in terms of this one convention. And what an astonishing variety of achievements they were able to get out of it! Using the same elementary classical units, successive generations produced a series of absolutely original and dissimilar works. Brunelleschi, Alberti, Michelangelo, Palladio, Bernini, Pietro da Cortona, Christopher Wren, Adam, Nash—all these architects worked in the same classical convention, making it yield a series of distinctive masterpieces, each utterly unlike the other.

These were all men of genius who would have done great things in any circumstances. What is still more striking is the achievement of the minor artists. During all this long period the work of even a journeyman had qualities which we look for in vain among the lesser artists of the present time. It was the absence of distracting knowledge that made possible this high level of achievement among the less talented men. There was for them only one possible convention. They concentrated their whole mind on getting the best they possibly could out of it.

How different is the present state of affairs! The artist of today knows, and has been taught to appreciate, the artistic conventions of every people that has ever existed. For him, there is no single right convention; there are a thousand conventions, which can all claim his respect because men have produced fine works in terms of all of them. Gone is the blessed ignorance, vanished the healthy contempt for all but one tradition. There is no tradition now, or there are a hundred traditions—it comes to the same thing. The artist's knowledge tends to distract him, to dissipate his energies. Instead of spending his whole life systematically exploiting one convention, he moves restlessly among all the known styles, undecided which to work in, borrowing hints from each.

But in art there are no shortcuts to successful achievement. You cannot acquire in half an hour the secrets of a style which it has taken the work of generations to refine to its perfection. In half an hour, it is true, you can learn what are the most striking superficial characteristics of the style; you can learn to caricature it. That is all. To understand a style you must give yourself up to it; you must live, so to speak, inside it; you must concentrate and steadily labor.

But concentration is precisely the thing which excessive knowledge tends to render impossible—for all, at any rate, but the most individually gifted, the most strong-minded of artists. They, it is true, can be left to look after themselves. Whatever their mental and physical environment, they will be themselves. Knowledge has had its most disastrous effects on the minor men, on the rank and file. These, in another century, would have worked away undistracted, trying to get the best out of a single convention—trying and, what is more, generally succeeding to the very limit of their natural capacities. Their descendants are trying to get the best out of fifty different conventions at once. With what results Munich most hideously shows. And not only Munich, but Paris too, London, New York, the whole knowledge-ridden world.

Still, the knowledge exists and is easily available. There is no destroying or concealing it. There can be no recapture of the old ignorance which allowed the artists of the past to go on working in one style for years, for centuries even, at a time. Knowledge has brought with it restlessness, uncertainty, and the possibility of rapid and incessant change in the conventions of art. How many styles have come and gone during the last seventy years! Pre-Raphaelitism, impressionism, art nouveau, futurism, post-impressionism, cubism, expressionism. It would have taken the Egyptians a hundred centuries to run through such a fortune of styles. Today, we invent a new convention—or, more often, resuscitate a combination of old conventions out of the past—exploit it, and throw it away, all in the space of five years. The fixity of the old traditions, the sure refinement of taste, born of ignorance and intolerant fastidiousness, have gone. Will they ever return? In time, no doubt, the artists will have inured themselves to the poison of the Pierian spring. The immense mass of knowledge which, in our minds, is still crude, will gradually be digested. When that has happened, some sort of fixity—or rather some slow and steady motion, for in life there is no fixity—will have been achieved. Meanwhile, we must be content to live in an age of dissipated energies, of experiment and pastiche, of restlessness and hopeless uncertainty.

The vast increase in our knowledge of art history has affected not only the artists themselves, but all those who take an interest in the arts. For *tout savoir est tout pardonner;* we have learned to appreciate and see the best in every style. To Voltaire and Dr. Johnson even Gothic art seemed a barbarism. What would they have said if we had asked them to admire the plastic beauties of a Polynesian statue, or the painting of an animal by an artist who lived millenniums before the dawn of history? Knowledge has enabled us to sympathize with unfamiliar points of view, to appreciate artistic conventions devised by people utterly unlike ourselves. All this, no doubt, is a very good thing. But our sympathy is so vast and we are so much afraid of showing ourselves intolerant towards the things we ought to like, that we have begun to love in our all-embracing way not merely the highest, in whatever convention, when we see it, but the lowest too.

We are not content with appreciating the good things which our ancestors condemned. Appetite grows with what it feeds on.

The good is not enough to satisfy our hungry appreciation; we must swallow the bad as well. To justify ourselves in this appreciation of what is bad, we have created a whole series of new aesthetic values. The process which began some time ago has gone on with ever-increasing speed and thoroughness, till there is now almost nothing, however bad, from which we cannot derive pleasure.

Historically, I suppose, the first stage in the breaking up of the old standards of taste was the invention of the "picturesque." A picturesque object may be defined as a thing which has some quality or qualities in excess of the normal. The nature of the excessive quality is almost a matter of indifference. Thus, even an excess of dirtiness is sufficient to render an object picturesque. The ideally picturesque object or scene possesses several excessive qualities in violent contrast one with another—for example, excess of gloom contrasting with excess of light, excess of magnificence with excess of squalor.

The quaint may be defined as the picturesque made smaller and touched with the comic. Those little old houses which Dickens so loved to describe—all holes and corners and curious accidents—are typical pieces of quaintness. There is always something snug and homely about the quaint, something even, in a comic way, slightly virtuous—funnily good, like Tom Pinch in *Martin Chuzzlewit*. It was the Victorian middle classes who erected quaintness into a standard of aesthetic excellence. Their love of it, coupled with their love of the picturesque, permitted them to admire a vast number of things which have practically no connection with art at all. What I may call "arty-craftiness" or "peasantry" is a Tolstoyan derivation from the quaint.

The great invention of more recent years has been the "amusing." In origin this is a highly sophisticated, upper-class standard of value. All bad art, whose badness is a positive and not a merely negative quality of respectable dullness, may be said to be amusing. For instance, Wordsworth, when he writes badly, is not at all amusing. Moore, on the other hand, is; for Moore's badness is of the period, highly colored, mannered and mincing. The badness of Wordsworth, like his goodness, is of all time. The Ecclesiastical Sonnets are absolute bathos, just as the finest passages in the Prelude and Excursion are absolute poetry.

A highly developed sense of the amusing in art is now extremely common. Few of those who take any conscious interest in the arts are now without it. Amusingness has even come to have a commercial value; dealers find that they can get good prices for the papier-maché furniture of the eighteen-fifties, for the wax flowers and statuettes of the age of Louis-Philippe. The people who collect these objects appear to derive as much satisfaction from them—for a time at any rate—as they would from the most austerely graceful Heppelwhite or the choicest fourteenth-century ivories. And there is no reason, of course, why they should not, provided that they continue to recognize the fact that Heppelwhite is better than Victorian papier-mâché and that medieval ivories are more beautiful than wax flowers. But the trouble is that this recognition is not always so complete or so prompt as it should be. That is the great danger attendant on the cult of the amusing; it makes its votaries forget that there are such things as the beautiful and the sublime. In the end Erasmus Darwin comes to be preferred to Wordsworth, Longhi to Giotto. Indirectly, it is the Pierian spring that is responsible.

[*Along the Road,* 1925]

The Mystery of the Theater

ONCE, in the course of an ill-spent life, it was my fate to go to the theater some two hundred and fifty times in one year.[5] On business, I need not add; one would hardly do that sort of thing for pleasure. I was paid to go.

By the end of the year—and, for that matter, long before our planet had completed its orbit round the sun—I had come to the conclusion that I was not paid enough; that, indeed, I could never be paid enough for this particular job. I gave it up; and nothing would now induce me to resume it.

Since then, my attendances at the theater have averaged perhaps three per annum.

And yet there are people who go to every first night, not because they have to, not because the griping belly must be filled, but because they like it. They are not paid to go; they pay, as though for a privilege. The ways of men are indeed strange.

5. Huxley was drama critic for *The Weekly Westminster Gazette* (1920–1921).

Concerning this mystery, I used often to speculate—abstracting myself as completely as I could from the environing horrors—during the most excruciating passages of the plays which I had to attend. Sitting all round me in the stalls—it was thus I used to reflect—are several hundred prosperous and, as education goes, well-educated people, who have paid money to see this driveling play (for I am assuming that the play is one of the nineteen driveling ones and not the rare twentieth *Heartbreak House* or *At Mrs. Beam's*). They are the sort of people who, in the privacy of their homes, would read the better class of novels, or at any rate not the worst. They would be indignant if you offered them a penny novelette. And yet these readers of respectable fiction will go to the theater (under no compulsion, be it remembered) to see plays which, as literature, are precisely on a level with the penny novelettes they scorn, very rightly and naturally, to read.

In their novels they demand a certain minimum of probability, truth to life, credible characterization, and decent writing. An impossible story, in which the personages are so many dolls, moving in obedience to the laws of an absurd and outworn convention, and expressing themselves in a grotesque, tumid, and ungrammatical English—this would disgust them. But to a play answering precisely to this description, they will flock in their thousands. They will be moved to tears and enthusiasm by situations which, in a novel, they would find merely ludicrous. They will let pass, and even fervidly admire, language which anyone with the slightest feeling for the use of words would shudder to see in print.

It was over this strange anomaly that I used to ponder during those hideous evenings at the theater. Why does the penny novelette disgust, in book form, those who delight in it when exhibited on the stage? Put succinctly, that was the not uninteresting problem.

Mr. Bernard Shaw has said that it is easier to write a novel than a play; and to show with what horrible facility a novelist can spin out into pages of thin description what the dramatist must compress into a few lines of dialogue, he re-wrote in modern narrative form a scene from *Macbeth*. Admittedly, Shakespeare stood the comparison very well. For it is certainly easier to write a bad novel than a good play. But on the other hand, it is much easier to write a bad play that will be successful—even with a quite intelligent and discriminating audience—than a bad novel that will take in readers of the same class. A dramatist can "get away with" a play in which there is no characterization subtler than caricature, no beauty of language less coarse than ranting rhetoric, no resemblance to life—only an effective situation. The novelist cannot.

This fact was recently impressed upon me (yet once more) when I went to the theater in Parma—not, alas, the great Estensian theater, but a gimcrack little modern playhouse—to see the Italian version of one of Sir

Arthur Pinero's plays—*His House in Order* it is called, if I remember rightly, in English. I confess that I thoroughly enjoyed the performance. English highlife, as seen through the eyes of an Italian touring company, was worth coming far—all the way from England—to study. And the comedians were admirable. But I marveled, as I listened, that a piece so entirely empty—for at Parma the unconscious humor and the good acting were merely accidental additions to the blank original—could have been, could still be, such a success. And as a hard-working novelist, I envied the lucky playwrights who can turn out a popular and even highly esteemed piece, in which the personages are either wooden puppets or caricatures, the language rant, and the plot a succession of those cheap epigrams of circumstance known as "situations." If I were allowed to make a novel out of only these ingredients, I should congratulate myself on having got off uncommonly cheaply.

What makes it possible for the dramatist to put so little into his plays, and yet successfully "get away with it," is, of course, the intervention of living interpreters. If he knows the trick, and one learns by practice, the dramatist can pass on to the actor the greater part of his responsibilities. All that he need do, if he is lazy, is to invent effective situations and leave the actors to make the most of them. Characterization, truth to life, ideas, decent writing, and all the rest he can resign to the writers for print, secure in the knowledge that the public will be too much taken up with the antics of the players to remark the absence of these merely literary trifles.

For it is the players, of course, who reconcile an otherwise relatively discriminating public to the sad stuff which finds its way on to the stage. It is for the sake of the comedians that occupants of the stalls who might, if they were sitting by their own firesides, be reading, shall we say, Wells or Conrad, or D. H. Lawrence, or even Dostoevsky, are content to put up with the dramatic equivalent of the penny novelette and the picture-paper serial story; for the sake of the living, smiling comedians; for the personal touch, the palpitating human note.

If acting were always first-class, I could understand people becoming hardened first-nighters—or shouldn't one rather say "softened"? for the contemporary theater is more relaxing than tonic, more emollient than astringent—becoming, then, softened first-nighters. A fine piece of acting is as well worth looking at as a fine performance in any other branch of art.

But good actors are as rare as good painters or good writers. Not more than two or three of the very best appear in every generation. I have seen a few. Old Guitry, for example. And Marie Lloyd, the marvellous, rich, Shakespearean Marie, now dead—alas, too soon; *car elle était du monde où les plus belles choses ont le pire destin.* And Little Tich. And Raquel Meller, marvellous both as diseuse and cinema actress, the most refined, the most nobly aristocratic interpreter of passion I have ever seen; *une âme bien née* if ever there was one. And Charlie Chaplin. All men and women of genius.

Such perfect performances as theirs are of course worth watching. And there are plenty of smaller talents, not to be despised. I am as willing to pay money to see these comedians interpreting nonsense as to pay to see a good play badly acted (and it is extraordinary how actor-proof a really good play can be). But why anyone should pay to see a poor, or even very competent but uninspired piece of acting in conjunction with a bad play—that is completely beyond my powers to understand.

Hardened—I beg your pardon—softened first-nighters to whom I have put this riddle have never been able to give me very satisfactory answers. Your true first-nighter, I can only presume, is born with a passion for the theater; he loves it always, for its own sake, blindly (for love is blind), uncritically. He pays his money at the box office, he leaves his judgment in the cloak-room along with his great-coat, hat, and walking-stick, and takes his seat, certain that he will enjoy himself, whatever may happen on the stage. The stuffiness and the crowd, the dark, expectant hush and then the apocalyptic rising of the curtain, the glitter and the shining, painted unreality—these are enough in themselves to make him happy. He does not ask for more. I envy him his easily contented mind.

[*Along the Road,* 1925]

II.

Music

Brahms

LAST MONDAY'S PERFORMANCE by the Symphony Orchestra of Brahms's C Minor Symphony gives one a pretext for talking about a composer whose attitude towards life and art are more than ever interesting today when that attitude has become, for the typical modern, remote and historical. Brahms and even the much greater Beethoven seem strangely grandiloquent, romantic, sentimental even, to a generation which has largely ceased to believe in the existence of the soul, finds the notion of spiritual conflict a bore, and sees human nature in terms of Freud rather than of Blake.

It is not our business in this place to analyze this modern attitude towards life. Is the present generation justified in thinking as it does? Is the old conception of the importance of the human spirit untenable? Can we halt at a compromise which would have us believe that the old faiths have little truth-value but great emotion-value? These are questions outside the scope of this article. What concerns us here is the empirical fact that the best art up to the present time has always had the old emotions and the old human values underlying it and that, so far at least, nothing of much significance has come out of negations.

Brahms was an artist whose work is based on the old values, a man who felt that the life of the spirit was something more than an affair of instinctive tics. His music is inspired by fundamentally the same sort of faiths, emotions, and spiritual experiences as those which underlie the art of Beethoven. He is a lesser artist than Beethoven, partly because he is a less resourceful and fertile musician and partly because there are certain weaknesses in his spiritual make-up from which Beethoven was free. There is, for example, that curious austerity which pervades so much of Brahms's music, an austerity which one feels to be forced, and which is in reality a consciously suppressed sentimentalism. At his best, however, as in the third and fourth movements of this C minor Symphony, in the Variations on the Chorale theme by Haydn, in certain movements of the Quintettes for piano and clarinet, he is as fine and full, as richly imaginative as anyone. The hostile criticisms which he now evokes are only to be expected from a generation whose mental outlook is so different from his. The succeeding criticisms of any enduring work of art form the best possible comment on the different epochs which produced them.

Technically Brahms represented the culminating elaborations of a long-developed tradition. He knew all there was to be known about his technique, and made the fullest use of his knowledge. The position that he occupied was much the same as that of an Italian painter in the seventeenth century, with the whole renaissance behind him. The artist who works in a great tradition in which great works have been produced in the past must be a man of real force if he is to express himself through his medium at all. A minor man disappears beneath the technique, and his work is but the empty husk of great art. Brahms was powerful enough to make himself felt through the traditional forms in which he worked. And he has had successors; Max Reger, for example, whose curiously acrid spirit is always strong enough to penetrate the dense masses of learning in which he enclosed his art. But think of the other contemporary musicians who have gone on using the traditional academic forms as their vehicle of expression. They have, almost without exception, sunk under the weight of tradition.

But this does not by any means imply that all those who rebel against tradition necessarily have something to say. Far from it. Good artists are rare whatever medium they use, and the important musicians of the present time may be numbered on the fingers of one hand. Brahms was the last great composer who worked in the traditional medium, and with him the great tradition became too much of a good thing. As in painting, so in music, there had to be a change, a simplification. Some, with rather affected rusticity, turned to folk-song for new inspiration; some, like Debussy, explored the more rarefied emotions and new, sophisticated techniques. Some, more recent—the dadaists of music—have tried to reduce all to the absurd. Our condition at the moment is one of considerable confusion. What we need is a musical Messiah, one who will make use of all the new-won liberties and the newly discovered technical means to build together a new form for the expression of great emotions and ideas.

And here we are, back again where we started from—back at the large, the noble, the spiritual emotions, and the clear intelligence which underlie all great art and which condition its technique. Brahms was a great composer because he had important emotions and beliefs.

[*The Weekly Westminster Gazette,* February 18, 1922]

Busoni, Dr. Burney, and Others

THE AMIABLE Doctor Burney[1] preferred Carl Philip Emanuel Bach to his father, John Sebastian. John Sebastian seemed rather old-fashioned in 1770; "for that venerable musician, though unequaled in learning and contrivance, thought it so necessary to crowd into both hands all the harmony he could grasp, that he must inevitably have sacrificed melody and expression." Emanuel was modern, a melodist, an emotional expressionist. Counterpoint, Emanuel thought, was too often mere music for the eye; he wrote for ears—and hearts. And Doctor Burney, albeit a great respecter of learning and the great tradition, was with the moderns of 1770. A stream of expressive melody blown in long, bright, wavering lines over a not too obtrusive foundation of harmony—that was the Doctor's ideal.

One wonders what he would have thought of Busoni's[2] *Fantasia Contrappuntistica* which was played last Saturday at the Wigmore Hall, on two pianos, by the composer and his pupil, Egon Petri. Here was old Bach, continued and developed in a great, massive, grimly intellectual piece of counterpoint. It was a notable work and fine enough for one to want to hear it again—which is more than can be said for some of Busoni's other compositions. The amiable Doctor, who had a very sound judgment, would certainly have admitted its merit; but he would as certainly have preferred something more modern and moving, something tender, perhaps, in the manner of Hasse, "the Raphael of music," something sublime in the style of its Michelangelo, the Cavaliere Gluck.

Dr. Burney's age was feeling out for a more dramatic, a more immediately emotional kind of music than had been possible in the age of counterpoint. Expressive melody, supported and emphasized by vertical harmonies, was taking the place of the old horizontal polyphony made up of a series of parallel airs, none of which was designed to produce any particular and immediate emotional effect.

Much later in the history of music, Wagner spent an evening listening to *Norma,* or was it *La Somnambula* or *I Puritani*? "I shall never forget," he wrote, "the impression made upon me by an opera of Bellini at a period when I was completely exhausted by the everlastingly abstract complications used in our orchestra, when a simple and noble melody was revealed anew to me." In Doctor Burney's day the development of expressive melody had been the result of a reaction against the over-elaborate pattern and surface texture of contrapuntal music. This time the revolt was against the rich romantic development of perpendicular harmony, which

---

1. Charles Burney (1726–1814). English organist and composer.
2. Ferrucio Busoni (1866–1924). Italian composer.

was threatening to blot out the clear lines of melody in a welter of mere color. The revolt against nineteenth-century romantic coloring has assumed several forms; there has been the naiviste revolt towards folk-song; the revolt of the highly sophisticated, like Debussy, who explored the possibilities of a new harmony and a new melodic line, and finally the revolt of such contrapuntists as Van Dieren and, in this *Fantasia,* Busoni.

Mlle. Suggia's concert on Monday night was a demonstration of the history of melody and harmony. Mozart's Haffner Symphony served as an admirable example of Doctor Burney's "modern music." The Saint-Saens Cello Concerto showed us expressive melody and romantic harmony in their feeble decay; the Dvorak Concerto showed a composer trying, not very successfully, to find salvation in folk-song melody. And then there was the sharp intellectual astringent of Bach's unaccompanied Cello Suite in C with the exquisite encore in E flat (played, we may add parenthetically, with consummate mastery by Mlle. Suggia). Listening to the program one could understand so well the reasons which made one generation turn from Bach to Dr. Burney's "modern music," which made another turn to romanticism and the next to the simplicity of folk-song and the austerity of the counterpoint from which the development started.

We today could do with a few more good melodists than we have. Where shall we find now that long, pure line of melody that gives to the best of Mozart's works an outline like the silhouette of a beautiful city of cones and towers? It is difficult, indeed, to think of any first-rate contemporary melodist, with the exception of Delius. He, however, most certainly possesses the gift of pure melody, as the long, beautiful lines of his "Village Romeo and Juliet" attest.

[*The Weekly Westminster Gazette,* February 25, 1922]

The Interpreter and the Creator

GRAMOPHONE RECORDS are classified in the makers' catalogues under the names of the performers, not the composers. It would be vain to try to discover from the catalogue index how many works of Beethoven have been recorded by Columbia and His Master's Voice. But you can see at a glance how often Caruso sang into the machine or the number of records made by Casals.

The fact is significant; the gramophone catalogue looks at the music from the same angle as does the general public, in whose mind the interpreter looms considerably larger than the creator. More people go to see Hamlet interpreted by Forbes Robertson. And when it comes to Chaliapine[3]—who goes to a Chaliapine concert for anything but Chaliapine? Who goes for the sake of Glazounov or Borodine, of Schubert and Schumann? Who goes for anything but the astonishing voice and the prodigious dramatic talent of the interpreter? Indeed, one cannot consciously go for anything else; for the program of music is not even announced before the concert begins. The public pays to hear Chaliapine sing whatever he chooses.

The program of Chaliapine's Albert Hall concert last week included a distressingly large proportion of musically worthless items. It is true that Chaliapine made them, by his singing, worth hearing; but one would have preferred something which bore a closer resemblance to real music. If only one could have a Chaliapine concert with a program as musically rich and varied as that which Mr. Egon Petri performed in his brilliant piano recital at the Wigmore Hall last Saturday! Beethoven's Hammerklavier sonata, César Franck's Prelude, Aria, and Finale, Brahms's Variations on a Theme by Paganini—find the vocal equivalents of these and induce Chaliapine to make a concert of them; we offer that as a recipe for a really agreeable evening. Enough is not as good as a feast.

The great interpreters of art—the artisans, shall we call them? as opposed to the real creative artists—have always been far more popular than the creators. The mere fact that they are seen and heard, that there exists a palpable and personal connection between themselves and the public, makes them more easily comprehensible and admirable than the retiring creator, who is only known impersonally by his works. Anyone possessing a talent that can be publicly and brilliantly displayed—whether he be a singer, a boxer, a tight-tope dancer, a conjurer—is sure of applause and contemporary fame.

The biographies of the great virtuosi make the most fascinating reading imaginable. They live in a strange world of ecstatic admiration, of roving adventures, of wealth and applause. Think of Paganini, who could play the most difficult of his rivals' works on one string, with a walking-stick instead of a bow; who imitated the braying of an ass with such perfection on his violin that he was almost lynched for it once at Bologna, a city in which, by tradition, this form of music was deemed peculiarly insulting; who was constantly assisted and inspired—so those who watched him playing declared—by a horned devil who stood at his elbow directing the movements of the bow. Or think of the still more fabulous Farinelli, described by a contemporary as being "to all other singers as superior as the famous horse Childers was to all other running horses." Like Saul, King

---

3. Fyodor Chaliapine (1873–1938). Russian operatic bass.

Philip V of Spain was possessed by a melancholy devil, and every night for ten years Farinelli was called in to sing the same four songs which alone could ease his master's chronic misery. Even the modern virtuoso is a prodigious figure. A few mellowing years will make Caruso as romantic as Paganini. Chaliapine himself is already almost a legendary hero, and we are delighted to see that an adventurous autobiography from his pen is about to make its appearance. Long live the virtuosi! But let us not make the mistake of confusing them with the real artists, the creators for whom they serve as interpreters.

[*The Weekly Westminster Gazette,* March 4, 1922]

Good-Popular Music

THE PEER GYNT SUITE is a musical work which one is not used to taking very seriously or enthusiastically. To appreciate it as it should be appreciated, one should go to see Ibsen's play, now being heroically performed at the Old Vic. All things one sees there are relative; and in the huge, void desert of Ibsen's dismal allegory Grieg's little tunes are like green palm trees and gushing springs. With what a thankful sense of relief one heard the familiar "One-and-two-and-three-and-four: one-and-two: three-and-four" of the Trolls' ballet! How eagerly one looked forward even to Anitra's dance! And as for Solveig's song—tears of gratitude came into one's eyes whenever Miss Stella Friston alleviated the appalling *ennui* of the last scenes by giving us a stave of it in her clear and unaffected tones. Four and a half hours spent at the Old Vic in the company of Ibsen and Grieg were enough to make one credit all the ancient stories of the soothing and medicinal powers of music. Orpheus could tame the beasts with song; David's harping eased the melancholy of Saul—one had no difficulty in believing these things seeing that Grieg had been able, momentarily at least, to exorcise a boredom which had, in Baudelaire's words, assumed "les proportions de l'immortalité."

And yet one cannot honestly say that Grieg's incidental music is particularly good. He is by no means among the best of the writers of good-popular music. In that most interesting and important category of musicians he occupies a respectable, but none too exalted, position—above the author of the *Indian Love Lyrics,* but some way below such a composer as, for example, the Tschaikowsky of *Casse-Noisette* and *Enchanted Princess.*

Many of the good-popular writers of the past are now only too seldom heard. There is Rossini, for instance. The overtures to his operas have become the prey of military bands; the operas themselves, with the exception of *The Barber of Seville,* are never heard at all. Rumor has it that a number of newly discovered quartets and trios by this amazing composer are about to be performed in Paris. Let us hope we shall soon be given a chance of hearing them here. And then, after Rossini, is Offenbach. There must be glittering treasures of popular music in all the many comic operas of his which our generation has never seen staged. There are Strauss and Waldteufel; there is the early Albéniz, who wrote good-popular for years before he began writing good-unpopular music. One could think of dozens more who combined the comprehensibility and direct emotional appeal of the ordinary-popular music of commerce with ingenuity, subtlety, and fertility of invention. Bad-popular music is tedious and monotonous, because it never escapes from a narrow circle of emotional and technical ideas. Good-popular music wanders over an enormous field of feeling and technique; it can only be written by a man of intelligence who is also a capable musician.

Good-popular music at the present time has many able exponents. There is Puccini, for example, who might easily go on ripening and improving as the aging Verdi did before him—ripening into goodness knows what, if he should happen to live as long as Verdi. On a less grandiose scale there are the many writers of songs and dances—the ragtime writers of North America, the tango writers of South America. It is from this last continent that one may probably expect the most interesting developments of good-popular music. The music of the *Boeuf sur le Toit*[4] is based on a medley of South American dance tunes, and very fine they are. But it will be the composers brought up in this Spanish-American tradition who will produce good music out of it, not the too sophisticated Frenchmen who use it for fun and to annoy the solemn. An astonishing Brazilian from Bahia is soon to be heard in New York. Will he bring a new revelation of good-popular music? It is pleasant to think so.

[*The Weekly Westminster Gazette,* March 11, 1922]

Instruction with Pleasure

THE ACT of combining instruction with entertainment results usually in the production of something monstrously boring. Nothing, for example, is more deplorable than a book of the *Sandford and Merton* pattern, where fiction serves as the jam that takes the taste from the didactic powder. But

---

4. A ballet by Jean Cocteau with music by Darius Milhaud.

in certain circumstances and for certain brands of instruction, the mingling of the two is tolerable and even exceedingly pleasant. The instructive concert is a case in point; it gives the right, the relevant sort of instruction. An instructive concert is not intended, like the didactic novel, to teach anything outside the sphere of its own art; it is a musical performance which gives pleasure as music and which is so arranged as to illustrate some fact in the history or the technique of the art.

Instructive concerts on a small scale are given fairly frequently. They might with advantage, it seems to us, be given much more often, and on a more ambitious and elaborate plan. Londoners at the present moment may take their choice between two or three series of instructive concerts. We take as our example the series which is being given every Sunday afternoon by Madame Levinskaya at her studios, 2 Leinster Gardens. Having made a beginning last Sunday, she is giving a series of chamber concerts, at which all the ten violin sonatas of Beethoven are being played through in chronological order. The beauty of the music would alone be enough to attract one to such weekly concerts; they possess the additional interest of showing in a series of concrete examples that steady, that almost ruthless development and improvement which characterizes the maturing Beethoven.

For the musical beginner Madame Levinskaya gives a few words of introductory explanation on the construction and musical form of each sonata; she picks out the first and second subject, shows where the development begins, and how the recapitulation differs from the first enunciation of the themes. The series promises to be a liberal education in Beethoven.

Others at the present time are doing the same sort of thing for different composers, different periods, different kinds of music; it is to be hoped that they will find numerous imitators. There are so many historical and technical facts which the ordinary musical layman, who has no time for systematic study, would like to learn—on the Montessori system, while he is enjoying himself—at his regular concerts. They are facts, a knowledge of which would make possible a fuller and more reasoned appreciation of what he hears; and they are facts which, by a judicious arrangement of concert programs and a very little explanation, it is easy to convey. All that is required is a little organization of our musical entertainments.

It is easy to think of innumerable concerts of instruction which it would be fascinating to hear. A brief history of chamber music, the evolution of the sonata form, the minor eighteenth-century composers, the story of harmony and melody, the history of the various musical scales, nationality in music—here are a few of the subjects for concerts or series of concerts which at once suggest themselves. These are subjects which may be illustrated by means of the piano, the voice, and a quartet of stringed instruments. With an orchestra at one's disposal—and there seems to me to be no good reason why the directors of our symphony orchestras should not arrange some of their programs with a view to instruction as well as entertainment—one would have a much wider range. The story of orchestration, for example, is a fascinating tale which could easily be told in a series of well-chosen works. And when that had been fully told, there are scores of other subjects which could be illustrated and explained in delightful programs. The ordinary uninstructive concert, with a program chosen for the sake of its entertaining variety is a good and refreshing thing, which it would be absurd to wish to abolish. Too much instruction would certainly be monotonous. But, side by side, with the uninstructive concerts, might one not have a few more of the didactic variety? They would help one to listen to the ordinary program with a greater understanding and a greater pleasure.

[*The Weekly Westminster Gazette,* March 18, 1922]

Emotional Contributions

SIGNOR RESPIGHI'S "Dance of the Gnomes," which was played at last Monday's Symphony Concert at the Queen's Hall, is a modern work which is only modern in its external form—in its harmonies and its orchestration. In its conception, in its range of emotions it belongs to Romanticism. In his extremely accomplished twentieth-century fashion, Signor Respighi is saying what Weber beautifully, what Meyerbeer a little meretriciously, were saying eighty, ninety, a hundred years ago. There is no reason, of course, why a contemporary should not try to thrill us with the horrid, the macabre, the supernatural, if he feels inclined to. No reason whatever. All we would say is this: that the romantically horrid emotions are not those which one would call characteristic of modern music; that these emotions have been turned into art by an earlier generation, and that the contemporary contribution to the store of musically expressed feelings is something different.

Nothing is more remarkable than the way in which hitherto unexploited emotions are perpetually finding their way into art, particularly music. Who could have guessed, for example, before the Fifth Symphony was written, that there could be an adequate musical expression for precisely those huge, tragic emotions about life and human destiny which were Beethoven's inspiration when he wrote? And how different these emotions are from the high intellectual well-being, far above any specific emotion, which is expressed in such works of Beethoven as the "Hammer-clavier" and Sonata III. In these works Beethoven passed into the transcendental region of pure art. Beethoven's emotional contributions to music were enormous. He expressed in sound a whole host of feelings which had never before found their musical expression. Many others have made contributions, not so great as Beethoven's, but of emotions equally novel to music, equally "unedited."

There was Chopin, for instance. He gave it romance—not the sugary, sentimental romance of the worse Schumann, the weaker Mendelssohn, and all the lesser romantics, down to the lowest drawing-room song writers—but the pure, fine, fiery romance which is a much nobler and more intellectual thing than sentimentality. Then came Wagner, who endowed music with the prodigious exultation and energy of the materially triumphant nineteenth century—a triumph, tinged with unrest and a certain nostalgic yearning for goodness knew exactly what. César Franck contributed something very different—the large, unpassionate serenity of religious faith. At a recent recital, Beethoven's "Hammerclavier Sonata" and Franck's "Prelude, Aria, and Finale" were played within the course of a single hour; it was profoundly interesting to compare the different serenities of these two great works. Beethoven's serenity is one in which the emotions have been intellectually digested and sublimated into pure art. Franck's is a serenity of calm, religious faith, beside which doubts and passions seem rather irrelevant and frivolous.

With Debussy we have the expression of late nineteenth-century *nostalgie,* that immensely intellectual sentimentalism which, with a love of pure beauty, was the inspiration of such poets as Laforgue and Mallarmé. It is a rare and subtle emotion that is expressed by the *Après Midi* and the Nocturnes; and once it has been expressed there is nothing more to say about it. Like Chopin's, Debussy's contribution is purely personal. It seems impossible for either to have spiritual disciples; they can only have technical followers.

These are but a few of the composers who have contributed new emotions to music. One could name many more. There are the Russians, for instance, to whom music owes a huge debt, the Spaniards, to whom the debt is small, but definitely established. One might even mention the ragtime writers and the niggers; for they have contributed new emotions, undreamed of before. And what is the contribution of our contemporaries? It is difficult precisely to say. But it is obvious that Stravinsky has given us something novel in the way of feeling, and that the younger Frenchmen are expressing a certain cheerful and buffoonish contempt for the grandiose which is characteristic of this generation. It is equally obvious (to return, rondo-fashion, to the theme from which we set out) that Signor Respighi contributes nothing with which we were not familiar before.

[*The Weekly Westminster Gazette,* March 25, 1922]

Light Opera and the New Stravinsky

A FEW WEEKS AGO I gave expression in this column to a desire which I did not for a moment expect to be satisfied: I wanted to hear some more Offenbach. Last week my wish was completely fulfilled. Quite suddenly, out of the blue, came the Stirling Mackinley Opera Society with an admirable production of Offenbach's *La Fille du Tambour Major.* I cannot help suspecting that this prompt answer to prayer has something to do with Monsieur Coué.[5] All unconsciously, no doubt, I had been autosuggesting Offenbach. "Every day, in every place, I am hearing more and more Offenbach." And naturally I heard it. But I divagate into metaphysics.

Last week's performance of *La Fille du Tambour Major* proved a number of things. It proved, to begin with, that the members of the Stirling Mackinley Opera Society have admirably trained voices, which would do credit to any company of professionals. It proved in the second place two more general propositions: that Offenbach was an exceedingly good composer—the opening chorus, the duet between Claudine and Riolet in the first act, the duet between the Duchess and the Drum Major in the third are little masterpieces of popular melody; and that good operas must have at least passable librettos. The libretto of *La Fille du Tambour Major* can never have been particularly brilliant. In its English translation it is really melancholy. The only reason why Sullivan's operettas hold the stage and Offenbach's do not is that Sullivan had a man of real talent as his librettist, and Offenbach—fully his equal as a writer of popular music—had not. It also proved, if that needed proving, that light opera or musical comedy is an art-form with immense potentialities. *The Marriage of Figaro* and *Don Giovanni* are entrancing even as they stand. What would they have been if Da Ponte had been more than the intelligent and respectable literary man he was—if he had been a real comic and poetic genius, like Aristophanes or the Shakespeare of *Twelfth Night*? Good comic art on a large scale and in the grand manner is far rarer than good serious or tragic art which has always, for some rather obscure reason, been considered superior to it.

5. Emile Coué (1857–1910). French psychotherapist, famous for the self-help formula, "Every day, and in every way, I am becoming better and better."

Some day, it may be, the combination of a super-Gilbert with a transcendent Sullivan may produce the perfect musical comedy. Meanwhile, we have Mozart to go on with, and the minor delights of Rossini and Offenbach and all their kin.

La Fille du Tambour Major came as a pleasant surprise. But the *divertimenti* by M. Massine's little band of dancers at Covent Garden were expected pleasures. Here, too, is to be heard some admirable, popular music. In the romantic passionate style we have Rubenstein's "Lezginka" and Brahms's "Czardas"; then there is a charming Pas de Deux to music by Cimarosa, that Offenbach of an earlier age, for the love of whose "Matrimonio Segreta" Stendhal would have walked ten leagues through mud; and finally we have a series of dance tunes—waltz, polka, mazurka, galop—by Johann Strauss. These, one felt, might have been better chosen from the musical point of view; they hardly did justice to the superb melodic gifts of the composer of "The Blue Danube" and "Fledermaus."

But the most interesting music to be heard at Covent Garden is Stravinsky's *Ragtime*. I cannot describe this odd work better than by calling it a piece of inverted transcendentalism. Beethoven was transcendental in the direction of heroism, of the soul, of infinity. But it is possible to transcend along other planes and in different directions. Stravinsky's *Ragtime* is transcendental in the direction of soullessness, of mechanics rather than heroics. In this respect the work is remarkably expressive of the contemporary *weltanschauung*. M. Massine's extraordinary mechanistic choreography was a perfect interpretation of the music. The chief defect in *Ragtime* is the fact that it is not large enough in conception, not vigorous, or certain, or emphatic enough. The heroic transcendentalism of the Ninth Symphony convinces by mere force of affirmation. *Ragtime* is small and dubious. One of these days, Stravinsky or someone else will write a work of inverted transcendentalism as prodigious and convincing as the Ninth Symphony—and there will be nothing to do, when one has heard it, but to go home and quietly commit suicide.

[*The Weekly Westminster Gazette*, April 8, 1922]

The Mysteries of Music

I WAS LISTENING, a few days ago, to a fragment from a suite for strings written by Mozart when he was fourteen. For beauty and originality of melodic invention, for musicianly skill in the writing, the thing was unsurpassable; in its small way it had achieved complete perfection.

What is this extraordinary art in which perfection—even limited—is possible at fourteen? What are the mental processes of a composer? And what is the relation between the composer's experience and his inspiration, between his life and his art? These are questions which must have suggested themselves at one time or another to all who love music without themselves possessing the gift of musical creation. Listening to that fragment of a Mozart suite I found myself speculating with more than ordinary perplexity over the mystery of music.

The infant prodigies of music have always been much more numerous than the prodigies in any other art. It would hardly be too much to say that musical prodigies are the only prodigies. The plastic arts very rarely produce a child exponent of any significance. Ingres, it is true, drew as well at the age of nine as the average accomplished art student of twenty: but that is not saying very much. Bernini, which is a good deal more remarkable, carved a pretty little marble tomb when he was fourteen. But in general it may be said that the age of real accomplishment is a good many years higher in the plastic arts than in music. The same is true of literature. In the whole history of literature there is only one infant prodigy of real importance: Rimbaud's achievement between the ages of seventeen and twenty is fully equal to Mozart's up to the same age; in its intellectual and emotional range it is, indeed, very much more remarkable. But Rimbaud, as we have said, is unique in his own art. Mozart's achievement is comparable to that of quite a number of other musicians, Beethoven, Liszt, Mendelssohn, Weber, Schubert—a surprising number of them started life as prodigious performers or precocious creators.

What, then, is the relation to life and ordinary experience of an artistic faculty that can achieve perfection even in the works of children? Here is a question which it is impossible for anyone who is not a composer to answer at all precisely. But it is sufficiently obvious that experiences, though they may not be directly translated and described, must always have a profound effect on music as on all other arts. The child Mozart could write a ravishingly lovely melody for strings: he could not conceivably have written the reflective, mysterious, almost tragic G minor Quintet of his late maturity. But the process by which an emotion or thought gets turned into music must always be obscure to the ordinary person.

What are the workings of a composer's mind? It is very hard to imagine. Most ordinarily musical people, I suppose, occasionally think of little tunes, or hear agreeable successions of chords in their heads. But the tunes are generally trivial and derivative, the successions of chords mere memories of something heard. This rudimentary musical imagination differs almost in kind, as well as in degree, from the imagination of a Mozart or a Beethoven. An ordinary mortal going for a walk on a fine, spring day experiences a sensation of well-being. A composer experiences the same well-being; but as likely as not it translates itself automatically in his mind into terms of pure music. The well-being of one becomes a bit of the Pastoral Symphony, of another the beautiful "On first hearing a Cuckoo in the spring."

Dogs and cats have very compact, efficient little minds; none the less, they must have a sadly imperfect understanding of the mental processes of those human beings with whom they live. To me, the mental processes of Einstein are almost as obscure as any soliloquy of mine on Shakespeare and the musical glasses would be to a listening audience of dogs. Between myself and the absolutely tone-deaf person, who may, in all other respects, be my superior in intelligence, there is, in the matter of musical appreciation, a gulf as great as that which separates me from Einstein; and to a Beethoven, musically, I stand in the relation of an intelligent cat to a man. The surprising thing is that there should be as much understanding and appreciation in the world as there is.

[*The Weekly Westminster Gazette,* April 15, 1922]

Some Easter Music

"THE WORLD," says Mr. H. L. Mencken, "has very little sense of humor. It is always wagging its ears solemnly over elaborate jocosities. . . . The case of Wagner's *Parsifal* is . . . remarkable. Even Nietzsche was deceived by it. Like the most maudlin German stockbroker's wife at Baireuth he mistook the composer's elaborate and outrageous burlesque of Christianity for a tribute to Christianity, and so denounced him as a jackass and refused to speak to him thereafter. . . . To this day *Parsifal* is given with all the trappings of a religious ceremonial. But try to imagine such a thumping atheist as Wagner writing a religious opera seriously. And if by any chance you succeed in imagining it, then turn to the Char-Freitag music and play it on your Victrola. Here is the central scene of the piece, the moment of most austere solemnity—and to it Wagner fits music that is so luscious and fleshly—indeed, so downright lascivious and indecent—that even I, who am almost anesthetic to such provocations, blush and giggle every time I hear it."[6]

Paradoxes are always amusing and often salutary. Let us be grateful for this cheerful specimen of its kind. It should be printed with the more solemn and orthodox analytical notes at the head of every *Parsifal* pro-

---

6. Huxley is quoting from H. L. Mencken's "Reflections on Monogamy" in *Prejudice: Fourth Series,* 107–108.

gram. That Wagner could deliberately have perpetrated on the Christian religion a practical joke of such weight, such vast proportions as *Parsifal,* is hardly credible. But the fact remains, none the less, that much of the *Parsifal* music is "luscious and fleshly" to a degree which makes it singularly unsuitable to celebrate the austere beauties of Christianity. Nobody could sit down in cold blood and compose a joke lasting five and a half hours; but a man like Wagner could very easily put so much unconscious humor into a seriously conceived work as to justify a paradox like Mr. Mencken's.

So, at least, it seemed to me as I listened on Good Friday night to the selections from *Parsifal* performed at the Queen's Hall. In its entirely different way, Wagner's music sounded as much out of harmony with the spirit of Good Friday as did the music of Rossini's *Stabat Mater,* to which I had been listening on the afternoon of the same day.

Rossini interpreted Good Friday in terms of the *Boutique Fantasque* and *The Barber of Seville.* A succession of ravishing sentimental airs and jolly choruses, interspersed with exquisite twiddly bits for the orchestra— his *Stabat* deserves all the applause it gets. It would get still more if the singers were costumed by Picasso and trained by Massine to give a graceful dance or two between the vocal numbers. Rossini's music is so completely divorced from Good Friday and all its associations that one cannot and does not regard it as religious music at all. It can give no offense.

But with *Parsifal* it is different. Here there is a studied attempt to express the religious emotions in solemn and splendid music. The emotions which Wagner actually does express—unconsciously or, as Mr. Mencken would have us believe, consciously and with a wink to the knowing few— are the emotions of sex; plain sex, unsublimated into anything appreciably nobler or finer than itself. Good Friday surely stands for something else than an agreeably sexual religiosity. The music that expresses the real sublimity and beauty of religion is not to be found in Wagner. One could have heard it on Good Friday afternoon at the Albert Hall—in Handel's *Messiah.* One can hear it in Bach, in a few of Mozart's delicious writings for the Church, in Beethoven's great Mass, in César Franck, and in many others. But in *Parsifal,* no. One hears there the musical equivalent of that sensually mystical St. Theresa of Bernini, whose swooning effigy amazes, delights, and disgusts all those who enter the church of Santa Maria della Vittoria in Rome.

[*The Weekly Westminster Gazette,* April 22, 1922]

Music and Machinery

THERE ARE STILL some people—they happily become fewer and fewer every year—who disapprove, on some strangely ill-founded William-Morrisish principle, of all mechanical devices for the making or reproduction of music. The gramophone disgusts them, the pianola makes them feel quite faint. Or rather, it is generally the mere idea of these machines that offends them; for, as often as not, you will find that these good people have never taken the trouble to listen to the devices which they condemn. It is enough for them that they are machines; machinery is a priori incompatible with music, which is an Art capital-lettered and high.

But in spite of the anti-mechanists, there can be no doubt that the mechanical inventions of the last few years are doing more to create an understanding musical public than anything short of compulsory musical education and forced concert-going could ever do. Between the gramophone and the pianola one can now hear a more or less adequate version of most of the world's best music in the comfort of one's own drawing-room; and, what is supremely important, one can hear it as often as one likes. For all but the very exceptional few who can take in an elaborate work at a single hearing, unlimited repetition is necessary for the thorough understanding and, consequently, for the perfect enjoyment of music. The machine makes that understanding and that enjoyment possible.

Few of us can afford the necessary time and energy to become more than very moderate amateur performers. Executant genius, in the words of Shestov, "must submit to cultivate an ass within itself." It must turn the mill, again, again, round and round, endlessly, with a "truly angelic or asinine patience." And even when one has cultivated and trained the ass into a Paganini-like accomplishment, one is really very little further with one's general musical education. Two hands playing on one instrument can interpret but a very small part of the world's music. Inevitably, one is brought back to the ideal of a labor-saving, all-competent machine. The ideal realizes itself more or less adequately today in the gramophone and the player-piano. In a perfectly organized society everyone would possess a specimen of both these machines. They are complementary to one another; each supplements the other's defects. Thus the pianola can only give you a piano transcription of music written for strings or orchestra or voices; but it can give a full-length version of that music. The gramophone on the other hand will record any kind of music with a fidelity that is often amazing; but it will only record it in little chunks of four or five minutes' duration. Jack Sprat's wife is needed as well as Jack Sprat, if the job is to be done really well.

What a test of musical merit the machines provide! There are the records and rolls that can be played again and again, every day, and that one enjoys as much or more each time one hears them. And there are the others—the ones that have constantly to be given a month's holiday. It is a test which mere concert-going, however regular, simply does not permit one to apply, except to a very few, well-known compositions. And even then it will take you twenty years to make your test instead of a few weeks.

The next forward stride in the mechanical dissemination of good music will come when the radio-telephone takes it place among the necessities whose mother is invention. On Armistice Day last year President Harding delivered an address at Washington; enormous trumpets attached to wireless receivers brayed out his words as he spoke them to a great crowd assembled in Madison Square Garden in New York. Since then no American home has been complete without a wireless telephone, and radio concerts and lectures are now a regular feature of trans-Atlantic life. Soon—can one doubt it?—we shall be listening, pillowed on cushions in a Thames-side garden or seated by the scarcely breathing sea, we shall be listening on the warm August nights to Monday's Wagner at the Proms, or Friday's Beethoven. Or, sharpening our electric ears, we may hear the Léner playing Ravel at Budapest or Toscanini conducting at Milan. Could anything be more delightful?

The only flaw one can detect in this Utopian state of things is the possibility that the new invention may throw many musicians out of work. One can imagine a great centralization of music with all Europe listening, when it cares to listen, to relays of singers, fiddlers, orchestras playing continuously day and night at some central point such as Munich or Vienna—all to the great disadvantage of the local *virtuosi*. However, this consummation is remote. Meanwhile, anything that will render it possible, in the remote and savage country and in some of the still more barbarous towns, to hear good music played by good performers should be welcomed with all our enthusiasm.

[*The Weekly Westminster Gazette*, April 29, 1922]

Beethoven's Quartets

IN THE COMPANY of a very respectable number of my fellow citizens, I spent the evenings of the last week in April at the Aeolian Hall, listening to the London String Quartet playing through the seventeen quartets of Beethoven—from Op. 18, no. 1, composed in 1800, to Op. 135, composed in 1826, the year before the composer's death—in their chronological order. It was, on the whole, an excellent performance; and if there seemed to be certain signs of weariness in the playing of some of the compositions of the middle period, this was compensated for by the brilliant rendering of the first and last quartets. But even if the playing were not so good as it actually is, the London String Quartet's Beethoven Festival Week is an institution which deserves all possible encouragement.

There is nothing more interesting or instructive than to watch the gradual unfolding of an artist's mind—particularly when the artist is a genius of Beethoven's magnitude, and when the development is as steady and as ruthlessly persistent as that which is exhibited in these seventeen compositions.

Listening to the six quartets of Op. 18, one wonders how, and in what direction, the composer is going to develop. Works like numbers 1, 4, and 5 of this opus seem already, in their own way, to have achieved perfection. We find that Beethoven is already the complete master of the world of Mozartian ideas and emotion. Take the Adagio of Op. 18, no. 1; it is comparable to what is perhaps the highest achievement of Mozart—the slow movement of the G minor Quintet, to which, in emotional conception and in musical execution, it bears more than a superficial resemblance. In some directions Beethoven has even overstepped the boundaries of the Mozartian world. Thus, in the Scherzo of the same quartet, he is expressing an emotion which is new to music, an emotion that was to play an important part in all his later writings; he is expressing that profound and beautiful humor which is something so different from the high-spirited gaiety of Mozart.

It is only when we hear the first quartet of the Op. 59 series, composed six or seven years later than Op. 18, that we find out how and whither he is developing. In the opening Allegro we are greeted with an emotional richness and intensity that are quite unlike anything in Op. 18. In the Adagio we hear another new note; we hear the authentic voice of romanticism, we hear the sobbing passion of the early nineteenth century, but kept in check, as it is in the work of all the romantics who count, by a severe intellectual discipline. The final Allegro introduces a daring new experiment in the expression of mixed, conflicting emotions.

The new emotional content is accompanied, in these quartets of the middle period, by new methods of musical expression. One cannot fail to be struck, for example, by the impressive rhythmical figure on one note which runs through the first movement of Op. 59, no. 1; it reminds one of the similar figures in the Fifth Symphony ("Fate knocking at the door"), in the G major concerto, in the Sonata Appassionata, and elsewhere in works of the middle period. By means of these strong and simple rhythmical figures, Beethoven is able to give dramatic interest to inner parts without obscuring the surface melody under a wealth of polyphonic detail. This was one of his musical inventions. Another remarkable achievement is to be found in the Introduction to the third of the Op. 59 series, in which we have a rush of free modulations, held together by a methodically progressive base.

The later works show an ever increasing richness and complexity of emotional content and of polyphonic writing. This polyphonic complexity culminates in the positively terrifying Grosse Fuge in B flat major, Op. 133, the most formidable piece of music that was ever written.

[*The Weekly Westminster Gazette,* May 6, 1922]

Singing and Things Sung

A GOOD VIOLIN is a rare and precious thing; so is a good violinist. The great singer—the singer who can reach and move a whole auditorium—is rarer still. For he must combine in his own person the fine and powerful instrument with the accomplished and sensitive performer. He must have rare physical as well as rare mental endowments.

It is very seldom that we hear a great singer in our theaters or our concert halls. Occasionally the lovely monster appears, and we are overwhelmed. In the intervals we have to content ourselves with the second-rate singers of the opera and the concert—a poor consolation, it must be confessed—or with those much more satisfying minor singers, whose instrument is too delicate for great ordeals, but perfectly adequate for producing a more intimate and private beauty.

The last few days have provided us with opportunities for listening to a good deal of singing. There has been the opening of the Covent Garden opera season; there have been concerts by two Italian celebrities of the first magnitude—Battistini and Ruffo; there has been a performance by the Philharmonic Choir of Beethoven's Mass in D.

Twice, and twice only, in this week of vocal music was anything like great singing to be heard. The perfect instrument and the accomplished performer came thrillingly together on only two occasions—in the performance of Miss Dorothy Silk in the Beethoven Mass and of Battistini in his recital of mixed Italian songs. Here we heard the real thing—tremendous voices of the purest and richest quality worked by singers who knew their business perfectly and who thoroughly understood the music they were singing. They gave one that peculiar and special emotion which only the perfect human voice can give.

Mr. Robert Radford followed them fairly close; but his voice, fine and

ample though it is, lacks some intangible quality of distinction, and so falls
short of the highest. Mr. Norman Allin proved himself at Covent Garden
to be an accomplished singer; but nature has not endowed him with a sufficiently powerful instrument, and he cannot claim a place among the
great ones. Titta Ruffo, on the other hand, has been very generously
treated by nature. He has an enormous voice that comes jetting out of
him, easily, effortlessly, like a fountain of some beerier liquor; a jet, shall
we say, of black and creamy Guinness. Now Guinness is a fine thing, but
somehow it cannot be associated with the highest flights of the human
spirit, except, possibly, with the comic flights. And the same is true of
Signor Ruffo's rich, thick voice. It is a voice for comic singing, a voice that
is made for nice, jolly, bad music. And he proved the fact by giving us, at
his last week's concert, a marvellous version of that popular tango-song,
"El Relicario."

Let us pass now from the singers to what they sang. The only novel
item in the National Opera Company's repertory, *The Goldsmith of
Toledo,* proved to be a great disappointment. This opera, which is reputed
to be by Offenbach, turns out in actual fact to be a work patched up by
two ingenious editors out of Offenbach's posthumous notebooks, with a
tune or two stolen from his other operas thrown in; the whole embedded
in a setting of dimly Wagnerian recitative that contrasts oddly with the
fragments of Second Empire melody. The work as a whole is completely
inartistic and undramatic, as the Offenbach fragments have no relation to
the plot—for which, of course, they were not originally written; and
though one enjoys some of the genuine tunes well enough, one is sadly
bored long before the end, and bored with an *ennui* that contains a strong
dose of irritation. Offenbach wrote a great many very amusing and agreeable operas, which it would be delightful to hear. Why the National Opera
Company should have chosen to perform this bad apocryphal work, when
they might have given everyone pleasure by reviving one of the good and
genuine operettas, passes all comprehension.

Parsifal was the other most important event in the first week of the
Covent Garden season. The singing was, on the whole, very sound and adequate, though it was never exciting. The acting was less good; but then, is
it possible to act in Wagner? As for the machines and the scenes, such as
the cottonwool swan and the flower maiden's pantomime garden, those
were as solemnly absurd as usual.

Writing a few weeks ago of Easter music, I had occasion to speak of
the somewhat unpleasant quality of the religious emotion in *Parsifal.* It is
a fine work, it is exceedingly effective (one thinks of the amazingly stage-
managed ceremonial scene in the first act); but it has uncommonly little to

do with real religion. Within the space of a few days one had the opportunity of hearing *Parsifal* and the Mass in D. Comparisons may be odious, but one couldn't help making them. Between the composer of the Mass and the composer of the opera a great gulf is fixed. Beethoven moves in a world of purity and sublimity, to which Wagner has no access. The composer of *Parsifal* is too much preoccupied with his eternal sex problems and his visions of material splendor to be able to find the way into it.

[*The Weekly Westminster Gazette*, May 13, 1922]

Patriotism and Criticism

PATRIOTISM is a virtue that should be practiced with discretion in matters of art. Let us by all means be patriotic about the home-grown art of which we can feel justifiably proud. Where the English product is definitely and absolutely good, let us say so—loudly and with, perhaps, a more than ordinarily emphatic jubilation. But our pride in the native product must not make us disparage or misunderstand foreign talent. Our ancestors' exclusive admiration for Italian opera and Italian singers was as silly and unreasonable as their exclusive admiration for English academic painting. The business of the enlightened critic is to recognize good work from whatever source it comes, and to educate himself into understanding all manifestations of art, however unfamiliar they may seem at first sight or hearing.

I am prompted to make these remarks by having read in last Sunday's *Observer* the comments of Mr. P. A. Scholes on the Vatican Choir and the British National Opera Company. To the Opera Company Mr. Scholes gives unreserved and copious praise; a loud, contemptuous sniff of disapproval is all he has for the Vatican Choir. Now all criticism is principally a matter of opinion and personal taste; but it is obvious that there are certain standards, certain universal notions about the good and the bad in art, fixed points to which the reader of the criticism can refer the taste and opinions of the critic. Mr. Scholes, it seems to me, has set up his patriotism in the place of these standards, and in speaking of the English opera company and the Italian choir he overpraises the one as unjustifiably as he disparages the other. To be able to say that the National Opera Company is in the front rank of excellence, one must first blot out from one's mind many memories. The best operatic organizations at home and abroad—one must forget how they sang and acted. One must forget Battistini, one must forget Frieda Hempel; for if one remembers them one will discover that there are no voices in the National Opera Company that can be compared with theirs. One must forget Chaliapine and the Russian crowds in

Boris; for if one remembers them, one will find that there are no great actors and no superbly trained choruses at Covent Garden today.

No, let us give the National Opera Company its rightful due, no less and no more. It is a sound, business-like, efficient organization, but it cannot be said to be particularly distinguished. Mr. Clarence Whitehill, recently recruited to its ranks, is the one great singer of the company, the only one whose voice gives one that peculiarly intense emotion which only the human voice—and the human voice at its very best—can give.

As for the Vatican Choir, it is dismissed by Mr. Scholes into the outer darkness for the not very adequate reason that it does not sing like an English church choir. One wonders why on earth it should. People of different races have different timbers of voice and different traditions concerning its proper use.

Mr. Scholes blames the Vatican Choir because the boys are trained to make a greater use of chest notes than our choir boys. They do. (It is worth remarking, by the way, that they were most chesty in the phrases of greeting with which the concert courteously began. In the religious music of which the real program consisted they used chest notes much less frequently.) The effect produced by the boys' chest notes and by the somewhat throaty tone of the tenors is certainly unfamiliar and un-English; but it is far from unpleasing, when one has grown used to it. It is an effect of passion and of force, not at all out of keeping with the music of Palestrina and Vittoria, in which the inspiring emotion is a strong and passionate religion. The tone of the lower men's voices is as rich and beautiful to English as to Italian ears; you do not have to get used to the basses in the Roman choir. I can hardly remember a more noble and splendid piece of singing than that of the men alone in Vittoria's *Tenebrae.*

Of Monsignor Casimiri's conducting one can be more justifiably critical. He has trained his voices to an extraordinary pitch of precision; there are few choirs, even in this choral England of ours, that can sing so consistently and so faultlessly in tune as his. It is a responsive instrument in his hands, and he uses it to get all the dramatic effects out of it that he can. It is here that criticism begins. The music of the great sixteenth-century masters is fundamentally dramatic under all its intellectual formalism, and a conductor is quite right to insist on this dramatic quality, particularly before an audience that is unfamiliar with the bewildering technicalities of the style. Monsignor Casimiri's fault is that he tries to be too often and too violently dramatic. Too much contrast defeats its own end; it ceases to be dramatic. Still, to any one unprejudiced by excessive patriotism, the performance was a very interesting one. And if it had been less remarkable than it actually was, one would have been grateful for the opportunity of hearing so much sixteenth-century music.

How wonderfully satisfying that music is! Intellectually and emotionally, as architecture and as drama, as pure music and as pure religion—it satisfies in every way. Which was the finest thing in last Saturday's program? It is hard to say. The most moving and emotional piece of music was certainly Vittoria's *Tenebrae*. Palestrina's *Improperium* followed very close. Perhaps the most perfect as works of art were the motets on words from the *Song of Solomon*. Written in 1582, at the moment of his completest maturity, these twenty-nine motets are among Palestrina's finest achievements. The three selected by Monsignor Casimiri last Saturday— *Vox Dilecti, Tota pulchra, Nigra sum*—served admirably to illustrate Palestrina's power of expressing the most delicate shades of emotion implied in the words. This expressionism, if we may be permitted to use a pleasantly meaningless and rather Teutonic locution, is carried to surprising lengths in the *Exultate Deo,* with which the program was brought to a close. Here, when the words exhort us to praise the Lord on various instruments, the music suggests the sound and quality of each instrument in turn. We hear the shawm, the harp, the tympanum, the hollow note of the trumpet. The voices are made to render the essential spirit of the orchestra.

In the Jubilee Year, 1575, a company of fifteen hundred people from the town of Palestrina, in the Campagna, marched in solemn state into Rome, singing as they went the music of their great townsman, who walked in the place of honor at the head of the procession. After listening to last Saturday's concert one cannot be surprised at their enthusiasm and their civic pride. There are only one or two greater names than Palestrina in all the history of music.

[*The Weekly Westminster Gazette,* May 20, 1922]

The Criticism of Music

THE PROBLEM which must be faced by anyone who would criticize music intelligibly, to his own and his readers' satisfaction, is a difficult one. There is no long-established tradition of musical criticism, and there are no supreme masters of his art to whom the musical critic can look for guidance. The reviewers of books can turn to Coleridge, to Sainte-Beuve, to Remy de Goncourt, and see how these masters did his particular job. But the critic of music has no patron saints to direct him; he finds no well-trodden path by which to approach his subject.

Two prime difficulties confront the musical critic; two pitfalls yawn, the horns of a dilemma dart their double prongs at him. To quote or not to quote? He is liable to get into trouble whichever way he answers that question. Suppose he decides not to quote—or, what is more frequently the case, suppose that his publisher, or his editor, or his printer decides that musical quotations take up too much space, are too expensive and give altogether too much trouble to be worthwhile: he is then in the position of a man who makes a statement, but who cannot bring evidence in support of it.

If, on the other hand, the critic does decide, or is allowed, to quote, he finds himself faced with dangers and difficulties of almost equal magnitude. To begin with, his quotations, if they are to be of real value, should be long and complete—and it is practically impossible, in the ordinary newspaper or book, that they should be. At best he can only quote snippets, at best a telescoped version of the score. In the next place, the majority of his readers will not be able to appreciate the full sense of his quotation by the eye alone. For while the sense of music is probably as widely, or as narrowly, distributed as is the sense of poetry, the amount of musical illiteracy is enormous, even among those who enjoy and understand music when they hear it. These are the difficulties of the musical critic who makes extensive use of quotations. His danger consists in a tendency to become too technically analytical in his quotations, too much preoccupied with the purely formal and constructional side of music. Formal analysis is interesting and instructive; but it is not enough, it is not criticism.

The ideal musical critic is a man who is perfectly at home with the technical part of music, but whose interest in it does not blind him to the larger emotional and intellectual aspects of composition. He must understand and he must be able to make other people understand; in a word, he must be able, like all other critics, to write well. Give this ideal man his ideal conditions and he will be permitted to quote at whatever length he likes, happily certain that his ideal audience will be able to follow wherever he leads them. However, the ideal conditions do not exist and the ideal musical critic still remains to be seen. Meanwhile, let us take a glance at a real critic of considerable interest whose book has recently been published in England.

Mr. Paul Rosenfeld, the author of *Musical Portraits, Interpretations of Twenty Modern Composers* (Kegan Paul), is one of those polyglottic, multicultured Americans who appear to be perfectly familiar with all languages, all arts, all knowledge. Mr. Huneker[7] was the most considerable of these critical cosmopolitans, Mr. H. L. Mencken is another; Mr. Rosenfeld threatens to carry on the tradition. *Musical Portraits* is an interesting book, and would probably be a good book if Mr. Rosenfeld possessed the

7. James Huneker (1860–1921). New York music and drama critic.

critic's first attribute—an ability to write well. Unhappily the interesting
things which Mr. Rosenfeld has to say are buried under layers of verbiage
so dense, so opaque, that we sometimes can hardly see the shape of his
thoughts. He aims, in his style, at being enthusiastic, picturesque, loud-
voiced. He is more often merely verbose and absurd. He tells us, for example, that Strauss's orchestra "has become a giant terrible bird, the great
auk of music, that seizes you in its talons and spirals into the empyrean."
Reference to the unenthusiastic pages of the encyclopaedia reveals the fact
that "in size the great auk was a little less than a tame goose," and that its
"most striking characteristic was the abortive condition of its wings . . .
proving its total inability to fly." But for those who take the trouble to ignore his great auks and his purple passages, Mr. Rosenfeld has plenty of
sound things to say. Very interesting, for example, are his comments on
Strauss's earliest music. "It was Nietzsche who had made current the
dream of a new music, a music that should be fiercely and beautifully animal, full of the dry good light of the intellect, of salt and fire. . . . And
though Strauss himself could scarcely be mistaken for the god, nevertheless he made Nietzsche's dream appear realisable." That is admirable; let
us give *Till Eulenspiegel* his due in spite of *Salome, Elektra,* and the un-
speakable *Joseph.* Admirable too is the gist, if not the actual form, of his
essay on Wagner, "the sign and symbol of the nineteenth century"; admirable his judgments on Moussorgsky, the musician through whom

> many long dumb voices,
> Voices of the interminable generations of prisoners
> and slaves,
> Voices of the diseased and despairing and of thieves
> and dwarfs,
> Voices of cycles of preparation and accretion,

are so grandly and so movingly expressed. Mr. Rosenfeld has something
true and something original to say about almost every one of his twenty
composers, who range from Berlioz and Liszt to Bloch and Ornstein. His
is a quotationless criticism, and one asks oneself, as one closes the volume,
whether it would not have been better for a few exemplary excerpts. Mr.
Rosenfeld might have given us a typical passage about the great auk. Or
he might have quoted from *Boris Godounov,* and reduced the dithyrambic
description of the human suffering in which Moussorgsky's music has its
roots. But even as it stands, his book is worth looking into.

[*The Weekly Westminster Gazette,* May 27, 1922]

A Problem of Musical History

THE HISTORY OF MUSIC abounds—for me, at any rate—with problems of a delightful obscurity, problems on which one may speculate with unending pleasure and with almost no practical fruit. I was recently discussing the most puzzling and the most absorbing of these problems with a friend of mine who is a good musician and a knowledgeable classical scholar. Our debate started with a question: What would have become of Beethoven if he had been born in Athens in the fifth century B.C.? And it rambled on into a general consideration of music at large—the birth, the growth, and the nature of the beast.

I am still wondering what would have happened to Beethoven if he had been born in the fifth century B.C.; what did happen, as a matter of actual fact, to the Greek equivalents of Beethoven, or even to the more modest musical geniuses, who must have been born as frequently in ancient Greece as they have been in modern Europe. It is something of a conundrum. We are putting the case of a man, capable potentially of writing the Mass in D and the Ninth Symphony, who comes into the world at a time when harmony does not exist, when there are no instruments more effective than a penny whistle and a rudimentary harp, when the singing voice is scarcely permitted to overstep, upwards or downwards, the limits set by the voice in ordinary speech. What does he do? The correct answer, I imagine, is: he doesn't. He doesn't—he can't, of course—write that Mass or that Symphony; he can produce nothing that is remotely comparable to music as we know it. In Greece one must do as the Greeks do, and in this matter of music they did very inadequately indeed.

One is astonished that so sensitive and artistic a people as the Greeks should have been able to work off their musical emotions in the monotonous tunes and the slavishly verbal rhythms of their singing. It was, no doubt, an unsatisfied craving for music that made them attach so much importance to the harmonious qualities of language. It is almost legitimate to believe that those fantastic sophists of the decadence, like Eunapius and Philostratus, those rhetoricians who cultivated language, not that they might express ideas or emotions, but for its own magically colored and melodious sake, were in some sort thwarted musicians; and the people who listened to them so greedily and with such a fine connoisseurship of style—they, surely, were the familiar figures whom one sees, night after night, in the concert rooms of contemporary London.

It is only for the last four or five centuries that music has existed as an independent and self-sufficient art. Why it ever emerged from its preharmonic childhood is a mystery; and why, considering the fact that the vast majority of human beings are now seen to be capable of appreciating the most elaborate forms of music, why the art did not grow up much earlier is a still greater mystery. One is appalled to think of the vast amount of genius which must have run to waste for lack of a shapely and sufficient artistic receptacle into which it might have poured itself. All preharmonious Beethovens were doomed from their birth to be mute and inglorious; for there was no way in which they could adequately express themselves. Fortunately, however, they were themselves unaware of the fact. We find it almost impossible to recreate in ourselves the state of mind of a Greek musician; but he would be absolutely totally incapable of even beginning to imagine how we felt about his art.

It took some ten or twelve generations for the musical faculty of modern Europe to evolve from a rudimentary hardly harmonic state to the elaborate perfection of Beethoven. In that short space of time a whole new spiritual universe was discovered and opened up. The seeds of what other faculties lie undiscovered or barely noticed within us, waiting to be cultivated? In five hundred years' time, it may well be, we shall all be clairvoyants, and the man who lacks second sight will be as rare and pitiable a figure as the man of today who cannot distinguish between *The Rosary* and *Rule Britannia*.

[*The Weekly Westminster Gazette*, June 17, 1922]

The Question of Form

THE DISINTEGRATION of the old traditions of form in music and in poetry has had the effect, among other things, of showing up very clearly the defects and dullnesses of the minor composers and the minor poets. The important artists have, of course, evolved new forms possessing as much validity, as much right to their existence, as much cohesion and unity within themselves, as the old. The lesser men have not had the capacity to make their own forms. Bereft of the support and guidance of the old conventions they are lost, and the ideas they have are expressed chaotically instead of in order. Furthermore, the mere working out of the old formal rules, if it was done skillfully and intelligently, did something, in the work of the lesser men, to make up for any inherent dullness or weakness in the root ideas. A Toccata by Galuppi, shall we say, may not be particularly profound in its emotional or intellectual import—though there always is, as a matter of fact, a curious little flavor about Galuppi which lingers very pleasantly on the palate—but there is, in its polished and patterned form a certain elegance, a style, a traditional swagger. It is, perhaps, an unreal, an extrinsic elegance, which the composer did not create. But an elegance it is, and it gives the hearer pleasure. This extrinsic elegance of tradition was, perhaps, the most remarkable characteristic of Purcell's incidental music to the *Amphitryon* of Dryden, produced so admirably by the Phoenix last Sunday. There was no great wealth of invention in it, but it possessed a neatness and a charm.

In contemporary works we have no extrinsic or traditional beauties to please us. Such formal, architectural satisfaction as we get is derived from the form evolved for the nonce by the composer himself. There is a great deal of architectural pleasure to be derived from Debussy's *Après Midi d'un Faune,* from the *Gibet* of Ravel, from Stravinsky's *Firebird,* or *Petrouchka.* But the form that pleases us in these works is created specially for them, and their elegance is an intrinsic elegance. The works that the lesser artists create outside the old formal tradition are automatically and by definition without extrinsic elegance (unless, of course, they are working in the new tradition of one of the modern masters); they are also, as we only too frequently find, lacking in intrinsic elegance, they possess no real form of their own.

This point, it seemed to me, was very well illustrated last week at M. Koussevitsky's second concert. The program on this occasion was divided into two distinct parts, the first of which consisted of old music, the second of modern music. In the first we had Handel's Concerto Grosso, Beethoven's first piano concerto, and a hitherto unperformed work by John Sebastian Bach's most accomplished son, that Charles Philip Emanuel Bach, whom Dr. Burney admired so much—perhaps too much— and Frederick the Great perhaps too little. The second part consisted of Ravel's choreographic fragment "The Valse," De Falla's "Gardens of Spain," and Rimsky-Korsakoff's "Capriccio Espagnole."

The emotions which one derived from this concert were as sharply contrasted as the two parts of the program. The first part gave the most exquisite pleasure; the second overwhelmed with an almost unrelieved boredom. It was nothing to do with the performance; for M. Koussevitsky conducted and M. Cartot played as brilliantly in the second as in the first part. It was simply that the music of the first part was (to use the useful Thomistic word) "informed," and that the music of the second was without form and chaotic. The Concerto Grosso is a fine work by one of the greatest masters and the First Piano Concerto is a poorish work by the supreme genius of music; it is perhaps unfair to compare the Ravel and the De Falla with these. But with C. P. E. Bach, that man of sound learning and respectable genius, they may be compared on equal terms. The fact that emerges from this comparison is that C. P. E. Bach said what he had to say very much more fully and completely and satisfyingly in his brisk contrapuntal allegro and his grave and penetratingly beautiful adagio than

Ravel and De Falla have succeeded in doing in the free and elaborate orchestral contrivances of the "Valse" and the "Gardens of Spain." Carl
Philip Emanuel's work has the extrinsic elegance of traditional form coupled with the intrinsic elegance of form that is born of the right, the inevitable expression of an idea. Ravel and De Falla have neither the one nor
the other. "The Gardens of Spain" is rambling, thin, and weak; the
"Valse" is diffuse and heavy. There is no emotional logic in either; they
have no inevitable shape. The result is that they bore one, as one listens to
them, most unconscionably.

What is the moral of all this? I hardly know. The pedagogues might deduce a moral obligation on the part of our contemporaries to write like
Carl Philip Emanuel. But that, of course, won't do. No, the only conclusion I can draw is the not very cheering one which follows. Those who,
working outside the old formal tradition, try to evolve new forms and who
fail in the attempt, must expect to be more boring than the older musicians
of no greater caliber, who had the extrinsic elegance of traditional form to
supplement their lack of ideas.

[*The Weekly Westminster Gazette*, June 3, 1922]

Literary Music

THE PROGRAM of Harold Bauer's recital last week included, besides
Schumann's curiously tedious Fantasia in C and the beautiful Prelude,
Aria, and Finale of Franck, the *Pictures at an Exhibition* by Moussorgsky.
Of Mr. Bauer's playing it is not necessary to say much; he remains what he
was when we last had the pleasure of hearing him, years ago—a soundly
excellent, solidly classical performer. It is of Moussorgsky's *Pictures* that I
propose to speak, of these and of the general ideas which the hearing of
them suggests.

For one cannot listen to a piece of progam music—and Moussorgsky's
suite of pictures is an admirable specimen of this musico-literary kind—
without reflecting a little on the relations of music to the non-musical facts
of existence. Ought music to be program music? Should it have an external literary theme? And does the best music, as a matter of historical fact,
belong to the literary or the unliterary variety? Let us consider the facts
first, and then go on to the theoretical principles.

The facts, on examination, would seem to be against literature. The
most tremendous and beautiful music that one can think of is not literary.
Take, for example, Beethoven's last piano sonatas and his last string quartets. They have no theme but themselves. One cannot say that this emotion

or this particular experience inspired them. They are, in a strange and transcendental way, inhuman. There are things in Ops. 109 and 111 that have no relation to our ordinary experience. They are not emotional; one cannot say that they are expressions of grief, or joy, or love, or despair. They are just music, the most prodigious music that has ever been written. This same inhumanity (I use the word in its current sense, according to which those qualities we share with the brute creation are "human" and those which belong uniquely to *Homo Sapiens*—the intellectual and spiritual qualities—are "inhuman")—this same inhumanity is found in the great fugues of Bach, in Mozart's symphonies, in certain things of Brahms, in much of Palestrina. A large amount of the supreme music of the world is not merely not written round any external literary subject; it is not even expressive of any particular emotion; it is, as we have said of Beethoven's latest work, just music.

But it is also true that a great deal of very beautiful music is literary, is immediately and dramatically expressive of emotions. The Moussorgsky *Pictures,* with which we started, are an example; they give one, all questions of musical values left out of account, a very great satisfaction as literature. Take the beautiful picture "Rich and Poor"—it is as moving, as truthful, as a chapter from Dostoevsky. It is a complete description and judgment of society. Strauss has given us wonderful musical renderings of characters and scenes; Wagner, the greatest of the literary composers, has created a whole epical system in terms of harmony and melody. One could lengthen the list almost indefinitely. As for the direct expression of emotion; that can be done more effectively in music than in literature. The direct expression and evocation of feelings is one of the principal functions of music. Between the poignant simplicity of folk-song and the poignant complexity of Debussy, music can express almost anything that can be felt.

But lovely as this literary and directly emotional music often is, it is never—one feels it without being able to give any very adequate explanation why—it is never quite so completely satisfying as this other music, which has no literary theme and expresses no specific or easily named emotion. Wagner is not so satisfying as Bach; one is quickly tired of Strauss's *Till Eulenspiegel,* never of Mozart's G minor Symphony; the directly emotional appeal of Tschaikowsky's "Pathetic" can be made too often, but there is forever a new exaltation, a new and indescribable source of life in the last sonatas and quartets of Beethoven.

[*The Weekly Westminster Gazette,* June 10, 1922]

A Few Complaints

FINDING MYSELF some few days ago in Paris, I went, piously and dutifully, to the Opera, to see the Russian Ballet, and to listen to Stravinsky's
new one-act musical comedy *Mavra*. My evening proved to be somewhat
depressing. Shorn of its best performers, M. Diaghileff's troupe made but a
poor show; Lopokova and Massine were only too conspicuously absent.
Their successors are hardly worthy of the supreme, the "absolutissimous"
position which they occupy. Idzikovsky has powerful legs but a feeble
head. And one can make the same criticism, in duly politer terms, of Mlle.
Trefilova; she has a great technique but no personality. At its best, dancing
may enrich music and adorn it; at its most subtle it may suggest interesting
interpretations. But dancing that is a mere display of agility adds nothing
to the music, and quickly grows tedious. Agility is one of the dancer's essential attributes, and we hold no brief for the amateurs who try to make
up for lack of muscle and defective training by excess of "temperament"
and "art." Technique is as necessary to the dancer as it is to the pianist—
and in both of them it is nothing without a directing intelligence, a controlling personality.

The other item in the evening's entertainment was even more depressing than the ballet. *Mavra* is depressing in spite of its gaiety, in spite of its
witty accomplishment—depressing because, in its prodigious triviality, it
simply isn't there, it doesn't exist. Like almost all the rest of Stravinsky's
most recent works, *Mavra* shows in a deplorable and unmistakable fashion the influence of the "young" French musicians. The dadaism which
does not permit the Frenchmen to undertake anything that is in the slightest degree serious, or vigorous, or noble, or strong, seems in some sort
to have infected Stravinsky. The man who wrote *L'Oiseau de feu, Petrouchka,* and the "Sacre," now occupies himself with little musical jokes
of no greater significance than *Ragtime* and *Mavra*.

It is a melancholy thing to see the worse and the sillier assimilate to itself the better and the more intelligent. That is what seems to have happened here. The French Six[8] are more "civilized" and urban, older and
possessed of a greater sophistication than Stravinsky. One can imagine
him feeling in their presence as a countryman might feel on finding himself
among a company of faultlessly well-dressed and correctly cultured men-
of-the-world in the dining-room of the Ritz. They have shamed the Russian out of his native seriousness and vigor. We shall soon see him, no
doubt, producing *Morceaux en forme de poire,* variations on Brazilian
tangoes, tone poems about goldfish and the like; and the result of this

---

8. The six are Durey, Honegger, Milhaud, Tailleferre, Auric, and Poulenc.

happy consummation will be the loss to Europe of one of its most interesting and original composers.

Having started this article on a note of complaint, I may as well go on in the same strain—for there are always plenty of things to complain about—to the bitter end. Let me make haste, then, to introduce a second subject as carpingly petulant as the first. I would complain of the dullness and lack of enterprise characteristic of so many concert programs at the present time, and of the introduction into otherwise excellent programs of utterly unworthy pieces of music. Let me give two recent examples. The program of Casals's recital last week included the noble Brahms cello sonata (played, it is almost unnecessary to add, superbly), a fine Handel, an unfamiliar Sammartini. All these were excellent. But what excuse was there for the Saint-Saëns, the two pieces by Fauré, the Florent Schmitt? There was none—except, perhaps, the fact that the repertory of cello music is unfortunately small. And why was it necessary to choose from among the six cello suites of Bach the almost too familiar C major? There are ten performances of the C major to one of the other suites; and yet they all are good. If we are permitted to listen to Casals only once in a season, may we not be allowed a program that is all good and, if possible, not too familiar?

My other example is the second recital of Harold Bauer, at which a very considerable time was taken up by a performance of Schumann's worst work, the *Scenes from Childhood*. Why Mr. Bauer should have chosen to waste our time and his talent on this almost imbecile stuff is a mystery. He has not even the cellist's excuse—limitation of repertory. When there are several hundred first-class piano pieces in existence, one is not justified in playing a work of the fifth class.

The dullness and staleness of many recent orchestral programs might also be illustrated, if this were necessary, by examples. The justification here is generally of an economic character. Rehearsals are expensive; it is cheaper to stick to the old familiar things. Still, that justification is not always and entirely satisfactory. Why, for example, do we so rarely hear any of the big symphonies of Mozart? They do not need very elaborate rehearsal by a competent orchestra; and yet how rarely these rapturously beautiful things figure upon our programs! But the fact remains that the financial problem of music has become serious. It will have to be solved somehow within the next little while, if we are not to be deprived of our orchestral concerts. What the solution should be, I am not competent to say. State support, reduction in the size of the band—these are two obvious ways out. Another alternative would be decentralization and the tapping of a larger musical public by means of concerts given in outlying quarters of London. There is something to be said in favor of all these proposals.

[*The Weekly Westminster Gazette,* June 24, 1922]

Mr. Lawrence's Marchioness

THERE IS a character in Mr. D. H. Lawrence's recent novel[9]—the Marchesa del Torre—who has ceased to be able to listen to harmonized music. The sound of two or more notes played simultaneously makes her feel sick. The fact that the hero of the novel is a flutist, and so can play only one note at a time, endears him to the Marchesa, and it is on the strength of the flute's limitations that they become lovers.

Now the Marchesa, Mr. Lawrence admits it, was a little neurasthenic; the violence of her reaction to a chord was not normal. Not many of us, I suppose, are made to feel sick by a harmony; but there are moments, nevertheless, when we can sympathize with the unfortunate Marchesa; moments when harmony, certain kinds of harmony in particular, seem strangely distasteful, almost nauseating. Listen, for instance, to those rich, glutinous chords which support on their pillars of treacle the sagging melodies of the ballad; one does not have to be one of Mr. Lawrence's Marchesas to feel revolted by harmonies such as these. And even the decent music, from which the popular sentimental stuff is ultimately derived, the romantic music of the nineteenth century, with its rich, perpendicular harmonies laid on to the musical canvas. In great masses of colored sound—even this may inspire us sometimes with a sudden sense of disgust. We find it all too sumptuous, too emotional and luscious. We pine for something much simpler—for the fine, pure melodies of Mr. Lawrence's flutist or else for something which, though it may be as highly complicated and sophisticated, is harder and clearer and purer in its sophistication; we pine for the austerer complexities of pure polyphony. An exclusive diet of nineteenth-century music is unhealthy in the long run. The best remedy for the qualms from which the poor Marchesa suffered is an occasional dose of folk-song and pure melody and a regular course of sixteenth-century choral music and eighteenth-century counterpoint.

The Oriana Madrigal Society is one of the organizations which benevolently dispenses the antidote to those sickly poisons which envenom, rankly or subtly, so much of the music of the last hundred years. They ad-

9. See chapter 16 of Lawrence's *Aaron's Rod* (1922).

ministered in their summer concert last Tuesday a stimulating and astringent dose of English sixteenth- and seventeenth-century music. The whole of the first part of their program was a tonic draft of pure polyphony. The concert opened with the fifteenth-century song of Agincourt, which was followed by two madrigals of Wilbye, a Psalm for Six Voices and Strings by Byrd, a religious Round by Lawes, a madrigal by Weelkes, a cheerful, prancing Ballet by Thomas Tomkins, and one or two other pieces belonging to the same period. Here was music that could not have offended even Mr. Lawrence's Marchesa. There was nothing which one could conceivably call sickly in the melancholy of Wilbye's "Draw on, sweet night," or in the rich, renaissance sensuousness of the same composer's "Sweet honey-sucking bee." The five or six parts slide over and through and across one another, each apparently aware only of its own rich variations of rhythm and changing phrases of melody, and together creating, almost accidentally, a harmony that is moving and expressive without being deliberately emotional. How exquisite, too, was Lawes's Round, "She weepeth sore to the night." Using a modified form of the "Three Blind Mice" principle, Lawes produces an effect of religious sadness that is incomparably pure and chaste. In this sort of music one gets the best of both worlds; one is given all the purity of melody coupled with all the complexities of harmony, and at the same time one is spared that conscious emotionalism which gives the sickly taste to so much of the perpendicular harmony of modern times.

I had hoped at the Oriana concert to hear some more than ordinarily choice folk melodies—something utterly fluty and single for the sake of that ghost of a neurasthenic Marchesa that was haunting me at the moment. But I was disappointed. Miss Patuffa Kennedy Fraser sang a number of Hebridean songs to the accompaniment of a Celtic harp. But I cannot say that I found them particularly satisfying. Readers of *Twenty Thousand Leagues Under the Sea* will remember the enchanting scene when Captain Nemo is discovered in the music saloon of his submarine playing Scottish tunes exclusively on the black keys of his organ. Miss Kennedy Fraser's performance reminded me a little of this romantic improvisation. None of the airs were particularly interesting or striking, and most of them had a certain softness and sentimentality which did nothing to assuage the Marchesa's sickness.

I looked forward, in the next section of the program, to hearing the Londonderry Air, that most penetratingly moving of tunes. What was my distress to find that it had been so sumptuously "arranged" in four parts by Mr. Percy Grainger[1] that its native beauty was entirely lost. The whole

---

1. Percy Grainger (1882–1961). Australian composer, pianist, and conductor.

beauty of the Londonderry Air consists in its long, clean, curving lines. Mr. Grainger's elaborate harmonization simply obscures those lines. Something simple, something beautiful in its way and moving has been turned, by this unnecessary exercise in harmonization, into something rather frowsy and dim and dull. The effect on the Marchesa, I may add, was deplorable.

[*The Weekly Westminster Gazette,* July 1, 1922]

Supplementing the Concerts

I GAVE VENT in these columns, not long ago, to certain complaints about the quality of our concert programs. I deplored the lack of novelty and variety, the admixture of dull, bad music with the good. Today I propose to show how gaps in the season's programs can be filled up, how concerts in the halls may be supplemented by concerts at home. I propose, in fact, to write a little treatise on the delights of the gramophone. Not, of course, that the gramophone is or should be our only home instrument. The piano or (for those who have no fingers but only feet) the pianola is indispensable. The fiddle is desirable; the enthusiastic amateur string quartet is a golden ideal. But the gramophone, with its faithful reproductions of instruments we cannot possibly be expected to play, of orchestras, of astonishing voices singing rarely performed works—the gramophone is also a necessary luxury for all musically minded people, whether they go to concerts or not. Let me describe a typical happy evening passed in the company of one of these beneficent machines.

I open my concert with a little Early English music—two madrigals sung by the English Singers. One is Weelkes's rollicking "Sing we at pleasure," with its beautiful changing rhythms; the other is a cradle song by Byrd, "Lullabye, my sweet little baby," a thing of long-drawn melancholy harmonies and haunting repetitions. A movement from Mozart's concerto for flute and harp follows. This ravishing work was played in its entirety some little time ago—at one of Mr. Goossens's concerts, I think it was. It is not likely that we shall hear it again for many a long day, and one is grateful to have this fragment of the delicate, pure, and passionless music preserved on a disc for post-prandial delectation. After the Mozart I feel that I should like, for a change, a little modern orchestration. What about Stravinsky's *Firebird,* conducted by Beecham? I follow this up with *Till Eulenspiegel* and the *Après Midi,* and I am only deterred from playing *Le poème de l'extase* by the thought of Scriabin's enormous pretentiousness.

By this time I have had enough of modern orchestration. I pine for pure melody and the human voice. Battistini in *La ci darem* is my next item. What a voice, what science and accomplishment! To hear Battistini in the recitative which leads up to the duet is a revelation. And now that we are started on Mozart operas and first-class singers it is difficult to stop. I put on Frieda Hempel as the Queen of the Night in *The Magic Flute.* It is the sort of record which makes one sadly realize that the recent opera season at Covent Garden was not all that it might have been, or all that its admirers said it was. More Mozart. I try Titta Ruffo in "Deh vieni alla finestra." His voice is naturally fine and powerful, but a little vulgar. Still, his rendering of the serenade, taken rather surprisingly slowly, is moving. From my German records I select Maria Ivogün in the marvellous air, "Martern aller arten" from the *Seraglio.* Her voice is a less powerful version of Frieda Hempel's—pure, flute-like, faultlessly on the middle of the note.

After this it is time for a little chamber music. I open the ball with the Flonzaley's splendid rendering (beautifully recorded) of the fugue from Beethoven's C major quartet, Op. 59, No. 3. That whets one's appetite for string music. I play through all the three discs on which Mozart's G minor quintet is recorded. Next, I take my choice from among Beethoven quartets recorded by the London. The noble Largo from Haydn's Op. 76, No. 5 is followed by the first movement of the Ravel quartet, which is followed in its turn by two movements from the Brahms quintet for strings and clarinet. And I end up this section of the concert by the amazing record made by Kreisler and Zimbalist of Bach's Concerto in D minor for two violins.

Feeling in need of a little relaxation after so intellectual a masterpiece, I listen to the Versatile Four playing "El Relicario" on banjoes. A real pick-me-up in moments of depression, this record. I follow it up by Tetrazzini singing the "Carnival of Venice," as arranged by Benedict from the violin solo of Paganini. These "Carnival" records must be heard to be appreciated; they are ravishingly comic. After this I put on a still more extraordinary record—Chaliapine and the chorus of the Scala in "Ite sul colle, o Druidi" from Bellini's *Norma.* The solemn romantic air, sung as only Chaliapine can sing, the romping chorus of the Druids—once heard, these are unforgettable. The combination of sublime singing and ridiculous song produces an astonishing effect.

Our minds being now sufficiently relaxed, we return to more serious stuff. Two fugues by Bach and two sonatas by Scarlatti played on the harpsichord by the most accomplished performer on that lovely instrument, Mrs. Gordon Woodhouse, have a bracing effect.

After that I listen to Mozart's "Ave Verum Corpus" and the "Kyrie" and "Gloria" from Palestrina's Mass *Aeterna Christi,* sung by the Westminister Cathedral Choir. And with this solemn and beautiful music in our

ears let us bring the concert to a close; for it is growing late. One last ciga-
rette and one last record while it is being smoked. I choose at random. It is
a French disc—a *chanteuse* singing "Je suis veuve d'un colonel," from Offenbach's *Vie Parisienne*. Mozart and Palestrina are forgotten in this gor-
geously grotesque anti-climax. What a song, and what a singer! Nobody
but Offenbach could have invented a tune so metallically vivacious, and
nobody but a French *chanteuse* could produce a series of such piercing little yelps as are uttered, to the accompaniment of castanets, in the couplet.

This is but one of many home concerts with which one may supplement the programs of the halls. One could compile plenty more of them
from the records of the two big English companies alone. And for those
who have the patience and the means to explore the foreign markets, there
are German and French and Spanish and Russian records; there are Hindu
and Chinese records. What matter if concert programs are dull? The gramophone offers us a remedy.

[*The Weekly Westminster Gazette,* July 8, 1922]

Orientalism in Music

I WAS PRESENT last week at a concert, given at the Royal College of
Music, where the program included, besides such large and monumental
works as the Brahms Variations on a theme by Haydn, a number of
smaller and lighter pieces. Among these airier morsels was a violin-solo
setting of Rimsky-Korsakoff's *La Chanson Hindoue* and Bizet's "Farewell
of the Arab Hostess," which comes, if I remember rightly, from the one-
act opera, *Djamileh*. Listening to these two pieces, which were performed
within the space of a few minutes, I could not help thinking of what is
comprehensively termed "The East," which was, indeed, just what the
composers had meant me to do. But they certainly did not mean I should
go on to speculate in a vague inaccurate way about Orientalism in general,
and its influence on Western music. That, however, was what I found myself doing; and since the subject seems not wholly uninteresting I shall go
on speculating about it here.

Orientalism was the vogue in literature and the arts long before it became anything like the fashion in the world of music. Lady Orford had
stuck up in the chastely Italian rooms of the Villa Medici her Cathayan
wall-papers, Voltaire had written Oriental tales, Chippendale had made
furniture in "the Chinese taste"—all the orientalizing writers and decorators of the eighteenth century had come and gone again before the spirit of
the east began to leak into music. Mozart, it is true, made beauty out of

abduction from the seraglio; many operas by Grétry and others had Oriental names; Turkish marches were frequently composed; but there was nothing in all this eastern music of the eighteenth century but the politest occidental culture.

It is not until well on in the nineteenth century that we find anything like a serious Orientalism in European music. In the Hungarian March from the *Damnation of Faust,* for example, one hears an early hint of it. A little earlier, that poorish but very serious composer, Félicien David, had published his Oriental Melodies, which were based, one imagines, on a real knowledge of Oriental music; for he had spent several year at Constantinople and Smyrna. His symphonic ode, *Le Désert,* obtained a prodigious success at its first performance in 1844, and it is from these middle years of the nineteenth century that Orientalism begins to be popular among the public and is taken seriously by the musicians.

The conscious nationalism of the Russian "Five" (composers, we may add parenthetically, of a very different order from the well-advertised "Six" of contemporary Paris) was inevitably an assertion of the right of Orientalism to be taken even more seriously than it had been before. For the native Russian music on which Moussorgsky and Borodine and Rimsky-Korsakoff (to say nothing of the other two, Balakireff and Cui) based themselves, was a largely Oriental music. The Russians made Orientalism classical and familiar.

What exactly is it that music has acquired by this assimilation into itself of the Oriental? It has acquired, in the first place, the power of expressing barbarity and savagery artistically. A new note of strange and poignant emotionalism is the other acquisition. The barbarity is chiefly expressed by the rhythms and the harmonies, the strange and poignant emotion by the melodies derived from Oriental music. *Prince Igor* is a good example of the eastern savagery, *La Chanson Hindoue* and the *Hymn to the Sun* of the new poignancy. The complicated and exciting rhythm of the tom-tom, the crude and unfamiliarly simple harmonies, and the queer wandering line of wailing melody have been taken from the East and incorporated into Western art.

The oriental contribution is a valuable one, and the fact that Orientalism has been horribly vulgarized in modern popular music in no way takes away from its value. The music to *Chu-Chin-Chow* could never have come to being if Rimsky-Korsakoff and Borodine and Moussorgsky had never existed. And in just the same way, the drawing-room songs of the nineteenth century would not have been what they were if Beethoven had never written the "Moonlight" and the "Appassionata" and *Adelaide*—if he had never opened up new possibilities of emotional expression. People are apt, in matters of art, to visit on the fathers the sins of the degenerate children. Nothing could be more unjust. Beethoven made romanticism and sentimentalism possible in music; but he was not a romanticist or a sentimentalist. And, in the same way, the introducers of Orientalism have made possible a hideous form of sophisticated savagery and naïveté, cheap exoticism. But that does not mean that Orientalism need always be cheap and flashy and insincere. Looking back we can see, indeed, that the East has done much towards the enlargement and enfranchisement of modern music.

[*The Weekly Westminster Gazette,* July 15, 1922]

Music in a Museum

CASUAL VISITORS to the National Gallery, last Tuesday afternoon, must have been struck, at about half past two, by the large concourse of people who were assembling in the four rooms which form a cross about the domed *rond-point* at the east end of the building. Chairs had been produced from somewhere in those capacious cellars in which the gallery keeps its superfluous masterpieces, and the assembly was waiting in comfort. For what? The stroke of three brought the answer. We were all waiting—to be precise and personal—for Mr. Loris Blofield, Miss Marie Wilson, Mr. Pierre Tas, and Miss Ida Starkie. These young musicians had come from the Royal College of Music to play quartets among the pictures, and the four or five hundred knowing or lucky people who had come to the Gallery that afternoon found that they had bought, for the price of their sixpences, something more than the privilege of looking at the pictures; they had bought an hour and a half of good music, most capably performed, as well. It was, even in this season of summer sales, a conspicuously good bargain.

The authorities in charge of the National Gallery and of the Royal College of Music are to be congratulated on their enterprise. Let us hope that the success of this first concert—for it was, most decidedly, a success, both as regards the numbers and enthusiasm of those who listened and to the quality of the playing—will encourage them to go on with the good work they have inaugurated. The more gratuitous music we can get, even though it be brass-band music, the better. And when this gratuitous music is chamber-music and the best of its kind, then indeed we have reason to be grateful and, at the same time, greedy for more. For of all kinds of music, the music of the string quartet is, I suppose, less familiar to the general public than any other kind of music. And—a fact to be deplored, when we consider how much of the world's most perfect music is written for the string combination. To be able to listen, as one could last Tuesday, to a quite satisfying rendering of Beethoven's nobly romantic Op. 95 (listen to it twice, for the players gave a welcome repetition of it), and to a characteristic specimen of one of Haydn's quartets, all for sixpence, is a privilege which should be granted frequently and to as many people as possible. That is why I hope that these free chamber concerts may become a regular institution at the National Gallery. The function of a museum is to spread gratuitously artistic and antiquarian knowledge. Why should they completely neglect the loveliest and most intimately moving of all the arts—music? The ideal museum, it seems to me, should be furnished as a matter of course with a music-room in which performances of a definitely instructive and historical character would regularly be given. This National Gallery concert (the first, let us hope, in a long series), marks a step towards the realization of this ideal. Let me commend the example of the authorities at the British and the Victoria and Albert. Even at Burlington House a little music would not be out of place, though it would require a good loud military band, rather than a poor little string quartet, to compete with the blaring vulgarity of most of the pictures which hang upon its walls.

Mr. Collins Baker of the National Gallery is reported, in last Sunday's *Observer,* as saying of this concert: "Music among pictures in a building of this sort must create an aesthetic atmosphere, and give a stimulus that the pictures by themselves may not produce." It is difficult to be quite certain what this means—unless it be a restatement of the well-known fact that more people can appreciate music with intelligence than can appreciate a work of visual art. People's attention is distracted from the real aesthetic point of a picture by the story and the associations, as it never can be from the essential beauty of a piece of music. (Only a few days ago, for example, I found myself, in a bus, sitting next to two young ladies who were discussing, very earnestly, whether it was possible for a picture to be beautiful if it did not represent beautiful scenes or persons. They decided that it was not possible. It did not occur to them, however, to go on arguing that music could only be beautiful when it imitated naturally beautiful sounds; and the fact that it should not, could not have occurred to them, explains why music is, on the whole, more intelligently appreciated, and by a larger audience, than painting.)

But to return to Mr. Collins Baker's somewhat cryptic sentence. Does he mean to imply, I wonder, that the "aesthetic atmosphere" created by the music will help people better to appreciate the pictures at the Gallery? That, after listening to Beethoven's Op. 95, one will see a new significance in the Piero della Francesca *Baptism?* If he does mean to imply this—which, of course, he may not—I think he is probably wrong. If the "pictures by themselves" do not produce the necessary stimulus, no amount of "aesthetic atmosphere" created by music will serve to make them do so. Either you enjoy pictures or you don't; and music is either a revelation or an irritating noise. The fact that you can appreciate one art will not help you to enjoy another to which you are congenitally blind or deaf. No, if we demand a place in our museums for music it is not that visitors may be stimulated by it into an appreciation of other kinds of art. Music should be represented in museums for the same reason as painting and sculpture are represented—because it is a fine art about which it is spiritually profitable for people to know something.

[*The Weekly Westminster Gazette,* July 22, 1922]

Popular Tunes—Past and Present

SOME five-and-twenty years ago, when I was a young man, I remember distinctly going to Hammersmith and listening to about half an act of one of the earliest performances of *The Beggar's Opera.* What it was that prevented me from sitting through the whole performance I have now completely forgotten; but the fact remains that, until last Monday, I was the only person in London who had not yet heard *The Beggar's Opera* in its entirety. On that date the good resolutions of a quarter of a century matured in action. For, since the musical season was dead, definitively dead without hope of resurrection till the beginning of the Proms in London, and the Festival Concerts in Salzburg, there seemed no further excuse for not going to Hammersmith—there was every reason, indeed, why I should go. I went.

When Rich first produced the Opera in 1728, its enormous success (the success which made "Rich gay and Gay rich") was largely due to its strong flavor of political satire. It will be remembered that the sequel, *Polly,* was suppressed by the Lord Chamberlain—and suppressed for political, and not, as one might have expected, for moral reasons. The hugely greater success of Mr. Playfair's production, two centuries later, has had nothing to do with politics. It is due to the fact that, in *The Beggar's Opera,* the post-war public has got something which, in its present spiritual condition, it wants. That a refusal to take things very seriously, or to be bothered with the moral problems, that cheerful *Je-m'en-fichisme* which are so typical of the after-war attitude towards life, have been very clearly reflected in the world of art. *The Beggar's Opera,* with its total disregard for morality, the horrifying flippancy (for the flippancy is horrifying, when one thinks of it in cold blood) of the way in which it treats such subjects as death, could only have achieved its success today. Ten years hence it will probably fall as flat as it would have fallen in the mid-nineteenth century. It represents us as we are here and now. Some of us may have preferred the subtler humor, the wittier and more brilliant music, the artistically finer setting of the *Boutique Fantasque*. But the *Boutique* is first cousin to the Gay-Playfair-Fraser-Austin production. In those two entertainments a great part of the contemporary spirit is, somehow, inextricably tangled.

The music of *The Beggar's Opera,* which consists of a pretty character-istic collection of early eighteenth-century popular airs, makes one marvel, as one listens to it, at the enormous gulf which separates the music-hall tune of today from the music-hall tune of two hundred years ago. The music of *The Beggar's Opera* is never glutinously emotional, is never las-civious, is never nervously noisy as contemporary popular music is. Why? Are we to suppose that the public of Gay's time was different from the public now? Clearly not. People were quite as sentimental, lascivious, and noisy then as they are at the present time, or as they will be at almost any future date before the millennium. They did not express these qualities in their music simply because they had, in 1728, no adequate musical meth-ods for doing so. Listen, for example, to any sentimental airs from *The Beggar's Opera,* and compare them with any capably written sentimental air of today; you will find that it simply does not express the things which the contemporary music expresses only too well. (The fact that the music is so unemotional is, of course, one of the reasons why the piece has been so successful with a public that is tired of emotions.) Handel and Gluck and Mozart and Beethoven had to experiment in the dramatic musical ex-pression of feeling; Chopin had to devise yearning sequences of chords; César Franck had to modulate richly and sumptuously and incessantly; Wagner had to be loudly passionate; and Debussy delicately, subtly melan-choly; two hundred years of incessant musical activity had to take place before the modern sentimental song could be as luscious, lascivious, and sweetly disgusting as it is.

When *The Beggar's Opera* was written, the mold into which most of the sentimentality of the last century has been poured had not even been invented. It was not till 1770 that the first waltz-tune was written—and a remarkably unsentimental, unlanguorous piece of music this primeval waltz was; for it was no other than that friend of all our childhoods, "Ach, du lieber Augustin," a piece of music to which the dancer must revolve at the rate of at least thirty-five revolutions a minute. Chopin's waltzes, though they bring their rich quota of emotionalism, are too complicated to be danced to, and the real creator of the popular sentimental waltz was the immortal Johann Strauss. In 1826, Strauss produced his first opus, the

"Täuben-walzer"; in 1837 he was all the rage during the brilliant London season which witnessed the young Queen's coronation; in 1849, on his return from his last trip to London, he was escorted down the Thames in triumph by a flotilla of decorated barges, from one of which a band brayed out the master's most celebrated dance tunes. The waltz had come to stay. Waldteufel and the younger Strauss kept up the grand Viennese tradition. Tschaikowsky, in his "Valse des Fleurs," and in his superb waltz-dance from the *Sleeping Princess,* introduced new languors and lusciousnesses. Since his day the popular waltz writers have been content to repeat his achievement, with variations. It remained for another Strauss, Richard this time, to increase once more its range of emotionality. And having reached the "Rosenkavalier" waltzes, how immensely far we find ourselves from the simple, straightforward, formal elegance of the little tunes in *The Beggar's Opera*! It is a great relief to turn back, every now and then, to these "unexpressive nuptial songs"; but there can be no doubt that the popular music of the future will develop an ever-increasing expressiveness, and that "The Rosary" is more truly in the movement than "How happy could I be with either."

[The Weekly Westminster Gazette, July 29, 1922]

Let Us Now Praise Famous Men

IN A RECENT ISSUE of the *Times,* Mr. Clutton Brock let fall the following statement: "William Morris is as great as Tolstoy." Reading these words I was a little startled. I looked to the head of the column to make quite sure that I had made no mistake about the name of the author of the article. The notion crossed my mind that I might have misread it, that perhaps the article was by Mr. Grock, not Mr. Brock, and that this pronouncement was a most exquisitely amusing piece of clownery. But no; the initial letter was decidedly B and not G. There could be no doubt, to anyone acquainted with Mr. Brock's writings, that the remark was intended quite seriously. Well, well. "De gustibus nil nisi bonum; tot homines, quot disputandum est." Let us leave it at that—the moral being that there is no certain, logical method by which one may detect a great man. Greatness is a quality to be apprehended, in the last resort, intuitively. How do we know, for example, that Mozart is a greater man than Rossini, or that the mystical writings of Jacob Boehme, unfamiliar and fantastic as they may often seem, are of enormous importance, while those of Joanna Southcote, or even of Mrs. Besant, are not? We don't know, except by a kind of inward certainty that William Morris is a great man—as great as one of the greatest of the men of letters. I sincerely hope that there are more people who feel my negative than feel Mr. Brock's positive certainty.

There is one man about whom, along with Shakespeare and a few others, a great many people have felt, intuitively, very certain indeed; that man is Beethoven. And since the musical season is now over, and there is nothing better to do than to praise famous men, let me string together a few reflections about the greatness of L. van B., even at the risk of being considered by the admirers of Erik Satie a witty clown or a hopeless imbecile.

It is not entirely apropos of boots, and because there is nothing else to talk about, that I write this article. What prompts me to choose Beethoven as an object of contemplation is the fact that I have recently wormed my way through the three dense volumes of Thayer's biography, which appeared not long since in its definitive English edition. Flushed with this triumph of endurance (for the book is as long and, in spite of its absorbingly interesting subject, almost as dull as Mr. James Joyce's *Ulysses*)! I turned back to another biography of the composer which I had not read for many years—the *Vie de Beethoven,* of Romain Rolland. Neither of the books is a satisfactory biography; but their unsatisfactoriness is interesting. For by studying the defects of these two books one sees, first, how the life of a great man should not be treated, and in the second place, how, ideally, it should be treated. In the present article I shall deal with Rolland's little study, reserving for another occasion a consideration of Thayer's huge amassment of facts.

One of the chief drawbacks of being a great man is the fact that, during your life and for long centuries after it, you are doomed to be the prey of innumerable small men who dissect you, re-invent you, use you as propaganda, slobber over you, abuse you, take the credit of you, make money out of you. Last year the Italians were celebrating Dante. The best thing they could find to say about the world's most intellectual poet was that he was an irredentist and an imperialist; the day of his birth was celebrated by an enormous review, the day of his death, more harmlessly, by bicycle races. On poor, defenseless, Shakespeare, the propagandists have fallen like hungry wolves. There is Mr. J. A. R. Marriot, the Oxford historian, who thinks Shakespeare is at his best, his truest, his most sincere, in *Henry V*; and there is Mr. Gerald Gould of the *Daily Herald,* who would have us believe that the same play is the most scathing satire on militarism and imperialism ever written. Pity the poor great men!

Romain Rolland's *Life of Beethoven* furnishes us with another example of the way in which men are used to make propaganda. The propaganda in this case is moral, and all on the right side. But that does not make us resent it any the less. For a biographer of Beethoven to use the man's life as an instrument for comforting the unhappy, as a peg from which to hang a moral doctrine, is not right. He ceases to be a biographer when he does so, and becomes a preacher. Rolland's book should not be called a "Life of Beethoven"; its title should be "A sermon suggested by certain aspects of Beethoven's life and character."

Rolland's main thesis is that men, including artists, are only great by force of character. He takes Beethoven as one illustration of this general law. Now, there is probably a good deal to be said for the notion that a great artist must be a man of character, a good man. It may well be impossible that a completely despicable man, however intelligent, should ever become a good artist. But we find as a matter of historical fact, that there have been good artists who were not particularly grandiose characters. Raphael, for example, was in no sense an inspired genius of the sort beloved by romantic M. Rolland; his sentiments, as expressed in his art, were often mawkish and insincere; the manner of his death was far from edifying. And yet he is an extremely great artist. Chaucer is another; a genial pleasant man, but not, one would say, a great character. Some of the few facts recorded about Shakespeare are not particularly creditable. And Beethoven himself, truly magnificent as he showed himself, in most ways, to have been, was capable of strange moral aberrations. We learn from Thayer (not from Rolland) that he was deliberately and with malice, dishonest towards his publishers—a venial offense, but still a turpitude. No, though there is probably something in M. Rolland's thesis (one feels, for example, that Beardsley would have been a better artist than he was, and he was most remarkable, if he had been interested in nobler themes), it has not anything like the importance which he attaches to it. It is the character which decides how the gift of genius shall be employed; but it is the gift, it is the talent and the mind that are really important in the making of the great artist.

And it is precisely these qualities which M. Rolland, in his moral fervor, ignores and leaves out of account. To read this book, you might imagine that Beethoven had no mind at all; that he was merely an unhappy man who, affected by poverty and deafness, bore up nobly against his afflictions, and was therefore a great man, and a great composer. Many humble beings have borne up grandly against adversity; but the fact has not made them great artists. What made Beethoven unique was his mind, and not, for all its nobility, his character. And a biography of Beethoven which omits even the most cursory analysis of his mental processes (oh, admittedly, the analysis of a musician's mind would be uncommonly difficult to make!) is really no more interesting than *Hamlet,* without the Prince of Denmark.

[*The Weekly Westminster Gazette,* August 5, 1922]

Thayer's Beethoven

CERTAIN AUTHORS possess the secret of a kind of reversed alchemy; they know how to turn the richest gold into lead. The most interesting subjects become in their hands so tedious that we can hardly bear to read about them. Leslie Stephen, in his less happy moments, was one of these authors. The man who wrote the *History of English Thought in the Eighteenth Century* knew the secret of the philosopher's stone; he touched *or* and it became the purest *plomb*. Many others have possessed this alchemical gift. (You will find dozens of them, relatively mute and inglorious, in every university and on the pedagogic staff of every school); among them was Mr. Alexander Wheelock Thayer, the biographer of Beethoven.

Thayer deserves almost all the commendatory epithets one can apply to him; he was patient, he was industrious, he was skeptical, he was indefatigable in the pursuit of evidence, he was judicial in his sifting of it. He had all the equalities of a good biographer, except the capacity of making his material interesting to the reader. His vast life of Beethoven, now at last concluded, boiled down and re-edited in English, is at one and the same time one of the most interesting and one of the dullest of books. It is interesting, because it contains a vast number of facts about an extraordinary man, and it is dull because those facts have been presented to us in an almost unreadable form by a dull writer, who seems, fundamentally, to have been not very much interested in his subject. That a man should spend the best part of fifty years in writing the life of another man and should yet have no real interest in the object of his long researches may sound absurd, paradoxical, impossible. But that is the impression which one derives from Thayer's book. Beethoven does not seem to have interested him.

His motive for writing the book would seem to have been, not an enthusiasm for Beethoven, as a great musician or as a strange and powerful character, so much as a kind of moral indignation provoked by the lies which other biographers had told about Beethoven. In his youth Thayer heard a number of anecdotes about the great composer—romantic, picturesque, Romain-Rollandish anecdotes—heard and with a skeptical good sense disbelieved. The disbelief provoked a reaction; he felt a desire to contradict these romantic anecdotes and replace them by well-documented truths. He devoted the next fifty years of his life to exploding the old fairy tales and grubbing up, out of the dustbins of Central Europe, the real facts. But it was not enthusiasm for Beethoven that inspired him. Nobody who was really interested in Beethoven could have succeeded so perfectly and consistently as Thayer did in separating the "man" from the composer. It was enthusiasm for facts and indignation against falsehood. That the facts happened to relate to the life of Beethoven seems really to have been accidental; the slightest change in Thayer's environment at Harvard might, one feels, have made him the indefatigable biographer of Pomponazzi or Sir Kenelm Digby or the Prince Consort.

However, let us be duly grateful that Beethoven, and not Pomponazzi or Prince Albert, was the man on whom Thayer's patience and moral fervor for truth elected to spend itself. His *Life* is an inadequate biography; but the documents he has so patiently collected together in his volumes have at least made it possible for the ideal biography to be written.

Thayer's preoccupation is, as we have already remarked, exclusively with Beethoven, the man. But fortunately the affairs of the man do sometimes throw considerable light on the composer. In his efforts to fix the chronology of Beethoven's earlier works—for it was part of Thayer's business to know precisely when and where the "man" did his writing—he shows pretty conclusively that many of the pieces published under the first Opus numbers while he was at Vienna were actually composed at Bonn. The old notion was that Beethoven's genius as a composer developed slowly, and that it was not till he was twenty-five or twenty-six that he began to write anything that was worthy of his later fame. Beethoven's tardiness of development is reaffirmed by Rolland, positively and with emphasis, as though it were an established fact. The notion happens to fit in very well with his conception of Beethoven in particular and of genius in general. He wanted to show that Beethoven was a great man because he bore up against suffering and conquered it. If Beethoven only began to write well after he had suffered, then this theory of genius gains in strength and solidity. So M. Rolland makes his affirmation; Beethoven did not compose well till he had suffered for a long time. Thayer's evidence, on the other hand, tends to show that Beethoven, like almost every other musical genius of the first order, was something of an infant prodigy, and that he had composed fine and characteristic works before he was twenty. That is really no more than one would expect. For music, in a strange way, seems to be independent of experience, and can be written by a child, provided he has the gift. M. Rolland, as I remarked in an earlier article, ignores the gift; he writes of Beethoven as though he had no mind, only a moral character. It is satisfactory to find Thayer reaffirming, by the means of his cautious chronological evidence, the supreme importance of the gift—of the divine thing that was in Beethoven from his birth, and that would have expressed itself triumphantly whatever his experience had been.

[*The Weekly Westminster Gazette,* August 12, 1922]

The Salzburg Festival—I

ENOUGH is as good as a feast: the proverb holds as true of a *musikfest* as of any other kind of feast, spiritual or gastronomical. Enough music is as good as an orgy of music—especially when the fare happens to be exclusively contemporary. I have been verifying the truth of the adage by personal experience in the Mozarteum at Salzburg. Twice every day I present myself at the Temple of Mozart, at seven in the evening and at half-past ten in the morning—for one must be an early worm in Salzburg if one would hear the singing of the musical birds—I take my seat (austerely wooden and unpadded), I listen to a generous program of at least three hours' duration, and I go out again into the night or the sunshine, whichever it may be, heavy with a certain sense of surfeit. There have been moments—dare I say it?—moments when, walking through the queer baroque streets, or over the picture-book mountains of Salzburg, I have revolted from the idea of spending another evening, another sunny morning in the hall of the Mozarteum, when I have almost wished that music had never been invented. After the feast comes indigestion; but a few days' abstention from music over the week-end, and a strong dose of Mozart opera next week will doubtless put me to rights again.

The trouble with a festival of nothing but contemporary music is that its programs cannot, in the nature of things, be all good. Genius is scarce; in four or five hundred years there have not been more than a dozen composers of indubitably the first rank; we cannot expect to find many among the musicians of only a single generation. It is not mere *passéisme*, not a perverse necrophily that makes one enjoy the music of the great masters more, on the whole, than that of one's contemporaries. It is simply that one prefers a work of genius, in whatever form, to something that is not a work of genius, even if its form be characteristically contemporary. I listen with pleasure, for example, to the Kreutzer Sonata; but at the end of the second movement of Mr. Leo Sowerby's violin sonata I must either leave the building or perish miserably of septic *ennui*. And I do so, not because I am a *passéiste*, but simply because Beethoven is a great musician and Mr. Leo Sowerby of New York is a very indifferent one. But to the music of more talented contemporaries one listens, of course, with pleasure and with, besides, that peculiar, personal interest which only the products of one's own age can inspire. The only trouble about contemporary talent is the fact that it is very scarce. A long feast of contemporary music may include the talent of the day; but, inevitably, it must also include a good deal of the mediocrity—and there will be more mediocrity than talent. And now, having explained why it is easy to be surfeited at the Mozarteum, let me go on to describe in detail the items of the feast—the good, the bad, and the indifferent.

I shall take the composers, for convenience sake, by nationalities, beginning, as it is only fitting, with the Austrians, our Salzburg hosts. The Viennese contingent consisted of Joseph Marx, Egon Wellesz, Anton Webern, Egon Kornauth, Rudolf Réti, Arnold Schönberg, and a number of song-writers whose works were performed at a concert at which, unfortunately, I could not be present. Most of these were more or less completely unknown to me before I came to Salzburg; and as it is obviously impossible to pronounce anything like a definitive judgment on an unfamiliar composer on the strength of a single work, I can only give my first impressions of the strangers, hastily, and without pretending that they are more than mere impressions.

Of Marx and Kornauth, then, I shall only say that they have written two brilliant and brightly colored piano-pieces which gave me, as rendered by the admirable Paul Weingartner, a reasonable amount of pleasure.

Herr Wellesz has made himself fairly familiar to the London musical public; his quartet, however, I had never heard before this week. It did not improve my previous opinion of his music. Herr Wellesz reminds me of one of those minor, modernist painters whose works adorn the walls of the Salon des Indépendents. But he is not the genuine article, and he has nothing really new to say, in spite of his consciously ugly modern methods of expression. He is an old-fashioned romanticist, using the new muddy colors: that is all.

Rudolf Réti I know by six "Liebesgesänge" of an exceedingly rich exotic character. As we reached the culminating paroxysm of the first song, the gentleman sitting next to me murmured, "Mein gott!" I cannot do better than repeat his comment: "Mein gott. . . ."

On Anton Webern's quartet the comments were more violent. The Austrians take their music seriously, and when they don't like it, they express their disapproval in the usual manner. Webern's Quartet was hissed; it was also violently applauded. Serene, like M. Rolland, I sat *au-dessus de la mêlée,* neutral and Swiss. I sympathized with both sides, finding it easy to understand why Webern's Quartet was hissed, and easy, though not perhaps quite so easy, to understand why it was applauded. It was hissed for two reasons: first, because it was largely inaudible, being composed for the most part of infinitely pianissimo pizzicati, and the faintest cat-like harmonics; secondly, because, when it was audible, it sounded not infrequently like the amours of cats. It was applauded because some of the audible fragments were interesting enough to prove that the composer was a serious musician, and because young experimenters ought on principle to be applauded rather than hissed. However, young experimenters may go too far, and perhaps, after all, the hissers were justified. Songs without words are all right—indeed, they are admirable, considering the words which musicians generally elect to set to music. But songs without sound—that is another matter. I have no objection to an occasional noise as of cats; but noise of some sort I must have, and if Herr Webern's innovation tends towards soundlessness, then hiss! I descend and take part in the battle.

The last of the Viennese musicians, Arnold Schönberg, is by far the most important of the lot. Indeed, after hearing his *Streichquartett mit Gesang*, one is inclined, in one's enthusiasm, to think him the most important of living composers. It is a really astonishing work. The learning, and the intellectual subtlety are as richly apparent in it as in all of Schönberg's works. The musical invention is wonderfully copious and varied. What is perhaps more surprising, in a work of Schönberg's, is the passionate emotional quality which informs it. The singer's declamation is profoundly moving. The long line of song, curiously curving through strange chromatics and modulations, is beautifully expressive of emotion. Played magnificently by the Amor-Hindemith Quartet, and sung by Fräulein Félicie Mhlacsek-Hünig, Schönberg's Op. 10 amply compensated for any defects in the rest of the feast, amply justified contemporary music. Schönberg's is one of the real talents of the present day.

[*The Weekly Westminster Gazette*, August 19, 1922]

The Salzburg Festival—II

I WROTE LAST WEEK of the Austrian composers represented at the Salzburg concerts of modern chamber music. Today I shall say something of the other nations and languages. Not that nations and languages have anything particular to do with music; they have not, fortunately. But since some system of pigeon-holing and docketing is necessary if one is to deal in an orderly fashion with a large subject, one had better make use of an arbitrary and irrelevant system than of none at all.

The Germans, then, were represented by Busoni, Paul Hindemith, Guido Bagier, and one or two others whose compositions I was unable, regretfully, to hear. Busoni's music is too familiar to English audiences to need description here. What was new, what was surprising among the German contributions was Hindemith's Quartet. Herr Hindemith, who plays the viola in the admirable string combination which bears the name, must be taken as seriously as a composer as he is, already, as a player. The quartet is a masterly piece of work, which takes its place, naturally and of right, among the modern classics. For classical it is—rooted firmly in the musical past, but flowering in the present; a contemporary and truly original work that is yet a development of the great style of the past. Let me enumerate its merits. To begin with, it is extremely ingenious and elaborate in construction; one realizes as one listens that its author is a man who knows all there is to be known about the potentialities of the four instruments, and who exploits them with an admirable virtuosity. In the second place, it is full of the most beautiful musical inventions. It is by his melodies one recognizes the truly inventive musician. Hindemith's Quartet is built up on melodic lines of a remarkable subtlety and originality. Another good quality of Hindemith's work is its strongly polyphonic system of harmony. He makes his parts move with a fine independence, reminding one of the horizontal harmonization of the sixteenth-century classics. I remember, for example, one striking passage in the second movement, in which the first violin outlines an eloquent flowing melody, while the second executes a series of curious downward-sliding chromatic figures, and the tenor and bass give out a striking pizzicato theme. Altogether, it is a most remarkable achievement. This quartet of Hindemith's and Schönberg's *Streichquartett mit Gesang* were certainly the best pieces of music performed at the Salzburg chamber concerts. If the programs had included nothing worse than these, then all would be very well indeed with modern music. But alas! Schönberg and Hindemith are the exceptions; the rule is represented by such not very transcendent personalities as Herr Wellesz and Mr. Arthur Bliss and M. Francis Pontenc, with Mr. Leo Sowerby as the exception (yes, fortunately, he is an exception!) at the other end of the scale.

Herr Guido Bagier is the third of the German composers whom I have mentioned. His variations on a theme of Schumann might have been written forty years ago by some very well-taught and efficient pupil of Brahms. There is really nothing more to be said about them. Learned and marked by a reasonable amount of originality—enough, at any rate, for the invention of some not uninteresting themes—they were pleasant enough to listen to, but just a little dull, just a little superfluous, too, in this year of musical grace, 1922.

So much for the Germans. It is the turn, now, of the Hungarians—Belá Bartók and Zoltán Kodály. Bartók's violin sonata, by which he was represented at Salzburg, was performed this summer in London by Miss Selby D'Aranzi and the composer. I have nothing to add to what I said of it on that occasion. It is a remarkable work, full of a sort of barbaric fervor. If I enjoy it less than the Schönberg and the Hindemith, it is because Bartók's "unrelated sonorities" (I believe that is the correct way of describing his harmonization) are not sufficiently systematic for my taste. One of the pleasures of music is the intellectual pleasure derived from following out the developing arguments of musical logic. It is a pleasure I cannot get from Bartók, whose music provides me only with a vigorous, emotional enjoyment.

Kodály's Serenade for two violins and viola is based on the classical system, its "sonorities" are not "unrelated"; it is possible to follow his arguments with intellectual pleasure. Not that the pleasure is purely intellectual; for the serenade is full of feeling, and contains passages of remarkable purity and beauty.

[*The Weekly Westminster Gazette*, August 26, 1922]

The Salzburg Festival—III

IT IS THE TURN in this article of the French, the Italians, the Spanish, the English, Americans, Scandinavians, Czechs, Dutch, and any other nationalities whom I may not previously have mentioned. About some of these contemporary musicians I cannot speak as intelligently as I could wish, since, for one reason or another, I was unable, at Salzburg, to listen to their compositions. The works of the French and Italian composers, for example, were mostly crowded into a single concert which I unfortunately missed. Not that I immensely regret not having heard Honegger's Rhapsody for two flutes, clarinet, and piano; Koechlin's Sonata for two flutes; Poulenc's Spanish Caprice for oboe and piano; and Magnard's Quintet for flute, oboe, clarinet, bassoon, and piano. No, I cannot imagine, from what I know of the French school, that this feast of woodwind would have been particularly sustaining—though it might occasionally have tickled the palate agreeably. But still, since the satisfaction of curiosity and the acquisition of knowledge are almost the only pleasures in life, I am sorry not to have heard this concert. And what makes me sorrier still is the fact that it included two songs by Pizzetti and five more by De Falla, all sung by Marya Freund. Now Pizzetti is an admirable musician, and the ablest of the contemporary Italians, and De Falla, though he can be feeble enough when he tries (witness those dreary "Gardens of Aranjuez" of his), can also be delightfully brilliant. A piano piece by him, performed at a later concert, proved this sufficiently well.

The English contingent included Dame Ethel Smyth, Mr. Bliss, Mr. Gustav Holst, Mr. Arnold Bax, Mr. Gerard Williams, and Mr. Armstrong Gibbs. On what principle the names of Elgar, Vaughan Williams, and, above all, of Delius were omitted; why, too, English music was represented almost exclusively by songs, I cannot imagine. Another year—for if political providence, in the shape of Poincaré and Lloyd George will refrain from destroying what little remains of Europe, the Salzburg Festival of modern music is to be annually repeated—let us hope that English achievement will be more completely represented. Not that the things we did hear were bad. The Holst songs were beautiful; those of Bax, though not up to that composer's best standard, were pleasant enough; the elaborate Odelette of Dame Ethel Smyth was extremely workmanlike in construction. But these things did not completely represent our music.

We now come to the Americans, represented (unrepresentatively, I hope) by Mr. Leo Sowerby. I have had occasion to mention Mr. Sowerby before. Indeed, his Violin Sonata threatens, I plainly see, to become my King Charles's head. Such a work! The violin maundered on interminably, fortissimo, with a hollow, stagey eloquence; while the piano, worked by the composer himself, emitted the most banal of rumbling accompaniments, that sounded like one of those dreary improvisations strung together by gifted amateurs who pride themselves on never having "learned music." Its effect on me was such that I had to leave the Mozarteum after the second movement. This is why I have nothing to say about the Scandinavian school, whose works immediately followed those of Mr. Sowerby. I am sorry to have done this injustice to Denmark and Sweden; but the fault, it will be seen, was not mine.

Only one Dutch composer made his appearance, and that was Mr. Willem Pijper, whose Sonata for violin and piano was a very refined (or should I say "refained"?) and discreetly sentimental piece of conventional music which might have been written for performance in a high-class—but excessively high-class—cinema.

The Czech songs of Messrs. Kricka, Vycpalek, and Vaclav Stepan were much more to the point. They were real music, of which one would have liked to hear more.

I have left to the last the consideration of one of the most interesting of the contemporary musicians heard at Salzburg. Bloch's nationality is, I suppose, American; at any rate, he has for a long time lived in the United States. But he was born and brought up, I believe, in Switzerland, and by race he is a Jew. This last fact has some significance, for Bloch has been ambitious to make himself the musician of the Hebrew tradition. His *Hebrew Melodies* are not the elegant shams of Byron; they are founded on the ancient Jewish chants. His *Psalms,* his *Schelomo,* are rooted in the Jewish musical past; even his portentous *Macbeth* has this same Jewish quality.

At Salzburg Bloch was represented by two considerable works—*Schelomo,* a Rhapsody for cello and piano, and the violin Sonata. *Schelomo* was played by that excellent cellist, Alexander Barjansky. (The piano part, unfortunately, was very poorly performed.) The Violin Sonata was given by Joseph Szigeti, with Carl Friedberg at the piano.

Bloch is a composer to whom one listens with mixed feelings. One cannot help admiring him, for he is a fine musician, whose conceptions are spacious and grandiose. At the same time, one cannot help (or at least I cannot help, for I speak only for myself) rather disliking his music, for all its workmanlike competence and the fine ideas and emotions that inspire it. There is a curious quality of clottedness about Bloch's music: it is, so to speak, overcharged, too heavily loaded with tragic emotions and conceptions. Bloch, one feels, is being too consciously the Michelangelo; the grandeur and tragedy are laid on too thick, and there is a certain impurity about them. This is particularly true of the *Schelomo*. For the first ten minutes it sounds extremely impressive. This, one decides, is the grand, noble, modern work for which we have all been waiting. But before it has come to its conclusion, the thing inspires a curious repulsion. It won't do: greatness, tragedy, heroism are not really like this—they are better, somehow; finer, purer, more transparent; this stuff is surcharged, its greatness is fundamentally theatrical.

The Sonata is a better work—finely constructed and full of exciting invention. But the same quality still lurks in it, tantalizingly spoiling what might be so tremendously good.

[*The Weekly Westminster Gazette*, September 2, 1922]

Mozart at Salzburg

AFTER SAILING so long on the troubled waters of modern music, after straining through its obscurities and groping down its tortuous channels, after lying stranded sometimes for hours on its arid sandbanks waiting for a new, generous high-tide of art to float one off, after all this beating about among unexplored archipelagos, it was a relief to find oneself once more in the familiar sunny Aegean of Mozart's operas. It was delicious to float on waves that rose and fell with the undulating grace of "Che soave Zeffiretto," to glide past neo-classical islands, from which deserted heroines complained, with an Ovidian sweetness and elegance, to the tune of "Dove son di bei momenti," and sirens with rich baritone voices tempted the frailer sex with "La ci darem" and "Deh, vieni alla finestra." It was delicious, this voyage in friendly and beautiful waters; it was rich. But a request for truth compels me to add that it was not quite so delicious as it might have been, not quite so sumptuously rich as the presence on board our pleasure boat of Dr. Richard Strauss and the Vienna Opera Company had led us to expect.

The company, take it all round—and that, after all, is the right way to take an opera company—is a good one. At Salzburg it was divided into two detachments, of which the first, consisting of the most accomplished performers, played in the best of the operas, *Don Giovanni* and *Figaro*, while the second detachment, less good on the whole, but containing one or two fine singers, such as Fräulein Schumann, dealt with *Cosi fan tutte* and *Seraglio*. There are no superlatively good singers in the company, no Battistinis, no Hempels; but all are reasonably good, and one or two are admirable.

The part of the performance of which I had expected most and which, in its quite remarkable badness, was most disappointing, was the setting. I had gone to Salzburg hoping to see a ravishingly witty, Goyesque setting to *Don Giovanni*; to see in *Cosi fan tutte*, a fantastic, eighteenth-century Naples; in *Figaro* a brilliant caricature of France at the end of its *ancien régime*. They order these things of the stage so well in Germany, or at any rate with so much care and pains, that I felt justified in expecting from the Viennese as much as I would expect from the Russian Ballet. What was my disappointment at finding, to all the operas, a setting that would not have done much credit to "Mother Goose" as performed by a traveling pantomime company in an English provincial town. The scenery was frightful in its old-fashioned vulgarity: the costumes were nothing at all—artistically nothing, I mean, for literally and ethically they were ample; and everyone was up to the eyes in Jaeger. And even if the scenery and the dresses had been perfect, it would have been difficult to enjoy them in the municipal Theatre of Salzburg, where they have a habit of leaving all the lights in the auditorium, aggregating the power of almost as many candles as there are crowns in a sterling pound, burning during the whole time of the performance. In the glare and the dazzle, it is impossible for the eye to take much pleasure in the objects presented to it on the stage.

The most remarkable thing about Strauss's conducting was his insistence on all that can be called sentimental in the operas. In *Don Giovanni*, for example, he took pains to tone down the comic asides of Leporello in the two scenes with the statue almost to inaudibility. They might not have been there at all for all the attention he paid to them; and yet how enormously they add to the dramatic intensity of the situation when they are fully and grotesquely insisted upon! This is a particularly obvious example of what I may call his sentimentalizing tendency; it could be paralleled by his treatment of many other passages. In a composer of so much dry, salty, and witty music as is Strauss, this tendency seemed rather surprising. But then one must remember that, besides *Till Eulenspiegel* and the

Rosenkavalier, Strauss has written plenty of music of a treacly sentimentality. The one thing comes as naturally to him as the other. One regrets,
however, that it should come naturally to him to treat *Don Giovanni* in
terms of *Ich Wollt ein Sträusslein binden* rather than of *Till Eulenspiegel.*

[*The Weekly Westminster Gazette,* September 9, 1922]

Popular Music in Italy

IN THE DAYS of the good Doctor Burney and of that exquisitely sophisticated Cocteau of the late eighteenth century, the inimitable Beckford,[2]
Italy was a land of never-ceasing music. Daily at the Misericordia in
Venice, Galuppi conducted his concerts, and behind their grille the clear-
voiced young orphans sang his cantatas and his embroidered airs, or with
nimble fingers called out of the harpsichord one of the master's crisp, tart-
flavored toccatos. At the other orphanage, Piccini presided; the churches
rang with new rococo masses and cantatas; at the San Moisé a score of
new operas were produced every year. And if you went to Bologna, there
was Father Martini, the most learned musician in the world; while on the
outskirts of the town stood an elegant little Palazzo, where the ancient cas-
trato, Farinelli, Grandee of Spain and Knight of Calatrava, lived on the
ghost of his own fabulous reputation, devoting his twilight existence to
good works and the education of an odious little nephew. You called on
him, and with great politeness he would show you his treasures—his harpsichords named after the great painters, Raphael, Correggio, Carlo Dolci;
his jeweled snuff-boxes from all the crowned heads of Europe; his portrait
by Amigoni (which would remind you of another less flattering portrait by
Hogarth). But his greatest treasure, the wonderful voice that was as far superior to all other voices as the racehorse "Childers" was superior to all
other horses—the voice he would not show off, that had departed forever.
From Bologna you hurried on to Rome, where Easter week, with Allegri's
Tenebrae attended you; thence to Naples, to listen to the cheerful card-
parties in the private boxes at San Carlo taking down the most powerful
soprano with their loud, incessant chatter.

Italy in 1922 is singularly different from the Italy of Burney and Beckford. Milan, it is true, has Toscanini, one of the greatest of living conductors; Rome has regular and excellent concerts—Malipiero, Respighi, and
especially Pizzetti are interesting composers. But there is nothing comparable to that incessant output of music—much of it possessing a real value—

2. William Beckford (1760–1844). English novelist.

that incessant performance, that universal preoccupation with the art which we find in the eighteenth century. Walking through the streets of an Italian town today you hear no itinerant musicians playing with that native taste which delighted Burney; you hear no charming voices singing charming songs. In the course of the last eighteen months I have been in many parts of Italy, and I do not remember more than two or three occasions when I have heard anything sung or whistled, in the streets or among the fields, that was not either the sentimental tune which is, I believe, called "Salome," or the marching song of the Fascisti; and of these two the Fascist air is enormously the more popular. In certain districts, no doubt, at Sonzana, for example, where the Fascisti last summer came to bloody disaster; in certain quarters of the big towns the strains of the "Red Flag" will be heard more frequently than those of the Fascist hymn. But everywhere in Italy the music of the streets, the music of whistling errand boys, and strollers who hum as they walk, is political music.

And what deplorable stuff this political music is! The Fascist hymn has the silliest and most irritating tune that has ever been written. Other famous political airs of history have justified their long-drawn-out popularity by their musical merit. "Trelawney," "Lilliburlero," "Rule Britannia," "The Marseillaise"—these are all excellent tunes. But the Fascist march is abject and infuriating; after the third hearing of it one becomes a convinced Communist.

Of all that rich and varied popular music which gladdened Dr. Burney on his Italian travels, the only thing that seems to be left is this one imbecile tune. Which simply means, I suppose, that the mass of Italians today are interested in other things than music. The energies which, in the past, were devoted to painting pictures and composing and executing music are now devoted to politics and business and engineering. Italy is a new developing country as well as a country with a past; the ubiquitousness of the Fascist tune signifies that the Italians are preoccupied with immediate and practical problems, and that they have not the leisure to devote themselves, like their fathers, to the arts. One evening, a week or two ago, I was sitting at a café table in the Piazza at Venice. A brass band belonging to the Royal Marines made its appearance in the center of the huge square and began to play. It opened its program with the Italian national anthem, that most gaily comic of patriotic hymns. Loyal, we rose from our tables before the glaring cafés—all except one man. A Socialist, evidently, a "subversive," a Communist. He was immediately assaulted; Fascisti knocked him down, officers trampled on him, the crowd yelled, and a stout old gentleman climbed on to a table and made a violent speech, to which nobody paid the slightest attention. In the end the Socialist was seized by a posse of carabiniere and dragged off to the Piombi, or wherever it is that prisoners of State are now confined in Venice. But the incident was by no means closed. The crowd continued to make patriotic demonstrations for at least half an hour—thereby rendering almost completely inaudible the "Tancredi" of Rossini which was being patiently played by the Marines in the center of the piazza, as though nothing had happened. As for me, I shed a silent tear. For that Venetians should prefer making a demonstration in favor of the House of Savoy to listening to a masterpiece by the son of a hornblower of Pesaro, seemed to me a melancholy and deplorable thing. But like the Fascist tune, it is symptomatic.

"Il Fascismo è lirismo."

Action, action! One can have too much of art.

[*The Weekly Westminster Gazette,* September 16, 1922]

Some Very Young Music

ON MONDAY LAST, at the Grand Theatre, Brighton, an audience that was at moments positively enthusiastic listened to the first performance of Mr. Adrian Beecham's musical setting of *The Merchant of Venice*. If rumor and the daily press are to be believed, Mr. Beecham is still very young. Not, indeed, exceptionally young as musicians go; for at Mr. Beecham's age of seventeen, your true infant prodigy has a long career behind him. Mozart composed a song at four, pieces for the harpsichord at five, and at twelve a work for strings which is still regularly played—a masterpiece. Beethoven, as Thayer's investigations show, had written large portions, at any rate, of some of the works attributed to his maturity before he was eighteen. And only a few weeks ago, I myself saw a child of four, the son of a great virtuoso, who could sing through most of *Parsifal*—he had heard it once—and who used to sit through long concerts of classical chamber music, listening with an absorbed and intelligent interest. So that Mr. Beecham is really quite old, after all. If he were destined to become a great musician we should have the definite proofs of it at seventeen. It is not absurd, as it would be if Mr. Beecham had appeared before us with a work of literature or painting, to pass a critical judgment. Part of the poet must certainly be born, but a great deal of him must also be made. A musician is so largely born that he can give proofs of his genius before he has had the formative experience which is necessary to the poet.

But to return to Brighton and last Monday night. Mr. Beecham, I think it is safe to assert, is not the Mozart of the future. But he is a young man with a definite gift which might, if it were cultivated, make him a writer of excellent musical comedies, or even a Sullivan, or, conceivably, even a minor Verdi. He has the gift of melody. His setting of *The Merchant of Venice* is nothing more or less than a long string of Italianate tunes, varied by reminiscences of Mozart and rollicking echoes of Sullivan. But always, in spite of the obvious derivativeness, there is a touch of individuality, a melodic style. The tunes, in spite of everything, are Mr. Beecham's own.

Tunefulness is his gift. It remains for him to discover that music is made up of other things besides tune—a compound not merely of sugar and spice and all that's nice, but having a strong admixture of snips, snails, puppy dogs' tails, counterpoint, harmony, development, tone, color, and many other things. The tunes in Mr. Beecham's opera come romping out one after another; the singers sing—generally one at a time, for Mr. Beecham is shy of tackling the intricacies of part writing; the orchestra tootles along vaguely. Before Mr. Beecham can become even a writer of musical comedies, he will have to learn a great many boring and disagreeable things.

Mr. Beecham's love of tunes makes him forget to be dramatic. Shakespeare's blank verse does not inspire the music; it gets jammed into the airs, anyhow; sound governs sense. There are lyrical Verdiesque passages about Shylock's rates of interest and the beginning of the trial scene is set to a tune that might be an old Piedigrotta prize-winner. The setting of "All that glitters is not Gold," was almost the only dramatically correct piece of music in the whole play. That was really excellent.

But the most remarkable thing about the performance was this: that, good or bad, everything in it was prodigiously old-fashioned. To have been able to ignore the existence of every musician since Sullivan, and of a good many who preceded him, is surely a very remarkable feat in one so young. One wonders in what monastic seclusion, apart from the musical life of the world, Mr. Beecham has spent his seventeen years. He has not the remotest conception how a dramatic effect can be obtained on the orchestra; he has never heard Strauss, nor even Wagner, or, for that matter, Meyerbeer. His boldest harmonic experiment is an arpeggio of major thirds expressive of horror. A young monk, brought up in a strange old tradition, has emerged upon the world. It is a curious spectacle. All the other young musicians of near Mr. Beecham's age whom I know are iconoclastically up-to-date. They like Italian tunes, but only for fun and because they are so comically mid-Victorian. They enjoy irony and intellectualism in music; they like amusing noises; they know all the orchestral tricks. They are, in fact, totally unlike Mr. Beecham in every possible way. Mr. Beecham might do well to borrow from his young contemporaries some of their hardness, their wit, their intellectuality, their knowledge of harmony and the orchestra. In return, these young contemporaries would be well advised to take from Mr. Beecham some of his simple, unironical singleness of purpose, his acceptance of common standards of sentiment, his love of melody, and his ability to make a good tune. Old-fashioned and new-fashioned—both would benefit.

[*The Weekly Westminster Gazette*, September 23, 1922]

Reflections in the Promenade

IT IS a melancholy thing to come back from a holiday, it is horrible to have to work, it is disgusting to breathe sooty air and to eat food cooked as only English restaurateurs can cook it. "Quel moine," exclaimed Saint-Amant, when he visited England in the 1600s:

> Quel moine au ventre bouffy,
> Accepterait le deffy,
> D'avaler leurs tripotages?

But still,

> Though (I do not thank God for it) I do hate
> Perfectly all this town.

London certainly has its compensations. It is pleasant, after an almost musicless month in Italy, to be able to stroll out every evening after dinner to the Queen's Hall and be sure, on any night but Saturday, of hearing something worth hearing, well played.

Some time ago, when writing of the chamber concert given under the dome of the National Gallery, I suggested in these columns that music should be given a place—its rightful place as the most moving of all the educative civilizing arts—in our museums; that there should be a department attached to all the great national and municipal repositories of ancient art, whose business it should be to give properly illustrated information about music in all its stages of development. I am delighted to find, by a recent correspondence in the Press, that other people are preoccupied with a similar idea. The suggestion that public libraries should stock gramophone records, whether for lending or for performance on the spot, is an excellent one. My only criticism of the scheme is that it is not sufficiently far-reaching. An adequate musical museum cannot be made up of the gramophone records issued by commercial houses. The museums and libraries must either make a great many new records of their own, or must supplement what they can buy on the market by instrumental performances on the spot. The first course would probably be the better of the two; you can duplicate gramophone records; a concert can only be heard by a few people in one place. The State already takes photographs of its art treasures. There is no reason why it should not make records of music.

Meanwhile, since there is not the slightest prospect that either the State, or the municipalities, or the public libraries, will do anything towards the creation of these highly desirable musical museums, we must be content with the nearest approach to a museum of good music which we have—the Promenade Concerts. At the cost of ten shillings a week, the regular promenader can become acquainted with practically all the masterpieces of nineteenth-century music, and with a certain amount of what is best in the eighteenth century. One can hardly expect more from something which is not professedly an educational institution.

But let us have done with this talk of education. After all, one goes to the Proms, not to be educated, but to enjoy oneself. And that one succeeds in so doing, in spite of having to stand, is a tribute to the charms of music as well as to the good conducting and the admirably chosen programs of Sir Henry Wood. And what a good empirical test of the merits of any piece of music this standing is! As long as you are thoroughly interested you feel nothing of the discomfort of your position. It is only when you are a little bored that you become aware of your feet and ankles, and of the ache that is developing in the small of your back. Lolling in the padded comfort of a seat one is ready to pass over an occasional *longueur*. But standing, one becomes exasperatedly critical; nothing but the very best, nothing but the most richly inspired will keep the ache from the leg.

For myself, I find that I can stand in comfort through most of a Friday evening's Beethoven and Bach. There are moments in the Pastoral Symphony, as I found last Friday, which was the first time, if I remember rightly, that I have ever stood through this particular work, there are moments in all the first movements when one becomes conscious of a distinct weakness in the ham. But what a tonic, and what an anodyne is the last movement! Similarly the first movement of the fifth Brandenburg seems, when one is standing, unjustifiably smug and self-complacent. You feel that Bach could do that sort of thing too easily, by force of habit. It is not till the slow movement begins that you cease to mind standing.

Brahms, I find, can be stood fairly well; the good and the bad quarters of an hour bring alternate discomfort and relief. But there is no considerable work of his, as there are so many of Beethoven, through the whole of which one can stand listening, unaware of physical distresses.

As for Tschaikowsky, I have in my time stood enthusiastically through his fourth, fifth, and sixth symphonies. Could I stand through them now? I confess that I have no particular desire to make the experiment.

What has always seemed to me the oddest thing about the Promenade public is the fact that Monday night has power to collect a large crowd and to keep it standing for hours, listening to nothing but Wagner. On Monday evenings I, personally, find myself aware of my legs very early in the performance. It would be interesting to know if the majority of people who go on Monday nights are hardened promenaders, thoroughly familiar with Wagner, and attending because of that familiarity; or whether the majority of them are new recruits, submitting themselves for the first time to the Wagnerian influence. That one should get a great thrill from Wagner the first times one hears him is very comprehensible. What I find hard to understand is that his music should be able to re-evoke the old *frisson* in people who know it well. Eloquence and emphasis may make you lose your head once; but surely not more than once. Are most of those who stand on Monday nights newcomers? Or are there many hardened concert-goers who find it possible to give themselves over to the intoxications of musical rhetoric with a Hippocratical regularity?

[*The Weekly Westminster Gazette,* September 30, 1922]

Busoni Again

BUSONI'S *Rondeau Arlequinesque* was given at last Thursday's Promenade Concert. I do not know if it has been previously performed in London; in any case, I have not heard it, if it has. For me it is a new work. That must be my excuse for talking about it at some length. For a new work by Busoni, even though it is certain not to be quite the genuine, splendid article, can scarcely fail to be interesting—more interesting, for example, than Mr. Waldo Warner's *Pixy Ring,* or the *Thanet* overture, which were the other musical novelties of last week.

In spite of his great talents—and, in a sense, because of them—Busoni is almost a pathetic figure. He is a tremendous executant—a little too arbitrary, perhaps, in his interpretations, and a little lacking, as an Italian pianist of my acquaintance complainingly expressed it, in the "quality of sensuality." But his power is formidable; his control over the instrument almost miraculous. He is a great interpretative artist.

But he has not been content to be merely that. He has been ambitious to become a great composer as well. Like his countryman, Alfieri, he has doggedly resolved to be a creative genius. He has come as near to making himself a good composer as Alfieri came to making himself a good tragedian—as near as anyone can come who possesses a great deal of learning, powers of appreciation, a keen intelligence, and an allowance of native talent that is not quite copious enough. But, however hard he tries, he will never come any nearer to the final triumph. That is his tragedy, the tragedy of all who want to be creative geniuses without nature's leave.

The *Rondeau Arlequinesque* is certainly one of Busoni's most successful attempts to achieve what is, for him, the impossible. It is, in its way and up to a point, excessively good. It is witty, dry, intellectual in conception; the themes are interesting (but, of course, never quite interesting enough); the construction is extremely ingenious and learned. With what an astonishing wealth of contrapuntal devices the parts are fitted together! How well it is orchestrated, and with what a masterly effect the voice part is introduced at the end! It is scholarly writing, and one can understand why scholars, like Mr. E. J. Dent, feel so tenderly for Busoni as a composer. But for the ordinary man, who is no scholar but merely fond of music, he will not do. Not that the ordinary man, who "knows what he likes" and not much more, is an infallibly good judge of a work of art; he is not. But, in the long run, he is probably a better judge than the scholar. For the scholar's attention is too often attracted by perfectly irrelevant things; he praises and blames because of details which have nothing to do with the main issue. The man who merely "knows what he likes," likes a great many vulgar and silly things; but he always likes for relevant reasons; he likes a work of art, not for its scholarly ingenuities, but for the sake of the life that is in the thing. Now, all manifestations of life are not necessarily beautiful or refined; but all that is really beautiful in art, all that has real lasting power, must be instinct with life in some manifestation or other. "You Made Me Love You" is a real manifestation of life; and so is the Fugue from Beethoven's Op. 59, no. 3, played by the London String Quartet last Saturday. Plenty of straightforward "know-what-they-like" sort of people sincerely admire both. The crowd at the Coliseum used to clap as loudly for Miss Florence Smithson as it did for the Russian Ballet. Both were alive. For reasons which it is really rather difficult to justify, we highbrows prefer the Ballet and the Fugue to Miss Smithson and "You Made Me Love You." We say that this manifestation of life is better, or at any rate more respectable, than that. But the *Rondeau Arlequinesque* is, somehow, not a manifestation of life. It is more than half dead. It would get no applause at the Coliseum—not because it happens to be difficult or "modern," but because it does not evoke in the listener any particular emotion, it does not bring him any new sense of life. The Fugue in Op. 59, no. 3, is complicated and ingenious and learned and intellectual; but it is also full of a life that flows into the spirit of the hearer and raises his store. Except where the methods of expression are so unfamiliar that they act as a kind of separating insulator, the man who "knows what he likes" feels and is moved by the life that is in a work of art. It does not matter whether

Busoni's *Rondeau* is insulated or not. Its battery is not charged; it will give
you no shock when you touch it.

[The Weekly Westminster Gazette, October 7, 1922]

Reflections in the Concert Room

LEEDS, not London, has been, during the last few days, the center of musical interest. A new Holst, a seldom-heard Delius were a sufficient attrac-
tion by themselves. Add to these a copious selection of the ancients from
Bach to Parry, the London Symphony Orchestra and the Yorkshire
choirs—and you have something worth going to Leeds for.

For those, however, who, like myself, didn't or couldn't go to Leeds
there were ample consolations at home. Music in London has been particularly rich and pleasant during the past week. The chief events have been
an interesting novelty in the shape of a work by Roussel, a Sunday afternoon performance by Cortot and Thibaud, and a Friday Prom that had
claims to being the Perfect Concert. An evening's entertainment which included Bach's Concerto for two violins in D minor, superbly played by
those most talented sisters, Miss Jelly d'Aranyi and Mrs. Adila Fachiri;
the *Water Music* and a couple of good arias by Handel, the Eighth Symphony of Beethoven; the third Brandenburg; and the Tragic Overture of
Brahms (which sounded, I may add parenthetically, a little dimly by the
side of the Bach, the Beethoven, and the Handel, each in its own way so
consummately beautiful)—this was something to make up for not being in
Leeds.

I was somewhat pained and astonished, at this concert, by an intelligent literary man of my acquaintance remarking, at the end of the *Water
Music,* that "Handel was the best writer of 'silly music.'" Now, the term
"silly music" is an admirable term which describes very succinctly a vast
quantity of the music of the eighteenth century, including all the Italian
operas. There was silliness in that elaborate singing for singing's sake, in
those meaningless rococo ornamentations that abound in one sort of
minor eighteenth-century music. There was silliness in the pedantic contrapuntal business that abounds in another variety. But Handel—can he be
labeled as belonging to either of these categories of silliness? In the forty-
one Italian operas which none of us have ever heard, and which Samuel
Butler, that strange and solitary prophet of a certain twentieth-century
spirit of anti-emotionalism, anti-seriousness, proclaimed as the perfect
kind of music, Handel exhibited, no doubt, almost as great a silliness as
any of his contemporaries. He accepted the fashionable form and was con-

tent to turn out specimens of it in the genial pot-boiling spirit of a Rubens. But see what happens when he is working in a form which gives him better scope than the opera; give him a chance with an oratorio. There is not much silliness in the *Messiah* or *Israel in Egypt*. What a sense of dramatic fitness, what ceaseless invention, what a feeling for vast architectural forms! But it is absurd to labor the point—almost as absurd as to say that Handel is a writer of silly music. As for the *Water Music,* which was the piece which actually provoked the comment—I can, I think, detect my literary friend's reasons for calling it silly. I can see that limpidity, simplicity and a disinterested delight in pure form might be interpreted as manifestations of silliness by someone who had come to listen to Wagner or even to the C minor Symphony. *Tout comprendre est tout pardonner.* Let us forgive and forget.

But before we leave the subject of silliness forever, I should like to state what I consider to be a truly and fundamentally silly piece of music. That is Scriabine's *Prometheus* to which I listened, for the first time for a good many years, at last Tuesday's Promenade Concert. *Prometheus* is silly in a totally different way from the Italian operas and the contrapuntal machines of the eighteenth century. It is not silly for lack of meaning or genuine emotional inspiration, not silly because of undue insistence upon form. It is silly because it tries to express too much in too violent a fashion, because it uses as its substance a form of material which is really no good for art. *Prometheus* is personal emotion, presented raw and quivering. It is the record of the sensations of an exposed nerve. Scriabine achieves in it perfectly what he set out to do in it. He expresses the exquisite torments and delights of a sensibility suffering from hyper-aesthesia with an appalling fidelity. But the record is not a work of art. Art cannot be made of raw sensibility and personal confessions. *Prometheus* reminds one of the most agonized passages of De Musset's *Confessions d'un Enfant du Siècle.* Like that fundamentally silly book, it is interesting as a document of emotionalism, not as a work of art. You cannot read Musset's book or hear Scriabine's music more than once. On a second examination these documents merely become rather disgusting.

> Tel qu'un morne animal, meurtri, plein de poussière,
> La chaine au cou, hurlant au chaud soleil d'été,
> Promène qui voudra son coeur ensanglanté,
> Sur ton pavé cynique, o plèbe carnassière!
> Pour mettre un feu stérile dans ton oeil hébété,
> Pour mendier ton rire ou ta pitié grossière,
> Déchire qui voudra la robe de lumière
> De la pudeur divine et de la volupté!

Leconte de Lisle's sonorous rhetoric rumbles in my memory (correctly, I hope). One need not, like de Lisle himself, make a supererogatory virtue of impersonality: one need not write exclusively of condors, elephants, Nordic warriors and similar wild fowl. But on the other hand one must not try, like Scriabine, to make works of art out of exposed nerves. The thing cannot be done. It is better to go to the dentist.

[*The Weekly Westminster Gazette*, October 14, 1922]

New Friends and Old

LONDON'S principal musical novelties during the last few days have been works which were performed this August at the Salzburg Festival, and which I have already described in these columns. Bloch's Schelomo was given at one of last week's Proms, a performance of the violin sonata took place last Tuesday. I see no reason for repeating my criticism of these works. Nor do I propose to reopen the painful subject of Mr. Leo Sowerby's sonata for violin and piano, which was given in London for the first time last week; it is enough to remark that I took some pains not to hear it a second time.

The other novelty of the week has been Mr. Rutland Boughton's opera, *The Immortal Hour,* produced by the Birmingham Repertory Company at the Regent. It is of this work that I shall write today. And now that I have engaged to write of it, I find myself at a loss how to begin. For *The Immortal Hour* is a work of which it is difficult to know what to say. The best method of criticizing it would be, I think, to write two articles, one in its favor and one in its dispraise. The good and the bad of the piece lie in distinct strata, like the layers of a Neapolitan ice; one could deal with each separately and apart from the other. The good stratum is Mr. Boughton's music; the bad is Fiona Macleod's libretto. The more independent and absolute the music is, the better; it is at its worst when it becomes most intimately involved with the play. The upper layer of the ice is an agreeable pink; but the color is spoiled wherever the sickly green of the lower stratum comes smudging across the line of demarcation. But this metaphor is becoming a trifle cloying; let us cease to speak in parables.

Mr. Boughton's music, then, compares very favorably with the libretto of his opera. Fiona Macleod's play is hazy and soft and dim, a thing compounded of fog and wool. (The word "dreams" occurs in it at least three hundred times—and we all know what "dreams" are when they get out of the clutches of the psychoanalysts and run amok in the Celtic twilight.) Mr. Boughton's music is clear, clean-cut, and definite; full of pleasant melodies and transparent instrumentation; not very grand, perhaps, but sound and workmanlike; in good taste but capable of making a popular appeal. There are one or two admirably effective musical inventions in the opera; the laughing chorus of the spirits in the first scene is an example. Mr. Boughton could do a great deal with his gifts; but not in conjunction with the secondary personality of the late William Sharp. One only wishes, as one listens to *The Immortal Hour,* that he would turn his talents to making music round themes more concrete and human, less windily dim. He might, for example, produce a charming comic opera if he tried. I do not make the suggestion with any desire to disparage or denigrate. Mozart, after all, created supreme beauty out of this light enchanting form; his comic operas are among the very, very few operas of any variety which one can take seriously as works of art. Mr. Boughton would be well advised to look for a competent Da Ponte (it cannot really be so hard to find one) who would write him a picturesque comic or serio-comic libretto of sufficient artificiality to allow it to sound reasonable when set to music. I can guarantee that we should all enjoy the resultant work of art a good deal more than we can enjoy *The Immortal Hour.*

The performance at the Regent is reasonably good. Mr. Arthur Cranmer's Dalua and Mr. Johnstone-Douglas's King are both pleasant, while there is a certain unsophisticated charm about the voice of Etain, played by Miss Ffrangcon-Davies.

But I must confess that I had been rather spoiled for ordinary singing when I listened to Mr. Boughton's opera. For I went to the Regent, on Monday, almost direct from the Queen's Hall, where I had been hearing Frieda Hempel in a program of lieder by Schubert, Schumann, and Brahms. What a voice! What effortless supple strength! What purity, what a flute-like roundness of tone! And, moreover, what is by no means invariable among Queens of Song, Miss Hempel possesses intelligence and refinement. Her interpretations are always in faultless taste, her phrasing is always clear and sensible. Miss Hempel's only defect as a singer of lieder is the too great purity, the fluty emotionlessness of her voice. Nature has given her that vocal agility, that silver coolness of tone which belong to the great coloratura singers. Exquisite as her rendering of lieder is, one cannot help feeling that it is almost a waste of her time and her voice to sing them. Quite a number of singers can make the songs of Schubert yield up their perfume of sentiment and charm. But how few can do justice to the flowing calligraphy of a Mozartian cadenza! We are to hear Miss Hempel in some of this calligraphic music next Sunday at the Albert Hall; it will be an experience that should not be missed.

[*The Weekly Westminster Gazette,* October 21, 1922]

Variations

OF ALL our numerous human limitations the inability to be in two places at the same time is one of the most galling and tiresome. Those of us who suffer concert halls gladly for the sake of the music that is to be heard in them feel, perhaps, more than anyone, the effects of this deplorable disability. When the Flonzaleys are playing in Wigmore Street, and the London Symphony Orchestra is giving a concert at the Queen's Hall—on the same night—what is one to do about it? In the bright H. G. Wellsian future it is sufficiently obvious what one will do; one will sit at home and, adjusting a little battalion of wireless telephone receivers to the requisite wave-lengths, one will listen simultaneously to all the concerts, sifting out with contrapuntistical ears, the Appassionata Sonata at the Aeolian from the Meistersinger Overture at the Queen's Hall and Bartók's string quartet at the Wigmore from the *Messiah* at the Crystal Palace. The conscientious critic will then be able in all good faith, to pass judgment on every single new performer as he or she appears, while the layman will find it possible to crowd into one glorious hour as much musical education as would have cost him, in the bad old days, a month's assiduous concert-going. But the present being what it is, one is compelled to make a choice. Flonzaley or London Symphony—it had to be one or the other last Monday night. In the end, I decided for London Symphony.

It was, more than anything, Brahms's *Variations on a Theme by Haydn* that drew me to the Queen's Hall. It is a work which, besides being superbly and absolutely good in itself, possesses for me certain sentimental and associative interests. For it was, I remember, a hearing of these *Variations* that first made me realize, as a boy, the enormous richness and complexity, the endless intellectual potentialities of music. After hearing them in the concert-room, I lived with these *Variations* for weeks at home, treading them out in the four-hand version on the pianola and poring over the printed music. I remember how I sat with the work, hours on end, trying to work out the ideal connections between variations and theme, trying to analyze and give a name to the logic which I could hear, as I listened to the music, but which I found it impossible to describe in words. In those hours spent with Brahms I began to find out a great many things about variations—how one can vary by quickening the tune with a hurry of ornament, how one can vary from the brass upwards, how one can vary by putting new melodies and harmonies into the rhythmic mold of the original. Incidentally, I learned a good deal about music in the process, and something, perhaps, about art in general. For the principle of the variation is one of the fundamental principles of all art. A theme, repeated with differences; a series of forms developing out of one another and having a recognizable relation to some primary form—you find these things in poetry and painting as well as in music. What is a painting by Raphael but a series of delicate variations on a number of plastic themes? The lines and the masses repeat themselves, balancing one another with a kind of symmetry. In the work of Raphael's friend, Fra Bartolommeo, the symmetry is too complete; the picture becomes almost a pattern. A Fra Bartolommeo is, as it were, a minuet and trio; a Raphael is the more subtly balanced set of variations. It would be interesting to reproduce such a picture as Domenichino's *Last Communion of St. Jerome* (one of the greatest masterpieces in the classical, Raphaelesque manner) and to show, diagrammatically, how the primary theme of the central arch, with its straight sides and semi-circular top, is repeated with variations in a series of marvellous curves, embracing the figures of the kneeling saint, the priest and his acolytes, the flying cherub overhead, and the architectural details in the background to right and left. It would be seen that the pictorial artist has built up in space a series of forms, varying from, but suggesting and recalling the original, in exactly the same way as the musician builds up in time his set of variations which differ from the original, simple theme (the equivalent of Domenichino's geometrically simple arch) while they evoke its memory in the mind of the listener.

I have wandered far from last Monday's concert—but perhaps not quite so far as might appear. Before I close this article I should like to thank Mr. Coates for the excellence of a program which included, besides the Brahms *Variations,* a Mozart Concerto for violin and the Eroica Symphony. For his conducting of these fine works I do not feel myself quite so grateful. It is a fine sight to see Mr. Coates wielding his baton as though he were fighting with the Prince of the Powers of the Air; but I must admit that I prefer, on the whole, the spectacle of his conducting to the sound of it. There is such a thing as being too dramatic, too violently energetic. Indeed, Mr. Coates's vigor on Monday night was such that, in the middle of the last movement of the Eroica, my nose suddenly started to bleed. I had always considered concert-going as one of the quiet diversions. Mr. Coates, it seemed to me as I tried, vainly, to staunch the flow of my life's blood, threatens to turn it into a dangerous sport.

[*The Weekly Westminster Gazette,* October 28, 1922]

Music and Politics

THE LAST FEW DAYS have contributed the customary quota of musical entertainments. But though it would be possible to say much about

Kreisler and the perfect violin tone (so different, it may be added parenthetically, from the soapy and somewhat rather medicinal tone of Mr.
Sammons's playing, of which we had a sample a few days before Kreisler's
coming); though the mechanical-piano concert at the Queen's Hall calls
for astonished comments (the Welte-Mignon and its successor, the Rondo-
Art, have been calling for them, for that matter, these many years); though
it would be possible to write of Mr. Holst's *St. Paul's Suite* and to discuss,
in this context, the whole question of the modern treatment and adapta-
tion of old themes—in spite of all that might be talked about here—I am
irresistibly drawn to another theme. It is the fault of the political situation.
On hearing, with that mixture of enthusiasm and righteous indignation
which is the appropriate emotion wherever Fascismo is concerned, of
Mussolini's *coup d'état* and the march of the Black Shirts on Rome, I felt a
passionate desire to listen to a little Italian music. Carl Rosa offered Puccini at Covent Garden; but on arriving at the theater on Monday night I
found that too many people had felt the same desire as I, and that I could
not get in. I took the disappointment philosophically. Those unheard, I reflected, are sweetest, particularly where the melodies of Puccini are concerned. I went home to think of Italian music in the abstract—to listen to
it also in the abstract, on the gramophone.

As I hoped, this spiritual contemplation of Italian music, assisted by
the gramophone and the sensuous ear, seemed to throw light on the whole
situation. Fascismo, one perceives, is something more than the two-
year-old reaction from Socialism. The Socialist tyranny only crystalized
something that was there before, in solution, so to speak, and diffused—
crystalized it into this particular shape. Caruso and the operas and the
Neapolitan tunes help one to perceive what Fascismo is made of.

This substance, which has crystalized into Fascismo, is a certain abstract ideal of passion and energy. You find it in the Italian music of the
last sixty or seventy years, you find it in Marinetti, you find it, transposed
to a rather different key, in the clotted eloquence of D'Annunzio. The best
way of realizing what this ideal of passion means in music is to listen to
the gramophone record on which Caruso sings the beautiful "Dieu s'a-
vance à travers la Lande" of César Franck. In no work by Franck is this
flawless purity of sentiment, his clear and limpid religious feeling, more
simply and beautifully displayed. Caruso sings it, and it becomes suddenly
quite unrecognizable. Not that it is a bad performance; it is superb, in its
way. But its way is very unlike Franck's way. It is no longer God advancing
across the lands; it is Benvenuto Cellini advancing across some warm,
dark piazzo in search of amorous adventures, a guitar slung over his
shoulder, and at his side a long and penetrating dagger. Caruso could in-
fect with his ideal of passionate energy a piece of music that was wholly

unpassionate. What he could do with Italian music that was itself passionate in conception and intention it is unnecessary to describe.

The oddest thing about this kind of music—from the best Verdi to the worst Piedigrotta popular song—is its relative novelty. The Italians have always shown themselves, if never quite so self-consciously as at the present time, passionate and energetic. Passion and energy were the ideals of the baroque art of the seventeenth century. They inspired to heights sometimes of sublimity, sometimes of vulgarity, the painters, the sculptors, even the architects of a whole age. But it is only of quite recent years that Italian music has been inspired by the same ideals. Stendhal, it is true, found a good deal of passion in Cimarosa; but then he had never heard "Celeste Aida" or "O sole mio." To us, who know these palpitating melodies of a later date, Cimarosa appears charming precisely because of his deliciously unpassionate, musical-boxy quality. Even in Rossini there is still very little of those qualities which had already appeared in the statuary of Bernini and the architecture of Borromini, and which were later to make Italian opera what we now know it to be—of those qualities which, later still, were to bring the Black Shirts tramping into Rome.

It is difficult to imagine musical life in the days before the existence of the Neapolitan song or of that more languishingly passionate South American product which most of us now prefer to the Italian article. In this context I may remark that there is a most interesting passage in Beckford's *Letters from Portugal,* written before the French Revolution, in which he speaks of the peculiar and strangely passionate airs imported from Brazil and sung by the fashionable Portuguese ladies of the period. Beckford declares that he had never heard anything like them, and that they were so ravishing as quite to undermine his morale. Can these strange Brazilian melodies have been the ancestor of the Tango? I like to think so. That Beckford should have anticipated the musical dadaists in discovering the lovely and delicately vulgar charm of South American music is delightful. Our English Jean Cocteau was born nearly a century and a half too soon.

[*The Weekly Westminster Gazette,* November 4, 1922]

An Orlando Gibbons Concert

OLD ENGLISH MUSIC is frequently talked about nowadays, but it is not nearly so often heard. Plenty of people can affirm, glibly enough, that England once possessed a school of music that was among the finest of the world; but few can tell one anything about the works which made that school so famous. Words without Songs were never a very satisfactory musical form; there has been too much conversation about the old English music and too little performance. Let us have more of the songs and less of the words.

There are, it is true, various individuals and corporate bodies who make it their business to perform our ancient music. The English Singers, the Oriana Madrigal Society, and Mr. Gerald Cooper—to mention a few of those who believe more in songs than in words—have all done excellent work in making this music known. It is to be wished that the organizers of popular concerts would arrange to include specimens of our old vocal music in their programs and that pianists would add to their repertory a few specimens of our sixteenth- and early seventeenth-century Virginal music. There is no question of forcing the musical public to listen to something too remote and unfamiliar to be enjoyed. There are plenty of Elizabethan madrigals which nobody can help liking at a first hearing; and there are few to which several hearings will not attach the listener. As for the Virginal music—anyone who listens to Bach with pleasure will find much to enjoy in the best of it. There is, in a word, no valid reason why our old music of every sort should not be given frequently and with applause. Why it should be so much neglected is a mystery.

How suitable Elizabethan keyboard music is for modern performance was proved last Friday by the recital of works by Orlando Gibbons, given at the Aeolian Hall by Miss Glyn and Miss Puttick, on the organ and piano. Gibbons, whom it is really incorrect to call an Elizabethan (for he was just reaching maturity when Elizabeth died and his works were all composed during the first quarter of the seventeenth century) was one of the composers who accepted the polyphonic convention as he found it, brought after long centuries of experiment to its ripe perfection, and who was content to use it without searching for new modes of expression. He exhibits all the beauties and ingenuities and intricacies of the style and all its limitations. The qualities of his work are the fine intellectual qualities of all good polyphonic writing; its chief defect is that incapacity to organize a large coherent structure which we find in almost all work of the period. It seems to us, familiar with the achievements of later music, an extraordinary thing that the composers of Gibbons's time should never have thought of the device of writing a piece of music round a series of central themes or subjects. Once grasped, the notion seems exceedingly obvious and altogether satisfying. The fact that this notion had not yet entered the mind of English musicians gives to the compositions of the period a curiously vague and rambling aspect. In the mind of one who lays feverishly awake at night, the sound of a dripping tap may form itself into a queer sort of inconclusive, never-finishing music. Much of the music before the invention of the theme-idea possesses, to our ears, something of this dripping tap quality; only, of course, each drip of the inconclusive tap is in itself a highly organized work of art, beautiful and intellectually stimulating to listen to. The counterpoint flows on, there are passages of fugue and imitation. But somehow, out of these rich elements, no completely satisfying whole is made.

On the evening of the day when I listened to this concert of Gibbons's works, I returned to the Aeolian Hall to hear Mrs. Adila Fachiri playing the Mozart Violin Concerto in A. It was a delightful performance of one of the most lovely works of the youthful Mozart. As I listened to it, I found myself remembering the music I had heard a few hours before in the same hall. If only Gibbons had had at his disposal the artistic materials which Mozart could command! If only he had known about the development of subjects, about the beauty of formal melody, about the relation of long movements to one another in a yet larger whole! What things he might have done! But even as it is, he is eminently worth listening to. There are plenty of modern composers who would do well to study the intricacies of polyphonic writing and to learn from it its lesson. There are no short cuts to perfection in polyphonic music. Brilliant orchestration, tone colour, impressionism—these things are no good in this sort of music. The composer of polyphony must lay all his cards on the table and must play them honestly and with all the skill and ingenuity he can command.

[*The Weekly Westminster Gazette*, November 11, 1922]

The Arnold Bax Concert

THERE WAS A FOG in the Queen's Hall last Monday night; the lamps were as moons in a pale mist, diffusing a gauzy radiance; the white-robed ladies of the Oriana Madrigal Society looked like a squad of banshees in the Celtic twilight and Mr. Goossens in the conductor's little dock was a dim silhouette gesticulating with a fabulous elegance. It was all very odd and unpleasant; but when the orchestra began to play Mr. Bax's *Garden of Fand,* it seemed, somehow, less peculiar; it seemed even apposite and suitable. In arranging that there should be a fog in the Queen's Hall on Monday night, the Clerk of the Weather showed that he possessed a sense of the fitness of things.

Comparisons are odious, but for the sake of intelligent criticism they must be made. Let us compare *The Garden of Fand* with a piece of music inspired by the same sort of lyrical feeling for the beauty and the exquisite melancholy of nature—the *Prélude à l'après-midi d'un faune.* The rich golden mist of sunset pervades Debussy's work; but the landscape is clearly seen through it. The powdery gold stippled over it serves but to enhance the beauty of its forms and contours. But through the radiant fog of Mr. Bax's work one sees nothing. The *Après-midi* has the logic and the fine composition of a landscape by Poussin.

But in speaking of music these analogies with other arts are, perhaps, a little dangerous; it is best to talk about music in terms of itself. When we look into the *Après-midi* we find that what makes it so perfect and coherent a work of art is its theme, which is developed in a long rhythmic line from one end of the piece to the other, holding it together. But in *The Garden of Fand* we find no real thematic coherence. The work is three times as long as the *Après-midi* and, therefore, requires, according to the laws of simple arithmetic, three times as much thematic material to bind it together. But, thrice as long, it seems to contain only a third of the substance of Debussy's work. There is no lack in *The Garden of Fand* of minor invention, no lack of ingenuity and beauty in the part-writing and the orchestration; almost any individual passage you liked to select from it would be interesting enough. What it does lack, however, is the major invention; it is without the central dominating idea which makes a mass of details into a work of art. It is a fog.

Foggy, too, was the Second Sonata for piano which followed it a little later in the program. The Sonata shows the same incoherence, the same absence of major invention, which characterize *The Garden of Fand*. But while the orchestral work is charming and interesting in its details, the Sonata is made up of a mass of rhetorical and rather disagreeably pretentious passages. There are moments, as one listens to it, when one is reminded of Liszt at his not very best. The fog which had been so soft and quivering-bright in *The Garden of Fand* had now become decidedly murky.

And then a strange thing happened; the fog which lay over the music suddenly lifted. In the Celtic twilight behind the orchestra there was a stir; the white banshees stood up and one became aware of certain black specters of the male gender who also rose. A new silhouette—Mr. Kennedy Scott's—appeared in the conductor's dock and waved at the specters; they began to sing an unaccompanied carol in a quite surprising number of parts. It was superb. The fog had lifted and we found ourselves in open country, surrounded by the clear and definite forms of a well-composed landscape.

If Mr. Bax always wrote so well as he does in *Mater ora Filium* and the other carols performed later in the evening, he would be a really admirable composer. The limitations imposed on him by the choir seem to act as a corrective to the vagueness and looseness which are his besetting weaknesses when he writes for the unshackled orchestra or piano. *Mater ora*

Filium is as clear and definite and logical as music can be; it has, at the same time, a rich emotional content, all the more moving because the work is so clear and definite. Mr. Bax knows how to use this most potent of musical instruments, the choir; he knows, as the great masters of choral writing have all known before him, how to make the voices sound as though they did not belong to respectable ladies and gentlemen, like you and me, but to disembodied spirits—angels or damned souls—demonically singing.

The next considerable item on the program was the concerto for viola, played by Mr. Lionel Tertis. I liked this work decidedly less than the choral music: not because it was foggy—it was remarkably definite—but because a good deal of the material out of which the piece was made seemed to me not of the most interesting. In this, as in so many other works, Mr. Bax employs Celtic themes. The sort of melodies that can be played on the black notes alone wander yearningly through his adagios; his jocular allegros take the form, as often as not, of some lively jig or reel. I must confess at once that I do not very much care for Celtic tunes and that a little of them goes, for me, a long way. The real trouble about these Celtic melodies is surely this: once the musical convention to which they belong has become familiar, they are altogether too easy and obvious and limited. It may be presumption on my part, but I believe that, with a little trouble, I could produce half a dozen excellent Celtic melodies that would respectably pass muster in a crowd. On the other hand, I know with a profound and unshakable certainty that I could never invent anything like the theme, shall we say, of the slow movement of Beethoven's quartet, Op. 18, no. 3, or of the finale of Mozart's G minor quintet. That an artist endowed with a talent I do not possess should content himself with doing things which I feel capable (possibly mistakenly) of doing myself, seems to me unsatisfactory. I feel, so to speak, that I am not getting my money's worth out of him. He possesses this talent which I do not possess; it is his business, therefore, to do things which I could not possibly do. *Argal* and in fine, I cannot feel much interest in Celtic melodies.

[*The Weekly Westminster Gazette,* November 18, 1922]

Temporaries and Eternals

IT IS POSSIBLE for a work of art, having little or no merit, to possess, on its first appearance at a given moment in time, a significance and an importance entirely disproportionate to its intrinsic value. Such works seem to the generation which witnesses their production enormously important, absorbingly interesting. A few years pass, and all the fire has died out of them; the new generation derisively wonders how its fathers could have been fools enough to take such nonsense seriously. Meanwhile, as likely as not, the men of the new generation are falling into ecstasies over something that is intrinsically no better.

It is easy to quote examples. There was Macpherson's *Ossian,* for instance—a book which exercised, during nearly half a century, a profounder influence upon more varied minds than almost any other single work of the eighteenth century. Who so much as tries to read *Ossian* now? To the art lovers of the beginning of the seventeenth century the painting of Caravaggio seemed a portent; and at the beginning of the twentieth Rostand and Maeterlinck possessed a significance which is far from being theirs today. It would be easy to lengthen the list almost indefinitely. Every age has produced these works of art which appear to be important, and which often are really significant at the moment. They differ from the eternal works of art in that it is possible to go on talking about these "eternal" things for hundreds of years—to talk about them and, what is more important, to say something new and significant in each generation; the non-eternal works do not stand re-examination. With the passing of time they prove to have lost entirely their point and savor.

One of these minor works of art, which forty years ago appeared to possess a considerable significance, was dragged, some few nights ago, out of a reposeful obscurity that should have been eternal, and galvanized by Mr. Coates's exuberant vitality into a semblance of life. There must have been many who, like myself, went to the London Symphony Orchestra's concert last Monday for the sole purpose of hearing what Bruckner's Fourth Symphony would sound like on revival. Most of them, I venture to believe, must have agreed with me that the poor thing was better dead, must even have budgeted it its allotted hour of re-existence; have wished long before the end, to see it safely under the tombstone once again.

At a time when it was complimentary in the highest possible degree to be compared with Wagner, Bruckner was called "the Wagner of the Symphony." People listened to his music with all the seriousness and good-will which he himself brought to the making of it. We who listen with forty years more experience in our ears than they, perceive that the Wagner of the Symphony was a man who wrote for the Wagnerian orchestra pieces of music which he believed to be in the form of Beethoven's symphonies. We perceive that his thematic invention was of a vulgar and commonplace character. (All his learning and ingenuity are lavished on themes that would not do any very great credit to a Gilbert and Sullivan opera.) We see that he has fallen heavily between his Wagnerian and classical stools; that he takes noise and climaxes from Wagner and cramping limitations from the classics, and that he makes of the two something that is at once curiously childish and pretentious.

Listening to this work, I found myself wondering which of our own esteemed composers will be regarded, a generation hence, as we regard Bruckner. Will they wonder why on earth we made all this fuss about Stravinsky, or how we were not disgusted by the emotionalism of Scriabin? I wonder. Of one thing, however, I do feel very certain. They will be astonished that anyone ever took the young Frenchmen of the nineteen-twenties as much more than a joke. Some of us are astonished even now. Darius Milhaud's sonata for two violins and piano, which was played by Miss Jelly d'Aranyi and Mme. Adila Fachiri at the Aeolinan Hall last Friday, did nothing to lessen that astonishment. It is pretty and elegant enough in its tenuous way. But for all practical purposes it does not exist. Milhaud's sonata sounds like the dry, evaporated essence of a piece of music by some not very original pre-Handelian composer. Mr. Newman recently printed an article on the difficulty of spotting winners for the artistic immortality stakes; it is less difficult, I think, to spot the losers. In M. Darius Milhaud we have a pretty certain Also Ran.

[*The Weekly Westminster Gazette*, November 25, 1922]

Verdi and Palestrina

ABOUT three and a half centuries ago the art of music had arrived at a pitch of excellence that was about as near to perfection as anything which is the work of men's hands or brains can be. It seemed as though a logical conclusion had been reached, as though the time had come to make a new start. The new beginning was made and a new music came in its turn—on several occasions in the course of the next centuries—very near to other kinds of perfection. And the old perfection was forgotten, the old music was almost as though it had never been, the lessons which it taught remained unheeded. It is a strange story—at once very creditable to humanity and rather discreditable; creditable inasmuch as it is a fine thing to be splendidly prodigal, to throw away old perfections for the dream of new; discreditable because it is rather stupid not to learn all that can possibly be learnt from the experience of past generations.

At the Albert Hall last Saturday we were given an opportunity of comparing the old perfection with one of the perfections (well, honestly, not quite a perfection!) of recent times. The Royal Choral Society gave a performance of Verdi's *Requiem* in the afternoon; in the evening Monsignor Casimiro Casimiri directed the Vatican Choir through a program consisting principally of Palestrina, varied by Orlando di Lasso and Vittoria. The contrast was extraordinarily interesting. The two programs mutually illumined one another, revealing each other's strengths and weaknesses and the beauties and defects of the two kinds of music which they represented.

Let us plunge straight into the details of this comparison and ask ourselves first of all which of the two kinds of music—Palestrina's polyphony or Verdi's monodic music, with its strongly accented rhythms, its recurring themes, its four-square melodies—is the more expressive, the more suitable for the conveyance of emotion? One's first impulse would be to answer in Verdi's favor. Polyphony, we are inclined to think, must be dry and intellectual; Verdi who had studied the passions in his operas; Verdi who knows how to write a languishing air, an air of passion, a tune full of rage and fury, Verdi surely knows better how to express emotion than did Palestrina. But listen to the music of the nineteenth-century master and then to Palestrina's. I venture to bet that, if you are a reasonably musical and sensitive hearer, you will have revised your first answer by the end of the second concert. It will seem to you that, in spite of polyphony, in spite of the absence of accented rhythms and recurring melodies (or even, perhaps, because of these things), Palestrina's music is really much more expressive than Verdi's. One cannot listen to those marvellous motets from the *Song of Songs,* to the *Improperia,* to the Offertory *Ad Te levavi,* without realizing that here was a man who knew admirably well how to express every emotion from sadness to exultation, from religious fervor to rage and derision. The *Tenebrae* of Vittoria, written in the same polyphonic convention, is even more directly and poignantly moving than the work of Palestrina. It is the consummately beautiful musical expression of sadness, despair, and darkness. In the *Tenebrae* as in the motets of Palestrina the music clings extraordinarily close to the sense of the words. Each word's full burden of significance is thoroughly analyzed, and every emotional implication it contains is expressed in the statements and repetitions by the various voices. The absolute flexibility of the polyphonic music, the absence of dominating and recurrent themes, make it peculiarly suitable for this close analysis and full exposition of emotion. It seems to me no exaggeration to say that words have never been set so well as they were by the great masters of sixteenth-century music.

Let us see now what Verdi does when he wants to express the emotions implied in the words he is setting. In that tender, plaintive section of the *Requiem,* the "Domine Jesu," he aims at obtaining his effect by stating a principal theme in strongly accented three-four time. We are given, in fact, a languishingly walloping waltz-tune. The *leit motif* of the "Dies Irae," for all that concerns the terrible aspects of the Last Judgment, is a sort of "William Tell" thunderstorm, full of descending chromatic figures, very loud and effective and brilliant. But do these bold themes really express all that is in the words? Are they not really absurdly crude when compared with those flexible melodies of the polyphonists, which follow every contour of the sense with absolute fidelity, which express every implication of emotion? It is difficult to pretend that they are not.

It would be absurd to say that the invention of recurrent themes and easily recognizable, accentuated rhythms has not, on the whole, been a good thing. It has enabled musicians to organize into coherent works of art much longer pieces of music than the sixteenth-century masters could conveniently put together. This by itself is something of immense importance. But there can be no doubt that for expressing fine shades of emotion, for setting specific words to music, the polyphonic convention, with its perfect flexibility and its independence of parts, is a better medium than the music of set melodies and rhythms.

On the question of the place of rhythm in music a great deal could be written. The nature of polyphonic music made it almost impossible for it to possess defined rhythms; nor did the Church, in whose service most of the great masters worked, approve of such rhythms, because they tended to distract the mind from religious thoughts by their almost physically stimulating nature. Nowadays we have carried the cult of rhythm to extremes. Our popular music is a banging of tom-toms. Even the writings of serious musicians—one thinks of Stravinsky's *Sacre*—are predominantly rhythmic, have rhythm rather than melody, whether monodic or polyphonic, as their backbone and framework. This excessive cult of rhythm is certainly a sign of barbarism; the sixteenth-century ladies and gentlemen who were educated to sing a part in a madrigal at sight, and who could listen to Palestrina's music familiarly and with pleasure, were certainly more civilized musically than their descendants today whose staple musical fare is provided by the jazz band. Still, one cannot regret the development of defined rhythms in serious music. They have given us the Fifth Symphony among other things. If the polyphonists had known as much about rhythm as, shall we say, Bach, their music would have been the finer. They teach us, however, that we have gone too far in our cult of what, after all, is a primitive and popular element of music.

[*The Weekly Westminster Gazette,* December 2, 1922]

Round About Don Juan

DON GIOVANNI at the Old Vic is not, perhaps, quite the same thing as *Don Giovanni* at Munich. But the performance is quite good enough to make an evening in the Waterloo Road extremely pleasant. And even if it were not so good as it is, Mozart's music is about as nearly performer-proof as any music can be. Given a reasonably faithful rendering of the notes, it can hardly fail to produce the desired effects upon the audience. The most serious thing that can happen to *Don Giovanni* is to be directed by someone who has the wrong ideas about the character of the play. When Strauss, for example, conducts the opera in such a way that Leporello's comic counterpoint to the high tragedy of Don Juan and the Statue is muted down out of existence, he does more to spoil one's pleasure in the piece than many indifferently good singers could do. Mr. E. J. Dent and Mr. Clive Carey have seen to it, however, that *Don Giovanni* at the Vic gets played and sung in the spirit in which it was written—as one of those rather appalling comedies of which our ancestors were so fond in the days before Rousseau invented humanitarianism.

To listen once again to *Don Giovanni* is to start wondering afresh wherein precisely lies the secret of the perfect melody. What is it, even when the elements that compose them—the turns, the melodic tropes and phrases—are the same, what is it that makes a good melody so vastly different from a bad one? What is it that makes an aria out of *Figaro* or *Don Giovanni* an unforgettably beautiful piece of music, while an aria out of Cimarosa's *Matrimonio Segreto* or *Astuzie Femminili*, made up of very similar melodic elements, is no more than a charming musical-comedy tune? The ultimate cause of the Mozartean superiority is, of course, extremely obvious; Mozart had genius and Cimarosa, in spite of Stendhal's enthusiastic admiration, had not. What is much more difficult to explain is the reason why one particular arrangement of common melodic phrases is exquisitely beautiful, while another and apparently not very different arrangement is either merely pretty or definitely dull. The principal cause for the badness of bad melodies is to be found, I imagine, more in their rhythm than in their pitch. Perfect melodies can be made out of a few adjoining notes so arranged that they imply the simplest tonic and dominant harmony. How many of Mozart's arias are to be found in this category! On the other hand, he often obtains some of his loveliest effects (as in "Deh vieni alla finestra") by an unexpected modulation in the midst of the simply harmonized air. Rhythm, however, seems to be the more important factor. Take the notes of a good melody by Mozart and change the rhythm in which they are arranged; you can produce a thoroughly bad melody. Take, for instance, the note of "Dove sono i bei momenti" out of *Figaro* and arrange them in waltz time to the rhythm: One, "One, "One, "three, One' ". The disgusting result might be a waltz out of any bad musical comedy. We have now to ask ourselves, what is a bad rhythm? Is any rhythm bad in itself? No, rhythms are only good or bad according to their position. It may, perhaps, be stated as a general rule, that any rhythm which is too insistently repeated tends to become a bad rhythm. The Fifth Symphony, it is true, provides a sufficiently striking exception to this rule. But it is surely owing to insistent repetition that the rhythms of popular dance tunes are so dull and fatiguing. It is the repetition of the very aggressive rub-dub, dub-a-dub of "Land of Hope and Glory" that causes what might otherwise be a very fine processional melody to sound so irritating. It is fairly easy, then, to see what a bad musical rhythm is; but to lay down any rule for the production of good rhythms is an impossibility. One finds oneself reduced to the old *argumentum ad hominem*: good rhythms are those invented by good composers.

[*The Weekly Westminster Gazette,* December 9, 1922]

Delius and the Nature-Emotion

OF ALL the contemporary English composers the man whose work one would like most frequently to hear is certainly Delius. But in point of fact how rarely one does hear it! The opera companies come and go, but *A Village Romeo and Juliet* is never on their repertories. Conductors, pianists, singers fairly tumble over one another in their anxiety to perform the works of Mr. Arnold Bax, but it is only once in a very long while that they think of Delius. And yet, it seems sufficiently obvious to anyone who has heard this pure and lovely music, *A Village Romeo and Juliet* is one of the very few good operas of recent times; and among the master's other compositions, choral and instrumental, there are things of extraordinary beauty, far more interesting and genuine as works of art than a great deal of modern music that is much more frequently heard. This being so, one is particularly grateful when any of the larger and more inaccessible works of Delius are performed. Our gratitude on this occasion (as on so many others) is due to the Philharmonic Society. At their last week's concert they gave us an opportunity of hearing once again Delius's big composition for chorus and orchestra, *The Song of the High Hills*.

The Song of the High Hills is by no means a faultless work; it tends to be a little diffuse, and it contains passages, particularly those of emphasis and climax, which one feels somehow, instinctively, to be not quite emotionally true, as though they had been forced artificially and consciously into their present shape for the sake of some dramatic idea in which the composer did not wholly believe. But the bulk of the work is good; it reveals to us, as we listen, the real Delius, the man who has said something in terms of music which no other composer has precisely said before, something beautiful and important and significant.

What is this new thing that makes itself heard in Delius's music? It is something which has long ago found expression in poetry, which has played an immense part in our English literature during the last century and more. It is what we may call, for lack of a better word, the "nature-emotion." It is that sense of exaltation tinged with melancholy, of a profound joy that is at the most piercing and exquisite of sorrows; it is, in a word, that complicated and nameless emotion which we feel in the presence of nature. It is the emotion to which Wordsworth was the first to give full expression in poetry, the emotion which inspired Edward Thomas (among all the modern babblers of green fields almost the only genuine "nature-poet") to write his bare and beautiful lyrics. Strangely enough, however, this nature-emotion seems never to have inspired any of the great composers who lived contemporaneously with the nature-poets of the nineteenth century. It cannot be said that Beethoven's Pastoral Symphony expresses anything comparable in complexity and serious import to the nature-emotion of some of Wordsworth's poetry. Beethoven, it seems to me, comes much nearer to capturing this particular emotion in the slow movement of the Ninth Symphony. His successors, so far as I know, never get anywhere near the Wordsworthian feeling. In Debussy's *Après-midi d'un faune* we find, it is true, something like it. But the emotion here, exquisite as it is and exquisitely expressed, is less full and beautiful than the real nature-emotion. The *Après-midi* is inspired by something simpler, something nearer to the old classical sentiments towards beauty and its transient fragility. A century has passed since the nature-emotion was first exploited in literature; it is only in our own times and in the work of a single composer that we find it inspiring music.

That composer is Delius. All his compositions, from the long-drawn-out *Village Romeo* to that small and perfect work of art, *On Hearing the First Cuckoo in the Spring,* are colored and pervaded by this nature-emotion. They are all of them expressions of that melancholy but at the same time intense and exalted joy which is the feeling of a man who walks alone among the "High Hills"—that melancholy joy which is to have known the nearest thing to happiness that is knowable on this earth. Delius has made a real contribution to music; he has extended the bounds of musical expression, has added a new province to that already vast and opulent empire. An artistic conquest is unlike a political conquest, in that everyone is the richer and happier because of it. Peru and Mexico were the destruction of Spain; a few more Mesopotamias, and England will be in ruins. But conquerors in the world of art bring back in the charming words of the hymn: "solid joys and lasting treasures." Alexander's empire was a frail thing; but Beethoven's will last for many a century to come. And the minor conquerors—the raiders into the intellectual unknown, the settlers of new colonies on the uttermost verge of art—their conquests are still with us, still enrich the public treasury. The Chopins, the Schumanns, the Debussys—they have all added a province; not large, perhaps, but none the less important. Delius is of their race, a conqueror.

[*The Weekly Westminster Gazette,* December 16, 1922]

Bad Music

THERE IS no experience more depressing than to listen to bad music played by a good executant. Well played, the bad music sounds, if anything, rather worse than it really is; its badness is fully and perfectly revealed. And what gloomy reflections are evoked by the contrast between the artistry and refinement of the player, and the coarse vulgarity of the work that is played! One thinks of the waste of the performer's talent and time (not to mention the waste of our time and the price of our tickets); one thinks of the minds of the people who like this sort of thing; one thinks of all the lovely works one might be hearing and isn't; one thinks of the spiritual hierarchy of man and makes the melancholy constatation that there are a great many Sudras in the world. And one comes away at the end of the concert—that is, if one hasn't had the wisdom to come out a good deal earlier—thoroughly cast down, damped and dejected.

Such, alas! was my experience at Madame Suggia's concert last Saturday afternoon. It started hopefully enough. A little piece by Boccherini opened the program—not a grand work, certainly, but graceful, charming, and thoroughly ingenious as the cello writing of that virtuoso-turned composer always is. A Haydn minuet followed, simple and single-minded; then the Bach suite in G, of which the last three movements, at any rate, reveal the real Bach at his best. It was in the second half of the program, in the section devoted to modern work, that the horrors of the afternoon began. Of the three pieces of which this section of the program consisted, the best (but that is not saying much) was a harmlessly melodious work by Max Bruch. Two empty little pieces by Sinigaglia followed. But the Symphonic Variations of Boëllmann, with which the concert ended, were more than negatively bad; they were positively dreadful. I am not familiar with many of the works of Mr. Boëllmann; but it would not surprise me to hear that he is the author of "Where my Caravan Has Rested." The *Symphonic Variations* are purely and simply cinema music, suitable for performance during the passion scenes of five-reel American drama. They would be tolerable enough if we could listen to them with the distracted ears of those who gaze absorbed at the Little Sweetheart of the World. But without the Little Sweetheart to divert our attention from the vulgarity of the original theme and the almost total lack of invention exhibited in the variations, Mr. Boëllmann's work is not easily to be listened to, particularly when it is played by a refined and accomplished artist like Madame Suggia.

There is no doubt that bad music is much more insufferable, more totally devoid of any value whatever, than bad literature. There are plenty of bad books which it is possible to read with patience and even pleasure, and plenty more which contain, among some barnyard litter, here and there something like a pearl. But bad music is in general altogether bad. (I am speaking here, of course, of the bad music which aspires to be good, not of the straightforward, popular tune of commerce which aims at producing what is scarcely more than a physical effect upon the hearer.) There is nothing in our *Symphonic Variations,* for example, to which one can listen with anything but pain. And yet, had the composer been a novelist possessing equivalent literary talents, he would in all probability have produced a book which we could in any case read through to the end.

At first sight all this seems rather curious, almost inexplicable. But a little reflection provides us with a very obvious reason for this inferiority of bad music to bad literature. The second-rate writer has this advantage over the second-rate musician: he can give a direct account of his experiences. Now, since interesting things constantly happen to not very interesting people, and since these not very interesting people frequently possess enough talent and education to write a sufficiently vivid account of their interesting experience, it follows that a book by a bad writer may be readable because it describes interesting events. In music, however, it is different. Interesting experiences may happen to an uninteresting composer; but he cannot give a direct, immediate account of them in his music. However descriptively a composer may try to write, his music must, in the fundamental nature of things, always remain a reflection of his private internal world; it cannot, as literature can, reflect only the external world. So it comes about, naturally enough, that the music of a man with an uninteresting mind can hardly fail to be as uninteresting as he is. In music nothing counts but the absolute, intrinsic genius of the composer; he can derive little or no assistance from what is outside him. What this thing "genius" is, what are its relations to morality, to the universe, to the fundamental reality?—these are questions which I prefer not to discuss. Christmas comes but once a year, and when it does come it is best to be merry and eat plum-pudding.

[*The Weekly Westminster Gazette,* December 23, 1922]

Music in the Encyclopaedia

THE MUSICIAN, it seems, like everybody else, takes a holiday at Christmas time. To all intents and purposes there have been no concerts in London for a full week and more.

> Only the carol-singer stalks
> Throughout the city's desolate walks
> At midnight and his carnage plies.

But by some almost miraculous stroke of good fortune I have not once heard his voice. Carols are extremely sweet; but unheard, at any rate for one season, they are sweeter still. Next year I shall listen to "Good King Wenceslas" with a renewed gusto. Meanwhile, in spite of the seasonal dearth of subject-matter, the poor critic is expected to write an article. Bricks without straw, words without songs ... the task is somewhat difficult.

As it happens, however, I spent a large part of Christmas Day turning over the pages of the three supplementary volumes of the *Encyclopaedia Britannica* which happened to have arrived, like a Christmas present (though, alas, I had paid for them) from the binders that very morning. After reading dutifully and with more profit than I generally derive from such literature, the article on Relativity, I turned—the tribute of ignorance to mathematics duly paid—with a good deal of curiosity and with mixed anticipations to the article on Music. Mr. Donald Tovey, to whose pen the Eleventh Edition of the *Britannica* owes its principal musical articles, is the author also of these pages on the music of the last decade. I was curious to see what he had to say—he, the learned scholar, and the preceptor, the accomplished musician—about the tumultuous present.

He says, in point of fact, remarkably and disappointingly little. For an article in an encyclopaedia—in an adult's guide to knowledge—Mr. Tovey's "Music" is non-committal and uninformative to a degree. A studious Japanese, having a conscientious desire to find out all about contemporary European music, might read and re-read the article and, literally, be none the wiser about the subject at the end of the process. Let us try to assess precisely what he would discover, this industrious Oriental of ours, from the pages of the *Britannica*.

To begin with, he would find that Mr. Tovey disapproved strongly of contemporary musical criticism. "The critics ... are now unanimous in condemning all that is under suspicion of being 'correct' and are desperately anxious that no *soi-disant* revolutionary tendency shall miss acclamation and that no dangerous outburst of normality shall escape damnation." A little later on he will discover that there has existed a musi-

cian called Scriabin, of whom he will gather, not very certainly, that Mr.
Tovey approves of his work. After that he will hear something about the
Russian ballet and two pieces of music entitled *L'Oiseau de feu* and
Petrouchka. Then follows a passage about large orchestras and Gustav
Mahler, of whom Mr. Tovey appears to approve. A passing reference to
Schönberg's *Gurrelieder* is followed by a discussion, couched in terms of
mixed admiration and dislike, of Max Reger. A few rather oracular references of Granville Bantock lead on to a passage in which Gustav Holst is
quite decidedly and definitely praised. After this Mr. Tovey goes back to
his old caution. How has the War affected music? "The wisest answer is
evasive." "If, however, any musical work is destined to impress posterity
as a noble expression and reaction of the World War, the choice, strange as
it may seem, might most desirably fall on Richard Strauss's 'Die Frau ohne
Schatten.'" The article ends with a description of Mr. Emanuel Moor's
"Duplex-Coupler" piano and a prophecy of the pianistic glories of the future. The interstices between these fixed points are filled up with historical
references and casual reflections, often interesting in themselves but doing
little or nothing to assist our poor Japanese to understand contemporary
European music. There are also a surprisingly large number of references
to the Crystal Palace Handel Festivals. This fact, however, is not surprising; for the Handel Festivals at the Crystal Palace are Mr. Tovey's King
Charles's head. References to them dot the pages of the Eleventh Edition;
it is delightful to find that the ten years which separate the Eleventh Edition from the Twelfth Edition have done nothing to dim that profound impression of horror which he must, one feels, have received as a child
beneath the arcades of Sir Joseph Paxton's gigantic greenhouse.

But seriously, our Japanese has cause to complain. This is not a good
article for an encyclopaedia. Not merely does it fail to give the facts (Mr.
Tovey, it must be admitted, disclaims any intention of making it a "catalogue raisonné of modern music"); it conspicuously fails in doing what it
sets out to do . . . to "put forward certain general principles [governing
music] that have become more clearly manifested during the decade."
There is scarcely a hint in the whole article of what it is that makes "modern" music different from older work. There is no word of any of the new
harmonic systems; no word of that introduction of barbaric rhythms
which is so striking a feature of much contemporary music; no word of
that reversion to polyphony which characterizes certain other work. There
is, indeed, nothing whatever in the article which would enable our hypo-
thetical Jap to form the faintest notion of modern music. For those of us
who are regular concert-goers, Mr. Tovey's article will signify something;
we can use our knowledge to catch references and fill in gaps.

[*The Weekly Westminster Gazette*, December 30, 1922]

Going to the Opera

LONDON is still on something less than quarter rations of good music. So serious has been the shortage that I was reduced, last Monday night, to listening to *Samson and Delilah* at Covent Garden. What an opera! I had forgotten what the thing was like, for it is a very long time since I last heard it; it will be longer still before I hear it again.

What is it, I kept wondering all through the evening, that induces people to go and listen—in quantities and, what is more, with apparent enjoyment—to things like *Samson and Delilah*? A kind of *snobisme* is, no doubt, a contributory cause of this strange state of affairs. People are hypnotized by the grandeur of Grand Opera, by the height of the High Art of which it is the shining symbol. For, by definition, everything that calls itself an opera and is produced at a great opera-house must be grand and must be a piece of High Art. To go to an opera, even if it happens to be *Samson and Delilah,* is to prove oneself to be interested in the higher life. So, unexpressed of course, the argument must run. But though this simple form of intellectual *snobisme* may have something to do with the crowding of Covent Garden, even on *Samson* nights, it is, after all, only a subsidiary cause. The real and cogent reason why people go to hear *Samson and Delilah* must obviously be that they enjoy it. The question is: why do they enjoy it? I really cannot imagine.

Without caring very much for the operas of Wagner, one can easily understand the reason for other people's devotion to them. The operas of Wagner were written by a man who was exuberantly alive. The violent energy with which they are charged infects the hearer and quickens his own sense of vitality. Like the sculpture of Bernini and his contemporaries, Wagner's music presents us with emotions caught at the very top of their gesture. Wagner was a baroque artist born out of his time and with a spirit somewhat unnecessarily complicated by the ideas and feelings of the nineteenth century. He worked on the principles formulated two hundred years before his time by the Cavaliere Marino:

E del poeta il fin la meraviglia,
Chi non sa far stupir vada alla striglia.

"The poet's aim is to surprise. He who knows not how to astonish, let him be whipped." Wagner certainly succeeds in astonishing, in carrying one off one's feet—at any rate on a first hearing, and when one is seventeen. It is easy to understand why *Tristan* fills Covent Garden and why the Monday evening Proms are always so well attended.

But Saint-Saëns is very far indeed from being a Wagner. He is not exuberantly alive—he is hardly alive at all. Nobody can come away from

Samson and Delilah with any feeling of renewed buoyancy and strength. Samson is a strong man who has no vitality to give away. Wagner would have made him a Lieutenant Muller of the spirit—fifteen minutes a day and a new zest for life guaranteed at the end of the week. But Saint-Saëns, with his eclecticism, his facile and vulgar and insignificant invention, his obvious theatrical sentiments, and the unfaltering technical competence with which he expresses the dreary things he has to say—Saint-Saëns does not whet the appetite for life; he turns its edge.

Samson's debility is most apparent when he tries to be most powerful. It is in the first act, where the music bases itself for the most part on the oratorio style of Handel and Bach, that we are most painfully aware of Saint-Saëns's shortcomings. The triviality and banality of all the themes becomes the more apparent when we think of those which the composer is trying to rival. From under the lion's skin of Handel the long ears most conspicuously project. When he is writing in the manner of Gounod or Meyerbeer, Saint-Saëns is more at home and his music does not suffer by odious comparison. It is relatively more satisfying because the frame of reference is different—Gounod instead of Handel.

And yet, extraordinary as it seems, people like this stuff. And what is more, they actually prefer it to works which are not only incomparably better, more original and dramatic, but which also possess in a far higher degree that most popular of musical qualities—tunefulness. The operas of Mozart abound with haunting melodies—melodies that stick in the mind and never lose their savor. *Don Giovanni* is far more melodious than *Samson and Delilah* and yet Saint-Saëns's masterpiece is much more frequently performed than Mozart's. This, I confess, completely mystifies me. That the obscurity and silliness of some of Mozart's libretti should deter a public that pays, when it buys an opera ticket, for two entertainments at a time—a play and a concert—is comprehensible. *The Magic Flute* and *Cosi fan tutte* are certainly not masterpieces of literature. But where can one find more neat and workmanlike libretti than *Figaro* and *Don Giovanni*? In these operas you really do get your money's worth—good plays, good tunes. And yet (we have to come back to this incomprehensible fact) there seems to be an immense number of people who prefer *Samson*—who incomparably prefer *Faust*. It is all very queer. However, the British National Opera Company is giving us a rare treat in the shape of a production of the *Seraglio*. Let us be duly thankful. Perhaps when the Samsonites listen to some of the miraculous tunes which find their way into the *Seraglio*, they may repent and become reformed characters. Let us hope so; it is about time.

[*The Weekly Westminster Gazette*, January 6, 1923]

Handel, Polly, and Ourselves

PEACOCK'S MR. ESCOT[3] (whose name, it will be remembered, was derived from *es skoton*, into the darkness) was a "pejorationist": he believed that things were steadily getting worse and worse. It is more fashionable nowadays to believe that they are getting better and better. The world has exchanged the undiluted pessimism of such products of the heroic age as Sir Philip Sidney and Lord Brooke, for the optimism born of an age of prosperity and expanding material life—an optimism which, tinged as it has been of late with more than a trace of doubt, still holds the field. Which is the truer view of life? It is absurd to attempt an answer. The most one can do is to suggest that certain aspects of contemporary life incline one to take the optimist's view, certain others the pejorationist's.

At the Albert Hall performance of the *Messiah*, last Saturday afternoon, I found myself on the side of Mr. Escot. It wasn't merely that the arena seats were possibly uncomfortable, that the hall was too large for the soloists, that the choir was too large for the music. No, these things contributed to my depression; but they were not the sole causes of it. What chiefly inclined me towards pejorationism was the thought that Handel has been dead a long time, and that we have not succeeded in producing anyone like him since. Nature seems to have lost the recipe which went to the making of such men. For some inexplicable reason, these gigantic creatures of inexhaustible energy and vitality, these grand men to whom the creation of grand art came naturally and easily, no more make their appearance among us. The portentous creatures of the renaissance seem now to be as extinct as pterodactyls; even the Christopher Wrens and Boscovitches of much later days have now no parallel. The universal genius is no more. We can account for that perhaps, by the fact that nowadays we know so much that no man has time to do more than one thing really well. If Wren had been born two centuries later than he was, he would have had no time, despite his ninety years of life, to make himself a first-class mathematician as well as a first-class architect; the mathematics would have kept him busy all the time. The universal genius then, is extinct, and we know the reason why. But why does the world produce no more specialized geniuses of the size and manliness, and vigorous humanity of Handel? Why has nobody the inexhaustible energy of these men of the past? or their capacity to be truly grand in an entirely simple and dignified manner? These questions are far more difficult to answer. Mr. Escot would say, of course, that it was just the normal process of pejoration: but that is too simple by half. No, we must leave the question unanswered—merely stat-

3. Escot is a character from Peacock's *Headlong Hall* (1816).

ing the fact that, so far as we can see, our age has produced nobody possessing these qualities of size, manliness, unaffected and spontaneous grandeur, lucidity, and intellectual force which are the peculiar characteristics of such a man as Handel.

What an extraordinary musician he is! The man who could write a melody like "The People that Walked in Darkness"—a melody that goes piercing and piercing in tireless undulations into the very heart of the emotion it has to express—surely deserved to be ranked by Beethoven as almost the greatest of his predecessors. And how refreshing it is, to ears accustomed to the theatrical grandiosities of Wagner or the Contemporary Block, to the neurasthenic crying and shouting of Scriabin, to hear something in which greatness is wedded to simplicity and dignity. What could give a nobler idea of the magnificence and grandeur of the human spirit than the great chorus, "For unto us a Child"? And yet what could be simpler and in every way less baroque? When he compares this spacious and serene greatness of Handel with the spirit which expressed itself today, Mr. Escot can only shake his head.

I can also imagine him shaking his head after an evening at *Polly*. Here is popular music, two hundred years old, which has to be listened to with a certain amount of intelligent attention if it is to be fully appreciated. The melodic phrases are long and gracefully curved. There is plenty of simple counterpoint in the orchestral accompaniment. Modern popular music need not be listened to at all. There is no counterpoint to follow and the melodic phrases are rarely of any length or intricacy. Instead, we have short obvious phrases, supported by lusciously colored chords which flare out at one like posters on a hoarding. One does not listen to this music; it is the music which comes up and hits one. *Argal,* Mr. Escot would conclude, there is also a pejoration among the audience.

He may be right, he may not. In any case, the audience is different. The producers of *Polly* have insisted upon the difference only too forcibly. They try to persuade us, by the oddities of their production, that there is something essentially quaint about the formalism of the old cut forms. The charming music is there to protest against this view. It is not quaint; it is merely beautiful.

[*The Weekly Westminster Gazette,* January 13, 1923]

Music Clubs

LAST TUESDAY EVENING the Chelsea Music Club inaugurated itself by giving, at the Chelsea Town Hall, one of the most satisfying concerts I have heard for a long time. The program was excellent and so were the performers, who included Mr. Goossens and his orchestra, with Mr. Harold Jones as solo pianist. The hall was commodious and cool, the audience intelligently appreciative. Altogether a charming evening's entertainment—and one which points a moral to every lover of music.

The Chelsea Music Club is one of the first of what ought in time to grow into a small army of similar clubs in London, and all over the country. It is a pioneer pointing the way towards hitherto unexplored possibilities, the prophet of a brilliant musical future in England. The astonishing thing is, surely, that clubs like this have not existed all over the country for years past and that music-lovers have been content to put up with a system which provides not very much music, frequently of an indifferently feeble sort, at high prices and in inconvenient places. Music at present is far too highly centralized. In London, for example, it can only be heard in four or five halls situated, for the most part, within a half-mile radius of Oxford Circus. Most of London's seven millions, however, live at a distance of anything from two to ten miles from this magic circle. Is it surprising, then, that the musical public which fills (or doesn't fill, as the case may be) these concert halls numbers perhaps seven thousand or .1 percent of the population? For certain kinds of music, it is obvious, centralization is necessary; it is difficult to transport a complete symphony orchestra from place to place, difficult to find a large enough hall to accommodate it, and difficult to collect a large enough audience at any non-central point, to pay for it. But with chamber music it is very different. A pianist, a singer, a violinist, a quartet, even a small orchestra can move from place to place easily and cheaply, and they are heard best in small halls. It is they who should go out to their audiences; it is absurd to expect the audience to come to them.

The performer will answer, no doubt, that they would be only too delighted to come to an audience if they knew precisely where to find it. They are not familiar with local conditions; they would be at a loss to know how to collect an audience in a country town or suburban borough; they would not even know where to play. That is why they go on giving performances in the central halls—despite the fact that such performances are sparsely attended, owing to their inaccessibility to the vast majority of the musical public, and often result in actual financial loss.

The Music Clubs are being founded to give the performers an opportunity of reaching a public which cannot come to the central halls and at the same time to give this music-loving public an opportunity of hearing the music it would like, but is unable to hear. In time, it is hoped, these Music Clubs will be federated together into a great association, which will arrange for players to give their performances all over the country. This will have the effect of ensuring a regular and dependable livelihood to many performers and will also encourage them in the rehearsal of new or unfamiliar works, the performance of which can scarcely ever be made to pay at a commercially organized concert at one of the central halls.

Last Tuesday's concert sufficiently proved that the idea of a Music Club is no idle dream. Here was a considerable audience, consisting entirely of subscribers, listening to an admirable concert. There is no reason why similar clubs should not exist in every London borough, there is no reason why Mr. Goossens and his orchestra should not play the same program every night for a fortnight to different, but equally appreciative audiences from Streatham to Hampstead, and from Greenwich to Twickenham. All that is needed is a little organization and some enthusiasm. The music-loving public, which exists potentially, will become an actual living army of men and women, eager to listen to the good things that are brought within their reach.

[*The Weekly Westminster Gazette*, January 20, 1923]

Cherubini—Emotion and Form

LISTENING the other day to that noble and beautiful piece of music, Cherubini's[4] overture to *Medea*, I found myself thinking about one of the paradoxes (or perhaps it is not a paradox at all, but only to be expected) of music and, indeed, of all art. I found myself wondering why it is that, as a general rule, the passions and the intenser emotions are most powerfully and movingly expressed in terms of the most austerely intellectual forms of art. A rhapsodical and disordered work of art, though it may accurately reflect in its form, or violent absence of form, the disorderliness of passion, rarely expresses that passion so effectively as does a work of severe formality. Nothing could be less *décousu*, nothing more severely concentrated and composed than the *Medea* overture. And yet it is a work of extraordinary passion and power. It expresses intense emotion; and it does so, in its clear, intellectual way, far better, one feels, than any wild patchwork of tumultuous harmony could ever do.

What is true of Cherubini's great overture is abundantly true of other works of art, plastic and literary as well as musical. The profound religious mysticism of Palestrina is expressed in terms of a music that comes about as near mathematics as any music could do. The finest of Bach's fugues have a great emotional content. Turn from music to sculpture; there

---

4. Maria Cherubini (1760–1824). Italian composer.

is a thousand times more passion and power in the studied repose of the statues that adorn the Medici tombs than in the wild gesticulation of Bernini's saints and angels and pagan gods. And yet Bernini's art reflects violent emotion with an extraordinary realism; he knew, as no one else has ever known, how to catch the passions at the top of their extravagant gesture. But the recumbent Night, but the Medicean warrior wrapped in his brooding quiet, express with an incomparably greater liveliness those infinities of passion within the soul which it was the ambition of the baroque artist to represent in all their force and grandeur. It is easy to think of similar examples in literature. Writers, like Balzac, who "protest too much" about energy and passion, do not, in most cases, give such adequate expression to these things as is given by writers who handle similar themes in a much more restrained and less feverish fashion. And a writer who canalizes his emotion into severe form will generally produce a more moving work of art than the man who lets his passion spill about in a flood. One feels more life and energy in a Shakespeare sonnet than in a wild rhapsody by Whitman.

In music this curious paradox has persisted during the last fifty years, in a very conspicuous fashion. For the commanding musical figure of the second half of the nineteenth century was one who, like Balzac, "protested too much," who tried, like Bernini, to give an absolutely direct artistic representation of passion and emotion. The music of Wagner is certainly moving. But does it move as much, at a repetition, as it did on a first hearing? Does it express passion in a manner that is permanently satisfying? The answer to both these questions is, surely, No. This music of emotionalism does not seem to express more than the surface, so to speak, of the emotions. It is *St. Theresa,* it is *Apollo and Daphne,* not the Michelangelesque *Night.* It is *Illusions Perdues,* not *Macbeth.* What is true of Wagner is true of most of his successors. The exultations and agonies of Scriabin's *Prometheus* are hysterical and insignificant compared with the exultations and agonies expressed with such logic, such formal lucidity in the Ninth Symphony.

Art that reflects life immediately and realistically tends to be less moving, less satisfying, at any rate in the long run, than art in which the passions of life appear at a further remove, and are expressed in terms of something that is not a realistic representation of life. Perhaps it is no paradox, but obvious and inevitable. Perhaps the process of artistic creation consists precisely in thus removing life into a different, formal world in which it is made to obey unfamiliar laws. Perhaps the men who insist so violently on passion and energy and who try to reflect these qualities immediately and realistically in their art—perhaps they are not artists at all.

[*The Weekly Westminster Gazette,* January 27, 1923]

Madrigals and Program Music

IF ALL CONCERTS were as interesting as that which was given, last Saturday afternoon, by the English Singers, how unadulteratedly delightful regular concert-going would be! But, alas! all concerts are not as good as this one; or, at any rate, they most certainly have not been during the last weeks. For, though Christmas is now long past, music still seems to be suffering from the effects of its holiday. A concert like the English Singers' stands out as an exception from among recent musical entertainments.

The bulk of last Saturday's program consisted of sixteenth- and seventeenth-century madrigals, canzonets, and ballets for three, four, five, and six voices. A hearing of these beautiful pieces of music, selected from the works of English, Flemish, and Italian masters, tends to confirm one in the opinion which a Palestrina concert always forces upon the mind: that for lovely and apposite setting of words, for richness of texture, for intricate beauty of the melodic lines in the separate parts, there is nothing in music that can compare with the motets and madrigals of the golden age. The principal defect of this music belonging to an epoch before the invention of the notion of themes and developments is the practical impossibility of organizing it into coherent forms of any size. Working on the principle of theme and development, the composer can construct a work of almost any length that shall still be recognizably balanced and symmetrical—a single, unified whole. The madrigalist composing, so to speak, not in a circle but along a continuous undulating line, cannot give his work formal symmetry and balance. Where the line is short, this does not matter; the perceiving mind can remember at the last undulation what the first was like. But prolong the line and the mind, fatigued, forgets, loses the clue. The modern *vers libriste* finds himself in very much the same position as the sixteenth-century madrigal writer. His continuous rhythmic line may follow the contours of his emotion with extraordinary fidelity; its undulations may be of the greatest beauty. But the mind cannot follow it, with any real satisfaction, for long. *Vers libre* is admirable in short pieces in which one can follow the line with ease from beginning to end. But an epic in *vers libre* is unthinkable. For longer works some definite meter with a norm to which periodical return is made is essential. The same, on a larger and more complicated scale, is true of music. The longer polyphonic works are, on the whole, less satisfactory, because less capable of being appreciated as single artistic units, than the shorter. The triumphs of the style are to be found, not in the long masses, but in the motets, the anthems, the madrigals, where a short line, which we can trace from beginning to end, is made to follow some specific emotion.

The Purcell songs, included by the English Singers in the second part of their performance, were interesting as being specimens—charmingly in-genuous—of early program music. "I spy Celia" follows what we may call an emotional program. "The Three Fairies" belongs to that class of music which is descriptive and imitative of natural phenomena. Both these kinds of program music were already old at the time of Purcell. Palestrina him-self gives spirited imitations in one of his motets of various instruments, while he often gives musical descriptions of physical acts suggested by the words he is setting—such as running, leaping, and the like. From the six-teenth century also date a number of battle pieces, imitations of birds, and so on. The seventeenth century developed the tradition of program music in the new art forms. Groves quotes the opening theme (in descending and rising semi-tones) of a four-part vocal fugue on the mewing of cats, written by Krieger in the latter part of the seventeenth century. Domenico Scarlatti is also the author of a cat's fugue.

In one of their charming little "Musikalische Stundenbücher" the Drei Masken Verlag of Munich have recently published two of the most inter-esting pieces of program music belonging to the early eighteenth century—Kuhnau's *Sickness of Hezekiah,* one of this curious composer's musical Bible-stories, and Bach's Capriccio in B flat, written on the occasion of his brother's departure from home. The Kuhnau sonata is a pleasant, thin lit-tle piece of music without much subtlety, but expressing sufficiently ade-quately the ups and downs of Hezekiah's emotions, from the *lamento* of the first movement to the *allegrezza del Re convalescente* of the last.

The Bach Capriccio is a very different affair. The first movement is an attempt to cajole the brother to put off his journey; in the second the dan-gers of the journey are set forth; the third is a general lament by the whole family; the fourth shows them resignedly saying good-bye; the fifth is the postilion's air; and the sixth is a fugue on the theme of the post-boy's horn. The music combines in an exquisitely subtle way a real tenderness of feel-ing with a joking touch of the comic. It is one of the most delightful pieces of program music ever written.

[*The Weekly Westminster Gazette,* February 3, 1923]

The Hymn and the Dream

MR. HOLST'S[5] *Hymn of Jesus* lasts, I should imagine, for little more than half an hour. And yet, when the Royal Choral Society performed it last Saturday at the Albert Hall as a pendant (a rather queer, incongruous pen-

---

5. Gustav Holst (1874–1934). English composer of Swedish origins.

dant, it must be admitted) to *The Dream of Gerontius,* there were a considerable number of old ladies and gentlemen, and even of young and middle-aged ones, who found that half-hour decidedly too long. Not to put too fine a point upon it, as Mr. Snagsby would have said, they left the building before the Hymn was half over. After the first five minutes they began putting on their coats and furs and collecting their umbrellas. A steady trickle of them flowed towards the doors through the whole of the rest of the performance.

I could not help speculating on the possible causes of this exodus. What was there, I wondered, in Mr. Holst's music so disturbing that old ladies found it impossible to listen to it? As the Hymn wore on towards its close I thought I could begin to understand the reason. The fact is that Mr. Holst's cantata is a very formidable piece of music. It expresses a kind of religious emotion that is passionate and hard and fiery—a kind of religious emotion, that is to say, not frequently associated with placid churchgoing once a week and mild, habitual good works. *The Hymn of Jesus* has disturbingly little resemblance to any Hymn A or M. Nobody brought up in a quiet way to round off Sunday evening with "Lead, Kindly Light" or "Abide with Me" picked out, with lots of expression but not too much technique, on the Broadwood or the harmonium, could listen to this surprising kind of hymn with equanimity. A Jesus so passionately alive, so strong, and of such abundant energy as this Jesus of Mr. Holst's Hymn has not much in common with the savior who speaks through the sagging cadences of "Art thou weary, art thou languid?" On the whole, when I come to consider the matter, I am surprised that more people did not leave the hall when Mr. Holst was let loose.

Archaistic and at the same time so up-to-date that it could not have been composed more than a few years ago, primitive and at the same time enormously sophisticated and based on profound musical scholarship, *The Hymn of Jesus* reminds me of one of those brilliant pieces of modern architecture in which the artist, working in some ancient style, has yet produced a novel and essentially contemporary work. It is the musical equivalent of Bentley's great cathedral. Westminster Cathedral, however, is a good deal nearer to genuine Byzantine architecture than is *The Hymn of Jesus* to Byzantine religious music. What Mr. Holst has done in this work is to show what Byzantine religious music ought to have been like if it had been as rich and as highly developed as the contemporaneous architecture. Like most other things in this world, these modern essays in ancient styles are justified by their success. Westminster Cathedral and Mr. Holst's Hymn are both abundantly successful. It is only in the case of the failures that we need question the rightness and advisability of making such essays.

Comparing *The Hymn of Jesus* with *The Dream of Gerontius*—and since they were both performed at the same concert it was difficult to avoid making the comparison—I was struck particularly by one fact: that for the expression of the emotions suggested by words an archaic form of setting is more effective than a less formal, "modern" setting. This same fact is strikingly illustrated by the different parts of *Gerontius* itself. In this work the long solo passages are set to a kind of recitative of an extremely "naturalistic" character. The words, that is to say, are not repeated, and there are no formal set pieces. Now, although it is natural in speaking to say a sentence only once, it does not follow that one ought, in music, to imitate the methods of speech. To do so is to abandon the greatest beauty that music possesses—the balanced symmetrical form. It might be worth-while to give up formalism if one were going to gain in force and truthfulness of emotional expression. But the curious fact emerges that, so far from gaining in emotional force by the abandonment of formalism, one actually loses. By repeating the same words on a series of slightly varying undulations the Handelian aria, at its best, expresses every possible emotion suggested in a single sentence; the recitative, which utters the word only once on a single musical line, cannot exhaust the whole emotional content of a pregnant sentence. It loses in expressive force as well as in formal beauty. In choral writing the lines described by the different parts give us a series of slightly different interpretations of the same set of words, so that even where the chorus is not worked up into a regular symmetrical form, with repetitions, one is likely to have a more expressive setting of words than in a recitative. One feels this very strongly in *Gerontius,* where the choruses are treated more formally than the solos—and are, in consequence, as it seems to me, both more beautiful in themselves and more expressive. Mr. Holst has no solos in *The Hymn of Jesus.* If he had, he could not have expressed what he wanted to express so tersely and so fully. His strangely harmonized counterpoint allows him to get the greatest possible amount of emotional expression out of his words in the shortest possible time.

[*The Weekly Westminster Gazette,* February 10, 1923]

Barbarism in Music

ON February 28th, 1894, the cult of Russian music in this country may be said to have definitely begun. It was on that day that Tschaikowsky's Pathetic Symphony was first performed in London. Intoxicated by this composer's exuberant and luscious self-pity, the public asked for more Russian music. They have been getting it in pretty large doses ever since. And though the Pathetic turned out not to be entirely characteristic of Russian music as a whole—for Tschaikowsky's emotionalism, as well as his musical talent, were unique and peculiar to himself—they were not at all disappointed by what they did get. A new revelation, comparable, it seemed, with the revelation of Wagner, had been manifested to the musical world. These all but thirty years which have elapsed since the discovery of Russia have put us sufficiently far above the turmoil to enable us to see things in their true proportions. We can begin to ask ourselves seriously what there is in this Russian music and what was the true nature of the revelation it unfolded before us.

On a first hearing of *Boris Godounov* it was possible to believe, particularly if Chaliapine was singing and one happened to be young at the time, that this was something of tremendous importance and significance. *Scheherazade* was a portent; and beside the *Capriccio Espagnol,* with its metallic high-lights, its aniline coloring, its chiaroscuro of Bengal lights and soot, all other music seemed at the moment of the first hearing singularly dim, neuter, and ineffectual. Time tends, however, to alter these estimates. Listening the other day for perhaps the twentieth time to Rimsky-Korsakoff's *Capriccio* I vowed that never, if I could possibly help it, would I listen to it again. A few weeks of regular ballet-going made *Scheherazade* seem absolutely intolerable, years ago. And even of *Boris* one has begun to doubt. How would it wear if it were performed as often as the Meistersingers? Badly, I am inclined to think. And what of Stravinsky? *Petrouchka* and the *Firebird* can certainly be listened to a good deal more often that most works by other Russian composers. On the lasting powers of the *Sacre* it is, perhaps, still too early to pronounce. But it may be permitted to doubt whether any of Stravinsky's works would stand the constant repetition which only tends to increase our admiration, as it enlarges our knowledge, of some favorite symphony or sonata of Beethoven.

The fact is that this Russian revelation was really a very poor apocalypse. The novelty of its melodic and harmonic conventions, based on those of native folk-song and religious music, wore off first of all. (I wish, by the way, that some of our younger composers would realize that the novelty of the Celtic convention had worn off some years before a note of Russian music had ever been heard in this country.) After that, those wild barbaric rhythms which had once been so intoxicating began to seem as irritating and as boring as the rhythms of last year's fox trots. And finally it was the dazzling orchestration that ceased to astonish and surprise. The aniline colors, the Bengal lights, and the soot came to look rather crude and uninteresting. The charm had rubbed off.

The Russian revolution was no more than a revelation of the charms of barbarism. To the highly civilized man the child of nature has always seemed a very attractive creature. The impossible noble savage was the delight of a past age. We who retain no illusions about the savage find the jovial ignobleness of the genuine article equally appealing. We like his high-spirited animalism; we admire, from the vantage point of our safe and orderly world, his wild energy and his passion. The Russians introduced the barbarian into music—naked but tattooed with the most brilliant colors, and furiously dancing to the accompaniment of the post-Wagnerian orchestra. Unfortunately, the appeal of the savage soon evaporates. Civilized beings may like barbarism for a change—for the weekends, so to speak. But they cannot stand it every day. A man in one stage of development cannot derive his staple intellectual sustenance from beings on another plane. Civilized men must have civilized art. Russian music was only for the corybantic weekend. The weekend has been unnecessarily prolonged, and we have, in consequence, grown heartily sick of Russian music. One thing, however, this weekend of barbarism has done for us; it has made us appreciate more highly than ever the qualities of civilized music. The Russians make us appreciate the qualities of orderliness and intellectual construction in Wagner's music; just a Wagner, in his turn (Wagner who, in Sir Hubert Parry's[6] words, "had unintentionally led public taste away from the purity of abstract art and created a craving which could only be satisfied with drafts of stimulants of ever-increasing strength"), makes us appreciate at their true value the great masters of the "abstract art." Russian music, meanwhile, will not disappear altogether out of our lives. It will only be kept for those occasions when we need something that is almost a physical tonic. For ordinary days, when we are in good mental and physical health and in no need of a pick-me-up, we shall stick to the civilized music of the past and to that contemporary work—there is, alas! very little of it—which, avoiding the seductions of barbarism, carries on the great tradition of civilization. We shall find that these products of civilized art are the only ones that can stand the test of repeated performance.

[*The Weekly Westminster Gazette,* February 17, 1923]

Notes on a Pianist and on Pianos

I LISTENED the other day to Mr. Walter Rummel playing a program of Beethoven sonatas—to be precise, Op. 109, the Moonlight, and Op. 110.

---

6. Sir Hubert Parry (1848–1918). English composer and author of *Evolution of the Art of Music* (1896) and vol. iii of *The Oxford History of Music* (1907).

It was a thoroughly enjoyable experience; for Mr. Rummel, besides possessing a very remarkable virtuosity, is a musician who plays with his head as well as his fingers. His performance of Op. 109, which next to Ops. 111 and 106, is perhaps the most superb and richly intellectual piece of piano music in existence, was really masterly. Mr. Rummel played it with a beautiful clarity; the themes stood out sharply and, as it were, stereoscopically; and at the same time all the parts were given their full proportionate value. Technically, too, the playing of the penultimate variation, in which a low G is shaken for pages at a time, was remarkably and unusually successful.

Interesting, too, though not quite so completely satisfactory, were his renderings of the Moonlight Sonata and Op. 110. The Moonlight was marred by the player's too conscious determination not to be sentimental in the first movement, and, in the last, by his desire for dramatic contrast, which caused him to take the pairs of loud chords very brutally and as though each of the pair were marked to be played with equal loudness—which they are not. The middle movement, however, was exquisitely performed. In the trio Mr. Rummel obtained an effect of striking beauty by imparting to the low F's a penetrating humming tone.

In Op. 110, a work which is, to begin with, a good deal less interesting in itself than Op. 109, Mr. Rummel seemed somehow not to do all that he might have done. The earlier movements were made to sound a little flat, and the main lines of the music were hardly sufficiently insisted upon. He was more at home with the fugues of the last movement; and the passage between the two fugues was played with a richness and subtlety and variety of tone that were absolutely astonishing. Mr. Rummel, it is obvious, is a pianist of whom we are going to hear much in the future. There are plenty of musicians who can ramp effectively enough through Rachmaninov concertos and such stuff; there are plenty more who can do Lisztian gymnastics with great ability; but there are precious few who can give a thoroughly satisfying rendering of pieces of real music, like Beethoven's Op. 109. Mr. Rummel is one of these few; it is sincerely to be hoped that he will stick to the real music and not take too many holidays among those "amusing" old-fashioned composers and not very amusing contemporaries whose names fill the program of his this-week's recital.

To listen to a first-class pianist, like Mr. Rummel, is to marvel at the extraordinary things that can be done with a piano. From an instrument, out of which even quite an accomplished amateur can get perhaps a dozen varieties of tone, these extraordinary players extract a whole enormous range of qualitatively different sounds. Sitting in front of an unresponsive piano one wonders ruefully how they do it. It is one of the miracles of the human hand, that least specialized and most universally efficient of organs. The great virtuoso is no more extraordinary than the electrical instrument maker who can tie knots in invisible filaments, than the juggler who balances billiard balls on the end of a cue, than the polisher of astronomical lenses whose fingertips are more reliable than the most precise measuring instruments.

The full richness of the modern virtuoso's technique has been rendered possible, to a very large extent, by the improvement of his instrument. The modern concert grand is a very different affair from the Erards of Beethoven's day, from the Broadwoods on which Chopin performed in his English recitals. The improved expressiveness of the modern instrument has been exploited by recent composers; the piano music of Scriabin, for example, is unthinkable apart from the modern piano, and the same is largely true of such different writers as Debussy, Albéniz,[7] and Ravel. We may be permitted to speculate whether a composer of the caliber of Beethoven would not have got much more out of the new instrument than have these lesser men. The modern piano is like the modern orchestra—an instrument of enormous range and power that still awaits its inspired player. The composers of the last forty or fifty years have shown us little more than that extra-ordinary things can be done with these new instruments. They have not yet done them.

[*The Weekly Westminster Gazette,* February 24, 1923]

A Mozart Program

IN ITS Saturday Evening "Pops," the Guild of Singers and Players aims at giving concerts of seldom-heard music at prices within the reach of everyone. The aim is a laudable one, and the Guild deserves all possible support—and a very much larger audience for its concerts than it actually got last Saturday when it gave at the Wigmore Hall an altogether admirable Mozart program.

That Mozart should rank among the seldom-heard composers seems an extraordinary thing. But the fact is as indisputably true as it is wholly deplorable. In musical circles at the present time no great name is more frequently invoked than Mozart's. And no first-class composer's music is less frequently heard in our concert halls. The great symphonies are given a performance, it is true, during the Promenade season; but how rare it is that they ever get an airing at any other time of the year! The beautiful piano concertos are played even less frequently. The operas, of course, have an assured position, and some sort of performance of them can be

7. Isaac Albéniz (1860–1909). Spanish pianist and composer.

heard reasonably often. A certain number of the string quartets are regularly played; but the pieces written for any less familiar combination than the four stringed instruments remain practically unknown.

No music is clearer or more exquisitely melodious than Mozart's; and it would be difficult to imagine a more sympathetic personality than that which reveals itself in his works. And yet he is not played. It is not easy to understand why Mozart should be so much neglected—particularly by a generation which professes, when it becomes at all sophisticated, to find his music transcendently beautiful and which uses his pure and comparatively unemotional art as a stick with which to beat poor Beethoven, condemned as a romantic and a sentimentalist. But the truth of the matter is, I suppose, that all these contemporary professions of love for unemotional and "abstract art" (nobody quite knows what the term means, but no resounding phrase was ever the worse for that) are singularly hollow. The strong alcohols of Wagner and his followers have tanned and hardened the modern palate; the most violent stimulants are the most highly appreciated, for the simple reason that they are the only stimulants to which most people can respond. It is impossible to be at the same time an admirer of *Parsifal* and of, shall we say, Mozart's motet, *Ave Verum Corpus;* of Scriabin's *Prometheus* and of the G minor Symphony. Nobody can simultaneously be genuinely fond of theatricality, pretentiousness, vulgarity, barbarism, and of unaffected sincerity, purity, refinement, and civilization. The eclectics who imagine that they have trained themselves to achieve this remarkable feat have merely trained themselves to suppress their instinctive reactions. They have ceased, as simpler minded people would say, to "know what they like."

The program last Saturday was designed to reveal Mozart at his best and most characteristic. The evening began with that amazingly beautiful quintet (for two violins, two violas, and cello) in G minor which one would be justified, if there were not so many other things quite as good, in describing as the best thing Mozart ever wrote. That profound melancholy which even in Mozart's most brilliant and seemingly gayest moments, comes ringing through the laughing harmony in a plaintive discord, which sends the melody drooping down through successive semitones; that melancholy which is the background of almost all Mozart's most beautiful music, finds in this quintet its most powerful, complete, and tragic expression. The first allegro is full of a kind of dancing sorrow.

Yea, in the very temple of delight
Veiled melancholy hath her sovran throne.[8]

8. From Keats's "Ode on Melancholy."

The second movement is a minuet—and surely the strangest minuet that was ever written; for it is one of the most masculine, powerful, and solidly thoughtful pieces of music in all Mozart's repertory. Those brief phrases of the opening theme, each closed by its savage sforzando chord, have a wonderful dramatic vigor. We have here that ideal music which is at once passionate and "abstract." The third movement, which is the slow movement, is the most directly emotional of them all. In the final movement, after a dark mysterious prelude, throbbing like a pain that quickens with every heart-beat throughout the night, the music bursts suddenly into hilarious gaiety—a gaiety that seems, alas! a little unreal and irrelevant after the melancholy of the first three movements.

Of the other pieces performed on the same evening, the most remarkable was the concerto for two pianos in E flat. This is a fine and spacious piece of music, containing passages that are almost as rich and substantial as the first movements of the quintet. The others—a sonata for two pianos and a quartet for three stringed instruments and oboe—were more "abstract," in the sense that they possessed less substance, that their beauty was more completely one of form and graceful line. If Mozart had been nothing more than a maker of such charming arabesques of sound, we should probably be justified in playing him as little as we do. We are emotional beings who cannot live by form alone, however beautiful that form may be. We need an art inspired by and in some sort expressive of emotion. The best art is that in which we recognize the inspiring and expressed emotion as being somehow qualitatively good (it is possible to know intuitively when an emotion is valuable or cheap, genuine or insincere); and in which the emotion is expressed in a form that satisfies the intellect by its symmetry and its logical coherence. Mozart is one of those composers who expresses something (in his most important works, at any rate) which one feels to be qualitatively valuable, as well as unaffected and having a certain purity and integrity. This thing he expresses in forms of the most amazing originality, beauty, and delicacy. And yet he is not played. I give it up.

[*The Weekly Westminster Gazette,* March 3, 1923]

Contemporaneousness

THEORETICALLY, it should make no difference to our enjoyment of it whether a work of art is new or old. There are standards of goodness and badness by which every work of whatever period may be judged. If it is good, then we admire it whether it was created this morning or three thousand years ago; if it is found to be bad, then we don't like it—and there is, or at any rate there should be, the end of the matter.

But this is true only in theory. When it comes to practice we find that this sublime disregard of time and space is not the obvious and easy thing we supposed it to be. Even when we are familiar and at home with every style and convention of art, we find that the period at which any given work was created does condition our appreciation of it. Literary scholars, and all those who for some reason have ever had to shut themselves up for any length of time in a library of nothing but ancient books, know what it is to be homesick from out of the past for the present. After a few weeks of unintermitted reading in the sixteenth century, what a blissful sensation it is to open a contemporary novel—even if it happens not to be a very good one, and even if our ancient reading has been of the choicest! At moments like these we infinitely prefer H. G. Wells to Shakespeare. He is contemporary, he breathes the same atmosphere as ourselves, his problems are our problems, and though his works may prove, in the words of the old poem, to be "damnably moldy a hundred years hence," when *King Lear* will still serenely remain what it is and always has been; though we know very well that, judged by any standard, they compare, to say the least of it, poorly with those of Shakespeare; we are ready, after too long a sojourn in the past, to turn to him with passionate avidity.

What is true of ancient and contemporary literature is true, though not, perhaps, to quite the same extent, of ancient and contemporary music. Literature tends naturally to become more easily "out-of-date" than music, because it is more intimately concerned with the external facts of life, which tend to alter very rapidly. Music, practically speaking, is never descriptive and reflects only the working of the human spirit, which is a relatively constant and unchanging thing. Emotions and thoughts do tend, however, to change with the passage of time; or to be more precise, one set of thoughts and emotions assumes more prominence at one epoch than at another, and new methods are discovered for the expression of these momentarily important feelings. Music which reflects that aspect of the spiritual life which seems at the moment most important tends naturally to satisfy us more than music that has a different inspiration and a different method of expression.

What is the aspect of spiritual life most forcibly insisted on at the present time? What is it in any contemporary piece of music that we feel to be essentially "modern"? Contemporary music is so various, so eclectic and experimental, that it is very difficult to answer this question. There are so many different composers doing so many different things that it depends on our personal taste which we choose to consider as typically "modern."

To a great many people, no doubt, the successors of the nineteenth-century emotional composers will seem most significant in their contemporaneousness. Scriabin, that Tschaikowsky *de nos jours,* will seem the most important of the modern masters; they will admire much of Bax and Bliss. They may even enjoy the more elusive emotions of Delius. Their favorite classic will, of course, be Wagner.

There will be others, however, who have reacted against the excessive and unrestrained emotionalism of the later eighteen-hundreds. These Protestants fall into two classes. Those in the first class react not only against the pretentious grand opera emotionalism too common at this period, but against all feeling and thought of a noble or spacious character. They like an art that is playful or excitingly barbarous. Stravinsky for them is the great master . . . the Stravinsky of *Pribaoutki* and the *Berceuses du Chat,* of the *Firebird* and *Le Sacre* (which last, by the way, does not improve, except in a few brilliant passages, with repeated hearing, as those who listened to it a few nights ago at the Queen's Hall can testify). There are signs, however, that this kind of music, wildly thrilling as it was when first performed, is losing its charm. The reactionaries of this class will either go back to the emotionalism from which they originally recoiled, or will affiliate themselves with those who have reacted from it in a rather different way. . . . They will join what we may call the intellectualist reactionaries; those who require that emotion (for they are not foolish enough to suppose that music or any other art can do without feeling) shall be fused with the intelligence, shall be controlled and molded and informed by the mind. For them the important contemporary composer is Schönberg.

I have indicated the three main types of contemporary music. Is there anything common to all three; any quality essentially contemporaneous belonging to every category? We shall find this common factor in their technique, in the medium rather than in the subject-matter of the music. Composers of every class agree in approaching harmony from a new angle; they ignore the formal, logical conception of harmony and regard the problem as simply a general problem of tone, having an infinite number of particular cases, each of which has to be solved individually as the process of composition goes on. The new harmony is still in the highest degree experimental and tentative, and it still remains to be seen what will be made of "this Freedom." But meanwhile the freedom, such as it is, exists; it is the refreshing contemporary thing to which we turn every now and then after too long a sojourn among the strait-laced tonic and dominant of earlier ages.

[*The Weekly Westminster Gazette,* March 10, 1923]

Bach and Handel

WITH THE APPROACH of Easter, concerts of religious music become frequent. Last week the London Bach Choir gave a performance of the Passion according to St. Matthew; the same work is to be repeated this Saturday at the Central Hall, Westminster, when Miss Dorothy Silk will figure among the soloists. Meanwhile, the joint Bach Choirs of Oxford and Cambridge are to give Beethoven's Mass in D at the Albert Hall; and the next fortnight will certainly see many other similar performances.

Before last week's performance of the Matthew Passion I had heard very little religious music since the last great feast of the Church, when it was not Bach but Handel who furnished the principal religious concert with music. It was with memories of the Christmas *Messiah* that I went to listen to Bach's paschal music. The two great composers of the early eighteenth century have very often been compared and contrasted. That is no reason, however, why we should not do it again. Comparison and contrast are the conditions of criticism.

On hearing the words "eighteenth century" most Londoners of today, I fancy, would conjure up a cheerful vision of the stage at the Lyric, Hammersmith: "eighteenth century"—why, that means wigs, pirouettes, quaint formality, boundless affectation, a schoolboyish cynicism, and a set of charmingly impersonal and unemotional tunes. That is surely the current popular view of an epoch which was, in fact, as much the age of Newton and Wesley as of Casanova and Pompadour. The past, for most of us, consists of a few little archipelagos of facts dotted sparsely here and there in the illimitable ocean of our ignorance. Our view of history depends on which set of facts happens to be most popular at the moment. Imagine two children, the one brought up exclusively on Handel's *Messiah,* the other exclusively on the Passion music of Bach; what would "eighteenth century" mean to them? Arrived at man's estate, how would each describe the period of which he had been told that his own particular great man was the typical representative?

The Handelian child, I imagine, would say something like this. "The first half of the eighteenth century was a time when people admired simple, epical emotions. They knew the secret, which nowadays appears to be lost, of being grand without affectation or pretentiousness. They were extremely objective in their art, which reminds one, at its best, a little of Homer's art. They were, however, highly cultured and took a great interest in the formal side of art. So much so, that they sometimes sacrificed substance for form, as, for example, in 'All we like sheep.' To conclude, these people of the eighteenth century seem to have been a simple, candid, unaffected people, who sincerely admired what was great and noble as well as what was purely beautiful and formally elegant."

The Bach boy would have a different story to tell. "The people of the first half of the eighteenth century," he would say, "were extremely devout. Their religion seems to have been a very personal and inward religion. They were accustomed to brood over it very tenderly, and at the same time with an extraordinary subtlety and refinement of emotion. This subtlety and refinement also characterized the form of their art, which was in the highest degree subjective and intellectual. They seem to have had very little epical faculty, and they were not very successful in giving objective descriptions of things. They had little histrionic sense, but were extremely lyrical."

I refrain from giving the various descriptions of the eighteenth century which would be made by other children brought up exclusively on *The Beggar's Opera,* on Dr. Arne's setting of *Comus* (which I heard with a mild pleasure at the Inner Temple Hall last week), on Domenico Scarlatti's harpsichord music. They would be, like biscuits, rich and mixed. All of which only shows how careful one should be before one makes any sweeping generalization about the past that is based on the achievement of a single man. For, however strict the tradition, however severely limited the means at their disposal, men of real individual genius will always find the means of being primarily themselves.

The epical, objective Handel is about as remote from the meditative, inward-looking Bach as any composer could well be from another. And yet they were contemporaries working within the same limits.

That Handel should ever have succeeded in achieving anything at all is astonishing, when one considers the circumstances of his life. He is surely the only man who has been able to combine the profession of impresario and provider of entertainments with that of great creative artist. He possessed the secret—if only it could be recaptured by our modern newspaper proprietors and theatrical managers!—of giving the public what it wanted, and giving it something supremely good. He worked for immediate success and immediate recognition, and he achieved a permanent and absolute triumph.

Bach's danger was not too much public recognition, but too much solitude, too little understanding. Men in his position have often relapsed into eccentricity. To have kept so much hold, as he did, on common life and on the common human emotions was his triumph.

[*The Weekly Westminster Gazette,* March 17, 1923]

Books About Music

"I LOVE MY BOOKS!" The journalist's single-minded, unsophisticated friend points with an air of paternal, of marital pride and affection towards his slowly expanding Globe-Wernickes. "I love my books!" But the journalist, who is a literary journalist and has survived a score of spring and autumn publishing seasons, smiles a little wearily. For he, too, like the earnest friend, once loved books—and still, perhaps, loves his own books, loves real books. But he has learned, in the course of those twenty spring and autumn seasons, to hate as vigorously as he loved; to hate with a real passion, with righteous indignation, with a bitter personal resentment. For he has seen the office tables groaning under the weight of new fiction; he has seen the shelves overflowing with memoirs and political economy and theology and psychoanalysis. Tons of ratiocination, with only a few ounces of sense in it; thousands of volumes and hardly a book to read among them. And yet they have all got to be read, or at any rate looked at. No wonder that he hates.

Among all these books which make their appearance round about the spring and autumn equinoxes, there are always, as might be expected, a certain number of books dealing with music. They come out rather unobtrusively into the light—and they soon go back, I imagine, with as little noise as they came, into the darkness. For books about music seem, as a general rule, to be rather less interesting than books on almost any other subject. Why should this be? I can only suppose that the general badness of musical books is the result of the peculiarly specialized character of the musical faculty. It is possible to be a fair, a good, even a great musician and yet to be, in other respects, quite remarkably unintelligent. At one time or another most of us must have come face to face with executant artists whom, on the concert platform, we greatly admired—to find that the man who gave us so astonishing an interpretation of, say, a late Beethoven sonata, appears, when we talk to him, to be a conceited imbecile whose ideas about music are so fantastically absurd that we cannot believe him capable, as we talk to him, of playing even Chaminade intelligibly. And yet, when he sits down to the piano, there he is again; the musician has come back. Which merely proves that the musical faculty is a separate, unattached faculty and that it does not work consciously in connection with the superficial reasoning faculties made use of in conversation. It is possible for a man to give a most subtle reading of Op. 111 and yet be able to furnish, in his conscious mind, only the most absurd explanation of his interpretation. It goes without saying, of course, that this is not true of all musicians. Many of them have critical and literary faculties almost as well developed as their musical faculties. Some, however, most undoubtedly have not.

It is these last, I suppose—the musicians who instinctively know what good music is, but have no well-developed faculty for saying why they appreciate it or in what way it is good—it is surely these last who are the authors of most of those very unsatisfying books about music which constantly make their appearance. I look at most books about music when they come out with a hopeful expectation; there is still so much to be said in literary form about music; almost everything, in fact, has still to be said. The titles of these books are always most alluring. *Spirit and Music, The Spirit of Music, The Heart of Music, How to Listen to Music*—these are the titles of a few books which have recently appeared. They are good titles; the great literary revelation about music might have lain between the covers of any of the volumes bearing them. But, alas! It did not. They all contained very much the same thing; bad writing, frequently pretentious; gush, often of a vaguely "musical" nature. They all lacked sensible, straightforward criticism; in one, at least, there were even inaccurate statements of fact.

Gush is one of the commonest literary vices of writers about music. In Mr. Alfred Swan's recent life of Scriabin we find the Russian composer constantly referred to as a Titan and a Messiah. The phraseology is only less rich in Mr. Lyle's life of Saint-Saëns, and in Mr. Porte's life of Macdowell.[9] Equally common is pretentious "mysticism." And yet the ideal book about music must certainly be written with a certain warmth and vehemence; nor can it ignore those qualities of music which certainly do impress themselves as being mystical. "Lilies that fester smell far worse than weeds." The bad book on music is a corruption of the ideal good book. It would, on the whole, be much better if these lovers of music who feel a need to write about it would confine themselves, not to the "spirit" or the "heart" of music, but to its body. There is so much useful writing to be done about that. Sir Charles Stanford's[1] recent *Interludes* contained some excellent pieces of practical, semi-technical criticism, worth a thousand volumes of vague outpourings and nebulous theorizings.

Of all books about music the most nearly ideal that I know are those of Sir Hubert Parry. In him the writer and the critic were combined with the fine musician. Books like his *Art of Music* and his *Musical Style* can be read with real pleasure and illumination. He could formulate theories without being vague; he could insist on the grandeur and the mystical

9. Edward MacDowell (1861–1908). American composer and pianist.
1. Sir Charles Stanford (1852–1924). Irish composer.

beauty of music without being gushing or pretentious. And he was also a most acutely critical analyst of what I have called the body of music. We are already in the midst of the spring publishing season; it is too late to do anything about that. But I should advise all who contemplate bringing out a book about music at the coming of the next equinox, to read Parry's critical writings and compare them with their own. If they are satisfied that their own are as well written, as sane in outlook, as learned, as penetrating, as finely analytic as Parry's—then by all means let them send the manuscript to the printers. If not—why, there are fires, and the city dust carts call at the back door at least once a week.

[*The Weekly Westminster Gazette*, March 31, 1923]

What Are the Wild Waves Saying?

MUSIC SEEMS, at the moment, to have migrated to Bournemouth, where Sir Dan Godfrey presides at a festival of which the mere bald accounts in the Press are interesting. "Would that we were there," as the beautiful old Lutheran hymn has it.

But what I am wondering is this: What is the difference between a festival week at Bournemouth and an ordinary week? For whenever I go down to one of our larger seaside resorts (to Bournemouth, as a matter of fact, I have not been for some time) I find evidence which makes me believe that every week in these places is a festival week. Not long ago, for example, I was at Hastings, where Mr. Dan Godfrey, Junior, directs the municipal music. There appeared to be a concert on six nights out of the seven; and what was more, four out of these six concerts were good concerts, with solid classical programs, and every now and then a contemporary novelty. During the winter months one can hear, I should imagine, more good orchestral music on St. Leonard's pier than in the concert halls of London. And one pays considerably less than in London for the privilege.

The secret of seaside music is summed up in the words, "small orchestra." "Small orchestra"—that is what, under the Palace Pier, the wild waves are saying, while Mr. Dan Godfrey, Junior, directs his concerts overhead. While the big orchestras are struggling, not very successfully, with the problem of increased costs and fixed incomes, the small orchestras can afford to exist; they may, I imagine, even make a profit.

There are, of course, certain aesthetic objections to the small orchestra. It is sufficiently obvious, for example, that you cannot get as great a volume of sound out of thirty performers as you can out of eighty. But a skillful conductor, performing in a hall of reasonable proportions, can do a great deal with his small orchestra. He can give, for example, a perfectly adequate account of all orchestral music written before 1800; he can give a sufficiently satisfactory idea of Beethoven's grandeur; and if he cannot do full justice to Wagner, Strauss, and Scriabin, does that, after all, vitally matter? He can at any rate give his audience quite a good idea of what these writers for the very large orchestra are aiming at. . . . In any case the reasonable music lover will prefer hearing an interpretation that is not absolutely perfect to hearing no interpretation at all. That is the choice with which, if the present difficult conditions continue to hold, he may be confronted.

The wild waves, it seems to me, have something useful to impart to us in London. "Small orchestra," they whisper. Why shouldn't we in this town have one or two small orchestras, no bigger than Mr. Dan Godfrey's, playing regularly every night of the week, all the year round—perpetual proms in miniature? Such an orchestra could play in one of the smaller halls. It might even—since there appears to be something so peculiarly attractive about anything in any way connected with water—it might even have a little pier built into the Thames to play on: a County Council pier— why not?—with an orchestra under County Council patronage.

As things are at present, we do not have nearly enough orchestral concerts. For a town with seven million inhabitants two or three orchestral concerts a week is absurdly few. The fifteen or twenty weekly recitals by aspiring soloists do nothing to make up for this paucity of orchestral concerts; they are mostly deplorably dull and uninteresting. The only way, it seems, by which we can get more orchestral concerts is to encourage the small orchestra. An enterprising conductor could do a vast service to the London musical public by organizing such a small orchestra and giving regular daily concerts in one of the smaller halls. The wild waves splashing under the Palace Pier know very well that the thing can be done; they have heard Mr. Dan Godfrey, Junior, doing it, daily, for the last I don't know how many months. There is really no reason why every week should not be festival week; it is so already at St. Leonard's. What stands in the way of its being so in London?

[*The Weekly Westminster Gazette*, April 7, 1923]

Brahms's Birthday

THE NINETIETH ANNIVERSARY of Brahms's birth was commemorated last Monday by Mr. Leonard Borwick in a recital of nothing but the master's works. I came away from the Aeolian Hall a little, it must be confessed, damped in my ardor for the "Last of the Classics," a trifle disappointed. Mr. Borwick's playing was in no way to blame; that was as technically sound, as clear and unaffected as it always is. The fault lay with the music; for, to be quite honest, a good deal of it was uncommonly dull. If we want to find fault with Mr. Borwick it must be for not selecting a more exhilarating program. For it could have been done; it was precisely the consciousness of that fact that made the concert seem so disappointing.

Brahms is one of those authors who look their best in anthologies. I can imagine a program of his works carefully selected by one of his enemies which should sound so dreary and lifeless that an audience would have difficulty in sitting through it.

But I can also imagine another program, selected this time by a friend of Brahms, which should be wholly delightful, grand, and beautiful. The two programs would have this in common: that both would consist, in the main, of works of great ingenuity and intellectual subtlety. But the works in the friendly selection would be endowed, over and above these qualities, with life; the others would be without it.

There is a notion, very dear to certain critics of literature, that the best, the only, poetry is a thing of native wood notes wild, and that education, a sound literary training, a conscious theory of art, are so many enemies to true poetry. It is a notion that looks sufficiently ridiculous even in literary criticism. Apply it to music and it is seen to be wholly absurd. There is no antithesis between inspiration and contrivance. A good training, a theory of art, a busy and ever-conscious intellect do not interfere with the workings of the native talent: they enrich it and they direct it. But there must, of course, be a talent to direct and enrich; contrivance is not a substitute for inspiration. In Palestrina, in Bach, in Beethoven we see the successful alliance, the perfect interfusion of talent and conscious intellect, of inspiration and contrivance. In composers such as Bruckner, on the other hand, we see contrivance trying to do without inspiration, we see education and careful thought setting themselves up as substitutes for native talent. In vain. For what can be more pathetically absurd than Bruckner's symphonies, with their trivial, silly, empty little themes and their elaborate developments, their huge climaxes evolving grandly out of nothing at all?

Brahms stands a little to the Brucknerwards of the greatest musicians. At their best his works teach the same lesson as is taught by those of Bach and of Beethoven: that inspiration can make use of contrivance to find its richest and most perfect expression. At their worst they prove what Bruckner's prove (though Brahms, even at his worst, is incomparably more interesting than "the Wagner of the symphony"); that ingenuity and knowledge will not make up for lack of inspiration.

A disproportionately large number of the piano pieces selected by Mr. Leonard Borwick for performance last Monday were calculated, it seemed to me, to teach the lesson of Bruckner rather than of Beethoven. The Variations on an original theme in D, for example, which he played after the beautiful Sonata in F minor, are surely a typical piece of uninspired subtlety. They contain everything but life. And the same seemed to me true of most of the Intermezzi chosen by Mr. Borwick.

The passacaglia in the finale of the fourth symphony, the variations on a theme of Haydn—to take only two examples—prove sufficiently clearly that Brahms knew how to enrich his inspiration with the contrivances of his educated intellect. But it is interesting to remember that he also had charming, noble, and beautiful inspirations, which he expressed with a remarkable degree of simplicity. Many of the songs, for example, are simple and of a genuine inspiration. The Scherzo in E flat minor, full and brilliant though it is, is direct and alive from beginning to end. His waltzes have a wonderful freshness and vitality, and, for Brahms at any rate, are expressed with no very great elaboration. I am sometimes inclined to think that it is in these shorter and more popular pieces that Brahms most completely "comes off." Few of his largest and most elaborately architected works seem entirely satisfactory from beginning to end; there are almost always dead bits in them, passages that do not sound inevitable. If I were compiling a Brahms program I should include as many of these lighter pieces as I possibly could.

[*The Weekly Westminster Gazette*, May 12, 1923]

Opera, Marionettes, and Battistini

THE OPENING of the British National Company's opera season gives a peculiar interest and significance to two musical events of the last days. I refer to the production of Rossini's *Gazza Ladra* at the Scala, by the marionette players, and the recital of Signor Battistini. Salutary lessons were to be derived from both of them.

Last Friday's production by the puppets suggested a number of things. It suggested, in the first place, that producers of opera in this country are too conservative in their choice of program; that there are plenty of good operas in the world which only too seldom get a hearing in England. Rossini's *Gazza Ladra* is one of them. It is a real musical comedy, with all the light sparkle and brilliance of Rossini at his best. Stendhal considered that Rossini was almost the greatest of composers; and that many of his contemporaries shared this opinion is proved by the fact that there was a period when the composer of the Ninth Symphony was neglected in favor of the composer of *The Barber of Seville*. We have got past this sort of thing now; we have also, in this year of grace 1923, outlined the reaction which followed on the heels of Rossini's success. We neither unduly exalt nor unjustly denigrate. Rossini, we perceive, was very good in his way and on his plane; quite good enough to make him worth hearing, if not every day of the week, at least occasionally; quite good enough, what is more, to take his place with the Donizettis, the Balfes, the Gounods, the Saint-Saëns, the Leoncavallos, the Puccinis of the orthodox opera company's program. He is a little vulgar, no doubt. (One of the reasons for Rossini's vast contemporary success is surely to be found in the fact that he invented, or as good as invented, the modern vulgar tune. Vulgar tunes had existed before, of course; but they had been vulgar in another style. Rossini invented a new type of tune, having a rich, immediately appreciable obviousness. Look, for example, at Moses' first solo in *Moses in Egypt*; it is built upon a short romping theme that might easily be taken as the basis of a good tune by Irving Berlin. The long, rather complicated phrases of the older melodies—phrases that needed a certain amount of listening to, if you were to hear them aright—have been replaced by very short phrases that require no listening to at all, phrases that come and embed themselves in your memory of their own accord, whether you want them to or not. It was surely the novelty of this sort of tune that specially captivated Stendhal and his contemporaries.) He is vulgar, yes; but no more so than any of the composers whose names I have mentioned above. And, vulgarity for vulgarity, I vastly prefer the light, gay, frank vulgarity of Rossini to the sickly and pretentious vulgarity of Saint-Saëns's mock grandeur.

So much for the first piece of good advice imparted by the marionettes. Their second hint refers to no single opera or composer; it refers, in general, to the production of all operas. It is the same hint as was dropped some few years since—more consciously and artistically—by the Russians under Diaghileff and Massine, in their production of Cimarosa's[2] *Astuzie Femminili*. Opera should be acted with no attempt at realism, but conventionally, symbolically, with the gestures of the dance, not the gestures of life. I do not suggest that all operas should be performed on the puppet-theater stage (though I should very much like to see, shall we say, *Parsifal*

---

2. Domenico Cimarosa (1749–1821). Italian composer.

and the *Valkyrie* duly "potted," of course, into reasonable proportions, staged in the Teatro dei Piccoli). The lesson to be learnt at the Scala is this: not that puppets should replace human beings on the operatic stage, but rather that human beings should behave more like puppets. The Russians' production of Cimarosa showed how delightful an opera could be when the ordinary conventional gestures of realistic acting were replaced by more carefully studied gestures of a richer and more significant convention specially worked out by a skilled choreographer for the occasion. It is not merely Rossini and Cimarosa who gain by being acted in this way. There is almost no opera, it seems to me, that would not make a better show if it were acted according to the rules of the ballet rather than the rules of the realistic stage.

Finally, there is the lesson of Battistini's recital. The gist of it may be summed up as follows: that operas sound best when they are sung by people who really know how to sing. Signor Battistini knows how to sing, and knows more thoroughly, I suppose, than any man alive. His performance last Saturday was a masterpiece of beautiful production. With an air of complete effortlessness he surmounted every difficulty, produced every desired effect. How long a training went to the perfecting of that voice? I have no idea; but I should guess that the answer would be somewhat discouraging to the young and impatient aspirant. When all singers know as much about their job as Signor Battistini knows, I shall be a very regular opera-goer. As things stand at present, however, my enthusiasm for this particular brand of musical composition is a tempered and sober enthusiasm.

[*The Weekly Westminster Gazette*, May 19, 1923]

Eclecticism

MR. HOLST'S *Perfect Fool* was performed for the second time last Friday; not by itself, as on the previous Monday evening, but in company with *Phoebus and Pan*. The directors of the British National Company would have shown themselves kinder to Mr. Holst if they had joined his opera with *Pagliacci*, shall we say, or *Cavalleria Rusticana*. To make it stand cheek by jowl with a first-class work by a very great composer was to invite the making of comparisons; and comparisons are odious, particularly to the party at whose expense they are made. Still, in the circumstances, it was impossible not to make them. Here were two composers who had set out to write, each in his own way, a short comic opera. Last Friday's performance at Covent Garden proved, I think, sufficiently cogently that one of them succeeded very well in his intention and that the other did not. Let us try to enumerate some of the reasons for Bach's success and Mr. Holst's failure.

Phoebus and Pan is a wholly delightful little opera which becomes better and better at every hearing. That is the important, the fundamental emotional fact. It is the business of the critic—and a rather wearisome business sometimes, for it is a blessed thing just to "know what one likes" and be able to say no more about it—it is the business of the critic to try and explain such a fact as this, to analyze the emotions produced in the mind by the contact of a work of art. If I were asked to say why I enjoy *Phoebus and Pan* so much, I should state my reasons in some such way as this: First, because it is the work of a completely single-minded artist, who knew how to give his work a perfect unity of feeling and style; like all good operas—like *Don Giovanni,* like *Tristan,* like *A Village Romeo and Juliet—Phoebus and Pan* is a single, self-sufficient, unified work. In the second place, because the music is beautiful, original, and appropriate—a very general, sweeping statement, but one which requires no further elaboration here.

Why, now, is *The Perfect Fool* not a good opera? For reasons precisely opposed to those which make *Phoebus and Pan* a good one. To begin with, it completely lacks any sort of single-minded unity. To a libretto consisting of a series of very imperfectly connected incidents, the composer has set a music that is as patchily without unity of style as the façade of the Victoria and Albert Museum. I leave out of account the passages of a deliberate parody, which are numerous. Parody is one of the best forms of criticism, and a composer has every right to turn critic if he wants to. But it must be admitted, I think, that parody, at least in quantity, does not mix well with original writing. The place of parody is in the text-book, not in the work of art. Those who have ploughed through the interminable chapters of parody in Mr. Joyce's portentous *Ulysses* will, I am sure, agree with this. It is not to the Wagnerian and Verdiesque passages that I would point as examples of patchy, disconnected writing—though I certainly think it a pity that so much Beckmesser fun should be admitted into a work of these small proportions. It is in Mr. Holst's own contributions that we find resemblances to the Victoria and Albert. In a good opera variety of effect is obtained within a certain general conception of musical style. The music of *Don Giovanni,* for example, is wonderfully dramatic, expressive, and appropriate; but it is all of a certain kind. Hence the beautiful artistic unity of the whole work. But now take an opera like *Samson and Delilah.* Here variety of effect is obtained by pastiching different kinds of music; a piece of sham Bach alternates with a piece of all too genuine Massenet. There is no unity. For contemporary composers, eclecticism offers even greater temptations; there is so much more to pick and choose from than ever there was before. Folk-song, Stravinsky, strict counterpoint, Rimsky-Korsakoff, Debussy, Wagner; Russia, Spain, Zululand, Ireland; Gregorian, ragtime—what a wealth there is to choose from! In *The Perfect Fool* Mr. Holst makes a modest selection; he writes now in one manner, now in another, according to the effect he wants to produce and the emotion he wants to express. The result is patchwork.

Eclecticism is the great danger to all contemporary art. Knowledge has been tabulated and made accessible as it never was before. We all know too much and can acquire knowledge easily. For upwards of three hundred years architects were content to exploit the possibilities of a single style— the Greco-Roman. They did it very thoroughly, and they did it very well. They were not distracted by too much irrelevant information. At the present day, an architect knows more or less thoroughly about every style that ever was, anywhere, and at any epoch. Result—unless he happens to be a great personality who can assimilate everything and yet remain himself— the Victoria and Albert. It is the same in music. *The Perfect Fool* is an example of the way in which a modern composer can be brought to grief by knowing too much.

As for the different elements of which the opera is made up—some are certainly charming. The round of the water-carriers is graceful and lyrical; the orchestral accompaniment to the shepherd's tale is a successful piece of pastoral music. But in a good many passages Mr. Holst's inspiration seems to have worn rather thin. From the composer of *The Hymn of Jesus* one had expected better things.

[*The Weekly Westminster Gazette,* May 26, 1923]

Music and the Interpretative Medium

DISGUISED IN RINGLETS and a white satin crinoline, Miss Freda Hempel gave a recital last Sunday of the songs that had been Jenny Lind's favorites. For the moment she was Jenny Lind (she is, I imagine one of the few living sopranos who could make that pretense with any degree of success). Even her accompanist looked like someone out of Dickens, and the flautists who played her obligatos were upholstered to match.

The masquerade was charming, no doubt, but a little superfluous, for the songs were not so definitely of the period that they could only be sung in fancy dress. Personally, indeed, I was rather disappointed that they were not more "old-fashioned." The songs with which Jenny Lind thrilled her world proved to be very much the same as those with which Miss Hempel is accustomed to thrill ours. A program containing three Schuberts, a Mozart, "The Last Rose of Summer," "Home Sweet Home," and "Way down upon the Swanee River" seemed hardly to demand the accompaniment of crinolines.

It was only in the aria from Meyerbeer's *L'Etoile du Nord* that one felt any real need for "period" environments. And it may be that the glassy perfection of Mendelssohn's "On Wings of Song" would have seemed less enchanting had the air been sung in a frock with the straight perpendicular lines of the present mode, instead of in the florid curves, rich as the outlines of the song itself, of the costume of the epoch.

But it is not of Miss Hempel's program that I mean to write here; it is of her voice and of voices in general, whether of human beings or of instruments. Music is unfortunate in this respect—that it cannot dispense with interpreters, and that it is, to a considerable extent, at the mercy of these secondary artists who must always come between the composer and his audience. A bad interpretation cannot, it is true, entirely ruin good music, no more than a good interpretation can reconcile us completely to music that is fundamentally bad. Still, good or bad, the interpreter can do a great deal. Personally I prefer good music not supremely well performed to a magnificent interpretation of poor stuff. A singer like Miss Hempel can make us listen with pleasure to almost anything; but she cannot quite succeed in turning bad into good. She cannot persuade us, for example, that the pointless gymnastics of the Meyerbeer aria she sang last Sunday are as interesting as those not dissimilar gymnastics, formally beautiful and dramatically opposite, in the Queen of the Night's song out of *The Magic Flute*. She can make each individual note of a bad song sound beautiful in itself, but she cannot cause the combination of notes to sound interesting; that only the composer can bring about. The indiscriminate and enthusiastic applauder of "Stars" is content with the beauty of each individual note, and does not demand anything much of the whole work of which they are the component parts.

Other instruments besides the human voice have power to enrich the individual note till its beauty in itself almost makes up for any lack of beauty in the arrangement of the notes. A good composer naturally exploits the beautiful quality of individual instruments; but he does not rely too much on them. It is a sign of weakness in a composer to depend more on his instruments than his invention. *L'Après-midi d'un faune* is a beautiful work, and it does, as a matter of fact, contain rather more imaginative substance than many of Debussy's works. But listening to it, I often wonder rather uneasily how much of the composition's beauty is really nothing more than the beauty of long-suspended notes of woodwind. It is difficult for a long-drawn note on an oboe to be anything but lovely; and combined with the sound of violins it is, in its individuality, and without considering its relations to other notes, almost heavenly. Blow these woody notes slowly and softly, weave them with strings into long tenuous bridges across the gulfs of silence and without going to the expense of much invention, you can produce beautiful and moving musical effects. Debussy often made up for his none too fertile invention by exploiting to their very limit the peculiar beauties of the instruments for which he wrote. Good composers naturally make use of virtuosity and the peculiar beauties of instruments; but not for their own sakes, not as a substitute for original thinking. They make use of them only when they happen to serve some significant purpose in the general scheme of composition. The Queen of the Night's song is as elaborate a piece of virtuosity as the aria out of *L'Etoile du Nord*; but one is a piece of music, and the other is only a piece of acrobacy.

[*The Weekly Westminster Gazette*, June 2, 1923]

Popular Music

THERE IS a certain jovial, bouncing, hoppety little tune with which anyone who has spent even a few weeks in Germany, or has been tended in childhood by a German nurse, must be very familiar. Its name is "Ach, du lieber Augustin." It is a merry little affair in three-four time; in rhythm and melody so simple, that the village idiot could sing it after a first hearing; in sentiment so innocent that the heart of the most susceptible maiden would not quicken by a beat a minute at the sound of it. Rum ti-tiddle, Um tum tum, Um tum tum, Um tum tum: Rum ti-tiddle, Um tum tum, Um tum tum, TUM. By the very frankness of its cheerful imbecility the thing disarms all criticism.

Now for a piece of history. "Ach, du lieber Augustin" was composed in 1770, and it was the first waltz. The first waltz! I must ask the reader to hum the tune to himself, then to think of any modern waltz with which he may be familiar. He will find in the difference between the tunes a subject richly suggestive of interesting meditations.

The difference between "Ach, du lieber Augustin" and any waltz tune composed at any date from the middle of the nineteenth century onwards, is the difference between one piece of music almost completely empty of emotional content and another, densely saturated with amorous sentiment, languor, and voluptuousness. The susceptible maiden who, when she hears "Ach, du lieber Augustin," feels no emotions beyond a general sense of high spirits and cheerfulness, is fairly made to palpitate by the luscious strains of the modern waltz. Her soul is carried swooning along, over waves of syrup; she seems to breathe an atmosphere heavy with ambergris and musk. From the jolly little thing it was at its birth, the waltz has grown into the voluptuous, heart-stirring affair with which we are now familiar.

And what has happened to the waltz has happened to all popular music. It was once innocent but is now provocative; once pellucid, now richly clotted; once elegant, now deliberately barbarous. Compare the music of *The Beggar's Opera* with the music of a contemporary revue. They differ as life in the garden of Eden differed from life in the artistic quarter of Gomorrah. The one is prelapsarian in its airy sweetness, the other is rich, luscious, and loud with conscious savagery.

The evolution of popular music has run parallel on a lower plane, with the evolution of serious music. The writers of popular tunes are not musicians enough to be able to invent new forms of expression. All they do is to adapt the discoveries of original geniuses to the vulgar taste. Ultimately and indirectly, Beethoven is responsible for all the languishing waltz tunes, all the savage jazzings, for all that is maudlin and violent in our popular music. He is responsible because it was he who first devised really effective musical methods for the direct expression of emotion. Beethoven's emotions happened to be noble; moreover, he was too intellectual a musician to neglect the formal, architectural side of music. But unhappily he made it possible for composers of inferior mind and character to express in music their less exalted passions and vulgarer emotions. He made possible the weakest sentimentalities of Schumann, the baroque grandiosities of Wagner, the hysterics of Scriabin; he made possible the waltzes of all the Strausses, from the Blue Danube to the waltz from *Salome*. And he made possible, at a still further remove, such masterpieces of popular art as "You Made Me Love You" and "That Coal Black Mammy of Mine."

For the introduction of a certain vibrant sexual quality into music, Beethoven is perhaps less directly responsible than the nineteenth-century Italians. I used often to wonder why it was that Mozart's operas were less popular than those of Verdi, Leoncavallo, and Puccini. You couldn't ask for more, or more infectiously "catchy" tunes than are to be found in *Figaro* or *Don Giovanni*. The music though "classical," is not obscure, nor forbiddingly complex. On the contrary it is clear, simple with that seemingly easy simplicity which only consummate genius can achieve and thoroughly engaging. And yet for every time *Don Giovanni* is played, *La Bohème* is played a hundred. *Tosca* is at least fifty times as popular as *Figaro*. And if you look through a catalogue of gramophone records you will find that, while you can buy *Rigoletto* complete in thirty discs, there are not more than three records of *The Magic Flute*. This seems at first sight extremely puzzling. But the reason is not really far to seek. Since Mozart's day, composers have learned the art of making music throatily and palpitatingly sexual. The arias of Mozart have a beautiful clear purity which renders them utterly insipid compared with the sobbing, catch-in-the-throaty melodies of the nineteenth-century Italians. The public, having accustomed itself to this stronger and more turbid brewage, finds no flavor in the crystal songs of Mozart.

No essay on modern popular music would be complete without some grateful reference to Rossini, who was, so far as I know, the first composer to show what charms there are in vulgar melody. Melodies before Rossini's day were often exceedingly commonplace and cheap; but almost never do they possess that almost indefinable quality of low vulgarity which adorns some of the most successful of Rossini's airs, and which we recognize as being somehow a modern, contemporary quality. The methods which Rossini employed for the achievement of his melodic vulgarity are not easy to analyze. His great secret, I fancy, was the very short and easily memorable phrase frequently repeated in different parts of the scale. But it is easiest to define by example. Think of Moses' first aria in *Moses in Egypt*. That is an essentially vulgar melody; and it is quite unlike the popular melodies of an earlier date. Its affinities are with the modern popular tune. It is to his invention of vulgar tunes that Rossini owed his enormous contemporary success. Vulgar people before his day had to be content with Mozart's delicate airs. Rossini came and revealed to them a more congenial music. That the world fell down and gratefully worshipped him is not surprising. If he has long ceased to be popular, that is because his successors, profiting by his lessons, have achieved in his own vulgar line triumphs of which he could not have dreamed.

Barbarism has entered popular music from two sources—from the music of barbarous people, like the negroes, and from serious music which has drawn upon barbarism for its inspiration. The technique of being barbarous effectively has come, of course, from serious music. In the elaboration of this technique no musicians have done more than the Russians. If Rimsky-Korsakoff had never lived, modern dance music would not be the thing it is.

Whether, having grown inured to such violent and purely physiological stimuli as the clashing and drumming, the rhythmic throbbing and wailing glissandos of modern jazz music can supply, the world will ever revert to something less crudely direct, is a matter about which one cannot prophesy. Even serious musicians seem to find it hard to dispense with barbarism. In spite of the monotony and the appalling lack of subtlety which characterize the process, they persist in banging away in the old Russian manner, as though there were nothing more interesting or exciting to be thought of. When, as a boy, I first heard Russian music, I was carried off my feet by its wild melodies, its persistent, its relentlessly throbbing rhythms. But my excitement grew less and less with every hearing. Today no music seems to me more tedious. The only music a civilized man can take unfailing pleasure in is civilized music. If you were compelled to listen every day of your life to a single piece of music, would you choose Stravinsky's "Oiseau de Feu" or Beethoven's "Grosse Fugue"? Obviously, you would choose the fugue, if only for its intricacy and because there is more in it to occupy the mind than in the Russian's too simple rhythms. Composers seem to forget that we are, in spite of everything and though appearances may be against us, tolerably civilized. They overwhelm us not merely with Russian and negroid noises, but with Celtic caterwaulings on the black notes, with dismal Spanish wailings, punctuated by the rattle of the castanets and the clashing harmonies of the guitar. When serious composers have gone back to civilized music—and already some of them are turning from barbarism—we shall probably hear a corresponding change for the more refined in popular music. But until serious musicians lead the way, it will be absurd to expect the vulgarizers to change their style.

[*Along the Road,* 1925]

III.

History,
Politics,
Social Criticism

Accidie

THE CENOBITES of the Thebaid were subjected to the assaults of many demons. Most of these evil spirits came furtively with the coming of night. But there was one, a fiend of deadly subtlety, who was not afraid to walk by day. The holy men of the desert called him the *daemon meridianus;* for his favorite hour of visitation was in the heat of the day. He would lie in wait for monks grown weary with working in the oppressive heat, seizing a moment of weakness to force an entrance into their hearts. And once installed there, what havoc he wrought! For suddenly it would seem to the poor victim that the day was intolerably long and life desolatingly empty. He would go to the door of his cell and look up at the sun and ask himself if a new Joshua had arrested it midway up to the heavens. Then he would go back into the shade and wonder what good he was doing in that cell or if there was any object in existence. Then he would look at the sun again and find it indubitably stationary, and the hour of the communal repast of the evening as remote as ever. And he would go back to his meditations, to sink, sink through disgust and lassitude into the black depths of despair and hopeless unbelief. When that happened the demon smiled and took his departure, conscious that he had done a good morning's work.

Throughout the Middle Ages this demon was known as Acedia, or, in English, Accidie. Monks were still his favorite victims, but he made many conquests among the laity also. Along with *gastrimargia, fornicatio, philargyria, tristitia, cenodoxia, ira and superbia, acedia or toedium cordis* is reckoned as one of the eight principal vices to which man is subject. Inaccurate psychologists of evil are wont to speak of accidie as though it were plain sloth. But sloth is only one of the numerous manifestations of the subtle and complicated vice of accidie. Chaucer's discourse on it in the "Parson's Tale" contains a very precise description of this disastrous vice of the spirit, "Accidie," he tells us, "makith a man hevy, thoghtful and wrawe." It paralyzes human will, "it forsloweth and forsluggeth" a man whenever he attempts to act. From accidie comes dread to begin to work any good deeds, and finally wanhope, or despair. On its way to ultimate wanhope, accidie produces a whole crop of minor sins, such as idleness, tardiness, *lâchesse,* coldness, undevotion, and "the synne of worldly sorrow, such as is cleped *tristitia,* that sleth man, as seith seint Poule." Those

who have sinned by accidie find their everlasting home in the fifth circle of
the Inferno. They are plunged in the same black bog with the Wrathful,
and their sobs and words come bubbling up to the surface:

Fitti nel limo dicon; "Tristi fummo
nell' aer dolce che dal sol s' allegra,
portando dentro accidioso fummo;

Or ci attristiam nella belletta negra."
Quest' inno si gorgoglian nella strozza,
chè dir nol posson con parola integra.

Accidie did not disappear with the monasteries and the Middle Ages.
The renaissance was also subject to it. We find a copious description of the
symptoms of acedia in Burton's *Anatomy of Melancholy*. The results of
the midday demon's machinations are now known as the vapors of the
spleen. To the spleen amiable Mr. Matthew Green, of the Custom House,
devoted those eight hundred octosyllables which are his claim to immortality. For him it is a mere disease to be healed by temperate diet:

Hail! water gruel, healing power,
Of easy access to the poor;

by laughter, reading and the company of unaffected young ladies:

Mothers, and guardian aunts, forbear
Your impious pains to form the fair,
Nor lay out so much cost and art
But to deflower the virgin heart;

by the avoidance of party passion, drink, Dissenters and missionaries, especially missionaries: to whose undertakings Mr. Green always declined to
subscribe:

I laugh off spleen and keep my pence
From spoiling Indian innocence;

by refraining from going to law, writing poetry, and thinking about one's
future state.

The Spleen was published in the thirties of the eighteenth century. Accidie was still, if not a sin, at least a disease. But a change was at hand. "The
sin of worldly sorrow such as is cleped *tristitia*," became a literary virtue,
a spiritual mode. The apostles of melancholy wound their faint horns, and
the Men of Feeling wept. Then came the nineteenth century and romanticism; and with them the triumph of the meridian demon. Accidie in its
most complicated and most deadly form, a mixture of boredom, sorrow,

and despair, was now an inspiration to the greatest poets and novelists, and it has remained so to this day. The Romantics called this horrible phenomenon the *mal du siècle*. But the name made no difference; the thing was still the same. The meridian demon had good cause to be satisfied during the nineteenth century, for it was then, as Baudelaire puts it, that

> L'Ennui, fruit de la morne incuriosité,
> Prit les proportions de l'immortalité.[1]

It is a very curious phenomenon, this progress of accidie from the position of being a deadly sin, deserving of damnation, to the position first of a disease and finally of an essentially lyrical emotion, fruitful in the inspiration of much of the most characteristic modern literature. The sense of universal futility, the feelings of boredom and despair, with the complementary desire to be "anywhere, anywhere out of the world," or at least out of the place in which one happens at the moment to be, have been the inspiration of poetry and the novel for a century and more. It would have been inconceivable in Matthew Green's day to have written a serious poem about *ennui*. By Baudelaire's time *ennui* was as suitable a subject for lyric poetry as love; and accidie is still with us as an inspiration, one of the most serious and poignant of literary themes. What is the significance of this fact? For clearly the progress of accidie is a spiritual event of considerable importance. How is it to be explained?

It is not as though the nineteenth century invented accidie. Boredom, hopelessness, and despair have always existed, and have been felt as poignantly in the past as we feel them now. Something has happened to make these emotions respectable and avowable; they are no longer sinful, no longer regarded as the mere symptoms of disease. That something that has happened is surely simply history since 1789. The failure of the French Revolution and the more spectacular downfall of Napoleon planted accidie in the heart of every youth of the Romantic generation—and not in France alone, but all over Europe—who believed in liberty or whose adolescence had been intoxicated by the ideas of glory and genius. Then came industrial progress with its prodigious multiplication of filth, misery, and ill-gotten wealth; the defilement of nature by modern industry was in itself enough to sadden many sensitive minds. The discovery that political enfranchisement, so long and stubbornly fought for, was the merest futility and vanity so long as industrial servitude remained in force was another of the century's horrible disillusionments.

A more subtle cause of the prevalence of boredom was the dispropor-

1. From Baudelaire's *Spleen* LXXVI.

tionate growth of the great towns. Habituated to the feverish existence of these few centers of activity, men found that life outside them was intolerably insipid. And at the same time they became so much exhausted by the restlessness of city life that they pined for the monotonous boredom of the provinces, for exotic islands, even for other worlds—any haven of rest. And finally, to crown this vast structure of failures and disillusionments, there came the appalling catastrophe of the War of 1914. Other epochs have witnessed disasters, have had to suffer disillusionment; but in no century have the disillusionments followed on one another's heels with such unintermitted rapidity as in the twentieth, for the good reason that in no century has change been so rapid and so profound. The *mal du siècle* was an inevitable evil; indeed, we can claim with a certain pride that we have a right to our accidie. With us it is not a sin or a disease of the hypochondries; it is a state of mind which fate has forced upon us.

[*On the Margin*, 1923]

Pleasures

WE HAVE HEARD a great deal, since 1914, about the things which are a menace to civilization. First it was Prussian militarism; then the Germans at large; then the prolongation of the war; then the shortening of the same; then, after a time, the Treaty of Versailles; then French militarism—with, all the while, a running accompaniment of such minor menaces as Prohibition, Lord Northcliffe, Mr. Bryan, Comstockery.[2] . . .

Civilization, however, has resisted the combined attacks of these enemies wonderfully well. For still, in 1923, it stands not so very far from where it stood in that "giant age before the flood" of nine years since. Where, in relation to Neanderthal on the one hand and Athens on the other, where precisely it stood *then* is a question which each may answer according to his taste. The important fact is that these menaces to our civilization, such as it is—menaces including the largest war and the stupidest peace known to history—have confined themselves in most places and up till now to mere threats, barking more furiously than they bite.

No, the dangers which confront our civilization are not so much the external dangers—wild men, wars, and the bankruptcy that wars bring after them. The most alarming dangers are those which menace it from

2. Alfred Charles Harmsworth (1865–1922). English newspaper editor and journalist. William Jennings Bryan (1860–1925). American lawyer, populist politician, and anti-Darwinist. Anthony Comstock (1844–1915). American crusader for morals and censorship, he authored the comprehensive New York statute suppressing ostensibly immoral works.

within, that threaten the mind rather than the body and estate of contemporary man.

Of all the various poisons which modern civilization, by a process of auto-intoxication, brews quietly up within its own bowels, few, it seems to me, are more deadly (while none appears more harmless) than that curious and appalling thing that is technically known as "pleasure." "Pleasure" (I place the word between inverted commas to show that I mean, not real pleasure, but the organized activities officially known by the same name) "pleasure"—what nightmare visions the word evokes! Like every man of sense and good feeling, I abominate work. But I would rather put in eight hours a day at a Government office than be condemned to lead a life of "pleasure"; I would even, I believe, prefer to write a million words of journalism a year.

The horrors of modern "pleasure" arise from the fact that every kind of organized distraction tends to become progressively more and more imbecile. There was a time when people indulged themselves with distractions requiring the expense of a certain intellectual effort. In the seventeenth century, for example, royal personages and their courtiers took a real delight in listening to erudite sermons (Dr. Donne's, for example) and academical disputes on points of theology or metaphysics. Part of the entertainment offered to the Prince Palatine, on the occasion of his marriage with James I's daughter, was a syllogistic argumentation, on I forget what philosophical theme, between the amiable Lord Keeper Williams and a troop of minor Cambridge logicians. Imagine the feelings of a contemporary prince, if a loyal University were to offer him a similar entertainment!

Royal personages were not the only people who enjoyed intelligent pleasures. In Elizabethan times every lady and gentleman of ordinary culture could be relied upon, at demand, to take his or her part in a madrigal or a motet. Those who know the enormous complexity and subtlety of sixteenth-century music will realize what this means. To indulge in their favorite pastime our ancestors had to exert their minds to an uncommon degree. Even the uneducated vulgar delighted in pleasures requiring the exercise of a certain intelligence, individuality, and personal initiative. They listened, for example, to *Othello, King Lear,* and *Hamlet*—apparently with enjoyment and comprehension. They sang and made much music. And far away, in the remote country, the peasants, year by year, went through the traditional rites—the dances of spring and summer, the winter mummings, the ceremonies of harvest home—appropriate to each successive season. Their pleasures were intelligent and alive, and it was they who, by their own efforts, entertained themselves.

We have changed all that. In place of the old pleasures demanding intelligence and personal initiative, we have vast organizations that provide us with ready-made distractions—distractions which demand from plea-sure-seekers no personal participation and no intellectual effort of any sort. To the interminable democracies of the world a million cinemas bring the same stale balderdash. There have always been fourth-rate writers and dramatists; but their works, in the past, quickly died without getting be-yond the boundaries of the city or the country in which they appeared. Today, the inventions of the scenario-writer go out from Los Angeles across the whole world. Countless audiences soak passively in the tepid bath of nonsense. No mental effort is demanded of them, no participation; they need only sit and keep their eyes open.

Do the democracies want music? In the old days they would have made it themselves. Now, they merely turn on the gramophone. Or if they are a little more up-to-date they adjust their wireless telephone to the right wave-length and listen-in to the fruity contralto at Marconi House, singing "The Gleaner's Slumber Song."

And if they want literature, there is the Press. Nominally, it is true, the Press exists to impart information. But its real function is to provide, like the cinema, a distraction which shall occupy the mind without demanding of it the slightest effort or the fatigue of a single thought. This function, it must be admitted, it fulfils with an extraordinary success. It is possible to go on for years and years, reading two papers every working day and one on Sundays without ever once being called upon to think or to make any other effort than to move the eyes, not very attentively, down the printed column.

Certain sections of the community still practice athletic sports in which individual participation is demanded. Great numbers of the middle and upper classes play golf and tennis in person and, if they are sufficiently rich, shoot birds and pursue the fox and go skiing in the Alps. But the vast mass of the community has now come even to sport vicariously, preferring the watching of football to the fatigues and dangers of the actual game. All classes, it is true, still dance; but dance, all the world over, the same steps to the same tunes. The dance has been scrupulously sterilized of any local or personal individuality.

These effortless pleasures, these ready-made distractions that are the same for everyone over the face of the whole Western world, are surely a worse menace to our civilization than ever the Germans were. The work-ing hours of the day are already, for the great majority of human beings, occupied in the performance of purely mechanical tasks in which no men-tal effort, no individuality, no initiative are required. And now, in the hours of leisure, we turn to distractions as mechanically stereotyped and demanding as little intelligence and initiative as does our work. Add such leisure to such work and the sum is a perfect day which it is a blessed relief to come to the end of.

Self-poisoned in this fashion, civilization looks as though it might easily decline into a kind of premature senility. With a mind almost atrophied by lack of use, unable to entertain itself and grown so wearily uninterested in the ready-made distractions offered from without that nothing but the grossest stimulants of an ever-increasing violence and crudity can move it, the democracy of the future will sicken of a chronic and mortal boredom. It will go, perhaps, the way the Romans went: the Romans who came at last to lose, precisely as we are doing now, the capacity to distract themselves; the Romans who, like us, lived on ready-made entertainments in which they had no participation. Their deadly *ennui* demanded ever more gladiators, more tightrope-walking elephants, more rare and far-fetched animals to be slaughtered. Ours would demand no less; but owing to the existence of a few idealists, doesn't get all it asks for. The most violent forms of entertainment can only be obtained illicitly; to satisfy a taste for slaughter and cruelty you must become a member of the Ku Klux Klan. Let us not despair, however; we may still live to see blood flowing across the stage of the Hippodrome. The force of a boredom clamoring to be alleviated may yet prove too much for the idealists.

[*On the Margin*, 1923]

Modern Folk Poetry

TO ALL THOSE who are interested in the "folk" and their poetry—the contemporary folk of the great cities and their urban muse—I would recommend a little-known journal called *McGlennon's Pantomime Annual*. This periodical makes its appearance at some time in the New Year, when the pantos are slowly withering away under the influence of approaching spring. I take this opportunity of warning my readers to keep a sharp lookout for the coming of the next issue; it is sure to be worth the modest twopence which one is asked to pay for it.

McGlennon's Pantomime Annual is an anthology of the lyrics of the panto season's most popular songs. It is a document of first-class importance. To the future student of our popular literature *McGlennon* will be as precious as the Christie-Miller collection of Elizabethan broadsheets. In the year 2220 a copy of the *Pantomime Annual* may very likely sell for hundreds of pounds at the Sotheby's of the time. With laudable forethought I am preserving my copy of last year's *McGlennon* for the enrichment of my distant posterity.

The Folk Poetry of 1920 may best be classified according to subject-matter. First, by reason of its tender associations as well as its mere amount, is the poetry of Passion. Then there is the Poetry of Filial Devotion. Next, the Poetry of the Home—the dear old earthly Home in Oregon or Kentucky—and, complementary to it, the Poetry of the Spiritual Home in other and happier worlds. Here, as well as in the next section, the popular lyric borrows some of its best effects from hymnology. There follows the Poetry of Recollection and Regret, and the Poetry of Nationality, a type devoted almost exclusively to the praises of Ireland. These types and their variations cover the Folk's serious poetry. Their comic vein is less susceptible to analysis. Drink, Wives, Young Nuts, Honeymoon Couples—these are a few of the stock subjects.

The Amorous Poetry of the Folk, like the love lyrics of more cultured poets, is divided into two species: the Poetry of Spiritual Amour and the more direct and concrete expression of Immediate Desire. *McGlennon* provides plenty of examples of both types:

> When love peeps in the window of your heart
> [it might be the first line of a Shakespeare sonnet]
> You seem to walk on air,
> Birds sing their sweet songs to you,
> No cloud in your skies of blue,
> Sunshine all the happy day, etc.

These rhapsodies tend to become a little tedious. But one feels the warm touch of reality in

> I want to snuggle, I want to snuggle,
> I know a cozy place for two.
> I want to snuggle, I want to snuggle,
> I want to feel that love is true.
> Take me in your arms as lovers do.
> Hold me very tight and kiss me too.
> I want to snuggle, I want to snuggle,
> I want to snuggle close to you.

This is sound; but it does not come up to the best of the popular lyrics. The agonized passion expressed in the words and music of "You Made Me Love You" is something one does not easily forget, though that great song is as old as the now distant origins of ragtime.

The Poetry of Filial Devotion is almost as extensive as the Poetry of Amour. *McGlennon* teems with such outbursts as this:

> You are a wonderful mother, dear old mother of mine.
> You'll hold a spot down deep in my heart
> Till the stars no longer shine.
> Your soul shall live on for ever,

On through the fields of time,
For there'll never be another to me
Like that wonderful mother of mine.

Even Grandmamma gets a share of this devotion:

Granny, my own, I seem to hear you calling me;
Granny, my own, you are my sweetest memory. . . .
If up in heaven angels reign supreme,
Among the angels you must be the Queen,
Granny, my own, I miss you more and more.

The last lines are particularly rich. What a fascinating heresy, to hold that the angels reign over their Creator! The Poetry of Recollection and Regret owes most, both in words and music, to the hymn. *McGlennon* provides a choice example in "Back from the Land of Yesterday":

Back from the land of yesterday,
Back to the friends of yore;
Back through the dark and dreary way
Into the light once more.
Back to the heart that waits for me,
Warmed by the sunshine above;
Back from the old land of yesterday's dreams
To a new land of life and love.

What it means, goodness only knows. But one can imagine that, sung to a slow music in three-four time—some rich religious waltz-tune—it would be extremely uplifting and edifying. The decay of regular churchgoing has inevitably led to this invasion of the music-hall by the hymn. People still want to feel the good uplifting emotion, and they feel it with a vengeance when they listen to songs about

the land of beginning again,
Where skies are always blue. . . .
Where broken dreams come true.

The great advantage of the music-hall over the church is that the uplifting moments do not last too long.

Finally, there is the great Home motif. "I want to be," these lyrics always begin, "I want to be almost anywhere that is not the place where I happen at the moment to be." M. Louis Estève has called this longing "Le Mal de la Province," which in its turn is closely related to "Le Mal de l'au-delà." It is one of the worst symptoms of romanticism.

Steamer, balançant ta mâture,
Lève l'ancre vers une exotique nature,[3]

exclaims Mallarmé, and the Folk, whom that most exquisite of poets
loathed and despised, echo his words in a hundred different keys. There is
not a State in America where they don't want to go. In *McGlennon* we
find yearnings expressed for California, Ohio, Tennessee, Virginia, and
Georgia. Some sigh for Ireland, Devon, and the East. "Egypt! I am calling
you; Oh, life is sweet and joys complete when at your feet I lay [*sic*]." But
the Southern States, the East, Devon, and Killarney are not enough. The
Mal de l'au-delà succeeds the *Mal de la Province*. The Folk yearn for ex-
tramundane worlds. Here, for example, is an expression of nostalgia for a
mystical "Kingdom within your Eyes":

Somewhere in somebody's eyes
Is a place just divine,
Bounded by roses that kiss the dew
In those dear eyes that shine.
Somewhere beyond earthly dreams,
Where love's flower never dies,
God made the world, and He gave it to me
In that kingdom within your eyes.

If there is any characteristic which distinguishes contemporary folk poetry from the folk poetry of other times it is surely its meaninglessness.
Old folk poetry is singularly direct and to the point, full of pregnant meaning, never vague. Modern folk poetry, as exemplified in *McGlennon,* is almost perfectly senseless. The Elizabethan peasant or mechanic would
never have consented to sing or listen to anything so flatulently meaningless as "Back from the Land of Yesterday" or "The Kingdom within your
Eyes." His taste was for something clear, definite, and pregnant, like
"Greensleeves":

And every morning when you rose,
I brought you dainties orderly,
To clear your stomach from all woes—
And yet you would not love me.

Could anything be more logical and to the point? But we, instead of
logic, instead of clarity, are provided by our professional entertainers with
the driveling imbecility of "Granny, My Own." Can it be that the standard

3. From Mallarmé's "Brise Marine" (*Poésies* 1898).

of intelligence is lower now than it was three hundred years ago? Have newspapers and cinemas and now the wireless telephone conspired to rob mankind of whatever sense of reality, whatever power of individual questioning and criticism he once possessed? I do not venture to answer. But the fact of *McGlennon* has somehow got to be explained. How? I prefer to leave the problem on a note of interrogation.

[*On the Margin*, 1923]

Democratic Art

THERE IS INTOXICATION to be found in a crowd. For it is good to be one of many all doing the same thing—good whatever the thing may be, whether singing hymns, watching a football match, or applauding the eternal truths of politicians. Anything will serve as an excuse. It matters not in whose name your two or three thousand are gathered together; what is important is the process of gathering. In these last days we have witnessed a most illuminating example of this tendency in the wild outburst of mob excitement over the arrival in this country of Mary Pickford. It is not as though people were really very much interested in the Little Sweetheart of the World. She is no more than an excuse for assembling in a crowd and working up a powerful communal emotion. The newspapers set the excitement going; they built the fire, applied the match, and cherished the infant flame. The crowds, only too happy to be kindled, did the rest; they burned.

I belong to that class of unhappy people who are not easily infected by crowd excitement. Too often I find myself sadly and coldly unmoved in the midst of multitudinous emotion. Few sensations are more disagreeable. The defect is in part temperamental, and in part is due to that intellectual snobbishness, that fastidious rejection of what is easy and obvious, which is one of the melancholy consequences of the acquisition of culture. How often one regrets this asceticism of the mind! How wistfully sometimes one longs to be able to rid oneself of the habit of rejection and selection, and to enjoy all the dear, obviously luscious, idiotic emotions without an afterthought! And indeed, however much we may admire the Chromatic Fantasia of Bach, we all of us have a soft spot somewhere in our minds that is sensitive to "Roses in Picardy." But the soft spot is surrounded by hard spots, the enjoyment is never unmixed with critical disapprobation. The excuses for working up a communal emotion, even communal emotion itself, are rejected as too gross. We turn from them as a cenobite of the Thebaid would have turned from dancing girls or a

steaming dish of tripe and onions. I have before me now a little book, recently arrived from America, which points out the way in which the random mob emotion may be systematically organized into a kind of religion.
This volume, *The Will of Song* (Boni & Liveright, 70 c.), is the joint production of Messrs. Harry Barnhart and Percy MacKaye. "How are art and
social service to be reconciled? . . . How shall the Hermit Soul of the Individual Poet give valid, spontaneous expression to the Communal Soul of
assembled multitudes? How may the surging Tides of Man be sluiced in
Conduits of Art, without losing their primal glory and momentum?"
These questions and many others, involving a great expense of capital
letters, are asked by Mr. MacKaye and answered in *The Will of Song,*
which bears the qualifying subtitle, "A Dramatic Service of Community
Singing."

The service is democratically undogmatic. Abstractions, such as Will,
Imagination, Joy, Love, and Liberty, some of whom are represented in the
dramatic performance, not by individuals, but by Group Personages (i.e.,
choruses), chant about Brotherhood in a semi-Biblical phraseology that is
almost wholly empty of content. It is all delightfully vague and non-committal, like a Cabinet Minister's speech about the League of Nations, and,
like such a speech, leaves behind it a comfortable glow, a noble feeling of
uplift. But, like Cabinet Ministers, preachers, and all whose profession it is
to move the people by the emission of words, the authors of *The Will of
Song* are well aware that what matters in a popular work of art is not the
intellectual content so much as the picturesqueness of its form and the
emotion with which it is presented. In the staging—if such a term is not irreverent—of their service, Messrs. Barnhart and MacKaye have borrowed
from Roman Catholic ritual all its most effective emotion-creators. The
darknesses, the illuminations, the chiming bells, the solemn mysterious
voices, the choral responses—all these traditional devices have been most
scientifically exploited in the Communal Service.

These are the stage directions which herald the opening of the service:

> As the final song of the Prelude ceases, the assembly hall grows sud-
> denly dark, and the DARKNESS is filled with fanfare of blowing
> TRUMPETS. And now, taking up the trumpets' refrain, the Orchestra
> plays an elemental music, suggestive of rain, wind, thunder, and the
> rushing of waters; from behind the raised Central Seat great Flashes
> of Fire spout upward, and while they are flaring there rises a FLAME
> GOLD FIGURE, in a cone of light, who calls with deep, vibrant voice:
> "Who has risen up from the heart of the people?" Instantaneous,
> from three portions of the assembly, the VOICES OF THREE
> GROUPS, Men, Women, and Children, answer from the dark in triple
> unison: "I!"

Even from the cold print one can see that this opening would be extremely effective. But doubts assail me. I have a horrid suspicion that that elemental music would not sweep me off my feet as it ought to. My fears are justified when, looking up the musical program, I discover that the elemental music is by Langey, and that the orchestral accompaniments that follow are the work of Massenet, Tschaikowsky, Langey once more, Julia Ward Howe, and Sinding.[4] Alas! once more one finds oneself the slave of one's habit of selection and rejection. One would find oneself left out in the cold just because one couldn't stand Massenet. Those who have seen Sir James Barrie's latest play, *Mary Rose*, will perhaps recall the blasts of music which prelude the piece and recur at every mystical moment throughout the play. In theory one ought to have mounted on the wings of that music into a serene acceptance of Sir James Barrie's supernatural machinery; one ought to have been filled by it with deeply religious emotions. In practice, however, one found oneself shrinking with quivering nerves from the poignant vulgarity of that *leit motif*, isolated by what should have united one with the author and the rest of the audience. The cenobite would like to eat the tripe and onions, but finds by experiment that the smell of the dish makes him feel rather sick.

One must not, however, reject such things as *The Will of Song* as absolutely and entirely bad. They are useful, they are even good, on their own plane and for people who belong to a certain order of the spiritual hierarchy. *The Will of Song*, set to elemental music by Massenet and Julia Ward Howe, may be a moving spiritual force for people to whom, shall we say, Wagner means nothing; just as Wagner himself may be of spiritual importance to people belonging to a slightly higher caste, but still incapable of understanding or getting any good out of the highest, the transcendent works of art—out of the Mass in D, for example, or Sonata Op. III. The democratically minded will ask what right we have to say that the Mass in D is better than the works of Julia Ward Howe, what right we have to assign a lower place in the spiritual hierarchy to the admirers of *The Will of Song* than to the admirers of Beethoven. They will insist that there is no hierarchy at all; that every creature possessing humanity, possessing even life, is as good and as important, by the mere fact of that possession, as any other creature. It is not altogether easy to answer these objections. The arguments on both sides are ultimately based on conviction and faith. The best one can do to convince the paradoxical democrat of the real superiority of the Mass in D over *The Will of Song* is to point out that, in a sense, one contains the other; that *The Will of Song* is a part, and a very small part at that, of a great whole of human experience, to which the Mass in D

---

4. Jules Massenet (1842–1912). French composer. Julia Howe née Ward (1819–1910). American writer and composer. Christian Sinding (1856–1940). Norwegian composer.

much more nearly approximates. In *The Will of Song* and its "elemental" accompaniment one knows exactly how every effect is obtained; its range of emotional and intellectual experience is extremely limited and perfectly familiar. But the range of the Mass in D is enormously much larger; it includes within itself the range of *The Will of Song*, takes it for granted, so to speak, and reaches out into remoter spheres of experience. It is in a real sense quantitatively larger than *The Will of Song*. To the democrat who believes in majorities this is an argument which must surely prove convincing.

[*On the Margin*, 1923]

Follow My Leader

FOR SUGGESTING that human beings ought to live without leaders or governments—virtuously, and by the light of pure reason—Shelley's father-in-law very nearly got himself clapped into jail. Luckily for him, the book in which he expressed these dangerous views was published at the price of three guineas. For those who could afford three guineas, this mild, millenarial anarchism would not, it was felt, be very harmful. Godwin[5] was not destined to see the inside of Newgate.

We may well wonder, today, why he was not ushered into Bedlam. The views which were then criminal, now appear merely a little imbecile. Man being what he is, we can see that it is biologically impossible for him to do without governments and leaders. A society of locusts or lemmings can dispense with leaders, because each individual is internally governed by instincts which allow him no freedom of action; at any given moment, there is only one thing he can do. A race of superior beings, like Milton's angels, for example, could equally dispense with leaders; they could be trusted in any crisis to do the virtuous and the rational thing. Men fall between two stools. Most of us are only too happy to shift the greater part of our responsibilities to other shoulders; we like to be told what to do, which way to go.

And, fortunately, there are always shoulders ready and eager to accept the burden. Guides offer themselves to us as importunately as those shady gentlemen who, in imperfect English, tender their services on the Boulevard des Italiens to every Anglo-Saxon who longs to see the night life of Paris. For among the innumerable many, whose destiny and desire it is to be led, there are always a few who have the ambition to lead.

---

5. William Godwin (1756–1836). English political philosopher and novelist.

What are the capacities which, in the world as we know it, qualify a man to become a leader? And what are the qualities which, ideally, he ought to possess? These are interesting questions, which I will try to answer to the best of my ability.

To begin with, there must be the ambition to become a leader. All of us, I imagine, have a certain lust for power. But the desire varies greatly in intensity, and the objects over which it is desired to exert power are not always the same. An artist, for example, lusts for domination, not over his fellow men, but over words, over colors, over bits of stone; above all, over his own thoughts. The philosopher, more ambitiously, longs to tyrannize over the whole universe. With a truly Procrustean love of neatness and symmetry, he chops and stretches the untidy facts of experience until they fit his favorite system. But philosophers and artists, after all, are rare monsters. The power most people desire is over their neighbors. When that desire is very strong—so strong that it does not shrink before any expense of labor or of thought—the man who feels it may be said to be ambitious to become a leader.

The ambition has now to be satisfied. To do that, it is almost essential that a man should be endowed with a good dose of what the quacks of an earlier age called "animal magnetism." This quality, which seems to belong in part of the graces of the body, in part to those of the mind, expresses itself in varying degrees of intensity. At its most amiable, we call it, charm. At its most formidable, it is that queer power which enables certain people to inspire confidence and, sure of obedience, to command. The would-be leader should also possess—the essential complement to this endowment—a certain gift of the gab. Eloquence enables him to exert his magnetism at long range and over a number of people at the same time.

Next, I may enumerate one or two of the common cardinal virtues. Without a few of them, no leader can hope to be successful. The two most important are courage and resolution. Chastity, in this age of virtuous public opinion, has great practical value. (Poor Parnell!) But prudence, the virtue which prevents one from being found out, will be found by some leaders the easier to practice. Finally, there is honesty. But this is by no means essential to success. Indeed, a would-be leader possessing no other quality but this, is almost inevitably doomed to failure. After a month or two of Mr. Baldwin's ingenuous honesty, we all began to sigh for a little of Mr. Lloyd George's[6] cleverness.

It is unnecessary here to do more than mention those adventitious aids

6. Stanley Baldwin (1867–1947). English Conservative politician and prime minister three times during the interwar decades. David Lloyd George (1863–1945). Politician and prime minister of England during World War I.

to success which, in one form or another, almost all leaders have employed. I refer to the distinguishing badges of office and, in more modern times, to the peculiarities of physique and dress which leaders always cultivate in order to make themselves easily recognizable. It is one of the achievements of democracy to have abolished the badges and liveries which were once worn by every man in the social hierarchy, from mechanic to king. Everybody now looks like everybody else; the Prince of Wales is no more than the type and model of *Vanity Fair*'s Well-Dressed Man.

In order to make themselves promptly recognizable—which is as important for a politician as it is for a patent medicine or a breakfast food—leaders are compelled to cultivate little personal eccentricities. Gladstone has his collar and his prophetic hair. The latter waves, a hereditary liberal symbol, from the skull of Mr. Lloyd George. Chamberlain had his eyeglass and orchid; so has his son. But Joe also happened to have political ability. Tirpitz has fabulous whiskers; Clemenceau has his drooping ones, and William Hohenzollern[7] his aspiring moustaches. The old method of dressing up the ruler in feathers, robes, and coronets was perhaps the more satisfactory; for these trade-marks of power had the advantage of being fixed and hereditary.

We have now to consider the intellectual qualities of the successful leader. These are, in the first place, a prompt and practical intelligence, and a touch of cunning. Almost equally essential, if success is to be steady and anything like permanent, is a good dosage of the current prejudices. Certain leaders, it is true, have been relatively free from the prejudices of the led, and have succeeded in imposing upon them unfamiliar, and therefore unpopular ideas. But their efforts, though often fruitful in the future, have rarely met with an untroubled success during their own lifetime.

The typical successful leader shares the prejudices, however platitudinous or false they may be, of the society in which he finds himself, and prefers the teaching of tradition to that experience. He belongs almost invariably to the class which Trotter has called the stable-minded. Successful leaders are rarely remarkable for their purely intellectual capacities; indeed, it is difficult for a man to be very intelligent and to accept the prejudices of the society in which he lives. They are rarely subtle or skeptical; they do not like the scientific suspense of judgment, preferring always to

---

7. Joseph Chamberlain (1836–1914). English statesman. Alfred P. Friedrich von Tirpitz (1849–1930). German admiral. Georges Clemenceau (1841–1929). French statesman and premier of France (1917–1920). William II of the Hohenzollern family was German emperor from 1888 to 1918.

believe one thing passionately, rather than another, and to make definite decisions even when they have no rational excuse for doing so.

Men possessing these qualities have succeeded in the past, and still continue to succeed. They are the leaders whom we know today. The state in which the world finds itself in the present year of grace is not, it must be confessed, a very glowing testimonial to their capacities. But while, acting as individuals, we dismiss incompetent and dishonest servants without a character, we continue, in our collective capacity, to employ the same rulers who, in the past, have reduced us to ruin.

The fact is, that we can find nobody else; the ruler shortage is even more acute than the shortage of servants. We are compelled, for lack of anyone better, to employ those whom experience has taught us to regard as bad. Tradition, however, which is more powerful than experience, still teaches us to respect them; so that the glaring stupidity of our action is not clear to us.

Tradition, too, makes us imagine that we are still living in the sort of world where these leaders could function without doing too much mischief; where they could even be positively beneficial. In a society of stable traditions, a stable-minded leader was entirely in his element. At the head of a relatively small, sparsely peopled, and self-supporting state, where social, economic, and intellectual change was slow, the most narrow-witted of traditionalists could do no harm; and, by consolidating the people in their traditional virtues, he could frequently do good.

But the leader who now comes to power finds himself at the head of a profoundly unstable society, large sections of which have lost their traditional respect for the established order of things. He finds enormous populations dependent for their livelihood on an industrial system, shaken by external events and unsteady from its own inward rottenness. He finds universal discontent. He finds, in every department of life, changes going on with a dizzying rapidity. He finds material unaccompanied by mental development—huge hordes, with the minds of neolithic men, armed with trinitrotoluene and tanks.

To rule such a society, a man should be a philosopher and a scientist. He should possess vast knowledge. He should be exquisitely sensitive to every lesson of experience. He should be quick to seize on every new idea, to judge it, and to assimilate the virtue contained in it. He should, in a word, possess all those intellectual qualities which the typical leader of the past—who is also, alas, the typical leader of the present day—does not possess.

And the worst of it is that it seems almost impossible for a leader to possess these intellectual qualities together with those other qualities which I have already enumerated as being essential to success. One set of qualities seems to exclude the other.

It is in the highest degree unlikely that the pensive introvert, who cultivates his mind until it becomes capable of philosophic breadth and scientific sensitiveness, can also be a man of action, endowed with resolution, practical cunning, animal magnetism, and the necessary pinch of charlatanism. In the whole of recorded history, there is scarcely one example of the philosopher king. Nor, until very recent times, was the need of such a type seriously felt. It is only now, when the world is immensely complicated, changeful, and unsteady, that he has become a necessity. But it would be unduly optimistic to believe that this new kind of leader will actually make his appearance, however much we pray for him.

And even if a lonely monster of this kind were to appear in one country, he could achieve little or nothing so long as the old type of leader remained in control of the surrounding states. One Poincaré[8] would be enough to reduce ten philosopher kings to impotence. A single, solitary nation cannot possibly afford to embark on schemes of disarmament while its neighbors retain their fleets and aeroplanes. Similarly, no state could afford to be governed by reason while the rest of the world was governed by the good old-fashioned light of unreasoning prejudice.

We are on the horns of a dilemma. There is every reason to suppose, on the one hand, that leaders of the old school will involve the new and complex and unstable world in fresh and even more appalling calamities. And on the other hand, there seems to be not the slightest probability of a new type of leader being evolved; at any rate, in the immediate and, for us, interesting future. The unstable-minded introvert (of whose literary subspecies I may modestly claim to be a member) has neither the initial desire, nor the capacity to turn himself into a busy extrovert.

In the long course of time, humanity will doubtless find some issue between the horns. Stable-minded men will always adhere to tradition and prejudice; but prejudice may as well be in favor of rational conduct as opposed to it. To face reality will become respectable; public schoolboys will be taught that it is a good form to learn by experience, to do and to believe nothing but what seems reasonable.

But the distant future can safely be left to look after itself. What we are most anxiously concerned with is the immediate future. It is still by no means respectable to face reality; to believe only what is reasonable; to suspend judgment about the things we do not and cannot know; to act in

8. Raymond Poincaré (1860–1934). French statesman and the premier of France (1922–1924) who ordered the occupation of the Ruhr in 1923.

an unprejudiced and sensible manner. And our leaders belong to the respectable classes. . . .

In the absence of good management, we can only pray for luck.

[*Vanity Fair*, January 1924]

The Dangers of Work

TOO MUCH is talked nowadays about the dignity of labor.

Not that labor isn't dignified or eminently worthy of all respect. The days when one could despise a man because he worked are passed—and passed, I should imagine, forever.

But too much is talked, all the same, about the dignity of labor. And what is worse, too many people listen to this talk and try to make themselves dignified by working. If I object to this talk about work, it is because it causes too much work to be done. Our age has many defects, and one of them is precisely this: that it works too much. Or rather, it would be more accurate to say, too many people work. For the average amount of work performed by the human individual today is probably less than it was in those high old times before trade unions, and eight-hour bills, and juvenile employment acts, and all the other checks upon the unlimited and tyrannous rapacity of the rich existed. But if the average amount of work performed has decreased, the number of workers, on the other hand, is greater than it was. Whole sections of the community which, in the past, devoted themselves to the cultivation of an unlimited leisure, have now taken to working. Time takes strange revenges: the rich and the aristocratic had to be restrained in the past from imposing excessive labor on the poor; today, they, too, are found among the workers—sometimes almost in the sweated class.

Twenty-five years ago, there were still countries in Europe in which it was socially impossible for anyone belonging to a certain section of society to work. A nobleman with no inclination to become a bishop, a soldier, or a diplomat was fairly compelled to do nothing at all. And the sons of the unaristocratic rich were inclined to imitate the scruples of their titled friends; they, too, felt an extreme repugnance for labor.

But today we have changed all that. Scions of the nobility show themselves only too eager to get jobs. You will find them in banks and insurance companies, growing rubber, refining oil, marketing automobiles, exposing themselves even on the stage. Poverty, no doubt, is the prime cause of this altered state of things. Confronted with the alternative of working or starving, our noblemen prefer to work. The hidalgos of old

Spain chose to be hungry. They satisfied their pride at the expense of their stomachs. More truly philosophic, the hidalgos of our generation prefer to eat at the Ritz.

But if more people work now than worked in the past, it is by no means always out of necessity. It is not merely the new poor who work; it is the new rich, too, and, still more surprising, the old rich. These people have been driven to work, sometimes, it is true, by avarice and a desire to increase their wealth, but more often because working is now regarded as the obvious and respectable thing. Contempt for work has been replaced by a new social convention which lays it down that labor is dignified, that the worker is noble, and the man of leisure rather ignoble. The manufacturers of Utopias look forward to an age when everyone will work—will have to work, whether he likes it or no. The man of leisure in that golden age will not merely be looked down on; he will be locked up.

Respect for work is one of the products of democracy. Being a worker myself, I am grateful to a system which entitles me to respect. But an appreciation of the laborer must not blind us to the utility of the man of leisure. One may approve of the democratic doctrine of labor's dignity, and at the same time deplore its wholesale practical application by the classes which once were leisured.

There are many, I know, who can see no virtues in a leisured class. And, indeed, it is certainly easier to see the vices of such a class than its virtues. In every society, the majority of the leisured people do, in point of fact, waste their opportunities in a fashion that is positively astonishing. Not knowing how better to occupy their endless spare time, they indulge in every kind of stupidity, silliness, and vice. By a routine of what is technically known as pleasure, they brutalize themselves as effectively as the sweated laborer does by his routine of work. In some countries, the leisured class has consisted almost exclusively of these people. But in other countries there has been a minority—and sometimes an influential minority—of leisured people who have devoted their leisure to the cultivation of their intelligences, their tastes, their sensibilities.

It would be absurd to claim for such leisured societies that they ever produced anything of epoch-making importance. La Rochefoucauld and Madame de La Fayette, Shaftesbury, Chesterfield, and Walpole[9]—these are the fine flowers of the leisured class. They are the best that such a class can produce, but they are also typical of it. The ideal leisured society—and it is an ideal which has not infrequently been realized—is one which culti-

9. Horace Walpole (1717–1797). English man of letters. Philip Chesterfield (1694–1773). English statesman and man of letters. Marie La Fayette (1634–1693). French novelist.

vates the graces of the spirit, which is at home in the world of thought, which is not shocked by unfamiliar ideas, and which protects the propounders of such new notions from the effects of popular prejudice. Leisured society, at its best, is detached and unprejudiced, has good taste, and an open mind; it may, it is true, regard the arts and the philosophies with insufficient seriousness—as mere pastimes—but, at any rate, it admits their existence; it interests itself in them, and in their practitioners. And it is able to do so because it is leisured.

Infatuated by a generous democratic enthusiasm, or, more often, intimidated by public opinion, our men of leisure have almost all abandoned their hereditary right to do nothing at all, and have plunged into the vortex of money-making labor. The results seem to me, on the whole, deplorable. For if a good many imbeciles who would otherwise have spent all their time drinking, wenching, and playing games are now compelled, for a certain number of hours in each day, to think soberly of the best way of making money out of their neighbors, a few intelligent men, who might otherwise have cultivated a taste for spiritual amusements, are caught up into the machine of business and made to devote their wits to purely practical and immediate ends. Honest work thus tends to rob society of its genial and unprejudiced skeptics, its refined appreciators, its setters of elegant standards. It can be no mere coincidence that the absorption of the old leisured class in practical and immediately profitable work should have been going on at the same time as the breakup of literary and artistic tradition and the general decay of taste. The passing of the old leisured class has, with equal certainty, helped to make possible the present state of things.

One immediate result of the modern mania for work has been to increase enormously the power and importance of women in society. The leisured class, such as it is now, consists entirely of women. In the past, their fathers and brothers, their husbands and lovers, would have shared their leisure. Now, as we have seen, they prefer to dignify themselves by working. Left to themselves, the women are free to dictate their own standards of taste; it is they who call the tune, and the minor, the fashionable, purveyors of spirituality give them what they want.

The leisured class today prizes sensation and warm immediacy above abstraction and logical thought. The most fashionable music of recent years has been the barbarous, exciting, non-intellectual music of Stravinsky. The drawing-room philosopher is Bergson. The new psychology, with its insistence on the importance of the primary instincts, has been received with joy, has been made the excuse for a wholesale disparagement of pure intelligence. There is not a novelist or female reader of novels who does not talk rapturously about Life with a capital L.

The leisured classes of the past certainly managed in practice to live quite as intensively as anyone does today; but they talked about reason, and cultivated their intelligence. In those days, there were still men of leisure; now there are only women of leisure. What a melancholy decadence! If only the women could have been infected with the mania of working. . . . Man's real place is in the home. It is there, at leisure and relieved from immediate, practical preoccupations, that he can exercise his native powers of abstraction. Woman's passion for the concrete, for immediacy, for Life should be exercised in the practical conduct of affairs; not, as at present, in the corruption of taste, the breaking up of standards, the de-intellectualizing of the arts, and the exaltation of the instincts at the expense of reason.

A recrudescence of male luxury would be an excellent thing. It would, to begin with, leave less money over to be spent by women. It would raise the male morale; man would see that he could outdo woman at her own game; at present, he is the abject grub, she the butterfly. It would bring him back, through a preoccupation with his own personal adornment, to a general interest in all matters of taste—to the infinite improvement of taste. It would distract him from his work and, indirectly, revive his appreciation for the leisured life. In time, we might even see the re-creation of a real leisured class.

[*Vanity Fair,* March 1924]

On Not Being Up-to-Date

I FEEL CONSTRAINED to begin this article with an apology; for to write in *Vanity Fair* about the pleasures of not being up-to-date is really rather an impertinence. For *Vanity Fair,* after all, is the incarnation (or should one say incartation, since these words are to be printed on paper and not tattooed on flesh?) the incartation, then, of up-to-dateness. Its function, the reason for its existence, is to tell the public about all the new, amusing things that are going on in the world. That is its mission.

And a very laudable mission, too. For without *Vanity Fair* we might be unaware, or only so vaguely aware that it wouldn't really amount to knowing, of a vast number of amusing and interesting contemporary activities. Some of these activities, it is true, when judged by the rather severe standards applied by posterity to the works of the past, will turn out not to be quite so important as we now think them to be. Indeed, there have been few works of art or ideas produced at any given time not destined to "look damnably moldy a hundred years hence."

But that consideration need not deter us from being interested in novelties; for, to us, it is precisely their novelty, their quality of contemporaneity, that is important. Contemporaneity pleases us in itself, even though it may not be combined with much artistic or intellectual merit. Thus, we like listening to jazz bands because the horrible noise they make is a contemporary noise. We read books about Freudian psychology, even though it is palpably obvious that nine-tenths of their contents are the purest balderdash; the nonsense is our nonsense. Anyone who has had occasion to spend several months in a library reading nothing but the literature of a dead epoch will know how eagerly, at the end of that time, one turns to almost any contemporary book, however bad. After a spell with even the best authors of antiquity, I have read even a first novel with infinite relish, not because the book was good (far from it), but because it had been written by a contemporary.

Yes, the pleasures of being up-to-date are certainly great. But, then, so are the pleasures of not being up-to-date. For the last six months, I have been living on the top of a small mountain in the neighborhood of Florence, seeing only one newspaper a week, going to no theaters, hearing no new music, reading no new novels or poetry. Every now and then, it is true, *Vanity Fair* breaks in upon my spiritual darkness. But it is, I confess, on the photographs of the ravishing young female comedians, not on the articles about the latest manifestations of Parisian art, that I now most lovingly dwell.

And yet, in spite of all this, I have passed a most agreeable and not unprofitable winter (albeit the worst, meteorologically, in these parts since Dante wrote the *Inferno*), so much so that I do not feel in the least tempted, as yet at any rate, to return to civilization, or exchange my quiet mental darkness for the dancing and dazzling lights of metropolitan life. The time will come, no doubt, when my mountain-top in Tuscany will seem intolerably flat (spiritually flat, I mean; for the physical height and steepness are such that one has to go into the lowest gear to get up to my hermitage). And when that time does come, I shall doubtless rush headlong to Paris and listen to M. Satie's[1] latest trio of two typewriters and a cat, look at M. Picabia's exquisite one-dimensional paintings, read with avidity the last and most trivially tedious of M. Cocteau's novels. Or I shall take the flying machine to London, so as to be in time for Mr. Drinkwater's latest and noblest play, *Guy Fawkes;* for the private view of the London Group; for the first audition, at one deliriously thrilling concert, of the most recent works by Arnold Bax and Arthur Bliss.[2]

Yes, I repeat, the time will doubtless come. But at present, I enjoy my

---

1. Erik Satie (1866–1925). French composer.
2. Sir Arnold Bax (1883–1953). English composer. Sir Arthur Bliss (1891–1975). English composer.

remoteness and serenity. I do not feel the slightest desire to be up-to-date. The thought that, at this very moment, while the enormous Italian stars are palpitating and tremolo-ing like passionate tenors in the blue sky outside my open window, the curtain may be rising on the first scene of Mr. Drinkwater's immortal *Guy,* leaves me perfectly unmoved; and the sound of my own typewriter quite consoles me for not being able to listen to the ticking counterpoint of M. Satie's two machines and the coloratura of his amorous cat; and as for the novels of M. Cocteau and all the thousands of other novels—well, I feel about novels that it is enough to write them; one ought not to be expected to read them, too.

In the old days, though I might have had the courage to slip away from time to time and live for a little in a serene ignorance of contemporary activity, I should never have had the courage to admit that up-to-dateness did not interest me and that I could get on very comfortably and happily without it. For I had the feeling, then, that I could not possibly afford not to be up-to-date, not to know the very latest things about everyone and everything. But now—and I suppose it is one of the results of growing a little older—I realize that I can afford, not only to live in a relative unawareness of contemporaneity, but even to admit it. I couldn't have afforded, in the old days, to shirk Mr. Drinkwater's *Guy Fawkes* or M. Satie's trio for two typewriters and a cat, because there were certain people in whose estimation I should seriously have declined if I had admitted my out-of-dateness to them. These people, it is true, still exist, and will certainly think the more poorly of me for not being up-to-date, and for admitting the fact. The reason why I feel that I can afford to be out-of-date is this: I have ceased to care two pins what these people—the intellectually smart, the leaders or follow-my-leaders of mental fashion—think of me, or indeed of anything else under the sun. I find it more agreeable to be, not fashionable, but myself.

When, from the depths of my calm solitude, I reflect on the many extraordinarily foolish and time-wasting things I have done for the sake of being up-to-date and earning the approval of the fashionable, I shudder and am amazed that I could ever have been so idiotic. Thus, I remember spending at least seventy-two precious now irremediably perished hours in reading Mr. James Joyce's *Ulysses.* I remember passing hundreds of evenings at the first nights of the most boring plays (though it is true I was paid for doing so). I remember listening to whole concerts of music by Mr. Arnold Bax, to a complete opera (though, luckily, a short one) by Mr. Gustav Holst. I remember passing whole afternoons among the landscapes of K. Marchand and his English followers. And for what? to whom is the benefit, as we used to ask in Latin? Merely that I might be able to say that I had read the portentous and boring book, heard the dim music, seen the plays, and thrilled aesthetically before the significance of those painted forms. Merely that the mentally smart might not despise me as a boor and a provincial for not having done so.

But now, I find that it really doesn't matter in the least what the mentally smart think. I find that I am quite as happy in my out-of-dateness as I was in my up-to-dateness; what is more, I find that I don't miss much. The distance at which I live from contemporary civilization acts, as it were, as a filter. The unimportant novelties stick on the way; the important ones, sooner or later, get through. Unlike most filters, my remoteness serves to strain away the gnat, but allows the camel to pass through.

To be free from the socially imposed necessity of knowing about novelties is to endow oneself with leisure and calm. It enables one to work; it leaves one at liberty to think—a process which, like almost everyone else, I used to detest, preferring to occupy my mind with the various substitutes for thought, from newspapers to the Freudian interpretation of dreams, which modern civilization provides in ever-increasing quantities for the relief of mind-haunted humanity. It leaves one at liberty, I repeat, to think (and once one is used to it, the activity is really quite agreeable); it gives one time and inclination to talk with the few people one likes, about interesting things; and excuses one from having to talk with the casually met many, about the things which one finds boring. It creates the leisure to read the books one always meant and wanted, but never had the time, to read, owing to the press of new novels, plays, and the like, a knowledge of which is essential, if one is to sustain a conversation in polite and intellectual smart society. These are the principal joys and advantages of not being up-to-date; and very considerable I find them.

I do not doubt, as I have said, that the time will come when I shall long to get back to contemporaneity, and when the sort of social life one can get in a metropolis (the very thought of which now fills me with a real horror) will seem to me once more infinitely alluring. Yes, I shall revert, no doubt, to up-to-dateness. But after a short spell of it, I shall as certainly renounce the joys of the contemporary world and, once more, on the top of this or of some other mountain, cultivate my own garden in peace and quietness.

[*Vanity Fair,* April 1924]

Fashions in Love

LA ROCHEFOUCAULD, who still holds the world's record for having said the greatest number of sensible things in the smallest possible number of words, remarked of love: that there are people who would never have been in love if they had never heard love talked about. We may extend the scope of the maxim and say that even the people capable of spontaneously falling in love would not fall in love in the peculiar ways they do, if they had never heard talk, or never read, of these particular ways of loving. For the fact is that there are fashions in love; fashions that last a little longer, it is true, than the modes in dress, but quite as tyrannous as these. It would be just as unreasonable to have expected a Roman of the empire to love in the same strain as Dante, as it would be to ask Beatrice to go about in a natty little tailor-made with a short umbrella under her arm.

Fashions in clothes are various, but not infinitely various—for the simple reason that the female form divine beneath the garments remains the same through all the centuries, while even the garments themselves are always expected to fulfil certain utilitarian functions, such as protecting the body from the elements and ensuring a greater or less degree of decency. So that, however charming aesthetically the effect might be, there have never been crinolines more than six feet in diameter or hats more than eight feet high. It is the same with love. There are limits within which the amorous fashions have always fluctuated in the past and presumably always will. But within the limits prescribed by the nature and functions of normal human love, there have been large and surprising variations. From Platonic love to love as practiced by the victims of Juvenal's satire; from love in the style of George Sand and Alfred de Musset to the contemporary love between earnest readers of the prevalent frank sex books of the psychoanalysts; from the Venetian cicisbeism of the eighteenth century to the Venetian passion of the fifteenth—the choice is sufficiently large and varied. In practice, however, choice is limited, so far as the majority of aspiring lovers at any given period is concerned, to those styles of love which happen at the moment to be fashionable. In love, as in every other human activity, it is only the very exceptional individuals who can go beyond the standards and conventions of their age.

Thus, to the intelligent Greek at the time of Plato, the possibility of a spiritual, idealistic, intellectual love affair with a woman would hardly have occurred. One married for the sake of progeny and because, in St. Paul's somewhat cynical phrase, it is better to marry than to burn. For all the rest it was natural—it was the fashion, then—to turn to romantic and passionate friendships with the youth of one's own sex. Today, this line of conduct is so decidedly not the fashion that a man can be put in jail for following it.

Similarly, it was clearly impossible for an imperial Roman, a Babylonian, a Lydian to practice ideal love of any sort—for the simple reason that it was impossible for these people, brought up to regard physical love as the most straightforward, natural, blameless, and easily obtainable of all diversions, to understand the nature of idealistic love or the reasons for its existence. Indeed, Platonic love, as we now know it and as it flourished in Europe in medieval and modern times, is a product of Christian rather than Platonic thought. An ascetic religion had condemned the care-free love-making of the ancients. Love, being something inherently sinful, it was only natural that thoughtful men, brought up in this belief, should look for some way of justifying their passions, affections, and instincts, should try to devise some scheme by which a sin might be turned into a virtue and the work of the devil be made to redound to the greater glory of God. It was to fulfil this purpose that Platonic love was called, or recalled, into existence. The theory of Platonic love is simple: the beauty of a loved object is a fragmentary manifestation of the Absolute Beauty, so that we can pass from love of the individual to the love of All, of God. Falling in love, if we do it in the right way, is thus as good as going to church. Thus is sin justified and made to serve religious ends. It is to be remarked that the great Platonic lovers of the Middle Ages—Dante and Guido Cavalcanti—made no attempt to come into personal contact with the objects of their ideal loves. Dante fell in love with Beatrice when they were both not more than nine years old and only saw her two or three times afterwards. In due time they both of them married—but not one another; the ideal did not interfere with the real love. And much the same is true of Guido and Monna Vanna. They were wise. One can only love ideally if one's lady is herself not quite real. It is hard to be at once Platonically and practically amorous. John Donne put the whole matter in a nutshell when he wrote:

Love's not so pure and abstract as they used
To say, who have no mistress but their Muse.

The fashion of Platonic love lasted throughout the Middle Ages. But parallel with the courtly and chivalrous panegyrics of the eternal feminine there runs a whole bourgeois literature, realistic, cynical, anti-feminist. You could take your choice of fashions then.

At a much later date we find a precisely similar co-existence of diametrically opposed fashions; and we find them both, which makes the contrast more striking still, worn at different periods of his career by the same man. Read the letters written by Alfred de Musset[3] first to George Sand, then to Aimée d'Alton. . . . The fashion of the first series is wildly, turgidly, romantic. It is all an affair of souls, an explosion of mystical religion; the lovers soar like eagles in a spiritual empyrean. But the letters to Aimée d'Alton are the letters of a gay and frivolously wise man of the eighteenth-

---

3. Alfred de Musset (1810–1857). French poet and dramatist.

century world. Love with Aimée is not a tragedy, not a religion; but a delightfully amusing and charming little diversion.

There is a superb account in Balzac's *Cousine Bette* of the change in amorous fashions which took place at the accession of Louis-Philippe—a change which corresponded to that which occurred in England at about the same time, at the accession of Victoria. He is describing the infatuation of the old beau of the Empire, Baron Hulot, for a young woman, Mme. Marneffe, brought up in the new Louis-Philippe mode of love-making. . . . The old gentleman, accustomed to the Empire style of love-making—it was a blunt and military style, extremely direct and frank and to the point, with no shilly-shallying since time was short between the battles—was naturally quite ignorant of the new style of love that had come into fashion since 1830. He had not so much as heard of the "pauvre faible femme," did not know that according to the modern convention she was always a self-sacrificing angel who immolated herself out of pure charity and Christian virtue on the altar of her lover's desires. "This new art of love," says Balzac, "consumes huge quantities of evangelical words in the devil's work. Passion is a martyrdom. Both parties aspire to the ideal, the infinite. Through love one desires to become better. All these fine phrases are an excuse for putting yet more ardor into the practice of love, more fury into the falls from virtue, than in the past. This hypocrisy, the characteristic of our age, has gangrened gallantry." No better or more succinct description of romantic love could be given. It is a masterly analysis. Balzac's only mistake is to suppose that this hypocrisy, which was to characterize the whole of the middle and later nineteenth century, had "gangrened gallantry." On the contrary, it had made it infinitely more interesting than it had been in the eighteenth century. For it is obvious that if love is taken as much for granted as eating, it becomes just as unexciting. It was surely in pure self-defense, that the nineteenth century took to hypocrisy and romanticism in love. Love, having been treated during the eighteenth century as being practically a non-moral affair of next to no consequence, had become most desperately dull. It needed the romanticism of George Sand and Alfred de Musset, coupled with hypocrisy, Mrs. Grundy, and the vast Victorian conspiracy of silence to make it interesting again.

It was a strange fashion, this Victorian mode; unique, indeed—for neither the Platonic-idealistic nor the puritanic convention had ever been pushed so far before. Unique: and yet those who were brought up in it seem to have imagined that their queer fashion was the natural norm and that the fashions current in every other age of history and pre-history, since the creation of man, were entirely unnatural and wicked. They might as reasonably have supposed that crinolines were the only natural dress, that the mode ought to persist forever and that the benighted ancients who had worn other garments were heathenish creatures, worthy of damnation.

The twentieth century has seen a very considerable reaction away from the erotic fashion of its predecessor. We are freer in speech and action than our fathers; we admit the facts of nature with less reluctance. But our frankness differs from the frankness of past ages in being largely medical and scientific, instead of cheerfully and spontaneously animal. Engaged couples discuss the steps they will take if their children-to-be grow up with Oedipus complexes or anal erotism. It is, to my mind at any rate, a rather dingy kind of frankness; better, no doubt, than the reticences it has superseded, but symptomatic of that general over-intellectualization of all our normal life which Mr. D. H. Lawrence so rightly deplores. We are becoming rather too self-conscious about our instincts. The attitude of Chaucer or of Brantôme is fundamentally saner and healthier than the attitude of Dr. Marie Stopes and the writers of Sane Sex Books. What the next fashion in love will be, it is difficult to foresee. Perhaps, to counteract the medical view and to rescue love from the tediousness with which the scientific and pseudo-scientific investigators have invested it, we shall have a new reaction towards romanticism and prudery. Perhaps, after the endless analyses of Proust, we shall demand a briefer, a hardier, less self-conscious literature. In any case, it will be interesting to watch.

[*Vanity Fair*, September 1924]

By Their Speech Ye Shall Know Them

WHEN THE EDITOR of this journal suggested that I should write an article on the difference between Oxford and Cambridge, I must confess that I thought twice before complying with his request. There is something tempting, it is true, about making sweeping generalizations of this sort; but the pleasure is not unattended by danger. Generalizations about corporate masses of human beings are generally wrong. The most intelligent writers, when they begin to talk about national characteristics, racial psychology, and class peculiarities, are apt to make fools of themselves. Dr. Jowett,[4] for example, who did not like what is known as the Latin spirit, was of the opinion that the motto written up over the gate of hell was: *Ici on parle français*. Lamartine thought that vanity was the soul of all English society and Montesquieu declared that an Englishman who loses his

---

4. Benjamin Jowett (1817–1893). English scholar and translator of Plato and other Greek authors.

fortune becomes either a murderer or a robber. None of these generalizations, it seems to me (though I, being an Englishman with a taste for French literature and French wines, may be prejudiced) has the slightest value. And yet their authors were all men of intelligence. You, on your side of the Atlantic, get some hearty laughs, no doubt, out of the slashing generalizations made by European visitors about the American mind. We find your comments equally amusing.

Generalizations deal pontifically with that purely mythical being, the average man or woman. None of us are average; we are all individuals. What applies to the average of fifty million individuals does not apply in its entirety to any one of the fifty million. Moreover the people who make generalizations about national character are never in a position to discover what the average really is. Generalizations of this sort are made on entirely inadequate data. A lecture tour in the Eastern states, a couple of evening parties in Dublin, are considered sufficient basis for making a generalization about the Irish or the American character.

If I have generalized at such length about the fallaciousness of generalizations, it is merely to excuse myself in advance for any gross blunders that I may make and to warn my readers against taking what I may say as gospel truth. At the most, I only profess to record personal impressions. Having made these preliminary reservations, let me get to work.

Before discussing the differences between Oxford and Cambridge, it may be as well to specify their resemblances. For the fact is (you see how confidently I already begin to generalize!) the fact is that the great mass of the alumni of these two venerable institutions are indistinguishable. They are Oxford or Cambridge men only locally, not mentally. For to be anything particular mentally one must first have a mind. Now the number of people who, for more than mere practical purposes, have a mind is small. It is only these few who will be influenced by the intellectual traditions of the places where they receive their education. The rest will be impervious to intellectual influences. Accordingly we find that the mass of Oxonians and Cantabs indistinguishably resemble one another. They are not strictly Oxford or Cambridge men at all. They are just Public School boys who happen to have gone on to one or other of the two universities. Their interests are those of all healthy and mindless young men . . . athletic sports, love (though their interest in this is tempered by the amount of violent physical exercise that they take), and the various social amusements. They are compelled, it is true, to read certain books, attend certain lectures, and pass certain examinations; every rose has its thorns and not even in the best-regulated universities is one allowed to devote one's time and energies exclusively to amusing oneself. But these things make only the slightest impression. Human memory is an admirable thing; but our capacity for forgetting is still more marvellous. The majority of young men can read, be lectured, and take a degree without being any the worse.

The examination once over, they forget everything they ever learned. It is only the things one desires to know, the things that were learned willingly, that one has any chance of remembering. Those who learn under compulsion can make sure of forgetting completely and at once. Thus we see that, for the majority of students the University means neither intellectual tradition nor the official curriculum, but simply leisure, sport, and amusement. But sports and amusements are standardized; one rows, one plays football or cricket in the same way at Cambridge as at Oxford. Hence, inevitably, the standardized type of young man who engages in these pursuits. The bulk of Oxford and Cambridge men are simply Public School boys of a larger growth. It is only by accident that they happen to be Oxonians or Cantabs.

So much for the resemblances between Oxford and Cambridge. It is with the blossoming of minds capable of absorbing the dissimilar traditions of the two universities that differentiation begins. In the past it was customary to sum up the difference between the two universities by saying that Oxford was literary and scholarly, Cambridge mathematical and scientific; Oxford retrospective, enthusiastic, mystical, the home of lost causes, and Cambridge rationalistic and dry. In process of time, however, these classical distinctions have come to be less true than they were. Science is very efficiently cultivated on the banks of the Isis, scholarship on those of the Cam. Nevertheless, these ancient generalizations do still retain a certain residuum of truth. There are still scholastics at Oxford who blandly ignore contemporary thought. Not long ago, I remember, Mr. Bertrand Russell unsheathed his sharpest pen against one of them who had written of the propositions of Euclid as though they were fundamental and necessary truths ... a notion that was very excusable in the eighteenth century but which, in the twentieth, does certainly look a bit superannuated and out of fashion. Rather cruelly, Mr. Russell remarked that there were probably only two universities in the world where such an opinion could still be held ... the universities of Oxford and of Lhassa. But then Mr. Russell is a Cambridge man. In justice to my own university I must insist that the number of Tibetan professors is small and, I trust, on the wane.

Still, I think it is true that there is still a certain difference between the intellectual traditions of the two universities. The fashionable mental tone at Cambridge is a dry, rather Gallic, rather eighteenth-century rationalism. An Epicurean philosophy, no prejudices, analysis carried everywhere ... these are the Cambridge watchwords. The so-called "Bloomsburies" are the most accomplished exponents of this point of view. Entrenched behind the mathematical works of Messrs. Russell and Whitehead (which, of course, they have never read), supported in the flank by such minor philosophers as Professor Broad,[5] they feel that they can safely defy the mystics, Christians, idealists, and all the other practitioners of mumbo-jumbery and occultism.

It is, perhaps, just a little unfortunate for them that the two greatest men of science produced by Cambridge, Sir Isaac Newton and James Clerk Maxwell, should both have been, in spite, or should we not rather say, because of their enormous intelligence, the most ardent of mystics. The fact has always seemed to me to take some of the bloom off Cambridge rationalism. But that is by the way. My business is to record anthropological facts, not to discuss the merits of philosophical theories or views of life.

At Oxford, this rationalism was never *de rigueur.* The more cloudy forms of metaphysics have always been popular beside the Thames, a fact which has led to the uttering, first and last, of a great deal of nonsense. The Oxford poets and novelists of the last few years have mostly inclined towards a mysticism varying from the genuine spontaneous article to the labored imitation made by those who feel intellectually that mystical emotion is desirable, but who are not gifted by nature with a capacity for feeling it.

But the more I generalize, the less secure my generalizations come to seem. I am appalled to think of all that I am leaving out. It is only ignorance or a deliberate omission of the outstanding cases that makes generalization possible. And after all it is the outstanding cases that are really interesting. In the case of an exceptional man it matters little, if at all, whether he went to Oxford or to Cambridge or to neither. He will be exceptional in any circumstances. So many exceptional cases occur to me, that it seems hopeless to lay down rules.

But this anthropological study would be incomplete if I did not give the readers of *Vanity Fair* some idea of the physical differences between Oxonians and Cantabs. For though the alumni of both universities are drawn from the same social class and have been educated at the same schools, it is frequently possible to tell them apart—not by the eye (though Mr. E. M. Forster, it is true, has differentiated between "tight little faces from Cambridge, little fish faces from Oxford"; but this is somewhat arbitrary), but by the ear. By the ear; for their speech betrayed them. The original speech from which the two dialects branch off is that version of the English language current in the Public Schools. It is a speech which you, in America,

5. Charles Dunbar Broad (1887–1971). English philosopher.

find just as comic as we find the dialect of New York. It should be noted, by the way, that it is not merely the sound of words which differentiates the English from the American dialect; it is, perhaps even more strikingly, the intonation. For Americans, as a rule—another generalization!—tend to speak on one note; their voices pursue a level course. Whereas an English-man of the Public School class is constantly modulating his voice from high to low—a process which seems wonderfully comic on your side of the ocean. This tendency towards modulation is exaggerated by the more brainy at both universities, but more especially at Cambridge, where the voice of an intellectual pronouncing that a picture by Marchand is "Too lovely" drops more than an octave between the words. At Oxford a cer-tain clerical rotundity of tone is apt to make itself heard in the voices of the best people. This tendency appears at its worst among Oxonian cu-rates, who pronounce the words "He that has ears to hear, let him hear" as though they were written: "He that hath yars to hyar let'm hyar." But the most certain shibboleth-test has yet to be described. It is by his method of breathing while he speaks that you can infallibly distinguish the Cam-bridge from the Oxford intellectual. Have you ever tooted a motor horn? You will have noticed that sometimes, when you loosen your squeeze of the rubber bulb, the instrument as it draws in breath makes a faint stran-gled sound in its throat. If TOOT is the noise made when you squeeze the bulb, then *toot,* in the smallest of letters, is the sound that is heard when you let go and the bulb replenishes itself with air. The conversation of Cambridge intellectuals is marked by precisely the same alternation be-tween TOOT and *toot.* First a word or phrase is spoken emphatically on an outward breath, to be succeeded by one faintly and stranglingly uttered on the intake. This test is infallible. If ever you hear a man speaking on the indrawn breath, you can be absolutely certain that he was educated at Cambridge and has pretentions to being an intellectual.

[*Vanity Fair,* December 1924]

The Importance of Being Nordic

NOT MUCH BALDERDASH is talked about organic chemistry. For the sim-ple reason that few people who do not know something of the subject are tempted, or have the impertinence, to talk about it. But about the infinitely more obscure and complicated subjects of human nature, heredity, racial characteristics, progress, and degeneracy, the majority of us feel no diffi-dence. Without possessing the slightest real, systematic knowledge of these matters, we are prepared to talk of them—to talk at length, confidently, and with fanatical passion.

Nobody imagines that, because his body is a walking chemical laboratory, he is therefore qualified to talk about chemistry; or that, being built up of atoms, he is for that reason an expert physicist. But we are all ready, on the mere strength of our humanity—just because we are human beings—to hold forth dogmatically on the subject of Man, or Sex, Race, Progress, and all the other glorious words which that curious race of beings known as publicists, love to spell with the largest capital letters. On the mere strength of our humanity, I repeat; not because we know anything. Just because we are men, we think ourselves qualified to talk about Man. Is it to be wondered at if our talk is, for the most part pure and unadulterated bosh?

On no anthropological subject have greater quantities of balderdash been uttered than on the subject of racial characteristics and racial degeneracy. The muddy stream of bosh flows intermittently, now fast, now slow, according to the pseudo-scientific fads and the political prejudices of the moment. At the present time it is in full spate, particularly on the American side of the Atlantic, where the political problems of immigration have stimulated the anthropological philosophers to tremendous efforts. In present-day America a handsome living is to be made by writing books about the racial characteristics of Europeans—solemn dogmatic books, full of perfectly groundless generalizations, which are immensely popular with thoughtful readers, because they happen to fit in with the political prejudices of the moment. From the books, some of this intellectual swill sloshes over into the newspapers. The journalists spice it with their sensationalism and the public greedily laps it up. So the great work of enlightenment goes on.

Successful nations, like successful individuals find it very difficult to believe that they are ever wrong; success, to them, is the sufficient proof of their intellectual and moral superiority. They therefore exalt the qualities in themselves which made for success, setting them up as a standard of absolute excellence. Races with different qualities, particularly if they happen not to be very successful at the moment, are regarded as lower races. Thus, the clever Greeks and the efficient, military Romans regarded all their neighbors as barbarians. But the word "barbarian" did not possess, for the two peoples, quite the same connotation. To the Greeks it signified primarily a stupid, unscientific unphilosophical man (a Roman, for example). To the Romans it implied lack of discipline, inefficiency, bad organization. In the course of history there have been many standards of racial virtue, set up by many races.

The Nordic races have now, in their own imagination, taken the place of the Greeks and Romans. All virtue and intelligence belong to them; all that is bad to the Mediterranean and Alpine races. Historians may venture to suggest that the Athenians were no fools, that Julius Caesar and Napoleon were remarkable men, that the Italians of the renaissance achieved a thing or two. "That was because they were all Nordic," the anthropological philosophers reply. "How do you make that out?" we ask in some surprise. "They must have been Nordic," the philosophers answer, "because they did such remarkable things." We sink beneath the weight of argument.

It is a very long time since I read Mr. Houston Chamberlain's[6] immortal work on these great subjects. But so far as I remember he contrived to prove decisively that not only Napoleon, but also Jesus Christ was of Teutonic origin. The Great War has been fought since Mr. Houston Chamberlain wrote his book. Naturally we can't expect anthropological philosophy to be the same today as it was in Houston's time. And it isn't. Since the war, certain American philosophers have made the epoch-making discovery that the Germans are not Nordic at all. Why not? Because, if they had been, they could not have behaved as they did. Q.E.D.

What nonsense it all is! Even the more cautious generalizations of those who did not go so far as to affirm the Nordicity of Napoleon and Jesus of Nazareth are still without foundation. These less extreme theorists are prepared to admit that the Mediterranean peoples were bright enough in their day; but they insist that they are now degenerate, and should not, therefore, be allowed to contaminate by their presence, the lands in which the all-virtuous, all-intelligent Nordics live. The compatriots of Dante, Michelangelo, and Galileo are permitted by the new immigration laws of the United States to send only a few hundreds of their annual increase of population into the great Nordic land. They are an inferior race; they are degenerates.

Degenerate. . . . It is a fine reverberating word. And a most convenient word to throw at people you don't like. For example, you don't like post-impressionism; therefore Matisse is degenerate. You think St. Francis was a fool because he didn't go on the Stock Exchange and make a large fortune; he was a degenerate. German beer gives you indigestion; you object to the rapacity of French hotel-keepers—these races (who can doubt it?) are degenerate. And so on. There are few more useful words in the whole dictionary.

Now if the word "degeneracy" means anything (beyond the fact, of course that you dislike the race or the individual to whom you apply it) it

6. Houston Stewart Chamberlain (1855–1927). English-born German author of *Foundations of the Nineteenth Century* (1899), a defense of Aryan supremacy.

connotes an inherited and heritable quality. In zoology, degeneration means the progressive simplification of forms. Thus many parasites are degenerates from non-parasitic ancestors having much more complicated and highly developed structures. When you say, therefore, that the Italians, for example, have degenerated from what they were in the days of Michelangelo, you mean—if you mean anything, which is in no way essential in these deep discussions—that they are now born different from what they were four hundred years ago, and that they are passing on this difference to their offspring. Now, if this is the case, the evolution of man must be utterly unlike that of all other animals. For in no other animals is the slightest specific change apparent after a lapse of only ten or twelve generations. If men degenerate so quickly, we might expect dogs and cats to do the same. But so far as I am aware, no cynological philosopher has arisen to denounce the abject degeneracy of the Irish terrier, the French bulldog, the sheep dog of the Maremma, the manifestly non-Nordic dachshund, and that sinister mixture of Teutonic and Mediterranean, the Alsatian wolf-hound.

The fact of the matter is that all the phenomena of so-called degeneracy are either imaginary—being invented by foreign observers who do not happen to like the characteristics of the race to which they attribute degeneracy—or, if real, are due to external causes which, although they may influence the life and habits of several generations of men and women, are quite powerless (acquired characteristics not being heritable) to affect the specific character of the race.

Let us take the obvious case of the Italians. The amateur anthropologists call them degenerate. Why? On the ground, chiefly, that they have failed to produce as many great artists during the nineteenth century as they did in the fifteenth and sixteenth. True; but the anthropologists forget to remark that during the first two-thirds of the nineteenth century the Italians were busily engaged in freeing their country from foreign oppressors and that since 1870 they have been at work on the exploitation of an, industrially speaking, brand new country, the gradual creation of a new European state, and the political education of a people habituated to foreign tyranny. These are labors requiring considerable ability to perform.

Ability is of two kinds—general and special. Special ability may be combined with general ability, or it may not. A man may be an extraordinary mathematician, painter, musician, or chess player, and in all other respects almost an imbecile. Claude Lorraine, for example, could not learn to read or write. The man with a highly developed special ability ought not and often cannot do anything but what he is peculiarly fitted by nature to do. But the man of general ability can do almost anything he chooses to set his mind to. His choice of a career is largely a matter of accident. Now, at the time of the renaissance, it happened that the political, social, and religious conditions in Italy were such that the greatest part of the existing general ability was turned into artistic channels. In the first two-thirds of the nineteenth century, almost all the general ability of the Italian people was absorbed in the struggle for liberty. Since 1870 it has been absorbed in the development of a politically and industrially new country. Nobody blames the Americans or the Australians for not having produced, within the first century of their existence, an Elizabethan or a Medicean age. It is recognized that they have had no time to do anything but develop the material prosperity of their countries. But to the Italian no such indulgence is allowed. And yet, they have had a far more difficult problem to solve than the Americans or the Australians. They have had to create an efficient government among the victims of century-long foreign oppression. They have had to develop, not a huge, rich, and unpopulated land, but a small, poor, and crowded one. All things being considered, it seems to me that they have done a difficult job remarkably well. And they have found time, in the midst of their labor, to produce a respectable quality of literature, music, and pure science. A little of that energy and ability which, in another epoch and in different circumstances, produced the artistic and speculative triumphs of the renaissance, still flows along the old channels. But the greater part of the ability has been diverted. The artists have turned into engineers, politicians, and business men. The ability which made the renaissance is now making modern Italy.

I have spoken dogmatically, as though I knew the whole truth about the Italian character, human ability, and all the rest. But of course, as a matter of fact, I know just as little of these matters as the philosophers who dogmatize about the degeneracy of the Mediterranean race and the supremacy of the Nordic—that is to say, precisely nothing. All that I claim for my dogmatisms is that they do not so obviously contradict the facts of history and the ascertained truths and probabilities of science as do theirs. The best would be, of course, not to dogmatize at all, until we know something about these fascinating and portentously difficult subjects.

The proper study of mankind, the poet tells us, is man. The proper *study*. He did not say that it was the proper subject to hold dogmatic and utterly unfounded opinions about. By all means let us study Man—study him patiently, scientifically, with humility and suspense of judgment, until we have some data on which to base reasonable opinions.

Meanwhile the ignorant dogmatists—such as myself and, on the other side, the numerous successors of Mr. Houston Chamberlain—would do well to hold their tongues. The noise we make distracts the serious students.

[*Vanity Fair*, March 1925]

The Horrors of Society

THE ENGLISH PHILOSOPHER, old Thomas Hobbes, was doubtless right; the life of savages *is* "nasty, solitary, brutish, and short." But the life of civilized men—however hygienic, relatively speaking, and long—is not all beer and skittles. Fate makes no free gifts; it sells, for a price. The price is heavy. Machine guns, cancer, slums, the penny newspaper—these are a few items of the tribute we pay to fate for the privilege of not being savages. It would be easy to lengthen the list. In this place, however, I shall confine myself to a description of one of the minor horrors of civilization—but a minor horror which, if it were not, providentially, escapable, would certainly deserve to be styled a major drawback to civilized life. I refer to what is called polite society.

Happily, as I have said, the horror is local and avoidable. It is not necessary to pass one's life in the literary drawing rooms of Paris or on the golf courses of the Riviera. There is no compulsion. If there was, there would be more suicides—mine amongst them.

Leisured society may be divided into two main classes. The end and aim of both is the same: to fill the intolerable vacuum of unlaborious existence. But the means they adopt are slightly different. The first relies mainly or exclusively on love, outdoor sports, and indoor games. Those belonging to the second class fill the void with love (perhaps of a rather more complicated variety) and the cultivation of letters and the arts. Both parties are snobs; the first exclusively of birth, wealth, and fashion, while the second tempers this exclusive allegiance with a half-hearted and rather insincere loyalty to brains and spirit. (I say insincere; for the rich can never honestly persuade themselves that a poor man, however manifestly a genius, is really their equal. They pretend, sometimes they even genuinely try, to believe it; but they never quite succeed.)

I find it difficult to decide which of these two subdivisions of the leisured class is the more to be avoided. Obviously, there are some charming people within the ranks of both. There are charming people everywhere—in convict prisons, in kitchens, in rectories. But that is no reason for not avoiding parsons, cooks, and convicts in general and as classes. Similarly, the charms displayed by individuals of the rich, polite, and leisured class must not blind us to the fact that the class, as a class, is one of the minor horrors of our civilization. As a class, it is obvious, doctors or lawyers, engineers, commercial travelers, or even novelists (any class of people, in fact, who pursue some regular and more or less rational occupation) are incomparably better worth seeking out and cultivating.

But to return to our question: which of the two types of leisured people is, on principle, the more to be avoided? It is a nice question. For the lowbrows it may be said that they are often simple folk, children of nature, happy, and almost unspoilt barbarians. Thoroughbred animals, high fed and well cared for, they prance about, made lively by their beans and oats, in the most diverting fashion. To the naturalist, the study of their sexual life—the courting, pairing, mating, separation, repairing, nest making, an occasional (discreetly occasional) production of young—is not uninteresting. Among these well-nourished and idle specimens, the instinct gets full rein and develops all its potentialities; with them, love romps and luxuriates with unheard-of vigor. A scientific observer of their habits remarks many phenomena worthy of record. Unfortunately, however, these delightful creatures do not devote the whole or even the major portion of their time to love. The greater part of the vacuum of their existences is filled with an infinitely less interesting stop gap—games. It is golf, and above all bridge and Mah Jong, that render lowbrow leisured society so profoundly distressing. I seldom venture, nowadays, into that society; but I can remember terrible occasions when staying in houses where time was murdered by the playing of bridge, I nearly died of a deep-seated, septic, and suppurating boredom.

So much for good society of the more lowbrowed variety. What now of the highbrow rich, the aristocratic intellectuals, the leisured patrons of the arts? What of these? They ought, of course, by definition to be superior to the lowbrows. Experience, alas, gives the lie to a priori definitions. I am inclined to think that, on the whole, the highbrows are almost worse than the lows. Those who sin after having seen the light and eaten of the tree of knowledge are more blameworthy than those who sin in pre-Adamite innocence and darkness.

You often hear people deploring the passing of that civilized eighteenth century when great ladies were interested in ideas and kept salons where, in the intervals of gossip, high-class subjects were discussed in a polished and elegant style by a mixed collection of dukes, marchionesses, and professional literary men. "If only," these backward-looking sentimentalists exclaim, "if only we had salons nowadays!" But we have. There are plenty of them in Paris, plenty. Genuine salons where you can go every day and be sure of meeting "interesting people," where you can sit and chat about the style of Paul Morand[7] and the inimitable drawings of Jean Cocteau, chat and sit—until all at once you find yourself wishing that you were sitting in the middle of the Sahara, or in a public house with a party of yokels, or even in one of those lowbrow drawing rooms where they play bridge. For bridge possesses at any rate this great merit; that while playing it, you cannot talk. In highbrow salons, on the other hand, you must

7. Paul Morand (1888–). Russian-born French novelist.

talk—of the latest pictures, the latest scandals, pornographies, and eccentricities, the latest books, the latest modes; the latest music, the latest religions, the latest psychologies of love, the latest theories of science and philosophy. And it is all, no doubt, very agreeable and diverting; but oh, if you happen to take anything at all seriously, how profoundly shocking and horrible! For to these polished beings, art is only another time killer, like bridge and flirtation; religion is something to be lightly chatted about over the tea and muffins—an amusing subject, but not, of course, so entertaining as a juicy piece of scandal. All fine and important things are degraded; all values are overturned. Men and ideas are prized in this polite society, not for their intrinsic merit, but because they happen, for one reason or another, to be fashionable. Literature is turned into a sort of elegant game, in which it is the object of the players to score points of "style" and "form"—as though form and style possessed any real existence apart from substance.

In these salons the professionals who are interested only in immediate successes, easy conquests and flattery, assemble in a company with the amateurs who find art a little more amusing than bridge and the cheapening of ideas as good a resource against boredom as gossip. What these places are now, they were—with a few changes in costume, manner, and idioms—in the past. The much regretted salons of the eighteenth century were just as frightful—I do not for a moment doubt it—as the salons one can find in Paris today. In some, it is true, where the proportion of serious professionals was high, the atmosphere was probably less suffocating than in those where a majority of aristocratic amateurs poisoned the spiritual air with their frivolity. D'Holbach's soirées were doubtless very decent; and even at Mlle. de Lespinasse's one could probably waste one's time very agreeably without being ashamed of oneself afterwards. The horrors really began when one penetrated into salons like that of Mme. du Deffand, where a few professionals gamboled obsequiously round the cultured duchesses and well-read counts; where scandal and that, in the long run, so desperately tedious analysis of love, which leisured ladies are never tired of making, alternated with discussions of the most recent poems and philosophies. One afternoon at Mme. du Deffand's might not have been so bad. But a hundred afternoons, a thousand, ten thousand. . . . One shudders. Every evening the same people, a day older than they were yesterday evening; every evening the same polite and witty conversation that touched indifferently, with the same light touch, on art, intrigue, fashion, and metaphysics; every evening for twenty, thirty, forty years. And none of the frequenters of the salon were really interested, lovingly interested, as friends, in one another; none were really and profoundly interested in the subjects discussed. The end and aim of all of them was the same—to escape from boredom, at any price. Lacking internal resources to keep that great enemy of leisure at bay, they came together in the hope of scaring him away by the sound of their voices united in chorus, in a propitiatory babble to the God of Tedium. Did they succeed? Of course not. But it is better to be bored in company than to be bored alone.

[*Vanity Fair,* June 1925]

The Psychology of Suggestion

COWS CANNOT BE PERSUADED that daisies are an unclean food; that they will die, lingeringly and agonizingly, if they marry their mother's bull calf by a different short-horn sire; that the meadows are greener in another hemisphere; that, if one can moo, one can be taught to sing like a nightingale. Cows cannot be persuaded of these things, because they are too stupid to be able to talk or to understand what is said to them. That is where they have a considerable advantage over us human beings.

For we human beings are so clever that we can understand what is said to us and not quite clever enough to resist the conviction that what is said three times is true. Tell the cow three million times that the daisy is an unclean flower, for the eating of which she will be punished eternally in some bovine hell; she will not believe it. But tell a man some few hundred times that pork and lobster are taboo and he will turn from them in horror. Cows can see no reason why they should not marry their half-brothers. Terrified by the word "incest" which they have invented and repeated to one another through centuries, human beings write agonizing five-act tragedies on the subject: to marry or not to marry, that is the question. Men can be persuaded that they will be happier if they frequently change their position on the earth's surface; cows cannot. Nor can the most specious arguments make cows believe that mere education and practice can render them proficient in arts for which they have no natural talent—a faith which is only too easily inspired in men.

True, in certain respects cows and other gregarious animals are highly susceptible to suggestion. The fear or rage of a single individual easily infects the whole herd. But this suggestibility of gregarious animals, though intense, is limited. Thanks to his invention of speech and letters, the suggestibility of man is absolutely without limits. By suitable suggestion, he can be made to believe or feel anything; he can be persuaded to act in the most manifestly irrational and preposterous ways. For him what is said three times is not only logically true, but actively compelling, like an enchantment.

The compulsive strength of religions, superstitions, and moralities has always consisted, and still consists, in suggestion by constant repetition. The extraordinary capers which primitive men have cut under the influence of suggestion are recorded in the text books of anthropology. The moral antics of the present day may best be studied in contemporary fiction. It must be confessed that, for fantastic queerness, Babbit rivals and often surpasses *The Golden Bough*.

Consciously (as when, in Roman days, a skeptical ruling class encouraged what Gibbon calls "useful prejudices" in order to keep their inferiors happy and submissive) or more often unconsciously, religion and morality have always ruled by the power of suggestion.

The technique of assertion and unwearying repetition has been employed in these two spheres of human activity from time immemorial. But the merit of having employed it in other spheres than religion and morality belongs to our own and, to a lesser degree, to the preceding generation. To us—whether British, European, or American—is due the credit of having invented and perfected the arts of political propaganda and advertisement. We have every right to feel proud of the achievement.

Of political propaganda I do not propose to speak. The official propagandists of wartime have given us ample descriptions of their methods—methods which we can see being put into practice all around us, wherever we choose to look. For propaganda is still with us, daily and almost hourly—propaganda of every political color, from revolutionary red to monarchic white and fascist black—in every newspaper we read. Lord Northcliffe, we are told by Dr. Chalmers Mitchell in his article on Propaganda in the supplementary volumes of the *Encyclopaedia Britannica,* "brought to his task (as Director of Propaganda) a limitless faith in the possibility of controlling public opinion." The faith was well justified—so well, indeed that it hardly deserves to be called a faith. It is not faith, for example, which makes one believe in the pressure of the atmosphere; it is the spectacle of the mercury rising in the tube of the barometer. The "possibility of controlling public opinion" can be proved, like the existence of atmosphere pressure, by experimental tests. Not to believe in that possibility would be a stupid denial of conclusive evidence. There was no great faith in Lord Northcliffe, only a very reasonable acceptance of proofs.

Perhaps the most convincing proof of the "possibility of controlling public opinion" is to be found in the existence—the flourishing, exuberant existence—of advertisement. That people should be induced by propaganda to change their political opinions is not, after all, so very extraordinary. It is only in rare, exceptional cases that the change of political opinions involves the slightest personal sacrifice. We can be convinced, shall we say, of Germany's war-guilt or of the paradisiacal nature of Soviet

Russia without having to spend a halfpenny. It is very different with advertisements. The process of being convinced of the excellence of A's loud speaker, B's straight eight limousine, C's chocolates, D's silk stockings, E's electric cigar lighter, F's spring models from Paris is a costly process. Our conviction, if it is really sincere, must find expression in the opening of pocketbooks and the signing of checks. Now, for most of us, parting with money is a most painful ordeal. And yet, at the bidding of advertisements, we are prepared to inflict this pain upon ourselves. Which only shows what strength there is in repeated suggestion. Lord Northcliffe made it his mission in life to give manufacturers and traders the opportunity of exercising repeated suggestion on the minds of an enormous number of potential buyers. He became, in the fulfilment of this mission, a multi-millionaire. It is not surprising that he had a "limitless faith" in suggestion; a limitless bank balance was its foundation.

Repeated suggestion is the essence of all advertisement. But the nature of the suggestion varies considerably according to the different parts of the mind, the various emotions or interests to which an appeal is made. The simplest form of advertisement consists in the mere endless repetition of the name of the object which it is desired to sell.

But when it comes to advertising hair lotions, or patent medicines, or steam yachts, or correspondence courses in the fine arts, the case is different. For these things are not naturally in universal demand. You have got to create a demand by persuading the public that it is in danger of going bald, that its liver needs tickling up, that it can afford a yacht, that it can make money by learning to paint landscapes. It is necessary to make an appeal to the conscious mind. This can be done in a variety of ways.

In the past, for example, much play used to be made with the appeal of mystery. Hair lotions, in those romantic days, were ancient secrets of the Egyptians, rediscovered; the recipe for cough drops had been brought back, at immense expense and fearful danger, from the jungles of Borneo.

Then there is the impressive citation of authority. In the past, tradesmen assured us that they were patronized by the nobility and clergy. The nobility and clergy have ceased to cut much ice; but there is still a certain lingering prestige about the patronage of a genuine monarch. But it is the authority of the acknowledged expert which counts most at the present time. Doctors who approve of patent medicines, novelists who recommend fountain pens—they inspire confidence.

And finally there is the frank, confidential manner, the appeal to reason and enlightened self-interest. You find the best specimens of the style in the advertisements of motor-cars. The makers put their case openly and reasonably. In the enumeration of the special merits of their machine, they even employ technical language. The reader does not understand, of course; but he is flattered by the advertiser's assumption that he does. I know, for example, how deeply I myself am always impressed when I read about automobiles which have crankshafts with seven bearings. I have no idea why there should be any great advantage in having seven bearings on a crankshaft instead of one or seventy. I am not even quite certain what a crankshaft bearing is. But that does not prevent me from saying knowingly, whenever that brand of car is mentioned: "Oh, an excellent machine, that! It has a crankshaft with seven bearings you know."

But there is another kind of advertisement, no less effective, which appeals, not to utilitarian reason but to the emotions. In these advertisements the merchant does not try to prove that you will be a gainer by purchasing his wares; what he suggests is that, if you don't buy them, you will be ridiculous, or eccentric, or old-fashioned, or even disgusting. He appeals to one or other of the many manifestations of the primary herd instinct which is in all of us—to our fear of public opinion, our snobbishness, or sense of shame.

It may be added that our wistful but hopeless desire is known to most advertisers, whatever type of suggestion they employ. Thus, the advertiser of soap, if he illustrates his appeal, shows his soap being used by ravishing young society beauties or strong and silent young men of an impeccable elegance, even in their underclothing. The utilitarian philosopher who sells you a brougham for the park does not disdain to append pictures of it with a man in a silk hat and a woman in pearls and sables stepping out of it. The vendors of patent medicines portray only Greek gods and fairy princesses. The figures inside the drawings of Paris models are beautiful and willowy. The people who listen to electric harps or wireless telephones are never out of evening dress. And when bath salts are advertised, there is always a marble bath in the picture, with a pretty young lady's maid in perfect uniform scattering the scented crystals, while the owner of the bath stands languidly looking on, dressed in a pink crêpe de chine dressing gown, swan's down slippers and golden hair, permanently waved. How right was Lord Northcliffe to feel that "limitless faith."

[*Vanity Fair,* August 1925]

Talking of Monkeys

OUR FATHERS were more logical than we, and more courageous. The conclusions to which their arguments led them might be manifestly idiotic or immoral; but that did not prevent them, once they were convinced that the premises were sound and the argument flawless, from drawing those conclusions and, if necessary, acting on them. Starting from the premises that everything in the Bible is literally true, Wesley was necessarily led to believe in witchcraft. The Bible is true; witchcraft is mentioned in the Bible as existing; therefore witchcraft exists. The argument is unimpeachable. In the century of Hume and Voltaire, Wesley believed in witches. If you abandon belief in witchcraft, he insisted, you abandon belief in the Bible. He was logical and had the courage of his opinions.

I do not happen to agree with Wesley; but I admire his spirit and his intellectual honesty. There is too much compromise nowadays and too little logical consistency. We are afraid of drawing the logical conclusions from the premises in which we profess to believe. We do not like to make any very definite or sweeping assertion for fear that by so doing we might be making fools of ourselves. The manifest contradictions which exist between different sections of our beliefs, between our beliefs and our actions, we vaguely harmonize, if we try to harmonize them at all, in some dim Higher Synthesis, where black is the same as white, good as evil and nonsense as sense. The Higher Synthesis is a most useful invention; it is part of the indispensable *confort moderne* of contemporary thought. No self-respecting philosophy is complete without it; as well imagine a hotel without bathrooms. The Higher Synthesis relieves all those who are conscious of contradictions from the necessity of doing anything about them. Those who are unconscious, whether deliberately or through mere unawareness, achieve the same end by simply ignoring logic. This age produces no Wesleys, no remorseless Calvins.

This reluctance to draw logical conclusions; at any rate the greatest possible number of logical ones, was shown in the most deplorable manner at the recent Monkeyville trial.[8] Here, in Tennessee, were a set of legislators who believed (a) that the whole of the Bible is literally true and (b) that it is impossible for anyone who does not believe in the literal truth of the Bible to be saved. From the first of these premises it would have been legitimate, it would have been logically necessary, to deduce innumerable conclusions of importance. The following are a few simple examples of the conclusions which should have been drawn. That the earth is flat; that the sun revolves around the earth; that the seat of intelligence is the heart and of the emotions, the bowels; that witches exist and have supernatural powers; that animals can talk; that at a given moment of history specimens of several million species of animals were accommodated by Noah in a vessel of the dimensions of a cross-Channel steamer. And so on and so forth. From the second premise, the logical mind of medieval inquisitors

8. John T. Scopes, a teacher of biology, was tried (July 1925) for teaching Darwinism in a Dayton, Tennessee, public school. William Jennings Bryan (1860–1925), American politician, assisted in the prosecution.

deduced the whole theory of persecution. Given the premise that belief in a certain doctrine is the only method by which an immortal soul can be saved from eternal torture, it follows that all those who tamper with that belief are criminals of a much more frightful and detestable sort than murderers. Murderers only kill the body; heretics destroy men's souls by making them believe false and damnable doctrines. It follows, therefore, that heretics should be treated even more severely than murderers. Moreover, we have motives of mere self-preservation for the stamping out of heretics. Heretics are, by definition, rebels against God. God, as we know by the Bible, is a jealous and choleric deity who has a wholesale way of punishing the innocent with the guilty. A society which tolerates heretics is therefore in imminent danger of being punished for the crimes of an iniquitous minority. Therefore, the minority must be extirpated. And this was what the Inquisition set itself to do—with complete success, it may be added, in more than one country.

These, then, are a few of the conclusions, practical as well as theoretical, which logically ought to have been drawn from the premises with which Mr. Bryan and the legislators of Tennessee set out. But they lacked logic and they were timid. The best they could do with their premises was to deduce that Darwinism should not be taught in schools and that Mr. Scopes should be fined one hundred dollars for having done so. Feeble and derisory conclusions! I must confess that Mr. Bryan disappointed me. The last act of his grandiose knockabout was an anticlimax. Only the very end was good. To perish suddenly, as he did, by a manifest judgment of the God of Evolution—that was magnificently dramatic. But the scenes which led up to this grand *dénouement* were of poor quality. I had expected more courage and more ruthless logic from Mr. Bryan.

No; for me, the Monkeyville trial was a failure; the Tennessee law inadequate. What I should have liked to see was a good swinging statute making belief, not only in Evolution, but also in the round earth, the Copernican system, the circulation of the blood, and all the other damnable innovations on the Bible, criminal offenses punishable by torture, incarceration, banishment, and death. I should have liked to see Mr. Scopes roasted over a slow fire, not let off with a paltry fine. Not that I bear any ill will to Mr. Scopes; far from it. I should be quite as happy, happier even, if he could be roasted in effigy. All that I demand is that the roasting should be public, solemn, and calculated to inspire the maximum amount of salutary terrors. The performance should be staged by a good producer, lavishly, and regardless of expense. Painted banners, penitential robes for the victim, mile-long processions of monks, thirty thousand Ku Klux Klansmen in full war paint, Billy Sunday on the scaffold administering extreme unction, Paul Whiteman's band playing suitable music, with all the other accompaniments of a really spectacular and up-to-date *auto da fé.*

This is really how the thing should have been done, with drums beating and flags flying, in the grand manner. The half-hearted, hole-and-corner persecution of Monkeyville was feeble and futile, a thing of compromise, a monstrous paralogism. I protest against it, on aesthetic grounds, because it lacked style; on intellectual grounds, because it was illogical; on moral grounds, because it was without courage; and above all on social grounds, because, grotesque and incredible as Monkeyville and the Tennessee statute are, they are not grotesque enough to make men realize, in a single, illuminating flash, the whole absurdity of the political system which made them possible. What I desire is that the Tennesseans should make their law as completely idiotic as it is possible for such a law to be. I want them to ban the teaching of all modern science, under pain of the most atrocious sanctions. I want them to imitate the Holy Office, to outdo Torquemada. I want them to commit every imbecility, every cruelty which the perverted ingenuity of intolerance can devise. Democracy must repeat and outdo the excess of tyranny and priestcraft. Only then will the fantastic, the impossible nature of the system, at any rate in the present state of human development, be made fully manifest.

Democracy is based on assuming that all men are equal. Now that assumption is true, but only in a mystical sense. Men are equal as being all the children of God—as being all endowed with a capacity for suffering, loving, and knowing good and evil. They are not equal in any of those abilities which make men fit to govern themselves or others. The mistake of the democrats has been to suppose that men are equal in every way and to base practical politics on this gratuitous and false assumption. Hence the Tennessee statute, the Monkeyville trial. The sooner political democracy reduces itself to the absurd, the better. That is why I desire to see the Tennesseans marching on from folly to folly.

It must not be supposed that, simply because the idea of the equality of man is mystical, it is therefore unimportant. On the contrary, it is of the highest significance. It is an idea which has already profoundly modified human society and which is destined to produce incalculable effects in the future. Humanitarianism is the expression of that idea. We are all humanitarians now, whatever our political opinions and wherever our social position. Even those who are in possession of wealth and power admit that those who possess nothing have certain rights. They are perpetually giving away little bits of their wealth and power to the dispossessed. Why? They are still the stronger. They could still resist the dispossessed, if they liked, they could still oppress them, even as their fathers resisted and oppressed. But somehow they are not able to do so.

Humanitarianism has become a part of them; it is impossible for them to ignore it.

It was this surrender of the powerholders to the dispossessed that outraged Nietzsche into propounding his new superman's morality—a morality indistinguishable, in truth from:

> The good old rule, the simple plan
> That he should take who has the power
> And he should keep who can.

He justified his anti-humanitarianism in the name of Natural Selection. The justification is quite invalid. Darwinism, as Benjamin Kidd pointed out long ago, justifies humanitarianism, not Nietzschean imperialism. It is by a ceaseless process of competition that the breed is improved, is even kept up to existing standards. In a tyrannical society, where humanitarian principles are not recognized, nine-tenths of the individuals composing that society are so unfairly handicapped by poverty, bad conditions, and inadequacy of education that they are not in a position to compete for any of the higher prizes of life. By ameliorating the lot of the dispossessed, humanitarianism removes this handicap, and thus, by multiplying the competitors, tends to create an intenser and therefore biologically more stimulating competition.

Humanitarianism, then, has a biological function—to render possible an intenser competition within society. When all men are free to compete and all start equal, the chance of getting able men at the head of affairs is obviously increased. That is the political justification of humanitarianism. Societies should be run on humanitarian principles because an increase in the number of competitors increases the chances of efficient leadership. To deduce from the mystical theory of universal equality that all men (not merely the best fitted to do so) should take a share in the government of society is absurd.

The defects of democratic government have long been apparent. It remains for the Tennesseans to make them so glaringly and grotesquely obvious that all the world may realize the impossibility of the system. A question arises; by what should democracy be replaced? None of the alternatives hitherto put into practice is very satisfactory. Fascism is as undesirable as Bolshevism. The lynch law and the professional philanthropy with which America tempers her democratic system are no better. All these alternatives err in their antagonism to personal freedom, their anti-humanitarianism, their hierarchical stiffness. In an ideal society, it is obvious, there must be the greatest possible suppleness and informality of organization. The ideal of all the anti-democrats up to the present has been an ideal of increased formality and rigidity. The system that is to replace democ-

racy has not yet been invented. I offer no suggestions, beyond the sufficiently obvious one that it would be a good thing if human societies could
be governed by their best and most intelligent members. Whether it will
ever be possible to induce the best and most intelligent men to take part in
an occupation as thoroughly discreditable as politics is another question.

[Vanity Fair, November 1925]

A Night at Pietramala

"WHAT I LOVE best in all the world," says Browning in *De Gustibus,* "is
a castle, precipice-encurled, in a gash of the wind-grieved Apennine." *De
Gustibus,* indeed. I take the hint and shall not argue the point. Suffice it to
say that, though I like the poem, I cannot share the poet's tastes. A castle
in the Apennines would come quite low in the list of the things I love. A
palace in Rome, a villa just outside the gates of Siena, even a motor caravan would stand higher. For the epithet which Browning applies to the
Apennines is only too appropriate. He himself, no doubt, enjoyed being
grieved by the wind. I can imagine him, with bent head, tunneling his way
through one of those hellish blasts which come hooting down, in spring
and winter, through the gashes between the hills. He would feel exhilarated by the effort; his struggle against the elements would elate him and
he would return to his castle to write some more than ordinarily hearty
paean in praise of passion and energy—passion for passion's sake, energy
admirable, not so much for its direction as for its volume. Such, I am sure,
were the effects of the wind on Browning; it confirmed him in his bluster-
ing optimism. In me, on the other hand, the wind of the Apennines begets
nothing but neuralgia and the profoundest depression. It is not *Prospice*
that I should write in the precipice-encurled castello; it is something in the
style of the *City of Dreadful Night.*[9]

That I am not exaggerating the horrors of the wind among the Apennines is proved by the fact that it has been found necessary, for the convenience and even the safety of travelers, to protect the most exposed places
of the principal passes with high walls. I remember in particular one section of the main road from Florence to Bologna which is flanked for hundreds of yards by an immense parapet, like the great wall of China. The
road at this point, which is between two and three thousand feet above the
sea, cuts across the head of a deep and narrow valley, through which there
sucks a perpetual draft. Even in summer, on halcyon days, you can hear as

---

9. Poem published in 1874 by James Thomson (1834–1882). Scottish poet.

you pass under the lee of the wall, a melancholy wailing of the winds over-head. But on rough days in winter, in the spring and autumn, the air is full of fearful noises, as though the gates of hell had been opened and the lost souls were making holiday. What happened to travelers who passed that way before, some hundred years ago, a beneficent Grand-Ducal government built the wall, I shudder to think. They must often have been, quite literally, blown off the road.

We passed that way once in March. The Italian spring, which is not so different from the spring in other countries, was inclement that year and icy. In Florence the sun shone fitfully between huge clouds. Snow still lay in patches on Monte Morello. The breeze was nipping. "Are the passes free of snow?" we asked at the garage where we stopped to fill our petrol tank. Animated by that typically Italian desire to give an answer that will please the questioner, the garage man assured us that the road was per-fectly clear. And he said it with such conviction that we imagined, as northerners would naturally imagine, that he knew. Nothing is more charming than southern courtesy, southern sympathy, and the southern desire to please. The heart is touched by the kindly interest which the Ital-ians take in your affairs; you love them for their courteous inquisitiveness; they make you at home immediately, treat you at once as a human being and do their best to please you. It is delightful. But sometimes they are really too sympathetic by half. For in order not to contradict you or give you a moment's pain by disputing the accuracy of your ideas, they will tell you what you want to hear rather than what it would be of real use to you to hear. At the same time their own self-esteem will not permit them to confess a blank ignorance; so that they will rather tell you something in-correct than tell you nothing at all. Thus, when the garage man told us that there was no snow on the road from Florence to Bologna, he said so first, because he saw that we wanted to go to Bologna and that we should have been disappointed if it had been impossible and, second, because it was pleasanter for him to say "No snow" with conviction than confess (which was the truth) that he hadn't the faintest notion whether there was snow or not.

We believed him and set out. The road rises steeply from Florence, climbs to twelve or fifteen hundred feet, and then plunges down again into that long flat-bottomed valley locked in the midst of the hills, the Mugello. By the time we had reached it the sun had entirely disappeared, and the sky above us was one vast yellowish-white snowcloud. Looking at the var-ious castelli one passes by the way, I found Browning's predilections more than ever incomprehensible.

Between Florence and Bologna there are two passes: the Futa and, five or six miles further on, the pass of Raticosa. It is near the top of the Futa

that the Grand Dukes built the bulwark against the wind. It was strength-
ened, that day, by heaps of driven snow. Below and above, the slopes were
deep in snow. In the midst of all this whiteness the road wound onwards
and upwards like a muddy snake.

Under the lee of the wall we halted and took photographs of the Italian
scenery. The air was calm where we stood and seemed in its stillness almost warm. But just above us, on a level with the top of the wall, was the
wind. The snowflakes that it carried made its speed visible. It filled the
ears with sound. I was reminded, as I stood there, of a rather ludicrous
and deplorable version of *David Copperfield,* which Beerbohm Tree[1] used
sometimes to stage at His Majesty's. Tree himself acted two parts—Micawber and Peggotty; the former, I may add parenthetically, very well indeed (for he was an admirable comedian), the latter, in his more pathetic
manner, with less success. But let that pass. Dressed as Peggotty, Tree never
made an entrance without the wind; it was in the bluff nautical part. Every
time he opened the door of his ship cottage on the sands of Yarmouth
there came from the outer darkness a noise like the witches' sabbath. It
never blew less than a full gale during the whole run of *David Copperfield.*
Whoo-oo-oo-oo-oo—crescendo and decrescendo. In the dress-circle ladies
reached for their furs, men turned up the collars of their coats. It was horrible. I had hoped then that I should never hear a wind like that outside
His Majesty's. And I never did till that icy March day when we paused beneath the Grand-Ducal wall on the road from Florence to Bologna. There,
for the first time, I heard nature rivaling Sir Herbert's art. A perfect site, I
reflected, for the Castello Browning.

At Pietramala, which lies just under the pass of the Raticosa, we
stopped at the little inn for lunch. The idlers who gathered immediately
and as though by magic round our machine—for even at Pietramala, even
in the snow, there were leisured car-fanciers to whom the arrival of a ten-
horse-power Citroën was an event—lost no time in telling us that the road
on the further side of the pass was blocked with wind-driven snow. We
went in to our lunch feeling a little depressed—a little annoyed, too, with
the garage man at Florence. The inn-keeper, however, was reassuring;
gangs of men, he told us, were to be sent out as soon as the dinner hour
was over from Pietramala and the village on the other side of the pass. By
four o'clock the road would be clear; we should be in Bologna before
dark. When we asked if the road by Firenzuola and Imola were open, he
shook his head. For the second time that day we believed.

The inn-keeper's motives for not telling the truth were different from
those that actuated the man at the garage. For the latter had lied out of

1. Sir Herbert Beerbohm Tree (1853–1917). English actor and stage manager.

misplaced politeness and pride; the inn-keeper on the contrary, lied merely
out of self-interest. He wanted to make us stay the night. He was perfectly
successful. At four o'clock we set out. At the top of the pass the snow lay a
yard deep across the road, and there was not a shoveler to be seen. We returned. The inn-keeper was astonished: what, no shovelers? He could
hardly believe it. But tomorrow morning the road would infallibly be
cleared. We decided to stay the night.

I had taken with me on that journey the second volume of the *Encyclopaedia Britannica—And.–Aus.* It is a capital volume from which one
can derive much useful knowledge about Angiosperms, the Anglican Communion, Angling, Anthrax, Aphasia, Apples, Arrowroot, Asia, Aurora
Borealis, and Australia, not to mention Anthropology, Archeology, Architecture, Art, Astrology, and Astronomy. I started hopefully on Animal
Worship. "The bear," I learned, "enjoys a large measure of respect from
all savage races that come in contact with it." From me, that evening, he
got a large measure of envy. I thought of Mr. Belloc's rhyme:[2]

> The Polar Bear is unaware
> Of cold that cuts me through:
> For why? He has a coat of hair.
> I wish I had one too!

For in spite of the fire, in spite of great-coats, it was appallingly cold.
"The products of the cow," I read on, and was charmed by the compen-
dious euphemism, "are important in magic." But I got no further; it was
too cold even to read. To this day I remain ignorant of the feelings of the
Thlinkit Indians towards the crow, of the Kalangs towards the dog, and
the Siamese towards white elephants. And if I do happen to know that the
Hottentot god, Cagn, is incarnated in the praying mantis, Ngo, that is due
to the fact that I took the same volume with me on another tour during the
summer, when the evenings were less inclement and the mind was free to
devote itself to higher things than the problem of mere self-preservation.

It was cold enough in the sitting-room; but the horror only really
began when we went to bed. For the bedrooms of the inn were without
fireplaces; there was no possibility of heating them. In those bedrooms one
could have preserved mutton indefinitely. Still dressed in all the woolly
garments we possessed, we got into our stony beds. Outside the wind continued to howl among the hills. While the sheets were yet unthawed, sleep
was out of the question. I lay awake listening to the noise of the wind and
wondering what would be the effect of the hurricane on those flaming jets
of natural gas for which Pietramala is renowned. Would the wind blow

2. Hilaire Belloc (1870–1953). French-born English poet.

out those giant will-o'-the-wisps? Or would they burn on in spite of it? The thought of flames was comforting; I dwelt on them with a certain complaisance.

They are not uncommon, these jets of fire, among the northern Apennines. Salsomaggiore, for example, owes its coat of arms, a salamander among the flames, to its fountains of natural gas. It is in this gaseous form alone that the hydrocarbons of the Apennines make their appearance at the center of the chain. On the outer slopes they are to be found in the more commercially useful form of petroleum, which is now extracted in small quantities from the foothills in the neighborhood of Piacenza, Reggio, and Modena. Who knows, we may yet live to see the towers of Canossa rivaled by the wooden castles of the derricks on the slopes below.

The shutters rattled, the wind howled. Decidedly, no fire could burn in the teeth of such a blast. Poor *ignes fatui!* How welcome we should have made them in this ice-house! How tenderly, like vestals, we should have cherished any name, however fatuous!

From thinking of those flames and wishing that I had them in the room with me, I went on to wonder why it was that the gas-fires of Pietramala should be so oddly familiar to me. Had I read about them? Had I recently heard them mentioned in conversation, or what? I racked my brains. And then suddenly I remembered; it was in Bence Jones's *Life and Letters of Faraday* that I had read of Pietramala.

One very wet day in the autumn of 1814 two rather queer English tourists alighted from their chaise in this squalid little village of Pietramala. One was approaching middle age, the other still a very young man. Their names were Sir Humphry Davy and Michael Faraday. They had been out of England almost exactly a year. For it was in the year 1813, just before the news of the battle of Leipzig had reached Paris, that they crossed into France. To us it seems in the natural order of things that science and religion should be national affairs, that clergymen should scream "Hurrah and Hallelujah" and chemists cheer for the flag and H_2SO_4. But it was not always so. God and the works of God were once considered international. God was the first to be nationalized; after the reformation he once more became frankly tribal. But science and even art were still above patriotism. During the eighteenth century, France and England exchanged ideas almost as freely as cannon balls. French scientific expeditions were allowed to pass in safety between the English fleets; Sterne was welcomed enthusiastically by his country's enemies. The tradition lingered on even into the eighteen-hundreds. Napoleon gave medals to English men of science; and when, in 1813, Sir Humphry Davy asked for leave to travel on the Continent, his request was granted at once. He was received in Paris with the highest honors, was made a member of the Institute, and in spite of the intolerable rudeness and arrogance which he habitually displayed, he was treated throughout his stay in France with the most perfect courtesy. In our more enlightened twentieth century he would have been shot as a spy or interned.

Restless and erratic, Davy hurried across Europe in search of scientific truth. All was fish that came to his net. At Genoa he made electric experiments on the torpedo fish. At Florence he borrowed the great burning-glass of the Grand Dukes and, with its aid, set a diamond on fire. At Rome he analyzed the pigments employed by the artists of antiquity. At Naples he made experiments on iodine and excursions up Vesuvius. With him went Michael Faraday as "assistant in experiments and writing." Lady Davy, however, tried to use him as courier and confidential servant as well. Young Faraday found the position a little trying. It was only the consciousness that he was being given an unrivaled opportunity to educate himself that decided him to keep his post. Sir Humphry's character might not be entirely estimable (indeed, Faraday was known to remark in later years that "the greatest of all his great advantages was that he had had, in Davy, a model to teach him what he should avoid"); but he was, undoubtedly, a mine of scientific learning. To be with him constantly, as Faraday was, during those eighteen months of travel, was a liberal education. Young Faraday knew it and put up with Lady D.

At Pietramala, then, they stopped in the pouring rain—and doubtless in the howling wind as well—to look at the natural fireworks. Specimens of the gas were bottled and taken down to Florence for analysis. Sir Humphry concluded, correctly, that it was a light hydrocarburet, pure.

To this desolate little village on the crest of the Apennines Faraday devotes a couple of pages in his journal. To Florence, except in so far as it was a town where there were facilities for making experiments, he gives no space at all. Faraday paid little attention to the works of man, however beautiful. It was the works of God that interested him. There is a magnificent consistency about him. All that he writes in his journal or letters is perfectly in character. He is always the natural philosopher. To discover truth is his sole aim and interest. His purpose is unalterably fixed. He never allows himself to be distracted—not by art, which he almost completely ignores; not by politics, which in the tremendous closing scenes of the Napoleonic drama he mentions casually once or twice, not at all by the delights of casual social intercourse, though he always found time for friendship—but pursues his course steadily, perseverantly, modestly, disinterestedly, and withal triumphantly as a conquering man of genius.

Outside science his great interest was religion. The battle between science and dogmatic theology, which was waged during the latter half of the nineteenth century, created an impression, which still survives, that there is a certain radical incompatibility between science and religion. History shows that, as a matter of fact, no such incompatibility exists. If we read the biographies of the three most genial (in the French sense) men of science that England has produced—Sir Isaac Newton, Faraday, and James Clerk Maxwell—we shall find that all three were profoundly religious. Sir Isaac devoted the greater part of a long life to the interpretation of Biblical prophecy. Faraday was an earnest and ardent Christian of the Sandemanian sect. Clerk Maxwell was a great mystic as well as a great man of science; there are letters of his which show him to have been of the company of Boehme and Swedenborg (himself, by the way, a scientific man of great distinction). There is nothing in all this that should surprise us. "An infidel astronomer is mad"; tempered, this piece of rhetoric is something like a truth. For it is certainly impossible to study nature at all closely without becoming convinced of the extraordinary strangeness and mysteriousness of the familiar world in which the mass of human beings unquestioningly pass their lives. The further our knowledge extends and the more completely we realize its implications, the more mysterious this universe is seen to be. A man must be crass and unimaginative indeed if he can study the intricacies of life, the movements of the stars, the intimate constitution of matter without feeling from time to time a sense of awe and amazement. In the ranks of the professional scientists such men undoubtedly find their place; there are unimaginative men in all professions, from that of the jockey to that of the bishop. But they are not, in general, the best at their jobs. Without imagination, without sensitiveness it is impossible to be a successful man of science. It would be difficult to find any great scientific man who had not been touched by this sense of wonder at the strangeness of things. It betrays itself in different ways according to the upbringing and temperament of those who feel it. In some, as quiet and orthodox religion; in others, unwilling to commit themselves definitely about the nature of the mystery which surrounds them, as agnosticism; in others again (Clerk Maxwell and Swedenborg are examples) the man of science is endowed with the peculiar mental qualities of the mystic; in yet other cases we find men possessing these same mystical qualities, but unrefined and somehow coarse (for there are good mystics and poor mystics just as there are good and poor artists), and then we have, not Clerk Maxwell with his delicate and beautiful mysticism, but Newton the interpreter of the prophetic books. For Faraday the corollary and complement of science was Protestant Christianity. His sense of wonder, his awe in face of the beautiful mystery of the world, expressed itself in the terms of Sandemanian[3] meetings and Bible reading. He stands in the scale of mystics some-

3. Robert Sandeman (1718–1771). Scottish sectarian.

where about half-way between Maxwell and Newton, not very highly gifted but at the same time not vulgarly gifted, a sort of Andrea del Sarto between Giotto on the one hand and Caravaggio on the other. A Cherubini between Mozart and Strauss.

That king who, in Anatole France's fable, was only to be cured of his melancholy by putting on the shirt of a happy man, would have been well advised to apply to Faraday. A shirt of his would have been specific against the king's malady. For if any man was happy it was surely he. All his life long he did, professionally, the things he desired to do. To know, to discover the truth—that was his desire. And it is a desire whose fulfilment does not lead to disappointment and boredom, as does the fulfilment of almost every other human longing. For there is no end to truth; each part of it reveals, when found, yet other parts to be discovered. The man who desires knowledge knows no satiety, for the knowable is perpetually new. He might live innumerable lives and never grow weary. True, the knowable world is not everything. There is also the world of feelings; there is also that which is humanly unknowable. In our relation to these two worlds there is plenty of scope for unhappiness. But Faraday was also emotionally happy. His marriage was an unqualified success; he had good friends; the tenor of his life was even and he did not desire more than what he possessed. He was equally fortunate in his relation to the unknowable. The problems of life, as they are called, never troubled him. The religion in which he was brought up offered a solution of them in advance; he passed through no crisis such as that which drove Tolstoy almost to suicide. It is interesting to note that he separated the domain of science sharply from that of religion, the knowable from the unknowable. "Not *how* the world is, is the mystical, but *that* it is," says Wittgenstein. And again: "For an answer which cannot be expressed the question too cannot be expressed. The riddle does not exist. . . . The solution of the problem of life is seen in the vanishing of this problem. (Is not this the reason why men to whom after long doubting the sense of life became clear, could not then say wherein this sense consisted?)" Faraday was happy in that he never doubted, never tried to put an inexpressible question for which there is no possible answer. How the world is, he set himself to discover, with more success than attends most investigators. He did not torture his intellect with the question why or what it is. His religion offered him the explanation why; or to be more exact (for there is no explanation) it helped him to "contemplate the world *sub specie aeterni,* as a limited whole." "The feeling of the world as a limited whole is the mystical feeling." Faraday had that feeling; not perhaps in its most exquisite form, but had it genuinely. His relations with the unknowable therefore were as satisfactory as his relations with what can be known.

Among the natural philosophers Faraday is by no means unique in his happiness. Indeed, as a class, I should say that men of science were happier than other men. A priori, and almost by definition, they ought to be. And when one reads their lives one finds that in point of fact they generally were happy. How satisfactory these lives of born men of science always are! There is an integrity about these men, a unity of purpose that to the rest of us poor distracted mortals seems wonderfully enviable and wonderfully beautiful.

If I could be born again and choose what I should be in my next existence, I should desire to be a man of science—not accidentally but by nature, inevitably a man of science. Fate might offer other alternatives—to have power or wealth, be a king or a statesman. These glittering temptations I should have small difficulty in rejecting; for my objection to the irritating turmoil of practical life is even stronger than my love of money or power, and since these cannot be obtained without plunging into practical life, I can sacrifice them cheerfully. It is easy to make a virtue of psychological necessity. The only thing that might make me hesitate would be an offer by fate of artistic genius. But even if I could be Shakespeare, I think I should still choose to be Faraday. True, the posthumous glory of Shakespeare is greater than that of Faraday; men still read *Macbeth* but not (even if they happen to be electricians) the *Experimental Researches in Electricity*. The work of a man of science is a creation on which others build; it has implications, it grows. If we want to know about electricity, we read what the contemporary successors and disciples of Faraday have to say about it. But *Macbeth* is a thing in itself, not a discovery on which other men can improve. There is no such thing as progress in art. Every artist begins at the beginning. The man of science, on the other hand, begins where his predecessor left off. Opinions and ideas change, under the weight of accumulated experience, from age to age. The instinctive, emotional side of man, being hereditary, remains the same. The man of science provides the experience that changes the ideas of the race; in course of time his discoveries are superseded. The artist does not go out-of-date because he works with materials that do not change. Lyrics composed by a Paleolithic poet would still be moving. But the views of a Paleolithic astronomer would possess, for us, a merely historical and academic interest.

And yet in spite of all this I would still rather be Faraday than Shakespeare. Posthumous fame brings nobody much satisfaction this side of the grave; and though the consciousness that one possesses a great artistic talent must be profoundly satisfying, though the free employment of it must be a source of happiness, it seems to me that the possession and employment of a scientific talent must be still more satisfying. For the artist, whose function is the apt expression and the conveyance to others of the common human emotions, must fatally pass much of his life in the emotional world of human contacts. His reflections upon the world, his personal reactions to contacts—these form the subject matter of his art. The world in which the man of science passes the professional part of his life is non-human, has nothing to do with personal relationships and emotional reactions. We are all subdued to what we work in; and I personally would rather be subdued to intellectual contemplation than to emotion, would rather use my soul professionally for knowing than for feeling.

One of the minor disadvantages of being a great artist is the fact that the artist enjoys a considerable social prestige. Art is the subject of snobbery to a far greater extent than science. The presence of a well-known poet or painter is felt to give distinction to a dinner-party. Hostesses rarely ask one to meet biochemists, however distinguished. The reason for this is simple; all men and women imagine that they can appreciate the arts—and up to a point, of course, actually can—while the number who can understand the technicalities of science is remarkably small. (Vainly, alas, I wish that I myself belonged to that minority.) To this is due the enviable immunity of the men of science from the intrusion of frivolous bores. The artist, on the other hand, is one of the favorite quarries of the unemployed rich; a good specimen is worth at least an ambassador, almost an Indian prince. If the artist is a man of strong character he will find the attentions of the lion-hunters not dangerous, indeed, but profoundly exasperating. They are only dangerous to those who allow themselves to be caught. It is pleasant to be flattered; and if one likes to waste time, there is no easier way of doing so than in casual social intercourse. The artist who succumbs to social temptations loses everything: his time, his integrity, his sense of proportion, the very hope of achieving anything important. He is the more unfortunate in being exposed to them.

Towards morning when, like a mutton chop on a cold plate, I had a little thawed my bed, the phantoms of Michael Faraday and Sir Humphry Davy departed, leaving me alone with my repressed wishes. What they may have been, I don't know. But at any rate they fulfilled themselves, ideally and symbolically, in a confused nightmare of motor-cars and snow-drifts.

The wind was still blowing when I woke up. We spent the forenoon shivering in the sitting-room of the inn. Every few minutes the landlord came in with fresh news about the state of affairs on the pass. Telephone messages had arrived from Florence and Bologna; an army of shovelers was being mobilized; now it was on the move; a man who had just come down from the pass had seen them at work; by two o'clock the road could not fail to be clear. After giving us each item of news, he bowed, smiled, rubbed his hands, and went back to his kitchen to invent the next. He had a fertile imagination.

Fitfully, I read about the Armenian Church. But my interest was languid. I was too cold even to feel a proper enthusiasm over the discovery that "the old sacrificial hymns were probably obscene and certainly nonsensical." Remembering that phrase in subsequent summers, I have been delighted by it. How well, how pithily it describes not merely the old sacrificial hymns of pre-Christian Armenia, but a whole mass of modern art and self-styled science—the greater part of psychoanalytic literature, for example, the music of Schreker, most expressionist painting, *Ulysses,* and so on. As for the less "modern" pseudo-sciences and pseudo-art, from spiritualism to commercial fiction—these do not even possess the saving grace of obscenity; they are merely nonsensical.

The morning passed; it was time for lunch. After a meal of spaghetti and broiled goat, we felt a little stronger and a little less cold. "How are things on the pass?" we asked. But our host seemed suddenly to have lost his omniscience and with it his optimism. He did not know what was happening and he advised us to wait for a little. By five o'clock, however, all would undoubtedly be well. And the road by Firenzuola? That was hopeless; he was certain of that. He left us wondering what to do; whether to wait, whether to return to Florence—what? We were still in a state of painful uncertainty when a heaven-sent messenger in the form of a man with a horse and trap stopped at the inn door. We appealed to him. A miracle! Not only did he know the truth; he also imparted his knowledge in a plain unvarnished way. No shovelers, he assured us, were working on the pass; nor would any be sent there till the wind had changed (for when the wind was blowing in this particular direction, the snow was carried back on to the road as soon as it had been taken off). The wind might change this evening, of course; but on the other hand it might only change next week. But if we wanted to go to Bologna, why hadn't we taken the Firenzuola road? Yes, why not? said the landlord, who had joined us and was listening to the conversation. Why not take the Firenzuola road? He had seen that the game was up and that there was now no further hope of getting us to stay another night. Why not? We looked at him significantly, in silence. He smiled back, imperviously good-humored, and retired to compile his bill.

We set out. The sky was white and full of cloudy movement. Here and there the white mountains were scarred with black, where the precipices were too steep to allow the snow to lie. From La Casetta we slid down the break-neck road that twists down into the valley of the Santerno. Within its walls Firenzuola was black, ancient, and grim. From Firenzuola the road follows the Santerno. The river has tunneled a winding passage through the mountains. The valley is deep and narrow; here and there road and river run between perpendicular walls of rock, banded slantwise with the lines of tilted stratification. Slowly the valley broadens out, the mountains degenerate into bare bleak downs. At the foot of the hills is the plain, narrowed here between the mountains and the sea, but expanding and expanding as one travels northwards into the immense unbroken flatness of the Po valley.

At Imola we turned into the great Via Emilia that runs in an undeviating straight line from Rimini to Piacenza. What cities are strung along that white stretched thread! Cesena, Forli, Faenza, Imola, Bologna, Reggio, Modena, Parma—bead after precious bead.

It was dark when we entered Bologna and the streets were full of maskers. It was the last day of carnival.

We nosed our way through the crowd, hooting. "Maschere!" the maskers shouted as we passed; and in our goggles and mufflers, we too seemed dressed for carnival. It was a feeble show; a few young women in dominoes, a few noisy students in fancy dress—that was all. I thought of the brilliant shows and masquerades of the past. Charming, no doubt; but one should not regret them. For shows and masquerades are symptoms of bad government. Tyrants pass all their lives at the center of a gorgeous ballet. An oppressed populace, too poor to pay for amusements of its own, is kept in good humor by these royal theatricals, which are free of charge. And in the course of periodical Saturnalia slaves are able to sublimate their revolutionary feelings in sportive license. If carnival has decayed, so too has oppression. And where people have pence enough to go to the cinema, there is no need for kings and popes to stage their ballets. Still, it was a very poor show; I felt they might have celebrated our arrival in Bologna a little more worthily.

[*Along the Road,* 1925]

Work and Leisure

REFORMERS LOOK FORWARD to a time when efficient social organization and perfected machinery will do away with the necessity for severe and prolonged labor, making possible for all men and women an amount of leisure such as is enjoyed at the present day only by a privileged few. Nobody, in that golden age, will need to work more than four or five hours a day. The rest of every man's time will be his own, to do with whatsoever he likes.

It is difficult for any sensitive person not to sympathize with these aspirations. One must be most arrogantly certain of one's own supermanhood before one can complacently accept the slavery on which the possibility of being a superman is based. Poor Nietzsche ended by signing his letters "Nietzsche Caesar" and died in a madhouse. Perhaps that is the price that must be paid—at any rate by the intelligent; for the placidly stupid never pay, just as they never receive, anything—for an unfaltering conviction of superiority.

But sympathy with an ideal need not make the sympathizer uncritical of it; one may feel strongly, but one must not therefore cease to think. The majority of human beings are oppressed by excessive labor of the most senseless kind. That fact may, and indeed should, arouse our indignation and our pity. But these emotions must not prevent us from criticizing the project of those who wish to change the present state of things. The social reformers desire to see a dispensation under which all men will have as much, or nearly as much leisure as is enjoyed by the leisured classes today. We may be permitted to doubt, for all our sympathy, whether the consummation is really, after all, so much to be desired.

Let us begin by asking one simple question: What is it proposed that human beings shall do with the leisure which social reorganization and perfected machinery are to give them?

Prophets of the future give fundamentally the same answer to this question, with slight variations according to their different tastes. Henri Poincaré, for example, imagined that the human beings of the future would fill their long leisures by "contemplating the laws of nature." Mr. Bernard Shaw is of much the same opinion. Having ceased, by the time they are four years old, to take any interest in such childish things as love, art, and the society of their fellow beings, the Ancients in *Back to Methuselah* devote their indefinitely prolonged existences to meditating on the mysterious and miraculous beauty of the cosmos. Mr. H. G. Wells portrays in *Men Like Gods* a race of athletic chemists and mathematical physicists who go about naked and, unlike Mr. Shaw's austerer Ancients, make free love in a rational manner between the experiments. They also take an interest in the arts and are not above playing games.

These three answers to our question are typical. Different prophets may differ in their estimate of the relative importance of the various activities which make up what is generally known as "the higher life"; but all agree that the lives of our leisured posterity will be high. They will eagerly make themselves acquainted with "the best that has been thought or said" about everything; they will listen to concerts of the classiest music; they will practice the arts and handicrafts (at any rate until the time comes when even these occupations seem childish); they will study the sciences, philosophy, mathematics, and meditate on the lovely mystery of the world in which they live.

In a word, these leisured masses of a future which there is no reason to believe enormously remote—indeed, our grandchildren may live to see the establishment of the four-hour day—will do all the things which our leisured classes of the present time so conspicuously fail to do.

How many rich and leisured people are there now living, who spend their time contemplating the laws of nature I cannot say; all I know is that I rarely meet them. Many of the leisured, it is true, devote themselves to the patronage and even the amateur practice of the arts. But anyone who has moved among rich "artistic" people knows how much of this cultivation of the arts is due to snobbery, how shallow and insincere their loudly voiced enthusiasms mostly are. The leisured classes take up art for the same reasons as they take up bridge—to escape from boredom. With sport and love-making, art helps to fill up the vacuum of their existence.

At Monte Carlo and Nice one meets the rich whose dominant interests are play and love. Two millions, according to my guide-book, annually visit Monte Carlo alone. Seven-eighths of the whole leisured population of Europe must concentrate themselves yearly on that strip of the coast. Five thousand jazz bands play daily for their delectation. A hundred thousand motor vehicles transport them from one place to another at great speed. Huge joint-stock companies offer them every kind of distraction, from roulette to golf. Legions of prostitutes assemble from all parts of the globe and enthusiastic amateurs of the gentle passion abound. For four months in the year the French Riviera is an earthly paradise. When the four months are over, the leisured rich return to their northerly homes, where they find awaiting them less splendid, but quite authentic *succursales* of the paradise they have left behind.

The leisured rich at Monte Carlo are those, I have said, whose chief resources against *ennui* or serious thoughts are love and play. Many of them are also "artistic." But it is not, I think at Monte Carlo that the best specimens of the artistic rich are to be found. To see them at their best one must go to Florence. Florence is the home of those who cultivate with an equal ardor Mah Jong and a passion for Fra Angelico. Over tea and crumpets they talk, if they are too old for love themselves, of their lascivious juniors; but they also make sketches in water color and read the *Little Flowers of St. Francis.*

I must not, in justice to the leisured rich, omit to mention that respectable minority of them who occupy themselves with works of charity (not to mention tyranny), with politics, with local administration, and occasionally with scholarly or scientific studies. I hesitate to use the word "service"; for it has been held up so frequently as an ideal and by such a riff-raff of newspaper proprietors, hard-headed business men, and professional moralists from the YMCA, that it has lost all real significance. The "ideal of service" is achieved, according to our modern messiahs, by those who do efficient and profitable business with just enough honesty to keep them out of jail. Plain shopkeeping is thus exalted into a beautiful virtue. The ideal of service which animates the best part of the English leisured class has nothing to do with the ideals of service so frequently mentioned by advertisers in American magazines. If I had not made this clear, my praise might have been thought, if not positively insulting, at least most damnably faint.

There exists, then, an admirable minority. But even when the minority and its occupations are duly taken into account, it cannot honestly be said that the leisured classes of the present time, or indeed of any historical period of which we have knowledge, provide a very good advertisement for leisure. The contemplation of richly leisured life in Monte Carlo and even in artistic Florence is by no means cheering or elevating.

Nor are we much reassured when we consider the occupations of the unleisured poor during those brief hours of repose allowed them between their work and their sleep. Watching other people play games, looking at cinema films, reading newspapers and indifferent fiction, listening to radio concerts and gramophone records, and going from place to place in trains and omnibuses, these, I suppose, are the principal occupations of the workingman's leisure. Their cheapness is all that distinguishes them from the diversions of the rich. Prolong the leisure and what will happen? There will have to be more cinemas, more newspapers, more bad fiction, more radios, and more cheap automobiles. If wealth and education increase with the leisure, then there will have to be more Russian Ballets as well as more movies, more *Timeses* as well as more *Daily Mails,* more casinos as well as more bookies and football matches, more expensive operas as well as more gramophone records, more Hugh Walpoles as well as more Nat Goulds. Acting on the same organisms the same causes may be expected to produce the same effects. And for all ordinary purposes, and so far as historical time is concerned, human nature is practically unchanging; the organism does remain the same. *Argal,* as Launcelot Gobbo would have said. . . .

This being so, we must further assume that increase of leisure will be accompanied by a correspondingly increased incidence of those spiritual maladies—*ennui,* restlessness, spleen, and general world-weariness— which afflict and have always afflicted the leisured classes now and in the past.

Another result of increased leisure, provided that it is accompanied by a tolerably high standard of living, will be a very much increased interest on the part of what is now the working class in all matters of an amorous nature. Love, in all its complicated luxuriance, can only flourish in a society composed of well-fed, unemployed people. Examine the literature which has been written by and for members of the leisured classes and compare it with popular working-class literature. Compare *La Princesse de Clèves* with *The Pilgrim's Progress,* Proust with Charles Garvice, Chaucer's *Troilus and Cressida* with the ballads. It becomes at once sufficiently evident that the leisured classes do take and have always taken a much keener and, I might say, more professional interest in love than the workers. A man cannot work hard and at the same time conduct elaborate love affairs. Making love, at any rate in the style in which unemployed women desire it to be made, is a whole-time job. It demands both energy and leisure. Now energy and leisure are precisely the things which a hard worker lacks. Reduce his working hours and he will have both.

If, tomorrow or a couple of generations hence, it were made possible for all human beings to lead the life of leisure which is now led only by a few, the results, so far as I can see, would be as follows: There would be an enormous increase in the demand for such time-killers and substitutes for thought as newspapers, films, fiction, cheap means of communication, and wireless telephones; to put it in more general terms, there would be an increase in the demand for sport and art. The interest in the fine art of lovemaking would be widely extended. And enormous numbers of people, hitherto immune from these mental and moral diseases, would be afflicted by *ennui,* depression, and universal dissatisfaction.

The fact is that, brought up as they are at present, the majority of human beings can hardly fail to devote their leisure to occupations which, if not positively vicious, are at least stupid, futile, and, what is worse, secretly realized to be futile.

To Tolstoy the whole idea of universal leisure seemed absurd and even wicked. The social reformers who held up the attainment of universal leisure as an ideal he regarded as madmen. They aspired to make all men like those rich, idle, urban people among whom he had passed his youth and whom he so profoundly despised. He regarded them as conspirators against the welfare of the race.

What seemed to Tolstoy important was not that the workers should get more leisure but that the leisured should work. For him the social ideal was labor for all in natural surroundings. He wanted to see all men and women living on the land and subsisting on the produce of the fields that they themselves had tilled. The makers of Utopias are fond of prophesying that a time will come when men will altogether abandon agriculture and live on synthetic foods; to Tolstoy the idea was utterly revolting. But though he was doubtless right to be revolted, the prophets of synthetic food are probably better seers than he. Mankind is more likely to become urbanized than completely ruralized. But these probabilities do not concern us here. What concerns us is Tolstoy's opinion of leisure.

Tolstoy's dislike of leisure was due to his own experience as an idle youth and his observation of other rich and leisured men and women. He concluded that, as things are, leisure is generally more of a curse than a blessing. It is difficult, when one visits Monte Carlo or the other earthly paradises of the leisured, not to agree with him. Most minds will only do work under compulsion. Leisure is only profitable to those who desire, even without compulsion, to do mental work. In a society entirely composed of such active minds leisure would be an unmixed blessing. Such a society has never existed and does not at the present exist. Can it ever be called into being?

Those who believe that all the defects of nature may be remedied by suitable nurture will reply in the affirmative. And indeed it is sufficiently obvious that the science of education is still in a very rudimentary condition. We possess a sufficient knowledge of physiology to be able to devise gymnastic exercises that shall develop the body to its highest attainable efficiency. But our knowledge of the mind, and particularly of the growing mind, is far less complete; and even such knowledge as we possess is not systematically or universally applied to the problems of education. Our minds are like the flabby bodies of sedentary city dwellers—inefficient and imperfectly developed. With a vast number of people intellectual development ceases almost in childhood; they go through life with the intellectual capacities of boys or girls of fifteen. A proper course of mental gymnastics, based on real psychological knowledge, would at least permit all minds to reach their maximum development. Splendid prospect! But our enthusiasm for education is a little cooled when we consider what is the maximum development attainable by the greatest number of human beings. Men born with talents are to men born without them as human beings to dogs in respect to these particular faculties. Mathematically, I am a dog compared with Newton; a dog, musically, compared with Beethoven, and a dog, artistically, compared with Giotto. Not to mention the fact that I am a dog compared to Blondin, as a tight-rope walker; a billiard-playing dog compared with Newman; a boxing dog compared with Dempsey; a wine-tasting dog compared with Ruskin's father. And so on. Even if I were perfectly educated in mathematics, music, painting, tight-rope walking, billiard playing, boxing, and wine-tasting, I should only become a trained dog instead of a dog in the state of nature. The prospect fills me with only moderate satisfaction.

Education can assure to every man the maximum of mental development. But is that maximum high enough in the majority of cases to allow a whole society to live in leisure without developing those deplorable qualities which have always characterized the leisured classes? I know plenty of people who have received the best education available in the present age and employ their leisure as though they had never been educated at all. But then our best education is admittedly bad (though good enough for all the men of talent and genius whom we possess); perhaps when it has been made really efficient, these people will spend their leisure contemplating the laws of nature. Perhaps. I venture to doubt it.

Mr. Wells, who is a believer in nurture, puts his Utopia three thousand years into the future; Mr. Shaw, less optimistically trusting to nature and a process of conscious evolution, removes his to the year 30,000 A.D. Geologically speaking, these times are to all intents equal in their brevity. Unfortunately, however, we are not fossils, but men. Even three thousand years seem, in our eyes, an uncommonly long time. The thought that, three thousand or thirty thousand years hence, human beings may, conceivably, be leading a lovely and rational existence is only mildly comforting and feebly sustaining. Men have a habit of thinking only of themselves, their children, and their children's children. And they are quite right. Thirty thousand years hence, all may be well. But meanwhile that bad geological quarter of an hour which separates the present from that rosy future has got to be lived through. And I foresee that one of the minor, or even the major problems of that quarter of an hour will be the problem of leisure. By the year two thousand the six-hour day will be everywhere the rule, and the next hundred years will probably see the maximum reduced to five or even less. Nature, by then, will have had no time to change the mental habits of the race; and nurture, though improved, will only turn dogs into trained dogs. How will men and women fill their ever-expanding leisure? By contemplating the laws of nature, like Henri Poincaré?[4] Or by reading the News of the World? I wonder.

[*Along the Road,* 1925]

4. Henri Jules Poincaré (1854–1912). French mathematician.

IV.

Travel

Tibet

IN MOMENTS of complete despair, when it seems that all is for the worst in the worst of all possible worlds, it is cheering to discover that there are places where stupidity reigns even more despotically than in Western Europe, where civilization is based on principles even more fantastically unreasonable. Recent experience has shown me that the depression into which the Peace, Mr. Churchill, and the state of contemporary literature have conspired to plunge the mind, can be sensibly relieved by a study, even superficial, of the manners and customs of Tibet. The spectacle of an ancient and elaborate civilization of which almost no detail is not entirely idiotic is in the highest degree comforting and refreshing. It fills us with hopes of the ultimate success of our own civilization; it restores our wavering self-satisfaction in being citizens of industrialized Europe. Compared with Tibet, we are prodigious. Let us cherish the comparison.

My informant about Tibetan civilization is a certain Japanese monk of the name of Kawaguchi, who spent three years in Tibet at the beginning of the present century. His account of the experience has been translated into English, and published, with the title *Three Years in Tibet,* by the Theosophical Society. It is one of the great travel books of the world, and, so far as I am aware, the most interesting book on Tibet that exists. Kawaguchi enjoyed opportunities in Tibet which no European traveler could possibly have had. He attended the University of Lhasa, he enjoyed the acquaintance of the Dalai Lama himself, he was intimate with one of the four Ministers of Finance, he was the friend of lama and layman, of all sorts and conditions of Tibetans, from the highest class to the lowest—the despicable caste of smiths and butchers. He knew his Tibet intimately; for those three years, indeed, he was for all practical purposes a Tibetan. This is something which no European explorer can claim, and it is this which gives Kawaguchi's book its unique interest.

The Japanese, like people of every other nationality except the Chinese, are not permitted to enter Tibet. Mr. Kawaguchi did not allow this to stand in the way of his pious mission—for his purpose in visiting Tibet was to investigate the Buddhist writings and traditions of the place. He made his way to India, and in a long stay at Darjeeling familiarized himself with the Tibetan language. He then set out to walk across the Himalayas. Not daring to affront the strictly guarded gates which bar the direct route to Lhasa, he penetrated Tibet at its southwestern corner, underwent prodigious hardships in an uninhabited desert eighteen thousand feet above sea-level, visited the holy lake of Manosarovara, and finally, after astonishing adventures, arrived in Lhasa. Here he lived for nearly three years, passing himself off as a Chinaman. At the end of that time his secret leaked out, and he was obliged to accelerate his departure for India. So much for Kawaguchi himself, though I should have liked to say more of him; for a more charming and sympathetic character never revealed himself in a book.

Tibet is so full of fantastic low comedy that one hardly knows where to begin a catalogue of its absurdities. Shall we start with the Tibetans' highly organized service of trained nurses, whose sole duty it is to prevent their patients from going to sleep? or with the Dalai Lama's chief source of income—the sale of pills made of dung, at, literally, a guinea a box? or with the Tibetan custom of never washing from the moment of birth, when, however, they are plentifully anointed with melted butter, to the moment of death? And then there is the University of Lhasa, which an eminent Cambridge philosopher has compared with the University of Oxford— somewhat unjustly, perhaps; but let that pass. At the University of Lhasa the student is instructed in logic and philosophy; every year of his stay he has to learn by heart from one to five or six hundred pages of holy texts. He is also taught mathematics, but in Tibet this art is not carried further than subtraction. It takes twenty years to get a degree at the University of Lhasa—twenty years, and then most of the candidates are ploughed. To obtain a superior Ph.D. degree, entitling one to become a really holy and eminent lama, forty years of application to study and to virtue are required. But it is useless to try to make a catalogue of the delights of Tibet.

There are too many of them for mention in this small space. One can do no more than glance at a few of the brighter spots in the system. There is much to be said for the Tibetan system of taxation. The Government requires a considerable revenue; for enormous sums have to be spent in keeping perpetually burning in the principal Buddhist cathedral of Lhasa an innumerable army of lamps, which may not be fed with anything cheaper than clarified yak butter. This is the heaviest item of expenditure. But a great deal of money also goes to supporting the Tibetan clergy, who must number at least a sixth of the total population. The money is raised by a poll tax, paid in kind, the amount of which, fixed by ancient tradition, may, theoretically, never be altered. Theoretically only; for the Tibetan Government employs in the collection of taxes no fewer than twenty different standards of weight and thirty-six different standards of measure. The pound may weigh anything from half to a pound and a half; and the same with the units of measure. It is thus possible to calculate with extraordinary nicety, according to the standard of weight and measure in which your tax is assessed, where precisely you stand in the Government's favor. If you are a notoriously bad character, or even if you are innocent, but live in a bad district, your tax will have to be paid in measures of the largest size. If you are virtuous, or, better, if you are rich, of good family and *bien pensant,* then you will pay by weights which are only half the nominal weight. For those whom the Government neither hates nor loves, but regards with more or less contempt or tolerance, there are the thirty-four intervening degrees.

Kawaguchi's final judgment of the Tibetans, after three years' intimate acquaintance with them, is not a flattering one:

> The Tibetans are characterized by four serious defects, these being: filthiness, superstition, unnatural customs (such as polyandry), and unnatural art. I should be sorely perplexed if I were asked to name their redeeming points; but if I had to do so, I should mention first of all the fine climate in the vicinity of Lhasa and Shigatze, their sonorous and refreshing voices in reading the Text, the animated style of their catechisms, and their ancient art.

Certainly a bad lot of vices; but then the Tibetan virtues are not lightly to be set aside. We English possess none of them: our climate is abominable, our method of reading the holy texts is painful in the extreme, our catechisms, at least in my young days, were far from animated, and our ancient art is very indifferent stuff. But still, in spite of these defects, in spite of Mr. Churchill and the state of contemporary literature, we can still look at the Tibetans and feel reassured.

[*On the Margin,* 1923]

Why Not Stay at Home?

SOME PEOPLE travel on business, some in search of health. But it is neither the sickly nor the men of affairs who fill the Grand Hotels and the pockets of their proprietors. It is those who travel "for pleasure," as the phrase goes. What Epicurus, who never traveled except when he was banished, sought in his own garden, our tourists seek abroad. And do they find their happiness? Those who frequent the places where they resort must often find this question, with a tentative answer in the negative, fairly forced upon them. For tourists are, in the main, a very gloomy-looking tribe. I have seen much brighter faces at a funeral than in the Piazza of

St. Mark's. Only when they can band together and pretend, for a brief, precarious hour, that they are at home, do the majority of tourists look really happy. One wonders why they come abroad.

The fact is that very few travelers really like traveling. If they go to the trouble and expense of traveling, it is not so much from curiosity, for fun, or because they like to see things beautiful and strange, as out of a kind of snobbery. People travel for the same reason as they collect works of art: because the best people do it. To have been to certain spots on the earth's surface is socially correct; and having been there, one is superior to those who have not. Moreover, traveling gives one something to talk about when one gets home. The subjects of conversation are not so numerous that one can neglect an opportunity of adding to one's store.

To justify this snobbery, a series of myths has gradually been elaborated. The places which it is socially smart to have visited are aureoled with glamor, till they are made to appear, for those who have not been there, like so many fabled Babylons or Bagdads. Those who have traveled have a personal interest in cultivating and disseminating these fables. For if Paris and Monte Carlo are really so marvellous as it is generally supposed, by the inhabitants of Bradford or Milwaukee, of Tomsk and Bergen, that they are—why, then, the merit of the travelers who have actually visited these places is the greater, and their superiority over the stay-at-homes the more enormous. It is for this reason (and because they pay the hotel proprietors and the steamship companies) that the fables are studiously kept alive.

Few things are more pathetic than the spectacle of inexperienced travelers, brought up on these myths, desperately doing their best to make external reality square with fable. It is for the sake of the myths and, less consciously, in the name of snobbery that they left their homes; to admit disappointment in the reality would be to admit their own foolishness in having believed the fables and would detract from their merit in having undertaken the pilgrimage. Out of the hundreds of thousands of Anglo-Saxons who frequent the night-clubs and dancing-saloons of Paris, there are a good many, no doubt, who genuinely like that sort of thing. But there are also very many who do not. In their hearts, secretly, they are bored and a little disgusted. But they have been brought up to believe in a fabulous "Gay Paree," where everything is deliriously exciting and where alone it is possible to see what is technically known as Life. Conscientiously, therefore, they strive, when they come to Paris, to be gay. Night after night the dance halls and the bordellos are thronged by serious young compatriots of Emerson and Matthew Arnold, earnestly engaged in trying to see life, neither very steadily nor whole, through the ever-thickening mists of Heidsieck and Roederer.

Still more courageously determined are their female companions; for they, mostly (unless they are extremely "modern"), have not the Roederer to assist them in finding Paris gay. The saddest sight I ever saw was in a Montmartre boîte at about five o'clock of an autumn morning. At a table in a corner of the hall sat three young American girls, quite unattended, adventurously seeing life by themselves. In front of them, on the table, stood the regulation bottles of champagne; but for preference—perhaps on principle—they were sipping lemonade. The jazz band played on monotonously; the tired drummer nodded over his drums, the saxophonist yawned into his saxophone. In couples, in staggering groups, the guests departed. But grimly, indomitably, in spite of their fatigue, in spite of the boredom which so clearly expressed itself on their charming and ingenuous faces, the three young girls sat on. They were still there when I left at sunrise. What stories, I reflected, they would tell when they got home again! And how envious they would make their untraveled friends. "Paris is just wonderful. . . ."

To the Parisians, the fable brings in several hundred milliards of good money. They give it a generous publicity; business is business. But if I were the manager of a Montmartre dancing saloon, I think I should tell my waiters to act their gay parts with a little more conviction. "My men," I should say to them, "you ought to look as though you believed in the fable out of which we make our living. Smile, be merry. Your present expression, which is a mingling of weariness, disgusted contempt for your clients, and cynical rapacity, is not inspiring. One day the clients might be sober enough to notice it. And where should we be then?"

But Paris and Monte Carlo are not the only resorts of pilgrimage. There are also Rome and Florence. There are picture galleries, churches, and ruins as well as shops and casinos. And the snobbery which decrees that one must like Art—or, to be more accurate, that one should have visited the places where Art is to be seen—is almost as tyrannous as that which bids one visit the places where one can see Life.

All of us are more or less interested in Life—even in that rather smelly slice of it that is to be found in Montmartre. But a taste for Art—or at any rate the sort of art that is found in galleries and churches—is by no means universal. Hence the case of the poor tourists who, from motives of snobbery, visit Rome and Florence, is even more pathetic than the case of those who repair for the same reasons to Paris and Monte Carlo. Tourists "doing" a church wear a mask of dutiful interest; but what lassitude, what utter weariness of spirit looks out, too often, from their eyes! And the weariness is felt, within, still more acutely because, precisely, of the necessity of simulating this rapt attentiveness, of even going hypocritically into raptures over the things that are started in the Baedeker. There come moments when flesh and blood can stand the strain no longer. Philistinism absolutely refuses to pay the tribute it owes to taste. Exasperated and defiant, the tourist swears that he won't so much as put his nose inside another church, preferring to spend his days in the lounge of the hotel, reading the continental *Daily Mail*.

I remember witnessing one of these rebellions at Venice. A motor boat company was advertising afternoon excursions to the island of Torcello. We booked our seats and at the appointed time set off, in company with seven or eight other tourists. Romantic in its desolation, Torcello rose out of the lagoon. The boatmen drew up at the side of a moldering jetty. A quarter of a mile away, through the fields, stood the church. It contains some of the most beautiful mosaics in Italy. We climbed on shore—all of us with the exception of one strong-minded American couple who, on learning that the object of interest on this island was only another church, decided to remain comfortably seated in the boat till the rest of the party should return. I admired them for their firmness and their honesty. But at the same time, it seemed to me rather a melancholy thing that they should have come all this way and spent all that money, merely for the pleasure of sitting in a motor boat tied to a rotting wharf. And then they were only at Venice. Their Italian ordeal had hardly begun. Padua, Ferrara, Ravenna, Bologna, Florence, Siena, Perugia, Assisi, and Rome, with all their innumerable churches and pictures, had still to be looked at, before—the blessed goal of Naples finally reached—they could be permitted to take the liner home again across the Atlantic. Poor slaves, I thought; and of how exacting a master!

We call such people travelers because they do not stay at home. But they are not genuine travelers, not travelers born. For they travel, not for traveling's sake, but for convention's. They set out, nourished on fables and fantastical hopes, to return, whether they avow it or not, disappointed. Their interest in the real and actual being insufficiently lively, they hanker after mythology, and the facts, however curious, beautiful, and varied, are a disillusionment. It is only the society of their fellow-tourists, with whom they conspire, every now and then, to make a little oasis of home in the foreign wilderness, coupled with the consciousness of a social duty done, that keeps them even moderately cheerful in the face of the depressing facts of travel.

Your genuine traveler, on the other hand, is so much interested in real things that he does not find it necessary to believe in fables. He is insatiably curious, he loves what is unfamiliar for the sake of its unfamiliarity, he takes pleasure in every manifestation of beauty. It would be absurd, of course, to say that he is never bored. For it is practically impossible to travel without being sometimes bored. For the tourist, a large part of almost every day is necessarily empty. Much time, to begin with, must be spent in merely getting from place to place. And when the sights have been seen, the sightseer finds himself physically weary and with nothing particular to do. At home, among one's regular occupations, one is never bored. *Ennui* is essentially a holiday feeling. (Is it not the chronic disease of the leisured?) It is for that very reason that your true traveler finds boredom rather agreeable than painful. It is the symbol of his liberty—his excessive freedom. He accepts his boredom, when it comes, not merely philosophically, but almost with pleasure.

For the born traveler, traveling is a besetting vice. Like other vices it is imperious, demanding its victim's time, money, energy, and the sacrifice of his comfort. It claims; and the born traveler gives, willingly, even eagerly. Most vices, it may be added parenthetically, demand considerable self-sacrifices. There is no greater mistake than to suppose that a vicious life is a life of uninterrupted pleasure. It is a life almost as wearisome and painful—if strenuously led—as Christian's in *The Pilgrim's Progress*. The chief difference between Christian and the vicious man is that the first gets something out of his hardships—gets it here and now in the shape of a certain spiritual well-being, to say nothing of what he may get in that sadly problematical Jerusalem beyond the river—while the second gets nothing, except, perhaps, gout and general paralysis of the insane.

The vice of traveling, it is true, does not necessarily bring with it these two particular diseases; nor indeed any diseases at all, unless your wanderings take you as far as the tropics. No bodily diseases; for traveling is not a vice of the body (which it mortifies) but of the mind. Your traveler-for-traveling's-sake is like your desultory reader—a man addicted to mental self-indulgence.

Like all other vicious men, the reader and the traveler have a whole armory of justifications with which to defend themselves. Reading and traveling, they say, broaden the mind, stimulate imagination, are a liberal education. And so on. These are specious arguments; but nobody is very much impressed by them. For though it may be quite true that, for certain people, desultory reading and aimless traveling are richly educative, it is not for that reason that most true readers and travelers born indulge their tastes. We read and travel, not that we may broaden and enrich our minds, but that we may pleasantly forget they exist. We love reading and traveling because they are the most delightful of all the many substitutes for thought. Sophisticated and somewhat rarefied substitutes. That is why they are not every man's diversion. The congenital reader or traveler is one of those more fastidious spirits who cannot find the distractions they require in betting, Mah Jong, drink, golf, or fox-trots.

There exist a few, a very few, who travel and, for that matter, who read, with purpose and a definite system. This is a morally admirable class. And it is the class to which, in general, the people who achieve something in the world belong. Not always, however, by any means. For, alas, one may have a high purpose and a fine character, but no talent. Some of the most self-indulgent and aimless of travelers and readers have known how to profit by their vices. Desultory reading was Dr. Johnson's besetting sin; he read every book that came under his hand and none to the end. And yet his achievement was not small. And there are frivolous travelers, like Beckford, who have gone about the world, indulging their wanton curiosity, to almost as good purpose. Virtue is its own reward; but the grapes which talent knows how to pluck, are they not a little sour?

With me, traveling is frankly a vice. The temptation to indulge in it is one which I find almost as hard to resist as the temptation to read promiscuously, omnivorously, and without purpose. From time to time, it is true, I make a desperate resolution to mend my ways. I sketch out programs of useful, serious reading; I try to turn my rambling voyages into systematic tours through the history of art and civilization. But without much success. After a little I relapse into my old bad ways. Deplorable weakness! I try to comfort myself with the hope that even my vices may be of some profit to me.

[*Along the Road,* 1925]

Wander-Birds

FAIR-HAIRED, bare-headed, with faces burned darker than their hair, they trudge along the dusty roads. They wear shorts; their Tyrolean knees are brown. Enormous boots, heavy with nails, click metallically over the flagstones of the churches into which, conscientious *Kunstforschers,* they penetrate. On their backs they carry knapsacks and in their hands, sometimes a stick, sometimes a stout umbrella; I have seen them making the ascent of the Viale dei Colli at Florence with ice-axes. They are the wander-birds, and they come, as their name (so romantic and applied so unironically), their Schillerian name too manifestly proclaims, from Germany. Many of them have walked all the way, across the Alps from Berlin to Taranto and back, with no money, living on bread and water, sleeping in barns or by the roadside. Adventurous and hardy youths! I feel the profoundest admiration for them. I even envy them, wishing that I possessed their energy, their hardiness. But I do not imitate them.

"The saints of old," says the hymnologist, "went up to heaven
With sorrow, toil and pain.

Lord, unto us may strength be given
To follow in the train."

For me, I confess, even the train has become a means of traveling too inconvenient to be much employed. I would amend the last two lines of the hymn to, "Lord, unto us may wealth be given to follow in the car." The prayer has been granted—partially, at any rate; for whether a ten-horse-power Citroën can really be called a car is questionable. Owners of Napiers, Vauxhalls, Delages, or Voisins would certainly deny it. I shall not argue the point. All I claim for the ten-horse-power Citroën is this: that it works. In a modest and unassuming way, not very rapidly, indeed, but steadily and reliably, it takes one about. This particular specimen has carried us a good many thousand miles over the roads of Italy, France, Belgium, and Holland; which, for all who are acquainted with those roads, is saying a good deal.

At this point, if I had any strength of mind, I should stop talking about Citroëns and return to higher themes. But the temptation of talking about cars, when one has a car, is quite irresistible. Before I bought a Citroën no subject had less interest for me; none, now, has more. I can talk for hours about motors with other car-owners. And I am ruthlessly prepared to bore the non-motorist by talking interminably of this delightful subject even to him. I waste much precious time reading the motoring papers, study passionately the news from the racing tracks, gravely peruse technical lucubrations which I do not understand. It is a madness, but a delightful one.

The spiritual effects of being a car-owner are not, I notice, entirely beneficial. Introspection and the conversation of other motorists have shown me, indeed, that car-owning may have the worst effect on the character. To begin with every car-owner is a liar. He cannot tell the truth about his machine. He exaggerates his speed, the number of miles he goes to the gallon of petrol, his prowess as a hill climber. In the heat of conversation I myself have erred in this respect, more than once; and even coolly, with malice aforethought, I have given utterance, on this subject, to frigid and calculated lies. They do not weigh very heavily on my conscience. I am no casuist, but it seems to me that a lie which one tells, expecting nobody to believe it, is venial. The motorist, like the fisherman, never really supposes that his vaunts will be believed. Myself, I have long ceased to give the slightest credit to anything my fellow-motorists may tell me. My last vestige of confidence was destroyed by the Belgian driver who told me that two hours were ample time to allow for the journey from Brussels to Ostend; he himself, he declared, did it constantly and never took more. I trusted him and did not consult the road book. If I had, I should have

found that the distance from Brussels to Ostend is something over seventy
miles, that the road is cobbled all the way and badly cobbled at that, and
that one has to pass through three large towns and about twenty villages.
As it was we started late in the afternoon and were hopelessly benighted.
Now, when motorists tell me how long it takes them to get from one place
to another, I add on, according to their character, from thirty to sixty percent to the figure they mention. In this way I reach approximate truth.

Another horrible sin encouraged by the owning of an automobile, particularly of a small automobile, is envy. What bitter discontentment fills
the mind of the 10 H.P. man as the 40 H.P. shoots silently past him! How
fiercely he loathes the owner of the larger machine! What envy and cov-
etousness possess him! In a flat country one envies less than in a hilly. For
on the flat even the little car can do quite creditably enough to keep up its
owner's self-esteem. It is in a mountainous country, like Italy, where the
roads are constantly running up to two or three thousand feet and down
again, that the deadly sin of envy really flourishes. For there the little car
must abjectly acknowledge its littleness. The superiority of 40 H.P. over 10
H.P. is only too painfully apparent. It was on the Mont Cenis that the cup
of our humiliation flowed over and the blackest envy filled our souls. We
had started from Turin. For the first thirty miles the road is perfectly flat.
We rolled along it in very dashing style; the smaller Fiats ate our dust. In
front of us, like an immense uneven wall, the Alps rose suddenly out of the
plain. Susa lies at the head of a long flat-bottomed valley that leads into
the heart of the hills. You pass through the town and then, suddenly, without warning, the road begins to climb, steeply. It goes on climbing without
respite for the next fifteen miles. The top of the pass is six thousand five
hundred feet above the sea. The Citroën went into second and remained
there; slowly we puffed up the long ascent. We had gone about a mile,
when we became aware of a noise coming up from the valley, a noise like
the noise of massed machine-guns. It grew louder and louder. A minute
later a huge red Alfa Romeo road racer, looking suspiciously like the machine that had just won the Grand Prix of Europe, roared past at a speed
that cannot have been less than fifty miles an hour. It was evidently being
driven by a genius; for, looking up, we saw the scarlet monster negotiating
turn after hairpin turn in the zigzag road above us without once abating its
speed by a mile an hour. In another thirty seconds it was out of sight. The
noise of it solemnly reverberated among the mountains, like thunder.
Slowly we puffed on. Half an hour later we met the red terror descending;
round the corners it showed the same disregard for the elementary laws of
dynamics as it had shown on the way up. We imagined that we had seen
the last of it. But waiting at the Italian custom-house while the officer in
charge examined our papers—a process which, as at all custom-houses,

took a very long time—we heard, far off, a familiar sound. In a few minutes the sound became deafening. Like a huge red rocket, trailing behind it a cloud of smoke, the Alfa Romeo passed at the head of its white dust. "They're doing hill-climbing tests," the soldier on guard explained. We set out once more. The custom-house is only half-way up the hill; we had another three thousand feet or so before we reached the summit. Slowly, on second, we addressed ourselves to the ascent. We were only a mile from the custom-house, when, for the second time, we met the Alfa Romeo descending. It disappeared, carrying with it a load of hatred, envy, and mixed uncharitableness of every variety.

The road mounted and mounted. We passed through the region of pine woods. Around and above us, now, the slopes were bare; quite close, among the nearer summits, across the valley, were patches of snow. For all that the season was summer, the air was uncommonly sharp and nipping. A wind blew; in the shade it was positively cold. But that did not prevent the car from boiling.

The hospice and the hotels of the Mont Cenis stand on the shores of a lake in the middle of a little plateau that lies, a miracle of flatness amid the surrounding perpendicularity. Towards the Italian side this shelf among the hills ends abruptly in what is nearly a precipice. For the last four or five hundred feet the road leading up to it is terraced out of the rock and rises with uncommon steepness. We were half-way up these final zigzags, when all at once, bursting with a roar round the corner of a bluff that had muffled the sound of its approach, the scarlet Alfa Romeo appeared at the bottom of the precipice up which we were painfully zigzagging. It came up after us, like a wild beast pursuing its prey, bellowing. Just as we reached the top, the monster overhauled us, passed, and went racing across the plain. Our humiliation was complete. Envy and discontent boiled up within us, like the water boiling in the radiator of our miserable little machine. "If only," we said, "if only we had a real car. . . ." We longed to exchange the passion of envy for the equally malignant and un-Christian passions of pride and contempt, to be those who pass exultantly instead of those who are passed. "Yea, also the heart of the sons of men is full of evil, and madness is in their heart while they live, and after that they go to the dead." When we reached the hotel, the Alfa Romeo had turned round and was just preparing to begin its third descent. "It's an ugly-looking car," we said.

Such are the moral consequences of being the owner of a small car. We tried to reason with ourselves. "After all," we said, "this little machine has done good service. It has taken us over bad roads, up and down enormous hills, through a variety of countries. It has taken us, not merely through space, across the face of the map, but through time—from epoch to epoch through art, through many languages and customs, through philology and anthropology. It has been the instrument of great and varied pleasures. It costs little, behaves well, its habits are as regular as those of Immanuel Kant. In its unpretentious way it is a model of virtue." All this we said, and much more; and it was comforting. But in the bottom of our hearts envy and discontent still lurked, like coiled serpents, ready to raise their heads the very next time that forty horses should pass us on a hill.

It may be objected that the small-car owner is not alone in envying. The wander-birds doing their four miles an hour, sweating, up the dusty hill, must envy indiscriminately both the ten- and the forty-horse-power man. True, some of them probably do. But it must not be forgotten that there are pedestrians who walk because they genuinely prefer walking to being carried effortlessly along by a machine. In my youth I used to try to pretend that I preferred walking to other means of locomotion. But I soon found that it was not true. For a little time I was one of those hypocrites of country heartiness (and they are quite numerous) who tramp and drink ale in little inns, because it is the right thing to do. In the end, however, I frankly admitted to myself and to other people that I was not one of nature's walkers, that I did not like hearty exercise and discomfort, and did not mean any longer to pretend that I did. But I still have the greatest respect for those who do, and I consider that they are probably a superior type of humanity to the idle and comfort-loving breed predominant at the present time. One of the great charms of mechanical progress is that it allows us to do everything quickly, easily, and comfortably. This is very agreeable; but I doubt whether it is, morally speaking, very healthy. It is not even very healthy for the body. It is in the civilized countries, where human beings eat most and take least exercise, that cancer is most prevalent. The disease spreads with every fresh expansion of Henry Ford's factories.

None the less I prefer to follow in the car. To the wander-birds whom we pass on our way, I take off my hat. It is a mark of my sincere esteem. But inwardly I repeat to myself the words of the Abbot in *The Canterbury Tales:* "Let Austin have his swink to him reserved."

[*Along the Road,* 1925]

The Traveler's-Eye View

I COULD GIVE many excellent reasons for my dislike of large dinner-parties, soirées, crushes, routs, conversazioni, and balls. Life is not long enough and they waste precious time; the game is not worth the candle.

Casual social intercourse is like dram-drinking, a mere stimulant that whips the nerves but does not nourish. And so on. These are respectable contentions and all quite true. And they have certainly had weight with me. But the final argument against large assemblages and in favor of solitude and the small intimate gathering has been, in my case, of a more personal character. It has appealed, not to my reason, but my vanity. The fact is that I do not shine in large assemblies; indeed, I scarcely glimmer. And to be dim and conscious of one's dimness is humiliating.

This incapacity to be bright in company is due entirely to my excessive curiosity. I cannot listen to what my interlocutor is saying or think of anything to say in answer to him, because I cannot help listening to the conversations being carried on by everybody else within earshot. My interlocutor, for example, is saying something very intelligent about Henry James and is obviously expecting me, when he has done, to make some smart or subtle comment. But the two women on my left are telling scandalous stories about a person I know. The man with the loud voice at the other side of the room is discussing the merits of different motor-cars. The science student by the fireplace is talking about the quantum theory. The distinguished Irish lawyer is telling anecdotes in his inimitable professional manner. Behind me a youth and maiden are exchanging views on love, while from the group in the far corner I hear an occasional phrase which tells me that they are talking politics. An invincible curiosity possesses me, I long to hear exactly what each is saying. Scandal, motors, quanta, Irish bulls, love, and politics seem to me incomparably more interesting than Henry James; and each of these is at the same time more interesting than all the others. Inquisitiveness flutters hopelessly this way and that, like a bird in a glass house. And the net result is that, not hearing what he says and being too much distracted to answer coherently, I make myself appear an idiot to my interlocutor, while the very number of my illicit curiosities renders it impossible for me to satisfy any single one of them.

But this excessive and promiscuous inquisitiveness, so fatal to a man who desires to mix in society, is a valuable asset to the one who merely looks on, without participating in the actions of his fellows.

For the traveler, who is compelled, whether he likes to or not, to pose as the detached on-looker, inquisitiveness is nothing less than a necessity. *Ennui,* says Baudelaire, "is *fruit de la morne incuriosité.*" The tourist who has no curiosity is doomed to boredom.

There are few pleasanter diversions than to sit in cafés or restaurants or the third-class carriages of railway trains, looking at one's neighbors and listening (without attempting to enter into conversation) to such scraps of their talk as are wafted across the intervening space. From their appearance, from what they say, one reconstructs in the imagination the whole character, the complete life history. Given the single fossil bone, one fancifully builds up the whole diplodocus. It is an excellent game. But it must be played discreetly. Too open a curiosity is apt to be resented. One must look and listen without appearing to be aware of anything. If the game is played by two people, comments should always be made in some language other than that of the country in which the game is played. But perhaps the most important rule of the game is that which forbids one, except in the most extraordinary cases, to make any effort to get to know the objects of one's curiosity.

For, alas, the objects of one's curiosity prove, once one has made their acquaintance, to be, almost invariably, quite unworthy of any further interest. It is possible at a distance to feel the most lively curiosity about a season-ticket holder from Surbiton. His bald head is so shiny; he has such a funny waxed moustache; he gets so red in the face when he talks to his friends about the Socialists; he laughs with such loud unpleasant gusto when one of them tells a dirty story; he sweats so profusely when it is hot; he holds forth so knowledgeably about roses; and his sister lives at Birmingham; his son has just won a prize for mathematics at school. At long range all this is fascinating; it stimulates the imagination. One loves the little man; he is wonderful, charming, a real slice of life. But make his acquaintance. . . . From that day forth you take pains to travel in another compartment.

How delightful, how queer and fantastic people are, at a distance! When I think of the number of fascinating men and women I have never known (only seen and momentarily listened to) I am astonished. I can remember hundreds of them. My favorites, I am inclined to think, were those male and female post-office clerks who lived *en pension* at the little hotel at Ambérieu where once I stayed for a week or so, finishing a book. They were fascinating. There was the oldish man, who always came in late for dinner, wearing a cap—a grim, taciturn fellow he was; there was the very young boy, not at all grim, but silent out of pure shyness; there was the very bright, lively, meridional fellow, who made jokes all the time and flirtatiously teased the young ladies; and the three young ladies, one ugly but tolerably lively, one rather pretty but limp and chlorotic, and the third so full of attractive vitality that she compelled one to think her pretty, such rolling black eyes, such a smile, such a voice, so witty! The shy young man gazed like a calf, blushed when she looked at him, smiled oxishly when she talked, and forgot to eat his dinner. Her presence thawed the grim and grizzled man and roused the meridional to yet higher flights. And her superiority was so enormous that the ugly girl and the chlorotic girl were not in the least jealous, but worshipped her. It is absurd to be jealous of the gods.

How I adored that party! With what passionate interest I overlooked them from my table in the little dining room! How attentively I eavesdropped! I learned where they had spent their holidays, which of them had been to Paris, where their relations lived, what they thought of the postmaster of Ambérieu, and a host of other things, all wonderfully interesting and exciting.

But not for the world would I have made their acquaintance. The landlady offered to introduce me; but I declined the honor. I am afraid she thought me a snob; she was proud of her pensionnaires. It was impossible for me to explain that my reluctance to know them was due to the fact that I loved them even more than she did. To know them would have spoilt everything. From wonderful and mysterious beings, they would have degenerated into six rather dull and pathetic little employés, condemned to pass their lives drearily in a small provincial town.

And then there were the millionaires at Padua. How much we enjoyed those! It was the waiter who told us they were plutocrats. In the restaurant of the Hotel Storione at Padua there is one special table, it appears, reserved for millionaires. Four or five of them lunched there regularly every day while we were in the hotel. Superb figures they were, and wonderfully in character like millionaires in an Italian film. In an American film, of course, the type is very different. A Hollywood millionaire is a strong, silent man, clean-shaven, with a face either like a hatchet or an uncooked muffin. These, on the contrary, had tremendous beards, talked a great deal, were over-dressed and wore white gloves. They looked like a little party of Blue-beards.

Another of my remembered favorites is the siren we saw at the Ristorante Centrale at Genoa. She sat at a neighboring table with four men, all desperately in love with her, talking, one could see by the way they listened and laughed, like all the heroines of Congreve rolled into one. One of the men was a Turk and had to have recourse periodically to the interpreter, without whose aid the majority of diners in that polyglot restaurant would be unable to order their macaroni. One—he was old and paid for the dinner—must have been her husband or her lover. Poor fellow, he looked rather glum sometimes, when she addressed herself too fascinatingly to the Turk, who was her principal victim, or one of the other men. But then she gave him a smile, she lifted her pale blue-grey eyes at him, and he was happy again. No, not happy exactly; happy is the wrong word. Drunk—that would be more like it, I imagine. Deliriously joyful on the surface; and within bottomlessly miserable. So we speculated, romantically, at long range. What we should have discovered on a nearer acquaintance I do not know—I do not want to know.

The most uninteresting human being seen at a little distance by a spectator with a lively fancy and a determination to make the most of life takes on a mysterious charm, becomes odd and exciting. One can work up a thrilling emotion about distant and unknown people—an emotion which it is impossible to recapture after personal acquaintance, but which yields place to understanding and consequent affection or antipathy.

Certain authors have exploited, either deliberately or because they could not do otherwise, their spectator's emotion in the presence of unknown actors. There is Joseph Conrad, for example. The mysterious thrilling charm of his characters, particularly his female characters, is due to the fact that he knows nothing at all about them. He sits at a distance, he watches them acting and then wonders and wonders, through pages of Marlow's winding narratives, why on earth they acted as they did, what were their motives, what they felt and thought. The God's-eye view of those novelists who really know, or pretend they know, exactly what is going on in the minds of their characters, is exchanged for the traveler's-eye view, the view of the stranger who starts with no knowledge whatever of the actors' personalities and can only infer from their gestures what is happening in their minds. Conrad, it must be admitted, manages to infer very little; he lacks the paleontologist's imagination, has little power of reconstructing thought from seen behavior. At the end of a novel, his heroines are as shadowy as they were at the beginning. They have acted, and Conrad has lengthily wondered—without discovering—why they have acted in this particular way. His bewilderment is infectious; the reader is just as hopelessly puzzled as the author and, incidentally, finds the characters just as wonderfully mysterious. Mystery is delightful and exciting; but it is foolish to admire it too highly. A thing is mysterious merely because it is unknown. There will always be mysteries because there will always be unknown and unknowable things. But it is best to know what is knowable. There is no credit about not knowing what can be known. Some literary men, for example, positively pride themselves on their ignorance of science; they are fools and arrogant at that. If Conrad's characters are mysterious, it is not because they are complicated, difficult, or subtle characters, but simply because he does not understand them; not knowing what they are like, he speculates, unsuccessfully, and finally admits that he finds them inscrutable. The honesty with which he confesses his ignorance is meritorious, not the ignorance. The characters of the great novelists, like Dostoevsky and Tolstoy, are not mysterious; they are perfectly well understood and clearly displayed. Such writers live with their creations. Conrad only looks on from a distance, without understanding them, without even making up plausible hypotheses about them out of his imagination.

He differs in this respect from Miss Katherine Mansfield, another writer who takes the traveler's-eye view of human beings. For Miss Mansfield has a lively fancy. Like Conrad, she sees her characters from a distance, as though at another table in a café she overhears snatches of their conversations—about their aunts in Battersea, their stamp collections, their souls—and she finds them extraordinary, charming beyond all real and knowable people, odd, immensely exciting. She finds that they are Life itself—lovely, fantastic Life. Very rarely does she go beyond this long-range café acquaintanceship with her personages, rarely makes herself at home in their flat everyday lives. But where Conrad bewilderedly speculates, Miss Mansfield uses her imagination. She invents suitable lives for the fabulous creatures glimpsed at the café. And how thrilling those fancied lives always are! Thrilling, but just for that reason not very convincing. Miss Mansfield's studies of interiors are like those brilliant paleontological reconstructions one sees in books of popular science—the ichthyosaurus in its native waters, pterodactyls fluttering and swooping in the tepid tertiary sky—too excitingly romantic, in spite of their air of realism, to be quite genuine. Her characters are seen with an extraordinary brilliance and precision, as one sees a party of people in a lighted drawing-room, at night, through an uncurtained window—one of those mysteriously significant Parties in Parlors of which we read in Peter Bell:

Some sipping punch, some sipping tea,
And all as silent as could be,
All silent, and all damned.

One sees them for a moment, haloed with significance. They seem fabulous (though of course, in point of actual fact and to those sitting in the room with them, they are nothing of the kind). Then one passes, they disappear. Each of Miss Mansfield's stories is a window into a lighted room. The glimpse of the inhabitants sipping their tea and punch is enormously exciting. But one knows nothing, when one has passed, of what they are really like. That is why, however thrilling at a first reading, her stories do not wear. Chekhov's do; but then he had lived with his people as well as looked at them through the window. The traveler's-eye view of men and women is not satisfying. A man might spend his life in trains and restaurants and know nothing of humanity at the end. To know, one must be an actor as well as a spectator. One must dine at home as well as in restaurants, must give up the amusing game of peeping in at unknown windows to live quietly, flatly, unexcitingly indoors. Still, the game, if it is kept as an occasional diversion and not treated as the serious business of life, is a very good one. And on a journey it is your only traveling picquet.

[*Along the Road*, 1925]

Guide-Books

FOR EVERY TRAVELER who has any taste of his own, the only useful guide-book will be the one which he himself has written. All others are an exasperation. They mark with asterisks the works of art which he finds dull, and they pass over in silence those which he admires. They make him travel long miles to see a mound of rubbish; they go into ecstasies over mere antiquity. Their practical information is invariably out-of-date. They recommend bad hotels and qualify good ones as "modest." In a word, they are intolerable.

How often I have cursed Baron Baedeker[1] for sending me through the dust to see some nauseating Sodoma[2] or drearily respectable Andrea del Sarto! How angry I have been with him for starring what is old merely because it is old! And how I have hated him for his lack of discrimination! He has a way of lumping all old things of one class together and treating them as if, being made at the same period, their merit were exactly equal. For example, the stained glass windows at Sens are treated by the guide-books as though they were just like all other stained glass of the fourteenth century, when in fact they are unique in boldness and beauty of design. Some very great artist made the series of Bible illustrations at Sens. The Baron speaks as highly of the competent craftsman's work at Chartres and Canterbury.

Similarly the monuments in the church of Brou and the choir screen at Chartres get as many stars as the tomb of Ilaria del Carretto at Lucca, or Della Robbia's bas-relief in the Opera del Duomo at Florence. They are all of them specimens of renaissance sculpture. There is only this slight difference between them that the Italian works happen to be consummate masterpieces, while the French are mere barbarisms—that at Brou positively and piercingly vulgar, that at Chartres well-meaning, laborious, and sincerely dull. And so totally does the Baron lack a sense of proportion that he gives as many stars to the church of Brou as to Bourges cathedral, recommending with equal enthusiasm a horrible little architectural nightmare

1. Karl Baedeker (1801–1859). German publisher best known for his series of guide-books which bear his name.
2. Sodoma was the sobriquet of Giovanni Bazzi (1477–1549). Italian painter.

and the grandest, the most strangely and fabulously beautiful building in Europe.

Imbecile! But a learned, and, alas, indispensable imbecile. There is no escape; one must travel in his company—at any rate on a first journey. It is only after having scrupulously done what Baedeker commands, after having discovered the Baron's lapses in taste, his artistic prejudices and antiquarian snobberies, that the tourist can compile that personal guide which is the only guide for him. If he had but possessed it on his first tour! But alas, though it is easy to take other people in by your picturesque accounts of places you have never seen, it is hard to take in yourself. The personal guide-book must be the fruit of bitter personal experience.

The only satisfactory substitute for a guide written by oneself is a guide which is copiously illustrated. To know the images of things is the next best to knowing the things themselves. Illustrations allow one to see what precisely it is that the Baron is recommending. A reproduction of those luscious Sodomas would enable one to discount the asterisks in the text. A few photographs of the tombs at Tarquinia would convince one that they were incomparably better worth looking at than the Forum. A picture of the church at Brou would excuse one from ever going near it. The best illustrated guide I know is Pampaloni's Road Book of Tuscany, in which the usual information is briefly summarized, the main routes from place to place described and nothing starred that is not reproduced in a photograph.

For some tastes, I know, Pampaloni seems a little too dry. All the cackle—even as much of it as gets into Baedeker—is cut, and one is left only with a telegraphic statement of facts and the photographs. Personally I have no great weakness for cackle (unless it be the cackle of a genius) and so find Pampaloni perfectly satisfying. Many tourists, however, prefer a more literary guide. They like sentiment, and purple passages and states of soul in front of the Colosseum by moonlight, and all the rest. So do I—but not from the pens of the sort of people who write chatty guides. To me, even Baedeker seems at times rather too lyrical. I like my guides to be informative, unenthusiastic and, where practical matters are concerned, up-to-date—which Baedeker, by the way (reluctant, I suppose, for patriotic reasons to acknowledge the fact of the late War) is not. If I want cackle I take with me a better stylist than the Baron or his gushing substitutes.

The only literary guides I enjoy are the really bad ones—so bad that their badness makes, so to speak, a full circle and becomes something sublime. Your ordinary literary guides are never bad in this superlative way. Theirs is that well-bred, efficient mediocrity for which there is nothing whatever to be said. It is only in obscure local guides that one finds the sublimely ludicrous. In any town it is always worth taking a look at the

local guide. If you are lucky you will find one in which a train is called
"Stephenson's magic babe." Not often, I admit (for it is not every day that
a genius is born who can hit on such felicities); but often enough to make
the search worthwhile. I myself have found some notable passages in local
Italian guides. This description of a sixth-rate "Venus rising from the Sea"
is juicy: *"Venere, abbigliata di una calda nudità, sorge dalle onde. . . . È
una seducente figura di donna, palpitante, vollutuosa. Sembra che sotto
l'epidermide pulsino le vene frementi e scorre tepido il sangue. L'occhio
languido pare inviti a una dolce tregenda."* D'Annunzio[3] himself could
hardly have done better. But the finest specimen of the guide-book style I
have ever met with was in France. It is a description of Dijon. *"Comme
une jolie femme dont une maturité savoureuse arrondit les formes plus
pleines, la capitale de la Bourgogne a fait, en grandissant, éclater la tu-
nique étroite de ses vieilles murailles; elle a revêtu la robe plus moderne et
plus confortable des larges boulevards, des places spacieuses, des
faubourgs s'égrenant dans les jardins; mais elle a gardé le corps aux lignes
pures, aux charmants détails que des siècles épris d'art avaient amoureuse-
ment ornés."*[4] Hats off to France! It is with alacrity, on this occasion, that
I accede to Lord Rothermere's request.

Old guide-books, so out-of-date as to be historical documents, make
excellent traveling companions. An early Murray is a treasure. Indeed, any
volume of European travels, however dull, is interesting, provided that it
be written before the age of railways and Ruskin. It is delightful to read on
the spot the impressions and opinions of tourists who visited a hundred
years ago, in the vehicles and with the aesthetic prejudices of the period,
the places which you are visiting now. The voyage ceases to be a mere tour
through space; you travel through time and thought as well. They are
morally wholesome reading too, these old books of travel; for they make
one realize the entirely accidental character of all our tastes and our fundamental intellectual beliefs. It seems to us axiomatic, for example, that
Giotto was a great artist; and yet Goethe, when he went to Assisi, did not
even take the trouble to look at the frescoes in the church. For him, the
only thing worth seeing at Assisi was the portico of the Roman temple. We
for our part cannot get much pleasure out of Guercino;[5] and yet Stendhal

---

3. Gabriele D'Annunzio (1863–1938). Italian writer and political leader.
4. "Like a pretty woman whose savory maturity rounds off the fullest shapes, the capital of Burgundy, by growing larger, has burst the constricting tunic of its old walls; she has
donned the more modern and more comfortable dress of wide boulevards, districts rippling
with gardens, but she has kept the pure lines of the body, the charming details which the
centuries, in love with art, had lovingly decorated."
5. Guercino (1590–1666). Italian painter.

was ravished by him. We find Canova[6] "amusing" and sometimes, as in the statue of Pauline Borghese, really charming in a soft, voluptuous way (the very cushion on which she reclines bulges out voluptuously; one is reminded of those positively indecent clouds over which Correggio's angels look down at one from the dome at Parma). But we cannot quite agree with Byron when he says "Such as the Great of yore, Canova is today." And yet after all, Goethe, Stendhal, and Byron were no fools. Given their upbringing, they could not have thought differently. We would have thought just as they did, if we had lived a hundred years ago. Our altered standards of appreciation and generally greater tolerance are chiefly the result of increased acquaintance with the art of every nation and period— an acquaintance due in its turn chiefly to photography. The vastly greater part of the world's art has been non-realistic; we know the world's art as our ancestors never did; it is therefore only to be expected that we should be much more favorably disposed to non-realistic art, much less impressed by realism as such than men who were brought up almost exclusively in the knowledge of Greek, Roman, and modern realism. These old books teach us not to be too arrogant and cocksure in our judgments. We too shall look foolish in our turn.

There are so many of these old books and they are all so characteristic of their epoch, that one can select them almost at random from the shelves of a well-stocked library, certain that whatever one lights on will be entertaining and instructive reading. Speaking from my own personal experience, I have always found Stendhal particularly agreeable as an Italian companion. *Les Promenades dans Rome* have accompanied me on many of my walks in that city and never failed to please. Very enjoyable too, when one is in Rome, is the too much neglected Veuillot.[7] I will not pretend that Veuillot is a great writer. Indeed, much of his charm and apparent originality consists in the merely accidental fact that his prejudices were unlike those which most travelers bring with them to Italy. We are so much accustomed to hearing that the temporal power was an unmixed evil and that the priests were the cause of Italy's degradation, that a man who tells us the contrary seems startlingly original. After the denunciations of so many Protestants and freethinkers we read his book, if it be tolerably well written (and Veuillot was a first-rate journalist), with a special pleasure. (It is, in the same way, the unusualness of the point of view from which it is written that makes *Les Paysans* of Balzac seem an even more remarkable book than it really is. We are used to reading novels in which

6. Antonio Canova (1757–1822). Italian sculptor.
7. Louis Veuillot (1813–1883). French author and extreme ultramontanist.

the humble virtues of the peasant are exalted, his hard lot deplored, and the tyranny of the landlord denounced. Balzac starts with the assumption that the peasant is an unmitigated ruffian and demands our sympathy for the unhappy landlord, who is represented as suffering incessant and un-merited persecution at the hands of the peasants. Balzac's reading of social history may not be correct; but it is at least refreshingly unlike that of most novelists who deal with similar themes.) *Les Parfums de Rome* shares with *Les Paysans* the merit of being written from an unexpected point of view. Veuillot tours the papal states determined to see in them the earthly par-adise. And he succeeds. His Holiness has only happy subjects. Outside this blessed fold prowl the wild beasts, Cavour, Mazzini, Garibaldi, and the rest; it is the duty of every right-thinking man to see that they do not break in. This is his theme and he finds in everything he sees excuses for recur-ring to it. *Les Parfums de Rome* is written with a refreshing intemperance of language. Veuillot, like Zimri,[8] was

> So over violent or over civil,
> That every man with him was God or Devil.

Moreover he was logical and had the courage of his convictions. How admirable, for example, is his denunciation of all pagan art on the ground that it is not Christian! While all the rest of the world grovel before the Greeks and Romans, Veuillot, the logical ultramontanist, condemns them and all their works, on principle, contemptuously. It is delightful.

Of the other old traveling companions who have given me pleasure by the way I can only mention a few. There is that mine of information, the Président des Brosses. No one is a better companion on the Italian tour. Our own Young is nearly as good in France. Miss Berry's journals of travel are full of interest. There are good things to be got from Lady Mary Mon-tagu. Beckford is the perfect dilettante. But plain Bible-selling Borrow[9] has the credit of being the first man to appreciate El Greco.

If pictures are not your chief interest, there is the admirable Dr. Burney, whose *Musical Tours* are as instructive as they are delightful. His Italian volumes are valuable, among many other reasons, because they make one realize what had happened, during the eighteenth century, to all the prodi-gious talent which had gone, in the past, to painting pictures, carving stat-ues, and building churches. It had all gone into music. The very street players were accomplished contrapuntists; the peasants sang divinely (you

---

8. Zimri is a character in John Dryden's *Absalom and Achitophel* (Part 1).

9. Arthur Young (1741–1820). English agricultural scientist and author of numerous tour-books. Lady Mary Montagu (1689–1762). English writer. William Thomas Beckford (1760–1844). English writer. George Henry Borrow (1803–1881). English writer.

should hear the way they sing now!), every church had a good choir which was perpetually producing new masses, motets, and oratorios; there was hardly a lady or gentleman who was not a first-rate amateur performer; there were innumerable concerts. Dr. Burney[1] found it a musician's paradise. And what has happened to Italian genius nowadays? Does it still exist? Or is it dead?

It still exists, I think; but it has been deflected out of music, as it was deflected out of the visual arts, into politics and, later, into business and engineering. The first two-thirds of the nineteenth century were sufficiently occupied in the achievement of freedom and unity. The sixty years since then have been devoted to the exploitation of the country's resources; and such energy as has been left over from that task has gone into politics. One day, when they have finished putting modern comfort into the old house, have turned out the obstreperous servants and installed a quiet, honest housekeeper, one day, perhaps, the Italians will allow their energy and their talent to flow back into the old channels. Let us hope they will.

[*Along the Road,* 1925]

Spectacles

I NEVER MOVE without a plentiful supply of optical glass. A pair of spectacles for reading, a pair for long range, with a couple of monocles in reserve—these go with me everywhere. To break all these, it would need an earthquake or a railway accident. And absence of mind would have to be carried to idiocy before they could all be lost. Moreover, there is a further safety in a numerous supply: for matter, who can doubt it? is not neutral, as the men of science falsely teach, but slightly malignant, on the side of the devils against us. This being so, one pair of spectacles must inevitably break or lose itself, just when you can least afford to do without and are least able to replace it. But inanimate matter, so called, is no fool; and when a pair of spectacles realizes that you carry two or three other pairs in your pockets and suit-cases, it will understand that the game is hopeless and, so far from deliberately smashing or losing itself, will take pains to remain intact.

But when, in any month after the vernal equinox and before the autumn, my wanderings take me southwards, towards the sun, my armory of spectacles is enlarged by the addition of three pairs of colored glasses—

---

1. Charles Burney (1726–1814). English musicologist.

two of lighter and darker shades of green, and one black. The glare from dusty roads, from white walls and the metallic, blue-hot sky is painful and even dangerous. As the summer advances or retreats, as the light of each day waxes or declines, I adjust to my nose the pale green, the dark green, or the black spectacles. In this way I am able to temper the illumination of the world to my exact requirements.

But even if I suffered not at all from excess of light and could perform without winking the feats of the eagle and the oxyacetylene welder, I should still take colored glasses with me on my southward travels. For they have an aesthetic as well as a merely practical use. They improve the landscape as well as soothe the eyes.

As one approaches the great desert belt which bands the earth with some thousand miles of aridity to this side of the tropic of Cancer, the landscape suffers a change which to us northerners at least seems a change for the worse. It loses its luxuriant greenness. South of Lyons (except among the mountains and the marshes) there is no grass worthy of the name. The deciduous trees grow with reluctance, yielding place to the black cypress and pine, the dark green laurel and juniper, the pale grey olive. The greens in an Italian landscape are either pale and dusty or glossily dark. Only when you climb to two thousand feet—and by no means invariably then—does anything like the brilliant, the seemingly self-luminous verdure of the English scene appear. The typical north Italian landscape is one of hills, the lower slopes grey with olives, the summits, when they are above the level of cultivation, bare and brown. It is a landscape that makes a not entirely satisfactory compromise between the northern type and the fully southern. The English scene is made rich and comfortable by the bosomy forms and the damply glowing colors of its luxuriant foliage. And its rather rotund earthiness is tempered and made romantic by the bloom of mist that half veils it from sight. The southern, Mediterranean landscape, which makes its first Italian appearance at Terracina, is bare, sharp-outlined, and austerely brilliant. The air is clear, and the far-seen earth seems itself to be made of colored air. The landscape of Northern Italy is neither northern nor southern—neither aerially bright and light nor, on the other hand, rounded, or softly, luxuriously green.

It is here, in this half-parched landscape that is not yet refined to a bright asceticism, that the judicious traveler will don his green spectacles. The effect is magical. Every blade of dusty grass becomes on the instant rich with juicy life. Whatever greenness lurks in the grey of the olive trees shines out, intensified. The dried-up woods reburgeon. The vines and the growing corn seem to have drunk of a refreshing rain. All that the scene lacked to make it perfectly beautiful is instantaneously added. Through green spectacles, it becomes the northern landscape, but transformed and glorified—brighter, more nobly dramatic and romantic.

Green spectacles make excellent wearing, too, on the shores of the northern Mediterranean. In the south the blue of the sea is beautifully dark, like lapis-lazuli. It is the wine-dark sea of antiquity in contrast with which the sunlit land seems more than ever light, clear-colored, and aerial. But north of Rome the blue is insufficiently intense; it is a china not a lazuline blue. The sea at Monaco and Genoa, at Spezia and Civitavecchia has the blue, glassy stare of a doll's eye—a stare that becomes very soon enraging in its enormous blankness and brightness. Put on green spectacles and this blank stare becomes at once the darkly glaucous, enigmatic gaze that shines up, between the cypresses, from the pools in the Villa d'Este gardens at Tivoli. From imbecile, the sea turns siren, and the arid hills that overhang it break into verdure as though beneath the feet of the spring.

Or if you like, you may put on black spectacles and so deepen the color till it approaches that of the wine-dark Mediterranean of Greece and Magna Graecia and the isles. Black spectacles do nothing, however, to make the land more southern in aspect. By the side of their dark sea, the southern coasts seem built of bright air. Black spectacles may darken the northern sea; but they also give weight and an added solidity to the land. The glass which shall make the world seem brighter, clearer, and lighter, put sunlight into the grey landscape and turn north into south still, alas, remains to be invented.

[*Along the Road*, 1925]

The Country

IT IS A CURIOUS FACT, of which I can think of no satisfactory explanation, that enthusiasm for country life and love of natural scenery are strongest and most widely diffused precisely in those European countries which have the worst climate and where the search for the picturesque involves the greatest discomfort. Nature worship increases in an exact ratio with distance from the Mediterranean. The Italians and the Spanish have next to no interest in nature for its own sake. The French feel a certain affection for the country, but not enough to make them desire to live in it if they can possibly inhabit the town. The south Germans and Swiss form an apparent exception to the rule. They live nearer to the Mediterranean than the Parisians, and yet they are fonder of the country. But the exception, as I have said, is only apparent; for owing to their remoteness from the ocean and the mountainous conformation of the land, these people enjoy for a large part of each year a climate, that is, to all intents, arctic. In England, where the climate is detestable, we love the country so much that we are prepared, for the privilege of living in it, to get up at seven, summer and winter, bicycle, wet or fine, to a distant station and make an hour's journey to our place of labor. In our spare moments we go for walking tours, and we regard caravaning as a pleasure. In Holland the climate is far more unpleasant than in England and we should consequently expect the Dutch to be even keener country-fanciers than ourselves. The ubiquitous water makes it difficult, however, for season-ticket holders to settle down casually in the Dutch countryside. But if unsuitable as building land, the soggy meadows of the Low Countries are firm enough to carry tents. Unable to live permanently in the country, the Dutch are the greatest campers in the world. Poor Uncle Toby, when he was campaigning in those parts, found the damp so penetrating, that he was forced to burn good brandy in his tent to dry the air. But then my Uncle Toby was a mere Englishman, brought up in a climate which, compared with that of Holland, is balmy. The hardier Dutch camp out for pleasure. Of Northern Germany it is enough to say that it is the home of the wander-birds. And as for Scandinavia—it is well known that there is no part of the world, excluding the tropics, where people so freely divest themselves of their clothing. The Swedish passion for nature is so strong that it can only be adequately expressed when in a state of nature. "As souls unbodied," says Donne, "bodies unclothed must be to taste whole joys." Noble, nude, and far more modern than any other people in Europe, they sport in the icy waters of the Baltic, they roam naked in the primeval forest. The cautious Italian, meanwhile, bathes in his tepid sea during only two months out of the twelve; always wears a vest under his shirt and never leaves the town, if he can possibly help it, except when the summer is at its most hellish, and again, for a little while, in the autumn, to superintend the making of his wine.

Strange and inexplicable state of affairs! Is it that the dwellers under inclement skies are trying to bluff themselves into a belief that they inhabit Eden? Do they deliberately love nature in the hope of persuading themselves that she is as beautiful in the damp and darkness as in the sunlight? Do they brave the discomforts of northern country life in order to be able to say to those who live in more favored lands, You see, our countryside is just as delightful as yours; and the proof is that we live in it!

But whatever the reason, the fact remains that nature worship does increase with distance from the sun. To search for causes is hopeless; but it is easy and at the same time not uninteresting to catalogue effects. Thus, our

Anglo-Saxon passion for the country has had the result of turning the country into one vast town; but a town without the urban convenience which makes tolerable life in a city. For we all love the country so much, that we desire to live in it, if only during the night, when we are not at work. We build cottages, buy season tickets and bicycles to take us to the station. And meanwhile the country perishes. The Surrey I knew as a boy was full of wildernesses. Today Hindhead is hardly distinguishable from the Elephant and Castle. Mr. Lloyd George has built a weekend cottage (not, one feels, without a certain appositeness) at the foot of the Devil's jumps; and several thousand people are busily following his example. Every lane is now a street. Harrod's and Selfridge's call daily. There is no more country, at any rate within fifty miles of London. Our love has killed it.

Except in summer, when it is too hot to stay in town, the French, and still more, the Italians, do not like the country. The result is that they still have country not to like. Solitude stretches almost to the gates of Paris. (And Paris, remember, still has gates; you drive up to them along country roads, enter, and find yourself within a few minutes of the center of the city.) The silence sleeps unbroken, except by the faint music of ghosts, within a mile of the Victor Emanuel monument at Rome.

In France, in Italy none but countrymen live in the country. Agriculture there is taken seriously; farms are still farms and not weekend cottages; and the corn is still permitted to grow on what, in England, would be desirable building land.

In Italy, despite the fact that the educated Italians like the country still less than the French, there are fewer complete solitudes than in France, because there are more countrymen. And how few there are in France! A drive from the Belgian frontier to the Mediterranean puts life and meaning into those statistics from which we learn, academically in theory, that France is under-populated. Long stretches of open road extend between town and town.

> Like stones of worth they thinly placed are,
> Or captain jewels in the carcanet.[2]

Even the villages are few and far between. And those innumerable farms which shine out from among the olive trees on Italian hillsides—one looks in vain for their French counterpart. Driving through the fertile plains of Central France, one can turn one's eyes over the fields and scarcely see a house. And then, what forests still grow on French soil!

2. From Shakespeare's Sonnet #52.

Huge tracts of uninhabited woodland, with not a weekender or a walking-tourist to be seen within their shades.

This state of things is delightful to me personally; for I like the country, enjoy solitude, and take no interest in the political future of France. But to a French patriot I can imagine that a drive across his native land must seem depressing. Huge populations, upon whose skulls the bump of philo-progenitiveness can be seen at a quarter of a mile, pullulate on the further side of almost every frontier. Without haste, without rest, as though by a steadily continued miracle, the Germans and the Italians multiply them-selves, like loaves and fishes. Every three years a million brand new Teu-tons peer across the Rhine, a million Italians are wondering where they are going to find room, in their narrow country, to live. And there are no more Frenchmen. Twenty years hence, what will happen? The French Govern-ment offers prizes to those who produce large families. In vain; everybody knows all about birth control and even in the least-educated classes there are no prejudices and a great deal of thrift. Hordes of blackamoors are drilled and armed; but blackamoors can be but a poor defense, in the long run, against European philoprogenitiveness. Sooner or later, this half-empty land will be colonized. It may be done peacefully, it may be done with violence; let us hope peacefully, with the consent and at the invitation of the French themselves. Already the French import, temporarily, I forget how many foreign laborers every year. In time, no doubt, the foreigners will begin to settle: the Italians in the south, the Germans in the east, the Belgians in the north, perhaps even a few English in the west.

Frenchmen may not like the plan; but until all nations agree to practice birth control to exactly the same extent, it is the best that can be devised.

The Portuguese who, in the later sixteenth and the seventeenth century, suffered acutely from under-population (half the able-bodied men had em-igrated to the colonies, where they died in war or of tropical diseases, while those who stayed at home were periodically decimated by famine—for the colonies produced only gold, not bread) solved their problem by importing negro slaves to work the deserted fields. The negroes settled. They intermarried with the inhabitants. In two or three generations the race which had conquered half the world was extinct, and Portugal, with the exception of a small area in the north, was inhabited by a hybrid race of Eur-Africans. The French may think themselves lucky if, avoiding war, they can fill their depleted country with civilized white men.

Meanwhile, the emptiness of France is a delight to every lover of na-ture and solitude. But even in Italy, where farms and peasants and peas-ants' children are thick on the land, the lover of the country feels much happier than he does in what may actually be more sparsely inhabited dis-tricts of the home counties. For farms and peasants are country products, as truly native to the land as trees or growing corn, and as inoffensive. It is the urban interloper who ruins the English country. Neither he nor his house belong to it. In Italy, on the other hand, when the rare trespasser from the town does venture into the country, he finds it genuinely rustic. The country is densely populated, but it is still the country. It has not been killed by the deadly kindness of those who, like myself, are nature's townsmen.

The time is not far distant, I am afraid, when every countryside in Europe, even the Spanish, will be invaded by nature lovers from the towns. It is not so long ago, after all, since Evelyn was horrified and disgusted by the spectacle of the rocks at Clifton. Till the end of the eighteenth century every sensible man, even in England, even in Sweden, feared and detested mountains. The modern enthusiasm for wild nature is a recent growth and began—along with kindness to animals, industrialism and railway traveling—among the English. (It is, perhaps, not surprising that the people which first made their cities uninhabitable with dirt, noise, and smoke should also have been the first to love nature.) From this island country sentiment has spread with machinery. All the world welcomed machinery with delight; but country sentiment has so far flourished only in the north. Still, there are evident signs that even the Latins are becoming infected by it. In France and Italy wild nature has become—though to a far less extent than in England—the object of *snobisme*. It is rather chic, in those countries, to be fond of nature. In a few years, I repeat, everybody will adore it as a matter of course. For even in the north those who do not in the least like the country are made to imagine that they do by the artful and never-ceasing suggestions of the people whose interest is that the country should be liked. No modern man, even if he loathed the country, could resist the appeal of the innumerable advertisements, published by railways, motor-car manufacturers, thermos-flask makers, sporting tailors, house agents, and all the rest whose livelihood depends on his frequently visiting the country. Now the art of advertising in the Latin countries is still poorly developed. But it is improving even there. The march of progress is irresistible. Fiat and the State Railways have only to hire American advertising managers to turn the Italians into a race of weekenders and season-ticket holders. Already there is a *Città Giardino* on the outskirts of Rome; Ostia is being developed as a residential seaside suburb; the recently opened motor road has placed the Lakes at the mercy of Milan. My grandchildren, I foresee, will have to take their holidays in Central Asia.

[*Along the Road*, 1925]

Montesenario

IT WAS MARCH and the snow was melting. Half wintry, half vernal, the mountain looked patchy, like a mangy dog. The southward slopes were bare; but in every hollow, on the sunless side of every tree, the snow still lay, white under the blue transparent shadows.

We walked through a little pine wood; the afternoon sunlight breaking through the dark foliage lit up here a branch, there a length of trunk, turning the ruddy bark into a kind of golden coral. Beyond the wood the hill lay bare to the summit. On the very crest a mass of buildings lifted their high sunlit walls against the pale sky, a chilly little New Jerusalem. It was the monastery of Montesenario. We climbed towards it, toilsomely for the last stage in the pilgrim's progress from Florence to Montesenario is uncommonly steep and the motor must be left behind. And suddenly, as though to welcome us, as though to encourage our efforts, the heavenly city disgorged a troop of angels. Turning a corner of the track we saw them coming down to meet us, by two and two in a long file; angels in black cassocks with round black hats on their heads—a seminary taking its afternoon airing. They were young boys, the eldest sixteen or seventeen, the youngest not more than ten. Flapping along in their black skirts they walked with an unnatural decorum. It was difficult to believe, when one saw the little fellows at the head of the crocodile, with the tall Father in charge striding along at their side, it was difficult to believe that they were not masquerading. It seemed a piece of irreverent fun; a caricature by Goya come to life. But their faces were serious; chubby or adolescently thin, they wore already an unctuously, clerical expression. It was no joke. Looking at those black-robed children, one wished that it had been.

We climbed on; the little priestlings descended out of sight. And now at last we were at the gates of the heavenly city. A little paved and parapeted platform served as landing to the flight of steps that led up into the heart of the convent. In the middle of the platform stood a more than life-sized statue of some unheard-of saint. It was a comically admirable piece of eighteenth-century baroque. Carved with coarse brilliance, the creature gesticulated ecstatically, rolling its eyes to heaven; its garments flapped around it in broad folds. It was not, somehow, the sort of saint one expected to see standing sentinel over the bleakest hermitage in Tuscany. And the convent itself—that too seemed incongruous on the top of this icy mountain. For the heavenly city was a handsome early baroque affair with settecento trimmings and additions. The church was full of twiddly gilt carvings and dreadfully competent pictures; the remains of the seven pious Florentines who, in the thirteenth century, fled from the city of destruction in the plain below, and founded this hermitage on the mountain, were coffered in a large gold and crystal box, illuminated, like a show-case in the drawing-room of a collector of porcelain, by concealed electric lights. No, the buildings were ludicrous. But after all, what do buildings matter. A man can paint beautiful pictures in a slum, can write poetry in Wigan; and conversely he can live in an exquisite house, surrounded by masterpieces of ancient art and yet (as one sees almost invariably when collectors of the antique, relying for once on their own judgment, and not on tradition, "go in for" modern art) be crassly insensitive and utterly without taste. Within certain limits, environment counts for very little. It is only when environment is extremely unfavorable that it can blast or distort the powers of the mind. And however favorable, it can do nothing to extend the limits set by nature to a man's ability. So here the architecture seemed impossibly incongruous with the bleak place, with the very notion of a hermitage; but the hermits who live in the midst of it are probably not even aware of its existence. In the shade of the absurd statue of San Filippo Benizi a Buddha would be able to think as Buddhistically as beneath the bo-tree.

In the grounds of the monastery we saw half a dozen black-frocked Servites sawing wood—sawing with vigor and humility, in spite of the twiddly gilding in the church and the settecento bell tower. They looked the genuine article. And the view from the mountain's second peak was in the grandest eremitic tradition. The hills stretched away as far as the eye could reach into the wintry haze, like a vast heaving sea frozen to stillness. The valleys were filled with blue shadow, and all the sunward slopes were the color of rusty gold. At our feet the ground fell away into an immense blue gulf. The gauzy air softened every outline, smoothed away every detail, leaving only golden lights and violet shadows floating like the disembodied essence of a landscape, under the pale sky.

We stood for a long time looking out over that kingdom of silence and solemn beauty. The solitude was as profound as the shadowy gulf beneath us; it stretched to the misty horizons and up into the topless sky. Here at the heart of it, I thought, a man might begin to understand something about that part of his being which does not reveal itself in the quotidian commerce of life; which the social contacts do not draw forth, spark-like, from the sleeping flint that is an untried spirit; that part of him, of whose very existence he is only made aware in solitude and silence. And if there happens to be no silence in his life, if he is never solitary, then he may go down to his grave without a knowledge of its existence, much less an understanding of its nature or realization of its potentialities.

We retraced our steps to the monastery and thence walked down the steep path to the motor. A mile further down the road towards Pratolino, we met the priestlings returning from their walk. Poor children! But was their lot worse, I wondered, than that of the inhabitants of the city in the valley? On their mountain top they lived under a tyrannous rule, they were taught to believe in a number of things manifestly silly. But was the rule any more tyrannous than that of the imbecile conventions which control the lives of social beings in the plain? Was snobbery about duchesses and distinguished novelists more reasonable than snobbery about Jesus Christ and the Saints? Was hard work to the greater glory of God more detestable than eight hours a day in an office for the greater enrichment of the Jews? Temperance was a bore, no doubt; but was it so nauseatingly wearisome as excess? And the expense of spirit in prayer and meditation—was that so much less amusing than the expense of spirit in a waste of shame? Driving down towards the city in the plain, I wondered. And when, in the Via Tornabuoni, we passed Mrs. Thingummy, in the act of laboriously squeezing herself out on to the pavement through the door of her gigantic limousine, I suddenly and perfectly understood what it was that had made those seven rich Florentine merchants, seven hundred years ago, abandon their position in the world, and had sent them up into the high wilderness, to live in holes at the top of Montesenario. I looked back; Mrs. Thingummy was waddling across the pavement into the jeweler's shop. Yes, I perfectly understood.

[Along the Road, 1925]

Patinir's River

THE RIVER FLOWS in a narrow valley between hills. A broad, a brimming, and a shining river. The hills are steep and all of a height. Where the river bends, the hills on one side jut forward in a bastion, the hills on the other retreat. There are cliffs, there are hanging woods, dark with foliage. The sky is pale above this strip of fantastically carved and scalloped earth. A pale sky from which it must sometimes rain Chinese white. For there is an ashen pallor over the rocks; and the green of the grass and the trees is tinged with white till it has taken on the color of the "Emerald Green" of children's paint-boxes.

Brimming and shining river, pale crags, and trees richly dark, slopes where the turf is the color of whitened verdigris—I took these things for fancies. Peering into the little pictures, each painted with a million tiny strokes of a four-haired sable brush, I laughed with pleasure at the beauty of the charming invention. This Joachim Patinir,[3] I thought, imagines deli-

---

3. Joachim (de) Patinir (1485–1524). Dutch painter.

cately. For years I was accustomed to float along that crag-reflecting river as down a river of the mind, out of the world.

And then one day—one wet day in autumn—driving out of Namur towards Dinant through the rain, suddenly I found myself rolling, as fast as ten horses ventured to take me through the slippery mud, along the bank of this imaginary stream. The rain, it is true, a little blurred the scene. Greyly it hung, like a dirty glass, between the picture and the beholder's eye. But through it, unmistakably, I distinguished the fabulous landscape of the Fleming's little paintings. Crags, river, emerald green slopes, dark woods were there, indubitably real, I had given to Joachim Patinir the credit that was due to God. What I had taken for his exquisite invention was the real and actual Meuse. Mile after mile we drove, from Namur to Dinant; from Dinant, mile after mile, to Givet. And it was Patinir all the way; winding river, the double line of jutting and re-entrant hill, verdigris grass, cliffs and pensile trees all the way. At Givet we left the river; for our destination was Reims and our road led us through Rethel. We left the river, but left it with the impression that it wound back, Patinir landscape after Patinir landscape, all the way to its distant source at Poissy. I should like to think, indeed, that it did. For Patinir was a charming painter and his surviving works are few. Two hundred miles of him would not be at all too much.

[*Along the Road*, 1925]

Portoferraio

THE SKY was Tiepolo's palette. A cloud of smoke mounted into the blue, white where it looked towards the sun and darkening, through the color of the shadowed folds in a wedding gown, to grey. In the foreground on the right a tall pink house went up, glowing like a geranium, into the sunlight. There was the stuff there for a Madonna with attendant saints and angels; or a scene from Trojan history; or a Crucifixion; or one of the little amours of Jupiter Tonans.

The earth was Mediterranean—a piece of the Riviera completely surrounded by water. In a word, Elba. The hills dived down into a handsomely curved bay, full of bright, staring blue sea. On the headland at one end of the bay Portoferraio was piled up in tiers of painted stucco. At its feet lay a little harbor bristling with masts. A smell of fish and the memory of Napoleon haunted the atmosphere inveterately. Conscience and Baron Baedeker had told us that we ought to visit Napoleon's house now, very suitably, a natural history museum. But we had hardened our hearts and would not go. It is very unpleasant not to have done one's duty. "How tedious is a guilty conscience," says the Cardinal in *The Duchess of Malfi*. He was quite right. We had walked the blazing streets groaning under conviction of sin.

And then, passing through a gateway in the walls of the old town, we found ourselves confronted by a scene that entirely relieved us of all our sense of guilt. For we were looking at something compared with which a house full of Napoleonic souvenirs was so obviously second-rate and dull that our rebellion against Baedeker ceased to be criminal and became positively meritorious.

Below us, on the further side of a blue inlet of the sea, and with the mountains behind it, lay a little piece of the Black Country. In the midst stood a group of blast furnaces with three huge chimneys rising from beside them like the bell towers of a cathedral. To the right of them were five or six more chimneys. Three huge cranes were perched at the water's edge, and an iron bridge led from the wharves inland to the furnaces. The chimneys, the cranes, the furnaces and buildings, the heap of rubbish, the very ground in this little area between the Mediterranean and the mountains— all were soot-black. Black against the sky, black against the golden-glaucous hills, blackly reflected in the shining blue water.

I should have painted the scene if I had known how. It was exceedingly beautiful. Beautiful and dramatic too. The mind delights in violent contrasts. Birmingham is frightful enough where it is, its body in Warwickshire and its sooty tentacles stretching out across the undulating land into Stafford. But set it down in Sicily or on the shores of Lago Maggiore and its frightfulness becomes at once more painfully apparent. In Warwickshire it is a full-length sermon on civilization, but one sleeps through sermons. Beside the Mediterranean it becomes the most bitingly memorable of epigrams. Moreover, the actual Birmingham of Warwickshire is too large to be taken in as a whole. This single piece of blackness between the blue sky and the blue sea was compactly symbolic. And because the sky and the grass were still visible all round it, the contest between industrialism and the natural beauties of the earth was much more vividly realized than where, as in the great towns of the north, industrialism has completely triumphed and one is not even aware of the existence of what has been conquered.

We stood for a long time, watching the smoke from the chimneys as it mounted into the still air. White gauze; white satin, glossy or shadowed; feathery grey—Tiepolo's angels hovered; and the blue sky was the Madonna's silken robe; and the tall pink house on our right was the color of one of those very handsome velvets to which, in the paradise of the last of the Venetians, the blest are so excusably partial.

[*Along the Road,* 1925]

The Palio at Siena

OUR ROOMS were in a tower. From the windows one looked across the brown tiled roofs to where, on its hill, stood the cathedral. A hundred feet below was the street, a narrow canyon between high walls, perennially sunless; the voices of the passersby came up, reverberating, as out of a chasm. Down there they walked always in shadow; but in our tower we were the last to lose the sunlight. On the hot days it was cooler, no doubt, down in the street; but we at least had the winds. The waves of the air broke against our tower and flowed past it on either side. And at evening, when only the belfries and the domes and the highest roofs were still flushed by the declining sun, our windows were level with the flight of the swifts and swallows. Sunset after sunset all through the long summer, they wheeled and darted round our tower. There was always a swarm of them intricately maneuvering just outside the window. They swerved this way and that, they dipped and rose, they checked their headlong flight with a flutter of their long pointed wings and turned about within their own length. Compact, smooth, and tapering, they seemed the incarnation of airy speed. And their thin, sharp, arrowy cry was speed made audible. I have sat at my window watching them tracing their intricate arabesques until I grew dizzy; till their shrill crying sounded as though from within my ears and their flying seemed a motion, incessant, swift, and bewilderingly multitudinous, behind my eyes. And all the while the sun declined, the shadows climbed higher up the houses and towers, and the light with which they were tipped became more rosy. And at last the shadow had climbed to the very top and the city lay in a grey and violent twilight beneath the pale sky.

One evening, towards the end of June, as I was sitting at the window looking at the wheeling birds, I heard through the crying of the swifts the sound of a drum. I looked down into the shadowy street, but could see nothing. Rub-a-dub, dub, dub, dub—the sound grew louder and louder, and suddenly there appeared round the corner where our street bent out of sight, three personages out of a Pinturicchio fresco. They were dressed in liveries of green and yellow—yellow doublets slashed and tagged with green, parti-colored hose and shoes, with feathered caps of the same colors. Their leader played the drum. The two who followed carried green and yellow banners. Immediately below our tower the street opens out a little into a tiny piazza. In this clear space the three Pinturicchio figures came to a halt and the crowd of little boys and loafers who followed at their heels grouped themselves round to watch. The drummer quickened his beat and the two banner-bearers stepped forward into the middle of the little square. They stood there for a moment quite still, the right foot a little in advance of the other, the left fist on the hip and the lowered banners drooping from the right. Then, together, they lifted the banners and began to wave them round their heads. In the wind of their motion the flags opened out. They were the same size and both of them green and yellow, but the colors were arranged in a different pattern on each. And what patterns! Nothing more "modern" was ever seen. They might have been designed by Picasso for the Russian Ballet. Had they been by Picasso the graver critics would have called them futuristic, the sprightlier (I must apologize for both these expressions) jazz. But the flags were not Picasso's; they were designed some four hundred years ago by the nameless genius who dressed the Sienese for their yearly pageant. This being the case, the critics can only take off their hats. The flags are classical, they are High Art; there is nothing more to be said.

The drum beat on. The bannermen waved their flags, so artfully that the whole expanse of patterned stuff was always unfurled and tremulously stretched along the air. They passed the flags from one hand to the other, behind their backs, under a lifted leg. Then, at last, drawing themselves together to make a supreme effort, they tossed their banners into the air. High they rose, turning slowly, over and over, hung for an instant at the height of their trajectory, then dropped back, the weighted stave foremost, towards their throwers, who caught them as they fell. A final wave, then the drum returned to its march rhythm, the bannermen shouldered their flags, and followed by the anachronistic children and idlers from the twentieth century, Pinturicchio's three young bravos swaggered off up the dark street out of sight and at length, the drum taps coming faintlier and ever faintlier, out of hearing.

Every evening after that, while the swallows were in full cry and flight about the tower, we heard the beating of the drum. Every evening, in the little piazza below us, a fragment of Pinturicchio came to life. Sometimes it was our friends in green and yellow who returned to wave their flags beneath our windows. Sometimes it was men from the other *contrade* or districts of the town, in blue and white, red and white, black, white and orange, white, green and red, yellow and scarlet. Their bright pied doublets and parti-colored hose shone out from among the drabs and funereal blacks of the twentieth-century crowd that surrounded them. Their spread flags waved in the street below, like the painted wings of enormous butterflies. The drummer quickened his beat, and to the accompaniment of a long-drawn rattle, the banners leapt up, furled and fluttering, into the air.

To the stranger who has never seen a Palio these little dress rehearsals are richly promising and exciting. Charmed by these present hints, he looks forward eagerly to what the day itself holds in store. Even the Sienese are excited. The pageant, however familiar, does not pall on them.

And all the gambler in them, all the local patriot looks forward to the result of the race. Those last days of June before the first Palio, that middle week of August before the second, are days of growing excitement and tension in Siena. One enjoys the Palio the more for having lived through them.

Even the mayor and corporation are infected by the pervading excitement. They are so far carried away that, in the last days of June, they send a small army of men down in the great square before the Palazzo Comunale to eradicate every blade of grass or tuft of moss that can be found growing in the crannies between the flagstones. It amounts almost to a national characteristic, this hatred of growing things among the works of men.

I have often, in old Italian towns, seen workmen laboriously weeding the less frequented streets and squares. The Colosseum, mantled till thirty or forty years ago with a romantic, Piranesian growth of shrubs, grasses, and flowers, was officially weeded with such extraordinary energy that its ruinousness was sensibly increased. More stones were brought down in those few months of weeding than had fallen of their own accord in the previous thousand years. But the Italians were pleased; which is, after all, the chief thing that matters. Their hatred of weeds is fostered by their national pride; a great country, and one which specially piques itself on being modern, cannot allow weeds to grow even among its ruins. I entirely understand and sympathize with the Italian point of view. If Mr. Ruskin and his disciples had talked about my house and me as they talked about Italy and the Italians, I too should pique myself on being up-to-date; I should put in bathrooms, central heating, and a lift, I should have all the moss scratched off the walls, I should lay cork lino on the marble floors. Indeed, I think that I should probably, in my irritation, pull down the whole house and build a new one. Considering the provocation they have received, it seems to me that the Italians have been remarkably moderate in the matter of weeding, destroying, and rebuilding. Their moderation is due in part, no doubt, to their comparative poverty. Their ancestors built with such prodigious solidity that it would cost as much to pull down one of their old houses as to build a new one. Imagine, for example, demolishing the Palazzo Strozzi in Florence. It would be about as easy to demolish the Matterhorn. In Rome, which is predominantly a baroque, seventeenth-century city, the houses are made of flimsier stuff. Consequently, modernization progresses there much more rapidly than in most other Italian towns. In wealthier England very little antiquity has been permitted to stand. Thus, most of the great country houses of England were rebuilt during the eighteenth century. If Italy had preserved her independence and her prosperity during the seventeenth, eighteenth, and nineteenth centuries, there would probably be very much less medieval or renaissance work now surviving than is actually the case. Money, then, is lacking to modernize completely. Weeding has the merit of being cheap and, at the same time, richly symbolic. When you say of a town that the grass grows in its streets, you mean that it is utterly dead. Conversely, if there is no grass in its streets, it must be alive. No doubt the mayor and corporation of Siena did not put the argument quite so explicitly. But that the argument was put, somehow, obscurely and below the surface of the mind, I do not doubt. The weeding was symbolic of modernity.

With the weeders came other workmen who built up round the curving flanks of the great piazza a series of wooden stands, six tiers high, for the spectators. The piazza which is shaped, whether by accident or design I do not know, like an ancient theater, became for the time being indeed a theater. Between the seats and the central area of the place, a track was railed off and the slippery flags covered parsimoniously with sand. Expectation rose higher than ever.

And at last the day came. The swallows and swifts wove their arabesques as usual in the bright golden light above the town. But their shrill crying was utterly inaudible, through the deep, continuous, formless murmur of the crowd that thronged the streets and the great piazza. Under its canopy of stone the great bell of the Mangia tower swung incessantly backwards and forwards; it too seemed dumb. The talking, the laughter, the shouting of forty thousand people rose up from the piazza in a column of solid sound, impenetrable to any ordinary noise.

It was after six. We took our places in one of the stands opposite the Palazzo Comunale. Our side of the piazza was already in the shade; but the sun still shone on the palace and its tall slender tower, making their rosy brickwork glow as though by inward fire. An immense concourse of people filled the square and all the tiers of seats round it. There were people in every window, even on the roofs. At the Derby, on boat-race days, at Wembley I have seen larger crowds; but never, I think, so many people confined within so small a space.

The sound of a gunshot broke through the noise of voices; and at the signal a company of mounted carabiniers rode into the piazza, driving the loungers who still thronged the track before them. They were in full dress uniform, black and red, with silver trimmings; cocked hats on their heads and swords in their hands. On their handsome little horses, they looked like a squadron of smart Napoleonic cavalry. The idlers retreated before them, squeezing their way through every convenient opening in the rails into the central area, which was soon densely packed. The track was cleared at a walk and, cleared, was rounded again at the trot, dashingly, in the best Carle Vernet style. The carabiniers got their applause and retired.

The crowd waited expectantly. For a moment there was almost a silence. The bell on the tower ceased to be dumb. Someone in the crowd let loose a couple of balloons. They mounted perpendicularly into the still air, a red sphere and a purple. They passed out of the shadow into the sunlight; and the red became a ruby, the purple a glowing amethyst. When they had risen above the level of the roofs, a little breeze caught them and carried them away, still mounting all the time, over our heads, out of sight.

There was another gunshot and Vernet[4] was exchanged for Pinturic-chio. The noise of the crowd grew louder as they appeared, the bell swung, but gave no sound, and across the square the trumpets of the procession were all but inaudible. Slowly they marched round, the representatives of all the seventeen *contrade* of the city. Besides its drummer and its two bannermen, each *contrada* had a man-at-arms on horseback, three or four halbardiers and young pages, and, if it happened to be one of the ten competing in the race, a jockey, all of them wearing the Pinturicchian livery in its own particular colors. Their progress was slow; for at every fifty paces they stopped, to allow the bannermen to give an exhibition of their skill with the flags. They must have taken the best part of an hour to get round. But the time seemed only too short. The Palio is a spectacle of which one does not grow tired. I have seen it three times now and was as much delighted on the last occasion as on the first.

English tourists are often skeptical about the Palio. They remember those terrible "pageants" which were all the rage some fifteen years ago in their own country, and they imagine that the Palio will turn out to be something of the same sort. But let me reassure them; it is not. There is no poetry by Louis Napoleon Parker at Siena. There are no choruses of young ladies voicing high moral sentiments in low voices. There are no flabby actor-managers imperfectly disguised as Hengist and Horsa, no crowd of gesticulating supernumeraries dressed in the worst of taste and the cheapest of bunting. Nor finally does one often meet at Siena with that almost invariable accompaniment of the English pageant—rain. No, the Palio is just a show; having no "meaning" in particular, but by the mere fact of being traditional and still alive, signifying infinitely more than the dead-born English affairs for all their Parkerian blank verse and their dramatic re-evocations. For these pages and men-at-arms and bannermen come straight out of the Pinturicchian past. Their clothes are those designed for their ancestors, copied faithfully, once in a generation, in the same colors and the same rich materials. They walk, not in cotton or flannelette, but in silks and furs and velvets. And the colors were matched, the clothes originally cut by men whose taste was the faultless taste of the early renais-

4. Horace Vernet (1789–1863). French painter of Versailles battle scenes.

sance. To be sure there are costumiers with as good a taste in these days. But it was not Paquin, not Lanvin or Poiret[5] who dressed the actors of the English pageants; it was professional wig-makers and lady amateurs. I have already spoken of the beauty of the flags—the bold, fantastic, "modern" design of them. Everything else at the Palio is in keeping with the flags, daring, brilliant, and yet always right, always irreproachably refined. The one false note is always the Palio itself—the painted banner which is given to the *contrada* whose horse wins the race. This banner is specially painted every year for the occasion. Look at it, where it comes along, proudly exposed on the great medieval war chariot which closes the procession—look at it, or preferably don't look at it. It is a typical property from the wardrobe of an English pageant committee. It is a lady amateur's masterpiece. Shuddering, one averts the eyes.

Preceded by a line of *quattrocento* pages carrying festoons of laurel leaves and escorted by a company of mounted knights, the war chariot rolled slowly and ponderously past, bearing aloft the unworthy trophy. And by now the trumpets at the head of the procession sounded, almost inaudibly for us, from the further side of the piazza. And at last the whole procession had made its round and was lined up in close order in front of the Palazzo Comunale. Over the heads of the spectators standing in the central area, we could see all the thirty-four banners waving and waving in a last concerted display and at last, together, all leaping high into the air, hesitating at the top of their leap, falling back, out of sight. There was a burst of applause. The pageant was over. Another gunshot. And in the midst of more applause, the racehorses were ridden to the starting place.

The course is three times round the piazza, whose shape, as I have said, is something like that of an ancient theater. Consequently, there are two sharp turns, where the ends of the semicircle meet the straight diameter. One of these, owing to the irregularity of the plan, is sharper than the other. The outside wall of the track is padded with mattresses at this point, to prevent impetuous jockeys who take the corner too fast from dashing themselves to pieces. The jockeys ride bareback; the horses run on a thin layer of sand spread over the flagstones of the piazza. The Palio is probably the most dangerous flat-race in the world. And it is made the more dangerous by the excessive patriotism of the rival *contrade*. For the winner of the race as he reins in his horse after passing the post is set upon by the supporters of the other *contrade* (who all think that their horse should have won) with so real and earnest a fury that the carabiniers must always intervene to protect man and beast from lynching. Our places were at a

---

5. French fashion designers. Jeanne Lanvin (1867–1946). Paul Poiret (1879–1944).

point some two or three hundred yards beyond the post, so that we had an excellent view of the battle waged round the winning horse, as he slackened speed. Scarcely was the post passed when the crowd broke its ranks and rushed out into the course. Still cantering, the horse came up the track. A gang of young men ran in pursuit, waving sticks and shouting. And with them, their Napoleonic coat tails streaming in the wind of their own speed, their cocked hats bobbing, and brandishing swords in their white-gloved hands, ran the rescuing carabiniers. There was a brief struggle round the now stationary horse, the young men were repulsed, and surrounded by cocked hats, followed by a crowd of supporters from its native *contrada,* the beast was led off in triumph. We climbed down from our places. The piazza was now entirely shaded. It was only on the upper part of the tower and the battlements of the great Palazzo that the sun still shone. Rosily against the pale blue sky, they glowed. The swifts still turned and turned overhead in the light. It is said that at evening and at dawn these light-loving birds mount on their strong wings into the sky to bid a last farewell or earliest good-morrow to the sinking or the rising sun. While we lie sleeping or have resigned ourselves to darkness the swifts are looking down from their watch-tower in the height of heaven over the edge of the turning planet towards the light. Was it a fable, I wondered, looking up at the wheeling birds? Or was it true? Meanwhile, someone was swearing at me for not looking where I was going. I postponed the speculation.

[*Along the Road,* 1925]

Views of Holland

I HAVE ALWAYS been rather partial to plane geometry; probably because it was the only branch of mathematics that was ever taught me in such a way that I could understand it. For though I have no belief in the power of education to turn public-school boys into Newtons (it being quite obvious that, whatever opportunity may be offered, it is only those rare beings desirous of learning and possessing a certain amount of native ability who ever do learn anything), yet I must insist, in my own defense, that the system of mathematical instruction of which, at Eton, I was the unfortunate victim, was calculated not merely to turn my desire to learn into stubborn passive resistance, but also to stifle whatever rudimentary aptitude in this direction I might have possessed. But let that pass. Suffice to say that, in spite of my education and my congenital ineptitude, plane geometry has always charmed me by its simplicity and elegance, its elimination of detail and the individual case, its insistence on generalities.

My love for plane geometry prepared me to feel a special affection for Holland. For the Dutch landscape has all the qualities that make geometry so delightful. A tour in Holland is a tour through the first books of Euclid. Over a country that is the ideal plane surface of the geometry books, the roads and the canals trace out the shortest distances between point and point. In the interminable polders, the road-topped dykes and gleaming ditches intersect one another at right angles, a crisscross of perfect parallels. Each rectangle of juicy meadowland contained between the intersecting dykes has identically the same area. Five kilometers long, three deep—the figures record themselves on the clock face of the cyclometer. Five by three by—how many? The demon of calculation possesses the mind. Rolling along those smooth brick roads between the canals, one strains one's eyes to count the dykes at right angles and parallel to one's own. One calculates the area of the polders they enclose. So many square kilometers. But the square kilometers have to be turned into acres. It is a fearful sum to do in one's head; the more so as one has forgotten how many square yards there are in an acre.

And all the time, as one advances the huge geometrical landscape spreads out on either side of the car like an opening fan. Along the level sky-line a score of windmills wave their arms like dancers in a geometrical ballet. Ineluctably, the laws of perspective lead away the long roads and shining waters to a misty vanishing point. Here and there—mere real irrelevancies in the midst of this ideal plain—a few black and white cows out of a picture by Cuyp browse indefatigably in the lush green grass or, remembering Paul Potter,[6] mirror themselves like so many ruminating Narcissi, in the waters of a canal. Sometimes one passes a few human beings, deplorably out of place, but doing their best, generally, to make up for their ungeometrical appearance by mounting bicycles. The circular wheels suggest a variety of new theorems and a new task for the demon of calculation. Suppose the radius of the wheels to be fifteen inches; then fifteen times fifteen times *pi* will be the area. The only trouble is that one has forgotten the value of *pi*.

Hastily I exorcise the demon of calculation that I may be free to admire the farm-house on the opposite bank of the canal on our right. How perfectly it fits into the geometrical scheme! On a cube, cut down to about a third of its height, is placed a tall pyramid. That is the house. A plantation of trees, set in quincunx formation, surrounds it; the limits of its rectangu-

---

6. Albert Cuyp (1620–1691). Dutch painter, particularly of cattle scenes. Paul Potter (1625–1654). Dutch painter.

lar garden are drawn in water on the green plain, and beyond these neat ditches extend the interminable flat fields. There are no outhouses, no barns, no farm-yard with untidy stacks. The hay is stored under the huge pyramidal roof, and in the truncated cube below live, on one side the farmer and his family, on the other side (during winter only; for during the rest of the year they sleep in the fields) his black and white Cuyp cows. Every farm-house in North Holland conforms to this type, which is traditional, and so perfectly fitted to the landscape that it would have been impossible to devise anything more suitable. An English farm with its ranges of straggling buildings, its untidy yard, full of animals, its haystacks and pigeon-cotes would be horribly out of place here. In the English landscape, which is all accidents, variety, detail, and particular cases, it is perfect. But here, in this generalized and Euclidean North Holland, it would be a blot and a discord. Geometry calls for geometry; with a sense of the aesthetic proprieties which one cannot too highly admire, the Dutch have responded to the appeal of the landscape and have dotted the plane surface of their country with cubes and pyramids.

Delightful landscape! I know of no country that it is more mentally exhilarating to travel in. No wonder Descartes preferred the Dutch to any other scene. It is the rationalist's paradise. One feels as one flies along in the teeth of one's own forty-mile-an-hour wind like a Cartesian Encyclopaedist flushed with mental intoxication, convinced that Euclid is absolute reality, that God is a mathematician, that the universe is a simple affair that can be explained in terms of physics and mechanics, that all men are equally endowed with reason and that it is only a question of putting the right arguments before them to make them see the error of their ways and to inaugurate the reign of justice and common sense. Those were noble and touching dreams, commendable inebriations! We are soberer now. We have learnt that nothing is simple and rational except what we ourselves have invented; that God thinks neither in terms of Euclid nor of Riemann; that science has "explained" nothing; that the more we know the more fantastic the world becomes and the profounder the surrounding darkness; that reason is unequally distributed; that instinct is the sole source of action; that prejudice is incomparably stronger than argument and that even in the twentieth century men behave as they did in the caves of Altamira and in the lake dwellings of Glastonbury. And symbolically one makes the same discoveries in Holland. For the polders are not unending, nor all the canals straight, nor every house a wedded cube and pyramid, nor even the fundamental plane surface invariably plane. That delightful "Last Ride Together" feeling that fills one, as one rolls along the brick-topped dykes between the canals is deceptive. The present is not eternal; the "Last Ride" through plane geometry comes to a sudden end—in a town, in forests, in the sea coast, in a winding river or great estuary. It matters little which; all are fundamentally ungeometrical; each has power to dissipate in an instant all those "paralogisms of rationalism" (as Professor Rougier calls them) which we have so fondly cherished among the polders. The towns have crooked streets thronged with people; the houses are of all shapes and sizes. The coast-line is not straight nor regularly curved and its dunes or its dykes (for it must be defended against the besieging waves by art if not by nature) rear themselves inexcusably out of the plane surface. The woods are unscientific in their shady mysteriousness and one cannot see them for all their individual trees. The rivers are tortuous and alive with boats and barges. The inlets of the sea are entirely shapeless. It is the real world again after the ideal hopelessly diversified, complex, and obscure; but, when the first regrets are over, equally charming with the geometrical landscape we have left behind. We shall find it more charming, indeed, if our minds are practical and extroverted. Personally, I balance my affections. For I love the inner world as much as the outer. When the outer vexes me, I retire to the rational simplicities of the inner—to the polders of the spirit. And when, in their turn, the polders seem unduly flat, the roads too straight, and the laws of perspective too tyrannous, I emerge again into the pleasing confusion of untempered reality.

And how beautiful, how curious in Holland that confusion is! I think of Rotterdam with its enormous river and its great bridges, so crowded with the traffic of a metropolis that one has to wait in files, half a mile long, for one's turn to cross. I think of The Hague and how it tries to be elegant and only succeeds in being respectable and upper middle class; of Delft, the commercial city of three hundred years ago; of Haarlem where, in autumn, you see them carting bulbs as in other countries they cart potatoes; of Hoorn on the Zuyder Zee, with its little harbor and seaward-looking castle, its absurd museum filled with rich mixed rubbish, its huge storehouse of cheeses, like an old-fashioned arsenal, where the workmen are busy all day long polishing the yellow cannon balls on a kind of lathe and painting them bright pink with an aniline stain. I think of Volendam— one line of wooden houses perched on the sea wall, and another line crouching in the low green fields behind the dyke. The people at Volendam are dressed as for a musical comedy—*Miss Hook of Holland*—the men in baggy trousers and short jackets, the women in winged white caps, tight bodices, and fifteen super-imposed petticoats. Five thousand tourists come daily to look at them; but they still, by some miracle, retain their independence and self-respect. I think of Amsterdam; the old town, like a livelier Bruges, mirrors its high brick houses in the canals. In one quarter an enormous courtesan sits smiling at every window, the meatiest specimens of

humanity I ever saw. At nine in the morning, at lunch-time, at six in the afternoon, the streets are suddenly filled with three hundred thousand bicycles; everyone, in Amsterdam, goes to and from his business on a pair of
wheels. For the pedestrian as well as for the motorist it is a nightmare.
And they are all trick cyclists. Children of four carry children of three on
their handle-bars. Mothers pedal gaily along with month-old infants sleeping in cradles fastened to the back carrier. Messenger boys think nothing
of taking two cubic metres of parcels. Dairymen do their rounds on bicycles specially constructed to accommodate two hundred quart bottles of
milk in a tray between the two wheels. I have seen nursery gardeners carrying four palms and a dozen of potted chrysanthemums on their handle-
bars. I have seen five people riding through the traffic on one machine.
The most daring feats of the circus and the music hall are part of the quotidian routine in Amsterdam.

I think of the dunes near Schoorl. Seen from a little distance across the
plain they look like a range of enormous mountains against the sky. Following with the eye that jagged silhouette one can feel all the emotions
aroused, shall we say, by the spectacle of the Alps seen from Turin. The
dunes are grand; one could write a canto from *Childe Harold* about them.
And then, unfortunately, one realizes what for a moment one had forgotten, that this line of formidable peaks is not looking down at one from
fifty miles away, over the curving flank of the planet; it is just a furlong
distant, and the chimneys of the houses at its base reach nearly two-thirds
of the way to the top. But what does that matter? With a little good will, I
insist, one can feel in Holland all the emotions appropriate to Switzerland.

Yes, they are grand, the dunes of Schoorl and Groet. But I think the
grandest sight I saw in non-geometrical Holland was Zaandam—Zaandam from a distance, across the plain.

We had been driving through the polders and the open country of
North Holland. Zaandam was the first piece of ungeometrical reality since
Alkmaer. Technically, Zaandam is not picturesque; the guide-book has little to say about it. It is a port and manufacturing town on the Zaan, a few
miles north of Amsterdam; that is all. They make cocoa there and soap.
The air at Zaandam is charged in alternative strata with delicious vapors
of molten chocolate and the stench of boiling fat. In wharves by the shores
of the river they store American grain and timber from the Baltic. It was
the granaries that first announced, from a distance, the presence of Zaandam. Like the cathedrals of a new religion, yet unpreached, they towered
up into the hazy autumn air—huge oblongs of concrete set on end, almost
windowless, smooth and blankly grey. It was as though their whole force
were directed vertically upwards; to look from windows horizontally
across the world would have been a distraction; eyes were sacrificed to this

upward purpose. And the direction of that purpose was emphasized by the lines of the alternately raised and lowered panels into which the wall spaces of the great buildings were divided—long fine lines of shadow running up unbrokenly through a hundred feet from base to summit. The builders of the papal palace at Avignon used a very similar device to give their castle its appearance of enormous height and formidable impenitence. The raised panel and the shallow blind arches, impossibly long in the leg, with which they variegated the surface of the wall, impart to the whole building an impetuous upward tendency. It is the same with the grain elevators at Zaandam. In the haze of autumnal Holland I remembered Provence. And I remembered, as I watched those towering shapes growing larger and larger as we approached, Chartres and Bourges and Reims: gigantic silhouettes seen at the end of a day's driving, towards evening, against a pale sky, with the little lights of a city about their base.

But if at a distance, Zaandam, by its commercial monuments, reminds one of Provençal castles and the Gothic cathedrals of France, a nearer view proclaims it to be unequivocally Dutch. At the foot of the elevators and the only less enormous factories, in the atmosphere of chocolate and soap, lies the straggling town. The suburbs are long, but narrow; for they cling precariously to a knife-edge of land between two waters. The houses are small, made of wood and gaudily painted; with gardens as large as table-cloths, beautifully kept and filled—at any rate at the season when I saw them—with plushy begonias. In one, as large, in this case, as two table-cloths, were no less than fourteen large groups of statuary. In the streets are men in wooden shoes, smoking. Dogs drawing carts with brass pots in them. Innumerable bicycles. It is the real and not the ideal geometrical Holland, crowded, confusing, various, odd, charming. . . . But I sighed as we entered the town. "The Last Ride Together" was over; the dear paralogisms of rationalism were left behind. It was now necessary to face the actual world of men—and to face it, in my case, with precisely five words of Dutch (and patois at that) learned years before for the benefit of a Flemish servant: "Have you fed the cat?" No wonder I regretted the polders.

[*Along the Road,* 1925]

Appendix

On the Margin: Notes and Essays
(Chatto & Windus, 1923)
Table of Contents as Originally Published

Centenaries
On Re-reading *Candide*
Accidie
Subject-Matter of Poetry
Water Music
Pleasures
Modern Folk Poetry
Bibliophily
Democratic Art
Accumulations
On Deviating into Sense
Polite Conversation
Nationality in Love
How the Days Draw In
Tibet
Beauty in 1920
Great Thoughts
Advertisements
Euphues Redivivus
The Author of *Eminent Victorians*
Edward Thomas
A Wordsworth Anthology
Verhaeren
Edward Lear
Sir Christopher Wren
Ben Jonson
Chaucer

Index

A NOTE ON THE EDITORS

Robert S. Baker is professor of English at the University of Wisconsin, Madison. He studied at the University of Western Ontario and at the University of Illinois, where he received a Ph.D. He has written *Brave New World: History, Science, and Dystopia* and *The Dark Historic Page: Social Satire and Historicism in the Novels of Aldous Huxley, 1921–1939.*

James Sexton teaches English at Camosun College in Victoria, British Columbia. He studied at the University of British Columbia, the University of Oregon, and the University of Victoria, where he received a Ph.D. With David Bradshaw he has edited an edition of Huxley's play *Now More Than Ever*, and has edited a collection of Huxley's Hearst essays.